MW01153771

– To Dwight Nesbit,
Best wishes,

RED CLAY TO RICHMOND

Trail of the 35th Georgia Infantry Regiment, C.S.A.

BY JOHN J. FOX, III

ANGLE VALLEY PRESS
WINCHESTER, VIRGINIA

 For information contact: Angle Valley Press, P.O. Box 4098, Winchester, Va. 22604.

www.anglevalleypress.com

FIRST EDITION

ISBN 0-9711950-2-1

LCCN 2004100204

Grateful acknowledgment is made for permission to quote extensively from *Letters to Amanda: The Civil War Letters of Marion Hill Fitzpatrick, A.N.V.,* edited by Jeffrey C. Lowe and Sam Hodges (Mercer University Press, Macon, Ga.: 1998). Reprinted by permission of Mercer University Press. Title page photograph by D. J. Bender, Winchester, Va. Georgia belt plate found at Millwood, Va. by Steve Baker. Plate owned by Harry Ridgeway and displayed at Old Court House Civil War Museum, Winchester, Va.

Publisher's Cataloging-in-Publication Data
(Provided by Quality Books, Inc.)

Fox, John J., 1959
Red clay to Richmond : trail of the 35th Georgia Infantry Regiment, C.S.A. / by John J. Fox, III.—1st ed.
p. cm.
Includes bibliographical references and index.
LCCN 2004100204
ISBN 0-9711950-2-1

1. Confederate States of America. Army. Georgia Infantry Regiment, 35th. 2. United States—History—Civil War, 1861–1865—Regimental histories. 3. Georgia—History—Civil War, 1861–1865—Regimental histories. I. Title.

E559.5 35th.F69 2004 973.7′ 458
QBI04-700022

DEDICATION

This book is dedicated to four very special people. My mother, Anne Gwinn Fox, who gave me a love of books; my father, John Joseph Fox, Jr., who gave me a love of history; my in-laws, Harry Tudor Jones, Jr., and Celetta Powell Jones, who have accepted me as their own son into their Georgia family.

*"...here the sun shone brighter, the skies were bluer,
the men nobler and the women purer and sweeter
than elsewhere under God's sun."*

*Brigadier General Edward Lloyd Thomas
in describing his native state of Georgia.
Quote attributed to him from
his obituary, Atlanta Journal,
March 10, 1898*

TABLE OF CONTENTS

ILLUSTRATIONS

PHOTOGRAPHS

CHAPTER 1

CHAPTER 2

CHAPTER 3

Chapter 4

Chapter 5

Chapter 6

Chapter 7

Chapter 8

Chapter 9

Chapter 10

Chapter 11

Chapter 12

Chapter 13

Chapter 14

Chapter 15

Appendix E

Appendix H

Roster A

Roster E

Roster F

Roster J

Roster T

MAPS

Chapter 1

Chapter 2

Chapter 3

PREFACE

The men of the 35th Georgia have been in my blood for over a decade now. After reading many letters and diaries, some of them stained with dirty fingerprints, I am in awe of what these men accomplished: the thousand miles or more of marching in incredible heat or bone-chilling cold; the sleeping on the ground amidst torrential rains without shelter; the surge of hunger pangs from shriveled stomachs; fighting the deadly effects of disease. Yet, they suffered all these things before the first enemy bullet came their way–and then the fighting began.

I read these wartime accounts as I sat in my comfortable home with all its modern niceties. My wife and children rested in the next room. I lacked nothing. The words in these letters created a complexity of thoughts and emotions in me. These men soon earned my complete respect and esteem. I truly wondered if I had the inner resolve to have served as a Confederate soldier–to have fought as a Georgia infantryman between 1861–1865.

However, these thoughts were far from my mind when I walked into *Frameworks,* a Columbus, Georgia frame shop, in 1987. There I met the owners, Jack and Dian Stroud. Dian found out I was interested in the Civil War and she showed me a framed original letter written by her eighteen-year-old soldier relative to his mother in 1863. Dian noticed my considerable excitement as I read the faded, but finely crafted script. I asked about other letters and Dian replied, "Oh, my great aunt in Alabama has two shoe boxes full that she keeps in her attic." My jaw hit the floor. I asked her to talk with her aunt to see if I could get a chance to look at the letters. She said she would try. Several months later, I finally held these treasured letters in my hands and made copies of them. What I thought would be a small project had only begun. I planned to transcribe the letters to outline only the experiences of Private James M. Garrett who enlisted in Company D,

35th Georgia Infantry Regiment in September 1861. Research revealed that Garrett was the oldest son of a Heard County widow. His photo shows a serious face perhaps due to his becoming the man of the house at age ten after his father died.

Initial research on the 35th Georgia showed the publication of only one book on the unit. John Frank Edwards, also a member of Company D, wrote *The Red Book - Army Life of Frank Edwards- Confederate Veteran 1861–1865.* Edwards recorded his account in 1906 just before he died and it appeared more of an effort to portray himself as a heroic soldier, than an actual wartime account of the regiment's activities. During a visit to the Georgia Division of Archives and History in Atlanta (now Morrow, Ga.), I came across other letters written by soldiers from the 35th Georgia. My curiosity then led me to visit other libraries and archives where I found more letters and even photographs of 35th Georgia soldiers. Then word of my research reached other families whose relatives fought in the regiment. I soon had more material related to the wartime lives of these men. I realized that the story of more than one Georgia soldier waited to be told. In fact, over 1,300 Georgia soldiers fought in the 35th Georgia during the four long years of struggle. These dedicated men and even some boys had spilled their sweat and blood all the way from their native state to Pennsylvania for a cause they thought was right. They willingly left their farms and their families and marched into an unknown future to protect their homeland.

These citizen-soldiers came from the red clay homesteads of ten different Georgia counties. They were mostly young farmers - the best each rural county could send. Brothers served next to brothers. Fathers served next to sons. Members of the same family dominated some of the companies like the eleven members of the Moon family in Company G from Walton County. These families had a significant blood stake in the daily grind of the war.

The soldier's shared experiences formed a bond that held them together through some of the heaviest fighting in Virginia, Maryland and Pennsylvania with General Robert E. Lee's Army of Northern Virginia. Their longing for home was so evident in their letters. These soldiers filled their paper with many questions. One father wanted to know how big his two-year-old son had grown. Another soldier wondered if his wife had trouble gathering in the crops before fall ushered in cool weather. Would the family be able to get by on the $22 sent home? Could the family send some peach brandy to help ease the cold nights? Could they send a coat before winter? Some men asked for cakes, cornbread and even fried chicken. One soldier, during the latter part of the war, persistently requested his younger brother come to the front to take his place. Many soldiers implored family members to write more often. Most heartbreaking of all was the love that many spilled out to their long unseen wives and children. The soldiers strained to find some way to keep their families from worrying. To overcome this worry, many of the men referenced the Lord in their letters because they truly believed He would work things out for the better in His own time. The war not only tested but also strengthened the spiritual faith of many Georgians and gave rise to a series of revivals that swept through Brigadier General Edward Lloyd Thomas' Georgia brigade beginning in the winter of 1862–1863.

The letters revealed the drudgery of daily army life: marching, cooking, parades, inspections, drill and picket duty. The soldiers abhorred all these tasks. The battles provided the excitement and escape from these dull soldierly duties; however, these same battles also brought the sober realities of war. What began for some as a great adventure changed during late 1861 after a disease epidemic struck the regiment. Most of these men had never experienced the horrors of war. The soldier's descriptive letters, like a photograph, captured the images of the dismembered bodies, the decimated landscape, the ravages of sickness and the unforgiving weather.

Fighting represented an extremely small percentage of the men's time in Confederate service. These letters tended to focus more on what happened in camp, what the soldiers really felt, their likes and dislikes, and who they respected. Many of the soldiers, not knowing these letters would be read beyond their families, wrote with brutal honesty about what was important to them and what was in their hearts.

This story describes the hardships and even the happiness that these men encountered. It describes the lasting friendships they formed and those cut short by bullets or disease. Most Georgians, in the fall of 1861, believed the conflict would last only a short time. These soldiers truly believed they would soon be back with their families performing as husbands, fathers and breadwinners. History shows this did not happen. The war continued on for four long years, and the toll of misery, destruction, illness, injury and death mounted for those back home as well as the soldier participants. In 1861 however, the realities of war stood a far distance away from these Georgia boys as they lined up to enlist in their hometowns while flag-waving family members watched with pride. Many of these men had never traveled outside their home counties, and they relished the future adventures of a trip to Atlanta and then Richmond.

The soldiers in the 35th Georgia were average men. Their leaders asked them to perform a Herculean task. The immensity of this task was not obvious at the beginning of the war. Sixty to eighty men filled each of the ten companies in the regiment. Each man had cares, needs and fears. The combination of all these emotions created many stories—some sad, some happy, some honorable, and some dishonorable. These men successfully carried the flag of the 35th Georgia from the red clay of their home state in 1861 until they tearfully furled the flag at Appomattox in 1865. The survivors in the 35th Georgia could proudly say that no enemy hand ever touched their banner during combat.

What began for me as a small project grew and carried me on expeditions to archives, historical societies, libraries, national battlefield parks and civil war shows from Gettysburg, Pennsylvania to New Orleans, Louisiana in search of anything that would help reveal their stories. I thank God for the opportunity to get to know these men on an almost personal level. Even though Georgia supplied the third highest number of soldiers to the Confederacy, only a handful of Georgia regimental histories exist. This is a small attempt to fill that void. Let us not forget the sacrifices made by these soldiers as well as their families, for if we do we lose a part of our heritage.

ACKNOWLEDGMENTS

A project of this scope is impossible without the dedicated help of many people. I am deeply indebted to these generous people for providing assistance and inspiration. This study has been a work in progress for quite some time–too long. Time, however, has been a friend. If this book had come out earlier a large amount of information would have been missing. Without fail, every time I thought I was finished, I discovered a new treasure trove of 35th Georgia facts. Some people have assisted me with research, some with proofreading and editing, while others have provided letters and photos of their relatives. I would especially like to thank my wife, Nancy, who has endured this project for most of our marriage. Her editing, insight and immense patience were indispensable and helped move this project to fruition.

I am thankful for the valuable time numerous distinguished historians gave in reviewing portions of this manuscript. Robert E.L. Krick, Frank A. O'Reilly, A. Wilson Green, Robert K. Krick, and Jeffry D. Wert all gave timely analysis that helped save me from errors of fact and of style. Their willingness to help an unknown author is especially noteworthy. Keith S. Bohannon, of Carollton, Georgia, continued to surprise and amaze me with the many 35th Georgia nuggets that he uncovered. This book would be laced with numerous holes without his steadfast detective work. Winchester's Brandon Beck provided rich inspiration and direction over an extended period.

I would like to thank Jack and Dian Stroud of Columbus, Georgia (*Frameworks*) for providing me with copies of the letters from their young relative, Private James M Garrett. The receipt of Garrett's letters provided inspiration for this project. Mark Pollard of McDonough, Georgia provided me with the photo of his great-great-grandfather, Private John Rigby, who graces the cover. Through the years, Mark has shared lots of Rigby information. Elaine and John Bailey of Douglasville, Georgia sent me the excellent photo and diary of his relative Major James T. McElvany. David Hollis of Lanett, Alabama provided me with the photo and diary of Corporal Hiram Hammond. Carl Summers of West Point, Georgia also provided me with a photo of Hammond and Captain George W. Hammond. Dennis and Emily Whitcomb of Oxford, Georgia sent me a photo of Edward L. Thomas' boyhood home. Arlene Shuler of West Columbia, South Carolina sent me a photo of Captain Graves B. Almand. Tom Aderhold of Stone Mountain, Georgia provided a picture of Private Jasper Webb. Bill Smedlund, of Sharpsburg, Georgia sent me copies of the letters written by George Pass and a list of period Georgia newspaper articles that mentioned Thomas' Brigade. The Charles Ray family of Marietta, Georgia provided access to the Daniel Jackson letters. Gwinnett County historian Alice Smythe McCabe provided answers to my many questions. Richmond's Jay Fox, my Dad and fellow history buff, provided research assistance as well as battlefield companionship. Atlantan Bob Price of the Georgia Civil War Commission provided research assistance in Athens, Georgia, and photos of Edward L. Thomas' grave in Oklahoma. Debbie Bender of Winchester, Virginia provided photographic advice and took photographs of pertinent Georgia relics. Culpeper County's John Bosserman and Byrd and Jack Inskeep allowed me access to the Cedar Mountain battlefield. Melissa Beck of Winchester, Virginia provided editorial advice. Steve Bayliss, Winchester, Virginia computer guru, helped restore my sanity and computer when both locked up. Anne Aschenbrenner of Winchester, Virginia gave editorial help. My sister, Sarah Liverance, read a poor manuscript from long ago and made positive suggestions. Jeanie Bechtol of Winchester's *Impressions Plus* gave me great graphics advice and helped convert my crude drawings into maps.

I would like to thank the following people for their research assistance: Heather Milne and Kara Griggs of the Museum of the Confederacy in Richmond; Dale Couch, Senior Archivist, Georgia Division of Archives and History and Charlotte Ray, now retired Senior Archivist; Steve Engerrand, Assistant Director of Archival Services, Georgia Department of Archives and History; Mary Thomason-Morris, Archivist, of the Clarke County (Berryville, Va.) Historical Association; Terry Reimer, Director of Research/Public Relations Coordinator, of the National Museum of Civil War Medicine in Frederick, Maryland; Mary Ellen Brooks, Director, and Melissa Bush, Archival Associate, at the Hargrett Rare Book and Manuscript Library, University of Georgia in Athens; Dorothy Olson, Director, and Travis Hutchins, Curator, Georgia Capitol Museum at the State Capitol building in Atlanta; Randall Allen and C.J. at the Troup County (LaGrange, Ga.) Archives; Laura Micham, Head of Public Services, and Anne Thomason, Reference Assistant, at Special Collections for Woodruff Library at Emory University in Atlanta; Miriam A.K. Syler, Archives Assistant, from the H. Grady Bradshaw Chambers County Library and Cobb Memorial Archives in Valley, Alabama; Teresa Roane, Archives Director, at the Valentine Richmond History Center; John J. Slonaker, Chief of the Historical Reference Branch, at the U.S. Army Military History Institute located at Carlisle Barracks, Pennsylvania; Dr. Thomas P. Lowry, of "The Index Project, Inc.," (database of Union and Confederate court-martial records) sent me the records for all court-martials in Thomas' Brigade; Anne Rogers, of Washington Memorial Library, in Macon, Georgia; all the patient personnel at the National Archives in Washington, D.C.; Jackie Kinzer at Rome Floyd County Library Special Collections in Rome, Georgia; Marc Jolley, Mercer University Press, who gave me permission to quote extensively from their excellent book (edited by Jeffrey C. Lowe and Sam Hodges) *Letters to Amanda: The Civil War Letters of Marion Hill Fitzpatrick, A.N.V.;* Jean Stubbs with the Chattooga (Summerville, Ga.) County Historical Society; Craig Lloyd, archivist and history professor, and David Daniell, at the Simon Schwob Memorial Library, Columbus State University in Columbus, Georgia; Harry Ridgeway who kindly allowed a photographer to record Georgia buttons and buckles from his extensive collection at the Old Courthouse Civil War Museum in Winchester, Virginia; Rebecca Ebert and Barbara Dickinson at the Stewart Bell, Jr., Archives Room, Handley Regional Library in Winchester, Va.; Archeologists Joe Balicki and Bryan Corle, of John Milner Associates in Alexandria, Virginia, who pleasantly surprised me with information about Camp French and then provided a walking tour of the 35th Georgia's well preserved winter camp; Kenneth R. Shobe, South Branch Valley Civil War Society, Inc., at Petersburg, West Virginia, who provided me information about Fort Mulligan. Ronald L. Smith, of Dumfries, Virginia, for giving me a copy of Mary Alice Wills' outstanding book, *The Confederate Blockade of Washington, D.C., 1861–1862,* and providing information pertaining to Camp French; Doris Maxwell and Fran Nifong with Manchester (Tx.) Historical Society; Mac Wyckoff with Fredericksburg—Spotsylvania National Military Park.

I have attempted to gather as much information as possible pertaining to the service of the men in the 35th Georgia. Certainly more primary information still exists that I missed. I would request that those people with knowledge of such items contact me at the publishers address listed in the front of this book.

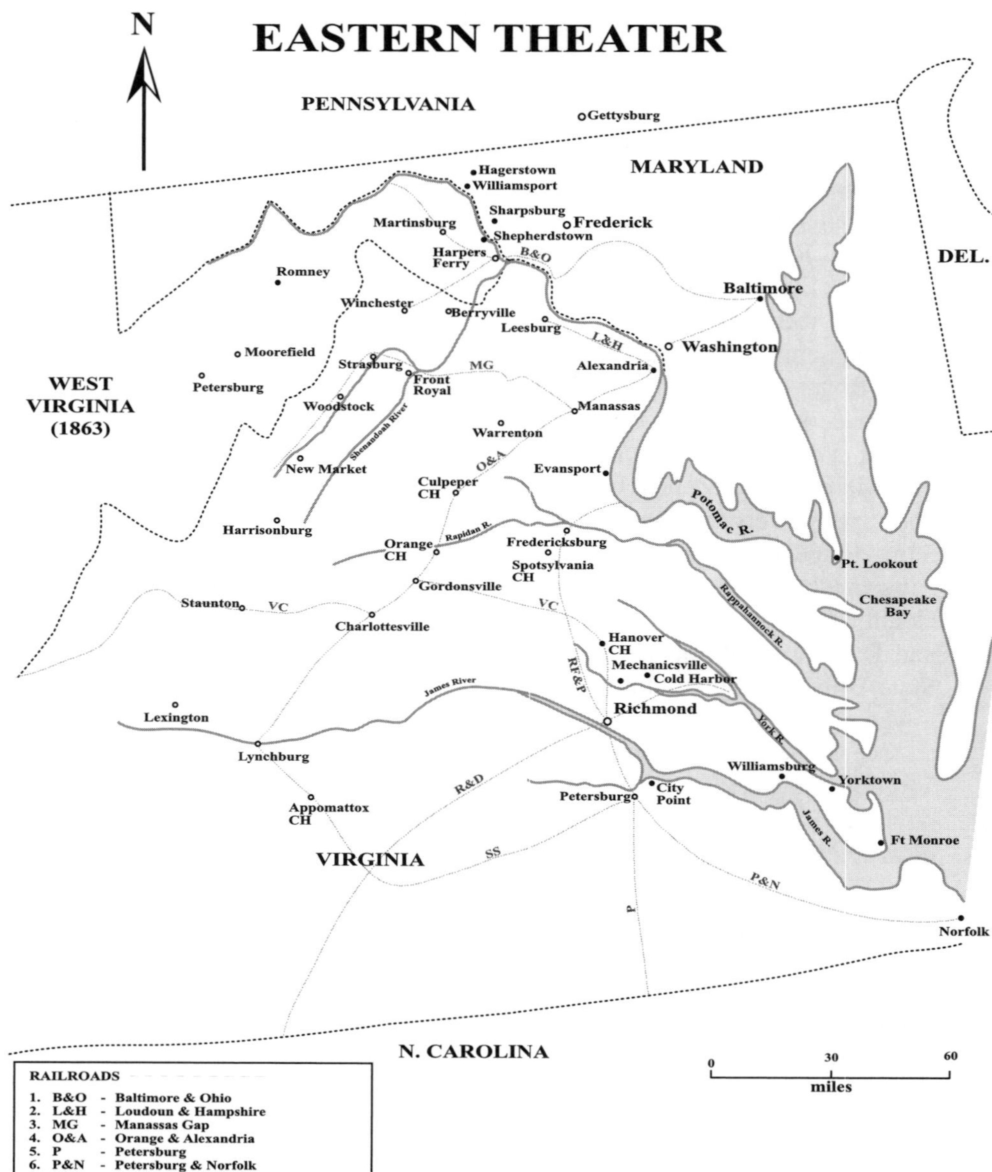

RAILROADS

1. B&O - Baltimore & Ohio
2. L&H - Loudoun & Hampshire
3. MG - Manassas Gap
4. O&A - Orange & Alexandria
5. P - Petersburg
6. P&N - Petersburg & Norfolk
7. R&D - Richmond & Danville
8. RF&P - Richmond, Fredericksburg & Potomac
9. SS - South Side
10. VC - Virginia Central

Chapter One

To Virginia

"Stand firmly by your cannon
Let ball and grape-shot fly
Trust in God and Davis
And keep your powder dry."
—Poem on front of envelopes sold by Starke & Cardozo to Confederate soldiers in Richmond, Virginia.

The War Between the States had entered its fifth month by August 1861. The Confederacy had won the first major battle of the war, at Manassas, Virginia the previous month. A newly formed Confederate government, located in Richmond, continued to call for more troops. Three companies of men from the Georgia counties of Haralson, Campbell and Harris accepted this call. When Georgia Governor Joe Brown failed to utilize the services of these companies in a timely manner, the three captains moved their men from the Atlanta area to Camp Lee in Richmond.

Meanwhile, a plantation owner from Newton County bypassed the Georgia capital and made a trip, at his own expense, to Richmond to offer his services to the fledgling army. Edward Lloyd Thomas wrote to Confederate Secretary of War Leroy P. Walker:

Richmond August 1 1861

Hon. L.P. Walker
Sir,
I can control companies sufficient in Georgia to form a regiment. I desire an order to organize them into a regiment—myself as Col. and have them mustered into service. If the Department cannot arm them also I desire them to be ordered into camp at such place as you may designate for the purpose of drill until arms can be furnished.

Yr. Able Servt.
E.L. Thomas

A War Department notation attached to the letter read, "Orders are not given to organize regt., nor permitted. If it were expedient to receive more regts. before arms are procured yours would be accepted but its not expedient."[1]

Several weeks later between September 10–18, seven other companies from Newton, Campbell, Heard, Troup, Gwinnett, Walton, Hall, and Chattooga counties arrived in Atlanta. They encamped at Walton Spring for training and awaited their orders.[2] The majority of these volunteers were farmers, teachers, lawyers, doctors, shopkeepers and artisans–all husbands, fathers, sons and brothers. Their departure left a serious void in each community.

Their enthusiasm for the Southern cause–a belief that they were doing something noble and right—was boundless. Twenty-six-year-old Gwinnett County schoolteacher James Thomas McElvany reflected on these thoughts in a letter he wrote to a family friend in February 1861, a month after Georgia seceded from the Union:

> Sir I have traveled farther since the first of January last than ever before, considering the conveyance I neither traveled by Rail Road nor Steam Boat nor by Telegraph nor by mail nor by land nor by Sea, But by the Powers of Government, I have gone clear out of the United States, and am now I hope, at my destination point, In a great and Independent Nation of which the history of the world gives us no account, however the prospect now is that it will become an asylum for the distressed and oppressed of all nations. I believe every Body is pleased with the new government and President and Vice President. If volunteers are needed Gwinnett will send her share.

The men in Company F elected McElvany to be their lieutenant.[3]

Private Benjamin Franklin Moody, of Company E, alluded to his own dedication and sacrifice in a letter to his family two months after his enlistment. The thirty-two-year- old farmer wrote:

> I know that the time is long and worrisome, but the more hardships we see the sweeter the country will seem to us when we gain it. I think when we gain our independence and get back home we will have a jubilee and say truly 'our country' and live a happy people! I want to see you very bad and spend some more pleasant hours with you. But I could not stay there until the war is over. I am glad that I did have the fortitude enough to come to the war, for I believe that it was my duty to come. I know that it is hard for you to do without me, but I think that it is better for you to do that than for our country to be subjugated and our children trampled in the dust forever.[4]

While in Atlanta these seven companies became the 4th Georgia Infantry Battalion. Some also referred to this group as the "Stephens Regiment." In October, some citizens presented a flag to the men in a ceremony at their Walton Spring camp. The civilians constructed the flag with fine blue silk. They painted on one side the Georgia state seal with "35th Georgia" written on the top arch above the three columns. On the opposite side they painted a likeness of Alexander Hamilton Stephens, the Confederate vice-president and former U.S. congressman from Georgia.[5]

These seven companies drilled for several weeks until they received Special Order No. 180, issued from the Confederate Adjutant and Inspector General's Office on October 15, 1861. The order read:

> The battalion of seven companies of Georgia Volunteers now at Atlanta, Ga. will proceed to this city (Richmond) as soon as practicable (not later than the 10th of November, proximo) and on arriving here will be united with the three companies now in this city commanded by Captains McCullohs (Co. K), Whitley (Co. E) and Head (Co. A), to form a regiment, the command of which is assigned to Col. E.L. Thomas.[6]

This order represented a successful culmination of Colonel Edward Lloyd Thomas' efforts to lobby Confederate officials for a command. His date of rank as colonel became effective on the same date as the order.

The thirty-six-year-old colonel arrived in Richmond with these seven companies during the first week of November 1861. They officially joined the Confederate army and united with the other three companies already at Camp Lee. The Georgians joined the thousands of other soldiers from all over the South at the training camp to await their orders.

Thomas had sent a letter to President Davis on October 26 from Atlanta. "In behalf of myself, officers and men, I respectfully request that my regiment may be united with the Wright Legion and made into a brigade, and that Hon. Augustus R. Wright be appointed to command it. I have known him long and intimately and have confidence in his prudence courage and skill." Wright was a former Georgia state superior court judge and U.S. congressman. At the time of this letter, the forty-eight-year-old Colonel Wright was in Atlanta training with his combined infantry, cavalry, and artillery unit commonly known as a legion. The Confederate President took no action on Thomas' request.[7]

The 35th Georgia initially numbered 692 enlisted men, 40 company officers and 9 staff officers for a total of 741 men. The following staff and ten companies comprised the 35th Georgia:

Colonel Edward L. Thomas, commander; Lieutenant Colonel Gustavus A. Bull; Major Bolling H. Holt; First Lieutenant

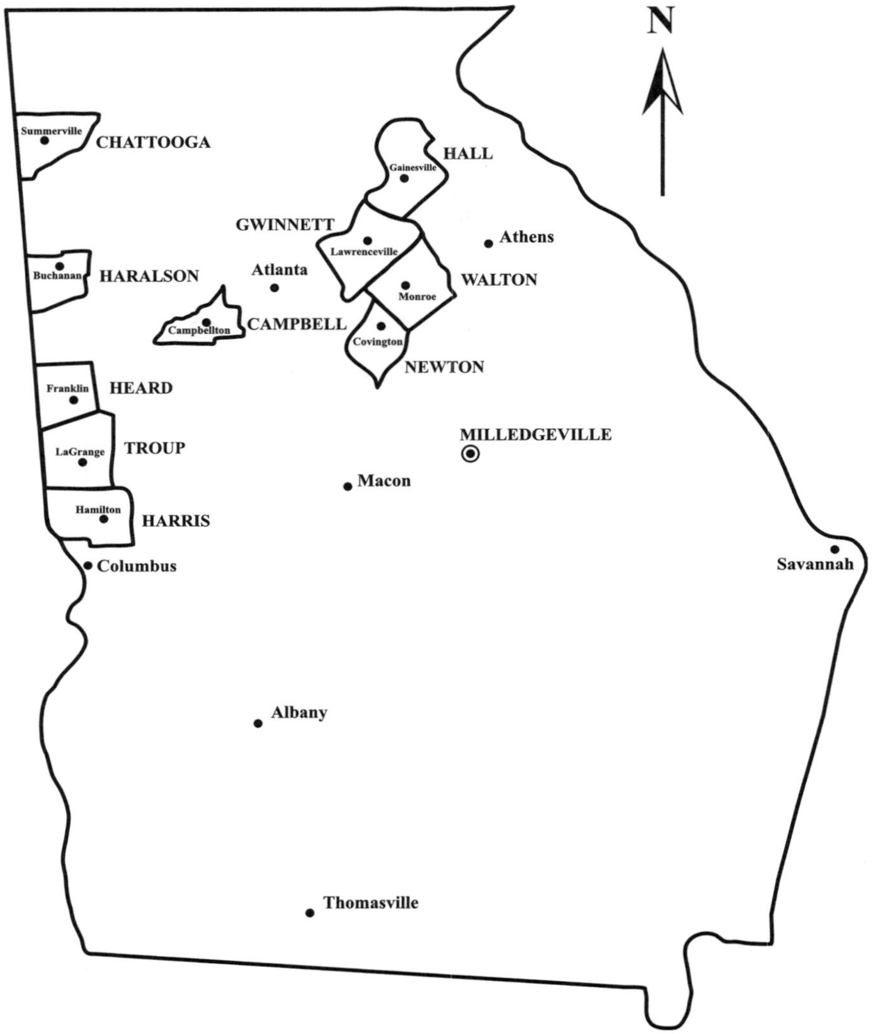

N

Summerville CHATTOOGA

Gainesville HALL

GWINNETT Lawrenceville

Athens

Buchanan HARALSON

Atlanta

Monroe WALTON

Campbellton CAMPBELL

Covington NEWTON

Franklin HEARD

MILLEDGEVILLE

LaGrange TROUP

Macon

Hamilton HARRIS

Columbus

Savannah

Albany

Thomasville

35th Georgia Enlistment Counties

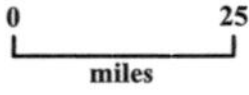

Colonel Edward Lloyd Thomas

This Mexican War veteran provided battle experience—a lacking ingredient for most Confederate regimental commanders in 1861. His leadership and fighting prowess earned him a promotion to brigade command in the summer of 1862. He survived the war and later served in the Indian Bureau in the Oklahoma Territory. He died and was buried in Oklahoma in 1898.

Georgia Division of Archives and History, Morrow, Ga.

James H. Ware, adjutant; Captain Lovick P. Thomas, quartermaster; Captain Virgil L. Hopson, commissary officer; Doctor James P. Hambleton, surgeon; Doctor Peter E.L. Jennings, assistant surgeon; Reverend George W. Yarbrough, chaplain.

Company A—Haralson Brown Guards from Haralson County. Enlisted August 15, 1861. Commanded by Captain William J. Head with 76 men.

Company B—Bartow Avengers from Newton County. Enlisted on September 21, 1861. Commanded by Captain James M. White with 79 men.

Company C—Campbell Rangers from Campbell County. Enlisted September 17, 1861. Commanded by Captain David B. Henry with 77 men.
Company D—From Heard and Troup Counties. Enlisted September 23, 1861. Commanded by Captain Lee A.J. Williams with 71 men.
Company E—Campbell Volunteers from Campbell County. Enlisted August 12, 1861. Commanded by Captain Evan R. Whitley with 78 men.
Company F—From Gwinnett County. Enlisted September 23, 1861. Commanded by Captain Robert M. Rawlins with 68 men.
Company G—Walton Sharpshooters from Walton County. Enlisted September 16, 1861. Commanded by Captain William S. Barrett with 64 men.
Company H—County Line Invincibles from Gwinnett and Hall Counties. Enlisted September 24, 1861. Commanded by Captain Aaron K. Richardson with 75 men.
Company I—Chattooga Mountaineers from Chattooga County. Enlisted September 25, 1861. Commanded by Captain William L. Groves with 67 men.
Company K—Harris Guards from Harris County. Enlisted July 4, 1861. Commanded by Captain William H. McCullohs with 77 men.[8]

These Georgians would soon realize the benefits of going into combat with a battle-tested leader. Experienced leaders represented a rare commodity among Confederate regiments in the early portion of the war. Edward Lloyd Thomas was born in Clark County, Georgia on March 23, 1825. He descended from the famous Thomas and Lloyd families of Maryland. His grandfather moved from Maryland to Virginia and then to Georgia in the early part of the 19th century. The younger Thomas graduated from Emory College in 1846. He enlisted the following year as a private in a Georgia battalion of mounted volunteers and went to fight in the Mexican War. During this war he received a lieutenant's commission for gallantry under fire. While making a daring charge, the young officer captured Iturbide, the son of a famous Mexican family and member of Santa Anna's staff. The Georgia Legislature commended him for bravery in 1848. The U.S. Army offered him a lieutenancy, but he declined. Instead, he married Jennie Gray who hailed from a prominent Talbot County family. The newlyweds settled on Thomas' plantation near Oxford, Georgia, about thirty-five miles east of Atlanta. He remained there until the outbreak of hostilities in 1861.[9]

The routine of daily drill at Camp Lee quickly grew monotonous for the soldiers in Richmond. Many men wondered when their first taste of battle would come. Eighteen-year-old Private Hiram W. Hammond, of Company E, mentioned in his diary that they relieved boredom by killing rats around the camp area. He also mentioned the five soldiers in his company who died of measles in Richmond.[10] Benjamin Moody, of the same company, expressed a combination of guilt, sadness and remorse when he wrote to his wife from Richmond on October 9:

> [M]y regret is the condishon of our company. [T]hair is 26 of our company sick and 24 of them has got the measules and 2 ded. J.T. Couch and J.M. Giles. [T]hey dide with the relaps of the measules. [O]ne dide this morning at 2 aclock and the other 9 oclock. I will say that I have had meny hard trials but this is one that beets all. [W]hen I think that Just a few days ago I was at home and James Couch was thare agong [a going] to school a harty brisk young man and it appears that I was the sole instegation of his coming outin camps and now hee is ded its all most more than I can bair.[11]

Moody expressed greater optimism in describing Richmond camp life in an October 20 letter:

> We have to lie on the ground and four sleep together under the width of one quilt. We have the nastiest cooking you ever saw and the nastiest arrangement that was ever put up. I do most of our cooking and I am just as nasty as a hog. I shall never be particular about cooking any more. We have potatoes a-plenty. We draw beef and trade them off for potatoes and cabbage and turnips. We have a-plenty to eat. We sometimes draw flour and sometimes draw bread. I am enjoying the best of health myself but the company is most all complaining. Some has the yellow jaundice and some the measles and some the bilious fever.[12]

Many of the men received their first pay as Confederate soldiers on October 31. Private James M. Garrett, from Company D, received $38.93. This broke down to $25 for an initial clothing allowance and $13.93 pay for service of one month and eight days as a private since his enlistment on September 23.[13]

The regiment endured Richmond for several more weeks and then the men suddenly drew three days rations on November 16. They departed the following morning on a northbound train along the Richmond, Fredericksburg and Potomac line. Rumors raced among the men that the regiment was headed to Manassas. The train rattled through Fredericksburg and stopped at Brooks Station, eight miles to the northeast. On November 19,

Boyhood Home of Edward Lloyd Thomas in Oxford, Ga.
Photo by Dennis and Emily Whitcomb of Oxford, Ga.

Company B and several other companies received altered muskets from a local armory at Dumfries to replace weapons carried from home. The other companies of the 35th Georgia also carried converted flintlock muskets, probably issued before they left Richmond.[14] Some of these weapons probably were .69 caliber smoothbore flintlocks altered by gunsmiths to use percussion caps. The Virginia Manufactory in Richmond originally made these weapons under a Virginia state militia contract in 1808. State officials had stored approximately 58,428 of these antiquated flintlocks in various state arsenals. When Confederate authorities seized the arsenals, they sent the flintlocks to gun shops to be retooled.[15]

The soldiers arrived at their new home around November 20. Camp French overlooked the Potomac River near the mouth of Quantico Creek at Evansport, Virginia.[16] Lieutenant Hope H. Roberts, of Company C, described the location of their camp midway between the mouths of Aquia and Occoquan Creeks: "Our camp is near a mile from the banks of the Potomac, surrounded by several large hills which hide us from the view of the enemy, stationed in large numbers, we presume, on the Maryland side of the river."[17] He recorded an avid description of the town of Dumfries located three miles north of their camp: "Every one of these old ruins that can be made to stand at all, is crowded with goods of some description, which are sold by these petty merchants to the soldiers at four times their actual worth: but the better part of Dumfries consists in the hospitals for the accomodation of the sick, which are neatly kept, provided with good nurses and under the direction of first class physicians."[18]

The 35th Georgia joined the brigade of Brigadier General Samuel G. French. Other units assigned to the brigade were the 2nd Arkansas Infantry Battalion; 22nd North Carolina Infantry; 47th Virginia Infantry; 2nd Tennessee Infantry; Braxton's Artillery Battery (Va.); Maryland Flying Artillery Battery; Caroline Light Dragoons (Va); and the Stafford Rangers Cavalry (Va). French's Brigade became part of the division of Major General Theophilus H. Holmes in the Aquia District. Holmes reported to General Joseph E. Johnston, commander of the Department of Northern Virginia.[19]

By the fall of 1861, the Federal army under Major General George McClellan had pulled back within the defensive confines around Washington. He reorganized and refitted the army after their defeat at the Battle of First Manassas in July 1861. The Confederate leadership believed that the Potomac River supply-route to Washington could be cut if they placed artillery batteries along a narrow portion of the river around Evansport. These batteries could shell any ship that attempted to sneak upriver. The depth of the river channel required boats to pass closest to the Confederate side of the river near Evansport. Once Confederate units arrived at Evansport, the Federal government feared they might cross the Potomac by boat and invade the Maryland countryside. Union Major General Joseph Hooker received orders during the last week of October 1861 to move his division toward the river to face this Southern threat. The 1st Massachusetts formed Camp Hooker at Budds Ferry directly across the river from the Confederate batteries at Evansport.

When the 35th Georgia arrived on the Potomac shore, they joined other infantry regiments to provide protection to the long-range batteries stationed at Evansport and at Shipping Point, north of Evansport. These gun crews failed to sink any Federal boats, but they successfully slowed maritime passage to a sporadic crawl. The five-month disruption of supplies to the Federal capital gave a psychological victory to the Confederacy. These Southern shore batteries fell under the combined control of the army and navy. The Federals established long-range batteries on the Maryland side too. Each side lobbed shells the one-and-a-half miles across the water on a frequent basis.

The Georgians established Camp French about one mile west of the Evansport batteries. This distance placed the site out of Federal artillery range. The soldiers initially slept in tents until they constructed winter quarters. They built their winter huts on the western slope of a wooded north-south ridge. This location enabled the men to bask in the longest period of

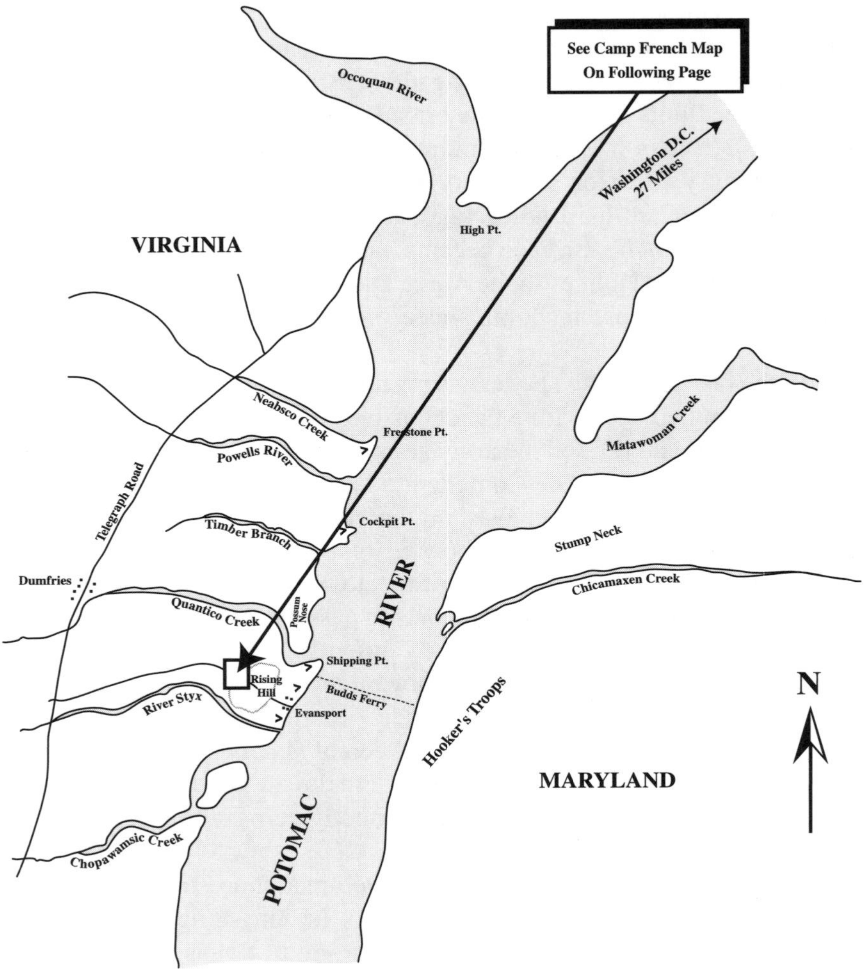

Potomac River Basin Near Camp French at Evansport, VA.

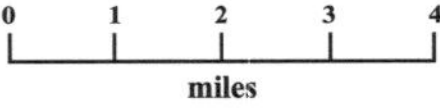

> position of Confederate heavy batteries

warm sunlight each day. Archeological research suggested that Colonel Thomas' men followed military protocol in their hut location. A site survey showed rows of huts extending from a cleared field upslope toward the ridge crest. Each company site comprised two enlisted hut rows. Company streets divided the ten company areas. This spot comprised at least 142 enlisted huts. Three to five enlisted soldiers lived in each structure. In the

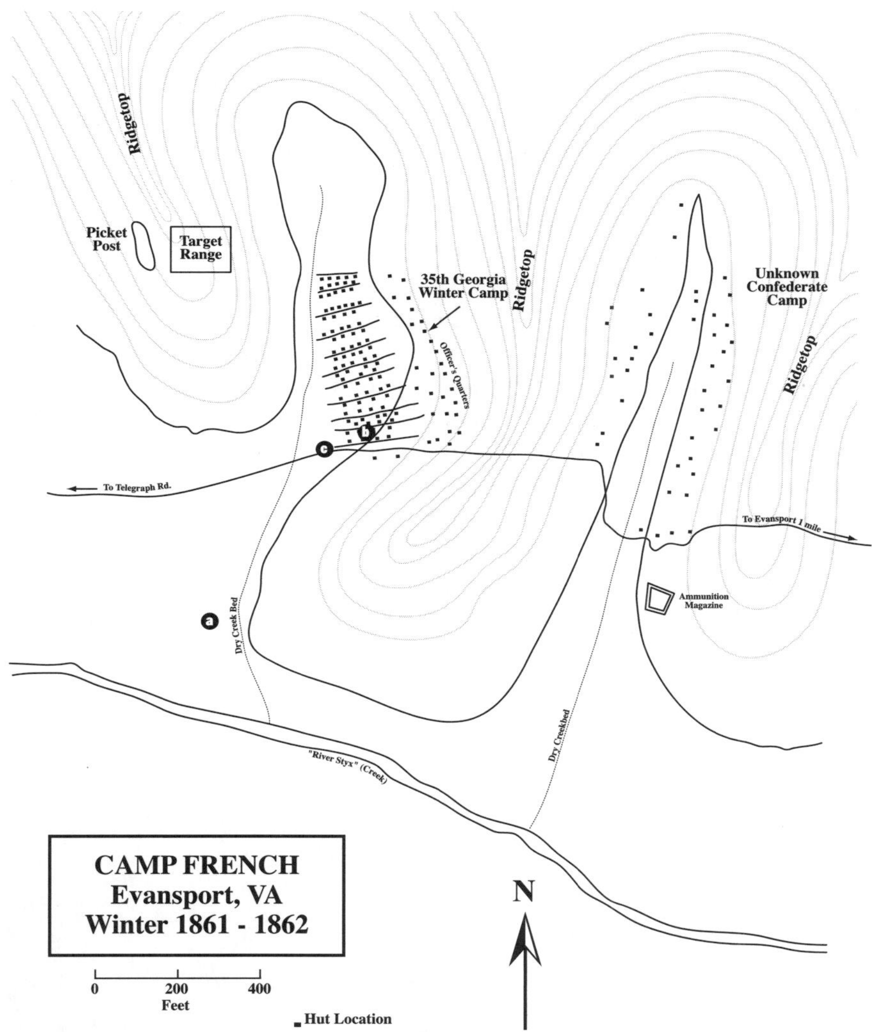

35TH GEORGIA 1861–1862 WINTER ENCAMPMENT AT CAMP FRENCH
Detail for this map courtesy of Joseph Balicki, John Milner Associates, Inc., Alexandria, Va.

woods east of the enlisted huts stood the larger officer's quarters. The road that ran from Evansport west to Telegraph Road bisected Camp French. Another camp rested in the steep valley on the east side from the Georgian's site. This area drained poorly and lacked adequate sunlight. The unknown soldiers in this camp built their huts in no discernible military order. A large 65x50 foot ammunition magazine cut into the steep slope. A drainage ditch surrounded this structure. The magazine stood a few yards south of the road and it separated the officer's and enlisted quarters.

The Camp French target range stood on a hillside west of the 35th Georgia site. A creek, just south of the Georgia area, flowed east to the Potomac. A war map labeled this creek the "River Styx", perhaps a reference to the mythological river that one crossed enroute to Hades.[20]

The unfamiliar and unpredictable Virginia weather created havoc among the Georgians. Illness continued to be a problem as the western winds ushered in the Virginia winter. Some of the men apparently had contracted measles while in camp in Atlanta. This particular illness spread to even more soldiers once the unit arrived in Virginia. The November 1861 regimental muster roll reported 655 enlisted men and 47 officers which totaled 702. The ravages of disease, however, lowered the number present and

a. Camp French at Evansport, Virginia
Looking north toward western slope of ridge. The 35th Georgia winter huts extended from the top of the ridge down into open area in left background.
photo by author

b. 35th Georgia Winter Hut

The western slope of this ridge is full of ground depressions that are the remnants of living quarters for three to four soldiers each. These huts were built into organized company areas. With a little imagination, the reader can picture this typical 12x12 foot hut site. The large tree stands on the left wall while the right wall was located to the right of the medium size tree.

photo by author

fit for duty. The cool weather, crowded living areas and unsanitary waste disposal enabled illnesses to spread. The roll listed 4 officers and 46 enlisted men present but sick. The regiment had left a trail of 6 officers and 108 enlisted men in Confederate hospitals from Richmond to Fredericksburg. Illness had downed twenty-three percent of the 35th Georgia by the end of November and yet conditions would get worse.[21] An ill Benjamin Moody, suffering from fever and diptheria, remained behind at the Soldiers Home in Richmond where ladies from the First Baptist Church tended to him. He wrote his wife from Richmond on November 25, "I have seene more suferin men her[e] then ever I saw before in my life. [T]hair sickness seemes to bee the hardis to git over that ever I saw. [I]t seemes to bee the most fatal. [M]en dies her[e] like sheepe with the rot." He further mentioned that so far five men in Company E had died from disease and many more were ill. He had failed to get a full night sleep in over a week because he was up every two hours administering medicine to Privates John C. Jackson and Berry S. Diggs. Diggs suffered from typhoid fever. Erysipelas, an ugly infectious skin inflammation of the head and neck, afflicted Jackson.[22]

c. Old Roadbed

This view looks east up the western slope of the 35th Georgia winter camp. The bank of the Potomac River stood about a mile away. The soldiers built winter huts on both sides of this road all the way to the top of the slope. The road ran from the Evansport batteries west to Telegraph Road.

photo by author

The weapons issued to the 35th Georgians created another problem. Some of the barrels on the altered muskets exploded when fired, creating injury. Colonel Thomas attempted to use his home-state influence in a letter to Confederate Vice-President Alexander Hamilton Stephens on December 2, 1861. Thomas asked the former U.S. congressman from Georgia for assistance in securing better weaponry for the regiment. He wrote, "I have made application to the Secretary of War to arm my regiment with some improved rifles or muskets. We have been armed with inferior muskets allowed upon the most dangerous and unreliable plan. Brigadier General French has indorsed the application and forwarded to the Secretary of War. The regiment being independent of any action of the Executive of Georgia. We must look to the Confederate government for everything."[23] It was unknown whether Stephens rendered any aid in this matter.

Lieutenant Colonel Gustavus A. Bull revealed the state of readiness in the 35th Georgia from his blunt inspection report of December 31, 1861. In Company D he remarked: "Discipline—Firm; Instruction—Good; Military Appearance—Fair; Arms—Altered Muskets; Accoutrements—Wanting; Clothing—Worn." Bull added more description in outlining the situation in Company E. He reported: "Military Appearance—Good looking men but not in high state of drill; Arms—Altered muskets of dangerous and unreliable style; Accoutrements—No wipors nor screwdrivers."[24]

Companies I and K picketed along the riverbank one night. Word spread among the men that a large enemy vessel, the "Pennsylvania," would try to sneak down the Potomac. As the dark foggy night wore on, the pickets failed to see or hear anything unusual. A short time before daybreak yells erupted from up the riverbank. The large vessel glided silently by under tow of a steam tug. The seconds ticked by and none of the batteries fired a shot. When the tandem of vessels reached the middle battery a cannon erupted. A fusillade of artillery fire followed. Some of the pickets fired their rifle muskets too. A solid shot hit one of the boats at the waterline and the vessels coasted to a stop about a mile below the Georgian's position. This thunder of noise surprisingly failed to bring either the battery commander or General French to the scene. The officer in charge of the guard detail and all the pickets received a reprimand a short time later. The battery's officers were arrested and tried by court martial. It was unknown whether senior officers issued the charges and reprimands because the boats escaped or because the battery and picket detail fired without orders from a senior officer. Lieutenant Colonel Bull, a LaGrange lawyer with a reputation for his oratorical skill, represented the artillerists. He quickly proved their innocence and they received an acquittal.[25]

Aggravating problems continued to mount for the regiment in December 1861. Colonel Thomas' older brother, Captain Lovick P. Thomas, was the quartermaster of the 35th Georgia. His responsibilities included procuring and distributing supplies and payroll to the troops, but many officers expressed dissatisfaction with his performance. The captains of all ten companies petitioned Colonel Thomas on December 10 to get the quartermaster to perform better. All ten captains, obviously unhappy with their colonel's response, breached military protocol on December 19 when they sent a letter that outlined the quartermaster's deficiencies to Confederate Secretary of War Judah P. Benjamin. They claimed that the quartermaster

Captain Lovick P. Thomas, 35th Georgia Quartermaster

He was Edward Lloyd Thomas' older brother. He created significant controversy in December 1861. All ten company commanders wanted him replaced for dereliction of duty. He was wounded at the Battle of Mechanicsville in June 1862 and resigned for a disability in October 1863. He was the father of Colonel Lovick P. Thomas, Jr., 42nd Georgia commander, and the father of Henry "Heck" A. Thomas, who later achieved fame as a U.S. Marshall. The 1970's television show "Hec Ramsey" was based on the postwar exploits of Heck Thomas

From *Sunny South,* Atlanta, Ga. May 2, 1891

had not filed a bond with the Confederate War Office in Richmond. The lack of this bond prevented the men from receiving any pay. "Many of the soldiers are barefoot without overcoats. The soldiers through his neglect are without money and clothes. The want of these things in this climate proves fatal to many." The captains further complained that the regiment did not have any baggage wagons or ambulances. They also claimed that the quartermaster "transacts business slowly and negligently." They asked that the secretary cancel his appointment as quartermaster captain. Colonel Thomas, in a letter to Secretary of War Benjamin on January 2, 1862, defended his brother by claiming that the captain had attempted to file the bond.[26] Judah Benjamin refused to take any action against Captain Thomas as he remained the regimental quartermaster until he resigned for a disability in 1863.

Hiram Hammond expressed his excitement at seeing the enemy for the first time in a diary notation on December 9. "I went on picket last night for the first time in my life and I heard the Yankees on the other side of the River. I went to the River and seen a balloon go up in Yankeedom. I saw the Yankees fire on our batteries." The firing Hammond heard came from a pair of Union gunboats that floated downstream from Washington. These vessels launched a fusillade against the batteries north of Evansport. The boats came close to the Confederate shoreline and perhaps even sent a landing party ashore to torch some storehouses.[27]

The ascent of the balloon tended to draw Confederate artillery fire. Union batteries on the Maryland shore then returned the fire. The records do not reveal any Confederate success in damaging the balloon. The chaplain of the 1st Massachusetts provided a close-up description of the tethered Federal balloon:

> The balloon was one of the largest size, with a handsomely-painted portrait of [George] Washington on the side, and capable of taking up two or three men at once. It was kept constantly filled, and, when raised a thousand feet or so, gave the aeronaut an uninterrupted survey of the enemy's positions, batteries, regiments, motions, forces, and, in fine, every thing a commander desired to know. Powerful glasses were taken up with the balloon, which showed the style of fortifications, the caliber of guns, and the locality of camps four and five miles off.[28]

Benjamin Moody in a letter to his family on December 10 expressed his joy at being well again and back with his comrades in Company E. He wrote, "I am whair I can hair [hear] the lowd canons roer thair fier at each other every day and nite. [L]ast nite thay was firing at a shup [ship] that was tr[y]ing to land and bastid [busted] a canon and broke one mans leg and wounded 3 more."[29] A Confederate cannon apparently exploded while firing at the Union gunboats. This accident injured several cannoneers.

Moody reported that Private Robert McMahan, Company E, died of disease. The men buried McMahan near the camp area at Evansport. The regulations had allowed shipment of dead soldiers back to Georgia accompanied by an escort soldier from the same company. New orders however specified that soldiers bury the body nearby unless a civilian relative came to Virginia to escort the deceased home. This change probably occurred because most units, especially the short-handed 35th Georgia, could not spare men from the front line to escort the dead back home. Moody let his wife know what he thought of this new order. "[I]f I should die I want them to bary mee deacent hear. [D]ue not send mee home."[30]

The Evansport area suited Moody. "I am very well satisfied hear. I think this is a helthey place. I had rather stay hear than richmond. [T]he boyes has fixet winter quarters hear. They have dug in the hill and bilt chimneyes to thair tents."[31] As the holiday season approached Moody's positive spirit contrasted with that of Hiram Hammond who wrote, "This is Christmas and a dull time too. I have just got through the Book of 2nd Chronicles in the Bible. I have eat some Chestnuts today. I have got the heartburn and must roast some corn to eat to cure it."[32]

Moody became a brigade wagoner on December 21. He left for Richmond the following day to get a wagon and team of horses. A week later he returned. He soon reported that the job did not suit him since the wagons never stopped rolling. He never had time to eat and in twenty-five days of driving through snow, sleet and rain he had ruined most of his clothes. The monthly pay he received of $18.50 was better than the $11 per month he had received as an infantry private, but Moody argued that the extra twenty-five cents per day was not worth it. He claimed this was why most of the white wagoners quit.

The first week of the New Year brought several sleet storms that made outside activity difficult. Hiram Hammond reported in his diary that during an arms inspection on Sunday morning, January 5, some of the soldiers took awful falls on the ice. The snow fell that night, and the soldiers had fun the next several days throwing snowballs at each other. The complaints against the quartermaster apparently yielded some results. Hammond helped build stables on January 8 for some mules issued to the regiment. The men of Company E drew overcoats from the quartermaster later that same day. [33]

The 35th Georgia gained notoriety in French's Brigade as the most disease-stricken regiment. French pleaded in a letter, written at the end of December to the Inspector General in Richmond, for more troops to guard the area between Chopawamsic Creek and Aquia Creek. He noted that the 35th Georgia only had 259 privates present for duty.[34] Secretary of War Benjamin addressed this problem when he wrote to their division commander on January 5, 1862. "I cannot further weaken your command, but humanity requires that I should try some way to prevent suffering and mortality among these troops just called from a southern clime and weakened by disease." Benjamin suggested that the 35th Georgia be removed from enemy fire and picket duty until they recovered from the measles and other camp diseases.[35]

Holmes apparently disregarded this request because Colonel Thomas wrote a letter to Benjamin on January 21, 1862, requesting that the 35th be moved to a post where its sick could be helped. He described the hardship of constant duty in the freezing elements. "Two companies from this Regt are organized for picket duty every night so that every officer and enlisted man must be thus exposed every fifth night and in addition to this small details are made daily for the police guard and fatigue duty. The few left able to discharge this duty precludes the possibility of the usual relief on guard duty. Almost invariably after a nights exposure on picket cases of violent sickness commonly attended with pneumonia symptoms arised."[36] Third Sergeant Isham Wallace, Company B, indicated the seriousness of the situation in a letter home the second week of January 1862. "I have nothing good to write to you only the health of hour company is improving after the loss of 7 fine boys. W.R. Owens and J.M. Wallis is in the hospital." The majority of these seven soldiers died from either typhoid fever or the measles. Private William R. Owens recovered from his illness, but Private James M. Wallace did not. James Wallace actually had died from ulceration of the bowels while in a Richmond hospital the day before Isham Wallace penned his letter.[37]

Hammond noted that after battalion drill on January 1, 1862, Company E held an election to replace Corporal John Brock who had died, presumably from disease, at Fredericksburg on December 29. Elisha B. Casey won the election.[38] A month later on February 1, Sergeant James M. Childs and Lieutenant George W. Hammond, of Company E, departed Evansport for Georgia to enlist more soldiers for their depleted company. They returned on March 19 with seven well-needed recruits.[39]

Benjamin Moody mentioned in a letter home dated January 20 that the men of Company E seemed in better health.[40] Moody noted several weeks later that he was sick again and had not left the tent in a week. He said he was trying to take care of himself and "I live on mush and milke when I can get the milk."[41] Then in another letter written five days later that surely must have further alarmed his family he described his worsening condition: "[I]f thair was eny way to get rid of ling [lying] on the ground I mout [might] recover but I dont no whether you wood no me or not if you was to see mee. I looked in the glass and I hardly new my self. [T]hey all told me that I looked bad but I had no thought that looked half as bad as I do."[42] He described the difficult living conditions of privates with a touch of humor. "I have to ly on the ground or the next thing to it. [T]hair is a litle straw lade on the ground and a quilt on that. [I]f you want to no how my bed looks jus lay som straw on the ground and red quilt on it and you can see it and if you want to see my fier [fire] place git som body to dig a hole in the ground and you can see it."[43]

Many soldiers still found ways to have fun and to get into trouble, despite the harsh living conditions in northern Virginia. Those soldiers who had not prepared winter quarters received orders on January 13 to begin construction. That night a heavy snow fell until around noon on January 14 covering the ground with four inches of powder. Hiram Hammond noted: "J.F. Nixon and Myself had a right smart of fun snowballing each other." Abner M. Shirley and John W. Webb celebrated a little too much. The provost marshal tossed the drunken pair into the guard tent for twenty-four hours.[44]

Some items issued by the quartermaster perhaps added to the disorderly conduct. Captain Virgil L. Hopson accepted an order of twenty gallons of whiskey and twenty gallons of molasses on an "Abstract of Extra Issues to the Troops." The last line of this document read, "I certify that the anti-scorbutics were necessary to the health of the troops. . . ." Assistant Surgeon William P. Hill and Colonel Thomas both signed the bottom of this document. The surgeon intended for the anti-scorbutics to prevent scurvy. It was difficult to understand how the whiskey and molasses would prevent scurvy except possibly to enable a soldier who had the disease to temporarily forget about his pain.[45]

A "Statement of Forage for Animals" signed by Captain Lovick P. Thomas in January 1862 revealed that quartermaster responsibilities extended to providing supplies to four-legged animals too. The 35th Georgia had sixteen horses and nine mules plus an additional six horses specifically assigned to the officers of the regimental staff. These six horses, like their officer counterparts, ate better than the regular horses of the regiment. The quartermaster issued 5,592 pounds of corn and 2,145 pounds of hay for the sixteen horses and nine mules. This equaled 224 pounds of corn and 86 pounds of hay per beast. The six regimental staff animals however received 2,160 pounds of corn and 2,790 pounds of hay. This averaged 360 pounds of corn and a whopping 465 pounds of hay per beast. When Hiram Hammond received orders at the beginning of the new year to build a stable for the regimental mules he did not mention if there was any soldierly resentment because the animals had better quarters than some of the men.[46]

Many men expressed feelings of homesickness in their letters sent to wives and children back in Georgia. Benjamin Moody described a sad, but touching dream in a letter to his family written on January 20. In the dream he held his wife's head closely to his breast, but when he awoke he was in his tent wrapped in the same old blankets and Martha's warm head was not there. He did not realize how much he really loved her until then as he burst into tears of sadness and longing. He failed to sleep another moment for the rest of the night.[47]

A heavy snow that began the night of February 2 and continued into the following day provided both joy and hardship. During daylight, Company E snowball battled against four other companies. Hiram Hammond described the difficult picket duty after dark on February 3:

> I had to stand for four hours. J.M. Hammond and myself stood on post together. We went to the tents to stay, stayed there about three hours and then went to the Bombproof. Stayed there the rest of the night. We only had one fireplace for two companys and we fared bad. The countersign was Lynchburg. It snowed and sleeted all night. I did not sleep more than ten minutes all night.[48]

Hammond and several of his friends entertained themselves as they trudged through the snow in search of rabbits for dinner. They failed to find any. On another night, several soldiers held a concert for tips. These men made little money and the rowdy audience nearly tore down their tent. A short time after the concert ended, the ground shook as the nearest battery fired forty to fifty rounds at several schooners headed up the river toward Washington. The next day a schooner passed down the river and then came about and headed past the battery again. The battery fired numerous salvos at the ship forcing its crew to drop her sails, but apparently no direct hits occurred.[49]

Measles struck Frank Edwards, Company D, during mid-February 1862. Doctors sent Edwards to a hospital in Richmond where he convalesced and recovered after about one month. Edwards discovered that Senator Benjamin Harvey Hill was scheduled to speak at the Capitol in Richmond on March 15. Edwards desired to hear the senator because they both called LaGrange home. The ever-resourceful Edwards described how he gained admittance into the Capitol chambers and the events of the night:

> I was not an officer, but I put a little red strip on my collar and in the dark you would have to look the second time to see whether I was an officer. The meeting was at night. I was there, one for Hill from LaGrange, Georgia. Everbody wanted to hear the great orator from Georgia. The great hall was full and overflowing. I considered myself fortunate indeed. Senator Hill arose to make his address; he certainly had the attention of that magnificent body of men. Just at that moment Col. Gus Bull, of LaGrange, and General Pettigrew, of North Carolina, entered the hall. As they arose the officers arose to greet them. The Hon. Alex Stephens was near the speaker's stand. Senator Hill motioned to Mr. Stephens to come over together with

General Joseph Johnston. They whispered together a few moments and then Senator Hill arose and said, 'The program for the present will be changed. Colonel Bull is one of my best counsels, and besides is from LaGrange, Georgia, the dearest spot on earth, my home. You will certainly be entertained.' Colonel Bull arose and said, 'I am certainly unprepared for this occasion.' About that time the whole house arose and cheered for Colonel Bull. Colonel Bull came around to the speaker's stand. It seemed that the building trembled, so great was the uproar in his honor. I desire to say this much for his home people and for the State of Georgia: The speech that he made that night has never been equaled but a very few times, if at all, in the great capitol building of Virginia, and you know some of the nation's greatest orators and statesmen have been reared in Virginia. I never heard such applause as was given Colonel Bull on that occasion. Do you have any conception as to how I felt? I was listening to the Colonel of the Twenty-fifth Georgia Regiment [35th Georgia], of which I was a member.[50]

Edwards liked Bull and freely admitted that the officer was strict, but always fair. He indicated that perhaps Colonel Thomas gave the responsibility for the daily drill and inspections to Lieutenant Colonel Bull. Edwards gave further description of Bull along with another anecdote:

A braver man never lived. One of the best drilled officers in the Army of Northern Virginia, it seemed his whole makeup was one of the greatest military talents. General Joe Johnston on general review at Fredericksburg, Va., in March '62, offered a new dress uniform to the best drilled regiment. The Thirty-fifth Georgia, Colonel Bull's regiment (and mine), won that suit. Colonel Bull was a very strict disciplinarian. He loved his command and we loved Colonel Bull. Though very strict while on duty, you certainly loved the man when off duty. He always cared for his men, to see that they received justice, and you my comrades, know that was lacking in a great many officers.[51]

The poor roads around Camp French made travel difficult. In a letter written on February 20, Lieutenant Hope Roberts recalled:

But the greatest difficulty with which we have to contend, is getting the sick from camps to the hospitals—the great quantity of rain and snow that has fallen during the last two months, and then the amount of transportation necessary for the use of the army combined, have rendered the roads almost impassable, though I trust ere long we will have no further use for hospitals, as the health of the Regiment

> is rapidly improving. Certainly we have had our proportionment of sickness; for today as I look out from my tent, my heart is sad when I behold upon a neighboring hill those rude pens marking the graves of so many departed Georgians.[52]

Benjamin Moody no doubt feared the "neighboring hill" might soon become his final resting place as he battled illness that would not let him loose. He decided to prepare his wife and four children for this possibility.

> "[T]he god of all the earth will doo rite by mee. I want you to not greeve a bout mee for I am in the hands of the lord and you no what I have often told you that the Lord has something for mee to doo and I beeleeve that I shall doo that work. [I]t may bee that it is his will that I should doo that worke on the Potomac river yet a killin yankeys. [R]est easy about mee. [I]f I should die hear I am just as clost to heavin hear as eny whair else and I am willin to die if it is the lords will.

He closed the letter with several missives for his children:

> To Robert you must bee a good boy and above all things obey your Mothers instructions and try to gane a good name at sch[o]oll and mind your teecher and git your lesons good and hurry home from scoole of a eavning and git wood cut to do all next day and lurn to do like a man for you dont no how soone you may have no father to instruct you and I want you to remember this. [T]o Comelar I have confidence to beleeve that you will doo rite. Lizy I no you air bad but I hope you will com of it whin you git older. Daniel I hope you will quit your bad wais [ways] and bee a good boy. [F]ar[e]well to all my famley if I never see you agan.[53]

Eighteen-year-old James Garrett provided more insight into camp life in several letters written to his mother in February 1862. "There is lots of Yankees on the other side of the river. [W]e can see their tents. I dont think they have a notion of attacking us at this place." He requested that she make a jeans coat for the upcoming summer and a dress coat because his present one appeared worn.[54] He wrote another letter a week later and mentioned to his widowed mother that he would send her twenty dollars. The eldest of five siblings, Garrett wanted to send as much money home as possible. Confederate soldiers normally received pay every two months. A private earned $11 per month. He reported: "It is raining tonight. [T]o morrow night will be our picket night. We go every 5 nights. [I]t rained all night last picket. [T]he night I had to stand four hours in the rain it was the darkest night I have ever seen." He described the table fare in optimistic terms.

Private James Marion Garrett, Co. D
The Stroud family's gift of copies of Garrett's letters started this project. Garrett was a Heard County native. This twenty-one-year-old was shot in the chest and hip at the Battle of Spotsylvania Court House on May 12, 1864. He died three days later and was buried near a field hospital. Years later the Confederate bodies buried in the area were disinterred and reburied at Spotsylvania Confederate Cemetery.
Courtesy of Dian Stroud, Columbus, Ga.

"[W]e get plenty of fresh beef to eat now and some salt to go with it. [W]e have coffee knight and morning and biscuits every morning." Shoes cost $5–$10 per pair. He found this expensive and asked his mother to send him a pair of " . . . large sixes or small sevens."[55]

On March 3, Hiram Hammond and three other soldiers struggled to help an artillery crew drag cannons through the mud to new positions. They labored from 6 P.M. until 4 A.M. in the darkness and driving rain. The temperature dropped in the early morning gloom. Icicles hung a quarter inch off the gun muzzles at sunrise.[56]

Passing Federal gunboats lobbed an occasional shell into the camp area. Soldiers scurried for cover when this happened. Camp life otherwise consisted of drill and picket duty, writing letters, playing cards, chopping firewood, hunting and avoiding exposure to sickness. Sometimes excitement came in an unusual way. Sergeant Isham Wallace noted in a letter in February 1862, "[I] have had a hard time for the last two weeks. 2 days after [I] got you're an[d] Johnthen letter the old man [I] was a liven was a foolin with a pistel and shot him self and mite of dide if [I] had not got to him in stop the bleedin."[57]

The monotony of camp along the banks of the Potomac River would be short lived. These same soldiers would soon be complaining of the long marches up and down the Virginia peninsula southeast of Richmond in search of McClellan's army as they anticipated their first real clash with the enemy.

Notes

Abbreviations:

CSR—"Compiled Service Records of Confederate Soldiers Who Served In Organizations From The State of Georgia," Thirty-fifth Infantry Regiment (National Archives Microfilm Publication M266) National Archives Building, Washington, D.C.

GDAH–Georgia Division of Archives and History, Morrow, Ga.

NMP–National Military Park

OR.—*War of the Rebellion: A Compilation of the Official Records of the Union and Confederate Armies.* 130 Vols.

1. Letter of E.L. Thomas to "Hon. L.P. Walker from Richmond, August 1, 1861," located in "Letters Received by Confederate Secretary of War 1861–65," (National Archives Microfilm Publication M437) roll #6, 2631–3130, July-Aug 1861, item 2780–1861. National Archives, Washington, D.C.
2. W.T. Irvine, *The Sunny South,* Atlanta, May 2, 1891, "Old 35th Georgia."
3. Letter of James T. McElvany to "Dear Mr. Dickson, Loganville, Ga Feb 25, 1861," located in "The Letters and Journal of Major James T. McElvany, Co.D, 35th Georgia Infantry Regiment."
4. Mills Lane, ed., *Dear Mother: Don't Grieve About Me. If I Get Killed, I'll Only Be Dead,* (Savannah, Ga. 1977) Letter of Benjamin F. Moody, "Dear Wife and Children from Richmond, Va. October 20, 1861." This is the only Moody letter in Lane's book. It appears with proper spelling and punctuation and I assume that Lane cleaned the letter up before publication. This letter does not appear with the rest of the Moody letters at the GDAH.
5. James E. Garman, "Bibliographical Material, Georgia CSA Units," 1960, located at GDAH; Irvine; *Southern Confederacy,* Atlanta, October 31, 1861. Note: W.T. Irvine in *The Sunny South,* Atlanta, May 2, 1891, "Old 35th Georgia," made reference to

these seven companies being called the 25th Georgia Battalion of Infantry. I think Irvine was either wrong or this was a typo in the article as I could find no other reference to this unit designation.

6. *OR.,* Vol.51, Part II, p.347.
7. Letter of Col. E.L. Thomas to "Mr. President, Atlanta Ga., October 26th, 1861," located in "Letters Received by the Confederate Secretary of War 1861–65," (National Archives Microfilm Publication M437) Roll 17, item 8040–1861, numbers 7921–8277, Nov.-Dec. 1861, National Archives, Washington, D.C.
8. Lillian Henderson, *Roster of the Confederate Soldiers of Georgia 1861–1865,* Vol.III, (Hapeville, Ga., 1960) p.843–929; Irvine; *CSR.*.
9. *Atlanta Journal,* Atlanta, March 10, 1893.
10. Hiram W. Hammond, "Confederate Diary of Pvt. Hiram Warner Hammond, private, Co.E, 35th Georgia Regiment Volunteers."
11. Letter of Benjamin F. Moody, "Dear Wife and Children from Richmond, Va. October 9, 1861," Benjamin F. Moody Folder, Civil War Miscellany, Personal Papers (Record Group 57–1–1) , GDAH. All of these letters are copied with the original spelling and lack of punctuation except I added periods at the end of sentences for clarity.
12. Lane. (Moody Letter)
13. CSR.
14. Philip Katcher, *The Army of Robert E. Lee.* (London, 1994) p.219.
15. Time-Life Books, *Echoes of* Glory*: Arms and Equipment of the Confederacy.* (Alexandria Va., 1991) p.33.
16. CSR. (Also on file GDAH). This area is present day Quantico, Va.
17. *Southern Confederacy,* Atlanta, February 12, 1862, Letter of Lt. Hope H. Roberts to "Editors, Southern Confederacy from the 35th Georgia Regiment, Camp French, Evansport Va., February 6th, 1862.
18. Ibid.
19. *OR..,* Vol.5, p.1031.
20. Warren H. Cudworth, *History of the First Regiment (Mass. Infantry)* (Boston, 1866) p.96&103; Joseph Balicki, "Camp French: Confederate Winter Quarters Supporting the Potomac River Blockade," 2003. This archeological paper was prepared by Joe Balicki of John Milner Associates, Inc., Alexandria, Va.—Note: Balicki contacted me with his information when he heard of my project. He and Bryan Corle were kind enough to give me an informative tour of the well preserved winter camp site at Camp French located at present day Quantico Marine Corps Base. Fortunately, Balicki and the Marine authorities are working to preserve Camp French as a permanent interpretive historical site. Balicki believed that Colonel Edward L. Thomas followed the *Revised Regulations for the Army of the United States* (1861) which diagrammed and directed the formation of a regimental camp. Balicki stated that two other nearby camps that fell under Confederate army leadership followed a similar pattern. He suggested that the disorganized pattern of the site just east of the 35th Georgia area was perhaps because that unit fell under Confederate navy command.
21. "Compiled Service Records- Captions and Records of Events," Thirty-fifth Georgia Infantry Regiment. National Archives Building, Washington, D.C. Also on microfilm at GDAH.

22. Letter of Benjamin F. Moody, "Dear wife and children from Richmond, Va. November 25, 1861," Moody Folder, GDAH.
23. Letter from E.L.Thomas to "A.H.Stephens from Evansport, Va. December 2, 1861," Alexander Hamilton Stephens papers, Special Collections Department, Robert W. Woodruff Library, Emory University, Atlanta, Ga.
24. "Compiled Service Records—Captions and Records of Events," National Archives.
25. Irvine. Note: Warren Cudworth, the chaplain of the 1st Massachusetts, described a similar incident on January 12, 1862, but he claimed the boat was named "Pensacola." See Warren H. Cudworth's *History of the First Regiment (Massachusetts Infantry),* (Boston, 1866) p.120–121. Mary Alice Wills in her book *The Confederate Blockade of Washington, D.C. 1861–1862* p. 112–115 described the successful passage of the large three-masted U.S.S. Pensacola in the foggy early morning hours. The ship passed the Confederate batteries at Cockpit Point without detection. Once the Pensacola and her escorts reached Shipping Point and Evansport the Confederate batteries fired numerous rounds. Irvine's description was probably of the Pensacola and he simply misnamed the boat Pennsylvania.
26. Letter from Officers of 35th GA to "Sec of War, Camp French Evansport, VA., Dec. 19, 1861," located in "Letters Received by the Confederate Secretary of War 1861–65," (National Archives Microfilm Publication M437) Roll 20, item 8966–9250, Dec 1861–Jul 1862, National Archives Building, Washington, D.C.; Letter of Col. E.L. Thomas to "Sec'y of War J.P. Benjamin Richmond, Va. January 2, 1862," located in "Letters Received by the Confederate Secretary of War 1861–65," (National Archives Microfilm Publication M437) Roll 20, item 8966–9250, Dec 1861–Jul 1862) National Archives Building, Washington, D.C..
27. Hammond; Cudworth, p.112.
28. Mary Alice Wills, *The Confederate Blockade of Washington, D.C. 1861–1862.* (Parsons, W.Va.., 1975) p.132–133; Ibid., Cudworth, p.99.
29. Letter of Benjamin F. Moody "Dear wife and children from Camp French near Evansport, Va. December 10, 1861," Moody Folder, GDAH.
30. Ibid.
31. Ibid.
32. Hammond.
33. Letter of Benjamin F. Moody "Dear Family from Evansport, Va. January 20, 1862," Moody Folder, GDAH; Hammond.
34. *OR..,* Vol.5, p.1013.
35. Ibid., p.1020.
36. Letter of Edw L Thomas to "Hon. J.P. Benjamin Sec of War from Col 35th Ga Regt, Evansport Jan 21st, 1862," located in "Letters Received by the Confederate Secretary of War 1861–65," (National Archives Microfilm Publication M437) Roll 20, item 8966–9250, Dec 1861–Jul 1862, National Archives Building, Washington, D.C.
37. Letter of Sgt Isham Wallis to "Mr. Anderson Owens from Camp French Evansport, Va 1/13/1862," Minnie Robertson Smith Collection, AC 33–031, Folder 5–06, GDAH.
38. Hammond.
39. Ibid.
40. Moody letter, January 20, 1862; Hammond.

41. Letter of Benjamin F. Moody "Dear wife and children from Evansport, Va. February 9, 1862," Moody Folder, GDAH.
42. Letter of Benjamin F. Moody "Dear wife and children from Evansport, Va. February 14, 1862," Moody Folder, GDAH.
43. Ibid.
44. Hammond.
45. CSR.
46. Ibid.
47. Moody letter, January 20, 1862.
48. Hammond
49. Ibid.
50. John Frank Edwards, *Army Life of Frank Edwards—Confederate Veteran–Army of Northern Virginia 1861–1865.* (1906) p.3–5.
51. Ibid., p.5
52. *Southern Confederacy,* Atlanta, February 1862, Letter of Lt. Hope H. Roberts to "Editors, Southern Confederacy from the 35th Georgia Regiment, Camp French, Evansport Va. The author has scoured his notes and apologizes for not being able to find the exact day in February 1862 this article was published. Since Roberts' letterhead date is February 20, 1862 the publication date in the *Southern Confederacy* would be at the very end of the month.
53. Moody letter, February 14, 1862.
54. Letter of James M. Garrett to "Dear Mother from Camp French, Feb. the 20th 1862," James M. Garrett Collection.
55. Letter of James M. Garrett to "Dear Mother from Camp French Evansport Va Feb. the 26th 1862," James M. Garrett Collection.
56. Hammond.
57. Letter of Isham Wallis to "Der Brother an Sister February 12 1862," Minnie Robertson Smith Collection, AC 33–031, Folder 5–06, GDAH.

Chapter Two

Initiation at Seven Pines

"I believe it to bee your dewty to be whare you are."
Martha Moody to her husband, Private Benjamin Moody

The Confederate defense line extended from the Occoquan Creek northwest to Centreville and then further north to Leesburg by winter's end 1862. Word had leaked to Joseph E. Johnston that George McClellan planned to leave a portion of his force to guard Washington, and the remainder of the Federal army would slip away by boat down the Chesapeake Bay. McClellan's troops would then attack northwest along the Virginia Peninsula and try to seize Richmond. Johnston also feared that the Federal army might cross the Potomac River and move west along Potomac Creek toward Fredericksburg. The Confederate commander responded by ordering an initial troop withdrawal from the banks of the Potomac on the morning of March 7, 1862.

This move made Captain Lovick P. Thomas a very busy man. As the quartermaster, he had to line up wagons and horse and mule teams to carry all the regimental equipment. The 35th Georgia additionally had received a large amount of provisions to cover the period from March 1–18. The list of provisions signed for by the commander, Colonel Edward Thomas, read as follows:

5,877 rations of beef
2,155 rations of bacon
4,807 rations of flour
3,204 rations of meal
6,710 rations of rice
1,326 rations of beans
4,017 rations of coffee
5,348 rations of sugar
6,717 rations of candles

4,017 rations of soap
12,042 rations of salt
2,690 rations of vinegar
1,617 rations of hard bread

Soldiers normally received three days rations prior to a march. Everything out of the above supply not previously issued or used would need to be carried by wagon or else abandoned.[1]

The 35th Georgia left Evansport around 5:30 A.M. on March 8. Hiram Hammond wrote about the twelve-mile march that day. "I am very sore and tired toating my knapsack."[2] The next day the Georgians continued their trek and bivouacked about three miles from Fredericksburg. They remained in the Fredericksburg area for just over one month.

Excitement raced through the Union ranks, camped near the Maryland shore, when they realized the Confederates had abandoned their lines. Union soldiers flocked to the Potomac riverbank to watch the smoke and flames roll skyward as the last Confederates torched the shelters and unused supplies. Chaplain Warren H. Cudworth, 1st Massachusetts, wrote, "The whole country, for miles up and down the Potomac, and far back to the rear, seemed to be in a perfect uproar. Every thing burnable was set on fire, guns spiked, gunpowder blown up; and soon dense volumes of smoke arose from all the camps, showing that they too had been fired and deserted. For over two hours, loud explosions were heard in the direction of this burning property, indicating that magazines and barracks were sharing the same fate." When Confederate soldiers exploded the Camp French ammunition magazine, the force of the blast ripped the northwest corner off. Bricks and artillery fragments rained down all over the area.

Teams of Union soldiers loaded into boats and crossed the river. They found sixteen heavy guns at Shipping Point. Closer inspection revealed that three of these guns were logs disguised to fool Federal balloonists. The Confederate gunners had previously spiked or burst their large guns and equipment. Federal scouting parties then moved inland and searched all the areas around Camp French.

Cudworth derided the uncivilized conditions found in the "Rebel" camps:

> They [Federals] found and brought away a considerable quantity of regimental papers and private letters, which were in hurry left scattered about the rebel quarters. The papers, for the most part, were poorly kept, and showed both a lax state of discipline among the troops, and gross ignorance on the part of officers. The private letters were of all descriptions, from almost illegible scrawls, with all

> the rules of grammar and spelling set at defiance, to delicate missives on gilt-edged paper, or verbose documents with rabid changes rung on the prevailing sentiment, 'Death to the Yankees!'.

Items left behind in the well-supplied Confederate camps at Evansport revealed the inhabitants had made a hasty departure. "The deserted camps were found supplied with every thing needed for winter quarters. The houses were built of logs, with floors and roofs of board, some having glazed windows; and one actually green blinds. Their cooking arrangements were on the most liberal scale; and utensils good as to quality, and plentiful in quantity; but houses, beds and every thing else, in fact, were filthy to the last degree." The Massachusetts soldiers gathered many war souvenirs during their inspection:

> Trophies of every conceivable variety were brought to camp, from a litter of bloodhound pups to a hundred and twenty-eight pound shell. Toothbrushes, buttons, Bibles, blankets, candy, tobacco, Underwood's Boston pickles, Ames's North Easton shovels and spades, wheelbarrows, chairs, camp stools, powder flasks, shot, gun sights, cap boxes, came over by the boat load. The Rebel camps were abundantly supplied with every thing needed for creature comfort; and if they had been neat or clean, and laid out with proper regularity, would have been very creditable to their late occupants; but they were filled with vile odors. The houses were infested with vermin, damp, and black with smoke; and most of our men would sooner sleep on the ground than in one of them.

Chaplain Cudworth continued: "The rebels seemed to have lived on the fat of the land. Beef, pork, flour, bread, salt, coffee, &c., were found among their stores, not to mention whiskey, and a large case of candy. In one instance, a table had just been set for dinner, the meat was already cut, and the cakes by the fire, showing, that from that place the occupants were in too much of a hurry to get away to stop for a lunch. The company rolls and morning reports of regiments showed that there had been great mortality among the men."

One Union captain found a large supply of fine boats along the banks of Quantico Creek. He sadly reported the Confederates had drilled holes or sawed the boat hulls in two. Cudworth reported discovery of a macabre hiding place for supplies:

> While pursuing their tasks, the members of the First [Massachusetts] came across numbers of graves. They were laid out in streets, carefully labeled, and contained pathetic remonstrances against disturbing the repose of the dead, and violating the sanctity of the tomb, so

> that suspicions were engendered that the sacred dead might be brought to life again, and made to see a little more service under the sun. Spades and shovels were accordingly brought into requisition; and speedily were exhumed, not the bodies of departed Confederates, but numbers of nice new tents, packages of clothing, mess-chests furnished with all the appliances of modern cookery, trunks of various articles, tools, &c. The grave diggers were complimented for the success of their first sacrilegious experiment, and recommended to try again.[3]

The men of the 35th Georgia received a new brigade commander at Fredericksburg. Brigadier General James Johnston Pettigrew, of North Carolina, replaced Samuel French at the end of March. Benjamin Moody reported the popularity of Pettigrew with the men. Some of the Georgians seemed glad to be finished with Brigadier General French.[4] Theophilus H. Holmes transferred to a command on the North Carolina coastline on March 22. Major General Gustavus W. Smith took over Holmes' Division.

Moody wrote a letter assessing the leadership qualities of some of his immediate officers. He apologized for his penmanship because he scribbled with a broom straw pen. The average soldier participated in numerous drills and became quite familiar with the stamina, fortitude and leadership skills of their officers. Moody felt confident following Captain Evan Riley Whitley, the Company E commander. "[W]e have got a captain that will doo in the time of batol [battle]. [H]ee will not flinch when the game is faling and that is the man for mee." In describing Colonel Edward L. Thomas, Lieutenant Colonel Gustavus A. Bull, and the regimental surgeon James P. Hambleton, Moody wrote: "I think also that wee have got a Kenuel [Colonel] that will due to tie to and our Lieutenant Kenuel is a mity crabie sort of a man but I thinke moore of him than eny of the staf oficers. Wee have got a meene doctor for a surgeon of the Regiment. [H]e gits drunk and you no that dont suit me."[5]

Colonel Thomas sent a letter concerning his two surgeons to the Confederate Adjutant & Inspector General's Office on March 13. The Georgia commander worried about the continued disability of Surgeon James P. Hambleton and Assistant Surgeon Peter E. Jennings. What part the doctor's drinking, referenced by Private Moody, played in this letter was unknown. Illness continued to plague both doctors and eventually forced their resignations by the close of 1862.[6]

Lieutenant Colonel Bull led a company drill in a steady rain on March 15. Benjamin Moody reported on March 24 that the men anticipated turning in their tents. He expected the quartermaster would issue smaller French tents the men could easily carry. Moody complained that his company would only be allowed to have four "messes" because of the small amount of cooking equipment available. The soldiers drilled three times a day: 8 A.M., 1 P.M., and 4 P.M. Moody disliked this schedule because it gave him little time to cook his food which he indicated for the time was plentiful. "[W]ee have a plenty of beef to cooke but you no I dont love it but it is the best beef I ever saw. [I]t is fed on corn and kepes [keeps] fat." Then in the next sentence he reflected on the shortages at home when he wrote: "I wish you had a quarter of it and my part of the cofey [coffee]. [W]e hant [haven't] drawed money yet but wil in a few days I thinke and then you must by you som cofey for sonday morning and I want you to by you $50.00 of shugar [sugar] and eny other thing you need. [I]f I cant be with you I want you to have just what you want." He decided to try to get his old wagoner job back for the higher pay. "I think I will take the wagon a gan [again] now as the winter is broke. I think I can stand it now and $18.50 is better than $11.00. [T]he od dollars wood pay the scooling of our children." Moody, ever romantic and lonely for his wife, ended the letter: "[G]ood by my lovely wife. [I]f I could see you I would kis your sweet lips a thousand times."[7]

Lieutenant George W. Hammond brought excitement to Company E on March 19 when he returned to camp with seven raw recruits from Campbell County, Georgia. Johnston Pettigrew marched the four infantry regiments of his brigade to a large field for drill on March 27. Edward Thomas drilled all ten companies of the 35th Georgia on April 5.[8]

Benjamin Moody became so proficient at cooking meals and washing clothes that he made a promise to his wife that must have pleased her. "I have bin washing my close [clothes] and I am a very good hand at the business. [Y]ou ot [ought] to see mee wash when I am well before I will pay 10 cents a garment. I washed 3 peeres [pairs] for Isah to day and when I git home I never will see you wash a nother time when you air not able neither shal you cook when you air not able to doo. I think that I will doo a heeper [heep] things when I com home."[9]

Moody expected a fight soon near their position at Fredericksburg. He reported that many soldiers believed when the battle started neutral Maryland would join the Southern cause. "I believe that when the yankeys leaves the other side of the river that Meriland [Maryland] will seceed and send her troops in the rear and help us whip the rasklers [rascals]. [T]hair a grate meny Meriland troops on our side and thay say that if thair state cood say so its self it would bee in our faver."[10] He wrote twelve days later that 65,000 Yankees advanced toward Fredericksburg and the Georgians still expected a fight. He expressed remorse to his wife that he had failed to write a last will and testament prior to his enlistment. In this difficult letter he described how he wanted his property divided if he died in battle or

Captain George Washington Hammond, Co.E
The Campbell County native was elected captain in January 1863 and resigned for illness five months later
Courtesy of Carl Summers, Jr. West Point, Ga.

from sickness. He acknowledged that this letter was not legally binding, but it would have to suffice.[11]

Moody expressed concern about his family's spiritual salvation as well as his own. He found it difficult to lead a clean Christian life while in camp:

> [T]hair is no one that can tell how thankful I feel to my kind maker for this kind faver he has shone mee in restoring mee to good helth agane tho I feel that I have his faver not that I am so rahios [righteous] tho I try to live as nere rite as I can. I can say that it is hard for a man to live in the discharge of his duty in camps. I hear at this time good spirtional [spiritual] sing and the sound of the railers and by looking a cros the street I cood see the gamblers plaing cards and various other sounds. [A] man may contend aganst improper conduct hear and thair is som that will becom afendid [offended] at him

> but I try to live so that my conduct will coreyspond with my perfeshon [profession]. I am cald a babptist [baptist] very often by strangers. I think that I can live rite hear if I will stach [stay ?] close against the evvil dooers. I dont want you to think that I am werthey to have prair for I feel as unwerthy as eny man on erth can. I no that I am a sinful beeing tho it grieve mee more now then it ever did before. I see so much sin hear that my own sines [sins] looke larger and worse than thay ever did before. I want to live so that I can have a clear conciene [conscience] but that is hard to doo hear.

He beseeched his wife to keep teaching the Bible to their four children:

> I want my childrin taught the scriptiers. I may never see them agane and if I dont I want to meet them in heaven whair parting will bee no more. [W]hair thair will bee no more wors [wars]. [W]hair Christ setith [sitteth] on the rite hand of the father.

Moody felt lonely and upset because there was nobody that he could speak with in camp about spiritual matters. He apparently could not or did not speak with Chaplain George W. Yarbrough. It was not known whether Yarbrough was absent or ill or Moody felt uncomfortable talking with the chaplain. Some of his fellow soldiers ridiculed Moody for his beliefs. He expressed frustration because when these spiritual matters came up, too many men made light of them and claimed "all things are fair in wars." He further scoffed at the notion that "[T]hair is a belief hear that if a man dies in the servis [service] of his country that his sole [soul] is safe and thus [this] is most comlly [commonly] believed and it is hard to convince them other wise. [T]hay tell mee that I will steeal and doo as others doo." He lamented the accusation that Christians sin in secret.[12]

The soldiers of the 35th Georgia marched northward with the rest of Pettigrew's Brigade early on April 7. The rain poured down as they crossed the Rappahannock River and slogged through the mud. Five miserable miles later the column halted. The men received orders to pitch tents. Twenty-four-year-old Lieutenant William C. Goggans, of Company A, wrote: "We continued our March through the day though owing to the inclemency of the weather we made but little progress. [A]rrived in four miles of the expected enemy when we taken up camp lying up on the cold and frozen woods With but few tents, and the bad clothes."[13] The enemy they hoped to meet had retreated northward. The next morning the Southerners struck their tents and marched back to their old camp near Fredericksburg. "We got to our camps at half past 4 A.M. and it set in to snowing and sleeting. The ground is perfectly white. It is verry rough time on us."[14]

Moody exhibited frustration too. "[W]ee felt much disappointed for wee was in hops [hopes] wee wood git a licke at them but the soldiers went out to meet the enmy singing and haling so that the curinel [colonel] had to stope them from it but as wee returned every man looked sad and not a holow [holler] was heard from our [men?] as we marched threw Fredericksburg. [W]ee was hailed by meny ladys and ofton hurd the sound of ladye voies [voices]." Some men circulated a rumor that the army would abandon Fredericksburg and move southward to Ashland. Moody disagreed with the idea because it would abandon fifty more miles of Virginia to the enemy.[15]

Moody made an uncannily accurate prediction; however, he would not live to see his prescience come true. The farmer-turned-soldier wrote on April 9: "I hope this war will end in a bout 3 years from now and not before. I thinke it will last as long as Linkon [Lincoln] is in office." He closed this letter by urging his wife to send him an ambrotype photograph of herself. "I want to see you and the childrin the worst I ever did. [O]fton when I wake up in the nite the tiers steeles down my cheake and some times I open my pockit book and looke in it to see the peace [piece] of hair that you sent mee and it is som satisfaction to mee but when I think of the caus that promped me to leeve you it creats courage in mee and I think that I can fite harder then eny body else."[16]

The rumor of a move south from Fredericksburg proved valid. Lieutenant Goggans revealed that Company A marched into Fredericksburg for city guard duty on April 11. The rest of the 35th Georgia joined them two days later. "We have again sent off a part of our baggage expecting to moove soon, our troops are being sent away by the thousand to Yorktown, The dispatches are that there is a fight in progress there." Goggans continued, "[W]e have all our sick out of camps. [T]hose that are unable to bear their knapsacks to the Railroad are sent off." The infirmed in his company had moved to Richmond except Privates Colvin Rowell and William A. Smith. These two men remained in a Fredericksburg hospital because of their weakened condition. Moody recorded the seriousness of Rowell's condition. Rowell died exactly two weeks later. Smith passed away two days after Rowell. The young Goggans found himself in a similar predicament just as the troops began to move toward Yorktown. Doctors ordered the young officer admitted to "an old desolated Hospital."[17]

Most soldiers expressed relief when they boarded the train. The cars rattled southward and arrived at Ashland, Virginia around 10 P.M. The town of Ashland stood twenty miles north of Richmond. Lieutenant Goggans' illness did not prevent him from making the trip because he recorded the uncomfortable train ride. "This was a very unpleasant trip though. [O]n the cars we were so crowded that a man could scarcely live." When the engine belched to a stop at the Ashland depot the troops stretched sore muscles and then marched to a camp about a mile from the town.[18]

Goggans astutely realized the tactical advantage of the railroads. "[O]ur force have given back and left a long scope of country in the eastern part of the state, The cars are running powerful a long the Fredricksburg and Richmond R. Road yesterday and to day. I will know [now] give you my opinion Relative to the Retreat. I learn that the Enemy are making a desperate re sistance with a force of two hundred thousand men. [I]n the Evacuation of this scope it will greatly strengthen our Army on the difirent Rail Roads so that the force can be run in event an attack is made."[19]

A rumor swirled through the Ashland camp that the regiment would leave in a few hours and start a march all the way to Yorktown—a distance of about 60 miles. Goggans reported, "[I]t will be a long march, but every train is crowded and all conveyance occupied so it is necessary to march." He recalled an order that drew a few chuckles among the men. "Our general has just sent in a laughable order but a very appropriate one that is as follows. [E]very man shall wash his feet without fail to knight, when expecting a march that is ever necessary to prevent blistering and sore feet." The young lieutenant made an accurate forecast at the end of one of his letters to his father: "[D]o not fail to write by our mooves for I look for us to be on the trot through the summer."[20]

The Georgians started a march toward Richmond on April 16. They reached the Confederate capital the next day. The men received three days rations of crackers and bacon.[21] Two days later, the soldiers marched to the docks at Rocketts Landing on the James River. They boarded boats bound for Yorktown to assist Major General John B. Magruder in the defense of the Virginia Peninsula. McClellan began massing his Federal army at Fortress Monroe on March 23. The Georgians reached the Yorktown area on April 19. Hammond noted in his diary on the same day, "We struck up the line of march this morning, marched about a mile and a half, went into entrenchments, stayed there about 6 or 8 hours and fell back about a mile and camped. There has been a great deal of bombardment going on today. We are in 3 or 4 miles of Yorktown. One of my legs has nearly given out." The following day they retraced their steps to the entrenchments and sent men forward of the main line on picket duty.[22]

On the following night the men scrambled into line of battle and waited. To their front lay a dense swampy forest:

> [W]ee was ling [lying] in the diches [ditches] last Sonday nite when an alarme broke out amungst the North Carolinens and they comenced firing and our rigement [regiment] all so and it continued

> on threw the hole brigad. [S]um fired 4 rounds befor thair pickets got in and thair was one killed and one wounded. [A]nd I dont no how eny escaped. I was a sleepe when the firing comenced and I got in the ditch in time to fire to. I saw the fireing as it com up the line and it looked like a streeke of fire or mor like litning.

The North Carolinians belonged to the 22nd North Carolina. Friendly fire struck and killed Private William Overby of Company H, 35th Georgia. The same fire wounded Private William J. Turner of Company B.[23]

Moody further elaborated on the situation in the same letter: "[T]imes is hard hear at this time. [W]e have nothing but bread and meete [meat] to eat. [T]hair is so meny men hear thay cant hall [haul] evry thing wee need. [W]e have got no tents hear to doo us eny good. [T]hay sent them off from hear. [W]hen wee left ashland wee left all wee had but 2 suits of under cloes [clothes] and 1 pair of pants and 1 blanket so as to make our lod [load] as lite as possible." Hiram Hammond reported that some of the men did have small open-ended tent flies for protection.[24]

Moody expressed surprise that a letter his wife wrote from Georgia took only five days to reach him in Virginia. He urged her to write every week and then described the Peninsula area of Virginia. "[T]his is a bad place to fite. [T]he pinenciler [Peninsula] is just like a swampe. [I]n fact it is a swamp and if we fight hear it will be mosley [mostly] small arm or artilery canonading."[25]

Boats laden with Federal troops and supplies continued to arrive and empty their holds. This massive reinforcement effort gave McClellan an advantage of 105,000 troops to Johnston's 60,000 Confederates. The Federal force additionally had superiority in naval, field and siege artillery. This situation demanded the Confederate withdrawal that commenced toward Richmond after dark on May 2. The Southerners moved only a few miles at a time over the next several days. The situation became so confused and unknown on the night of May 3, the soldiers slept along the march route with all their equipment still buckled on to be prepared to move or fight at a moment's notice.[26]

Pettigrew's Brigade formed part of the reserve in Major General Gustavus W. Smith's Division on the movement up the Peninsula. Company B received orders to provide the guards for Smith's headquarters. The 35th Georgia and most of the Confederate column passed through Williamsburg on the afternoon of May 4. The following day the men heard heavy firing to the rear of the column. A courier arrived moments later with orders for the 35th Georgia to hustle back to the fighting at Williamsburg. Raindrops pelted their backs as the firing grew louder, but less frequent.

When they reached the battlefield, the fighting had ceased. Bodies of soldiers from both sides littered the ground. The soaking rain made their uniforms indistinguishable.

The frustrated soldiers in the 35th Georgia had traveled a long distance and again had failed to taste battle.[27] Then two days later, on May 7, they dropped their knapsacks to the ground and double-quicked over a mile to assist Brigadier General John Bell Hood's Texas brigade in a brief fight at Eltham's Landing on the York River near West Point, Virginia. As they approached the scene of the brief fight, it too ended.[28]

Many soldiers in the 35th Georgia expressed irritation over the long marches in wet weather. Sergeant Isham Wallis of Company B wrote home: "[W]e have got in two miles of Richmond which makes about 40 days we have been marching. [W]e have marched a bout 15 days and nights. [W]e hardly sleep any or eat any. [W]e eat about half meal every two days and sleep about 2 hours in 24. [W]e ain't been in nary a fight yet." He said that if a friend could get him a lieutenant's or sergeant's position in a new company that would see some fighting he would join.[29]

Sergeant James M. Kimbrough of Company K added, "The service at this particular time was very severe, the weather was bad and rations were scarce and hard to get. For three days we had little to eat on account of the continued rains. The mud in the roads was almost up to the axels of the wagons and cannons."[30]

Moody perhaps described the anger of a tired foot soldier the best:

> There is a great deal of sickness here and more men dying with it than ever will get killed in the battles of the Confederacy. I think that if Lincoln has to account for all the bloodshed and misery and death he is the instigation of he will be damned world without end. I think this is the most unholy war. The sufferings and miseries of this war will never be forgot by us that is engaged in it. The miseries of being absent from our families and fathers and mothers and sickness and exposure to rain, mud and dust, cold and heat, lying and rolling on the ground in the dirt without the change of clothes, sleeping without blankets, suffering under hard and rigid officers, suffering scornings from commanding bearings, driven from pillar to post by commanders that dont understand their business.

He explained his thoughts on the officers in Company E versus the officers of the regimental staff:

> Now don't think I am particular faulting my officers for they are very good enough. I reckon they are as good as we deserve. Our Captain

> is just as kind as he can be. There can be nothing said against him in that respect. In fact our company officers are all good enough for me. But the regimental officers are very rigid in marching. They are very tight. I dont know that [I] ought to speak of these things but I thought you wanted to know some of the trials in this life. I want to see you so bad that I could eat a fried chicken if I had it.

The frustrated farmer apologized for his absence from home. "I am sorry that you have to go to the field to make a living, but I can't help it. If ever I get home then I will relieve you of that trouble, and I long to see the time come to be with you."[31]

The same time that Moody penned the above lines he received a dispiriting letter from his wife. She described the hardships of many of the women left to run the farms in Campbell County. The Confederate Congress had increased the difficulties for these women when it passed the first draft in American history on April 16. The Conscription Act required the military service of every white male between the ages of eighteen and thirty-five for three years service. Martha Moody wrote:

> [T]he neighbors is all well at this time but the worst distrest peple [distressed people] you ever saw. Crow left yesterday and merion Lee is going to start this eavning and evry man that is able under 35 years old will leave this weak [week] and you know that it is serious times hear.

She told her husband of another family friend leaving later in the week:

> [T]hare will bee another broke up famley. [Y]ou never saw the like. [I]t ant worth while for me to mention thare names for you can ges [guess] at thar [their] ages. [T]har has bin the most detles [deaths] among the wemin [women] this year I ever herd of and I dont think no wonder if truble [trouble] can cill [kill] any bady [body]."

She justified the suffering when she wrote, "[I]f we cold [could] be resined to it it wold [would] be beter for theem and mee too but I cant altho I believe it to bee your dewty to be whare you are." She gave a first hand account of the lack of supplies and food in the area and their own poor wheat crop:

> I cant see what will become of the wimin [women] and children. [I]f peas ant [peace ain't] made before what they have is eat up. [I]t looks hard that the poore farmers is all gon [gone] and thare famlies left and the speculaters [speculators] are giting evry thing off of them they can now and if they ever have to by [buy] all they eat I dont think they will git it. I no [know] that I am in beter sircumstance than aheap [a heap (many)]. I believe if I can have seasons I can make

> bread if I ceap [keep] my helth and Robert ceaps his. Wheat looks sory. [I]t is red with the rust on the blade. I am afraid I wont make mutch but I have got old wheat aplenty to do me if I bee saveing.

Martha Moody closed her sad letter by saying that she would send some clothes to her husband and she urged him to check the pants pocket because she would put a piece of her new dress there.[32]

Captain James M. White received orders on May 18 relieving his Company B as Major General Smith's headquarters guard due to sickness among all the company's officers. Illness gripped Lieutenants Samuel H. Dean, Graves B. Almand and Nathan C. Carr. Ten days later, an emaciated and gaunt White would also be admitted to a hospital for debility. Edward Thomas sent Lieutenant John Duke from Company A to assume temporary command of Company B.[33]

Captain White soon found himself embroiled in controversy. Some accused White of faking illness to avoid battle. This accusation began

Captain Graves Bennett Almand, Co. B

The Newton County men elected Almand to succeed Captain James White in mid-June 1862. Almand was hospitalized in Lynchburg, Va., and died of typhoid fever there in June 1864. He was buried in the city's Confederate cemetery

Courtesy of Arlene F. Shuler, West Columbia, S.C.

because of a letter written back to home by one of White's lieutenants. White defended himself against these charges in his own letter printed on the front page of the *Southern Confederacy,* an Atlanta newspaper. "I went with my company down on the Chickahominy, on picket. I was so feeble I could no longer drag myself after them, and on the night of the 27th [May], they left me and other sick men, to get back to camp as best we could. We had no desire to fall into the hands of the Yankees, so we made an effort to follow them to camp, and arrived there on the 28th in time to see the regiment start again." White reported to the 3rd Georgia Hospital in Richmond on May 29 and remained there through the Battle of Seven Pines two days later.[34]

Lieutenant Dean wrote the controversial letter to W.U. Almand and J.F. Almand back in Georgia. The Almands apparently misinterpreted the letter. When the problem surfaced, Dean wrote a letter defending White that the same newspaper published. Dean described his Captain: "You were in a state of debility, produced by great hardship and poor food. I regarded you as much disqualified for the performance of your duties in camp, as you would have been had you had a seated disease." He further explained:

> If there was anything in my letter to Mr. A. that could be used to your injury, by any legitimate construction of the language, I regret it exceedingly. I perhaps spoke too lightly of your case, if so, it was that I might not give unnecessary uneasiness to your family. As you are thus rudely assailed at home, I am glad that you will be there so soon, that your emaciated appearance, and worn and almost haggard expression of countenance may give the lie to your assailants and prove to the public that you have given your best energies and strength to your country. But few men would have remained at their posts so long. Captain Rawlins (Co.F) did, but it cost him his life.[35]

The J.F. Almand mentioned as the recipient of the first Dean letter was probably Sergeant James F. Almand, who had received a discharge for a disability in April 1862.

Captain White queried Dean whether he thought Colonel Thomas and the soldiers in Company B would accept his resignation for disability. Dean responded in a letter written from camp on June 8:

> Col. T. said he was sorry to give you up, but says that as your health is failing, and you are growing old, he is willing for you to do as you please about it. He says you will have to get a certificate of your inability for service. Some of the company say they can not give you up, but most of the company present (about 40) say they are, and will be satisfied for you to do as you think best. If your health was

> good they would not like for you to leave them. All the company say they want you to come see them before you go home.[36]

A reading between the lines showed some members of Company B probably considered their captain a burden. Lieutenant Dean ironically resigned from his post on June 13 for illness. This same day Captain White resigned for debility. Dean died a month later in Richmond.

As the Confederate army neared Richmond, Gustavus Smith assumed command of the left wing and his senior brigadier general, William H. Chase Whiting, moved to temporary command of Smith's Division. The 49th Georgia arrived from Goldsboro, North Carolina to reinforce Pettigrew's mixed brigade composed of the 2nd Arkansas Battalion, 22nd North Carolina, 47th Virginia and 35th Georgia.[37] McClellan's army simultaneously inched its way northwest toward Richmond. Five Federal corps halted on May 25 around Bottoms Bridge on the Chickahominy River, a mere thirteen miles east of the capital. McClellan ordered the Third and Fourth Corps to cross to the south side of the river. His other three corps remained north of the river.

Those present on both sides knew that a mighty fight would soon occur. Moody wrote his wife on May 27, "The canons air [are] roring loud and fast. [W]ee air in a tite hear. [T]he yankeys air in a mile of us and in 3 or 4 miles of Richmond. [W]ee air lying ready to fite at eny time." He expressed fear that the enemy might capture Richmond and he might not survive. "I cant say that this will bee the last leter I shall rite to you but it may." Moody, like many soldiers, nervously wondered how he would stand up to the challenge of battle. "I hear the gratest roring that I ever heard them [make] and I thinke that wee will son [soon] be in gaged [engaged]. [W]ee have to fite this time. I [want] you to doo the best you can. I aint a fraid to fite. I am anxios to get threw with it. [Y]ou no that when I comence a thing I am mity impatient tell [until] I git it don [done]."[38]

Joseph Johnston developed a plan to launch an aggressive attack against the two enemy corps south of the Chickahominy River. He believed the river barrier would prevent the rapid crossing of Union reinforcements. The recent heavy rains had pushed the waters of the Chickahominy out of its banks and increased the Confederate advantage. A heavy rainstorm blew in late on the afternoon of May 30. Driving rain and hail fell all night and added to the swollen creeks and rivers. The soldiers of the 35th Georgia prepared to move out of their soggy bivouac between the Meadow Bridge and Mechanicsville Roads in the early morning darkness of May 31. They marched eastward through mud and water along Nine Mile Road to the intersection with the New Bridge Road. They waited to support the initial attack of Major General Daniel H. Hill and Major General James Longstreet.[39]

The Georgians sought shade near Old Tavern, at the road intersection, as they waited for sounds of a battle. They waited and waited, but nothing happened. Chase Whiting finally received orders between 4 and 5 P.M., to move his division southward along Nine Mile Road to meet Longstreet's urgent request for assistance. Hood's Brigade moved along the right of the Nine Mile Road. These Texans rushed south of the Richmond and York River Railroad to aid Longstreet's left. Whiting's former brigade, commanded by Colonel Evander M. Law, followed the rapid march along the Nine Mile Road. Pettigrew's Brigade with the 35th Georgia came next. The soldiers moved at the double-quick along the muddy road. Gunfire erupted ahead as the Southerners approached the village of Fair Oaks on the Richmond and York River Railroad. Hood's Brigade veered off the Nine Mile Road to the right to cross the railroad. Cannon fire suddenly shook the ground. Smoke swirled upward across a wheat field about one thousand yards to the left rear. The crew of a Union long range artillery battery scrambled to reload their guns and send more iron into the exposed flank of the Confederate column. Union Captain James Brady stood nearby the Parrott rifles of his Battery H, 1st Pennsylvania Light Artillery. He watched the chaos unfold in the Confederate ranks on the Nine Mile road.[40] Colonel Law moved his Southerners across the field to seize the battery. They soon found that an enemy infantry brigade supported these cannons.

Johnston Pettigrew received an order to move his brigade to the left of Law's men. He ordered Colonel Thomas to take the 35th Georgia into some nearby woods to flank the enemy battery. The 35th Georgia, as the initial regiment in the brigade to enter the wheat field, bore the brunt of the enemy fire.

Federal Lieutenant Edmund Kirby's Battery I, 1st U.S. Artillery rolled up with the first of his three 12-pounder Napoleons and not a moment too soon. This battery had miraculously crossed the swaying flooded Grapevine Bridge over the boiling waters of the Chickahominy. The artillerymen had followed Brigadier General Willis A. Gorman's brigade across the decrepit structure. Gorman's men represented the lead elements of a Federal Second Corps reinforcement effort. The fact that these troops crossed the swollen river provided one of the biggest surprises for the Confederates on this day. The soldiers aptly named this bridge because when the Union engineers who built it ran out of rope they used thick grape vines abundantly growing along the riverbank to lash the corduroy planking together. The name also may have originated from a nearby pre-war bridge of the same name. Kirby described the situation as his cannons and caissons rolled toward the fighting. "At about 4:45 P.M. I was ordered by General Sumner to place the battery in position, the right resting on a strip of woods and the left about 70 yards from Adams' house, facing nearly south and towards Fair Oaks Station. The enemy advanced through an open field, and was about 1,000 yards away from the battery when I commenced firing with spherical case and shell. They immediately tried to cover themselves in the woods on my right."[41]

The enemy that Kirby referred to was probably the 35th Georgia as they sought cover from the rapid fire of both batteries. When Kirby saw Confederate soldiers charging toward his guns from the woods on the right, he ordered the barrels turned westward to meet the threat. At that moment two more of his guns rolled up and he placed them on his left. "All of the spherical case and shell were exhausted. I sent two limbers to the rear, where the caissons were buried in the mud, to bring up a fresh supply of ammunition.

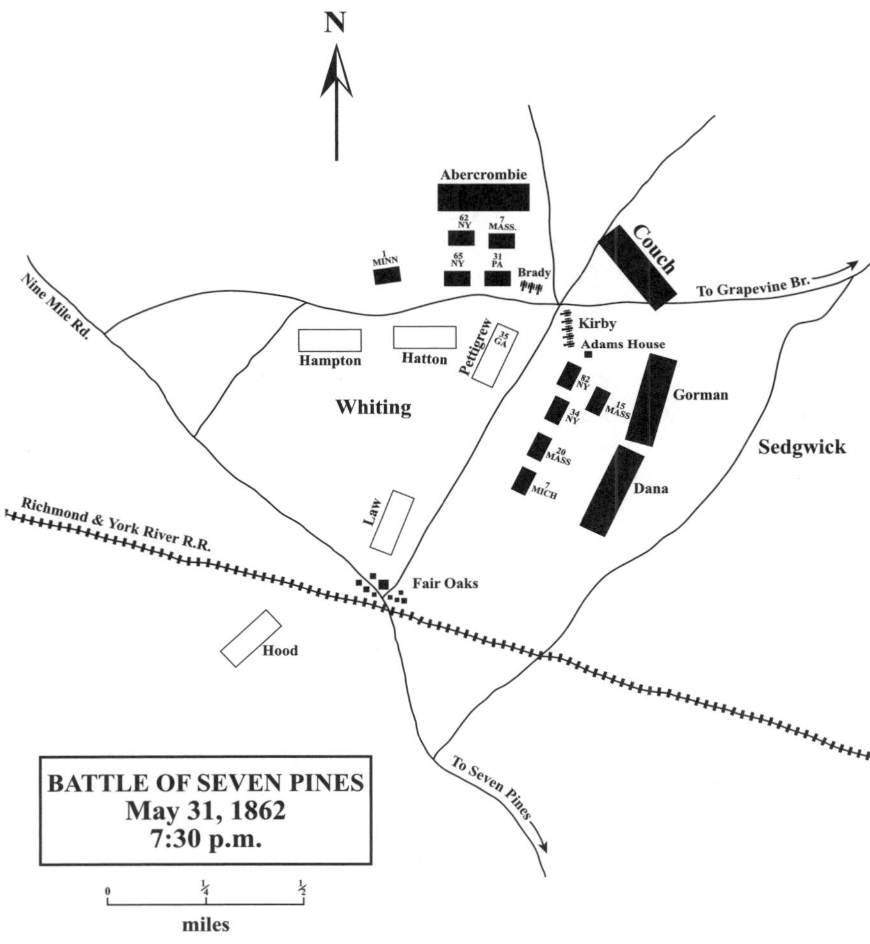

As the enemy were beyond canister range, I fired a few rounds of solid shot to occupy them until I could obtain more shell. As soon as the ammunition arrived I ordered shell and spherical case to be fired until the enemy were within 500 yards of my right flank, when I opened with canister."[42]

When the 35th Georgia approached the Union line, the intense artillery and infantry fire coming from behind the enemy rifle pits and breastworks stopped them. Lieutenant Kirby described the Confederate approach: "They came down a road which was on my right when the firing commenced, and when they emerged from the woods found themselves in front of the battery instead of on the right, as they expected, and were consequently subjected to a tremendous fire of canister from five light 12-pounder guns, which they were unable to stand. They retreated in disorder into the woods."[43]

Pettigrew saw the 35th Georgia bogged down. He ordered the rest of his infantry regiments to move across the field to support the 35th and capture the two enemy batteries. Meanwhile, Gorman's brigade reinforced the Union line to the left of Kirby's battery.[44]

The time was about 5:30 P.M. as the 82nd New York double-quicked into the line by the Adams house. The men of the 34th New York moved into a position on the left of the 82nd New York. The 15th Massachusetts meanwhile halted just to the rear of these two regiments. The commander of the 82nd New York, Lieutenant Colonel Henry W. Hudson, wrote what happened moments later. "At this time the enemy had charged to within about forty or fifty rods [275 yards] of the battery and received a most terrific fire from my command, which evidently staggered him and caused him to fall back with heavy loss."[45]

Captain Brady recalled the intense Confederate musket fire from the woods only fifty yards to his front. The left section of his battery commanded by Lieutenant Andrew Fagan spewed a rapid enfilade fire each time the weary Confederates in Pettigrew's Brigade rallied for a charge. Brady wrote: "This section, after exhausting canister, played upon the enemy's lines with spherical case and shell without fuse, bursting the shell as it left the gun, as determined by the yellow sulphurous smoke, sweeping its broken fragments before it, eliciting the remark from the enemy that nothing could stand up before such 'rotten shot'."[46]

The Union artillery caught the 35th Georgia in a deadly crossfire. The Georgians had clawed there way to fifty paces from the Union artillery, but the men started to fall back. Benjamin Moody described the action: "[W]e was throde in a dangrious place. [W]ee tried to charge a batry but faild. [W]ee charged up in twenty or 30 yards of the canon and lay down on the grownd a bout 10 minutes when wee was ordered to retreet which was don with speed. [O]ur regiment got most up with the 49 ga Reg and got scatered very bad. I give out on dobel quicke and retierd from the field. [T]hair was a grate meny give out and got scatered so it was hard to git them to gethor [together]."[47]

Casualties along the Confederate line rose, especially at the command levels. Johnston Pettigrew fell with a gunshot to the chest. He believed himself mortally wounded and refused to allow any soldier to leave the ranks to carry him rearward. Something slammed into the side of the 35th Georgia's Lieutenant Colonel Gustavus Adolphus Bull. Adjutant James H. Ware's horse went down from under him. Ware, once on the ground,

Lieutenant Colonel Gustavus Adolphus Bull

This carte de visite shows Lieutenant Bull with the 4th Georgia prior to his resignation and election as second in command of the 35th Georgia. The LaGrange teacher and lawyer was wounded and captured at the Battle of Seven Pines on May 31, 1862. He died in Federal hands and was buried in an unmarked grave.

Courtesy of The Museum of the Confederacy, Richmond, Va. Copy photography by Katherine Wetzel

attempted to carry Pettigrew to safety. The general scolded the young lieutenant and ordered him to leave. A shell exploded near Major Bolling H. Holt knocking him senseless and forcing him to the rear.[48] Another explosion tossed General Joseph Johnston from his horse. Staff members surrounded the unconscious army commander.

As confusion swirled all around, Colonel Thomas, on horseback, seized the moment. Thomas, in a dash of bravery, "with a daring which brought back the courage and confidence of his wavering troops, seized the colors of his regiment in his hand, rode in advance of his troops, and called on them to rally and follow their leader. Struck by the devoted conduct of their Col., the men rallied with enthusiasm under the banner, and again charged . . . ."[49] Somehow, Thomas remained unscathed. The same could not be said of many others. Lieutenant Hope Roberts, of Company C, wrote, "It was in this second charge we sustained our heaviest loss, losing in killed and wounded one-fourth the number carried in the field."[50] Another soldier described the difficulty in locating targets to shoot. "A brilliant blaze was even before the eyes of our brave men. They were being mowed down by the scores. Not an enemy could be seen nor any sign of them but this prolonged flash, proceeding as it were from the ground, where he was concealed."[51]

Roberts continued his description of the second charge: "after our forces composed of two or more brigades had been forced to retire through the skirt of woods fronting the batteries and rifle pits of the enemy, this regiment was rallied, and by its heroic Colonel led the second time into the woods, which they penetrated as far as the center–met the enemy–fired into him, and forced him again to take shelter behind his fortifications." However, because of the continued withering enemy cannon and small arms fire they fell back again.[52]

Thomas rallied the Georgians for a third charge right about the time that two more Union regiments arrived from Brigadier General Napoleon J. Dana's brigade. The 20th Massachusetts and the 7th Michigan linked up on the left of the 34th New York to extend the left flank. It was now about 7:45 P.M. The Union reinforcements helped turn the Georgians rearward again. Moody described the intense fire, "I have hived bees but they want [were not] haf [half] as thicke as the bals [balls]."[53] Now as darkness approached, there was a terrific yell from the Union line. Pettigrew's men looked over their shoulders as the entire left wing of the Union line rushed forward with fixed bayonets.[54]

Colonel James A. Suiter, of the 34th New York recorded: "About a quarter of 8 o'clock I was ordered to charge the enemy with the bayonet in the woods, which they did in good order, pouring into them a withering and deadly fire as they charged, the enemy standing their ground till my command mounted the fence on the skirt of the woods, when they broke and ran in great confusion. We followed them about twenty rods [110 yards], when we lost sight of them in the darkness. I was ordered to withdraw my command, which I did, and formed it in the field just outside the wood, when we rested for the night."[55] The 82nd New York's Lieutenant Colonel Hudson expressed surprise at how much ammunition his men fired. "My command entered the action with an average of 60 rounds of ammunition, and at the close had barely 6 rounds each left."[56]

Senior Confederate commanders failed to order their artillery support forward during this fight. This represented a glaring oversight! Without the intense rapid fire of the two Union batteries the outcome of the battle might have turned out differently. The large number of shells fired by just Kirby's five-gun battery evidenced the intensity of the artillery fire faced by Pettigrew's men. "Expended during the action 70 rounds shell, 210 rounds spherical case, 48 rounds canister, and 15 rounds solid shot; total 343 rounds."[57]

Pettigrew's Brigade pulled back with the fall of darkness. The 35th Georgia spent the night about 300 yards from the Union line. Many men wondered how Edward Thomas remained untouched while countless other officers became casualties. This list included Pettigrew and Bull who were both missing.[58] One observer commented on Thomas' good fortune. "How the chivalrous Colonel of the 35th escaped death seems a miracle. Exposed to the hottest of the fire from first to last, his position on horseback making him a conspicuous mark for the enemy's sharpshooters, frequently in advance of his regiment, encouraging his men, he escaped strange to say without the smell of fire on his clothes."[59]

Colonel W. Raymond Lee of the 20th Massachusetts in Dana's brigade described the end of the fight. "It was now getting dark and the enemy soon ceased firing, seemingly retiring. We occupied the field on which we halted after the last movement to the front, all night under arms, engaged mainly in securing prisoners and collecting and providing as best we could for the enemy's wounded who were numerous, and scattered on the field around us. Among the latter were Brigadier General Pettigrew, of South Carolina, and Lieutenant Colonel Bull, of Georgia."[60]

Benjamin Moody reported that an enthusiastic Armistead R. Bomar made three charges during the day–two with the 35th Georgia and one with the nearby 19th Georgia. The young Bomar had enlisted as a musician which made his bravery more remarkable. Bomar would be discharged more than eighteen months later for being underage.[61]

The 35th Georgia inflicted moderate casualties on the enemy. The 82nd New York reported 23 killed, 71 wounded and 3 missing. The 34th New

York tallied 10 killed and 61 wounded. Brady counted 6 wounded while Kirby had 5 wounded men.[62]

The Battle of Seven Pines cost the 35th Georgia 23 killed and another 50 wounded. They left more of their comrades dead on this battlefield than any other during the war. Lieutenant Colonel Bull survived his wounds for only one day in Federal hands. The final resting place of his body was unknown. Private Thomas L. Baker, of Company D, died and his older brother, Sergeant Charles N. Baker, suffered a disabling wound.[63]

A letter written by General Robert E. Lee and sent through Union lines to the commander of the 20th Massachusetts, Colonel W. Raymond Lee, is of interest. "I have the honor to acknowledge the receipt of your letter of the 15th June, announcing the death of the late Lt. Col. Bull 35th Ga Regt.

Sergeant Charles N. Baker and his younger brother Private Thomas L. Baker

Enemy fire at the Battle of Seven Pines wounded Charles Baker. He was again wounded at the Battle of Fredericksburg six months later. Thomas Baker was killed in action at the Battle of Seven Pines on May 31, 1862.

Courtesy of Keith Bohannon

I have caused your kind and considerate communication to be transmitted to the father of the deceased, to whom I doubt not it will afford a great satisfaction to know that his son, in his last moments, enjoyed the care and attention of a humane and generous enemy. I thank you Colonel, for the kindness you have manifested to this deceased officer, and trust that a like spirit will always mark the treatment of the unfortunate wounded who may fall into the hands of either army."[64]

Edward Thomas saluted his men in a note written to an officer in the regiment. "At Seven Pines, your regiment made one of the most gallant charges on record during the war, and when the other commands were melting away on your right and left, you stood like a wall and breasted the full shock of a full division, and acquitted yourselves like men."[65] Another observer bestowed rich accolades upon the 35th Georgia for their first real fight. "Recruits but half drilled fought with the coolness and courage of veteran soldiers, and the officers seemed to vie with each other which should dare the greatest dangers–sharing all the exposure of the soldiers under them."[66]

Private Frank Edwards gave his perspective on the fight many years after the war:

> We were in a dangerous position and remained longer than we should. We were in a very thick forest. Finally overwhelming numbers compelled us to give way, just as Colonel Bull predicted before entering the battle. He said it was a bad move, and hesitated before advancing, but he advanced to his death. I knew a great many of our private soldiers could maneuver an army more successfully than some of the leaders. Lack of judgment by the men in power caused many of our poor boys to lose their lives.[67]

On June 1, President Davis made a critical decision that had a lasting effect on the conduct of the war in the eastern theater. He needed an immediate competent replacement for Joseph Johnston. Davis chose Robert Edward Lee. The men of the 35th Georgia soon found themselves fighting for arguably the finest and most famous commander either side produced during the four long years of the war.

Notes

Abbreviations:

CSR—"Compiled Service Records of Confederate Soldiers Who Served In Organizations From The State of Georgia," Thirty-fifth Infantry Regiment (National Archives Microfilm Publication M266) National Archives Building, Washington, D.C.

GDAH–Georgia Division of Archives and History, Morrow, Ga.

NMP—National Military Park

OR.—War of the Rebellion: A Compilation of the Official Records of the Union and Confederate Armies. 130 Vols.

1. CSR.
2. Hiram W. Hammond, Confederate Diary of Pvt. Hiram W. Hammond, Co.E, 35th Georgia Regiment Volunteers.
3. Warren H. Cudworth, *History of the First Regiment (Mass. Infantry)* (Boston, 1866) p127–132; Joseph Balicki, "Camp French: Confederate Winter Quarters Supporting the Potomac River Blockade," 2003. This archeological paper was prepared by Joe Balicki of John Milner Associates, Inc., Alexandria, Va.
4. Letter of Benjamin F. Moody to "Dier wife camp nier Fredericksburg Va. April the 1st 1862," Benjamin F. Moody Folder, Civil War Miscellany, Personal Papers (Record Group 57-1-1), GDAH.
5. Letter of Benjamin F. Moody to "Dier wife an childrin from Evinsport Va, March the 4th 1862," Moody Folder, GDAH
6. "Adjutant & Inspector General's Office Register of Letters Received," (National Archives Rare Book Room, Vol.48, item 164T (1862), p.472) National Archives Building, Washington, D.C. The original of this letter disappeared and only a brief description of the letter exists in an old leather-bound book at the National Archives.
7. Letter of Benjamin F. Moody to "Dier wife and childrin from Fredericksburg va, March the 24th 1862," Moody Folder, GDAH.
8. Hammond.
9. Letter of B.F. Moody to "Dier wife and children, Fredericksburg Va. March the 22 1862," Moody Folder, GDAH.
10. Ibid.
11. Letter of B.F. Moody to "Deer Wife and Childrin Campe near Fredericksburg Va. April the 4 1862," Moody Folder, GDAH.
12. Letter of B.F. Moody to "Wife and childrin Fredericksburg Va. March the 30th 1862," Moody Folder, GDAH.
13. Letter of Lieut. W.C. Goggans to "Dear Father from Fredricksburg Virginia April 11th 1862," William C. Goggans Civil War Letters, courtesy of Hargrett Rare Book & Manuscript Library/ University of Georgia Libraries, Athens Ga.
14. Hammond.
15. Letter of Benjamin F. Moody to "Dier Wife and Childrin, Camp near Fredericksburg Va, April the 9th 1862," Moody Folder, GDAH.
16. Ibid.
17. Letter of Lieut. W.C. Goggans to "Dear Father from Fredricksburg Virginia Appril 11th 1862," William C. Goggans Civil War Letters, courtesy of Hargrett Rare Book & Manuscript Library/ University of Georgia Libraries, Athens Ga.
18. Hammond; Letter of Lieut. W.C. Goggans to "Dear Father from Camp near Ashlen Virginia April 14th 1862," William C. Goggans Civil War Letters, courtesy of Hargrett Rare Book & Manuscript Library/ University of Georgia Libraries, Athens Ga.
19. Ibid., Goggans.
20. Ibid., Goggans.

21. Hammond.
22. Ibid.
23. Letter of Benjamin F. Moody to "Dier wife from Campe nier yorke towne va, April the 25th 1862," Moody Folder, GDAH; W.T. Irvine, *The Sunny South,* Atlanta, May 2, 1891, "Old 35th Georgia".
24. Ibid., Moody; Hammond.
25. Letter of Benjamin F. Moody to "Dier wife and childrin from Camp nier Yorktown va, April the 29th 1862," Moody Folder, GDAH.
26. Hammond.
27. James Folsom, *Heroes and Martyrs of Georgia–Georgia's Record in the Revolution of 1861,* (Macon, Ga.,1864) p.137.
28. Irvine.
29. Letter of Sgt. Isham Wallis to "Anderson Owens from Camp Near Richmond, 5/21/1862," Minnie Robertson Smith Collection, AC 33–031, Folder 5–06, GDAH.
30. J.M. Kimbrough, "My War History 1861–65", typescript at Chickamauga-Chattanooga NMP, Ga.
31. Mills Lane, ed., *Dear Mother: Don't Grieve About Me. If I Get Killed, I'll Only Be Dead,* (Savannah, 1977) Letter of Benjamin F. Moody to "Dear Wife from Richmond, Va, May 22, 1862," This is the only Moody letter in Lane's book. It appears with proper spelling and punctuation and I assume that Lane cleaned the letter up before publication. This letter does not appear with the rest of the Moody letters at the GDAH.
32. Letter of Martha Moody to "Dear husban Georgia Campbell Co. May the 12 1862," Moody Folder, GDAH.
33. *Southern Confederacy,* Atlanta, July 5, 1862.
34. Ibid.
35. Ibid.
36. Ibid.
37. Folsom, p. 127.
38. Letter of Benjamin F. Moody to "Dier Wife from Richmond Va. May the 27th 1862," Moody Folder, GDAH.
39. Letter of J.P. Jones to "The Editors of the Dispatch, Gen. Pettigrew's Brigade, Camp Four Miles from Richmond June 7th 1862," *Columbus Enquirer,* Columbus, Ga., June 24, 1862.
40. *OR* ., Vol.11, Pt. I, p.989–992.
41. Ibid., Vol.11, Pt. I, p.795; Richmond National Battlefield Park Historian Robert E.L. Krick brought to my attention the pre-war Grapevine Bridge that may have been the name source.
42. Ibid.
43. Ibid., Vol.11, Pt. I, p.795–796.
44. Ibid., Vol.11, Pt. I, p.880, 990, 791, 798–799; *The Daily Intelligencer,* Atlanta, July 2, 1862, "The 35th Georgia In the Battle of Seven Pines"; Jones, *Columbus Enquirer.*
45. Ibid., Vol.11, Pt.I, p.805. note: Webster's Dictionary defines a rod as 16 1/2 feet. Lieutenant Colonel Hudson's estimate of 50 rods would equate to 275 yards which is deadly range for canister.

46. Ibid., Vol.11, Pt. I, p.904.
47. Letter of Benjamin F. Moody to "dier wife from Richmond Va. June the 3d 1862," Moody Folder, GDAH.
48. Letter of Lt. Hope H. Roberts to "Editors of the Dispatch, Thirty-fifth Ga. Regt., Camp Near Richmond, June 14th 1862," *Southern Confederacy,* Atlanta, June 26, 1862.
49. *The Daily Intelligencer.*
50. Roberts.
51. Jones, *Columbus Enquirer.*
52. Roberts; *The Daily Intelligencer.*
53. Ibid., *The Daily Intelligencer;* Moody letter, June 3rd 1862.
54. *OR .,* Vol.11, Pt. I ,p.809–810.
55. Ibid., Vol.11, Pt. I, p.804.
56. Ibid., Vol.11, Pt. I, p.805.
57. Ibid., Vol.11, Pt. I, p.796.
58. Ibid., Vol.11, Pt. I, 909–993; *The Daily Intelligencer.*
59. Ibid., *The Daily Intelligencer.*
60. *OR.,* Vol.11, Pt. I, p.810, note Pettigrew was from North Carolina.
61. Letter of Benjamin F. Moody to, "Dier wife, Richmond Va, June the 11th 1862," Moody Folder, GDAH.
62. *OR.,* p.758, 761.
63. Folsom, p.136; CSR for Baker.
64. Letter of RE Lee to "Col W. Raymond Lee Comdg 20th Mass Regt from HdQu Dep. N.Va. 19th July 1862," located in "Papers of the Association of Officers of the 20th MA.," Vol.2, p.37, Rare Books and Manuscripts Dept., Boston Public Library.
65. Irvine.
66. *The Daily Intelligencer.*
67. John Frank Edwards, *Army Life of Frank Edwards—Confederate Veteran–Army of Northern Virginia 1861–1865.* (1906) p.6.

Note: the entire area of the fighting north of the Fair Oaks station has been decimated by development. Houses and apartments occupy the battlefield.

Chapter Three

Seven Terrible Days

"I believe that thair will bee a heep of hard fiting before long."
Corporal Benjamin Moody to his wife

Robert E. Lee held a meeting with his commanders on June 2. He decided that the army would maintain and fortify the present line. The twelve-mile Confederate defensive line extended from Chaffin's Bluff on the James River northward across the Darbytown, Charles City, Williamsburg, and Nine Mile Roads. The line continued up to New Bridge on the Chickahominy and followed that river to Meadow Bridges. The 35th Georgia and the rest of Chase Whiting's Division occupied the Confederate left between New Bridge and the Mechanicsville Bridge. Benjamin Moody wrote on June 3, "I cant rite much now for wee are looking for a big fite every minut." He ended this letter to his wife with, "I will rite agane before meny days if I live."[1]

Moody warned his wife that she might receive a report of his death from the Seven Pines fight. A wounded Private Wiley Milam, upon reaching a hospital in Richmond, reported to Sergeant James M. Childs that he had stepped over the body of Moody, dead on the field. Moody feared this misinformation might make it back to Campbell County. He stressed to his wife that he was still very much alive on the picket line, and he still expected a fight any moment. He further described the situation: "President Davis ses [says] that hee will nuvar serander [never surrender] the sity as long as hee can hold it and I believe that thair will bee a heep of hard fiting before long." Moody was right. He pleaded with his wife, as he had in previous letters, to send him an ambrotype of herself. He wrote that when he saw fellow soldiers receiving likenesses of their wives he moved away from the crowd and cried.[2]

A command change occurred on June 11 in Company G. Captain William S. Barrett, a Walton County medical doctor, had originally organized the company at the Walnut Grove schoolhouse. Illness afflicted

Barrett, in spite of his profession, causing his resignation. The men elected First Lieutenant James P. Wilkinson to become the new captain. Second Lieutenant John Y. Carter also moved up one spot.[3]

Illness infected the Mobley men in the same company. Corporal David Harrison Mobley's father visited Richmond in June to see two of his hospitalized sons and a brother. The father stood by the bedside of Private Daniel I. Mobley when he passed away on June 13. The doctors sent David Mobley home to Georgia on furlough a few days later. His father remained behind to nurse along Private Henry Mobley, the father's brother. Henry Mobley died of his illness on July 24.[4]

The 35th Georgia received a reassignment to Brigadier General Joseph R. Anderson's Georgia brigade on June 16. They joined the 14th, 45th and 49th Georgia Infantry Regiments, and the 3rd Louisiana Infantry Battalion. Anderson was born in Fincastle, Virginia on February 16, 1813. He graduated fourth academically in the West Point class of 1836. Anderson held the rank of cadet captain, the highest leadership rank among his peers, during his final year. He served a brief stint in the regular army and then he accepted a position under Colonel Claudius Crozet, the designer of the Virginia turnpike system. Crozet placed Anderson in charge of construction for the Valley Turnpike from Staunton to Winchester. Anderson changed to a job with the Tredegar Iron Works in Richmond in 1841. He moved up through the ranks to become the owner of this indispensable Southern company as the war approached. This factory on the James River was the leading producer of Confederate cannon and heavy ordnance during the war.[5] Anderson, although a successful forty-nine-year-old businessman, lacked battle experience.

Anderson's Brigade joined the recently formed division of Major General Ambrose Powell Hill. Brigadier Generals Lawrence Branch, Charles W. Field, Maxcy Gregg, James J. Archer and William D. Pender commanded the other brigades in the division. Hill's Division anchored Lee's left from the Richmond, Fredericksburg and Potomac Railroad north of Richmond southeastward to a link with Longstreet's Division near the New Bridge Road. In a June 1 communiqué, Hill referred to his division as the Light Division—and the name stuck for the remainder of the war.[6]

Morale suffered under General Lee during the middle of June 1862. The long Confederate defense line required large numbers of soldiers to brave the elements on picket duty. The men gained such proficiency digging defensive positions that some derisively referred to their new army commander as the "King of Spades."

Newly elected Corporal Benjamin Moody proudly wrote his wife on June 11 that Colonel Thomas appointed him to be the color corporal for the

General Robert Edward Lee
Photo by Julian Vannerson, 1863 Library of Congress

regiment. He described the trust that Thomas placed in him. "I can informe you that this is a very responseble persishon [position] and is very dangerous one. The curnol [colonel] required it of mee that if the culars [colors] fell to take them and keep them spred and if the culair barer falls or gits killd or is absent I have to take them." He stated that the flag had three holes shot through it in the Seven Pines fight.[7]

Moody reported on June 16 the prevalence of illness in Company E, including Captain Evan R. Whitley. He reported only ten soldiers fit for duty and four of them displayed signs of sickness too. That same morning, stretcher-bearers carried five men from the company to the hospital. To make matters worse, Moody had worn out his clothes. "I am giting most nakid for close [clothes]." He had not changed his pants or shirt since the regiment left Ashland on April 16. This was a period of sixty days! Most of the men had no other clothing to wear. The quartermaster had previously gathered all the soldiers' extra clothing and personal items and had shipped them to Richmond for safekeeping. Moody discovered that washing his filthy clothes without soap in the nearby creeks proved futile. His sense of humor showed when he wrote his wife, "I want you to change clothes and think of me." He further fretted about not being paid since the end of February. This left little money in his pocket and even less to send home.[8]

The thirty-three-year-old Moody was a prolific letter writer during his short military career. This dedicated husband and father dated his last letter to the family on June 22. He referred to his persistent ill health, but he insisted that he would remain with his company. This dedication unfortunately would soon lead to his downfall. "I am in bad helth at this time. I have had a bad time of it for about 5 weeks or more tho [though] I hope that I shal soone git well agane. The Captin wants mee to go to a hospitle but thair is and has bin so meny of the company at the hospitle that I wont go. I dont take no medson [medicine]." He complained of a severe pain in his breast–so bad that he could hardly eat any food. He described the unappetizing food. "[A]ll wee draw is fat midling [middling] bacon and flour and it is baked as hard as a rocke if posable and wee git it cold. I thinke if I could bee at home to eat som of your buiskets [biscuits] and buter I thinke I wood git well." Moody wrote this last letter over a several day period. He noted on June 25 that he felt a little better. "[W]e air looking for a battle hear before meny days and I thinke it will be a monstrous one when it coms on. I thinke it will have something to doo with setling the wore [war]." Then in the next line he moved from the war to the salt shortage. "I can tell you that salt has most give out and I cant tell how the armey will bee kept up with out salt. I dont thinke wee could live long here without that article. [W]ee may fite the wore [war] on tell [until] all the men die and air buried and that wont bee long for thay die very fast in richmond and evry whare else that I can hear from."[9]

Lieutenant Josiah Blair Patterson shed more light on army conditions in a letter written on June 13. He complained of constant picket duty that started ten days prior to the Battle of Seven Pines and ended the previous day:

> The weather has been unusually cold and wet. We have no shelter save what we lug on our shoulder, no bedding except what we transported in the same manner. Our rest has been short and frequently disturbed, our meals scant, irregular and badly cooked, as we were allowed but little pine and cypress (to cook with). When standing we were in a bog of mud; when lying down to refresh ourselves in sleep we were in a pool of water. Constant excitement added to the uneasiness of our condition, as an occasional explosion of a bomb indicated plainly that we were within the range of the enemy's battery,

> while the whistling balls of the enemy's infantry pickets warned us to keep both eyes scanned.[10]

Each day they came under the bird's eye view of enemy observers launched aloft in tethered balloons on the other side of the Chickahominy River. An officer in the 45th Georgia thought the balloons gave the enemy quite an advantage, and he expressed surprise that his army did not have any.[11]

Lee decided to take the offensive during the third week of June. The Confederate commander held another meeting with his subordinates on Monday, June 23. Most officers expressed astonishment when Major General Thomas J. "Stonewall" Jackson rode up because he had recently been thwarting Federal efforts in the Shenandoah Valley, about 120 miles to the west. Lee planned to attack the Federal right flank near Mechanicsville and to disrupt Federal supplies coming from White House on the Pamunkey River. Union Major General Fitz John Porter's Fifth Corps occupied the area around Mechanicsville. The plan hinged on Jackson's ability to move his men from the Shenandoah Valley into position for the attack across the Chickahominy River. Jackson agreed to have his troops in position on the morning of June 26.

The 35th Georgia and the rest of Anderson's Brigade marched to Meadow Bridges on the Chickahominy River west of Mechanicsville on Wednesday evening, June 25. The next morning warmed as the expectant troops peered down from the hilltops that overlooked the river. They waited, yet nothing happened.

Unbeknownst to Hill, Jackson's troops marched forward, somewhere to the northwest—six hours behind schedule. At 3 P.M., a frustrated A. P. Hill boldly ordered his troops to seize Meadow Bridges and cross the river.

Charles Field's Brigade led the Light Division across the river. They encountered only slight opposition as Federal troops fell back toward Mechanicsville. As the Georgians neared Mechanicsville cannon shot of all sizes rained down from the left. The fire came from enemy batteries east of town. Captain D.G. McIntosh's Pee Dee (South Carolina) Battery, assigned to Anderson's Brigade, rolled across a field to take position and to draw the Federal artillery fire. Anderson moved his Georgia brigade to the northeast through some woods to flank the enemy batteries. With the 35th Georgia in the lead, Colonel Thomas found a local man to guide the brigade. The troops ran across fields and into dense woods for almost a mile. This made it difficult to judge the brigade's position relative to the Federal batteries. The guide finally assured them they stood behind the enemy. When Edward Thomas peered out of the wood's edge, the Georgians still stood in front of the enemy line. The enemy's fortified position lined with abatis rested on the other side of Beaver Dam Creek. A long line of Union infantry supported the batteries.[12] A line of enemy skirmishers stood in front of the works near the east bank of the creek.

Brigadier General George McCall, commander of the Third Division of Pennsylvania Reserves, observed Anderson's movement in the distance to flank his right. He wrote, "I, however, was not long in discovering that his principal effort was directed on my extreme right, whereupon I ordered Kerns' battery to that point, and at the same time moved forward Sickel's regiment (Third) to support it." Captain Mark Kerns moved two sections of his Battery G, 1st Pennsylvania Light Artillery (four 12-pound howitzers) into some woods just north of the Old Church Road. They occupied a position to the right of two sections of Battery B, 1st Pennsylvania Light Artillery commanded by Captain James H. Cooper. Another gun section from Captain John R. Smead's Battery K, 5th U.S. Artillery occupied some small earthworks on the south side of Old Church Road. The men from Brigadier General John Reynolds' brigade manned the right part of the Union line next to the batteries. Reynolds' line from right to left consisted of: the 1st Pennsylvania Reserves, 2nd Pennsylvania Reserves (7 companies), 1st U.S. Sharpshooters (2 companies), the 1st Rifles (a.k.a.13th Pennsylvania Reserves or the Bucktails, 6 companies), the 5th Pennsylvania Reserves, and the 8th Pennsylvania Reserves. Truman Seymour's brigade stood to Reynolds' left.[13]

The 35th Georgia occupied Anderson's right with the 14th Georgia and the 3rd Louisiana Battalion formed into line of battle on the left flank. Archer's Brigade lined up to the right. Anderson's line advanced out of the woods across a field toward the enemy while the 45th and 49th Georgia remained behind in reserve. Lead whizzed through the air like hornets. Edward Thomas led the troops downhill toward the creek, which at this point in the line more closely resembled a pond because of a dam further downstream. Pockets of quicksand throughout the marshy area presented another threat. A relentless fire of musketry continued from the Federal entrenchments to the right of the batteries. The Confederate soldiers in the lead reached the creek bank and slid into the cool water. The creek stood fifty yards wide and from two to four feet deep. Wounded soldiers dropped into the water, evidence of the accurate enemy fire. Crimson slicks of blood stained the surface and many of the wounded drowned where they fell, unable to hold their heads above water. Those soldiers still unscathed struggled to reach the east bank. The men of the 49th and 45th Georgia soon came forward to give supporting fire on the right, but neither of these regiments actually crossed the creek.[14]

Enemy fire struck Lieutenant Colonel Robert W. Folsom, commanding the 14th Georgia, just before he crossed the creek. In the ensuing confusion, only a few of Folsom's men crossed. Colonel Thomas fell to the ground with a wound, but he remained at the head of his troops. Thomas described the situation once across the creek. "We attacked the enemy in the woods on their right, and after a severe conflict drove them from the woods and some distance through a field." The enemy Thomas described probably represented the skirmish line that gave way as the Confederates approached. The Southerners gazed up at the fortified Federal position and realized the difficulty of their task. They found themselves "separated from the enemy's main work by a deep ravine and their [enemy] position strengthened by abatis at the foot of the hill, while its crest was strongly supported by extensive rifle pits, manned with sharpshooters." Thomas immediately sent a request for reinforcements.[15]

The 1st Pennsylvania Reserves arrived on the scene and moved to anchor the Union right. The commander, Colonel R. Biddle Roberts, described the sudden appearance of the Georgians and Louisianans: "The regiment had scarcely gained this position when the enemy, concealed in the woods below, opened upon me a galling fire of musketry, which was particularly severe upon the right of the line. The fire was returned by the regiment promptly and most effectively, and in less than an hour we had driven them from the woods and silenced their musketry. Occasional shots were, however heard, though no injury was done by them."[16] Double-charges of canister greeted the Georgians when they charged toward Kerns' guns. Captain Cooper whose battery stood beside Kerns' wrote: "At intervals during the engagement we fired canister into the woods on our right and left, assisting the First Regiment on our right and the Fifth on our left in repelling the enemy, who were engaging these regiments at short musketry-range."[17] A terrific noise roared on this part of the line. General McCall wrote, "Here for a long time the battle raged with a great fury. The Georgians rushed with headlong energy against the Second Regiment, only to be mowed down by the steady fire of that gallant regiment, whose commander soon sent to the rear some 7 or 8 prisoners taken in the encounter."[18]

Thomas waited some time for reinforcements, but the help never arrived. He now found his right flank open. He ordered his men to pull back as the creeping darkness cast long shadows over the grisly site. They reluctantly sloshed back across the creek and joined with the rest of the brigade as it moved toward a bivouac on the eastern edge of Mechanicsville.[19] The men of the 35th and 14th Georgia and the 3rd Louisiana Battalion represented the only Southerners to place their feet on the enemy's eastern side of the creek during the late afternoon fight.

General McCall feared another attack further to his right. He dispatched more Union troops to that point, but the assault never came. The Federals suffered light casualties because of their fortified positions. The

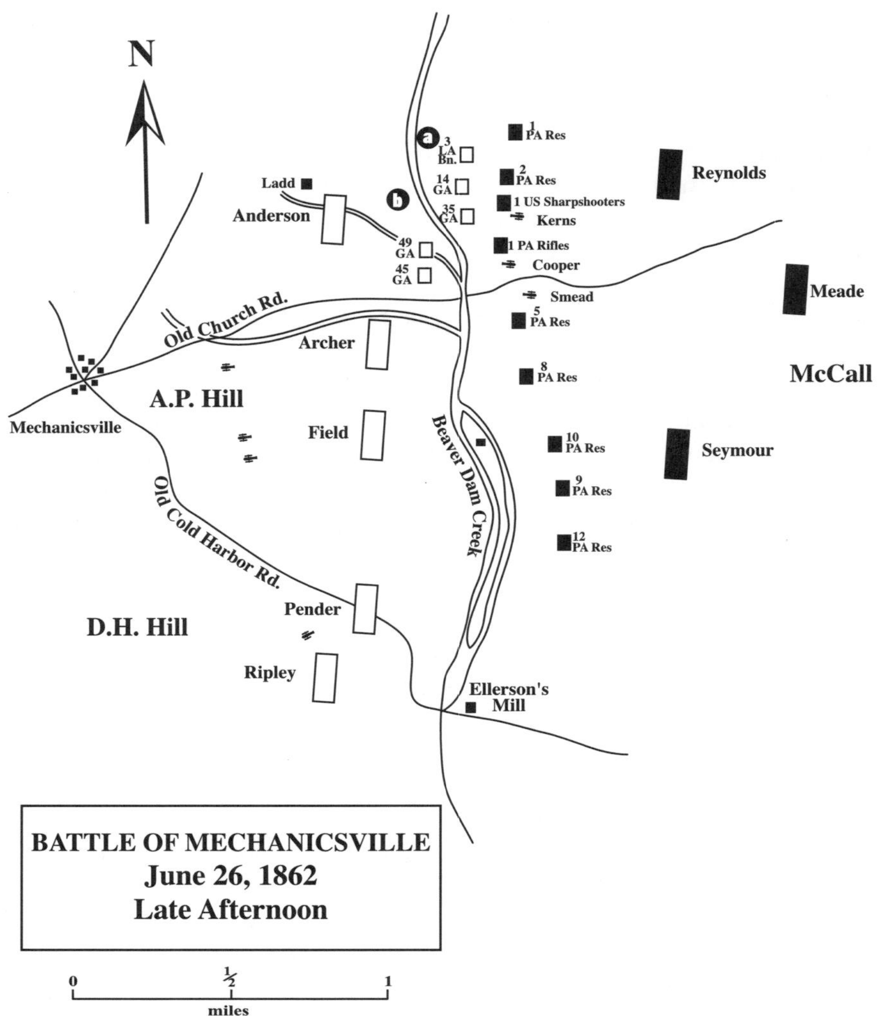

casualties for the 1st and 2nd Pennsylvania Reserves and 1st Pennsylvania Rifles, which received the brunt of Colonel Thomas' attack, amounted to a combined 16 killed and 66 wounded. Cooper's battery reported 5 wounded and Kerns' battery suffered no casualties. Lieutenant Frank Amsden, of Kerns' battery, recorded that his four guns fired 78 rounds of spherical case, 60 rounds of shell and 16 rounds of canister.[20]

The situation on the other side was different. The 35th Georgia had 18 killed and 61 wounded in this regiment alone during the Battle of Me-

a. Beaver Dam Creek
This modern day view, located just north of the I-295 cloverleaf, looks southwest along creek. In 1862 the area on both sides of the creek was more open. The 35th Georgia waded across the creek from right to left under heavy enemy fire.
photo by author

chanicsville. Benjamin Moody fell trying to protect the regimental flag. First Sergeant Isaiah Hembree, of Company E, wrote Moody's widow that nobody in the company saw Moody after he fell. Corporal William J.T. Long organized some men to search for his body. They could not find it. A brigade burial detail probably buried the farmer somewhere along Beaver Dam Creek in an unmarked grave.[21] Martha Moody apparently wrote a letter to Hembree to see if there was any chance her husband's body had been found and sent home. In a second letter to the widow, Hembree told her there was no new information about her husband. He insisted that he would have personally looked for the body if he had not been wounded himself. "[I]f I could I would have sent him home. But tha ant [there ain't] No chance for pore privets to be Sent home Be cause tha [there] are so meny kill." Hembree shed tears over a letter from Moody's wife and children that arrived after his death. He closed his note by assuring her that he would gather all of Moody's clothes in camp and in Richmond and box them up to send back home.[22]

Company C took a hard hit on this day. Captain David B. Henry fell on the eastern side of Beaver Dam Creek in front of the Federal line. His

b. Position of Kerns' Federal Battery

Looking east across creek toward entrenched Federal position. The 35th Georgians crossed the creek at this spot and charged uphill into the muzzles of Battery G, 1st Pennsylvania Light Artillery's four 12-pound howitzers. The 35th Georgia and elements of the 14th Georgia and 3rd Louisiana Battalion were the only Confederate units to cross Beaver Dam Creek on this day.

photo by author

men never located his remains. A Union burial detail probably buried this officer. The next in command of the company, First Lieutenant Hope H. Roberts, also died. The twenty-year-old Roberts had written such a descriptive narrative only twelve days before of the regiment's participation in the Battle of Seven Pines for the Atlanta newspaper, *Southern Confederacy.* The company's junior officer, Second Lieutenant Orlando S. Cochran, fell too. His men carried him rearward with a compound fracture of his left ankle. Later that night, Cochran's troops elected him to be their new captain.[23]

Colonel Thomas and his brother, Captain Lovick P. Thomas, both rode to a hospital for their wounds. General Anderson in his brigade report wrote:

> I would especially notice the conduct of Col. E.L. Thomas, commanding Thirty-fifth Georgia, who evinced fearlessness and good judgment not only in this affair, but throughout the expedition. He was wounded on this occasion, but remained always on duty at the head of his regiment. His adjutant, too, Lt. Ware [1st Lt. James H. Ware, Company K] was conspicuous for gallantry, and sealed with

Lieutenant General Ambrose Powell Hill
Hill was a major general while he commanded the Light Division.
Photo by Julian Vannerson, Library of Congress; Print courtesy of The Museum of the Confederacy, Richmond, Va.

> his life his devotion to the cause of his country, as did other valuable officers.

He continued: " . . . nor can I omit to call special attention to the gallant conduct of Capt. L.P. Thomas, quartermaster of the 35th Ga., who volunteered his services for the occasion in the field, seeing his regiment deficient in field officers. He rendered valuable service until he was seriously wounded."[24] Lieutenant Ware's loyal servant, David, scoured the battlefield in the darkness until he found the fallen officer. David escorted Ware's body back to his parent's house for burial in Columbus, Georgia.[25]

The ground again shook in the early morning darkness of June 27. The beginning of a two-hour Federal artillery barrage jolted the Georgians awake. This artillery fire helped to mask an enemy withdrawal. The bombardment ended around sunrise. The threat of Stonewall Jackson's arrival against the Federal right flank caused Porter's Fifth Corps to move to a plateau about a mile east of Gaines' Mill that overlooked Boatswain's Creek.[26]

The Light Division moved at 8 A.M.and one Georgian reported a sight that roiled his stomach. "While passing through Mechanicsville I saw arms and legs, which had been amputated in a temporary hospital, piled outside as high as the window sill."[27] There was no resistance as the troops waded across Beaver Dam Creek. Lieutenant Patterson of the 14th Georgia described the scene. "Soon after daybreak of the 27th we took up our march in pursuit of the enemy every footstep was marked with deserted pits and fortifications that yesterday gleamed with the glitter of bayonets. Guns, pistols, sabres, knapsacs, haversacks, canteens, shoes, blankets, overcoats scattered all along the road indicated that the Yankees were in a hurry to get to some place of safety. Soon the smoke rising from their burning camps were visible and as we approached we discovered that waggons, provisions, guns, medicines in fact every thing that could be fired they attempted to burn yet much of these were saved by our forces."[28] Members of Company G, 35th Georgia, reported that they were able to enjoy "Yankee bread, meat, apples and cooled parched throats with Yankee ice, and appropriated Yankee coffee already ground and sweetened. Tents had been cut to ribbons and as much equipment destroyed as haste of the flight permitted."[29]

Gregg's Brigade led the Light Division eastward across Beaver Dam Creek and past Ellerson's Mill, the scene of heavy fighting the day before. Anderson's Brigade followed. A.P. Hill and Longstreet received orders to attack the Federal center. Lee believed Porter's Unionists had dug in on the east side of Powhite Creek. This creek powered a grain mill known to all the locals as Gaines' Mill. The Confederate commander hoped to push the enemy into the waiting guns of Jackson and D. H. Hill coming in from the north. Porter's men actually had formed entrenched defensive positions beyond Powhite Creek along Turkey Hill. This wooded precipice overlooked swampy Boatswain's Creek. The Confederate generals failed to realize the strength of the new Union position. The Southern leadership's lack of accurate maps coupled with the unfamiliar terrain caused this lack of foresight. The Union's Turkey Hill position in fact was stronger than their Mechanicsville line of the previous day.

Meanwhile, on the Federal side of Boatswain's Creek the men used the few axes on hand to strengthen their line. Some felled trees. Others hacked at the ground and piled up fence rails and knapsacks to prepare for the inevitable attack. Brigadier General Charles Griffin's brigade held the right flank of Brigadier General George Morell's division. Griffin's brigade lined up from right to left as follows: 9th Massachusetts, 14th New York, 4th

Michigan. Griffin held the 62nd Pennsylvania in reserve. Brigadier General John H. Martindale's brigade stood on Griffin's left. Martindale's 2nd Maine occupied a position to the left of the 4th Michigan. Several companies of the 1st U.S. Sharpshooters armed with breech-loading Sharps rifles crossed to the north side of Boatswain's Creek as skirmishers.[30]

Maxcy Gregg's South Carolinians moved past Gaines' Mill down the road toward New Cold Harbor. They soon encountered heavy artillery fire. When Anderson's Brigade followed down the same road, it too came under artillery fire. Anderson sent out an advance guard with flankers into the woods. As the Georgians veered off the road to the right, the advanced guards saw enemy pickets and captured two of them. Anderson reported, "I then filed to the right, marching through the woods by the right flank until my right reached the field in which General Pender's battery was posted and playing on the enemy. Here I faced to the front and marched forward in line of battle, driving the enemy's skirmishers before us, while I was supported by General Field's brigade, a few paces in rear." A.P. Hill dispatched forward more artillery while the brigades of Branch, Pender, Anderson, Field and Archer formed on Gregg's right. These batteries quickly bogged down because Hill failed to realize the muddiness of Boatswain's Creek plus the steepness of the large ravine along the northern creek bank.[31]

Colonel Hiram Berdan, commander of the 1st U.S. Sharpshooters, described the efforts of his skirmishers as the Confederate line of battle approached his position in the woods north of Boatswain's Creek. "About 1:30 P.M., the enemy advanced in line of battle the whole length of the woods. My men had good cover, and so rapid was our fire from our breech-loading guns we repulsed the enemy with great loss."[32] Berdan's men probably drove back a Confederate skirmish line and not the main line of battle.

Hill gave the order to advance around 2:30 P.M. Federal artillery from the plateau and long-range guns south of the Chickahominy roared to life. The gray troops moved across the quarter mile of open field about two hundred yards from the enemy skirmishers. The Confederates again encountered the fire of the enemy sharpshooters. Anderson ordered his men to charge forward across this field at the double-quick. The soldiers hustled to reach the protection of a narrow wood line that stood on the crest of a hill and swept downward to the northern edge of the swamp. The soldiers reached the hill and they thought the wood line would provide some protection. They quickly discovered this was a bad place. Anderson wrote, "Here the brigade encountered a very hot fire, both of musketry and shell, which brought us to a halt from the double-quick in which I had commenced the charge." Large gaps immediately appeared in the ranks, but the troops continued on over the crest and downhill toward Boatswain's Creek.[33]

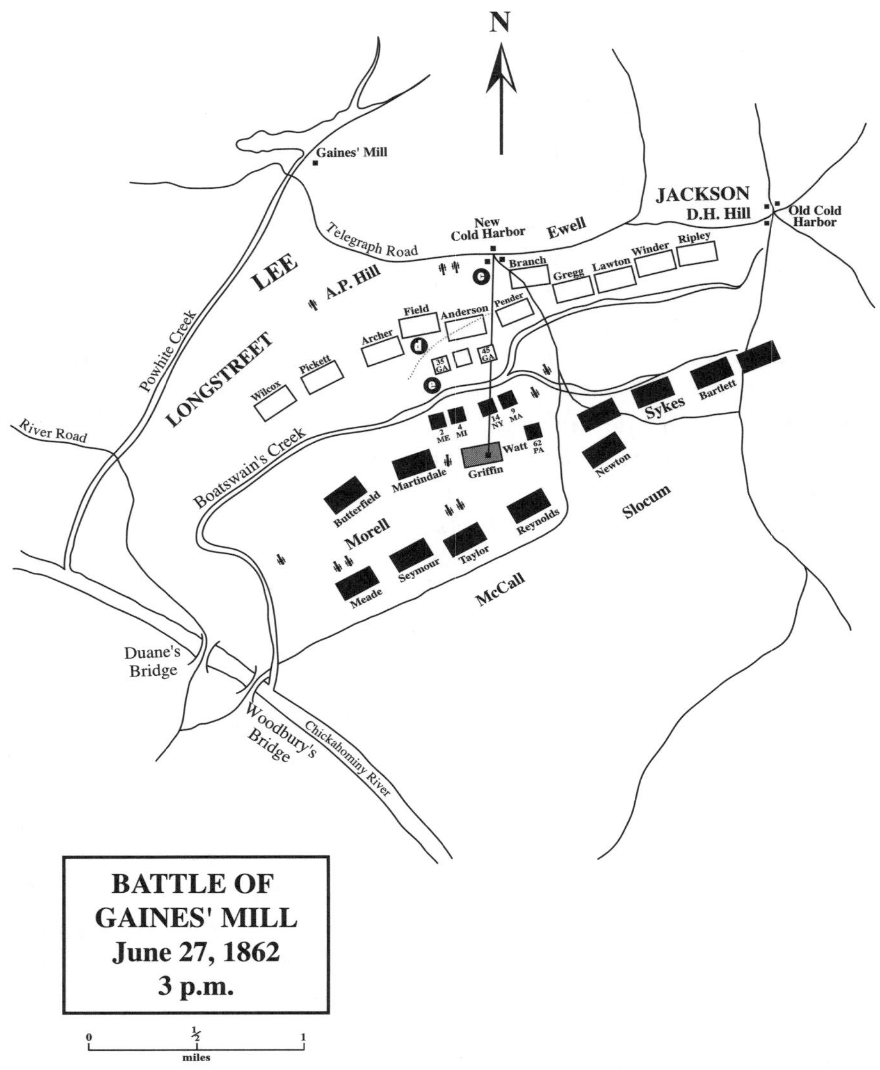

The 35th Georgia anchored the right and Colonel Thomas Hardeman's 45th Georgia anchored the left of Anderson's Brigade. The exact disposition of the 14th and 45th Georgia Regiments and the 3rd Louisiana Battalion was unknown. Field's Brigade moved forward on the right flank of the 35th Georgia. Field recalled the charge of both brigades: "Giving the command to charge, we rushed forward and opened fire within 100 yards of the enemy, which was continued until forced by an overpowering fire from greatly superior numbers to fall back for support, which was received."[34]

c. Field North of Boatswain's Creek
View looking SSW (200 degrees). Road to Watt House in left of photo. Joseph Anderson's Brigade came out of wood line on right and crossed field toward distant trees under fire from Berdan's Sharpshooters and enemy artillery. The terrain at distant tree line slopes down toward Boatswain's Creek and main Federal position.
photo by author

Colonel Thomas had returned to duty earlier in the day. As he led the 35th Georgia into the woods he discovered that they would have to go down a steep ravine and then cross the creek at the bottom to reach the enemy's position. The attack floundered as the accurate Federal fire increased. The Georgians made three charges against Griffin's blue line in an attempt to cross the swampy morass. Each time they rushed past the bloody bodies of their fallen colleagues the heavy enemy fire stopped them. The center of Anderson's Brigade wavered on the third charge. Scared men headed to the safety provided by the opposite slope of an elevated wagon road. Joseph Anderson seized the colors of one of his regiments and "he planted it near the crest of the hill, and, by entreaty and example, soon gathered around it the more intrepid of his command." Because the center units had pulled back, Anderson's Brigade line became a concave arc facing south. The alignment left the 35th Georgia extended toward the enemy on the right and the 45th Georgia in the same dangerous position on the left. This left both flanks of the 35th Georgia in the air. Edward Thomas described his situation: "After receiving and returning the fire of the enemy for some time, it was discovered that the troops both on the right and left of this regiment

d. Downhill Toward Boatswain's Creek

View looking SE (130 degrees) from top of old wagon road down steep hill. Boatswain's Creek runs from left to right just beyond downed tree rootball. This was the right flank of the 35th Georgia. The enemy's entrenched position stood along the opposite slope.

photo by author

had retired." Anderson attempted to rectify his situation. He ordered the center units to lie on the ground at the wood's edge. A courier went forward to order the 35th and 45th Georgia Regiments to pull back until even with the center and then lie in position on the ground as well. The hot fight had sapped Anderson's men.[35] A.P. Hill liked the valiant effort exhibited by the 35th Georgia. The Light Division commander embellished their accomplishments when he wrote eight months after the battle, "The Thirty-fifth Georgia, Colonel Thomas, also drove through the enemy's lines like a wedge, but it was all of no avail."[36]

Charles Griffin described the staunch defense of his Union brigade against the repeated attacks of the Georgians. "The right wing of the Fourteenth (N.Y.) and the Ninth (Mass.) and the Sixty-second (Pa.) held their position in the wood, resisting repeated attacks by fresh troops of the enemy, until they were relieved . . . ."[37] A section of Captain William B. Weeden's Battery C, 1st Rhode Island Light Artillery, commanded by Lieutenant W.W. Buckley rested at the edge of the woods between the flanks of Griffin and Martindale. This gun section probably had the greatest effect on pinning the 35th Georgia down and preventing its

e. Boatswain's Creek

The creek flows from left to right in the foreground. This was the view of the 35th Georgia soldiers as they struggled three times under heavy fire to cross the creek. Federal soldiers from the 2nd Maine, 4th Michigan and the guns of Battery C, 1st Rhode Island Light Artillery fired from their entrenched positions into the hapless Georgians.

photo by author

crossing of the swamp. Captain Weeden described the efforts of his men: "Lieutenant Buckley opened fire with shrapnel, bursting in the enemy's line as they appeared on the crest beyond the ravine. The practice with the guns was excellent, and the fire was continued until the enemy retired. He advanced and was repulsed three times, the section firing shell and shrapnel."[38]

With A.P. Hill's attack stalled, Longstreet launched a probe to relieve pressure on the Confederate center. His attack on the far right ran into the same difficulties experienced by Hill's men. Jackson's troops finally arrived and joined the attack too. Lee believed one more decisive push could drive Porter's Union corps from the field. Whiting's Division from Jackson's corps replaced the exhausted Light Division in the final assault. This Confederate attack moved forward as the sun dropped in the west. Brigadier General John B. Hood's Brigade finally pierced the middle of Morell's line. Federal troops retreated from their positions all along the line as darkness arrived. Panicked blue-clad soldiers crowded every nearby bridge that led to the south side of the Chickahominy.

Brigadier General Joseph R. Anderson

This native Virginian and West Point graduate was wounded at the Battle of Frayser's Farm on June 30, 1862. He owned Tredegar Iron Works in Richmond. This industry was the leading provider of cannon and heavy ordnance for the Confederacy. Anderson resigned his brigade command in July 1862 and returned to Richmond to smooth out manufacturing problems at Tredegar. His departure opened the door for Colonel Edward L. Thomas' ascent to command the Georgia brigade. Anderson posed for this post-war photo in 1865.

Photo by Mathew B. Brady, Library of Congress

Precise casualty figures for the 35th Georgia at the Battle of Gaines' Mill could not be found. General Anderson reported that his brigade suffered 364 killed, wounded and missing, but there was no breakdown by regiment.[39] A search through the "Compiled Service Records of Confederate Soldiers Who Served In Organizations From the State of Georgia" (CSR) revealed four soldiers wounded and another two killed outright. Two of these wounded men subsequently died. The records of these six soldiers specifically mentioned Gaines' Mill as the place where they received their wounds. These numbers are certainly too low and thus misleading because the CSRs list many more soldiers with the phrase "Seven Days Battles around Richmond" as the place where they were killed or wounded. These figures of course include all the battles around Richmond from June 25 to July 1. The casualties for the two Union regiments in Griffin's brigade that probably took the brunt of the attack of the 35th Georgia included: 4th Michigan, 16 killed (including 4 officers), 41 wounded, 32 captured/missing; 14th New York, 12 killed, 73 wounded, 16 captured/missing. The 2nd Maine lost 4 killed, 36 wounded, 49 captured/missing [40]

The soldiers of Anderson's Brigade cared for their wounded comrades and buried their dead on the following day. General Lee realized that McClellan would be most vulnerable while he moved his Federal army through White Oak Swamp. This quagmire lay directly between the Federal position and the James River. Lee decided he would attempt to halt McClellan from three sides: Jackson from the north; Huger and Magruder from the west; Longstreet and A.P. Hill from the southwest. This plan meant that the men of Longstreet and Hill would undergo a long forced march around the Union right and attempt to get in their front. If successful, they could cut McClellan's army off from its new base of supply on the James River.

The Light Division followed Longstreet's troops across the New Bridge over the Chickahominy River on Sunday, June 29. The march was hot and tedious as the column snaked along the narrow roads west of White Oak Swamp. The men finally halted around 9 P.M. The 35th Georgia bivouacked along the Darbytown Road at Atlee's Farm.

The next morning, June 30, dawned clear and hot. The Longstreet-Hill column reached the intersection of the Darbytown and Long Bridge Roads and turned northeast along the Long Bridge Road. Hill halted about one mile from Willis Church Road. Longstreet halted about three-quarters of a mile further ahead. Scouts reported that a strong line of Federal troops stood along the high ground near Frayser's Farm. Hill moved forward to support Longstreet.

Federal artillery rounds fell amidst the Confederate ranks around 2:30 P.M. Hill reported, "The fight commenced by fire from the enemy's artillery, which swept down the road, and from which his Excellency the President narrowly escaped."[41] President Davis had arrived on the battlefield to view the performance of his new army commander and several artillery rounds landed dangerously close. Hill ordered a soldier's escort to hustle Davis to the rear.

Enemy artillery continued unabated as the afternoon grew long. Minutes became hours as Longstreet and Hill waited for orders. Lee waited for word from either Jackson or the Magruder/Huger force. Lee finally ordered Longstreet to attack the numerically superior Federal force at 5 P.M. The

Confederate commander hoped the other units would soon arrive. Longstreet's troops surged back and forth in a seesaw battle with George McCall's division of Pennsylvania Reserves. Darkness approached as commanders on both sides sent fresh troops into the fray. Anderson's Louisianans and Georgians became the last brigade held in reserve on the Confederate side.

Hill ordered Anderson to send his troops forward along the Long Bridge Road at about sunset. He urged Anderson in the gathering darkness "to advance cautiously and be careful not to fire on our friends."[42] The brigade formed into two wings with the 3rd Louisiana Battalion and the 14th Georgia on the left of the road under the direction of a Louisianan, Lieutenant Colonel Edmund Pendleton. This left wing moved forward at the double-quick ahead of the right wing that comprised the 45th, 35th and 49th Georgia Regiments. The 45th Georgia probably occupied the left side of this right wing.

The Georgians hustled about a half-mile up the Long Bridge Road when suddenly out of the twilight galloped an entourage of horsemen headed away from the battle. When someone recognized that one of the horsemen was President Davis a vociferous cheer spread all along the brigade column. As the right wing moved through an open field, muzzle flashes to the left of the road revealed the enemy's front. Anderson ordered the men to form into line of battle and he steered the right wing toward the left side of the road to link with the left wing. He ordered that "no musket was to be fired till we came up with and recognized our friends in front."[43]

They climbed a fence and Anderson halted them about seventy yards from a brigade-size unit ahead. The Southerners aimed their guns toward the murky figures. Were they friend or foe? Anderson was confident they were foe, but several voices yelled out from across the field, "For God's sake, don't fire on us; we are friends." Several soldiers realized the voices didn't have Southern drawls. Suddenly an enemy soldier bellowed out the order to "fire." The resultant fusillade of balls cast aside all doubt about the allegiance of the troops ahead. Another report stated the unknown voices to the front called out, "Don't shoot; friends in front." A Confederate officer, probably from the 14th Georgia, moved forward to investigate. Enemy soldiers quickly captured him. Moments later Union soldiers rushed forward in a bayonet charge against the left of the brigade line. Anderson's men repelled the attackers. When the sun rose the following morning, the light revealed a gruesome scene. Piles of enemy dead, stacked two and three deep, covered the ground in front of the 3rd Louisiana, the 14th Georgia and the 45th Georgia. One Georgian in the burial detail recounted his attempts to assist a stubborn wounded enemy soldier. "I came upon a Yankee soldier sit-

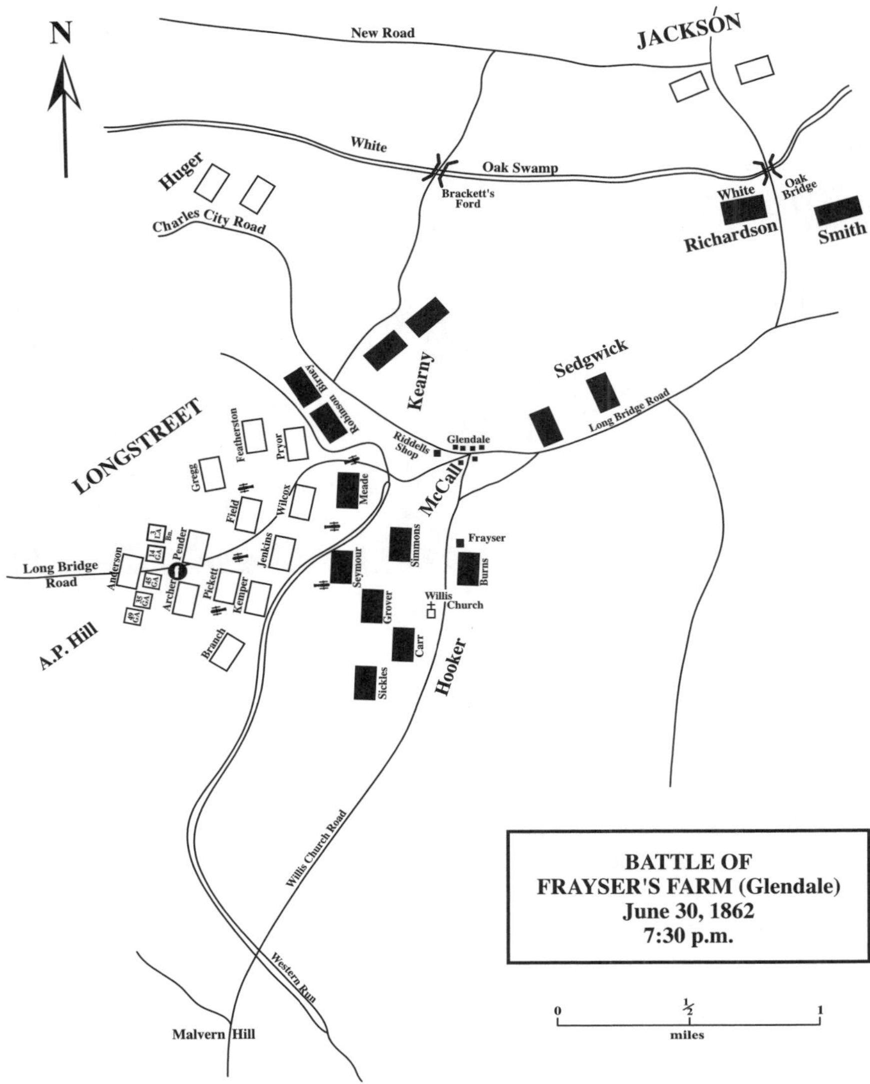

BATTLE OF
FRAYSER'S FARM (Glendale)
June 30, 1862
7:30 p.m.

ting beside a tree, mortally wounded, and offered him water from my canteen, but he refused it and cursed me and the Confederacy for everything he could think of. I tried to persuade him to let me help him, but he firmly refused and died shortly afterward."[44]

The 45th Georgia suffered the brunt of casualties during the confusing fight, including their commander, Colonel Thomas Hardeman. Some type

f. Long Bridge Road
View looking NE (070 degrees) across road. Joseph Anderson moved his right wing across the road at this point to assist the left wing. As darkness fell, the muzzle flashes in the woods to the left front revealed some of the enemy positions. A short time later, Anderson was struck in the head and knocked unconscious.
photo by author

of projectile struck Joseph Anderson on the head and he dropped to the ground unconscious. Colonel Thomas, as the senior regimental commander, assumed command of the brigade.

The 35th Georgia saw little action during the Battle of Frayser's Farm. They received word that Pender's Brigade stood in their front thus caution prevented them from firing forward. The Georgians remained in the same position until 10 P.M. when they found that enemy troops actually occupied their front. This Federal unit had added to the confusion because earlier they mistakenly had fired into another adjacent Federal unit. The firing ceased after 10 P.M. and the Union troops quietly withdrew. Anderson's Brigade moved toward the rear and bivouacked on another part of the field.[45]

Sluggish Confederate troop movements again had foiled Lee's attempt to annihilate McClellan's army. The Federal army moved closer toward the James River and the safety of their gunboats.

The divisions of Hill and Longstreet moved into a reserve position to rest their decimated regiments prior to dawn on July 1. Lee met with his commanders at Willis Methodist Church on the Willis Church Road just south of Frayser's Farm. Lee stressed that they had to destroy the Union army before it reached the James River.

The rising sun shed light on another hot, humid day. Federal troops occupied the crest of Malvern Hill, flanked on either side by creeks that ran through steep ravines. Willis Church Road ran right down the middle of Malvern Hill from north to south. Federal artillery officers placed their guns side by side with clear fields of fire northward over open ground that sloped down to woods and swamp. Fitz John Porter commanded the Federal defense with orders to protect the trains and reserve artillery until they reached Harrison's Landing, the army's new base on the James River.

The Confederate attack commenced after 5 P.M. The day turned out badly for Lee's troops because of accurate concentrated Federal artillery fire. Darkness fell on over 8,000 casualties and more than 5,000 of them wore gray.

A.P. Hill sent the brigades of Branch and Anderson (henceforth referred to as Thomas' Brigade) to assist John Magruder's Division on the Confederate right during the latter part of the battle. Edward Thomas moved his brigade by the flank to an open field. He formed them into line of battle, but they received orders to halt well to the rear. They waited in their lines, but did not actively engage the enemy. The big problem for the Georgians became the massive onslaught of large artillery projectiles fired from the Federal gunboats that floated on the James River. Darkness put a temporary end to the ugly sights in the fields of Malvern Hill. The firing soon ceased and the Georgians withdrew to their camp of the previous night.[46]

One Georgian described the carnage he witnessed at Malvern Hill in a diary notation: "the most terrible sight I ever saw I witnessed hear which I cannot find words to describe, thousands of dead men and horses in every direction and some of them torn with bombs so you could not tell what they were. . . ."[47]

A letter to the *Columbus* (Ga.) *Enquirer* on August 5, 1862, from the regimental adjutant, Winfield Scott Thomas, listed casualty returns for all the battles near Richmond. He reported the loss in the 35th Georgia at 14 killed, 94 wounded, and 2 missing. James Folsom stated in his book that the 35th Georgia suffered 21 killed and 74 wounded in the same battles. Folsom's numbers appear low based on the eyewitness reports. Lieutenant William C. Goggans reported similar numbers to those of Winfield Thomas in a letter he wrote at the end of July. "The loss our Regt was 114 killed and wounded about one third that was engaged. I do not think our killed including those Died from their Wounds since the Battle to amount to more than 25. [M]any that were slightly wounded are with us in camps ready for another combat."[48]

A.P. Hill recognized Colonel Thomas, Lieutenant Colonel Folsom of the 14th Georgia and several other officers from the Light Division for "conspicuous gallantry" in his Seven Days Battle report. A notation in Thomas' report created a mystery. The new brigade commander wrote: "I have the honor to send the inclosed reports from Lieutenant Colonel Manning, Forty-ninth Georgia Regiment; Lieutenant Colonel Folsom, Fourteenth Georgia; and Major Grice, Forty-fifth Georgia Regiment, in reference to the conduct of officers in their several regiments." An asterisk after this sentence indicated that the compilers of the *Official Records* could not locate the reports of these three officers. These missing reports from commanders of the other Georgia regiments certainly would have shed greater light on troop movements and battle conditions. The taciturn Edward Thomas ended his report: "Regretting that I cannot make a more complete report . . . ."[49] This telling line foreshadowed the brevity of his reports for the remainder of the war. Thomas' style contrasted with most of his colleagues who wrote long descriptive accounts of their exploits.

The Battle of Malvern Hill ended the Seven Days Battles and the Peninsula Campaign. The men of Lee's army, after fighting six battles in seven days while on the march, stood at the brink of physical and mental exhaustion. Lee therefore, allowed McClellan to escape down river without another fight. His Southerners had achieved the objective of keeping the Federal army out of Richmond. With one foe momentarily stymied as he retreated away from Richmond, another formidable opponent with fresh troops appeared in central Virginia. The much-needed rest for Lee's troops on the east side of Richmond would not last long.

Notes

Abbreviations:

CSR—"Compiled Service Records of Confederate Soldiers Who Served In Organizations From The State of Georgia," Thirty-fifth Infantry Regiment (National Archives Microfilm Publication M266) National Archives Building, Washington, D.C.

GDAH- Georgia Division of Archives and History, Morrow, Ga.

NMP–National Military Park

OR.—War of the Rebellion: A Compilation of the Official Records of the Union and Confederate Armies. 130 Vols.

1. Letter of Benjamin F. Moody to "dier wife from Richmond va, June the 3d 1862," Benjamin F. Moody Folder, Civil War Miscellany, Personal Papers (Record Group 57-1-1), GDAH.
2. Letter of Benjamin F. Moody, "Dier wife, Richmond Va, June the 11th 1862," Moody Folder, GDAH
3. Anita B. Sams, *Wayfarers In Walton.* (Atlanta, 1967) p. 434–435.

4. Ibid.
5. Charles B. Dew, *Ironmaker To The Confederacy–Joseph R.. Anderson and the Tredegar Ironworks.* (New Haven and London, 1966) p.7–9; *Biographical Register of the Officers and Graduates of the United States Military Academy, Volume I.* (Boston and New York, 1891) p.631.
6. *OR* ., Vol. 11, Pt. III, p.567.
7. Moody letter, June the 11th 1862.
8. Letter of Benjamin F. Moody to "Dier wife from Camp ner Richmond, June the 16th 1862," Moody Folder. GDAH.
9. Letter of Benjamin F. Moody to "Dier wif from Camp nier Richmond Va, June the 22d 1862," Moody Folder. GDAH.
10. Mills Lane, ed., *Dear Mother: Don't Grieve About Me. If I Get Killed, I'll Only Be Dead,* (Savannah, 1977), Letter of Josiah B. Patterson (14th Ga.) to "Family from Camp On the Chickahominy, Virginia, June 13, 1862."
11. *The Georgia Historical Quarterly,* Vol. XLVI, 1962, Georgia Historical Society, p.182. In fact, Lee's army used balloons on a limited basis starting in June 1862. For more on this see E. Porter Alexander's, *Fighting for the Confederacy,* edited by Gary Gallagher, University of North Carolina Press, 1989, p.115–116.
12. *OR.,* Vol. 11, Pt.II, p.877.
13. Ibid., Vol. 11, Pt.II, p. 263,385,399.
14. Ibid., Vol. 51, Pt.1, p.117; W.T. Irvine, *The Sunny South,* Atlanta, May 2, 1891, "Old 35th Georgia"; Ibid. Vol. 11, Pt. II, p.877–878.
15. Ibid., Vol. 11, Pt. II, p.836, 878; Ibid, Vol. 51, Pt. I, p.117.
16. Ibid., Vol. 51, Pt. I, p.110.
17. Ibid., Vol. 11, Pt. II, p.410–411.
18. Ibid., Vol. 11, Pt. II, p.385.
19. Ibid., Vol. 51, Pt. I, p.117–118; Ibid, Vol. 11, Pt.II, p.877–878.
20. Ibid., Vol. 11, Pt. II, p.38, 411. note: The 1st Pennsylvania Rifles were also known as the 13th Pennsylvania Reserves. This combined casualty figure does not include the 3 officers and 72 enlisted men from the 13th Pennsylvania/1st Pa. Rifles that were captured earlier in the day when the first Confederate units crossed Meadow Bridges.
21. First letter of 1st Sgt. Isaiah Hembree to "Mrs Moody," no date/place. Moody Folder. GDAH. This letter was probably written in July 1862 from Richmond before the regiment marched north to join Stonewall Jackson.
22. Second letter of 1st Sgt. Isaiah Hembree to "Mrs Moody," no date/place. Moody Folder GDAH. This letter was probably written in July 1862 from Richmond before the regiment marched north to join Stonewall Jackson.
23. Nancy Jones Cornell, *Campbell County, Georgia Miscellaneous Records.* (Riverdale, Ga. 1983) p.15–16.
24. *OR* ., Vol. 11, Pt.II, p.878.
25. *Columbus Daily Enquirer,* Columbus, Ga. July 8, 1862, available on microfilm at GDAH.
26. *OR.,* Vol. 11, Pt.II, p.853.

27. Report of Lt. David Champion, Co. G, 14th Georgia. "Confederate Reminiscences and Letters 1861–65," Vol. 1 ,1995, Georgia Division United Daughters of the Confederacy, p.6, GDAH.
28. Carroll R. Patterson, "The Incomplete Correspondence of Lt. Josiah B. Patterson and the 14th Georgia Volunteer Infantry- An Outline of Its History," Atlanta Historical Society, Atlanta.
29. Sams, p.138.
30. *OR.,* Vol.11, Pt.II, p.273,278,313.
31. Ibid., Vol. 11, Pt. II, p.879, 900.
32. Ibid., Vol. 11, Pt. 11, p.278.
33. Ibid., Vol. 11, Pt.II, p.836–837, 841–842, 879.
34. Ibid., Vol. 11, Pt. II, p.879, 842.
35. *The Confederate Veteran,* Volume XXXI, p.450; Ibid, Vol. 11, Pt.II, p.879; Ibid, Vol. 51, Pt. I, p.117–118.
36. Ibid., Vol. 11, Pt. II, p.837.
37. Ibid., Vol. 11, Pt. II, p.313.
38. Ibid., Vol. 11, Pt. II, p.282.
39. Ibid., Vol. 11, Pt.II, p.982–983.
40. CSR; Ibid., Vol. 11, Pt.II, p. 39, 987–988.
41. Ibid., Vol. 11, Pt. II, p.838.
42. Ibid., Vol. 11, Pt. II, p.838.
43. Ibid., Vol. 11, Pt.II, p.879–880.
44. Ibid., Vol. 11, Pt. II, p.879–880; Champion, p.9.
45. Ibid., Vol. 51, Pt.I, p.118.
46. *The Confederate Veteran,* Vol. XXIII, 1915, p.162; Ibid., Vol. 51, Pt.I, p.118; Ibid., Vol. 11, pt. II, p.839.
47. Diary of George W. Hall, 14th Georgia, Hargrett Rare Book and Manuscript Library, University of Georgia Libraries, Athens, Ga.
48. *Columbus Enquirer* (Weekly). Columbus, Ga., 8/5/1862; James Folsom, *Heroes and Martyrs of Georgia—Georgia's Record in the Revolution of 1861.* (Macon, Ga. 1864) p.136; Letter of Lieut Wm C Goggans to "Dear Father from Camp near James River South Virginia July 27th 1862," William C. Goggans Civil War Letters, courtesy of Hargrett Rare Book & Manuscript Library/ University of Georgia Libraries, Athens Ga.
49. *OR* ., Vol. 11, Pt. II, p.839; *OR..* ,Vol. 51, Pt. I, p.118.

Chapter Four

WITH STONEWALL AT CEDAR MOUNTAIN

"I can also bear testimony to the gallantry and good conduct of Colonel Thomas and the officers and men of his brigade . . . ."
Brigadier General Jubal Early

The threat posed by Major General John Pope's new army caused Robert E. Lee to send Stonewall Jackson's command toward Gordonsville, Virginia on July 13. At the same time, a dispute between A.P. Hill and James Longstreet over each other's accomplishments during the Seven Days Battles reached a climax when Longstreet placed Hill under arrest. A solution to this command conflict occurred when Jackson requested reinforcements. Lee sent Hill orders on July 26 transferring the Light Division to Jackson's corps. Portions of the Light Division left Richmond on July 27. Edward Thomas' Georgians marched to the rail depot in Richmond and boarded a Virginia Central train bound for Gordonsville in mid-afternoon on July 30.[1]

The Georgians also lost their brigade commander. Joseph Anderson, still recovering from wounds suffered at Frayser's Farm, resigned via a letter to Robert E. Lee on July 15. While in the hospital, Anderson had received word of significant manufacturing problems at the Tredegar Iron Works. Anderson stated in his letter that he needed to resume his duties as head of the company to prevent disaster to the Confederate munitions effort.[2] Lee replied that he would regretfully forward and recommend acceptance of the resignation to higher authority. "I know that all your energies and abilities will be devoted to the Cause of the Country and that it is your desire as well as mine, that they should be applied where they can be of most benefit."[3]

Colonel Thomas officially became the new brigade commander, and twenty-one- year-old Lieutenant Colonel Bolling Hall Holt took charge of the 35th Georgia Infantry Regiment. Holt, a Columbus, Georgia native and former University of Virginia student, had enlisted as a private in Company G, 2nd Georgia Infantry on April 16, 1861. He had received a discharge from that unit on October 14, 1861 and his new men had elected him major of the 35th Georgia on the same day. After the Battle of Seven Pines and the death of Lieutenant Colonel Gustavus A. Bull, Holt had received a promotion as his replacement.[4]

The hot summer fanned controversy among men at the lower command levels too. Captain William Jefferson Head, Company A, had lent $200 to his men some time prior to June. Head became sick and went to Richmond for treatment and convalescence on or about June 1. Several days later Head's father appeared in camp with the debt papers to collect payroll money from the soldiers. Both Lieutenants William C. Goggans and John Duke refused to honor the debt papers without the permission of the individual soldiers. Some of these men had died or still lay wounded in area hospital beds and thus obviously were not available. Goggans revealed his smoldering resentment toward Head. "Head made no effort to see the men consequently we felt under no obligation to take the papers neither did we feel bound in any way as there was no promise made relative to us taking them."[5]

Captain William Jefferson Head, Co. A

This Haralson County lawyer turned officer became frustrated with the slow-moving Georgia Governor Joe Brown. Head and two other company commanders took action and moved their men to Richmond in September 1861. He resigned for illness and fatigue on July 3, 1862.

From *Sunny South,* Atlanta, Ga. May 2, 1891

Captain Head then wrote a letter wrought with frustration to his two lieutenants. This letter so angered Goggans that he hand-copied part of Head's message and inserted it into his letter mailed to his own father in Haralson County. Goggans no doubt hoped to influence public opinion against Head at home. Head wrote, "Sirs when I made the arrangement with you I did it in good faith. I am not so hide bound yet that I cannot risk a few Dollars on the Haralson Brown Guards. [T]rue they may get Killed or a large portion of them yet when they can risk their lives I can certainly risk my Dollars."[6]

Goggans cited Head's offenses:

> We think this letter to be uncalled for, ungentlemanly and without cause, for which he is liked none the better for by us. [H]e remained better than one month in few miles of the company Previous to his leaving but never visited us. [H]is excuse was not able. We learn he reached home in about the same condition as to Health. I do not know how he stands in Haralson, but one voice speaks here. [S]o I will close. [Y]ou need not make this public as I have written it but have the better right to be leave [believe] when others tell.[7]

Head resigned on July 3 and returned home. It remained unclear whether Goggans' anger stemmed from the debt collection attempt or about Head's departure without a proper farewell to the men. The men elected thirty-year-old John Duke to succeed Head. Duke, a former Tallapoosa lawyer, failed to indicate his thoughts about the controversy.[8]

William Goggans wrote another letter from Richmond on or about August 5. Doctors had discharged him from a hospital for illness and he planned to take a train the following morning to catch up with the regiment near Gordonsville. He had lost a lot of weight and described how loosely his shirt fit. Just days before, weakness had prevented him from sitting up in bed forcing him to pen a letter while the paper rested on his knee. He expressed concern because his friend, Corporal Reuben Ayers, had recently died.[9]

Goggans had learned to turn a skeptical eye on what he read in the local press. "To days paper give inteligent News if only true which we hope is though not given as such. To days Dispatch give news that Secretary Seward has resigned also that three of the most Leading Northern states have refused to furnish any more troops to fight The rebelion." The paper to which he referred, the Richmond *Daily Dispatch,* had the largest circulation of the city's four daily newspapers. While these reports made for good talk around the local camps and taverns, they in fact turned out to be unfounded. These rumors, however, brought a sense of hope to the young officer. "[I]f these things are so, I think there will be some changes for the better soon. [H]ope it will be so." He also wrote that many Richmonders expressed relief because the threat of attack on the capital city had subsided with the withdrawal of McClellan's forces down the James River. "I have no news to write at this time only the citty is releaved of their Doleful expectations. [M]any are going to their Residences in the Country."[10]

The Light Division marched north from Gordonsville toward Orange Court House on August 6. Stonewall Jackson wanted to strike several scattered Union divisions in the vicinity of Culpeper Court House before Pope could consolidate them. Jackson, in customary fashion, failed to inform his commanders of the plan, the objective, and the route of march.

August 7 dawned hot and humid. Grimy choking dust filled the air along the march route. The troops finally reached the outskirts of Orange Court House around midnight. Most soldiers, although famished, succumbed to exhaustion and fell asleep beside the road. The following day, because of confusion in marching orders, a tremendous traffic jam of sweaty bodies collided at Barnett's Ford on the Rapidan River. The Light Division only marched one mile out of Orange Court House and halted. A courier arrived with subsequent orders for Hill's men to retrace their steps. Tempers rose with the temperature and many soldiers scrambled for shade on both sides of the road. Some failed to get up again because of sunstroke.

The 35th Georgia sergeants awakened their men at 1 A.M., on the morning of August 9. Thomas' Brigade led the march of the Light Division. They trailed the divisions of Ewell and Winder northward toward Culpeper. The dust still hung thick in the air, and as the sun came up, soldiers again collapsed by the roadside. Many hours later, the blurred hazy outline of Cedar Mountain slowly crept into view of the winding column.[11]

The men heard the distinct reports of artillery far ahead. Edward Thomas quickened the pace. Sharp volleys of musketry added to the noise. Around 3 P.M., Hill ordered Thomas' men moved to the right of the Orange-Culpeper Road and to report to Jackson.

Jackson's corps had stumbled into units from Major General Nathaniel P. Banks' corps six miles south of Culpeper Court House. Thomas reached Jackson who ordered the Georgia brigade to move into a reserve position in the woods by the intersection of the Orange-Culpeper Road and the Fordsville Road. They remained there only a short time. The situation at the front became dire. Union troops threatened to envelop the Confederate right flank, anchored by Jubal Early's Brigade. Several artillery pieces also faced capture.

Thomas' Georgians first moved to support Taliaferro's Brigade located on Early's left. Thomas halted his men in a strip of woods to the left rear of Taliaferro. Early's Brigade had initially stopped in the woods west of the

Crittenden Lane while skirmishers moved forward. Early then posted Captain William Brown of the Chesapeake (Md.) Battery with one gun and Captain William Dement's Maryland Battery with three guns in front of a clump of cedar trees on his right. A short time later, enemy skirmishers followed by several regiments of infantry plodded through the cornfield to his front. As Early surveyed the scene, what he saw on the right struck him with fear. "A body of infantry also commenced moving up toward my right, which rested near the clump of cedars where the guns of Brown and Dement were posted. The hill there falls off rather abruptly to the right, and as infantry could have come up under cover of this hill very near to me, I sent to General Jackson for a brigade to support my right, which was promised."[12]

Jackson soon delivered on that promise. The time was about 5:45 P.M. as he caught up with Thomas and sent the brigade farther to Early's right with orders to hold the position. The Georgia brigade rushed southward through the woods and down the Crittenden Lane. Suddenly, they ran into panicked Southern soldiers storming toward the rear. These men belonged to one of Taliaferro's regiments. In the ensuing chaos, Colonel Thomas ordered the 14th Georgia, at the brigade rear, to halt and try to stem this breakthrough. The 14th Georgia stopped in the right place to plug the gap and force back the Union troops that had broken Taliaferro's line.[13]

The remainder of the Georgians continued ahead. They broke out into a field and rushed southeastward, amidst heavy fighting from the proximity of Taliaferro and Early's beleaguered line on the left. A concerned Early had spurred toward the right end of his line to anchor the position of his right flank unit, the 12th Georgia. He expressed surprise a short time later when he observed Thomas' Georgians rushing behind the 12th Georgia to his aid. His concern now turned to jubilation. He wrote, "I immediately proceeded to post this brigade to the right of the Twelfth Georgia Regiment and at right angles with it, where it also had a strong position."[14]

Thomas' men dashed across the open field toward the clump of cedar trees. They lined up at almost a right angle to Early and crouched behind a wooden fence that bordered a cornfield. Captain Washington T. Irvine wrote that the 35th Georgia occupied the extreme right side of the line. The 49th Georgia stood in the middle while the 45th Georgia held the brigade left next to the clump of cedar trees.[15]

Two lines of Federal Brigadier General Henry Prince's brigade moved ahead in the chest-high corn. Prince's left flank, held by the 102nd New York, passed along the Georgian's entire front. The 109th Pennsylvania moved on the New Yorker's right. The 3rd Maryland and the 111th Pennsylvania came in order further to the right. Thomas' Georgians

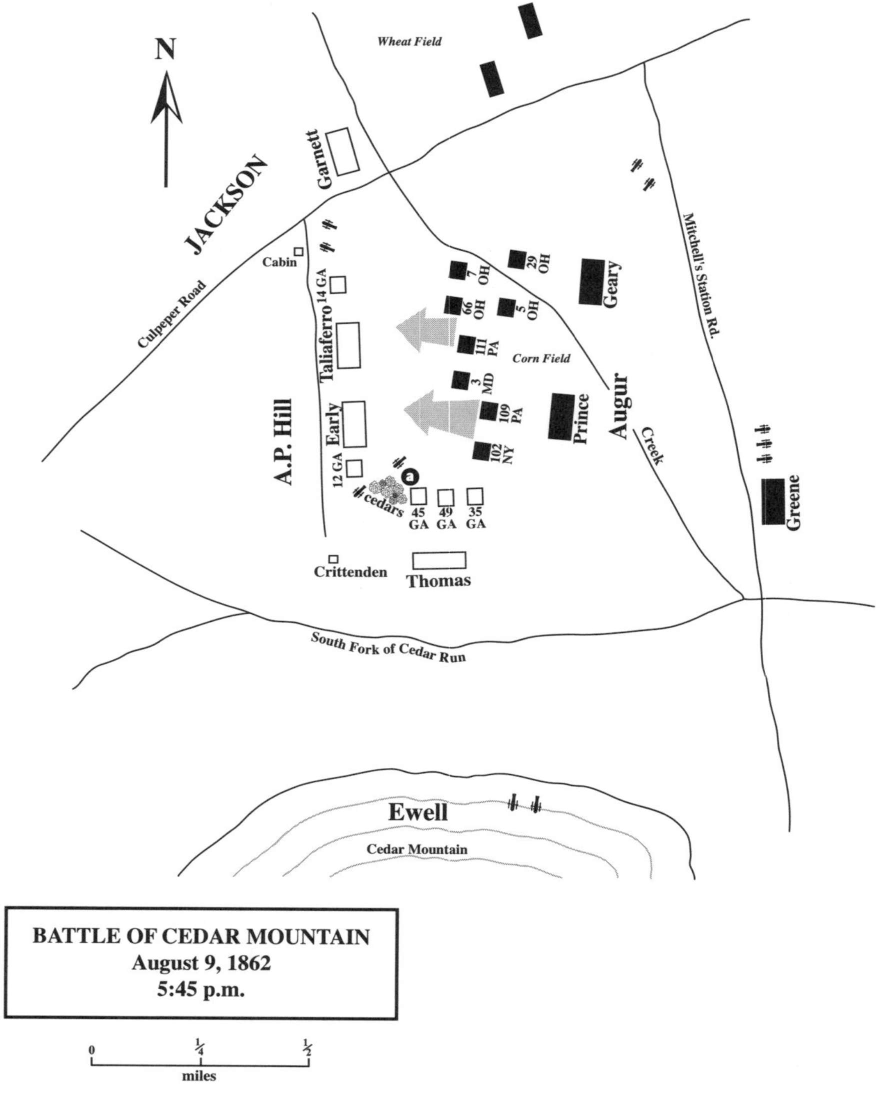

BATTLE OF CEDAR MOUNTAIN
August 9, 1862
5:45 p.m.

poured deadly fire into the left flank of the New Yorkers as they moved toward the 12th Georgia. This onslaught caught the Empire Staters by surprise. Most of the Georgians used up their ammunition as the battle continued. Reports stated that many men fired from 25–40 rounds and had to scavenge amongst the dead and wounded of both sides for more ammunition. The Southerner's rapid shooting overheated many gun barrels. Soldiers exchanged the hot guns for ones lying on the ground. Other sol-

a. Thomas' Left Flank At Cedar Trees
Looking north from cedar knoll downhill into cornfield. Cedars trees are no longer present. This position enabled the Georgians to decimate the left flank of the 102nd New York and 109th Pennsylvania. Thomas' timely arrival to this position saved the day for Jubal Early's Brigade.
photo by author

diers poured canteen water on their weapons to cool them down. An explosion suddenly rocked the ground amidst Company F. Several soldiers rushed to the aid of their dazed company commander, Captain James McElvany. Blood poured from his left temple. His men rushed him off the field.[16]

Early soon felt confident with the security of his right. He moved toward the left of his line, hidden from view by the rolling terrain, to view the situation. As he rode northward, the scene that came into view gave him another shock—even greater than the earlier fear that his right could be turned. Blue-clad soldiers raced all along his line. The enemy most definitely had turned his left! He quickly realized that the key to holding his line was for the regiments in his center plus the 12th Georgia and Thomas' men on the right to make a stand. He knew that these units were "isolated and in an advanced position, and had they given way the day in all probability would have been lost." He sent an aide to attempt a rally of his left and remained with his anchored troops urging them to hold the line.[17]

This line held. Prince's Union troops advanced no farther than the western boundary of the cornfield. Confederate fire mowed them down

Major James Thomas McElvany, Co. F

This Gwinnett County school teacher turned officer was elected captain by his men in May 1862. He was wounded by a shell fragment in the left temple at the Battle of Cedar Mountain on August 9, 1862. This picture was probably taken in Richmond while McElvany convalesced. Note the bare spot on the left side of his head probably from his wound. He survived the war, but buried three brothers. He served as a Gwinnett sheriff and a state representative after the war.

Courtesy of John Bailey, Douglasville, Ga.

each time they tried to rally for a charge out of the scant protection provided by the browning green cornstalks. Early and Taliaferro's wavering units, on the left, finally mounted a staunch counterattack with the aid of the 14th Georgia and drove the invaders back through the cornfield toward Mitchell's Station Road.

Even with this Federal repulse on Early's left, portions of the 109th Pennsylvania and the 102nd New York maintained a position in the corn and traded sporadic fire with the Georgians. Early described what he found upon his return toward the right of his line. "I rode off to the right again and found the troops there maintaining their ground against a body of infantry in front of Colonel Thomas' brigade, which kept its position for some time. The ammunition of my own regiments being nearly exhausted, as was that of Colonel Thomas' brigade, I directed them to maintain their ground at all hazards and use the bayonet if necessary, and they did not waver for a moment." This standoff on the south edge of the cornfield continued for some time as the Georgians hugged the ground with fixed bayonets. Early stated that he did not believe that a charge into the cornfield to rout these stubborn New Yorkers and Pennsylvanians would be successful because it would invite an attack from Brigadier General George S. Greene's fresh troops on Thomas' right.[18]

It was now almost dark as the men of the 109th Pennsylvania found there was no longer any support on their right. The Pennsylvanians turned toward the rear and the New Yorkers followed.[19] Both regiments joined the rest of Pope's troops in a withdrawal back toward Culpeper Court House. Jackson ordered a pursuit, and the Light Division led the chase. Thomas' men, lacking ammunition, joined the advance with fixed bayonets. They continued forward for a little over one mile when a scout reported the proximity of the enemy in some woods only a few hundred yards ahead. Confederate artillery shelled the woods which drew return fire. The artillery duel continued for some time. Jackson interrogated some prisoners who convinced him that Pope had received reinforcements. Jackson wrote, "Believing it imprudent to continue to move forward during the darkness, I ordered a halt for the night."[20] Thomas' Brigade bivouacked that night on ground previously held by the enemy. The next day, August 10, the Georgians pulled back a short distance and formed a defensive line.

Jackson described his actions: "On the following morning (10th), having reason to believe that the Federal Army had been so largely re-enforced as to render it imprudent for me to attempt to advance farther, directions were given for sending the wounded to the rear, for burying the dead, and collecting arms from the battle-field." Later in the morning, Jackson utilized Major General Jeb Stuart's cavalry for a reconnaissance. Based on Stuart's report, Jackson correctly deduced that reinforcements had reached Pope. Jackson believed in the strength of his position, so he elected to keep his soldiers in the line. The Federal troops asked for and received a flag of truce to remove and bury their dead on August 11. Jackson granted the request until 2 P.M. and later extended it until 5 P.M. He withdrew that night under cover of darkness and moved his troops back toward Gordonsville.[21]

The Union casualty reports for Prince's left flank reflected the effective fire from Early's and Thomas' infantry plus the nearby artillery. The 102nd New York suffered the highest losses in the brigade with 15 killed,

85 wounded and 15 missing for an aggregate of 115. The 109th Pennsylvania lost 14 killed, 72 wounded and 28 missing for a total of 114.[22]

In Jubal Early's report of the Battle of Cedar Mountain, he paid tribute to Thomas' Brigade. "I can also bear testimony to the gallantry and good conduct of Colonel Thomas and the officers and men of his brigade, whose timely arrival rendered my right secure, and whose deadly fire contributed largely to the repulse of the enemy."[23] A.P. Hill also lauded the Georgians warmly: "Much credit is due Thomas' Brigade for the admirable manner in which they acted under discouraging circumstances."[24]

A Georgia newspaper correspondent wrote that the Battle of Cedar Mountain represented the twenty-fourth time that Colonel Thomas had withstood enemy fire. "His conduct in action is characterized by great coolness and unflinching bravery." No doubt this number included his combat forays during the Mexican War.[25]

The 35th Georgia reported 9 killed and 17 wounded at Cedar Mountain. The wounded Captain McElvany spent the next two months in a hospital.[26]

Many regarded this battle as one of Stonewall Jackson's greatest victories. It represented the last battle in which he exercised independent command. Pope's army had only received a bloody nose. This force represented a threat that Lee wanted to destroy, but the Confederate commander needed the right opportunity. Both armies glared at each other and jockeyed for position along the banks of the Rapidan and then the Rappahannock River for the next two weeks.

NOTES

Abbreviations:

CSR—"Compiled Service Records of Confederate Soldiers Who Served In Organizations From The State of Georgia,"- Thirty-fifth Infantry Regiment (National Archives Microfilm Publication M266) National Archives Building, Washington, D.C.

GDAH- Georgia Division of Archives and History, Morrow, Ga.

NMP–National Military Park

OR.—War of the Rebellion: A Compilation of the Official Records of the Union and Confederate Armies. 130 Vols.

1. Diary of George W. Hall, 14th Georgia, Hargrett Rare Book and Manuscript Library/University of Georgia Libraries, Athens, Ga. p.5.
2. Charles B. Dew, *Ironmaker To The Confederacy–Joseph R. Anderson and the Tredegar Ironworks.* (New Haven and London, 1966) p. 150–151.
3. Letter of R.E. Lee to "My Dear General 15 July 1862," Joseph R. Anderson Papers 1861, 1862 & 1867, # 26167, Virginia State Library, Richmond, Va.

4. Robert K. Krick, *Lee's Colonels: A Biographical Register of the Field Officers of the Army of Northern Virginia.* (Dayton, Oh., 1979) p.179–180; CSR of Colonel Bolling Hall Holt, M266.
5. Letter of Lieut Wm. C. Goggans to "Dear Father from Camp near James River South Virginia July 27th 1862," William C. Goggans Civil War Letters, courtesy of Hargrett Rare Book and Manuscript Library/ University of Georgia Libraries, Athens Ga.
6. Ibid.
7. Ibid.
8. Ibid.
9. Letter of Lieut. W.C. Goggans to "Mr. Josiah Goggans from Richmond Va July 5th 1862," William C. Goggans Civil War Letters, courtesy of Hargrett Rare Book & Manuscript Library/ University of Georgia Libraries, Athens Ga. note: Lee did not direct A.P. Hill's Light Division to transfer to Jackson at Gordonsville until July 26, so there is no way Goggans would be writing of such a transfer three weeks before the fact. The date of this letter has to be wrong. It must be later in the month and possibly was written August 5 and Goggans mistakenly wrote the previous month at the head of the letter. More evidence that the date of this letter is incorrect is that Goggans mentioned that he wrote in a previous letter about the death of his friend Reuben Ayers and this soldier did not die until July 5.
10. Ibid. note: U.S. Secretary of State William H. Seward did not resign. He actually served in this position from 1861–1869.
11. *OR* ., Vol.12, Pt.II, p.215.
12. Ibid., Vol. 12, Pt.II, p.229–230.
13. Ibid., Vol. 12, Pt.II, p.215, 219.
14. Ibid., Vol. 12, Pt.II, p.230–231.
15. W.T. Irvine, *The Sunny South,* Atlanta, May 2, 1891, "Old 35th Georgia"; Captain S.T. Player, 49th Georgia, *Central Georgian* (Sandersville, Ga.), August 27, 1862, "Report of Battle of Cedar Mountain."
16. Letter of Capt. M.R. Rogers of Gresham Rifles, 45th Georgia Infantry, *Weekly Enquirer (*Columbus, Ga). August 26, 1862; "The Letters and Journal of Major James T. McElvany, Co.D, 35th Georgia Infantry Regiment."
17. *OR* ., Vol. 12, Pt.II, p.231.
18. Ibid., Vol. 12, Pt.II, p.231.
19. Ibid., Vol. 12, Pt.II, p.168–169.
20. Ibid., Vol.12, Pt.II, p.184–185.
21. Ibid., Vol. 12, Pt.II, p.184–185.
22. Ibid., Vol.12, Pt.II, p.137.
23. Ibid., Vol.12, Part II, p.233.
24. Ibid., Vol.12, Pt.II, p.216.
25. *Central Georgian* (Sandersville, Ga.), August 27, 1862, "Georgians At the Battle of Cedar Run."
26. James Folsom, *Heroes and Martyrs of Georgia—Georgia's Record in the Revolution of 1861.* (Macon, Ga. 1864) p.136; McElvany.

Chapter Five

Second Manassas

"If I did not have money I would be in a bad fix here and every thing is so high it takes a heap of it to do a man."
Private James M. Garrett

James Garrett lay far from the danger of battle on the eve of the climactic fight with John Pope's army. However, a Richmond hospital bed did not guarantee the young private's safety. Disease and infection coupled with grievous wounds ensured that Confederate hospitals witnessed far more deaths than all the battlefields combined.

Physicians sent the ill Garrett to a medical facility on August 1. Records indicated his admission to Richmond's Winder Hospital on or about August 18. There the doctors diagnosed his loss of strength and energy as debilitus. He wrote his mother in Heard County, eight days later, that he felt better and his appetite had returned. Unfortunately, there was not a lot to eat. "I will tell you what we get. [B]read and coffee for supper and the same for breakfast and a little fat bacon boiled and for dinner we have a little fat bacon and bread that is not fitten for a sick man to eat." Garrett longed for home and he hoped to get a furlough soon. He promised to send some of his pay home soon to help his mother and four younger siblings [Sophronia, 17; William (Bud), 15; Mary (Ellen), 13; and John, 10] on their farm. The Georgian wrote that due to the current high prices of food in Richmond "I have to keep it [money] to live on hear. If I did not have money I would be in a bad fix here and every thing is so high it takes a heap of it to do a man." In frustration he listed the exorbitant prices for various goods in the capital city:

> [Y]ou cant buy a chicken her[e] for less than a dollar; butter is a dollar a pound; roasting ears [corn] fifty cts a doz.; cabbage $1.00 a head; little plate pies fifty cts a piece; ginger cakes 25 cts a piece; watermelons $2.00 to $2.50 a piece; peaches 50 cts a doz.; apples the same; sweet milk ten cents a glass; fresh meat is fifty cents a

> pound; irish potatoes 25 cents a quart; eggs $1.00 a doz and corn bread 10 cents a pone. [S]mall pity at that. [Y]ou cant get a meals vitiuals [victuals] hear for less than a $1.00.[1]

The inflation problem had spread from southern cities to the countryside. Several things caused this crisis: an effective Federal naval blockade of Confederate ports; decreased farm output because most military age farmers wore a gray uniform; and overcrowding in southern cities, especially Richmond.

Garrett pleaded with his family to send him some home cooking:

> I would like very much to get a box of vituals [victuals] from home if you can get the chance. I want you to send me a nice piece of ham. [T]he best you have got as soon as possible and anything else you can send that is to eat. [A]nybody can find me at Winder Hospital Second Division and ward No. 47. [M]aybe you can send it by railroad and it would not cost much. I would like to have a baked chicken or some fried chicken. [A]nything that is good will do me.[2]

Garrett changed his attitude about his hospital environment in the same letter. Maybe he feared alarming his family or perhaps he read the Cedar Mountain casualty reports. "[I]f I dont get a furlough I am going to stay hear all winter as I have a good bed to ly [lie] on and a good house to stay in and a plenty to eat. [S]uch as it is I can make out on it.[3]

All of the brigade commanders in the Light Division had received their brigadier general's star by mid-August 1862 with the exception of one officer. Colonel Edward Thomas' lack of promotion created a controversy because he commanded the only Georgia brigade in the division. Many soldiers perceived this lack of recognition as a significant slight in an era where appearances carried great weight. The officers of Thomas' Brigade wrote a letter in mid-August to both the Confederate Adjutant & Inspector General and the Secretary of War George W. Randolph urgently requesting Thomas' promotion. Two more months would pass before Thomas received his promotion.[4]

Robert E. Lee recognized another opportunity to attack Pope's army. The Light Division moved on August 15 from their bivouac on the Crenshaw Farm located halfway between Gordonsville and Orange Court House. They marched with the rest of Jackson's corps north about twenty miles to Mountain Run, west of Clark's Mountain. The men remained in this area for several days. Due to confusion in orders, the Light Division failed to begin a march early on the morning of August 20 according to Jackson's timetable. The troops sloshed across the Rapidan River at Somerville Ford and despite the delay, they still covered nearly twenty miles. They camped that evening near Stevensburg.

Lieutenant General Thomas Jonathan "Stonewall" Jackson
Carte de visite taken by Rose in Winchester, Va., 1862.
Copy print courtesy of The Museum of the Confederacy, Richmond, Va.

Jackson met with Lee on August 24. The commanders decided to leave Longstreet's troops along the western bank of the Rappahannock River just northeast of Culpeper to mask Jackson's sweep northwestward. Jackson would march west of the Bull Run Mountains using the terrain to screen his move and then turn east through Thoroughfare Gap and destroy Pope's supply line. This move, if successful, might pull Pope away from the Rappahannock River and a consolidation with McClellan's army.

Jackson's troops prepared three days cooked rations. Orders specified the men could only carry haversacks. Officers refused to allow the men to carry knapsacks nor would supply wagons follow the column. Each soldier knew the minimal provisions signaled some rough, rapid marching. Jackson's corps moved several miles toward their unknown destination by sunrise on August 25. Ewell's Division led the march followed by the divisions of Hill and Taliaferro. Jackson allowed only his chief engineer, Lieutenant

James Keith Boswell, to know the destination. The hot, dusty march continued all day and into the night. The column finally stopped just south of Salem, known today as Marshall, Virginia.

The troops pulled their sore bodies off the ground before dawn on August 26. When the column reached Salem, it turned sharply eastward. They soon passed through White Plains, Virginia as the Bull Run Mountains loomed larger to the east. The hungry soldiers stripped the edges of the numerous apple orchards and cornfields along the route. When Jackson's "foot cavalry" reached Thoroughfare Gap they found a surprise. Pope's men had failed to defend the mountainous pass. The Southerners trudged through the gap and their enthusiasm grew. They had marched undetected into the rear of Pope's army.

Jackson's column met slight picket resistance at Hay Market and Gainesville. When the men halted for the night, the soldiers of the 35th Georgia found themselves in a field about four miles east of Gainesville, Virginia. Jackson's corps of 23,500 men had marched fifty-four miles in barely thirty-six hours, achieving total surprise.[5]

Meanwhile in Richmond, Captain Evan R. Whitley penned a note on August 27 to Benjamin Moody's widow in Campbell County. The Company E commander failed to explain why he was not with his men on the march. Whitley had received a power of attorney to collect Moody's back wages. The Confederacy owed Moody two-month's pay as a private at $11 per month and one month and twenty-six days as a corporal at $13 per month. His total pay for this period amounted to $46.26. He owed the Confederacy $7.75 for a uniform coat and cap so the actual balance due the dead soldier was $38.51. Whitley explained to Martha Moody that her husband, who had made the ultimate sacrifice, missed eligibility for a one-year enlistment bounty by only forty-six days.[6]

Jackson's men continued the march toward Manassas Junction early on August 27. After a mile Colonel Thomas halted his troops to watch the torching of two Federal trains. A Confederate artillery battery unlimbered its guns and fired into a nearby detachment of Union cavalry sending the enemy dashing for cover.[7] The march resumed a short while later, and the Georgians reached the Federal supply depot at Manassas Junction around noon. Two regiments from Isaac Trimble's Brigade and Stuart's cavalry had seized this depot on the previous night. A beggar's dream unfolded before the members of the Light Division. Federal boxcars stretched for a half-mile. Warehouses and wagons, full of essential military and luxury items, stood in every direction. The dirty, hungry soldiers quickly overwhelmed the guards who Jackson had posted to prevent pillaging. Hill's troops tore into the boxcars and wagons and gorged themselves on lobster

Captain Evan Riley Whitley, Co. E

This Campbell County officer, frustrated with the slow-moving Georgia Governor Joe Brown, was one of three company commanders who moved their men to Richmond in September 1861. He resigned for a disability on January 23, 1863.

From *Sunny South,* Atlanta, Ga. May 2, 1891

salad, sardines, vegetables, corned beef, cakes, fruits, pickles and mustard. The joyous men washed the feast down with champagne, whiskey and wine. Pockets bulged with handfuls of cigars. Trimble noted in his report, "It was with extreme mortification that, in reporting to General A.P. Hill for orders about 10 o'clock, I witnessed an indiscriminate plunder of the public stores, cars and sutler's houses by the army which had just arrived, in which General Hill's division was conspicuous, setting at defiance the guards I had placed over the stores."[8] General Jackson officially reported that the seized items included: "50,000 pounds of bacon, 1,000 barrels of corned beef, 2,000 barrels of salt pork, 2,000 barrels of flour, quartermaster's, ordnance, and sutler's stores deposited in buildings and filling two trains of cars."[9]

The approach of Colonel Gustav Waagner's 2nd New York Heavy Artillery, a green artillery-turned infantry unit, briefly interrupted the Manassas Junction party. A. P. Hill moved the Light Division east to meet the threat. Waagner expected to subdue the reported "small band of guerillas" who had captured the depot. Colonel William S. Baylor's Stonewall Brigade unleashed the initial gunfire on Waagner's troops. When the Light Division arrived, Hill placed Branch's Brigade to the left and then the brigades of Archer, Pender, Thomas and Field to the right. Waagner ordered a retreat because of the hot fire. A short time later, Brigadier General George Taylor's New Jersey brigade arrived by train one mile north of the depot. The New Jersey soldiers formed into line of battle and marched into the same problem recently vacated by Waagner. The Confederates routed Taylor's brigade capturing about two hundred prisoners. Some of Hill's exuberant men burned the train and a nearby railroad bridge.[10]

When A.P. Hill's men returned to the depot, they found that Jackson had ordered the guard increased. Jackson, after much cajoling, finally agreed to let the troops help themselves before he ordered the remains burned. Hill ordered the two brigades of Thomas and Gregg moved south of Manassas Junction at dark. The men formed a rear guard position to protect against an attack from Bristoe Station.[11] The rest of Jackson's men continued their drunken revelry. Jackson ordered the depot torched after dark. The bright flames reached the ammunition magazines around 10 P.M. The powder and shells exploded with a deafening roar as flames leaped high into the air.[12] One Georgian enjoyed being able to eat until he was full, but he lamented watching the majority of the needed supplies go up in smoke.[13]

Jackson knew that Pope's numerically superior army was not far from the smoldering ashes of Manassas Junction. The daring commander studied his map to locate some defensible terrain. He selected Stony Ridge northwest of the town of Groveton, Virginia.

Jackson's early morning march on August 28 towards Stony Ridge became a navigational disaster. Many soldiers drunkenly stumbled along the dark roads. Most men had stuffed themselves, both internally and externally, with as much as their bodies could carry. Lieutenant Henry Kyd Douglas, from Jackson's staff, remarked:

> The appearance of the marching columns was novel and amusing. Commissary, quartermaster, and sutler store, enough for an army and a campaign, were carried along on the backs of soldiers wearied with excessive marching the days before. Here one fellow was bending beneath the weight of a score of boxes of cigars, smoking and joking as he went, another with as many boxes of canned fruits, another with coffee enough for a winters encampment, or perhaps with a long string of shoes hung around his neck, like beads. It was a martial masquerade by night.[14]

Taliaferro's Division, in the lead, became the only unit to reach the area along Stony Ridge as scheduled. The Light Division departed Manassas Junction about 2 A.M.The flickering light given off by the conflagration of boxcars and assorted supplies initially aided Hill's men.[15] A guide, sent by Jackson, soon became disoriented in the darkness and led the division to Centreville some seven miles to the east. Ewell's Division also became lost on another road. The tired men grumbled to each other as the sun crept into the eastern sky. Hill pushed his men quite hard until the Light Division finally located the Sudley Springs Ford along Bull Run around 12 noon. The planned eight-mile march had turned into sixteen. The confusion during the march ironically worked in Jackson's favor because Pope could not determine Jackson's location or his intentions.

Elements of the Light Division moved into the woods adjacent to Sudley Springs Ford. Fighting broke out later in the day to the southwest. A portion of Ewell's and Taliaferro's divisions attacked the flank of Brigadier General Rufus King's division which unwittingly marched northeast along the Warrenton Turnpike toward Centreville. Thomas' Brigade, although not directly engaged, remained in reserve and endured a severe shelling. The indecisive but bloody Battle of Groveton ended around 9 P.M. when Union troops withdrew under cover of darkness.[16] This fight left Jackson with A.P. Hill as his only experienced division commander because both Taliaferro and Ewell fell with serious wounds.

The Light Division moved into position on the vulnerable left flank of Jackson near the Sudley Springs Ford early on August 29. The brigades of Gregg, Thomas and Field occupied the line from left to right behind an unfinished railroad bed. The brigades of Archer, Pender and Branch stood a short distance to the rear. Hill placed his artillery in the open field behind the infantry, but he admitted, "the nature of my position being such as to preclude the effective use of much artillery."[17]

Gregg's Brigade, on the extreme left, occupied a position on a knoll west of the rail bed. His line curved northward at an angle where the railroad crossed the Manassas-Sudley Road. On Gregg's right, Thomas' troops formed a line in heavy woods about sixty yards behind the railroad. Federal cannon fire suddenly shook the ground along the rail bed around 7 A.M.[18] Soon afterward, Union troops from Franz Sigel's First Corps led by Carl Schurz's division attacked Gregg and attempted to turn his left. Thomas' skirmishers probably traded shots with the 75th Pennsylvania and the 58th New York of Colonel Wladimir Krzyzanowski's brigade as it moved northward. Gregg's troops initially succeeded in halting the Union move and even pushed some of the enemy units back a few hundred yards. A short time later, the South Carolinian ordered his regiments back to their original line.[19]

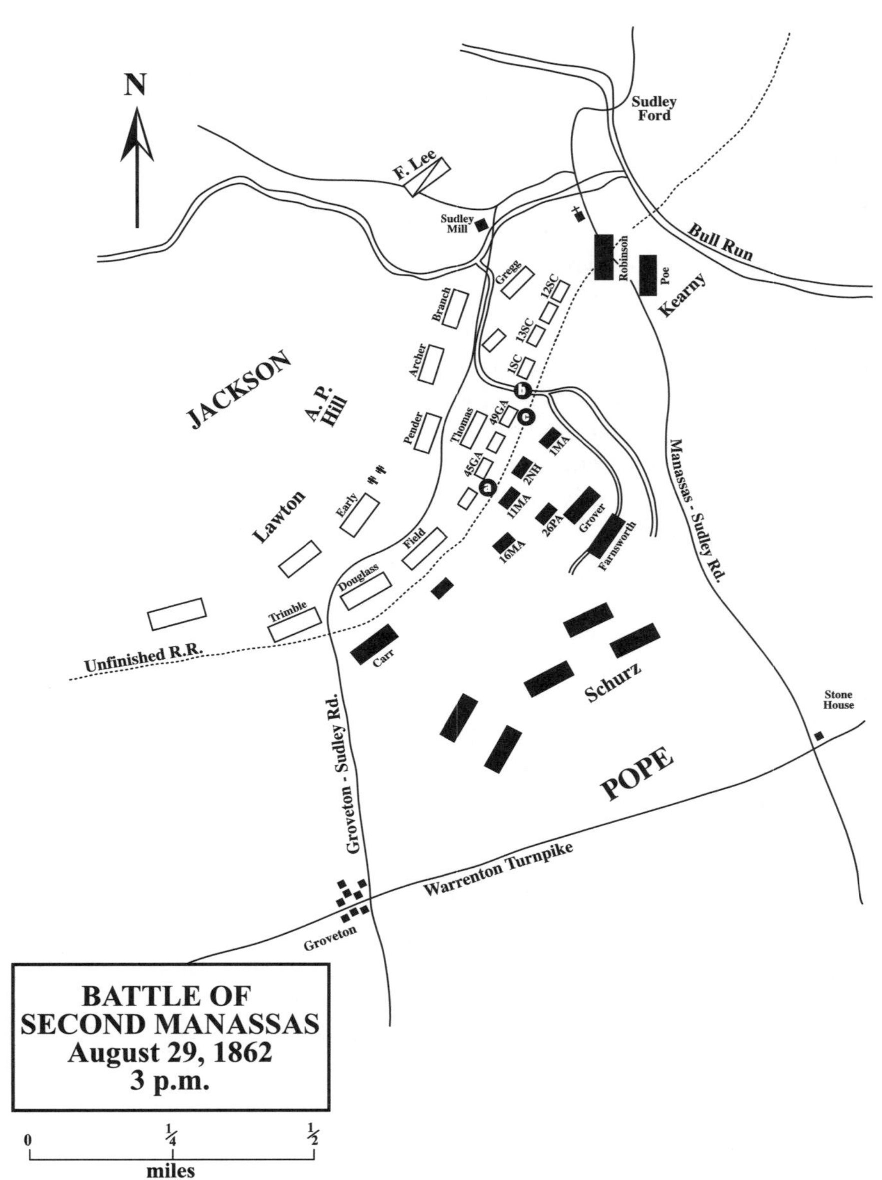

BATTLE OF SECOND MANASSAS August 29, 1862 3 p.m.

0 ¼ ½
miles

a. Railroad Cut Along Thomas' Line
Looking NE along middle of Georgia line occupied by 45th Georgia. Notice steep angle of slope on both sides. Brutal hand-to-hand combat broke out here when Grover's Federals dropped in on the heads of the Georgians as they reloaded their weapons.
photo by author

A renewed Federal attack against Gregg brought the enemy into full contact with Thomas' Georgians. The fire from Gregg's right combined with Thomas' guns caused the men of Krzyzanowski's brigade to think better of crossing the rail bed. The men of the 75th Pennsylvania and the 58th New York probably bore the brunt of the Georgia effort again. These Federal soldiers sought cover and traded fire with their Southern counterparts. This sporadic fire continued between both lines until mid-afternoon.[20]

Seven hours of fighting had exhausted Schurz's Unionists as well as their ammunition. A small brigade commanded by Colonel Addison Farnsworth from Brigadier General Isaac I. Stevens' division moved forward. Farnsworth placed his men into position at around 2 P.M., well behind Schurz's line along the rail bed. Farnsworth's troops began a sporadic and ineffective fire after Schurz's fatigued men passed behind the new Federal position.

Edward Thomas immediately noticed the slackening Federal fire when Schurz's men pulled back. The Georgia commander ordered his men forward. They took possession of the unfinished railroad, but the 49th Georgia on the left of Thomas' line failed to make contact with the right of Gregg's

b. Rail Bed On Thomas' Left Flank

View from gap looking SW at Thomas' left flank occupied by the 49th Georgia. Notice how rail bed slopes away on each side where wooden steps stand. Federals moved through this low undefended area from left to right and turned the flanks of two Confederate brigades.

photo by author

Brigade. This left an unguarded low wooded gap about 175 yards wide. The dense foliage prevented the Georgians from viewing this area. The 49th Georgia's position next to this gap soon proved to be an unhealthy place. The men from this regiment hugged the west side of the rail embankment because the ground sloped away on both sides of the bed. The center of the Georgia line was different. There the bed ran through a deep cut. The steep ten-foot slope spilled into the rail bed from both sides. The 45th Georgia occupied the center, but it was unclear where the remaining two regiments stood. The 35th Georgia possibly occupied a position to the right of the 49th Georgia. Thomas could have also held the 35th in reserve and later thrust them into the hottest part of the line during the enemy breakthrough that occurred later. Whichever position the 35th Georgia held, they suffered the highest brigade casualties of the day.[22]

Farnsworth's attack fizzled into nothing more than skirmish fire. Portions of the divisions of Major General Joseph Hooker and Major General Phil Kearny moved against Jackson's line at around 3 P.M. Hooker ordered Brigadier General Cuvier Grover's brigade to launch a frontal attack against

c. Gap Between Thomas and Gregg

View looking NE down into gap. Small wooden bridge in middle of photo crosses a small creek. The lush summer foliage enabled enemy soldiers to move undetected from right to left through the 175 yard wide gap.

photo by author

the center of Jackson's line. Grover hesitated and then reluctantly agreed. Grover moved his brigade forward through the Groveton Woods. When he reached the Groveton-Sudley Road and saw the open space his men would have to cross, he ordered his troops to move further right using the woods as a screen. Grover's men followed the woods for several hundred yards until they reached the area near the gap between Thomas and Gregg.[23]

Grover paused to reorganize his lines. He used some advice received earlier from another brigade commander, Brigadier General Robert H. Milroy. Because of the thick woods, Grover advised his men to move at a walk until the Confederate troops fired a volley. Then he wanted his men to rush forward, fire once, and use the bayonet.[24] He placed his three veteran regiments on the front line. The 11th Massachusetts occupied the left with the 2nd New Hampshire in the middle. The 1st Massachusetts came on the right. The 16th Massachusetts took the left and the 26th Pennsylvania took the middle in a second line. Both lines moved forward in the thick woods. They aimed right at Thomas' position and the gap to his left. Thomas' skirmishers heard the enemy approach and peppered them with rifle fire before rapidly falling back to the main line. The heavy picket fire gave ample warning of the impending attack. The Georgians hugged the railroad bank for concealment. Georgia officers urged their men to stand only to fire.[25]

Grover's brigade came within yards of the rail bed before they saw it, but it was too late. The Georgians popped up from their concealed positions and delivered a staggering fire into the Yankees. The volley surprised and slowed the first line of blue-clad soldiers. An excited Cuvier Grover, on horseback, waved his sword with his cap on the tip. He ordered a charge and spurred his horse forward. The animated officer made a tempting target. The horse stumbled. Grover leaped to the ground as the severely wounded animal raced into the Georgia line. The Federal soldiers bellowed a roar and rushed forward into the excavation of the unfinished railroad.[26]

The next surprise fell on the Georgians. Most of the Confederates had dropped back down to the safety of the railroad embankment after delivering their initial volley. They must have expected the enemy to reload and fire too. Thomas' men instead, found Union soldiers pouring over the edge of the embankment into their midst. Other enemy troops clambered up the sides of the undefended gap. The 49th Georgia found its flanks turned. This forced these Georgians to peel rearward amidst the noise and smoke. This move exposed the flank of the sister regiment on the right. The flying powder and lead caught the dry underbrush on fire. Hand-to-hand combat ensued as the soldiers blindly swung their rifles like bats in the swirling smoke.[27]

The commander of the 11th Massachusetts, Colonel William Blaisdell wrote:

> Here for two or three minutes the struggle was very severe, the combatants exchanging shots their muskets almost muzzle to muzzle and engaging hand-to-hand in deadly encounter. Private John Lawler, of Company D, stove in the skull of one rebel with the butt of his musket and killed another with his bayonet. The enemy broke in confusion and ran, numbers throwing away their muskets some fully cocked and the owners too much frightened to fire them, the regiment pursuing them some 80 yards into the wood, where it was met by an overwhelming force in front. . . . [28]

The 11th Massachusetts hit the right center of Thomas' line occupied by the 45th Georgia and a sister regiment. Sergeant Marion H. Fitzpatrick described their precarious spot as the 45th Georgia attempted to make a stand. "Our Regiment was in the center. The first we knew both wings had given away and the 45th was nearly surrounded. The last fire I made I stood on the embankment and fired down amongst them just as they were charging up the bank about fifteen ranks deep. I turned and saw the whole Regiment getting away, and I followed the example in tripple quick time."[29]

As pressure mounted on both flanks and low on ammunition, most of the Georgians rapidly moved about eighty yards rearward. With Grover's pursuers hot on their heels, the Georgians had very little time to form a defensive position other than locating the nearest tree. The Confederates unleashed another strong volley, but the Yankees again charged. A soldier in the 2nd New Hampshire described the carnage: "Here occurred the most desperate fighting of the day, a hand-to-hand melee with bayonets and clubbed muskets. Such a fight cannot last long. New Hampshire won."[30]

The remaining Georgians again scampered to the rear closer toward the Groveton-Sudley Road. A New Hampshire soldier reported that he shot the color-bearer of the 49th Georgia at some point during the attack.[31]

The situation on Jackson's left turned desperate. Confederate hope dwindled along with ammunition. The enemy had turned Gregg's right flank and Thomas' left. This threatened to cut off the South Carolinians. One of Grover's men later wrote, "Victory appeared to be certain."[32] Grover however, needed to have some support for him to capitalize on this breakthrough. He expected help from Phil Kearny's division pushing into Gregg's left flank. Grover's drive into the Georgia and South Carolina lines had created disorganization among his men. Edward Thomas' troops added to his problems because they continued to fight. Fifteen percent of Grover's men lay scattered along the ground as casualties. He needed Kearny to attack soon. Kearny however, failed to act decisively this day.

Kearny's tardiness enabled Maxcy Gregg to pull the 12th South Carolina away from his extreme left and double quick them to the right to assist the 1st and 13th South Carolina Regiments in plugging the gap. The 12th South Carolina plunged into Grover's men with their bayonets. An intense firefight interspersed with more hand-to-hand combat ensued in the gap.[33] Gregg brought the 14th South Carolina up from their reserve position and hurried them into the gap. Colonel Thomas rallied the 49th Georgia and sent them back in on the right of the 14th South Carolina. Soldiers fired at each other from less than ten yards away. The 35th Georgia and the remainder of Thomas' Brigade formed a ragged defensive position near the Groveton-Sudley Road. A.P. Hill jumped into the middle of the fray to offer encouragement while his staff officers scurried around filling their pockets and haversacks with ammunition for the front.[34]

Relieved Georgians heard more noise and looked rearward to see Pender's Brigade running forward. Pender had previous orders to support Thomas if needed. He wrote, "it seeming to be the time to go to his assistance, I ordered my brigade forward." The North Carolinians moved into position on the right of the 49th Georgia.[35] These reinforcements plus the addition of an artillery battery changed the balance in the fight. Grover's men now found themselves receiving fire from three sides. Both second line regiments, the 16th Massachusetts and the 26th Pennsylvania, could not push past the railroad because of accurate artillery fire. The 2nd New Hampshire, which had advanced the furthest, now found themselves pinned down in front of Thomas' Brigade.[36] Grover's troops, unsupported, could not last long. His brave survivors, within thirty minutes of initiating their attack, briskly withdrew. Pender's and Thomas' men closely followed on their heels. A soldier in the 2nd New Hampshire recalled the Union retreat: "As they recrossed the railroad bank, they were exposed to a murderous fire from each flank, to say nothing of the bad language used by the rebels in calling upon them to stop."[37] The Georgians and North Carolinians chased Grover's men for a short distance and then returned to the safety of the rail bed.[38] John Pope had squandered a great opportunity to exploit Lee's army.

Colonel Thomas in his very brief report paid tribute to Pender's Brigade: "when General Pender's brigade advanced promptly and in fine order to the assistance of the Third [Thomas], most of which joined General Pender's, and together they drove back the enemy some distance beyond our previous position, which was held until night, the brigade bivouacking on the field."[39]

The casualty figures in Cuvier Grover's front line attested to the deadly Confederate fire and the ferocity of the close-quarter mayhem. The 2nd New Hampshire made the furthest penetration into Thomas' line and lost sixteen killed, eighty-seven wounded and thirty missing for a total of 133, the highest in the brigade. The 11th Massachusetts suffered ten killed, seventy-seven wounded and twenty-five missing for a total of 112. The 1st Massachusetts had five killed, sixty-six wounded and seven missing for an aggregate of 78. The 16th Massachusetts on Grover's left flank lost four killed, sixty-four wounded and forty-two missing for a total of 110 men.[40]

A.P. Hill worked during the lull to reorganize his tired troops. His front line had fought the enemy since early that morning. Most of the exhausted men lacked ammunition, and yet to the east the blue lines formed again. This signaled the arrival of Kearny's division and some Ninth Corps troops. The time was after 5 P.M.The 101st and 40th New York regiments from Brigadier General David Birney's brigade ran into the skirmishers from Thomas' and Gregg's brigades. The 40th New York deployed to the right of the 101st New York. The heavy skirmish fire forced the New Yorkers to charge forward at the double-quick. A sharp firefight erupted as the Yankees approached the unfinished railroad. Birney's regiments exchanged several volleys with the Confederates and then charged with their bayonets. The Georgians and South Carolinians found themselves in another bloody close quarter melee. This attack soon forced both Southern brigades to yield ground. Thomas' and Gregg's men scampered away from the railroad with the New Yorkers swarming on their heels. Dead and wounded Confederates littered the western bank of the cut. Lieutenant Colonel Nelson A. Gesner, commander of the 101st New York, wrote, "We continued to drive them before us, stopping now and then to fire a volley into them, until we had driven them clean out of the woods into the clear space beyond. Here we received a heavy cross-fire from the left at a distance of about 200 paces."[41]

The situation turned gloomy again on the Confederate left. Branch sent two regiments to help, but A.P. Hill needed more troops to patch his broken line. Brigadier General Jubal A. Early received orders to move his large seven-regiment brigade to Hill's assistance. The 13th Georgia and the 8th Louisiana also joined Early's force. These reinforcements added about 2,500 more soldiers to Hill's line. Early's troops belted out a loud rebel yell as they raced through the open fields behind Thomas and Gregg.[42]

Relief again swept over the men in Thomas' and Gregg's brigades.[43] Early's soldiers punched into the Union thrust slowing the enemy effort. Nelson Gesner's New Yorkers had suffered numerous casualties and they had fired most of their ammunition. Gesner reported they remained at their breakthrough position for thirty minutes until "I found that their [Confederate] fire was increasing and working more to our rear. Not seeing any support on our left, and finding that the combined strength of the Fortieth and One hundred and first would not amount to over 250 men, I deemed it prudent to retire, and we fell back in good order, at quick-time."[44]

This Confederate counterattack drove the Unionists back several hundred yards past the unfinished railroad. Jackson's left had held, but a high toll of blue and gray bodies covered the charred, smoky ground. Darkness fell and both sides agreed to a ceasefire so soldiers could search for and assist their wounded comrades.

The 101st New York lost seventy-nine killed or wounded. Specific casualty figures for the 40th New York could not be found.[45]

Young Henry "Heck" Andrew Thomas and his father Captain Lovick P. Thomas had met the 35th Georgia several days before the battle. The elder Thomas, wounded two months prior at Mechanicsville, had convalesced at home. He had returned to his command with two servants and his twelve-year-old son. The young Thomas soon became a regular sight as a drummer boy or courier, delivering messages between regimental headquarters and his uncle, Colonel Edward L. Thomas. The grisly Manassas fight provided a lifetime of memories for the impressionable youngster. "Heck" Thomas described the sights along the unfinished railroad: "For 400 to 500 yards on the edge of that cut you could have walked on dead men–some places two and three deep. Nearly all of these men were shot in the neck, face or head. I well remember going over that part of the battlefield after the engagement."[46]

Jackson's troops rose on August 30 with replenished ammunition and energy. The soldiers in Thomas' Brigade continued to wait for any sound that might signal an attack. There was still no discernable enemy movement to the east at noon. Brigadier General Charles Field had suffered a wound the previous day. Hill placed his brigade in reserve. Archer's

Henry "Heck" Andrew Thomas

At age twelve, Thomas served as a regimental courier and drummer. His father, Captain Lovick P. Thomas brought the boy to Virginia just days before the Battle of Second Manassas. In later life, Heck Thomas ventured out West and became a Texas Ranger and U.S. Marshal. He served as a role model for the 1970's NBC series "Hec Ramsey." See Appendix E.

The Constitution, Atlanta, Ga., "Bruff's Column", March 9, 1908.

Brigade took Field's former position on the right front while Thomas remained in the middle and Gregg on the left.

The bark of cannon fire erupted around 3 P.M.from the Confederate right. The men soon heard the rattle of intense rifle fire. All those along Jackson's left prepared for the fight, but nothing happened. This noise came from Fitz John Porter's Fifth Corps attack against Jackson's right. Jackson's units repulsed the initial Union attack. Porter sent a second and third wave of blue-clad troops forward. Heavy Confederate artillery fire slowed this move. James Longstreet's corps, hidden to the west, suddenly plowed into Porter's unprotected left flank, caving it in. The time was about 4 P.M.

Two precious hours passed before Jackson ordered his left brigades forward. The Light Division poured out of the woods and down the railroad embankment toward the confused Federal lines. Branch's Brigade occupied the left and next in order came Archer, Thomas, Pender and Brockenbrough. Gregg's Brigade brought up the rear to protect the left flank. The combined charge swallowed up two enemy batteries and a number of prisoners.[47] Sergeant Fitzpatrick of the 45th Georgia recorded the relatively easy day the Georgians had: "There was hard fighting done that day but our Brigade was not engaged till nearly dark when they charged a battery and took it by firing only a few shots."[48]

A few Federal units made a determined stand around the Henry House, a landmark from the battlefield of a year before. This effort saved Pope's army from annihilation. Thomas' Brigade broke off the chase about 10 P.M. and bivouacked with their sister brigades among the dead and dying of the enemy. The toll in the 35th Georgia amounted to eighteen killed and fifty-five wounded during the Second Battle of Manassas.[49]

Destruction and mayhem littered the plains of Manassas for the second time in thirteen months. First Sergeant Draughton S. Haynes of the 49th Georgia recorded his impression of the Manassas battlefield. He passed through on foot three days after the battle as he searched for Thomas' Brigade. Haynes had missed the fight as he recovered from illness in Richmond. "I passed through the battlefield of Manassas and found dead and wounded Yankees by the hundred, it was the most horrible sight I beheld. There was not a Yankee left with a pair of shoes on and a few had every rag of clothes taken off. Many of our men are barefooted therefore I would not condemn them for taking shoes off the dead. Many of the Yankees bodies had turned perfectly black, and to pass them would almost make a person vomit."[50]

Lee developed another plan to destroy Pope. He believed Jackson's wing could swing north and launch a flanking attack against the retreating Federal army near Fairfax Court House.

The soldiers in Thomas' Brigade awoke the following morning (August 31) at 3 A.M. The men marched to a spot where the brigade commissary had butchered and barbecued a cow for the early morning meal. One Georgian failed to note how the beef tasted, but he quickly pointed out the lack of bread. Thomas' troops joined the rest of the Light Division around 5 A.M. The march started across Bull Run at Sudley Ford and continued north toward Little River Turnpike.[51] A pesky rain started to fall and continued the entire day. The head of A.P. Hill's column reached the Little River Turnpike and turned southeast toward Germantown and Fairfax Court House. Confederate scouts reported Pope's location near Centreville. Pope actually had moved six miles east of Centreville closer to the Germantown-Fairfax Court House area. The muddy roads slowed and disrupted Jackson's march. Hill received orders at 10 P.M. to halt for the night. The Georgians had only reached Pleasant Valley Baptist Church on the Little River Turnpike, barely ten miles from where they had started.[52]

The march started again at 7 A.M. on September 1. A gloomy sky threatened a downpour. The slow cautious advance continued along the muddy road. Thomas received orders, around noon, to put skirmishers on the right side of the turnpike. The column continued forward until about 4:15 P.M. when Hill's lead unit bumped into Federal troops near Ox Hill, southeast of Chantilly. [53] Heavy skirmish fire erupted while the soldiers formed their battle lines. Hill sent forward the brigades of Branch and Brockenbrough. A tremendous thunderstorm erupted just as these brigades ran into Major General Isaac Stevens' division of the Federal Ninth Corps. A.P. Hill reported, "This battle commenced under the most unfavorable circumstances—a heavy, blinding rain-storm directly in the faces of my men."[54]

Rain and hail pounded the men and the ground. Visibility dropped to a few yards. The momentary glitter of lightning flashed off the trees while thunder drowned out the rattle of musketry. The moisture soaked unprotected cartridges making them worthless. Several opposing units stumbled into each other because of poor visibility, and hand-to-hand combat ensued. Hays' Louisiana brigade broke under pressure from Stevens' Federal troops. Thomas' Georgians, initially held as reserve behind Gregg's brigade, moved in to plug this gap. The 35th Georgians slid into position behind a worm rail fence screened in front by thick sassafras bushes. They anchored Thomas' left. The 45th Georgia stood to the right of the 35th. The other two Georgia regiments manned Thomas' right. The Federal pressure in front of Thomas eased when Isaac Stevens fell to the ground with a bullet in his head.[55]

In the gathering darkness, a lone horseman approached the right side of the Georgia line, manned by the 14th and 49th Georgia Regiments. The horseman queried several Confederate soldiers as to what unit stood in his front.

When he heard there answer he turned and spurred his horse to escape. A volley of gunfire followed him, and a single bullet removed him from the saddle. Several Georgians carried the body of Union Major General Philip Kearny back to their line. The one-armed Mexican War hero had died before his body struck the ground. Several Georgians took credit for the fatal shot, which sparked argument. Colonel W. L. Goldsmith, who at the time commanded Company K, 14th Georgia, believed a soldier from his regiment killed Kearny. Other soldiers reported Sergeant John McCrimmon, Company B, 49th Georgia, fired the fatal shot.[56] A newspaper account from Columbus, Ga., mentioned that Kearny rode in front of the 49th Georgia, so one could assume from this account that a soldier from this regiment shot Kearny.[57]

Union troops did not actively engage the 35th Georgia during the Battle of Ox Hill (Chantilly) although the regiment lost five men killed or wounded [58] The combination of Phil Kearny's death and complete darkness brought the fight to a close. This battle signaled the end of the Second Manassas Campaign as Pope's disgruntled soldiers retreated to safety near Washington.

That night, "Heck" Thomas stood with several of his uncle's servants in the brigade rear area. They guarded the baggage of the brigade staff. A lone soldier walked up leading the reins of a saddled black horse. The soldier turned over a sword and the horse to the young Thomas with orders to care for them. They belonged to Phil Kearny.[59]

Robert E. Lee worked through the night to develop a new offensive. He wanted to move the war out of Virginia and pull the Federal army away from Washington. His new plan ensured that the Army of Northern Virginia would be on the march again soon.

Notes

Abbreviations:

CSR—"Compiled Service Records of Confederate Soldiers Who Served In Organizations From The State of Georgia," Thirty-fifth Infantry Regiment (National Archives Microfilm Publication M266) National Archives Building, Washington, D.C.

GDAH- Georgia Division of Archives and History, Morrow, Ga.

NMP–National Military Park

OR.—War of the Rebellion: A Compilation of the Official Records of the Union and Confederate Armies. 130 Vols.

SHSP- Southern Historical Society Papers.

1. Letter of JM Garrett to "Dear Mother from Winder Hospital Richmond, Va Aug the 26th 1862," James M. Garrett Collection.
2. Ibid.

3. Ibid.
4. "Adjutant & Inspector General's Office Register of Letters Received," Vol 52, item 619T and 620T (1862), p.343; item 752T p.352 and 764T p.353. (National Archives rare book room) National Archives Building, Washington, D.C.
5. *OR.,* Vol.12, Pt.II, p.670.
6. Letter of Captain Evan R. Whitley to "Mrs. B.F. Moody from Richmond Va August 27th 1862," Civil War Miscellany, Personal Papers (Record Group 57–1–1), Benjamin F. Moody Folder, on microfilm at GDAH.
7. Diary of Capt. John W. Dozier, Co.B, 45th Georgia, "Reminiscences of Confederate Soldiers—Stories of the War 1861–65," Vol. VIII, compiled by Georgia Division, United Daughters of the Confederacy, p.75,. Located at GDAH.
8. *OR.,* Vol. 12, Pt.2, p.721.
9. Ibid. Vol. 12, Pt.2, p.644.
10. Ibid. Vol. 12, Pt.2, p.670.
11 Ibid. Vol. 12, Pt.2, p.679.
12. Dozier.
13. Marion Hill Fitzpatrick, *Letters to Amanda.* (Macon, Ga., 1998) p. 24–26 (edited by Jeffrey C. Lowe and Sam Hodges), Letter of M.H. Fitzpatrick (45th Ga.) to "Dear Amanda from near Fairfax CH, Va September 2nd 1862." Reprinted by permission of Mercer University Press, 1998.
14. Henry Kyd Douglas, *I Rode with Stonewall.* (Chapel Hill, N.C., 1940) p.138.
15. Edward McCrady, *SHSP,* "Gregg's Brigade of South Carolinians in the Battle of Second Manassas," Vol.12. 1885. p.13.
16. Dozier.
17. *OR.,* Vol.12, Part 2, p.670, 702 .
18. McCrady p.14–15.
19. *OR .,* Vol. 12. Pt. II, p. 298–299, 311–315, 686–687.
20. Ibid. Vol.12, Pt.2, p.309–312, 687. A casualty count for these two Federal regiments for the fighting that took place in front of Thomas' Brigade on August 29th could not be determined. The only count available was the "Return of Casualties in the Union forces commanded by Maj. Gen. John Pope, during the operations August 16–September 2, 1862" which covers the entire period of the Battle of Second Manassas as well as the Battle of Chantilly. During this more than two-week period the casualty count in the 75th Pennsylvania was 20 killed, 113 wounded, and 17 captured/missing. The count in the 58th New York was 14 killed, 32 wounded, and 11 captured/missing.
21. J.F.J. Caldwell, *The History of a Brigade of South Carolinians First Known as 'Gregg's' and Subsequently as 'McGowan's' Brigade.* (Philadelphia, 1866) p.63.
22. *OR .,* Vol. 12, Pt.II, p.454, 459, 460, 462, 464, 646, 680; Letter of Mark Newman (49th Ga), *Central Georgian* (Sandersville), October, 15, 1862; Fitzpatrick, p. 24–26.
23. *OR .,* Vol.12, Pt.2, p.680–681.
24. Ibid. Vol.12, Pt.2, p.315, 320, 439.
25. Ibid. Vol.12, Pt.2, p.439.
26. Ibid. Vol.12, Pt.2, p.441; Henry N. Blake, *Three Years in the Army of the Potomac.* (Boston, 1865) p.128; Warren H. Cudworth, *History of the First Regiment (Massachusetts Infantry).* (Boston, 1866) p.272–273.

27. *OR.*, Vol. 12, Pt.II, p.670–671, 439, 440, 702–703.
28. Ibid. Vol.12, Pt.2, p.441.
29. Fitzpatrick, p.24–25; Dozier.
30. Martin A. Haynes, *History of the Second Regiment, New Hampshire Volunteer Infantry in the War of the Rebellion.* (Lakeport, NH, 1896) p.132; Blake. p.128; *OR.*, Vol.12, Pt.2, p.441.
31. Ibid. M.A. Haynes, p.127.
32. Blake, p.128.
33. McCrady. p.28–30.
34. *OR* ., Vol.12, Pt.II, p.670–671, 702–703, 645–646; Caldwell, p.36.
35. Ibid. *OR* ., Vol. 12, Pt. II, p.698, 703.
36. M.A. Haynes. p.132.
37. Ibid. p.132.
38. *OR* ., Vol.12. Pt.II, p.697–698.
39. Ibid. Vol.12, Pt.II, p.703.
40. Ibid. Vol. 12, Pt. II, p.439.
41. Ibid. Vol. 12, Pt. II, p.431, 681.
42. Ibid. Vol. 12, Pt. II, p.712.
43. McCrady. p.34–35.
44. Ibid. Vol. 12, Pt. II, p. 431.
45. *OR* ., Vol. 12, Pt. II, p.257. The 101st New York took 153 enlisted men into the fight and suffered 74 killed or wounded plus an additional 5 wounded officers. Casualty figures in the 40th New York for the period from August 16th- September 2nd, showed this unit suffered a combined 12 killed, 107 wounded and 28 missing for a total of 147 men.
46. Bruff's Column, *The Constitution,* (Atlanta, Ga.) March 9, 1908.
47. Ibid. Vol.12, Pt.II, p.671.
48. Fitzpatrick, p. 25.
49. James Folsom, *Heroes and Martyrs of Georgia–Georgia's Record In The Revolution of 1861.* (Macon, Ga., 1864) p.136.
50. Draughton Stith Haynes, *The Field Diary of A Confederate Soldier–Draughton Stith Haynes–While Serving With the Army of Northern Virginia, CSA.* (Darien, Ga. 1963) p.14 (Edited by William G. Haynes, Jr.)
51. Newman, *Central Georgian* (Sandersville, Ga.) October 15, 1862.
52. Ibid.
53. Ibid.
54. *OR* ., Vol.12, Pt.II, p.672.
55. *Confederate Veteran,* Vol. XV, no. 6, June 1907, p.264; Ibid. Vol. 12, Pt.II, p.647, 677; *SHSP,* Vol. XXV, 1897, p.99.
56. Ibid. *Confederate Veteran,* p.264–266; Folsom, p.130.
57. *Columbus Enquirer* (Weekly). Columbus, Ga. "Battle of Chantilly", September 30, 1862.
58. *Columbus Enquirer* (Weekly). Columbus, Ga. "Casualties from 35th Georgia", October 7, 1862.

59. Bruff's Column. "Heck" Thomas claimed that he cared for Kearny's horse and equipment for several weeks until the Georgia brigade reached Harper's Ferry. The youngster claimed that Robert E. Lee requested the horse be brought forward to Sharpsburg, Maryland to be sent through Federal lines under a flag of truce for Kearny's widow. Thomas brought the horse forward and he stated how excited he was to successfully perform a task under the commanding general's watchful eye. "Heck" Thomas might have been mistaken on the time frame for this incident because Lee was certainly busy trying to extricate his army from the Sharpsburg disaster and had little time to worry about a dead mans horse.

Chapter Six

To Maryland

"Monday will be a day never forgotten by the boys that were at Harpers Ferry."
Lieutenant William C. Goggans

Robert E. Lee decided a bold move into Maryland could bring international recognition and aid from Britain and France—a move that could spur on the mood for peace in the North. The fertile landscape would also provide forage for the army. Neutral Maryland might also be brought into the Southern fold, which would isolate Washington.

The Army of Northern Virginia soon moved northward. On September 3, the Light Division spent the night just north of Dranesville, Virginia. Thomas' Brigade led the march the following morning. Stonewall Jackson expressed displeasure because the march failed to begin at 4 A.M. as ordered. Captain Washington T. Irvine stated that the 35th Georgia led the column as the dusty troops approached Leesburg around noon. Jackson rode up from the rear and dismounted. He walked over to Captain Winfield Scott Thomas, the regimental adjutant, and asked him if he knew how to march. Thomas stated, "he ought to know, as he had done a good deal of it." Jackson said, "I will show you," and then the general stepped out in front of the column. After a short distance he turned and ordered the troops to halt for a rest. A.P. Hill rode ahead of his men. When he looked back in the saddle and saw his column halted without *his* orders he angrily turned his horse and spurred back. Hill approached the head of the column and confronted Colonel Edward L. Thomas. He demanded to know who ordered a halt. Thomas pointed a finger in the direction of Jackson standing nearby. The infuriated Hill apparently felt Jackson challenged his command authority. He dismounted and offered his sword to Jackson. Jackson replied, "Put up your sword General Hill and consider yourself in arrest."[1] This incident marked the second time in two months that the thorny Jackson had placed A.P. Hill under arrest. Temporary command of the Light Division fell to Brigadier General Lawrence O. Branch.

On September 5, the main body crossed the Potomac River at White's Ford. The Light Division marched in the lead with General Jackson at its head. The Confederates reached Frederick, Maryland and spent five days bivouacked just east of town. Lee intended to use the Shenandoah Valley for a supply route and a line of communication. It would also make a good escape route if needed. Lee however, needed the town of Harper's Ferry under Confederate control. This picturesque town represented a strategic location at the confluence of the Potomac and Shenandoah Rivers. The Baltimore & Ohio Railroad's main east-west line crossed the river there. A 14,000 man Federal garrison occupied the area between Harper's Ferry and Martinsburg. All these blue-clad soldiers prevented the safe use of this northern part of the valley for Lee's army.

Lee decided to divide his forces. This decision harbored risk because Pope's army had joined with McClellan's army. This combined Federal force moved toward Frederick. Lee planned for three groups led by Stonewall Jackson, Major General Lafayette McLaws, and Brigadier General John G. Walker to surround and capture Harper's Ferry; then they would rejoin with the rest of Lee's army near Boonsboro, Maryland, twenty miles north of Harper's Ferry. Command of this mission fell to Jackson. Lee wanted the Harper's Ferry mission accomplished in three days.

Jackson started his move on September 10. Robert E. Lee's orders stated the troops would march no faster than three miles per hour unless there was an emergency. There would be a ten-minute rest period every hour. The sick and sore-footed would be carried in ambulances. This new order differed from Jackson's previous marching orders when his men fought in Virginia. There, Jackson demanded the foot weary be left by the roadside where sympathetic civilians might help them.[2]

Jackson changed his mind about A.P. Hill. He restored Hill to command after realizing the benefit of having his best division commander available for the upcoming battle. Jackson's faction of 14,000 men represented the largest of the three groups converging on Harper's Ferry. His group consisted of his old division now commanded by Brigadier General John R. Jones, Richard Ewell's division commanded by Colonel Alexander R. Lawton, and the Light Division. They marched west across Maryland, on September 11, and crossed the Potomac River at knee-deep Light's Ford near Williamsport, Maryland.

The following day the column approached the outskirts of Martinsburg, Virginia. Lieutenant William C. Goggans recalled that they:

> [C]ontinued our march in direction of Martinsburg where we learned the yankees were waiting to give us a happy reception but Lo! when our cavalry come in sight of the citty they found the enemy to be

> gone however there was a few left to burn and destroy the property left be hind. [T]he result was the capture of several prisoners with one thousand barrels of crackers weighing 80 *lbs* each, some flour and bacon, several boxes of fine improved Rifles, some shoes, boots etc. The Army marched by the Depots. [M]any Halted to fill Haversacks of crackers & then continuing our march after the foe that were skedaddling for safety. The enemy were making for Harpers Ferry. [O]ur front over halled [overhauled] many of their straglers while pursuing them.[3]

The Light Division arrived near Harper's Ferry on September 13. The men waited for the signal that McLaws' Division had seized Maryland Heights and Walker's Division had seized Loudoun Heights. These two mountains towered over the eastern side of Harper's Ferry. Jackson's success required control of both precipices. Goggan's men were "much fatigued and worn down from the excessive march we had taken. We then began to wake them [enemy] by occasionally giving them a bum [artillery shell] merely to interest them, while our forces were gathering."[4]

Both Loudoun Heights and Maryland Heights stood under Confederate control by Sunday afternoon, September 14. Goggans wrote, "The Times lively untill late sunday evening. When we saw our Colors flying on the Maryland Hights also on the Bolivar or Virginia Heights which commanded the whole town. [O]ur Division marched up the Shanadoah River." He mistakenly referred to Loudoun Heights as Bolivar or Virginia Heights.[5]

A.P. Hill wrote, "I was ordered by General Jackson to move along the left bank of the Shenandoah and then turn the enemy's left flank and enter Harper's Ferry."[6] Confederate artillery fire crashed into the woods between Hill and the Shenandoah River to clear it of Federals. Hill's troops moved along the river and located some high ground that anchored the extreme left of the Federal position on Bolivar Heights. This prominent ridge guarded the western approach to Harper's Ferry. Sharpened points of abatis ringed the Federal position on the south end of the Bolivar Heights line, but the infantry had failed to build any protective earthworks. No artillery guarded this position either. What an oversight! The brigades of Pender, Archer, and Brockenbrough moved to seize the hillcrest and they quickly drove the small infantry force away. Goggans reported on this action. "During the evening a brisk engagement insued which lasted but a short time driving the enemy back to the citty. [O]ur loss was but few in fact the loss of both sides killed was but few. We lay in line of Battle for the knight."[7]

Another Union position further ahead looked very strong. Their soldiers had dropped logs and large tangles of brush in front of the breastworks. Abatis faced the Confederate lines. Hill waited until after dark and

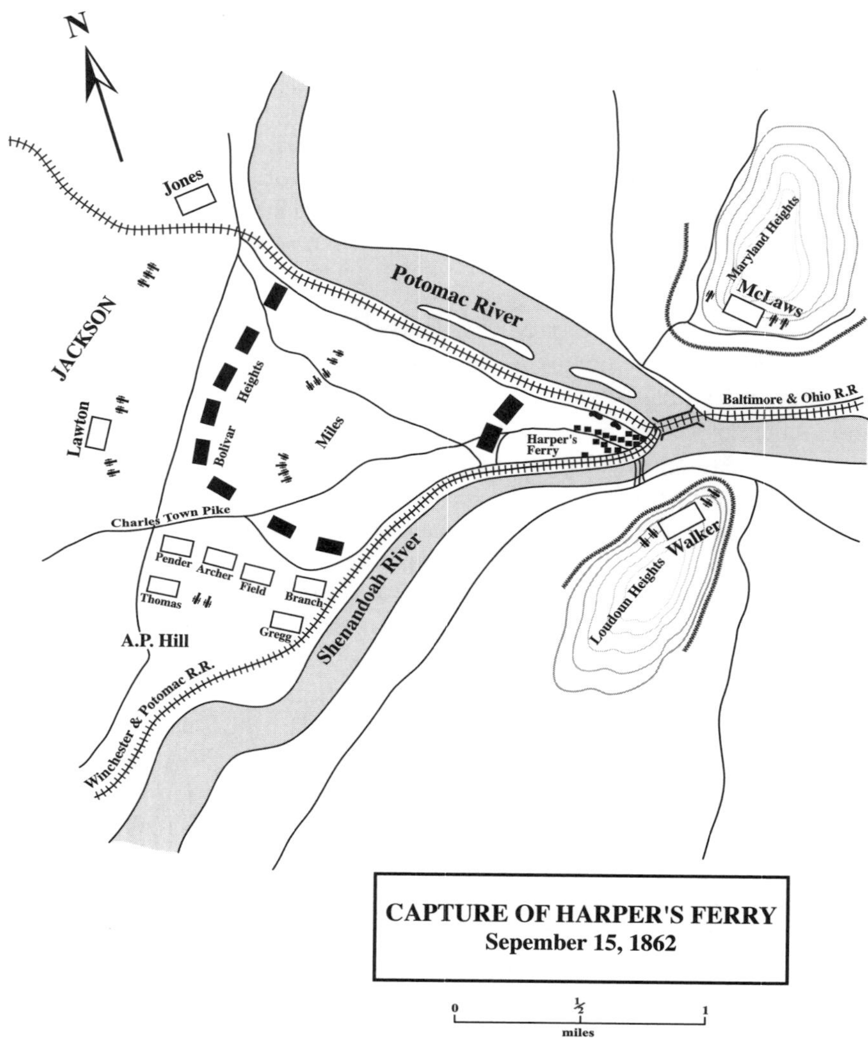

CAPTURE OF HARPER'S FERRY
Sepember 15, 1862

then ordered artillery strategically placed to enfilade this enemy line. Pender's Brigade, supported by the Georgians, crept to within 150 yards of the Federal works.[8]

Thick fog covered the ground at dawn on September 15. "Early next morning a terrible fire of Artillery was opened by us soon replied to by the enemy," recalled Lieutenant Goggans. "[A]s the fire then opened from the Heights The enemy could not stand such Terrific fire." The noise from the

Federal side weakened after an hour, and the Confederate guns ceased firing. Pender's troops moved forward and the Federal batteries again erupted. Confederate counter-battery fire quickly subdued this problem.[9]

Colonel Dixon Miles, the Harper's Ferry garrison commander, held a council of officers at 9 A.M. The officers reached a unanimous decision to surrender. Brigadier General Julius White wrote, "The long range ammunition had now almost entirely failed, and it became evident that, from the great preponderance of the enemy's artillery and his ability to keep up a fire at long range to which we were no longer able to reply, our ability to hold the position became a mere question of time, and that our defense could only be continued at a great sacrifice of life without any corresponding advantage."[10]

A white flag soon waved from the Federal side. William Goggans wrote, "The air was rent with the missiles of Death for 2 hours that morning when the enemy Hoisted the white flag and seased their fire. [O]ur brigade were drawn up ready to charge the Battery and would have done

Captain Washington T. Irvine, Co. I

The Chattooga County men elected the twenty-six-year-old Irvine in November 1862 as their new commander. He replaced the promoted Major William L. Groves. Irvine survived the war and surrendered at Appomattox, Va in 1865.

From *Sunny South,* Atlanta, Ga. May 2, 1891

so if the flag had not been reared." He was one of many who expressed relief over the surrender: "[O]ur men were much revived for my self I did not feel to rejoice over the conquered but Rather Pity them."[11]

Sergeant James M. Kimbrough knew that many Georgians would have been maimed or killed if they had been forced to storm the enemy position. "I was near up to the breastworks. I never was so glad as I was when I saw the white flag go up."[12] A 49th Georgia soldier described his elation: "How thankful we ought to feel the Yankee batteries have surrendered-the position is very strong." He then wrote, "Gen Hill has just passed (in his shirt sleeves as he always goes) with three Yankee officers dressed as fine as could be, quite a contrast."[13]

A.P. Hill rode forward with his staff to arrange the terms of surrender. He expressed surprise at the total confusion that existed among the enemy. He reported, "When I entered the works of the enemy, which was only a few moments after the white flag had shown, there was apparently no organization of any kind." The seizure of Harper's Ferry not only gave Lee undisputed access to the Shenandoah Valley, but it also provided much needed supplies and equipment for his army. The Harper's Ferry operation netted 12,419 prisoners consisting of 12 infantry regiments, 3 cavalry companies and 6 artillery batteries; some 13,000 long and small arms; 73 artillery pieces consisting of 49 cannon and 24 mountain howitzers; 200 wagons; and 1,800 horses, commissary, quartermaster and ordnance stores.[14]

Pride and elation filled William Goggans over the capture of this key town. "Here the greatest Victory known to the world was accomplished," he wrote. He described in detail the number and types of captured weapons. "With Ammunition in a bundance in fact an immence quantity of Arms Stores, almost enough tents for our whole Army. Provisions in a bundance. [M]onday will be a day never forgotten by the boys that were at Harpers Ferry." The officer described: "There was many Horses, Mules, Waggons, Ambulances of the finest prize captured." The captured soldiers appeared in good spirits. Thomas' Georgians issued parole papers to these prisoners and sent them to Washington with the stipulation they could not serve again until officially exchanged for an equal number of Confederate prisoners.[15]

Goggans happily reported no casualties in Company A though he did describe a near escape by Private Francis M.B. Stripling and Corporal Robert Summerville. A fragment from an artillery shell struck Stripling's gun. The metal then ricocheted into Summerville's canteen and tore a hole in the side. Water spewed all over his pants leg and the ground. The half- pound piece of metal remained inside the canteen.[16] The 35th Georgia suffered light casualties at Harper's Ferry with only four soldiers reported wounded.[17]

A scene at Harper's Ferry reflected the affection most Confederates had for Stonewall Jackson. After the town's capture, Jackson gathered his forces to link back up with Lee near Sharpsburg, Maryland. Hill's Division remained in town to guard the prisoners and captured equipment. A Georgia officer wrote: "Before leaving Harper's Ferry, Jackson rode down the lines, with little black cap in hand, and with his knees-on account of his short stirrups-sticking up at a high angle and his head bobbing up and down in acknowledgement of our greetings. His presence electrified the whole army; men jumped up and down, threw hats into the air and yelled themselves hoarse. A Yankee officer who had been captured asked who it was on the bay horse and, when told, remarked, 'You can never whip soldiers who love their leaders as you do'."[18]

At dawn on September 17, A.P. Hill received an urgent request for assistance from Lee at Sharpsburg, Maryland, a distant fourteen-mile march. Hill quickly assembled five of his brigades and rushed north toward the battle. Thomas' Georgians remained at Harper's Ferry to complete the removal of the captured equipment and to parole the prisoners. James Kimbrough enjoyed the light duty during his stay at Harper's Ferry. "We had a great time there, plenty to eat and but little to do."[19] Meanwhile, the timely arrival of the rest of Hill's Division at Sharpsburg prevented Lee's right flank from being rolled back.

The Battle of Sharpsburg ended under the cover of darkness on September 17. The next night Lee withdrew his battered troops from the Maryland town and crossed the Potomac at Boteler's Ford. Thomas' Brigade moved north to cover the crossing. The Georgians bivouacked on September 19 about five miles from Shepherdstown. Three Federal brigades from the divisions of Major General George W. Morell and Brigadier General George Sykes followed Lee's army. The Federal pursuers crossed Boteler's Ford while supported by about seventy Federal cannons on the north bank. The accurate Federal fire drove off Brigadier General William N. Pendleton's Southern artillerists on the south bank and resulted in the capture of four Confederate cannons.[20]

Jackson dispatched the Light Division, at 6:30 A.M. on September 20, to take care of this problem. Hill's troops rapidly retraced their path and formed a line of battle in a cornfield about one-half mile from the ford. Open ground lay to their front with golden piles of freshly cut wheat scattered about. Blue-clad infantry lined the riverbank about one thousand yards away. Thomas' Georgians anchored the right in the front rank. Gregg's Brigade stood in the middle with Pender on the left. The brigades of Brockenbrough, Archer and Lane manned a second line. Robert E. Lee anxiously joined Hill to survey the situation.[21]

Hill gave the command and the gray masses moved forward. Fire and smoke belched forth from the enemy artillery on the north bank as soon as the first line entered the field. Seconds later, large gaps appeared in the

Confederate ranks.[22] A 14th Georgian noted, "Cannon balls exploded all around us; the shrapnel and canister whipped the shrub oak in front of us to a frazzle."[23] Hill expressed awe and pride when he said, "This advance was made in the face of the most tremendous fire of artillery I ever saw, and too much praise cannot be awarded my regiments for their steady, unwavering step. It was as if each man felt that the fate of the army was centered in himself." First Sergeant Draughton S. Haynes, 49th Georgia, concurred with his division commander's assessment of the enemy artillery deluge when he wrote, "We are under the severest cannonading I ever heard . . . ." The young officer ended that day's diary passage: "May God protect us is my prayer."[24]

Thomas and Gregg swept the Union troops in their front back. Pender and Archer mounted a charge on the left and drove the pursuers into the river. The Light Division occupied a position over Boteler's Ford and sent a tremendous fire into the enemy soldiers who tried to swim to safety. Hill wrote, "Then commenced the most terrible slaughter that this war has yet witnessed. The broad surface of the Potomac was blue with the floating bodies of our foe."[25] William Goggans described what he saw as he raced with his men toward the river:

> On Saturday last early in the morning we marched briskly some 5 miles near Shepherds Town where we were again placed in line of Battle throwing out skirmishers and marching on in the direction of the enemy. [S]oon our pickets began to fire which continued to the River that were about 1 mile off where one Brigade of our Division charged them, taken between 3 & 4 hundred prisoners, Killing many almost bloodying the water of the Potomac from the slain while crossing. [O]ur loss was but few. [W]e routed and drove them from our side.[26]

The 35th Georgia missed most of the heaviest fighting that took place on the left in front of Pender's men. The regimental casualty figure stood at nine wounded, mostly from the accurate enemy artillery fire.[27]

Hill expressed exuberance over the complete beating he had given the enemy troops at Shepherdstown. "This was a wholesome lesson to the enemy, and taught them to know that it may be dangerous sometimes to press a retreating army."[28] He expressed appreciation to his troops, on September 24, when he issued a written proclamation commending his men for their fine efforts from the Battle of Mechanicsville to the most recent conflict.[29]

Edward Thomas' brief report mentioned all the regimental commanders by name except one. He wrote they "led their commands with a skill and gallantry honorable to them." Thomas failed to mention his old regiment, the 35th Georgia, or its young commander Lieutenant Colonel Bolling H. Holt. Thomas continued: "With few exceptions the officers and men of this command conducted themselves on the field in a manner highly honorable to them." This omission probably was not an oversight. What could have so displeased Colonel Thomas that he would completely disregard in writing his old unit during such a grueling campaign? No evidence hinted at a personality conflict between Thomas and Holt.[30]

The Light Division moved southward and bivouacked in the Bunker Hill area along the Opequon Creek. Bunker Hill was located twelve miles north of Winchester, Virginia. Sergeant John William Sharp Morgan, Company K, expressed delight over the letter he finally received from his wife. The long campaign had disrupted the mail. In a return letter to her, he expressed his weariness of war:

> Oh My Dear it does me so much good to hear from you it is much pleasure to me to read after your pen but it would be a grate deal more pleasure to talk to you in person. I could listen to you and Charley [young son] talk forever but I cant tell when that time will ever com. [C]an you tell me when this war will com to a close, if you do I wish you would tell me, I hear nothing butt the roar of the Cannon and the wistle [whistle] of the balls and I tell you my dear I am tired of the war. I want it to com to an end so that I can com home to those that I love so well.[31]

The constant marching and fighting since early spring had decimated the ranks of Lee's Army of Northern Virginia. The number of 35th Georgia soldiers present for duty on September 22 totaled only 240. This figure represented an average of twenty-four soldiers per company. When the regiment had formed one year earlier the rolls had listed 741 men, and each company had an average strength of seventy-two. Yet, these numbers do not reflect the true story. Company recruitment officers had trekked back to their Georgia communities during the previous year to enlist more soldiers.[32]

Lieutenant Goggans stated on the same day that he was one of only four officers present in the whole regiment. He expressed relief the following day: "I am revived this morning. Capt Duke has come in with three other officers. Capt Duke has had a long spell. [H]e left us about 12 of Aug. [H]e is well at Present." Company A numbered twenty men present in camp.[33]

A South Carolinian described the condition of the men in the Light Division. "They were sunburnt, gaunt, ragged, scarcely at all shod, spectres and caricatures of their former selves." He continued: "They now stood, an emaciated, limping, ragged, filthy mass, whom no stranger to their valiant exploits could have believed capable of anything the least worthy." Fleas and lice created an army-wide itching problem. Whole companies marched into Opequon Creek to rid the soldiers of these constant companions.[34] Sergeant Kimbrough went back to Georgia during this period to gather badly needed supplies for the 35th Georgia.[35] The division's condition significantly improved by mid-October because of rest, food and new recruits. The Light Division's size doubled from 4,700 troops at the end of September 1862 to 9,400 men a month later.

The large quantity of captured supplies from Harper's Ferry helped Lee's army during this rebuilding period. These stores probably benefited Thomas' soldiers the most because the Georgians had remained behind at the captured town. They had time to pick and choose what they wanted. Goggans exhibited pride in his loot. "I am some what better situated for traveling than I have been in former times. Our Mess have a horse and little Wagon which we carry a long with us to hall our Plunder in & I have me a very fine yankee overcoat, hat and pants. A navy Pistol and sword all setting up know [now]."[36]

Late in October, Hill's troops marched south ten miles toward Berryville. The 35th Georgia and other units received orders while on the march to destroy the nearby tracks of the Baltimore and Ohio Railroad near Harper's Ferry. The Union Twelfth Corps had reoccupied the river town.[37] William Goggans wrote, "We marched out near the Rail Road that is the Baltimore & Ohio R.R. when we stoped. During our stay there we destroid the Rail Road. Torn up the Cross tyes piled them with the Iron and Burned the Iron so as to render it of no servise."[38]

The "Report of Sick and Wounded, 35th Georgia Volunteers" for the month of October listed the number of ill soldiers and their specific malady. This report signed by Assistant Surgeon A.L. Durrett at Berryville listed fifty-three sick soldiers. The mean strength for the 35th Georgia stood at thirty-six officers and 420 enlisted men for a total of 456. The number of men present since the end of September had increased ninety percent. Thirty-eight of the sick men suffered from diarrhea. Doctors diagnosed one soldier with smallpox (variola), three with rubeola, two with typhoid fever, and four with other types of fevers. The remainder of the ill men suffered from a variety of lesser diseases.[39]

On October 25, an irate Gwinnett County father wrote a letter to Confederate Secretary of War George W. Randolph demanding his son's discharge from Company H. James Tuggle stated that his son had enlisted the previous year at age sixteen without his permission. The elder Tuggle insisted that Private Sanford Tuggle be discharged and returned to Gwinnett County. Confederate officials refused this request.[40]

William Goggans gave a warning on October 28: "Winter is comming on and our Army ill prepared to meet it. [M]any are destitute of shoes perfectly Barefooted be side [besides] ill clad otherwise. The Weather is cold. [T]he last week has reminded me of our coldest weather of Ga. We have had no snow but ice etc. Our Regiment has been separated from the Brigade on account of a case of small pox that were among us or so said the Physician." Doctors sent this ill soldier off to a hospital in Winchester. "[A]ll of the Regiment has been Inoculated from which there are many sore Arms. [I]t has taken no affect up on me as yet. I have been tried twice and shall a gain in few days if I hear of any other cases."[41]

Civil War era surgeons attempted to prevent smallpox outbreaks by two methods: inoculation or vaccination. The method of inoculation was invented in the 1720's. Doctors introduced diseased agents to the body producing a mild onset of the disease. The surgeon took pox scabs from an infected person, then made cuts to the arm of a healthy individual and placed the scabs into the cuts. In 1798, doctors developed the vaccination process. This method introduced weakened or dead disease agents to the body. The doctors vaccinated with cowpox serum because cowpox was similar to smallpox and created a resistance to the more deadly disease. Medical personnel also administered cowpox serum via cuts to the arm. The official form of treatment and prevention of smallpox during the war was via cowpox serum vaccination. Many soldiers in other units inoculated themselves by using scabs from diseased people. One reason doctors shied away from inoculation was the ease of infection from smallpox, erysipelas or even venereal diseases.[42]

William Goggans sent his father a list of items he needed to help ward off the cold weather:

> 1 Close bodied coat made in Uniform stile. 2 pair of jeans pants lined. [B]e careful not to have them made too large. 4 shirts, 2 nice and 2 plain. 2 pair of Drawers. 3 or 4 pair of socks. One pair of heavy home made Boots as the Winter is severe. [T]hese things will be of great Benefit too me. [A]lso a head-cover to sleep in. [M]y Pants & Coat I want to be made of Gray cloth or one pair of the pants Gray and the other Brown. [A]lso a good Heavy Vest. [Y]ou may think strange of me for sending for so much but I am tyred of being unclothed. I had forgot to say a cover led [coverlet] to sleep under & some Potatoes, chestnuts with some [of] that good old Brandy that my lips are watering for. I hardly thing [think] that I

> should get to come Home During the Winter. I send to you the best Over Coat the Yankees ever wore. I do not mean they have worn this but this is my prize of Harpers Ferry. [I]t is fine and I want you to ware it and think of your boys at Harpers Ferry and other Battles. I hope it may suit you. [I]t is worth $75.00 hear but I gave it to you to remind you of your boy.[43]

The Georgians marched fourteen miles to the Berryville area on or about October 29. They established camp near the Shenandoah River. Whether the 35th Georgia remained quarantined from the rest of the brigade was unknown. Company A reported thirty-six men present, with ten soldiers on the sick list. These ill soldiers remained in camp. William Goggans' believed only one of these soldiers, Private Charles P. Head, was really sick. "The others I spoke of being on the sick list have long since proved to me that the old soldier could be plaid [played]. That is to say there is but little ailding [ailing] of those." The officer described Head's condition: "I fear he is taking Typhoid Fever, he seems greatly reduced for the last few days, he is able to walk a bout camps but I fear we shall have to send him off to a Hospitle shortly." This soldier died on November 8.[44]

The latter part of 1862 brought a flurry of promotions. The most significant of these promotions affected Colonel Thomas and Lieutenant Colonel Holt. Thomas received his overdue promotion to brigadier general on November 1. Thomas had remained the only brigade commander in the Light Division still ranked as a colonel since Joseph Anderson's resignation on July 15. A.P. Hill had recommended Thomas for promotion immediately after the Seven Days Battles, but it had been delayed. Bolling H. Holt received a promotion the same day to colonel. Major William H. McCullohs (promoted to Major July 3, 1862), originally captain of Company K, moved to lieutenant colonel. Captain William L. Groves, commander of Company I, became a major. The men of Company I elected First Lieutenant Washington T. Irvine to captain and he assumed Groves' old spot. James P. Johnston, originally from Company D, remained the regimental sergeant major. Edward Thomas had appointed Johnston to that position on July 28, 1862.[45]

By the beginning of November, Federal troops controlled Snicker's Gap. This mountain pass sat on the Blue Ridge, east of Berryville. The Light Division held Castleman's Ferry over the Shenandoah River just west of the gap. William Goggans described the events of November 2 and 3:

> On sunday morning last We were called in line and hastily marched to the River where we expected a fight. We supposed from the movements of the enemy that they would make a great effort to

Lieutenant Colonel William H. McCullohs

The Harris County native and former Company K commander received rapid promotions during the first two years of war. McCullohs, frustrated with the slow-moving Georgia Governor Joe Brown, was one of three company commanders who moved their men to Richmond in September 1861.

From *Sunny South,* Atlanta, Ga. May 2, 1891

> cross the River at this place. The enemy occupying the Gap of the Mountains from which they occasionally threw their bums [artillery shells] during the day. [T]he Result of Which was three men wounded by a shell that fell near them. We did not reply with our cannon as it would have been in vain. Our Brigade remained on the River till 12 oclock on Monday when we were relieved.

Archer's Brigade arrived to replace the Georgians at the river crossing. The happy Georgians hustled back to their camp where they could make a fire and warm up. The high wind and the low temperature had made the previous night difficult. William Goggans described the frigid conditions:

> [T]he weather is getting very cold. I suffered greatly last sunday knight while in an open old field with but one Blanket and destitute of fire. We have become reconciled to hardships and have but little murmuring while many of our Brave soldiers on the Tinted field

> destitute of shoes to protect their feet from the many heavy frost that we have long since be come acquainted with.[46]

The men eagerly scoured the forest around their camp for tinder and firewood. Smoke soon wafted upward. The heavy sound of artillery suddenly echoed along the valley. It came from the direction of the river. The Georgians quickly gathered their weapons and raced back to Castleman's Ferry to assist Archer's Brigade and two artillery batteries. The Federal troops overlooking the river apparently thought there had been a Confederate withdrawal when Thomas' Brigade moved back to camp. Archer's men and the artillery had remained concealed from the enemy's eyes behind a ridge along the river. Goggans reported: "[S]o they [enemy] mooved some of their troops near the River and stacked their Arms. [A]bout this time our Artillery oppened upon them killing between thirty & forty of the yankees, wounding a bout the same number. [W]ith no loss to us whatever, the enemy fled for safety." The beleaguered Union force comprised approximately 1,000 men.[47]

These soldiers came from the 1st Massachusetts Cavalry, 7th U.S. Infantry, and elements of the 6th and 14th U.S. Infantry Regiments. Lieutenant Colonel Horace B. Sargent, commander of the 1st Massachusetts Cavalry, led a reconnaissance from Snickers Gap westward down the mountain to ascertain Confederate strength. As his men neared the river they spotted some Confederate cavalry and gave chase. The gray cavalrymen sloshed back across the river and disappeared. Sargent described what happened when his men rode into the open: "A severe fire of small arms opened upon us from every window of a house on the opposite bank and from the shore, which killed a captain and wounded 3 men of my cavalry force, and a severe fire of shell from one or two heavy guns on the ridge compelled me to withdraw the cavalry under cover, and advance the infantry skirmishers to protect it, and make the enemy display his force." The 14th U.S. Infantry charged out of the woods and down to the riverbank. Confederate fire killed five men and wounded another twenty-seven. Union officers feared that because of the severity of the injuries, many of the wounded would soon die. The rocky ground along the banks of the Shenandoah contributed to the Federal injuries. The bursting shells threw jagged pieces of stone as well as metal through the air. The men of the 14th U.S. Infantry quickly retreated for cover. The Federals sent a flag of truce forward a short time later so ambulances could retrieve their wounded.[48]

The Georgians heard a steady thump of cannonading in the distance. Lieutenant Goggans believed this sound signaled another engagement soon. He wondered why the enemy seemed so anxious to cross the Blue Ridge Mountains in such difficult weather.[49]

The first winter snow blanketed northern Virginia on November 7. At this time a major command change occurred in the Army of the Potomac. Abraham Lincoln, disgruntled over George McClellan's lack of movement, replaced him with General Ambrose E. Burnside. The Federal president expected immediate results. Burnside made plans for the first winter campaign in the east.

NOTES

Abbreviations:

CSR—"Compiled Service Records of Confederate Soldiers Who Served In Organizations From The State of Georgia," Thirty-fifth Infantry Regiment (National Archives Microfilm Publication M266) National Archives Building, Washington, D.C.

GDAH—Georgia Division of Archives and History, Morrow, Ga.

NMP—National Military Park

OR.— War of the Rebellion: A Compilation of the Official Records of the Union and Confederate Armies. 130 Vols.

SHSP—Southern Historical Society Papers

1. W.T. Irvine, *The Sunny South,* Atlanta, May 2, 1891, "Old 35th Georgia." Another version of the same story is found in James I. Robertson's book *General A.P. Hill: The Story of a Confederate Warrior* (pg. 131). Robertson states that A.P. Hill set a faster than normal pace probably to make up for the late start.The faster pace strung the column out. This may explain Jackson's query to Captain Winfield Scott Thomas, 35th Georgia adjutant, asking if he knew how to march. Jackson grew infuriated when A.P. Hill failed to halt his men for a mandatory ten-minute rest period. Jackson ordered Edward Thomas to stop his brigade. Hill and his staff rode well ahead of the column. When Hill saw the column halted he raced back and the confrontation with Jackson occurred.
2. J.F.J. Caldwell, *The History of a Brigade of South Carolinians First Known as 'Gregg's and Subsequently as 'McGowan's Brigade.* (Philadelphia, 1866) p.69–70.
3. Letter of Lieut W.C. Goggans to "Dear Father from Camp Jackson near Martinsburg North Virginia Sept. 23rd 1862," William C. Goggans Civil War Letters, courtesy of Hargrett Rare Book & Manuscript Library/ University of Georgia Libraries, Athens Ga.
4. Ibid.
5. Ibid.
6. *OR* ., Vol.19, Part I, p.980.
7. Goggans letter, September 23, 1862.
8. *OR* ., Vol.19, Part I, p.980; Report of Lt. David Champion, Co. G, 14th Georgia, "Confederate Reminiscences and Letters 1861–65," Vol. 1 ,1995, Georgia Division United Daughters of the Confederacy. p.11. Located at GDAH.

9. Goggans letter, September 23, 1862.
10. *OR* ., Vol. 19, pt.I, p.528
11. Goggans letter, September 23, 1862.
12. J. M. Kimbrough, "My War History, 1861–1865," typescript at Chickamauga-Chattanooga NMP, Georgia.
13. Draughton Stith Haynes, *The Field Diary of A Confederate Soldier—Draughton Stith Haynes—While Serving With the Army of Northern Virginia, CSA.* (49th Ga.) (Darien, Ga. 1963) p.14 (Edited by William G. Haynes, Jr.)
14. *OR* ., Vol.19, Part I, p.980, 951, 955, 960–961, 980–981; *Columbus Enquirer* (Weekly), "Latest from Harpers Ferry," Columbus, Ga., September 30, 1862.
15. Goggans letter, September 23, 1862.
16. Ibid.
17. James Folsom, *Heroes and Martyrs of Georgia-Georgia's Record in the Revolution of 1861.* (Macon, Ga., 1864) p.136. (reprinted by Butternut and Blue, Baltimore, 1995)
18. Champion. p.11.
19. Kimbrough.
20. *SHSP,* Vol. XII, Jan-Dec 1884, p.533–534.
21. *OR* ., Vol.19, Part I, p.982.
22. Caldwell, p. 81.
23. Champion., p.12.
24. Haynes, p.14.
25. *OR* ., Vol.19, Part I, p.982.
26. Goggans letter, September, 23, 1862.
27. *OR* ., Vol.19, Part I, p.982; Folsom, p.136; *Columbus Enquirer* (Weekly). Columbus, Ga., October 7, 1862.
28. *OR* ., Vol.19, Part I, p.982.
29. Ibid., Vol. 51, Part 2, p.626.
30. Ibid., Vol.12, Part 2, p.703.
31. Letter of J.W.S. Morgan to, "My Dear Nittie, Camp Near Bunkers Hill, Va. this the 30th of Sept 62," typescript in bound Volume 205, Fredericksburg-Spotsylvania NMP, Virginia.
32. Goggans letter, September 23, 1862.
33. Ibid.
34. Caldwell, p.53.
35. Kimbrough.
36. Goggans letter, September 23, 1862.
37. *Richmond Daily Dispatch,* Richmond, Va., October 30, 1862; Folsom, p.138.
38. Letter of W.C. Goggans to "Dear Father from HDQ 35th Regt Ga. Vols Camp A.P. Hill 4 miles south of Smithfield Va Oct 28 1862," William C. Goggans Civil War Letters, courtesy of Hargrett Rare Book & Manuscript Library/ University of Georgia Libraries, Athens Ga.
39. "Report of Sick and Wounded, 35th Georgia Volunteers Near Berryville, VA. October 1862," Eleanor S. Brockenbrough Library, The Museum of the Confederacy, Richmond, Va.

40. Letter of James Tuggle to Confederate Secretary of War, October 25, 1862. "Confederate Secy of War Letters Recd," National Archives, Washington D.C., on microfilm roll m437, roll 75, item 476-T-1862.
41. Goggans letter, October 28, 1862.
42. C. Keith Wilbur, *Civil War Medicine: 1861–1865.* (Old Saybrook, Conn.1998), p. 84; Medical information received by author from Terry Reimer, Director of Research/ Public Relations Coordinator, National Museum of Civil War Medicine, Frederick, Md.
43. Goggans letter, October 28, 1862.
44. Letter of Lieut WC Goggans to "Mr. Josiah Goggans from Camp Hill near Buryville Northern Va. Nov 5th 1862," William C. Goggans Civil War Letters, courtesy of Hargrett Rare Book & Manuscript Library/ University of Georgia Libraries, Athens Ga.
45. CSR; Lillian Henderson, *Roster of the Confederate Soldiers of Georgia 1861–1865,* Vol.III, (Hapeville, Ga., 1960) p. 842–844, 874, 914, 922.
46. Goggans letter, November 5, 1862.
47. Ibid; *OR.,* Vol.19, Pt.I, p.982; Carroll R. Patterson, "The Incomplete Correspondence of Lt. Josiah B. Patterson and the 14th Georgia Volunteer Infantry—An Outline of Its History," Atlanta Historical Society, p.60.
48. *OR*., Vol.19, pt.II, p.133–135.
49. Goggans letter, November 5, 1862.

Chapter Seven

FREDERICKSBURG: THE WORST KIND OF WEATHER

"I was sorry to learn that you had heard that I was Dead, butt I am hapy to inform you that this is a lie. . . ." Sergeant John Morgan

On November 11, Edward Thomas' Brigade moved eight miles west toward Winchester, Virginia. Captain Charles A. Conn, commander of Company G, 45th Georgia, believed the move came because his division had chased away the Federal troops at Snicker's Gap. The soldiers had denuded their old bivouac area of firewood too. Conn wrote a letter on November 12 and described a smallpox outbreak in the 35th Georgia. "I understand 'tis reported, at home, that the small pox is in our Regiment–'tis not so, though there is a case or two in the 35th Ga in our Brigade, they are not allowed to encamp near any other troops and are under quarantine, none of them have died from its effect." Probably the lone patient afflicted with smallpox, listed in the October "Report of Sick and Wounded, 35th Georgia Volunteers", had infected other men. This patient might have been Private Jasper Webb, Company G. Doctors admitted Webb to a Winchester hospital some time in October or early November. He died in the same hospital on November 16.[1]

The quarantine of the 35th Georgia near Winchester lasted a short time because the Light Division received orders to march toward central Virginia. Meanwhile, Ambrose Burnside's Army of the Potomac moved toward Fredericksburg. There Burnside planned to cross the Rappahannock River on pontoon boats and head for Richmond before Lee could block his move.

The Light Division marched through Winchester at 2:30 A.M. on November 22. A Winchester woman who witnessed the move described the sorry scene. "They were very destitute, many without shoes, and all without overcoats or gloves, although the weather is freezing. Their poor hands looked so red and cold holding their muskets in the biting wind."[2]

A.P. Hill's men moved south along the Shenandoah Valley to New Market where they turned eastward. The soldiers crossed Massanutten Mountain at Luray Gap and entered the Luray Valley. They turned southeast and climbed the western slope of the Blue Ridge Mountains at Fisher's Gap. The troops somehow held up under the strain of the elements. Snow and sleet made the mountain crossing difficult and dangerous. Many soldiers left bloody footprints as the sharp rocks and ice pierced their rag-wrapped feet. The men plunged their chapped hands deep into pockets or under armpits as the relentless wind tore at their clothing. The weary soldiers shuffled down the eastern slope and passed through Madison Court House and then Orange Court House. They finally arrived in Fredericksburg on December 3 after marching 140 miles in twelve days. The weather in Fredericksburg failed to improve. Four more inches of snow covered their sleeping bodies on the night of December 4.[3] Sergeant John Morgan's shoes, during the long march, either completely disintegrated or fell into tatters because he wrote his wife on December 8: "My feet are on the ground and I don't know when I will get any more [shoes]. I am tolerbly supplied with clothes. I have now drawers only what I have on at this time and I have been wearing them six month. [T]hey are covered with lice. [T]hey nearly eat me up."[4]

The late arrival of the pontoon boats delayed Burnside's crossing of the Rappahannock River. Federal soldiers lined a ridge known as Stafford Heights, which overlooked Fredericksburg on the other side of the Rappahannock. James Longstreet's First Corps occupied the hills to the rear of Fredericksburg. Jackson spread his Second Corps troops in a thin line, farther downstream from town. Burnsides pontoon boats finally arrived on December 11. Union engineers wrestled the pontoon boats down to the river. Soon Federal artillery crashed into buildings in town. The Confederates realized Burnside planned to cross the stream. Jackson sent a courier southeastward to have the divisions of A.P. Hill and William Taliaferro concentrate at Prospect Hill, south of town.[5]

The Light Division, at 6:15 A.M., on December 12, hustled to bolster the defenses on the extreme Confederate right. Hill placed Brockenbrough's Brigade on the right along the wooded slopes of Prospect Hill. The brigades of Archer, Lane and Pender moved into position on Brockenbrough's left. John Bell Hood's troops had cut a military road along Prospect Hill, and here Hill placed his reserves which included Thomas' Brigade. The Georgians spent the night along the road in support of Pender's Brigade, which anchored Jackson's left.

Soldiers from both sides knew a great clash was near. Captain Conn described the anticipation behind the Southern lines. "Our line of battle extends about ten or twelve miles up and down the river—every one seemed to be on the 'que vivi', and great activity prevailed among our troops. Generals Lee, 'Stonewall', Longstreet, (A.P.) Hill and others, who have been often tried, were on hand; Surgeons riding around hunting up a suitable

Private Jasper Webb, Co. G

This Walton County soldier was part of a smallpox outbreak in October 1862. Doctors vaccinated all the 35th Georgia soldiers and then quarantined the regiment. Webb died of the disease in mid-November at Winchester, Va.

Courtesy of Tom Aderhold, Stone Mountain, Ga.

place to establish Hospitals for the wounded—Medical waggons and Ambulances (hundreds of them) driving around or standing close by—all eagerly expecting the conflict to begin . . .".[6]

A chilly fog coated the area at dawn on Saturday, December 13. Confederate pickets strained to see through the mist. They distinctly heard the eerie sound of movement from the Union side. Jackson strengthened his reserve by placing the divisions of Taliaferro, D.H. Hill and Early behind the Light Division. The fog lifted like a curtain, at around 10 A.M., to reveal a massive Federal force. The enemy line extended from Hill's front far to his left toward town. A.P. Hill noted, "They were deployed in three lines, with heavy reserves, behind the Port Royal Road (Old Richmond Road). Soon their lines, accompanied by ten full batteries (six on their left and four on the right) moved forward to the attack." The Federal movement halted when a one-gun section of Stuart's Horse Artillery led by Major John Pelham bravely rode forward of the Confederate line along the Federal left flank and hit them with accurate enfilade fire. Pelham soon received orders to retire when his position drew heavy enemy artillery fire. The Federal batteries then directed their fire at Prospect Hill and A.P. Hill wrote, "All their batteries, right and left, opened a terrible fire upon the positions occupied by my batteries and shelled the woods promiscuously."[7]

Major General George Meade's troops again advanced after an hour of unanswered artillery fire upon Hill's position. The forty-seven guns from A.P. Hill's artillery spewed their fiery iron when the Federals reached a distance of 500 yards. The Federal lines buckled and wavered as gaps rapidly appeared, but they kept coming.[8]

Generals Hill and Jackson soon realized that a previously discussed gap in the line would prove significant. This gap existed between Archer's left and Lane's right. Incredibly, this gap was nearly 600 yards wide in a low wooded swampy area. Meade's troops steered directly toward this spot. A.P. Hill had perhaps thought that this tangled morass would not allow for a Federal penetration. Jackson had surveyed this area prior to the fighting and he apparently felt comfortable with Hill's decision.

The regiments on Lane's right and Archer's left suddenly found themselves overwhelmed by exuberant Union infantrymen. With their flanks turned and their rear threatened, these Confederate regiments fell back.

The anxious Georgians awaited orders in the woods along the military road. They could not see the battlefield, but they certainly heard the noise. Sergeant Marion Hill Fitzpatrick wrote, "About half past one o'clock the deafening roar of thousands of small arms and the whistling of bullets all around us told us that the ball had opened in earnest."[9]

An anxious staff officer from Lane's Brigade rode up to Edward Thomas and requested assistance about 1:45 P.M. The Georgians rushed in column formation down an off-shoot of the military road for about three-quarters of a mile. The 14th Georgia led the way followed by the 49th, 45th and 35th Georgia Infantry Regiments respectively. Fitzpatrick remembered, "We doublequicked the most of the way and when we reached the place, formed a line of battle or tried to, in a thick low cedar growth and marched into it. We had gone but little distance before the bullets came whistling thick and fast and the heart rending cries of the wounded were constantly heard."[10]

Smoke from the weapons cut visibility even further in the thick trees. General Thomas wrote that he would have preferred moving through the woods directly to Lane's assistance but he was "unable, on account of the density of undergrowth, to advance in line." The brigade then moved by flank off the road into the woods and advanced toward the noise.[11]

The Georgians struggled through nearly five hundred yards of fallen trees, vines and briars. The loudest sounds of fighting came from the right. Thomas formed his regiments into line of battle and moved them in the direction of Lane's Brigade. The 14th Georgia located the enemy first and beat them back, but the Federals pushed forward again. The 49th Georgia, amidst the smoke and confusing clatter, became separated from the left flank of the 14th Georgia. The 49th suddenly faced attackers on their own front. Confusion swirled further along the Georgia line as the 45th and 35th Georgia Regiments lost touch with their sister units. Then Union soldiers hit these two regiments. The 45th Georgia finally located the 49th Georgia. The 45th and 35th Georgia soldiers slid to the right and strengthened Thomas' left flank. This sudden increased firepower from Thomas' left caused the blue clad troops to melt back into the woods. Fitzpatrick recalled, "On we went but still could see no Yankees—but soon the right wing of our regiment fired a deafening volley which told that they were in sight of the bluecoats. In a moment we could see a plenty of them. I raised my rifle, took deliberate aim and fired, loaded and fired again."[12]

The Georgians ran head long into Colonel Adrian Root's brigade from Brigadier General John Gibbon's division. The center of Root's line, the 104th and 105th New York, probably struck the area where the 35th and 45th Georgians struggled to link their flanks. Root's line comprised from right to left: the 16th Maine, 94th New York, 104th New York, 105th New York, and 107th Pennsylvania. Gibbon had initially sent Brigadier General Nelson Taylor's brigade forward at 1 P.M. When this line bogged down, Gibbon had sent Colonel Peter Lyle's brigade ahead to force a breakthrough. The Confederate fire had halted Lyle's troops too. Gibbon next ordered Root's men forward as Lyle's soldiers fell back in confusion. The fiery Union commander expressed frustration with the lack of success of his first two brigades despite the fact that Lane's North Carolinians initially entrenched in a strong position behind the rail bed. "Finding we were making but little impression on the enemy's position, sheltered as he was, I ordered up Root's brigade and directed it to take the position with the bayonet."[13]

Root described what happened when his men reached the position vacated by the previous two Union brigades. He wrote, "the fire of the enemy became so incessant and galling, and so many of my men fell killed or wounded, that the front line of the brigade slackened its pace, and the men, without orders, commenced firing. A halt seemed imminent, and a halt in the face of the terrific fire to which the brigade was exposed would have been death; or, worse a disastrous repulse." Three of Lyle's regiments returned about this time to bolster Root's line. The 90th Pennsylvania and the 26th New York moved on the left while the 12th Massachusetts moved to the right. All three of these regiments had spent most of their ammunition.[14] Root and his officers vociferously implored the men to halt their premature firing and ordered a charge. "The brigade resumed its advance, and as the men recognized the enemy, their movement increased in rapidity until,

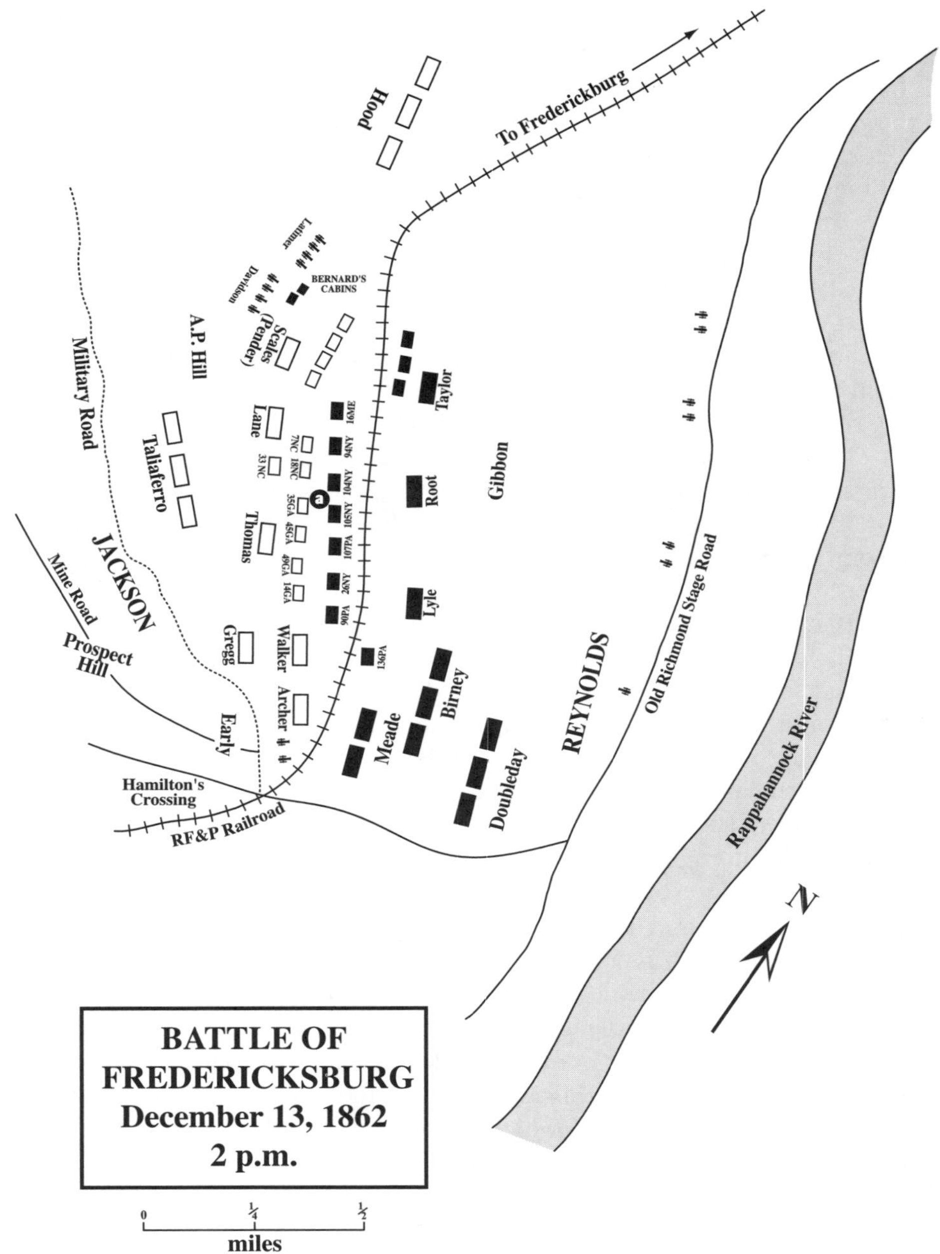
To Fredericksburg
Hood
Latimer
Davidson
BERNARD'S CABINS
A.P. Hill
Scales (Pender)
Military Road
Taylor
Lane
16ME
7NC
94NY
18NC
33 NC
Taliaferro
Gibbon
Root
35GA
104NY
105NY
Thomas
45GA
107PA
49GA
26NY
14GA
90PA
JACKSON
Mine Road
Lyle
Old Richmond Stage Road
Gregg
Walker
136PA
Prospect Hill
REYNOLDS
Birney
Archer
Early
Meade
Doubleday
Rappahannock River
Hamilton's Crossing
RF&P Railroad
N
BATTLE OF FREDERICKSBURG
December 13, 1862
2 p.m.
0
¼
½
miles

a. RF&P Railroad

This view looks ESE (120 degrees) across tracks from position of 35th Georgia. Nearby trees east of tracks did not exist in 1862. Right distant tree line was area that Meade's troops had earlier guided toward when they crossed tracks and entered wide undefended gap between Archer and Lane. The 35th Georgia, 45th Georgia, 18th North Carolina and 7th North Carolina helped push the attackers from Gibbon's division across the tracks near this point and chased them through fields eastward. Low ammunition and Federal artillery halted their chase and they returned to the railroad.

photo by author

with a shout and a run, the brigade leaped the ditches, charged across the railway, and occupied the wood beyond, driving the enemy from their position, killing a number with the bayonet, and capturing upward of 200 prisoners." Root reported that most of the captured soldiers came from the 33rd North Carolina in Lane's Brigade.[15]

The renewed Union line struck Lane's North Carolinians as his two right flank regiments fired their last ammunition. Lane's men fell back from the railroad into the woods to await reinforcements. The Union soldiers entered the edge of the woods but halted. They stopped perhaps because of the thickness of the woods and their own dwindling ammunition. Colonel Root reported that the charge over the railroad had caused the brigade to "become somewhat broken." Root, unsure of his next move, spurred his horse to find General Gibbon, who directed him to continue the assault. When Root returned, he found the situation had changed. "On returning to the wood, I found that the enemy had rallied in superior force, and were vigorously pressing the front and flank of my brigade."[16] This superior force was Thomas' Georgians.

Root, dismayed over the changing situation, again raced off to find reinforcements. Root learned of John Gibbon's wounding and he sought the next most senior officer. Brigadier General Nelson Taylor directed Root to withdraw from the woods when he deemed it necessary. The beleaguered Union commander returned to his men only to find some of them already pulling back. Confederate soldiers from Thomas' Brigade poured out of the woods turning his flanks. Root believed his position tenable, but he needed support to hold his men's hard-fought gains. The infantry support failed to arrive.[17]

Confederate fire had dropped Major Daniel Sharp, commander of the 105th New York, before the Union charge began. Captain Abraham Moore took Sharp's place. Moore noted the numerous casualties in his regiment from the charge across the tracks. This left too few men to make a stand in the woods once Thomas' men arrived. The Georgians pushed the New Yorkers back beyond the railroad tracks. Moore's dejected men found themselves in their original starting point from earlier in the morning.[18]

Colonel Gilbert G. Prey, commander of the 104th New York, described some confusion as his line became intermixed with the 94th New York and the 16th Maine as they approached the railroad. Prey restored his line after his men rushed across the railroad tracks and chased Lane's North Carolinians into the woods. He said that after the firing had continued for some time an order passed down the line to fall back. His men withdrew to the edge of the woods where they discovered that the fall back order had been false. Prey then urged his men forward again, and they moved back into the woods.

Adrian Root sensed the peril of his brigade as the fire to his front increased with the arrival of the Georgians. He described his position with no support in sight as "simply murderous to my command." Root unwillingly gave the official order to fall back. When he issued this order he wrote, "The officers and men received it with surprise and grief, and retired so reluctantly that the enemy was enabled to close upon the rear of the brigade and inflict loss exceeding that incurred during the charge itself."[19]

Prey described the orderly withdrawal of the 104th New York: "Retiring across the railroad, the regimental line was reformed, and came in good order off the field." Captain Moore failed to describe any disorder in the 105th New York as they retreated. These descriptions conflict with the Confederate reports of what happened next.[20]

Edward Thomas sensed the slackened Union fire and realized that this could only mean two things: the enemy lacked ammunition or had ordered

Brigadier General Edward Lloyd Thomas

Thomas' delayed promotion incensed most of his officers who launched a letter writing campaign on his behalf to Confederate authorities. A beardless Thomas dressed in a new brigadier general's uniform presented a contrast with an earlier photo (see Thomas photo in chapter 1).

Courtesy of Valentine Richmond History Center, Richmond, Va.

a withdrawal. He seized the initiative and ordered an attack. The Georgians supported by Lane's and Scale's brigades moved forward through the woods and struck with a fury that pushed Gibbon's division back across the railroad tracks. The 35th and 45th Georgia Regiments did not stop their pursuit at the rail bed. These two Georgia regiments, supported on the left by the 18th and 7th North Carolina, pushed the enemy farther eastward for several hundred yards until hitting Federal infantry and artillery fire.[21] Soldiers from the 35th Georgia boasted they "blued the ground for a quarter mile with Yankees." One observer estimated by his watch that the Georgia brigade engaged the enemy for only thirty-three minutes. Another witness described how the 49th Georgia "piled up the blue coats as they were retreating across the field a little thicker than you ever saw pumpkins in a new ground."[22] Edward Thomas maintained control over his zealous troops. He recalled, "We pursued for some distance across the railroad, when, seeing no support either on the right or left, and my ammunition being reported to be well-nigh exhausted, I concluded to fall back to the railroad. Forming at this place I determined to hold the position. . . ."[23] Accurate enemy sharpshooters from a distance of seven to eight hundred yards dropped a number of Georgians along the rail bed. Corporal David Harrison Mobley reported that as he held the regimental colors he lay down at the crest of a hill, and Private George W. Briscoe and Rolly Needham rolled over dead within three feet of him.[24] That evening, Thomas' troops moved a short distance to defensive positions in the woods as pickets patrolled along the railroad tracks. The men of Colonel Edward T.H. Warren's Brigade moved in, early the following morning, to give the Georgians a well-needed rest in the rear.[25]

Thomas' Brigade with help from the brigades of Lane, Scales (Pender), and Walker had stopped the Union breakthrough at the north end of A.P. Hill's line. Other Confederate brigades helped stem the enemy push into the center and right side of Hill's position. General Hill cited the admirable job performed by Thomas' Brigade in his report. "The enemy having thus been repulsed at all points, my brigades remained in their original positions save General Thomas' (Fourteenth, Thirty-fifth, Forty-fifth, and Forty-ninth Georgia), which was not recalled from the position it had so gallantly won in the front line. . . ."[26] Lane recalled, "General Thomas came to my assistance, but too late to save my line. He encountered the enemy in the edge of the woods, drove them back, and with the Eighteenth and the Seventh Regiments of my brigade on his left, chased them to their first position."[27]

The 14th Georgia, on Thomas' right, took the brunt of the brigade's casualties, but the 35th Georgia suffered the second highest casualty rate. Captain James McElvany, commander of Company F, reported to his family, "To tell you of the dangers through which I have passed and through which I am likely to have to pass again would be anything but pleasant to you." He then described the effects of the fight on his Gwinnett County men. "We had a hard fight last Saturday, out of my company we lost ten men killed and wounded, only two (J.M. Plummer and J.S. Wilder) were killed, out of our Regiment we lost ninety-three killed and wounded. Our Division is commanded by A.P. Hill, and it suffered worse than any other Division of the Whole Army."[28] William Fox claimed, in *Regimental Losses In The American Civil War,* the 35th Georgia had 10 killed and 79 wounded during the battle. James Folsom claimed, in *Heroes and Martyrs of Georgia,* a very low casualty rate at 14 killed and 41 wounded. The *Official Records* stated the Georgians lost 7 killed and 82 wounded. McElvany's figures, which approximated William Fox's and the *O.R.'s* , are probably the most accurate. A newspaper article in the *Columbus* (Ga.) *Enquirer* additionally reported that the 35th Georgia lost about 100 out of 400 soldiers that went into the battle.[29]

Root's brigade suffered the highest casualties in Gibbon's division. The 105th New York reported 10 killed, 62 wounded and 6 missing for a total of 78 men. The 104th New York suffered 5 killed, 45 wounded and 2 missing for a total of 52. The 107th Pennsylvania had 3 killed, 47 wounded and 6 missing for a total of 56. The 94th New York lost 2 killed, 49 wounded and 7 missing for a total of 58.[30]

Confederate troops waited in line of battle through Tuesday morning, December 16. During this time, pickets from both sides stood within talking distance. Burnside's troops finally moved back across the river to safety. The Georgians moved to Hamilton's Crossing near the spot where they had fought several days before. Captain McElvany compared food over the previous week: "We get very good fare where we are Stationed, but while we were in line of Battle, where we lay four days, we had rough fare." He gave some details of their bivouac area: "We are camped in the Woods about Six miles from Fredericksburg. We have no tents and but one Blanket each. The ground is now frozen hard and you can guess what kind of Camp fire we have." Illness plagued many of the men in Company F because of these conditions. Captain McElvany displayed the inner strength developed by soldiers of both sides as they fought the elements. "I have had a bad cold myself, but I am only surprised that I am not down sick, nobody knows what a man can stand until he tries it." Confederate troops speculated in camp about the enemy's intentions. Many believed that Burnside would try to cross the river again below Fredericksburg at Port Royal. McElvany spread a camp rumor: "[D]own here it is reported that twelve thousand of them have crossed at that place but we dont know the truth of the matter.[31]

The wife of John Morgan had suffered through several difficult weeks. She received a report that her husband had died prior to the fight at Fredericksburg. Morgan wrote back to her on December 18: "I was sorry to learn that you had heard that I was Dead, butt I am hapy to inform you that this is a lie and I knew it was a lie as soon as I heard it." Later in the same letter he lamented, "My Dear Nittie I was glad to hear that you all think anuff [enough] of us as to pray for the poor Soldier for my Dear we need the prares of the good. I some times think that fighting will never end this war. We have flogged the Yankees every time we have fought them and it seemes that the war is no near the end then it was when it first begun."[32]

Frustration was rampant all along the lines. While the soldiers tried to stay warm, many wondered if there would be more fighting. Most of the men wanted to construct winter quarters. The hardships of an uncertain winter campaign taxed the troops of both sides.

The month of December 1862 ended and both armies finally settled in for the winter. Union troops occupied Stafford Heights, and Confederate troops eyed them from the south bank of the river.

The first mail call after the battle was a welcome escape from the previous days of hard marching and fighting. Many soldiers received clothing from home. Some packages occasionally arrived after a soldier had died in battle. Company members normally opened these packages. The boxes usually contained items of food, clothing, drink or divine providence that could sustain the well-being of a living comrade.

Private James Plummer, Company F, suffered wounds at the Battle of Fredericksburg. He died in a hospital two days later without seeing the suit and boots sent from home. Members of the company opened his package and distributed the clothing. Captain McElvany mentioned in a letter to his own family that Plummer's new boots fit his feet very well. The officer also listed a number of clothing items that he needed. These items included shirts, socks, drawers and a hat. He wanted a new overcoat and a drop coat too. He hoped that his father would visit soon and bring some supplies from Gwinnett County for the men of Company F. This company numbered about fifty men fit for duty as another Christmas away from home approached.[33]

Sergeant James Kimbrough returned from Georgia at the end of December 1862 or early January 1863. He brought a large amount of supplies that included shoes, blankets, and assorted clothing. Colonel Bolling Holt's father, Hines Holt of Columbus, assisted with the supply drive. The senior Holt, a lawyer by trade and an 1824 Franklin College graduate (now University of Georgia), served as a Georgia congressman in the First Confederate Congress from 1862–1864.[34]

Thomas' Brigade had constructed winter quarters at Camp Gregg by the beginning of January 1863. The men named the site in honor of Brigadier General Maxcy Gregg. The South Carolinian had succumbed to wounds suffered in the previous battle. The camp sat near the Rappahannock River, halfway between Fredericksburg and Port Royal. The soldiers usually built their log huts either on the southern slope or on a hilltop to receive the sun's warmth. The water of a creek or river was never far away. Usually a group of up to six soldiers, called a "mess," gathered available tools and worked to assemble their shelter. Many men dug a floor about two feet below ground level. This provided more warmth as well as headroom. Sometimes they placed a wooden floor over the ground. The men wrestled pine logs into place to form the walls. They used more logs and

Tombstone of Private Henry S. Barnes, Co.A

This Haralson County soldier enlisted at the beginning of 1862. He was wounded ten months later at the Battle of Fredericksburg and died the following day. He was buried at Spotsylvania Confederate Cemetery.

Photo by the author

woven brush for the roof. Some soldiers even placed their rubber blanket on the roof to help with waterproofing. A stove or fireplace with a chimney stood at the far end. The men smeared lumps of mud and clay into the cracks between the logs to seal in the warmth.[35]

When the 35th Georgians completed their huts, they settled into the relative safety but boredom of winter camp life. With so many soldiers camped close together, picket duty occurred infrequently—once every twelve days for twenty-four hours. Orders prohibited picket firing. Some soldiers crossed the river against orders to swap tobacco, knives, clothing, newspapers, coffee and other items with Union pickets. Private Joseph T. Johnson, Company H, described his violation in a letter to his niece: "We went on picket last week down on the Rappahannock River where it is not more than one hundred yards wide—the Yankees on one side and me on the other and I went over to them and swapt tobacco to them for coffee and swapt knives with them and one of them give me a fine pipe. . . ." He sent the pipe home to his mother as a souvenir. Johnson bragged about his prowess as a soldier. "Tell Noah that I have seen lots of Yankees sins [since] I saw him and that they have tried to kill me two-but they did not quite make the trip and that I am very certain that I have killed several of them and wounded a great many."[36]

Captain McElvany reflected on his Christian beliefs and his desire for the war to end so he could return to his loved ones:

> I would be glad to see this war end but I cant see where it will stop. I trust in God that it will be brought to a close before long. In his own good time He will have all things right. We have been a stiff necked and Rebelious people and are being chastised for our conduct. It does appear that we have suffered a great deal but when we have suffered enough Peace will smile on us again and we will be suffered to return to our homes and firesides, to spend the remainder of our days with the friends and loved ones we have left behind. That will be a happy, happy day for the poor soldier who has been truged [trudged] about during this unnatural war. Many have fallen and perhaps many more will fall before it comes to a close, but if I am spared to see these troubles over it will certainly be the happiest hour of my life. But if it be my lot to fall in the conflict I can only wish to meet my friends in a Brighter and Better world than this, where the war whoop will not be heard where the wicked cease from troubling and the weary are at rest.[37]

The captain would soon have his faith severely tested. As the war lengthened it was not unusual for a family to be robbed of more than one male. McElvany's world shattered when told of the death of his younger brother, Second Lieutenant Samuel Jacob McElvany, Company I, 16th Georgia. He died of smallpox on January 1, 1863. Three weeks later, John Franklin McElvany, another brother in the 16th Georgia, succumbed to smallpox too.[38]

Frustrated by not being able to console his family in person, McElvany tried to bring them comfort with his pen:

> Then let us content ourselves with that happy reflection that they have gone to rest, gone to that world above, which John spoke of in one of his letters home, where he said, there would be no wars. He desires to meet us all there. He has gone to meet Sam there. And I hope we will all meet there. And although two Bright Stars have been taken from our family circle on Earth, At that day they will all be replaced and shine more Brilliant than ever. Yet I hope I can be spared to meet you all again on earth, but if it should please our

> Heavenly Father not to Suffer it, I hope I shall go to my poor Brothers in Heaven, and be ready to greet you when you come.

He perhaps pictured his family gathered around the kitchen table as they agonized over the difficult news. He pleaded with them as he probably pleaded with himself:

> What shall we do! I could only answer by repeating, What shall we do! It will do no good to weep. We can't benefit the dead. We can only injure ourselves. Then let us content ourselves with the consoling thought that a better time is Coming, That Sam and John are in Heaven, where we all hope to meet them.[39]

Light Division soldiers gathered money during the first week of January 1863 to help the many families of Fredericksburg who had lost homes and possessions during the battle. Captain Conn reported the 45th Georgia raised $760 and he expected the brigade to raise about $2,000. The division collected $10,000 in cash, all from men who had very little themselves.[40] The citizens of Fredericksburg, in fact, made a significant sacrifice. Betty Herndon Maury, daughter of the famous mariner Matthew Fontaine Maury, described the unpleasant scene that a neighbor probably relayed to her:

> Almost every house has six or eight shells through it, the doors are wide open, the locks and windows broken and the shutters torn down. Two blocks of buildings were burned to the ground. Our house was a hospital. Mr. Corbin says every vessel in the house (even the vegetable dishes and cups) are filled with blood and water. There are large pools of gore on the floor, the table in the parlor was used as an amputating table and a Yankee (Byron Pearce of New York) is buried at the kitchen door.[41]

Another civilian who remained in Fredericksburg during the battle described the destruction of private property wrought by the Union soldiers:

> All discipline was gone. They pillaged every house in the town, ransacking the whole from garret to cellar-smashing the windows, doors, and furniture of every description-and committing every species of outrage. They broke the chinaware, smashed the pianos, and annihilated the chairs, tables, and bedsteads. They cut open the beds, emptied the contents in the street, and burned the bedticks. They stole all the blankets, sheets, counterpanes, and everything they could use. They broke into the cellars and drank all the liquors they could find, so that the whole army became a drunken and furious mob.[42]

Meanwhile in Richmond, Lieutenant William Goggans fought for his life. He was bedridden with typhoid fever, probably in a house converted into a hospital that belonged to the Taylor family. "Since then I have been quite Sick and I am not improving any yet. I am not helpless. I can set up in bead [bed] and get up by my self-but am not able to get out of the house." He wrote an urgent letter to his father on January 14, 1863 soliciting his immediate visit. "Father I want you or Brother to be shure to come and see me immediately. I think you can do me the most good by visiting me now than before and if you come, come to stay with me. Mrs and Mr Taylor are verry kind to me and I Supposed I am doing as well as I could any where else from home—My disease is Typhoid fever." He closed this last letter home with, "I am now looking for you or brother and will continue to look until I see you. I intend to go home as soon as able and if you was hear perhaps You would make it lighter on me getting off." Whether family members made it to Richmond in time was unknown. The twenty-four-year-old student-turned officer died on February 27.[43]

Religious revivalism took root in many Confederate camps around Fredericksburg during the winter of 1862–63. The movement gained momentum as the warm weather of spring returned. Several reasons existed why it took eighteen months for an organized religious movement to gain momentum. Many original regimental chaplains lacked moral fiber. Numerous Confederate soldiers came from small communities where the church exerted a strong presence and revivals were common. Countless soldiers realized their mortality as the war grew longer. They wanted to make their peace with the Lord. When new army chaplains arrived to replace the deficient ones, the soldiers easily accepted revivals as a way to reach God.[44] The preacher selected his meeting spot in the woods, usually on a hillside. The soldiers chopped down trees for benches and they erected a platform for a pulpit. The men drove stakes into the ground and placed baskets filled with wood chips on top of the stakes. A designated soldier torched the baskets after dark. These crude lanterns cast a rosy glow across the hillside. Chaplains held prayer meetings in at least ten brigades, including Thomas' Brigade, during this period. These meetings began around mid-day and continued into the night.[45]

The regimental chaplains in Thomas' Brigade frequently combined their efforts and held brigade size meetings. Around February 1, 1863, one of the most powerful revivals of the winter occurred in the brigade. Chaplain John J. Hyman from the 49th Georgia preached from four to six times each day and "was about to break down, when Reverend Edward Benjamin Barrett came to his help and was soon commissioned chaplain of the Forty-Fifth Georgia Regiment." Barrett was a Baptist preacher from Irwinton, Georgia.[46]

Tombstone of Private Sheldrick Brown, Co.K

This Harris County soldier enlisted in March 1862. He was killed in action at the Battle of Fredericksburg on December 13, 1862. His body was buried at Spotsylvania Confederate Cemetery.

Photo by the author

Barrett and Hyman served as the only chaplains in Thomas' Brigade during early 1863. Chaplain George W. Yarbrough had resigned from the 35th Georgia due to ill health in September 1862. Hyman mentioned in a letter to Reverend J. William Jones that he (Hyman) was the only chaplain in Thomas' Brigade after the Seven Days Battles. This indicated that Yarbrough must have been too sick to perform his duties months before his resignation. Chaplain William P. Reed refused to accept an appointment to the 35th Georgia in December 1862. Hyman wrote that after the brigade transferred to Stonewall Jackson's command, little time existed for religious services because of the rapid marching and severe campaigning. This changed after the brigade went into winter quarters at Camp Gregg near Fredericksburg in mid-December 1862. Hyman opened regular night services for the troops at this time. They met outside when the weather permitted and crowded into tents when it rained. Hyman wrote, "often I have seen large numbers leave the door of the tent, unable to get in, when the snow was all over the ground." The overworked John Hyman preached regularly three times a week to each regiment in the brigade. He described the revival of February 1, 1863: "the good Lord poured out His Spirit upon us; hundreds were seeking the Lord for pardon of sins; almost daily there were some going down into the water, being buried with Christ in baptism." Chaplain A.W. Moore received an assignment to the 14th Georgia and he soon joined Hyman and Barrett.[47]

George W. Hall, 14th Georgia, remarked, "I was happier when I met around our rude seats to hear the beloved chaplains of our Brigade than I ever was before during this terrible and wicked war."[48] Numerous soldiers trekked to local churches to worship on Sundays. Stonewall Jackson, a fiercely devout Presbyterian, no doubt greeted revivalism with open arms for his troops.

Gray clouds obscured the sky on January 29. Snow started to fall, and soon fourteen inches coated the ground. The troops in the 35th Georgia engaged several other regiments in a snowball fight. This fight quickly escalated and soon numbered several thousand Confederate soldiers. The thud of snowballs smacking against bodies and huts echoed throughout the camp. The fight produced no major injuries.[49]

The knee-deep snow brought elation for another reason too. John Morgan wrote on January 30, "I tell you it is very Cold but then we have one Concolation [consolation] that is this. That they cant fight as long as it snowes. [T]he boys say that they wish it would snow always." His humor was evident as he expressed his frustration with being unable to obtain a furlough because he could not obtain an enlistee to take his place. "I Could com home if I had aney [any] one to work for [me]. [M]r butt black John is not rich and so I have to stay hear untill the war brakes." He then reminded his wife that this day, four years before, had been the happiest day of his life. It probably was the day they married. "I wish that I could See you. I would tell you Something that wont do to write." He thanked her for sending a box by way of Jim Kimbrough who returned from Georgia with supplies. The box contained an odd combination of salt and shoes and perhaps some new underdrawers.[50]

In January, Private James M. Garrett returned to Company D from his home in Houston, Georgia. Doctors had sent him home to recuperate from debilitus. This illness caused feebleness and a loss of strength. He reported in a letter to his mother that he found things in the 35th Georgia much different from when he had departed in August 1862. He found many new faces in the ranks, but expressed sadness over the familiar faces that were gone. "The health of the company is better than I ever saw it before." He reflected on how different the Virginia weather was from Georgia's. "It snowed all day yesterday and it is raining today. We have had bad weather ever since I have been here."[51]

The food situation in Lee's army was still far from perfect. The men received food only twice a day and they quickly gobbled up the sparse portions. One officer in the brigade felt the troops should get more beef to eat. He wrote, "The men have eaten beef till they like it so much better than bacon. A beefs liver is a very rare dish." He expressed dissatisfaction at the high prices Confederate officers paid for their rations—forty cents for a pound of bacon, and twenty cents per pound for beef. "The government is issuing plenty of sugar now, but we have done without it until we do not care much about it."[52]

James Garrett expressed optimism when he wrote, "Whisky is cheap here. $80 a gallon." He mentioned the upcoming Company D election to replace Fifth Sergeant Robert D. Dansby who died three days after being wounded at Fredericksburg.[53]

Meanwhile, on the other side of the river, dissatisfaction with Burnside ran from Union privates all the way to President Lincoln. Major General Joseph "Fighting Joe" Hooker replaced Burnside at the helm of the Army of the Potomac on January 25. Lincoln no doubt wondered if Hooker could live up to his nickname and bring victory and honor to the eastern army.

NOTES

Abbreviations:

CSR—"Compiled Service Records of Confederate Soldiers Who Served In Organizations From The State of Georgia,"—Thirty-fifth Infantry Regiment (National Archives Microfilm Publication M266) National Archives Building, Washington, D.C.

GDAH—Georgia Division of Archives and History, Morrow, Ga.

NMP—National Military Park

OR.—War of the Rebellion: A Compilation of the Official Records of the Union and Confederate Armies. 130 Vols.

SHSP—Southern Historical Society Papers

1. "Letters of Two Confederate Officers: William Thomas Conn and Charles Augustus Conn," (45th Ga.) edited by T. Conn Bryan, *The Georgia Historical Quarterly,* Vol. XLVI 1962, p.185; "Report of Sick and Wounded, 35th Georgia Volunteers Near Berryville, VA. October 1862," Eleanor S. Brockenbrough Library, The Museum of the Confederacy, Richmond, Va.; CSR of Private Jasper Webb.
2. Cornelia McDonald, *A Diary With Reminiscences of the War and Refuge Life in the Shenandoah Valley, 1860–65.* (Nashville, Tn. 1934) p.107.

3. James Folsom, *Heroes and Martyrs of Georgia-Georgia's Record in the Revolution of 1861,* (Macon, Ga.,1864) p.118. (reprinted by Butternut and Blue, Baltimore, 1995)
4. Letter of John W. S. Morgan to "My Dear wife, Camp Near Fredericksburg Dec 8th/62," typescript in Volume 205, Fredericksburg-Spotsylvania NMP.
5. *OR* ., Vol.21, p.645.
6. "Conn-Brantley Letters 1862," edited by T. Conn Bryan, *The Georgia Historical Quarterly,* Vol.LV, 1971.
7. *OR* ., Vol. 21, p.645.
8. Ibid., Vol. 21, p.637–39, 645–46, 649, 656–57, 511, 515.
9. Marion Hill Fitzpatrick, *Letters to Amanda.* (Macon, Ga., 1998) p. 37 (edited by Jeffrey C. Lowe and Sam Hodges). Reprinted by permission of Mercer University Press, 1998.
10. Ibid., p.37; *OR* ., Vol. 21, p.654–655.
11. Ibid., Vol.21, p.653.
12. Fitzpatrick, p.37; Jasper, "Letter From Thomas' Brigade," *Augusta Daily Constitutionalist,* Augusta Ga., January 14, 1863.
13. *OR* ., Vol. 21, p. 480.
14. Ibid., Vol. 21, p.496–499.
15. Ibid., Vol. 21, p.487.
16. Ibid., Vol. 21, p.487, 655.
17. Ibid., Vol. 21, p.487.
18. Ibid., Vol. 21, p.492–493.
19. Ibid., Vol. 21, p.487.
20. Ibid., Vol. 21, p. 492–493.
21. Ibid., Vol.21, p.616.
22. *Columbus Enquirer,* Columbus, Ga., December 12, 1862. "A.P. Hill's Division in the Fight."; Jasper; Veritas, "The Battle of Fredericksburg-Third Georgia Brigade," *Augusta Daily Constitutionalist,* Augusta, Ga., December 23, 1862.
23. *OR* ., Vol.21, p.653.
24. Anita B. Sams, *Wayfarers In Walton,* (Atlanta, Ga., 1967) p. 435; CSR, No military record could be found of a soldier named Rolly Needham in Company G.
25. Jasper; *OR* ., Vol. 21, p.653.
26. Ibid., Vol.21, p.647.
27. Ibid., Vol. 21, p.655.
28. Major James T. McElvany, "The Letters and Journal of Major James T. McElvany of the 35th Georgia Infantry Regiment."
29. William G. Fox, *Regimental Losses in the American Civil War 1861–65,* (Albany, NY, 1898) p.566; Folsom, p.136; *Columbus Enquirer,* Columbus, Ga., December 30, 1862, "A.P. Hill's Division in the Fight."
30. *OR.,* Vol. 21, p.138. The 16th Maine, on Root's far right, suffered a disproportionate share of the brigade casualties with 27 killed, 170 wounded, and 34 missing for a

total of 231 men. The high Maine casualty rate probably resulted from their proximity to the Confederate batteries of Latimer and Davidson.

31. McElvany, p.4–5.
32. Letter of John W. S. Morgan to "My Dear nittie, On March from Fredericksburg, Dec 18/62" typescript letter in Vol. 205, Fredericksburg-Spotsylvania NMP.
33. McElvany, Letter to "My Dear Mother from Camp In the Woods near Fredericksburg Va Dec. 19, 1862," p.5–6.
34. J. M. Kimbrough, "My War History 1861–1865," typescript at Chickamauga-Chattanooga NMP.
35. Howard Crouch, *Relic Hunter,* (Fairfax, Va. 1978) p.129.
36. Letter of Joseph T. Johnson to "Judith Beard from Camp of 35th Georgia Near Fredericksburg, January 4, 1863". John H. Boyce Collection, microfilm, GDAH.
37. McElvany, p.6–8.
38. Ibid., p.8.
39. Ibid., p.8–9.
40. Conn, *The Georgia Historical Quarterly,* Vol. XLVI 1962, p.188; Jedediah Hotchkiss, *Make Me A Map of the Valley.* (Dallas, Tx., 1973) p.107.
41. Betty Herndon Maury, "Diary of Betty Herndon Maury-Daughter of the Pathfinder of the Seas, 1861–1863," microfilm (21/41), GDAH.
42. *Augusta Daily Constitutionalist,* Augusta, Ga., December 23, 1862, "Yankee Doings In Fredericksburg." For an eye-opening study of the Union desecration of private property at Fredericksburg see Frank O'Reilly's excellent book *The Fredericksburg Campaign: Winter War on the Rappahannock.* O'Reilly dedicates a full chapter, "The Most Gothic of Gods: The Sacking of Fredericksburg," (p. 102–126) to the ugliness.
43. Letter of WC Goggans to "Dear Father from Richd Va Jany 14th 1863," William C. Goggans Civil War Letters, courtesy of Hargrett Rare Book & Manuscript Library/ University of Georgia Libraries, Athens Ga.
44. J. William Jones, *Christ In the Camp.* (Richmond, Va., 1888) p.490.
45. John H. Worsham, *One of Jackson's Foot Cavalry.* (New York, 1912) p.181.
46. Jones, p.306; Conn, *The Georgia Historical Quarterly,* Vol.XLVI, 1962, p.186.
47. Ibid. Jones, p.504–505.
48. "Diary of George Washington Hall, 14th Georgia Volunteers, CSA, 1861–1865," courtesy of Hargrett Rare Book and Manuscript Library/ University of Georgia Libraries, Athens, Ga., p.41.
49. Sams, p.151.
50. Letter of John W.S. Morgan to "My Dear Nittie, Camp Gregg, Jan the 30th/63," typescript from Vol. 205, Fredericksburg-Spotsylvania NMP.
51. Letter of James M. Garrett to "Dear Mother from Camp Gregg, Feb the 6th 1863," James M. Garrett Collection.
52. Letter of Captain Simeon B. David (14th Ga.) to "My dear parents from Camp Gregg near Fredericksburg, VA March 12, 1863," copy in possession of Fredericksburg-Spotsylvania NMP.
53. Garrett Letter of February 6th, 1863.

Chapter Eight

A Bold Gamble Near Chancellorsville

"I saw men with their heads and arms shot off."
Private James M. Garrett

Joe Hooker spent February and March 1863 rebuilding the strength and morale of his army. Robert E. Lee's men watched and waited on the other side of the Rappahannock River.

A court-martial panel settled a case, on March 1, involving an officer in the 35th Georgia. The panel found Lieutenant John F. Morris, Company E, not guilty of cowardice. Morris allegedly hid behind a stump during the Battle of Seven Pines in May 1862. The notes from his case stated that the officer falsely used a surgeon's certificate to escape duty at the Battle of Mechanicsville. Morris reportedly "hid 130 yards behind his company," at the Battle of Cedar Mountain, and may have purposely wounded himself to avoid the fight. The court-martial panel found Morris not guilty despite these scathing accusations. Whatever happened to Morris was unknown since his military file indicated no further record after August 1862.[1]

A happy James Garrett wrote his mother on March 3 that he had drawn $187. The Confederate paymaster owed Garrett a large amount of back pay because of his sick furlough. This large chunk of cash included a $50 reenlistment bonus plus $2.21 for a clothing allowance. Garrett planned to send her $160 of the pay by way of Captain Lee A.J. Williams.[2]

Sergeant John Sloper, Company D, returned to Camp Gregg on April 4 from furlough. He probably carried a letter from Mrs. Garrett for her son. James Garrett wrote a letter home the following day expressing thankfulness for his mother's recent but tardy note. He softly chastised her though it was unclear whether the delay belonged to her or to the mail service. "I have received a letter from you after so long a time I had begun to think you had all blowed away or gone dead or something. The Snow is nearly a foot deep now. [T]here is know [no] sine of spring here yet." Garrett did not envision a move by either side any time soon because of the weather. He indicated that some of the camp rations were plentiful. "[W]e draw rice all the time. [W]e draw sugar enough to sweeten our coffee all the time. [W]e make coffee out of flour rice or anything."[3]

Later in April, Captain James McElvany reported, "Provisions are somewhat scarce. 1/4 lb Bacon constitutes a mans Ration of meat. This is small fair." The officer also reported that he heard two sermons preached by Chaplain A.W. Moore, a Methodist from the 14th Georgia. He witnessed the baptism of a soldier by Chaplain Edward Barrett, the Baptist minister from the 45th Georgia.[4]

Private Nathaniel D. Knight, Company D, returned from Georgia with a box for Garrett from his family. Garrett wrote, "I got the things you sent by Knight and have just cut my sliver off of that ham. I am enjoying health now and pray I will remain so. [W]e have some very nice weather for the last few days. [T]he peich [peach] trees have just commenced putting out."[5]

Camp life presented numerous ways for enterprising entrepreneurs to make money. James Garrett earned extra money by washing other soldiers' clothes at twenty-five cents per garment. He described the profitable efforts of Corporal Henry L. Harris. "Mr Harris is doing good business now. [H]e bought one hundred and fifty three fish the other day and made one hundred dollars off of them. [T]hey were white shade [shad]." Garrett decided he wanted to take advantage of this opportunity too. He wrote his mother: "I want you to get me a fish hook and put a long line to[o] in and send it to me in a letter. [D]ont roll it up. [D]ouble it around so it will ly flat in the letter. I can put a sinker on it after it gets here. [B]e sure to send it." He also wanted his sister to know that he was well from the "itch."[6]

The weather improved toward the end of April. Soldiers on both sides knew that a fight would come soon. Hooker developed a solid plan to defeat Lee. He ordered Major General John Sedgwick to remain with 40,000 Federal troops at Fredericksburg to hold Lee's attention. On April 27, Hooker slipped northwest with 54,000 men from three corps hoping to flank Lee's army.

Meanwhile, a problem had developed in Company K, 35th Georgia. Lieutenant G.W. Jones had lost the confidence of both the enlisted men plus at least one senior officer. The frustrated Jones resigned. He claimed the enlisted men and the officers conspired against him. Lieutenant Colonel William H. McCullohs, Jones' first company commander, supported the resignation. McCullohs recommended that the resignation be accepted and he wrote, "believing that there are other men of this same company who are better qualified for the position than said Lt. G.W. Jones."[7]

A cannonade from up the river awoke the Georgians, early on April 29. Confederate cavalry reports poured in describing Union movement. Lee correctly guessed that Hooker would try to flank him. The Georgians received orders to march at a moment's notice. Camp Gregg became a flurry of activity as soldiers rapidly packed while others cooked rations for the move. However, no sooner were these preparatory orders issued than new orders arrived to fall in. The grumbling Georgians stepped into formation with empty stomachs and haversacks. The 35th Georgia departed Camp Gregg for Fredericksburg. Rain began to fall adding to their misery. The Light Division neared town and then received orders to slosh back through the mud to the military road near Hamilton's Crossing. They had fought near this spot the previous December. This countermarch of about 25 miles took sixteen soggy, miserable hours. The men formed a skirmish line near Hamilton's Crossing. Enemy soldiers stood in another skirmish line about four hundred yards away. The Georgians remained in line of battle for two nights with orders not to remove any accoutrements and be ready to move at a moment's notice.[8]

The Georgians listened to the distant rumble of artillery on April 30. Marion Hill Fitzpatrick, 45th Georgia, walked through a nearby field and noted the numerous graves from the Battle of Fredericksburg, four months before. "I saw the arm of a dead Yankee sticking out of a grave that had not decayed."[9]

Confederate skirmishers found empty Union lines early on May 1. The enemy troops had withdrawn across the river. Thomas' Brigade headed west, before sunrise, toward Chancellorsville. Hooker's army simultaneously approached the vicinity of the Chancellorsville crossroads. The Federal lines extended westward along the Orange Turnpike into an area of matted vines and dense forest known as the Wilderness. This thick underbrush restricted a unit's ability to see and maneuver. The Wilderness comprised an area about twelve miles long and six miles wide.

As the Georgians approached the area from the east, they heard sounds of heavy skirmishing and artillery fire ahead. At nightfall, they bivouacked along the Orange Plank Road without moving closer to the fighting.

Lee composed his most daring and brilliant plan to date. With Early's Division still at Fredericksburg, he planned to divide his army again. Lee would remain southeast of Chancellorsville with only 14,000 troops to occupy Hooker. Jackson meanwhile, would sneak away to the west with 28,000 troops and fold in Hooker's right flank and rear. If the bold gamble worked, Lee would beat Hooker at his own game. If Hooker realized the situation, he could destroy Lee's army one piece at a time.

Jackson needed speed and stealth for this mission. He wanted his troops on the road at 4:30 A.M., on May 2. Brigadier General Robert E. Rodes' Division, the lead unit, failed to move until almost 7 A.M. Brigadier General Raleigh E. Colston's Division and then A.P. Hill's men trailed. Thomas' Brigade protected the rear of Jackson's long serpentine file.

Archer's Brigade marched ahead of the Georgians. The column reached a small industrial development, known as Catharine Furnace, and turned south. A man named Charles B. Wellford, who lived on the property, agreed to guide the Jackson wing. Recent rains kept the dust down, but the sun made the sweat flow.

Thirty minutes after Thomas' Brigade had passed Catharine Furnace, artillery and rifle fire erupted from that direction. Minutes later a courier galloped down the road and requested help from Edward Thomas. Elements from the Federal Third Corps threatened to capture a wagon train as the 23rd Georgia fought to hold them off.[10]

Thomas immediately turned one regiment back to help. He soon received another plea for assistance. The rest of the brigade performed an about face and double-quicked back. Brigadier General James J. Archer's Brigade followed the Georgians. These soldiers reached the scene and repelled the attackers with little fight. General Thomas reported his troops "remained until the train had passed and the demonstration of the enemy had ceased, when we moved on to overtake the division, which we did about 11 o'clock at night."[11]

Jackson rode at the head of his column miles away, oblivious to the problems in his rear. He halted at the intersection of the Brock Road and the Orange Turnpike, late in the afternoon. His men had marched more than twelve weary miles. They occupied a line just west of the unsuspecting Federals. As Jackson ordered the forward units into line of battle the brigades of Thomas and Archer hustled to catch back up for the fight. Since Jackson opened the attack at 5:15 P.M., prior to darkness, these two brigades missed the initial fighting.[12]

The troops of Oliver O. Howard's Eleventh Corps anchored the Federal right flank. Most of these men, preoccupied with their cooking fires, stared in disbelief as wild animals raced out of the woods. Their looks changed to horror as the first wave of Jackson's troops stormed out of the wood line behind the animals. A resounding rebel yell roared along the Confederate ranks. The blue-clad troops fired a few shots and then ran for the rear as the Federal right flank collapsed. Confederate units, thrilled by the ease of their success, pushed farther into the dense jungle of the Wilderness. The cloak of darkness halted Jackson's attack. Clusters of Confederates stopped amid confusion as different units tried to untangle themselves from the undergrowth as well as each other. The light of a full moon guided the brigades of Thomas and Archer toward the fighting. They reached the Brock Road-Orange Turnpike intersection shortly before midnight. Edward Thomas located the Light Division staff and received a surprise. Henry Heth commanded the Light Division replacing the wounded A.P. Hill. Heth ordered Thomas' Brigade into position north of the Orange

Plank Road on the Confederate left. Thomas guided his men as they slowly crept through the dark woods. The 45th Georgia gingerly linked their right flank with the 13th North Carolina on Dorsey Pender's left. The 35th Georgia then fell in on the left of the 45th Georgia while the 49th and 14th Georgia Regiments guarded Thomas' left flank.[13]

Captain John Duke, Company A, temporarily commanded the 35th Georgia. Numerous reports spread along the Confederate line of active Federal cavalry roaming the area. The Georgians heard the dull thud of axe against wood and the murmur of voices in the foliage ahead, but the men could see nothing. Frank Edwards wrote of his nervousness: "I was on the

Private John Frank Edwards, Co. D

Edwards wrote The Red Book—Army Life of Frank Edwards—Confederate Veteran, 1861–1865. Edwards penned his book in 1906 and until now it was the only published account of the 35th Georgia. Edwards fought alongside 300 Confederates at bloody Fort Gregg on April 2, 1865. They held off 5,000 determined Union soldiers at what many called the "Confederate Alamo." Edwards was one of the few Confederates left standing when the fort finally fell. His capture led to several unpleasant months spent at Point Lookout, Md., prison.

From *The Red Book—Army Life of Frank Edwards—Confederate Veteran, 1861–1865.*

skirmish line that night, close to the enemy. We lay very still all night. It was a cold night. I was wet with perspiration and I was so cold or excited it seemed that I could see the leaves on the bushes shake. The lines of the opposing armies were only from fifty to one hundred yards apart."[14] A soldier in the 45th Georgia recalled, "The night was clear and the moon shone bright but we could not sleep, the enemy could be heard very plainly in front throwing up breastworks and we knew we had to run them out in the morning."[15] Another 45th Georgian went into more detail about that long night:

> We formed a line of battle in his rear and lay all night long listening to the axes hard at work building breastworks for us to charge next morning. Here again the Pickets kept up almost incessant fireing. [I]t was a dreadful night. [A]ll knew well that the Stronghold that we could so plainly hear them building had to be charged the next morning in the very mouth of 12 lb. Cannon beside a world of small arms. [O]ften in the night we were aroused put on our accouterments expecting an advance but this night wore away like all the other nights and the next morning just as the first red rays of the Sun could be seen our Pickets were reinforced and ordered to advance and our line of battle likewise.[16]

Most Georgians did not realize their corps commander, Stonewall Jackson, lay gravely wounded. Nervous soldiers of the 18th North Carolina from Lane's Brigade mistakenly had fired into Jackson and A.P. Hill's entourage. The shots killed or wounded twelve of the nineteen horsemen. A short time later, artillery fire had wounded A.P. Hill. Jeb Stuart, the cavalry chief, received orders to assume command of Jackson's corps for the rest of the battle.[17]

Major General Hiram Berry's troops from Major General Dan Sickles' Third Corps occupied the area to the north of the Orange Plank Road. These men had rushed to their present position to stem the disorderly retreat of the Eleventh Corps earlier. Brigadier Generals Joseph B. Carr and Joseph W. Revere commanded the two brigades that faced the Georgians. Hiram Berry's chief of staff, Captain John S. Poland, had led Revere's Excelsior Brigade into the woods north of the road and pointed out their positions. Berry ordered two regiments from Carr's brigade, the 1st Massachusetts and the 26th Pennsylvania, to form on the front line alongside Revere's men. Two batteries occupied the clearing at Fairview along the road southeast of Berry's line.[18]

The 72nd New York and the 26th Pennsylvania occupied the northern end of the first Union line, opposite the 14th and 49th Georgia Regiments. Captain Poland described his frustration with the alignment that Joseph Revere assigned to the Pennsylvanians. Despite repeated orders to place the 26th Pennsylvania directly on the front line, Revere had them "nearly perpendicular to the rear."[19] Aligned to the left of the 72nd New York in order came the 70th New York, 71st New York, 120th New York, 74th New York and the 1st Massachusetts, with their left flank touching the Orange Plank Road. On the south side of the road stood the 3rd Maryland from the Eleventh Corps. In a second line, about 150 yards to the rear, stood the 16th Massachusetts, 11th Massachusetts and 11th New Jersey.[20]

Revere's brigade encountered difficulty moving north of the Orange Plank Road into the thick woods because of confusing orders. His men finally aligned themselves and began to prepare defensive positions. Skirmishers and scouts crept forward to locate the Confederate line. The scouts found the Confederate pickets from Lane's and Thomas' brigades a short distance ahead. The Federal infantry scratched at the ground with what was available because they lacked entrenching tools. They built a low breastwork of logs and formed an abatis with downed bushes, logs and debris.[21]

Union Lieutenant William G. Tackabery, 70th New York, commanded a company of skirmishers. Two other companies moved forward in the darkness after they completed their breastwork construction. A company of 72nd New Yorkers crept ahead to connect their skirmish line with Tackaberry's line on the left. The remainder of the 72nd New Yorkers spent all night chopping, digging and cutting to strengthen their breastworks. They completed their work at daylight.[22]

Major Robert Bodine, 26th Pennsylvania, failed to note the alignment problem mentioned by Captain Poland. Bodine wrote that his men anchored the front line to the right of Revere's Excelsior Brigade. Perhaps, the Keystone Staters at some point stood perpendicular to the main line, but then they later moved forward to align themselves with the other regiments. Joseph Revere's handling of his brigade during this fight brought great criticism from his fellow officers, and for good reason.[23]

No more friendly units moved in on the left of the 14th Georgia during the night. They anchored the left flank of Robert E. Lee's army. Thomas' skirmishers slowly inched forward in the gathering light of May 3. The pickets exchanged fire for about thirty minutes. Then the main Confederate line moved forward. The 35th Georgia probably collided with the Union line on Joseph Revere's right side occupied by the 71st New York, 70th New York and the left flank of the 72nd New York.

Revere gave a descriptive account of what happened on his Union front:

> At early daylight, the enemy drove in our pickets, and commenced the battle with a terrific fire of artillery and musketry, while his sharpshooters were also actively engaged. Our gallant soldiers, however undauntedly returned their fire from behind their low defenses, and defiantly

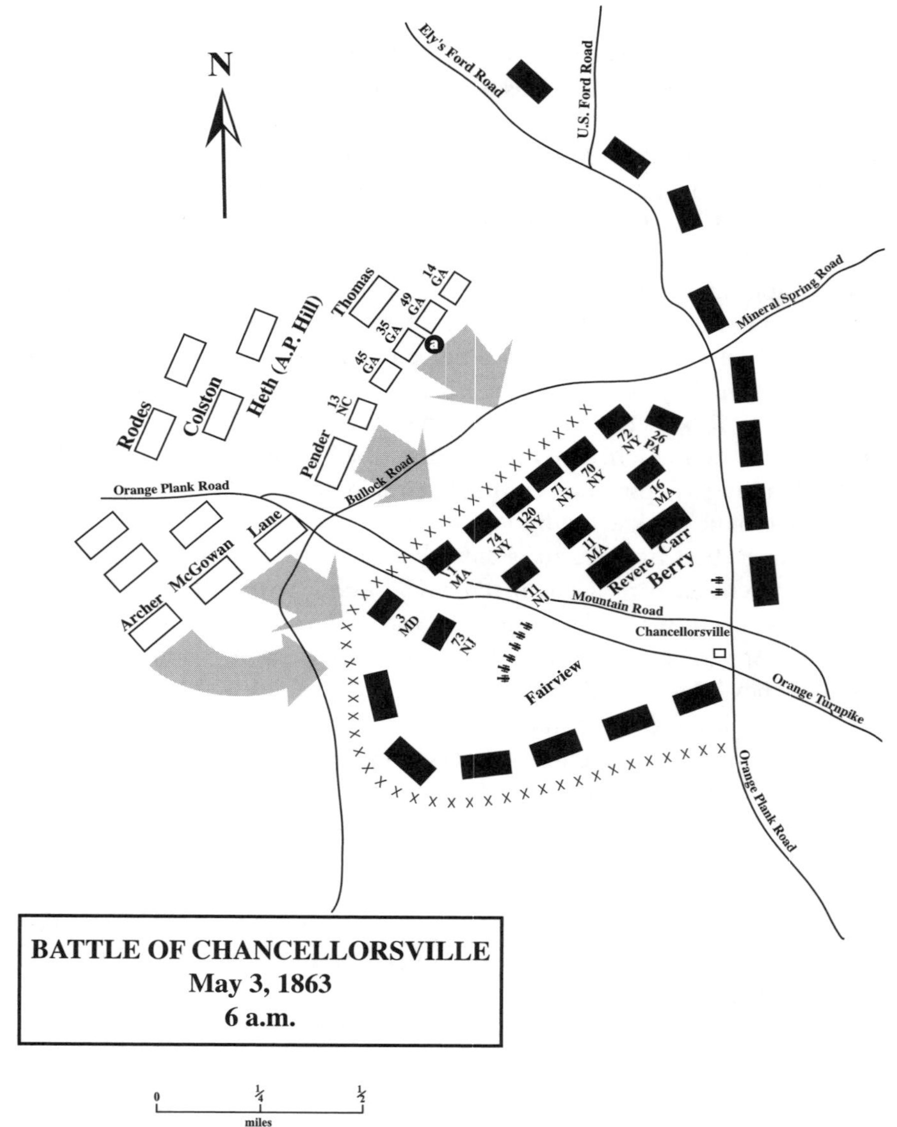

BATTLE OF CHANCELLORSVILLE
May 3, 1863
6 a.m.

a. Georgia Trench Line
Looking SE toward Bullock Road. The Georgians scraped these shallow trenches in the early morning hours of May 3, 1863 while they listened to the enemy building their own trenches only a few hundred yards to the left.
photo by author

answered their savage yells by hearty cheering, and for several hours maintained their position, when, the enemy having turned our left flank and enfiladed the breastworks, the brigade broke off gradually, regiment after regiment, from the left, and reluctantly yielded their ground to a vastly superior force, which was, however, well punished by our men. Owing to the practice of the enemy firing so low, the breastwork was a great protection, which will account for the comparatively small number of casualties in the brigade. Our brigade, however, lost all its knapsacks, shelter-blankets, and rations, which were left at the bivouac near the cross-roads, and which we were forced to abandon during the enemy's assault upon our position.[24]

Reports by soldiers on both sides failed to validate Revere's claim that his men maintained their position behind their breastworks for several hours.

Confederate Frank Edwards claimed that a cannon in the middle of the line fired to start the advance. He dreaded this advance because he had not slept all night and was in no hurry to start the move. "When we arose the skirmish line of the enemy fired. We didn't pay any attention to that. We went right on until we came to the main line of the enemy, fired, gave a yell and charged. Their whole line gave way against the charge of our skirmishers. We lost a good many killed and wounded in that charge."[25] Edward Thomas wrote, "At an early hour on Sunday morning, the brigade was ordered to advance and attack the enemy. We advanced at once, driving a very heavy force of skirmishers before us. After proceeding about 250 yards, we found the enemy in strong force in our front, behind breastworks. The brigade charged with promptness and energy, and at the first charge drove the enemy, utterly routed, from their intrenched position."[26] Captain S.B. David, 14th Georgia, described the charge of the brigade: "With a tremendous shout that almost made the earth tremble," the dreaded rebel yell fell on the ears of the Union line. Captain David continued, "In fifteen minutes the enemy's whole line had broken and fled in the wildest confusion our boys scaling the breastworks and rushing on with the impetuosity of an avalanche."[27] Indicative of the decreased visibility in the woods, the adjutant for the 49th Georgia recorded, "The charge on the enemy's breastworks by this regiment and in fact by the whole brigade was a movement worth looking at. So quick and well executed was the charge that the Yankees who were captured expressed their surprise at having seen us mounted on their works before they had any idea of our being anywhere near them."[28]

Union Major John Leonard reported that to the front of his 72nd New York the Confederates opened a severe fire at 6 A.M. His pickets crashed back through the underbrush for the protection of their breastworks in the main line. The Georgians followed close on their heels and a "severe engagement ensued" that he claimed lasted for at least forty-five minutes.[29]

All the Federal reports noted the strength of their first line until the left flank caved in. Captain Poland described this front line when he wrote, "the enemy's attack began with heavy columns against our single line, which, by the aid of its rude defense, held its own successfully until the premature and precipitate withdrawal of the Third Maryland Regiment." Brigadier General Carr described the cause of the first line fall back as "an injudicious retreat of a Maryland regiment . . . ."[30]

Colonel J. Egbert Farnum, 70th New York commander, described the unraveling of his left flank: "The regiment maintained its position firmly until our left was turned, and then, being greatly outnumbered, and the regiments on our left having abandoned their position, we fell back without more disorder than the nature of the dense woods warranted."[31] To the right, Colonel William O. Stevens, 72nd New York commander, ordered his men to change front to the left to face the sudden threat from their left flank. This difficult maneuver in the face of a charging, exuberant enemy was probably the reason this regiment suffered the highest casualties in Revere's brigade. While trying to wheel his men leftward into position, Stevens dropped to the ground mortally wounded along with three of his lieutenants. Major Leonard reported what happened next:

> In consequence of the nearness of the enemy and the severity of the engagement, it was impossible to carry him [Stevens] from the field. After the fall of our noble colonel, the enemy rendered bold by their momentary success, advanced more rapidly on our flank and front, and attempted to capture our color, but the steadfast devotion and bravery of my regiment repelled their attempt, and, although the conflict was hand to hand, and their force far superior in numbers to our own, the four who successively seized our colors were made to bite the dust, and the colors of the regiment were borne in safety from the field.[32]

The 26th Pennsylvania's Major Robert L. Bodine reported that his men, upon finding their left turned, retired in "good order, the men keeping up a constant fire, leaving all the dead and some wounded on the field." The wounded included their commander, Colonel Benjamin C. Tilghman.[33]

The length of time the first and second Union lines held back the Confederate attack north of the Orange Plank Road varied among the Union accounts. The time each individual regiment stayed their ground before they retreated probably varied too. The men in the second Federal line, only a short distance behind, became the best witnesses to the attack. Lieutenant Colonel Waldo Merriam, 16th Massachusetts commander, reported:

> I was placed on the extreme right of the brigade as a reserve for the Twenty-sixth Pennsylvania Regiment. The enemy soon attacked in force to the left of us, moving by degrees toward our right. The front line broke and fell back on my left, immediately followed by the enemy. I threw back my left wing to cover the retreat of the Twenty-sixth, which regiment retired to my line, and after about ten minutes of hard fighting we were obliged to give way. The attack of the enemy was very furious, and the regiment has never lost so many men in so short a time.[34]

Colonel William Blaisdell, 11th Massachusetts commander, recalled that the battle raged for two hours along the front line before the troops fell back to his second line. Lieutenant Colonel Porter D. Tripp, 11th Massachusetts, wrote that when the front line did break, anxious fugitives streamed back through their position. His frustrated men had to hold their fire until the first line troops passed through their ranks. Then, his men commenced firing and "offered a desperate resistance, and only fell back when no hope remained to make a successful effort to hold the ground."[35] The 11th New Jersey's commander, Colonel Robert McAllister, wrote that for some time the front line held their place until their left wing began to fold. As the fight fell back to his men, the line see-sawed back and forth until he too was forced to retreat.[36]

JUDGE SAMUEL B. LEWIS.

Corporal Samuel Bailey Lewis, Co.E

This Campbell County native surrendered at Appomattox at the end of the war. He returned to Georgia and served as a postmaster and judge in Fayette County.

From *Confederate Veteran,* Feb. 1925.

Brigadier General Edward Thomas reformed his troops at the first line of Union breastworks. In few words he wrote, "Advancing still further, we found a second line of the enemy, which we at once drove from its position." They continued the advance with Pender's Brigade to their right and found a third enemy line. This line probably comprised Colonel Samuel S. Carroll's brigade from Major General William H. French's division. Carroll had received orders to move into the woods about 7 A.M., to shore up the withdrawal on the right flank. As the fighting heated up, this third Union line also withdrew. The Georgians followed in hot pursuit, but they apparently outran their support. Thomas reported, "At this point, finding that there were no troops on my left and none in supporting distance on my right or rear, and the enemy were advancing in very heavy force on my left flank, and making demonstrations on my right, I ordered the brigade to move back, and took position near the line of the enemy's breastworks, where we remained until the whole line advanced."[37] Carroll reported that his Union men forced the Confederate line back in confusion. Whether any confusion existed in the ranks of Thomas' and Pender's men was not reported. Both Confederate brigades pulled back to the first line of Union breastworks they captured when the advance began.

During this lull, Frank Edwards suffered a close call. He wrote:

> The enemy's batteries were throwing shells in all directions. One shell struck an oak limb close to my foot; the limb flew back and tore off the sole of my shoe. About that time I heard the most terrific firing on our right about five hundred yards away. It seemed to be in front of the Chancellorsville House. In about an hour the whole line was engaged. The enemy began to give way all down the line, with our boys pushing them. [38]

The heavy fighting Edwards described on the right was the drive of the two North Carolina brigades of Lane and Pender.

Reinforcements came forward and a general Confederate attack began again around 10 A.M. The Federal troops hastily withdrew in the direction of the Rappahannock River at U.S. Ford because of the renewed strength of this push.[39] George Hall, 14th Georgia, described the prizes the men in the brigade found among the enemy works: "Thousands of them having left their arms and accoutrements behind in our possession, while the battlefield was literally covered with knapsacks, haversacks, blankets, oilcloths, frying pans, overcoats and clothing of various kinds, us tired and hungry soldiers feasted ourselves sumptiously on the Yankees well filled haversacks of crackers, Beef, coffee and sugar in them." The 1st Massachusetts commander reinforced the image of a hasty retreat when he made the embarrassing admission that "We lost 157 knapsacks, 110 haversacks, 51 canteens, 49 woolen blankets, and 96 rubber blankets."[40]

The fighting touched off a brushfire that burned up a number of the dead and wounded of both sides. Screams of agony mixed with the musketry. Many of the wounded fought a race to out-crawl the flames and lost. The 35th Georgians saw ghastly sites in every direction. James Garrett provided a sobering view of battle in a disturbing letter to his mother. "I tell you it was the greatest fight that I ever seen. [T]he woods caught on fire and burned up lots of dead and wounded. I saw men with their heads and arms shot off."[41] A soldier in the 45th Georgia described the brushfire: "One of the most horrible and heart rending things happened Sunday evening and I scarcely trust I may never see the like again. The woods which were full of dead and wounded were fired by the explosion of a shell and the fire swept over the poor fellows burning many of the wounded to death. The poor fellows tried to get out of the way but could not do it. It was the worst thing I ever saw in my life and I have seen many bad sights."[42] A South Carolina officer contrasted the beginning of the day with the subsequent destruction around him. He wrote:

> It was pitiful to see the charred bodies, hugging the trees, or with hands outstretched, as if to ward off the flames. We saw around some of them little cleared circles, where they had evidently raked away the dead leaves and sticks, to stay the progress of the fire. And there were ghastly wounds there-heads shot off or crushed, bodies and limbs torn and mangled, the work of shells. The smoke and stench were stifling. This was May 3, as beautiful and bright a day as one could desire, even for a Sabbath.[43]

Frank Edwards surveyed the scene later. He saluted the heroic efforts of the North Carolinians who charged the enemy batteries along the Orange Plank Road at Fairview. "The brave North Carolinians charged and moved the enemy from those guns. That was one of the most daring charges ever made by our troops. I never saw such destruction; the undergrowth and stumps were torn all to pieces. The boys from North Carolina suffered; their dead were lying as close as I ever saw them; but they captured, I think, sixteen of those fine guns." Edwards heard some riders approach and he recognized two of the soldiers as Generals Lee and Stuart. The entourage slowed because of all the debris and bodies along the road. He wrote:

> When they came up, the men cheered. They halted about two minutes for our men to move the dead and wounded out of the road. I

> saw men raise their hats to them, though they were lying there with their life blood flowing away, and never expected to be moved alive; men would raise their hands that never saw either of the generals, though their faces and hands were covered with blood. Generals Lee and Stuart could not hold back their emotions. When the road was cleared they rode away with their hats off.[44]

Edwards described his encounter with several enemy soldiers:

> I passed over the hill to get a drink of cool water. I saw a great many of our boys and of the enemy lying about. I noticed out to the left a blue coat sitting up against a tree. He seemed to be unconscious. I went out that way to see if I could aid him in anyway. I saw he could not possibly live but a few minutes. I raised his hat and saw his skull was broken all around. I stepped down and filled up my canteen full of water and went back and bathed his head in cold water. It seemed to relieve him to some extent. I bathed his lips. Then I went for the second canteen of water. As I was bathing his face and lips again, I saw two Yankees coming. I grabbed my gun and said, 'Surrender, sir.' They seemed to be very obedient.
>
> 'We have a passport from General Lee to look after the dead.' Knowing the regulations of war, I took the pass and read it.
>
> 'All right,' I replied.
>
> 'We would like to see this man.' They stepped up and looked at the man, then came back and gave me their hands.
>
> 'We have been looking for our brother that was wounded in your lines. This is he. We desire to thank you for the kindness you have done.'
>
> I gave them my name and address, by request. They were from Pennsylvania.[45]

The Georgians remained in line of battle on the Confederate left and awaited an attack. Around midnight, the crack of musketry broke out among the skirmishers, but failed to escalate. The following morning, May 4, the men improved their positions with breastworks and abatis, but then grudgingly moved to another spot and built more breastworks.[46] A heavy rain fell on May 5. That night, under cover of darkness, Hooker withdrew his troops back across U.S. Ford.

The men in Joseph Revere's brigade who manned the Union front line in the area where the 35th Georgia attacked suffered light to moderate casualties. The 71st New York lost 1 killed, 15 wounded and 23 captured/missing for a total of 39. The 70th New York lost 4 killed, 11 wounded and 17 captured/missing that totaled 32. The 72nd New York took the brunt of the brigade losses with 11 killed (including their commander plus three lieutenants), 31 wounded and 58 captured/missing for a combined loss of 101 men. Revere received severe criticism for his actions after his men retreated from their front line of breastworks. This officer, without orders, led his men, miles to the rear in search of ammunition and rations. He was promptly relieved from command and subsequently court-martialed. The Union men in the second line composed of Joseph Carr's brigade suffered moderate casualties while those men in Samuel Carroll's brigade suffered light to moderate losses.[47]

The 35th Georgia reported 8 killed and 27 wounded during the Battle of Chancellorsville.[48] Edward L. Thomas, in his report, mentioned by name all the regimental commanders including Captain Duke of the 35th Georgia. "All officers and men of my command who were present acted with the utmost coolness and the most daring courage before the enemy."[49] After a short time of reflection, James Garrett reported on the difficulties of the march and the toll it took on Company D. "[I]t was the longest and hardest fought battle that has ever been fought in Virginia. It was the hardest marching that I ever saw. [W]e started from camp with 42 men and 15 got into the fight."[50]

Lee gained his boldest victory yet at Chancellorsville. However, the most significant Confederate casualty of the battle, Stonewall Jackson, lay fighting for his life some twelve miles away to the southeast, at Guinea's Station.

Notes

Abbreviations:

CSR—"Compiled Service Records of Confederate Soldiers Who Served In Organizations From The State of Georgia," Thirty-fifth Infantry Regiment (National Archives Microfilm Publication M266) National Archives Building, Washington, D.C.

GDAH—Georgia Division of Archives and History, Morrow, Ga.

NMP—National Military Park

OR.—War of the Rebellion: A Compilation of the Official Records of the Union and Confederate Armies. 130 Vols.

SHSP—Southern Historical Society Papers

1. "Army of Northern Virginia General Orders, August 11, 1861-March 27, 1865," (National Archives publication M921, roll 1, file 0634) National Archives Building, Washington, D.C. I wish to thank Dr. Thomas Lowry with "The Index Project, Inc." (Woodbridge, Va.) for providing me with all the court-martials on file for Thomas' Brigade.
2. Letter of James M. Garrett to "Dear Mother from Camp Gregg March 3d 1863," James M. Garrett Collection.

3. Letter of J.M. Garrett to "Dear Mother from Camp Gregg April the 5 63," James M. Garrett Collection.
4. Letter of JT McElvany to "Mr & Mrs Dickson from Camp Gregg Va April 20th 1863," James T. McElvany Collection.
5. Letter of JM Garrett to "Dear Mother from Camp Gregg Va Apr the 20th 1863," James M. Garrett Collection.
6. Letter of James M. Garrett to "Dear Mother from Camp Gregg March 3d 1863," James M. Garrett Collection; Letter of JM Garrett to "Dear Mother from Camp Gregg Va Apr the 20th 1863," James M. Garrett Collection.
7. CSR, also on microfilm at GDAH.
8. D.S. Redding, "Diary of Capt. Daniel S. Redding, 45th Georgia", "Reminiscences of Confederate Soldiers—Stories of the War 1861–65," Vol.15 Compiled by United Daughters of the Confederacy, p.13, GDAH; Letter from Jasper A. Gillespie, Co. B, 45th Georgia, to "Dear Sallie, Saturday Morning, May 9th 1863, Camp Gregg Va," Jasper A. Gillespie Civil War Papers (photocopies), AC. 65–404, GDAH.
9. Ibid., Redding; Marion Hill Fitzpatrick, *Letters to Amanda.* (Macon, Ga., 1998) p. 67 (edited by Jeffrey C. Lowe and Sam Hodges). Reprinted by permission of Mercer University Press, 1998.
10. *OR.,* Vol.25, Part II, p.912.
11. Ibid. Vol. 25, Pt.II, p.912.
12. *OR.*, Vol.25, Pt.I, p.941.
13. *OR* ., Vol.25, Pt.I, p.912–915, 890–891.
14. John Frank Edwards, *The Red Book-Army Life of Frank Edwards-Confederate Veteran.* 1906, p.100.
15. Letter of Francis Solomon Johnson (Co.F, 45th Georgia) to "My Darling Emmie from Camp 45th Geo. Regt, May 9th 1863," Special Collections, MS 243, Hargrett Rare Book & Manuscript Library/University of Georgia Libraries, Athens Ga.
16. Gillespie letter, May 9th 1863, GDAH.
17. *SHSP.* Vol.VI, 1878, p.279; Robert K. Krick, *The Smoothbore Volley That Doomed the Confederacy: The Death of Stonewall Jackson and Other Chapters On the Army of Northern Virginia,* (Baton Rouge, 2002) p.17–18.
18. *OR.,* Vol. 25, Pt.I, p.387–390.
19. Ibid. Vol. 25, Pt. I, p.449.
20. Ibid. Vol. 25, Pt. I, p.451–472.
21. Ibid. Vol. 25, Pt. I, p.461.
22. Ibid. Vol. 25, Pt.I, p.463–464, 466–467.
23. Ibid. Vol 25, Pt. I, p.459.
24. Ibid. Vol. 25, Pt.I, p.462.
25. Edwards., p.101.
26. *OR.*, Vol. 25, Pt. I, p.913.
27. Letter of Capt. S.B. David (14th Ga.) to "My Dear Parents from Camp Near Fredericksburg, VA May 9, 1863," copy in possession of Fredericksburg-Spotsylvania NMP.
28. Letter of Mark Newman (49th Ga.) to "Editor, Georgian from A.P. Hill's Division Hospital, May 6th 1863," *Central Georgian* (Sandersville, Ga.), May 20, 1863.

29. *OR.,* Vol. 25, Pt. I, p.467.
30. Ibid. Vol. 25, Pt.I, p.445, 450.
31. Ibid. Vol. 25, Pt. I, p. 464.
32. Ibid. Vol. 25, Pt. I, p.467.
33. Ibid. Vol. 25, Pt. I, p.459.
34. Ibid. Vol. 25, Pt. I, p.456.
35. Ibid. Vol. 25, Pt. I, p.455.
36. Ibid. Vol. 25, Pt. I, p.456–458.
37. Ibid. Vol. 25, Pt. I, p.913.
38. Edwards. p.101.
39. *OR* ., Vol. 25, Pt. I, p.892.
40. "Diary of George W. Hall, 14th Georgia Volunteers, CSA, 1861–1865," Hargrett Rare Book and Manuscript Library/ University of Georgia Libraries, Athens, Ga., p. 40; Ibid., Vol. 25, Pt. I, p. 454.
41. Letter of James M. Garrett to "Dear Mother from Camp Gregg, VA May the 15th 1863," James M. Garrett Collection.
42. Johnson.
43. J.F.J. Caldwell, *The History of a Brigade of South Carolinians Known As 'Gregg's, and Subsequently As 'McGowan's Brigade.* (Philadelphia, 1866) p.83–84 (Morningside Press reprint, p.120).
44. Edwards. p.101.
45. Edwards, p. 102–103.
46. "Diary and Memorandum kept by Capt. Daniel S. Redding, Co.D, 45th Georgia," compiled by UDC, Vol. 15, p.14, typescript held by Fredericksburg-Spotsylvania NMP, Va.
47. *OR.,* Vol. 25, Pt. I, p. 177–179, 186.
48. James Folsom, *Heroes and Martyrs of Georgia—Georgia's Record in the Revolution of 1861.* (Macon, Ga., 1864) p.136. (reprinted by Butternut and Blue, Baltimore, 1995)
49. *OR* ., Vol.25, Part II, p.913.
50. Letter of James M. Garrett to "Dear Mother from Camp Gregg, VA May the 15th 1863," James M. Garrett Collection.

Chapter Nine

Northward to Gettysburg

"They charged under one of the most galling fires that ever came from an enemy's line . . . ."
Captain James McElvany

Edward Thomas' Brigade marched through the rain and mud back to Camp Gregg after Joseph Hooker's army escaped to the north bank of the Rappahannock River. On May 10, word quickly spread through camp that the formidable Stonewall Jackson had died.

To offset the loss of Jackson, Robert E. Lee believed that three corps would make his army more maneuverable. Richard Ewell received a promotion to lieutenant general and the command of the Second Corps. James Longstreet remained the commander of the First Corps. A day later, A.P. Hill received a third star and assumed command of the newly formed Third Corps.

Major General Dorsey Pender became the new commander of the Light Division, which consisted of the brigades of Edward Thomas, Dorsey Pender, James Lane and Samuel McGowan. The brigades of James Archer and Henry Heth moved from the Light Division into a newly formed division commanded by Heth.

Private James Garrett wrote in the middle of May that they expected to draw money in a few days. He described his satisfaction with the supply system. "I got me a pair of pants yesterday. I drew them from the government. [T]hey are good pants. I have got clothes enough to do me this summer if I dont hapen to no bad luck."[1]

Garrett happily reported on May 26 that the situation was quiet on their front. He voiced concern over the Union siege around Vicksburg, Mississippi, and expressed disdain for the Confederate troops in the West. "[W]e are listening with great angsiety to hear the result from Vicksburg. I dont think that army is doing its duty know [no] how. [T]he Yankees never can drive this army like they have that [one]." Garrett sent his letter home via Corporal Orin H. Roberts. He also sent a small axe and a ring. The ring was a gift for his sister Ellen. He instructed that if it failed to fit her finger, then the ring be given to his other sister, Sophronia. He again reported that he had all the summer clothes he needed, but he advised them to get some wool to make him some clothes for the following winter.[2]

Lee decided to take the offensive to northern soil again. On June 3, Ewell's corps departed Fredericksburg west toward the Shenandoah Valley, followed by Longstreet's men. Hill's new Third Corps remained near Fredericksburg to deceive Hooker, who soon unleashed artillery fire into Hill's area. A short time later, a Federal scouting party crossed the river on a pontoon bridge to assess Confederate intentions.

General Lee issued an order on June 5, for Hill "to occupy the position of Fredericksburg with the troops under your command, making such dispositions as will be best calculated to deceive the enemy, and keep him in ignorance of any change in the disposition of the army." The order further stated that should the enemy make a move across the river, then Hill was to stop him. If he needed to withdraw, Hill should retreat along the Richmond, Fredericksburg, and Potomac Railroad to protect the line of Confederate communications and present an obstacle to an enemy advance toward Richmond. Hill could request reinforcements if needed at Hanover Junction.[3]

Hill issued movement orders for his corps on the same day. When orders reached Thomas' Brigade to begin the march north, Chaplains Hyman and Barrett stood in the water of Massaponax Creek baptizing forty-eight converts.[4] The men hastily finished their ceremony and then gathered up their gear. The Georgians departed Camp Gregg about 11 P.M. George Hall of the 14th Georgia wrote, "we were aroused from our slumbers and ordered to fall into line immediately. We scarcely had time to do up our things and we marched off in the direction of Fredericksburg. We marched the remainder of the night and arrived at Hamilton's Crossing a little before daylight." The Georgians marched along the railroad tracks for thirteen miles before reaching Hamilton's Crossing. They formed into line of battle and continued north along the railroad for a short distance. Edward Thomas ordered his regiments to post skirmishers along the riverbank to the right.[5] The next morning several tethered observation balloons rose into the air along the Federal side of the river. These provided good sport for the skirmishers to shoot.[6]

First Lieutenant William Boswell, Company K, sent a letter to his wife from camp at Hamilton's Crossing. He wrote that they had waited in line of battle for five days. The pickets from both sides stood within shouting distance of each other, but he reassured her that neither side had fired at the other since the first day. He assumed a more somber tone when he wrote:

Lieutenant William Boswell, Co.K
This farmer turned officer from Harris County was brother-in-law to Lieutenant Colonel William McCullohs. Boswell was wounded three separate times during the war. He survived the war and moved to Mansfield, Texas in the 1880's.
Mansfield (Texas) Historical Society

> Missouria, don't let my present condition trouble you, try to console yourself that if I fall I shall fall in the defense of my country and in the discharge of my duty and at my post. I hope if it is my lot to sacrifice my life on the battlefield that God will take me to that happy world where there will be no more wars, but all will be peace and harmony. I pray God will spare my life to see the end of this war that I may return home to my loved ones. Last night while at prayer meeting I could imagine that I saw you and Ma bended over my little children while asleep before you retired, asking God to have mercy upon them while their father was far away from them in defence of their liberties, their home, their all in the world. The tears were made to run down my cheeks while these thoughts were in my mind. I hope that we shall soon have peace so we may enjoy each others society as we have in bygone days.

He ended his letter with a touch of humor as he apologized for his dirty writing paper. "You must not laugh at this paper because it is black, for it is a mile to the water. I have nothing to sit on or lay on but the ground, and broiled meat on the coals, I get my hands greasy, and then the dirt sticks to them until they don't look like they are mine then when I go to write I am perspiring all the time, it rubs off on my paper."[7]

Boswell apparently had decided to be baptized and he expressed his thoughts on salvation in a letter. Unfortunately, only a small torn portion of this letter was available. The officer wrote:

> have seen me baptized and heard what I had to say to the church, but God commanded me to take up my cross immediately and follow him, and I was afraid to put off until I came home for fear I should never be permitted to get home. We have no promise of tomorrow. Today is the only time we have any promise of. We had a good meeting today in our Regiment. There was not more than fifty people at meeting, but we had a good meeting indeed. There was 9 joined the church. 7 of us the Baptist, 2 the Methodist. We can be at prayer meeting every night somewhere in the Brigade.

He then mentioned that the only person in his company that joined the church that night was Private Esley M. Wilson.[8]

Boswell wrote a letter to his mother asking her prayers to help him deal with an unnamed problem:

> I wish to write you a few lines requesting you to pray for me, pray in faith, nothing doubting. I am so afraid I have been deceived. Pray God to strengthen my faith, and pray that I may never bring disgrace or reproach upon the profession I have made. Pray that I may hold out faithful to the end, that if we are never permitted to meet on this earth, we may meet in heaven where there will be no parting. Ma, if I should not see you again, teach my little children in the way they should go, and encourage Missouria to attend to her souls salvation immediately. May God guide, direct, and protect you is the prayer of your unworthy son.[9]

Corporal Stephen LaFayette Moon, Company G, wrote a letter on June 14 to his mother. He described the religious services that continued in Thomas' Brigade:

> God has begun a good work here among the soldiers, they are coming to Christ daily. The Chaplains are doing all in their power to carry on the good work. I have seen several baptised. The Chaplain

> of the 49th Ga. went out the other day and baptised 30 odd. There is a meeting held here every day while we are in line of battle. Mother, I have been living dissatisfied for several years. I thought that I wanted to be with the people of God, but I thought I was not good enough, and kept putting it off until yesterday the 13th of June, and I came out and joined the church and was baptised by the Chaplain of the 49th Ga. His name is Mr. Highman [Hyman]. We have no chaplain in our regiment.

A spiritually revived Moon wrote, "I feel a great deal better satisfied, my mind was continually wondering about the welfare of my soul hereafter, but I could not see the way. I have had a change of heart for several years, but I could not give up my old ways, still I felt like I wanted to be with Christians and from this time I am going to forsake all my evil ways and try to live a Christian life the balance of my days and I desire to be a member of Old Sharon Church and I wish I could be there with you all."[10]

Private Dock Knight, Company G, decided the time had arrived for his baptism. Chaplain John Hyman performed the ceremony. It probably occurred in the spring of 1863 and the end result provided laughs throughout the brigade. When Knight talked, many soldiers had difficulty understanding him because of his hair lip. The private came forward out of the crowd and:

> As the Chaplain let him into the water he [Knight] spied a mocassin snake over the place where he was to be baptised and began to pull back and say, 'Don't you see that ockerson [water moccasin] overthere?' The Chaplain not knowing what he said told him to come along, the water would not hurt him - by this time Dock was getting too close to the snake so he jerked loose and said, 'O! Damn it, don't you see that Okerson?' The Chaplain finally understood what he said and realizing that he needed to be baptised, stepped and put him under.

Dock Knight had quite a reputation throughout the regiment and brigade. In another undated incident, Stephen Moon saved Knight from a firing squad at the last moment. Everybody knew that Knight would run away whenever the 35th Georgia engaged the enemy. "He was finally court martialed, blindfolded and ready to be shot when LaFayette Moon [Stephen L. Moon] pleaded for his life, telling them that he was not bright and could not help from running when the bullets began to whistle." Apparently, Moon issued a persuasive argument to spare Knight's life, and the nervous soldier became a free man. "He [Knight] was one of the happiest men you ever saw. He always said that the first $25 in gold that he ever got, he was going to give it to 'Tate' ([Stephen] Lafayette Moon) for saving his life, but Dock never succeeded in getting the gold." One reason was probably because authorities halted Knight's pay for twelve months in November 1864 for a general court-martial.[11]

James Garrett spent the first weeks of June at Chimborazo Hospital in Richmond recuperating from bronchitis. He knew the 35th Georgia was on the march, but he could only speculate where. "I guess our regiment will go back up in the Valley again this summer. [M]ost of our troops have gone up there all ready. [W]e can get things cheaper up there than we can any where else."[12] On June 21, Garrett wrote from the Georgia Soldiers Home in Richmond that he expected to leave the following morning with two other Company D soldiers:

> I will have to take a long march before I get to the regiment. I expect it is in Maryland before this time. I have three days rations and one dollar to start on. I expect to live on Virginia chickens and honey as I go on. I am going to press it in the night or day time either if I cant get it any other way. There is two more of my company along with me. Redding and Strickland [Privates E.W. Redding or George W. Redding and Wilson Strickland] and we will have a fine time of it certain.

Garrett missed another pay period because of his illness. This forced the young Georgian to request money from his mother. "If you have got plenty of money by you I expect you had better send me about ten dollars for I dont know when we will draw again and I will need some." He described his thriftiness. "I have been staying here at the hospital over two weeks spending a half dollar a day for milk. I bought a pint at night and morning. [I]t is fifty cents a quart. I was obliged to have it for I could not drink the tea they had at the table." He reiterated to his family that he had plenty of clothes including a new pair of shoes. These would serve him well on his upcoming trek. "So you kneed not give your self any uneasiness about me if you dont hear from me again soon. [A] part of our army is now in Pennsylvania and I may have to go there two."[13]

By the evening of June 13, Joseph Hooker realized that he had been duped. His army raced off in pursuit of Lee. A.P. Hill sent Richard H. Anderson's Division northwest followed by Heth's on June 15. At 4:30 A.M., on June 16, Pender's Light Division followed the well-worn path westward. Hill's corps followed the same route as Ewell.[14] The Georgians passed the Chancellorsville battlefield. The more than thirty day's passage of time had failed to cleanse the area of its grisly sights.

"Dead horses and men are buried by the hundred. Many of each are not half covered, and not infrequently portions of the latter can be see, where the beasts and birds of prey have eaten the flesh from the bones. The scent is awful."[15]

On June 16, the men of the 35th Georgia splashed across the Rapidan at Ely's Ford, before they stopped for the night. The high heat and humidity made the march tough on June 17 and 18. Captain James McElvany, Company F, reported in his diary the high temperature on June 17. "Many men fell by the way, some died on the road." He noted the following day that Private Hardy J. Benafield, Company F, fainted in the road and fellow soldiers had to carry him to the hospital. The troops bivouacked at Gaines Crossroads on June 19. This intersection sat four miles from Flint Hill, on the eastern face of the Blue Ridge Mountains. A steady rain made sleep difficult. The following morning, at 4:30 A.M., the march continued in a torrential downpour.[16]

Captain Thomas W. Latham, Co.E

Latham hailed from Campbell County. The men elected him captain on June 10, 1863 prior to the regiment marching north to Gettysburg. He replaced the disabled George W. Hammond. Latham surrendered at Appomattox in 1865.

From *Sunny South,* Atlanta, Ga. May 2, 1891

This change in weather provided a respite from the terrible heat, but it failed to make the march any easier as aptly described by an officer in the 49th Georgia:

> This has been a trying day to the soldiers. It commenced raining just as we marched off and continued till we arrived here on the Blue Ridge at Chester's Gap-the march was very heavy, and there was no small amount of straggling. From Gaines Crossroads to this place is a distance of 12 miles is one mud hole. We passed through Flint Hill, a little village. Gen. Lee has marched us everywhere and has even taken us above the clouds.[17]

The night of June 20, brought no relief from the elements as they camped on top of a mountain between Flint Hill and Front Royal. The men found themselves in the midst of a dark thunderstorm. Over the next several days, the column passed through Front Royal and Berryville. By June 24, they reached Shepherdstown after nine grueling days on the march. The following morning the tired men waded the Potomac and crossed into Maryland again. They entered Sharpsburg and Thomas' men viewed the old battlefield for the first time. The column passed Hagerstown and Leitersburg, on June 27, and by mid-morning set foot into Pennsylvania.[18] Late that evening the weary soldiers of the 35th Georgia stopped about four miles east of Chambersburg. They had covered twenty-three miles that day.[19] One soldier reflected on his pain: "we marched farther that day than we had before on this campaign and I was so tired and sore that it would have been impossible for me to have went much farther and my feet had swelled considerable."[20]

Dorsey Pender seemed impressed with the strength, stamina and morale of his Light Division troops. He conveyed his men's dedication in a letter written shortly before his death. "I never saw troops march as ours do; they will go 15 or 20 miles a day without leaving a straggler and hoop and yell on all occasions."[21]

These tired Georgians remained in bivouac on June 28 and 29. During this period, the various Confederate quartermasters seized all the beef cattle and horses from the surrounding farms. Pennsylvania's lush green Cumberland Valley provided a stark contrast to the battle-scarred landscape of Virginia. George Hall, 14th Georgia, wrote, "Every thing looked as though war had never been in a thousand miles of it, the vandal foe had laid wast [waste] to the beautiful fields of Virginia and other states of our beloved South, while their own country lay as peaceful as if there had been no war, but I guess the region our army visited felt something of the weight of war, something they will not soon forget."[22] Army scavengers gathered enough beef to supply Lee's army for several months. Captain McElvany wrote that the quartermasters rounded up 5,000 head of cattle.[23] Many soldiers gorged themselves on this rarity. Not owing an allegiance to the Union side, many Pennsylvania farm horses found themselves conscripted and hitched to a Confederate artillery or commissary wagon.

The latter part of June saw a command change in the Army of the Potomac. Major General George Meade replaced Joseph Hooker because of Hooker's ineptness at Chancellorsville. The last few days of June 1863 created a dilemma for Robert E. Lee. His army had moved through enemy territory with only infantry to screen the flanks and front. Major General Jeb Stuart's cavalry had departed on June 25 on a circular raid around the Federal army and had not been heard from since. Without cavalry to screen far enough ahead of the main body, the danger existed that Lee's army could be lured into battle on unsuitable terrain before it was ready to fight.

The Georgians moved eastward at 4:30 A.M., on June 30. They passed Greenwood, Pennsylvania. James McElvany noted that they saw the burned shells of ironworks buildings owned by abolitionist Congressman Thaddeous Stevens along the Chambersburg Pike. Confederate soldiers farther ahead in the march had torched this property.[24]

On July 1, the 35th Georgia marched off at 7 A.M. Several hours later Hill's Third Corps approached Gettysburg, Pennsylvania, from the west. He believed that only a small detachment of enemy cavalry occupied the small town. Heth's Division led Hill's column. Pender's Light Division followed about three miles behind. As Thomas' Brigade joined their place in the march, Colonel Bolling Holt received orders detaching the 35th Georgia to guard a wagon train. Shortly afterward, the distant sound of artillery drifted westward from the direction of Gettysburg.[25]

A courier soon galloped up and reined to a halt on a winded horse. He gave new orders to Holt. The young colonel issued instructions to several staff officers and within moments the 35th Georgia raced toward Gettysburg. The men double-quicked for nearly three miles as the crash of artillery became louder with each bound. They joined Thomas' Brigade located north of the Chambersburg Pike and west of Herr Tavern. The Georgians provided infantry support for two artillery battalions, commanded by majors David G. McIntosh and William J. Pegram. This position sat approximately one mile northwest of Gettysburg.[26]

George Hall, from his position behind the artillery, gave a description of what he saw: "We can see the Yankee's flag flying in the breeze. Onward our brave goes with a yell that seems to rend the air, we can see the Yankees in the edge of the woods, see the thick clouds of smoke that flies forth and their numerous batteries belched forth fire and death into our ranks."[27] Thomas' Brigade spent the entire first day of the battle in the frustrating position of dodging artillery shells while they witnessed the action to their front. Pender's other brigades moved forward in the afternoon to support Heth's second attack. The men of these units suffered tremendous losses. Thomas' men, in addition to providing artillery support, anchored the left flank of Hill's corps. Ewell's Second Corps arrived from the north and helped to push the enemy back through Gettysburg to Cemetery Ridge. This move brought temporary relief to the Georgians from the enemy artillery. McElvany described the accomplishments of the other brigades: "Our men captured the place, with a great many prisoners. The dead lay thick on the field. Our loss heavy."[28]

Troops from both sides poured into the area as the sun dropped in the west. It became obvious to all present that a great clash would shake the ground the following day. In the darkness, Pender ordered Thomas' brigade forward to support Pegram's artillery battalion. This new position stood in the woods about seven hundred yards south of the Hagerstown Road, southwest of the McMillan Farm. The ground around the new spot shook as enemy artillery unleashed a torrent of fire that caused little injury to the Georgians. The 35th Georgia anchored the brigade left with the 14th, 45th, and 49th Georgia regiments in line to the right. One Georgian wrote, "We lay in line of battle that night, the night was unusually still no sound disturbed dead silence that reigned over the terrible Battlefield where a few hours before the thunders of artillery and roar of small arms, and the shouts of antagonists as they rushed madly forward upon each other and the shrieks of the wounded and dying could have been heard several miles but now all was still and silent. Save once and awhile a stray gun shot from some out post picket."[29]

Bolling Holt, early on July 2, left three companies to support the artillery batteries. The rest of the regiment inched forward in the darkness, almost six hundred yards. They formed a skirmish line in the area of Long Lane. This narrow road poked in a straight line southwest out of Gettysburg. The road made an almost ninety degree turn to the west, about two hundred yards north of an orchard and farm owned by the Bliss family. The Blisses had previously abandoned their property as the soldiers arrived. Their frame house stood on the east side of the orchard. A large stone and brick bank barn stood south of the house. Thomas' right flank regiment, the 49th Georgia, anchored the right of Thomas at the north end of the orchard. Over the next two days, fighting over possession of these farm buildings seesawed back and forth between both armies.

The 35th Georgia soldiers endured the heaviest skirmishing of the war during this hot day. "Charge after charge was made, and in one assault the skirmishers advanced within a short distance of the enemy's batteries."[30]

The Confederates stationed on the Long Lane line faced skirmishers from two divisions of the Federal Eleventh Corps. Brigadier General Adolph von Steinwehr and Major General Carl Schurz commanded these divisions. The capture of several Georgia skirmishers revealed the proximity of opposing lines. Some of the captured men like Private Samuel Henry Starr came from Company F. Others like Second Lieutenant Robert C. Carter, Corporal Martin M. Dial (died at Ft. Delaware Prison on January 16, 1864), and Private Charles B. Roberts belonged to Company G. Captain Charles M. Tuggle, Company H, fell into enemy hands and he died in captivity four months later at Johnson's Island, Ohio. Eighteen-year-old Private Sanford Tuggle was captured and he spent the next eight months at Point Lookout prison. That experience prompted him to go AWOL shortly after his exchange in March 1864. Corporal David H. Mobley reported that the enemy caught several men in Company G around the Bliss barn. He also reported that his uncle, Private John Ephraim David Mobley, was struck on the hatband by a spent ball, but remained in line. Federal artillery fired into the Georgia brigade area around 5 P.M. The ground reverberated under the weight of this severe shelling. An officer in the 45th Georgia described their difficult position when he wrote: "In addition to supporting our batteries we had to furnish a picket or skirmish line. The skirmishing was the heaviest I ever heard of, being almost equal to a pitch battle all the time. I was in command of the line of skirmishers from our Regt and I think twas the hottest place I have yet been in."[31]

Major General Dorsey Pender's short command of the Light Division came to an abrupt end on this day. As he rode along his line, a shell fragment knocked him from his horse leaving a gaping hole in his thigh. Hill replaced his best commander with Brigadier General James Lane.

More soldiers moved forward on the night of July 2 to reinforce the Long Lane line, in anticipation of a rare night assault. Thomas' men took position along a fence in an open field about 300 yards from the Federal line. The Georgians supported the right flank of Robert Rodes' Division. The brigades of Colonel Abner Perrin (McGowan) and Brigadier General Stephen D. Ramseur lined up on Thomas' left. The 35th Georgia still occupied Thomas' left with the 14th, 45th, and 49th Georgia regiments in order to the right. Confederate authorities soon cancelled the assault, but these brigades remained in their position along Long Lane. The firing of nervous pickets continued throughout the night.[32]

With the first glint of morning on July 3, skirmishers peppered each other's silhouettes. Federal cannon fire from nearby Cemetery Hill soon added to the noise. Confederate sharpshooters stationed in the Bliss barn and house exacted a heavy toll on the Union artillery gunners. A small force

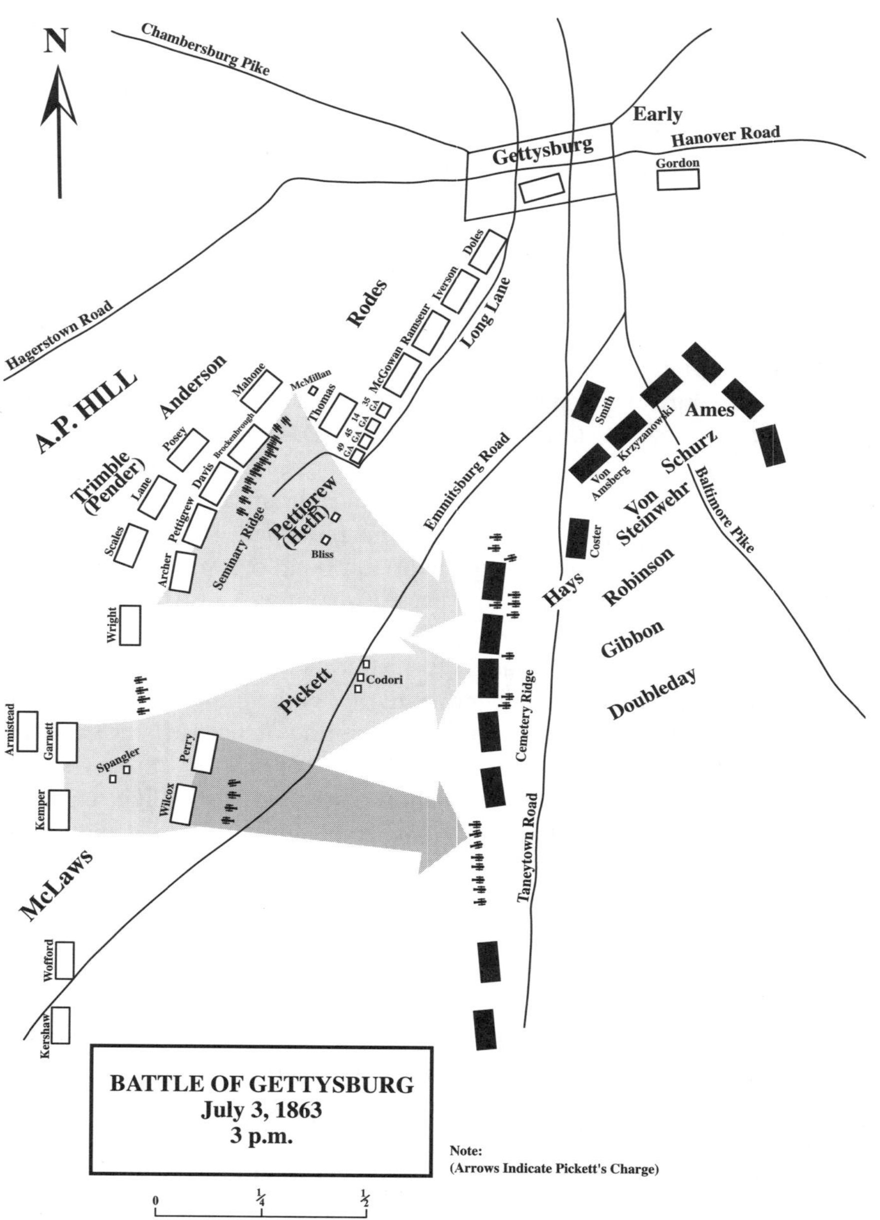
N
Chambersburg Pike
Gettysburg
Early
Hanover Road
Gordon
Hagerstown Road
Rodes
Doles
Iverson
Ramseur
McGowan
Long Lane
A.P. HILL
Anderson
Mahone
McMillan
Thomas
Posey
Brockenbrough
Trimble (Pender)
Lane
Davis
Pettigrew
Scales
Archer
Seminary Ridge
Pettigrew (Heth)
Bliss
Emmitsburg Road
Smith
Krzyzanowski
Ames
Von Amsberg
Schurz
Baltimore Pike
Von Steinwehr
Coster
Hays
Robinson
Gibbon
Doubleday
Wright
Codori
Pickett
Armistead
Garnett
Spangler
Perry
Kemper
Wilcox
Cemetery Ridge
Taneytown Road
McLaws
Wofford
Kershaw
BATTLE OF GETTYSBURG
July 3, 1863
3 p.m.
Note:
(Arrows Indicate Pickett's Charge)
0
1/4
1/2
miles

of Federal infantry charged the barn and house sending the Confederates fleeing west. Possession of these buildings changed hands at least twice more that morning. The last group of Federal soldiers stormed the buildings and set them afire, perhaps around 10 A.M. Thick flames and dark smoke soon rolled high into the air.

Captain McElvany reported being under a severe fire all day. Another Georgian recalled, "[W]e were between our artillery and the enemy's and what time we were not engaged with the enemy we had to lie flat on the ground and it seem the hottest I ever experienced. [T]here was no shade to protect us at all. [T]he vertical rays of the sun pored down upon us and the explosion of so much gunpowder heat the air and rendered the heat more hot than it would have been otherwise."[33] Lieutenant Draughton S. Haynes, 49th Georgia, described the day as, "The most terrific shelling I was ever under-my brigade was stationed midway between our own and the enemy's batteries. We charged the last but were repulsed."[34] Brigadier General James Lane reported that the heavy skirmishing along Long Lane required the deployment of entire regiments to throw back the enemy.[35]

The enemy captured several more soldiers from Company G on this day. Private Solomon Dabney Edwards spent the rest of the war at Fort Delaware prison. He finally gained his release on June 16, 1865. Private Elisha L. Smith died of smallpox at Fort Delaware on October 22, 1863. Private Cordy W. Hogan died of chronic bronchitis at the same prison on February 21, 1864.[36]

At 1 P.M., a pair of Confederate signal cannons fired. What followed shook the ground along the entire front. More than one hundred Southern cannons unleashed an intensive bombardment designed to soften Union resistance for an impending attack. The Federal batteries responded in sporadic fashion. The Confederate artillery fire continued for almost two hours. Robert E. Lee had planned an attack against the Federal center. Near mid-afternoon, some 13,000 gray infantrymen stepped forward in line of battle. The focus of their attack was a small copse of trees some three-quarters of a mile to the east on Cemetery Ridge. These soldiers represented nine brigades. Brigadier General Johnston Pettigrew commanded the wounded Henry Heth's Division with four of the brigades. Major General Isaac Trimble commanded the wounded Dorsey Pender's Division with two brigades. Major General George Pickett's Division comprised three brigades.

Colonel John M. Brockenbrough's Brigade held Pettigrew's left flank. When the attack began these Virginians brushed by Edward Thomas' right flank on their trek toward Cemetery Ridge. Evidence suggested that some Georgians joined the attack while others watched as the long lines moved forward. Within an hour, the discouraged participants stumbled back toward Seminary Ridge heckled by exultant Union cheers. This ill-fated attack galvanized itself in history as Pickett's Charge.

Edward Thomas did not mention in his report that any of his regiments participated in Pickett's Charge. Indications however, existed that some of his soldiers did go forward from their Long Lane position on that fateful day. Captain James McElvany reported, "General Heth's Division with Thomas's Brigade charged the enemys Battery at 5 o'clock. They charged under one of the most galling fires that ever came from an enemy's line, but were Repulsed and had to retreat under the same fire."[37] James Folsom referred to Pickett's Charge in *Heroes and Martyrs of Georgia.* "When the grand charge was made some brigade [Brockenbrough] in its advance passed near Thomas' Brigade and seemed disposed to stop; but that it might have no excuse for halting, General Thomas ordered his brigade forward. The Thirty-fifth being near him heard the command and led by Lieutenant Colonel McCullohs, participated in that memorable charge of Pickett and Heth." Captain Washington T. Irvine in a newspaper article written almost 28 years after the battle gave almost a verbatim description of the 35th Georgia's involvement on July 3 as the Folsom account. However, because Irvine's article is strewn with inaccuracies it should not hold a great amount of validity on its own.[38] John O. Andrews, 14th Georgia, stated, "I was wounded the afternoon of the 3rd in Pickett's charge, laid on the battlefield in a wheatfield until eleven o'clock that night."[39] George W. Hall, 14th Georgia, recalled: "about 3 o'clock P.M. our corps charged the enemy in order to try to rout them from their strong position, but we had to charge them so far across the old field, and the weather was so hot a great many of our men fainted and the remainder were exhausted so we had to fall back to our old position."[40]

If portions of Thomas' Brigade did participate in Pickett's Charge, perhaps Thomas did not want it known that his Georgians had moved forward without orders. This would explain his failure to mention Pickett's Charge in his report. Several reasons existed that might have prompted elements in the brigade to move forward from Long Lane without orders. The first and foremost reason stemmed from the Georgian's position. Their location was an infantryman's worst nightmare. Little cover existed behind the wooden fence on Long Lane. As enemy shot and shell ripped holes in the fence and the bodies behind it, many men probably wanted to move. Some of these men perhaps believed joining the grand charge could be no worse than standing still and dying.

Thomas reported his brigade line stood only 300 yards from the enemy. It was quite possible that amidst the noise and confusion, part of his line merged with Brockenbrough's Brigade, which passed mere yards from Thomas' right flank.[41] The casualty report listed a large number of soldiers in the 35th Georgia as missing in action. The regiment reported the highest MIA figures of the war from the Battle of Gettysburg. If the 35th Georgia provided mostly a support role during the battle, as the official reports indicated, then why were so many soldiers listed as MIA? The close proximity of the 35th Georgia to Federal lines on July 2–3, resulted in the capture of many Georgia skirmishers. The casualty list should have logged their names as captured in action not MIA. Those Georgians listed as missing in action may have fallen while participating in Pickett's Charge.

On the evening of July 3, Thomas pulled the brigade back to the same area near the McMillan farm that they had occupied on July 2. Company commanders attempted to ascertain their losses in the darkness. The 35th Georgia totaled 9 killed, 53 wounded and 57 missing. Many of the missing were presumed dead or else they would subsequently die in Federal prisons. This regimental loss amounted to 119, just less than half of the brigade's 250 casualties.[42] A newspaper dispatch signed by Colonel Holt indicated that the 35th Georgia suffered a total of 103 soldiers killed or wounded at Gettysburg.[43] These numbers reflected the highest casualty figures that the 35th Georgia suffered in battle during the war.

That night, all along the Confederate line, the men prepared their positions to repel a certain Federal assault the following day. A 14th Georgia officer described the difficulty of sleep that night: "On every side rose the shrieks of wounded and dying men and pitiful neighing of horses. Lying on our guns the whole night, we were kept awake by the cries for help from the wounded between the lines."[44]

The skirmishing continued at daybreak on July 4. Relief from the overbearing heat came that morning as a hard rain attempted to cleanse the fields of their grisly sights. The scenes around the battlefield of Gettysburg forged an unforgettable impression on the senses of those still living. George Hall, 14th Georgia, remembered, "I was in part of the town that day and saw some of the havoc the Battle had made on it. Some of the finest buildings I ever saw tore to pieces and demolished by cannon balls and shells and our troops had taken Shelter in some of them out of the rain, and the most desolating sight I ever saw, I saw there, all the furniture had been torn down and trampled under foot, ward robes, bureaus, sofas, trunks, librarys, torn open and their contents Scattered in every direction, our troops done bad there for they ought not to have destroyed the homes of helpless women and children. . . ."[45]

A strong stench from the carnage permeated the area for miles. The soldiers of both sides had fired some 569 tons of iron and lead between the short distance of Seminary Ridge and Cemetery Ridge. Many of the projectiles found warm flesh, but the soldiers were not the only victims. Between 4,500 and 5,000 horses fell at Gettysburg and their death poses added to the macabre landscape.[46]

When the anticipated Federal attack failed to occur on July 4, Lee had an important decision to make. Should he try to withdraw his battered troops or stay to fight?

Notes

Abbreviations:

CSR—"Compiled Service Records of Confederate Soldiers Who Served In Organizations From The State of Georgia," Thirty-fifth Infantry Regiment (National Archives Microfilm Publication M266) National Archives Building, Washington, D.C.

GDAH—Georgia Division of Archives and History, Morrow, Ga.

NMP—National Military Park

OR.—War of the Rebellion: A Compilation of the Official Records of the Union and Confederate Armies. 130 Vols.

SHSP—Southern Historical Society Papers

1. Letter of James M. Garrett to "Dear Mother from Camp Gregg, VA May the 15th 1863," James M. Garrett Collection.
2. Letter of James M Garrett to "Dear Mother from Camp Gregg Va May the 26 1863," James M. Garrett Collection.
3. *OR.,* Vol. 27, Pt.III, p.859.
4. J. William Jones, *Christ In the Camp.* (Richmond, Va., 1888) p.254, 306.
5. "Diary of George W. Hall, 14th Georgia Volunteers, CSA, 1861–1865," Hargrett Rare Book and Manuscript Library/ University of Georgia Libraries, Athens, Ga., p.42.
6. Draughton Stith Haynes, *The Field Diary of A Confederate Soldier-Draughton Stith Haynes-While Serving With the Army of Northern Virginia, CSA.* (49th Ga.)(Darien, Ga. 1963) p.26–27 (Edited by William G. Haynes, Jr.)
7. Letter of Lt. William Boswell to "My Dear Wife from Hamilton's Crossing, Va. June 11th 1863," William Boswell Collection, Mansfield (Texas) Historical Society.
8. Partial letter of Lt. William Boswell to persons unknown on unknown date. William Boswell Collection, Mansfield (Texas) Historical Society.
9. Undated letter of Lt. William Boswell to, "Ma". William Boswell Collection, Mansfield (Texas) Historical Society.
10. Letter of Stephen Lafayette Moon to "Dear Mother from Camp near Virginia, June 14, 1863," "Reminiscences of Confederate Soldiers and Stories of the War 1861–65," Volume XIII. Collected by Ga. Division, United Daughters of the Confederacy, p.108–109. GDAH.
11. Anecdote about Doctor O. Knight. "Reminiscences of Confederate Soldiers and Stories of the War 1861–65," Volume XIII.Collected by Ga. Division, United Daughters of the Confederacy, p.107, 104. GDAH. The author assumes that the baptism

incident occurred in spring of 1863 for several reasons. Dock Knight looked up to Corporal Stephen L. Moon since Moon apparently kept Knight from facing a firing squad for desertion. Moon was not baptized until June 13, 1863 so Knight probably would have waited until the same time frame to be baptized. The baptizing chaplain was John Hyman from the 49th Ga. and the spring of 1863 was a time when the 35th Ga. did not have a regimental chaplain. Water snakes will not be out of hibernation unless the weather has been warm for an extended period of time. Knight's court-martial and forfeiture of pay in 1864 may have been his punishment for being spared the firing squad.

12. Letter of JM Garrett to "Dear Mother from Chimbarazo Hospital Richmond June the 17th 1863," James M. Garrett Collection.
13. Letter of James M. Garrett to "Dear Mother from Richmond Va June the 21 63," James M. Garrett Collection.
14. *OR* ., Vol.51, Pt.II, p.723.
15. Haynes, p. 28.
16. "Letters and Journal of Major James T. McElvany, 35th Georgia Infantry Regiment," p.15.
17. Haynes, p.30. This route from Gaine's Crossroads is 12 miles of almost all uphill road. Gaine's Crossroads is where present day Massie's Corner is located at the intersection of Virginia State Route 211 and 522, southeast of Front Royal.
18. McElvany, p.15; Hall, p.42.
19. Ibid., McElvany, p.16.
20. Hall p.42–43.
21. William Dorsey Pender, *The General to His Lady: the Civil War Letters of William Dorsey Pender to Fanny Pender.* (Chapel Hill, N.C., 1962) p.254–255.
22. Hall, p.43.
23. McElvany. Letter to "My Dear Father and Mother from Valley of Virginia near Shepardstown June 24th 1863".
24. Ibid., p.16.
25. James Folsom, *Heroes and Martyrs of Georgia-Georgia's Record in the Revolution of 1861,* (Macon, Ga., 1864) p.140. (reprinted by Butternut and Blue, Baltimore, 1995); Hall, p.43.
26. Ibid., Folsom, p.140.
27. Hall, p.43.
28. McElvany, p.17.
29. Hall, p.43–44.
30. Folsom, p.140.
31. McElvany, p.18; Anita B. Sams, *Wayfarers In Walton.* (Atlanta, Ga., 1967) p. 169, 435; Haynes, p.14; "Letters of Two Confederate Officers: William Thomas Conn and Charles Augustus Conn" (45th Ga.), *The Georgia Historical Quarterly,* Vol. XLVI, 1962, p.189.
32. *OR.,* Vol. 27, Part 2, p.659, 668–669; Hall, p.44. Note: unfortunately the pristine appearance of the Long Lane position occupied by Thomas' men has disappeared. Long Lane is now occupied by numerous houses.

33. McElvany, p.18; Ibid., Hall, p.44.
34. Haynes, p.32
35. *OR.,* Vol. 27, Pt.II, p.666.
36. Sams, p.169.
37. McElvany, p.18.
38. W.T. Irvine, *The Sunny South,* Atlanta, May 2, 1891, "Old 35th Georgia".
39. Folsom, p.140; J.O. Andrews, 14th Ga., "Letter of John O. Andrews", "Reminiscences of Confederate Soldiers and Stories of the War 1861–65," Vol.3. Collected and bound by the Georgia Division—Daughters of the Confederacy, p.258, 1940. GDAH.
40. Hall, p.45.
41. *OR.,* Vol. 27, Pt.II, p.668–669.
42. Folsom, p.119, 140.
43. *Columbus Enquirer,* Columbus, Ga., July 21, 1863. microfilm 210/55, GDAH.
44. Lt. David Champion Co.G, 14th Ga., "Confederate Reminiscences and Letters 1861–1865," Ga. Division UDC, Atlanta 1995, p.15. GDAH
45. Hall. p.44–45.
46. Luther W. Minnigh, *Gettysburg, What They Did Here.* (Gettysburg, Pa., 1922) p.126–127.

Chapter Ten

RETREAT BACK TO VIRGINIA

"War is not the thing it is cracked up to be."
Private James M. Garrett

Robert E. Lee made the difficult decision to withdraw from Gettysburg under cover of darkness on the night of July 4. He left behind thousands of wounded Southerners. The 35th Georgia's Assistant Surgeon William P. Hill probably remained behind to treat the wounded because Union soldiers captured him on July 5. Lee ordered A.P. Hill's corps to lead the retreat west along the Hagerstown Road. Captain James McElvany, Company F, reported the 35th Georgia began their march just after nightfall. The march continued through a driving rain until daylight the following day.[1] The roads turned into quagmires making the going slow. Barefooted soldiers made better time marching in these conditions. Men with shoes, frequently halted to grope through the muck searching for brogans sucked off their feet.[2] One Georgian wrote, "The mud was from ankle to knee deep all the way. The march was awful. . . ."[3]

Thomas' Brigade passed through Hagerstown, Maryland on July 7. His men set up camp about two miles out of town. The Georgians remained there for several days. Four days later, on July 11, the 35th Georgia formed in line of battle with the rest of the brigade to meet an enemy threat in the army's rear. They occupied the line of battle over the next several days amidst sporadic heavy skirmishing. On the night of July 13, they marched toward the Potomac River in the mud and rain.[4] In the early morning hours of July 14, the 35th Georgia crossed the Potomac River on a pontoon bridge at Falling Waters, four miles below Williamsport, Maryland.

Lee's army arrived back in Virginia in poor physical shape. The long marching and heavy fighting had exacted a heavy toll. Witnesses noted the bad condition of the men in Hill's corps. Many of these troops walked barefooted and nearly naked. That evening the 35th Georgia drew rations for the first time in three days. Early the next morning, the march continued until they bivouacked at Bunker Hill, Virginia, where they had spent the fall of 1862. McElvany mentioned that on July 16 they rested and cleaned their filthy bodies for the first time in over a month.[5] He wrote a letter on July 19, from Bunker Hill, expressing thankfulness to still be alive after the difficult campaign:

> I seat myself to drop you a few lines from which you will learn I still live and Breathe as natural as ever. I have good health and a good appetite. We get plenty now but we were a little scarce a few days about the time we crossed the River coming out of Md. You have heard a great deal about our trip in Pennsylvania but you have not heard half, I know. We have been marching for more than one month, and have seen hard service I assure you. I thought we saw hard times last year but we certainly seen harder service this summer than we did last. The hardest Battle that we ever fought was fought at Gettysburg Pa. I cant attempt to describe the fight, for it would take too much time and space. We fought three days the 1st 2nd & 3rd of this month. I lost four men wounded and five missing. If I could see you I could tell you the great deal about it and I hope I shall be spared to see you all again and I am sure I shall never forget much that I have seen, heard and felt since we crossed the river.[6]

Hill's corps suffered another blow to its leadership on July 17. Johnston Pettigrew, wounded during the fighting near Falling Waters, died. The following day, Dorsey Pender died shortly after having his leg amputated. The fortunes of war had failed to smile on the six original brigade commanders in the Light Division. Joseph Anderson had resigned and was replaced by Thomas; Lawrence Branch was dead; Charles Field was severely wounded; Maxcy Gregg was dead; Pender was dead; and James Archer was a prisoner of war.

Private James Garrett, meanwhile, finally located the 35th Georgia near Hagerstown, Maryland after he and two friends had trekked north from Richmond. He wrote a letter from Bunker Hill on July 18 to let his mother know he was still alive. "I expect you are getting very uneasy about me as you have not heard from me in some time. I have not had the chance to write to you. I have marched about two hundred miles since I wrote to you last." He reported the regiment was still absent a chaplain, but apparently, different pastors preached during meetings hoping to qualify for the job. "Mr Cumby is here now. [H]e preached for us today. [H]e is trying to get to be Chaplain of our Regt."[7]

The 35th Georgia broke camp, after four days' rest, and marched two miles south from Bunker Hill. The next day they continued through Winchester and bivouacked about two miles south of town on the Valley Pike. On July 24, while crossing Thornton's Run near Sperryville, Federal cavalry appeared and unlimbered their horse artillery. The enemy lobbed shells into the gray column, but these Union troopers quickly departed after they received a hail of lead. The Confederates captured several of the cavalrymen.

The march continued to the Hazel River, northwest of Culpeper Court House. Some troops crossed the small stream on an unfinished bridge while others waded across to cool off. The Georgians bivouacked south of the river. The entire 35th Georgia assumed picket duty. The soldiers received reports of enemy cavalry in the area. This news kept the men vigilant until the march resumed at 4:30 A.M., on July 25. Hill's corps reached Culpeper Court House late that afternoon.[8]

A favorite part of any soldier's day was mail call. The mail from June and July caught up with the soldiers while the army halted at Culpeper. Many of the letters from home expressed worry about Southern setbacks at Gettysburg and Vicksburg as well as the harsh living conditions in Georgia. Farm help remained scarce at home. A salt shortage made preservation of meat difficult. Other foods and essential items also remained in short supply. Sick soldiers spread disease while they recuperated at home. These home-front problems added to the burden many soldiers carried on their shoulders as they yearned to help their families so far away.[9]

James McElvany expressed worry about what the future held for his country as well as himself personally. "I suppose Vicksburg has fallen and Charleston is in great danger. Times look gloomy I assure you. I hope things will Brighten up soon, but I cant tell what will be." When one of McElvany's siblings wrote that she planned to move into the country, the officer described the beautiful land he had marched through. "I have seen so much good country that I am in favor of looking for a better country than I have been in heretofore. This is a great country for grain. People generally lives well in this Portion of Va and in Maryland and in Pennsylvania. There is no end to the Wheat that is now being harvested in these countries. I think surely there is a better country for me than old Gwinnett is. I don't know that I shall ever go to it but, I am satisfied that I could do well to go Somewhere."[10]

Hill's entire corps moved south to Orange Court House during the first week of August 1863. The 35th Georgia bivouacked north of the town. North Carolinian Cadmus M. Wilcox, an 1846 West Point graduate and former regular army officer, assumed command of the Light Division. Wilcox was thirty-nine-years-old. Lee had considered Edward L. Thomas for the vacancy. Lee apparently wanted to avoid internal command disagreements since Thomas commanded a Georgia brigade in a division that also had two brigades from North Carolina and one from South Carolina. Lee wrote in his letter to President Davis recommending Wilcox, "Gen. Lane the senior brigadier is not recommended for promotion-Gen. Thomas the next in rank, a highly meritorious officer if promoted it is thought might create dissatisfaction."[11]

Private George Pass, Company H, wrote several desperate letters from Richmond's Camp Lee to his wife in August. Confederate authorities probably had conscripted the thirty-seven-year-old Pass in the spring of 1863. They had sent him for training to Camp Randolph at Decatur, Georgia. Illness had struck Pass by the time he reached Richmond in June. Medical authorities detained the soldier and sent him to convalesce at Richmond's Camp Lee. The depressed Georgian wanted to come home to escape the rampant illness he saw at the Richmond camp. "To think what I suffer with affliction and yet I have to be punished by living here in these nasty camps

Major General Cadmus M. Wilcox
This West Point graduate was promoted over Edward L. Thomas to command the Light Division after Dorsey Pender's death.
Photo courtesy of Library of Congress.

and a way from a peaceful and loving home." More than a month after his arrival Pass referred to the large number of soldier deaths at Camp Lee. "Thare has been hundreds died here since I have been here and I am yet Living. Thare is two or three dies Every day in this Little camp." The last few lines of an August 8 letter revealed the soldier's sense of foreboding and desperation. "I had rather go home and live on Bread and Water than to stay here. Francis, I cannot discribe how bad I want to see you and the children. I want you to pray for me that I may be preserved to get home one time more but if I do not have the pleasure I hope you will meet me in heaven." Pass informed his wife three days later that he expected to leave Richmond to go find the 35th Georgia. He recognized the South's manpower shortage when he wrote:

> I think the Confederacy needs soldiers migty bad or they would not keep such as I am. I have been suffering with my old diseas and it has settled in my Back so I cannot hardly get up when I am down. I donot no how I will get along a traveling but I will do the best I can. Francis I will say to you that if anything should befall me so that I should never get Back I want you to do the best you can and put your trust in a higher power and try to Rais the children Right and probable we may all meet in a better Country Whare thare will be no more parting.

It was not known how long Pass remained with the 35th Georgia at Orange Court House before illness incapacitated him. Doctors sent him to a Lynchburg hospital where he died of chronic diarrhea on November 11, 1863.[12]

James Garrett chastised his mother in a letter at the end of August. "I have received a letter from you at last. [I]t was a long time coming. I wrote six letters to you before I received a single one from you." This delay was probably Garrett's own fault because he had earlier requested that his mail be directed to Richmond and then forwarded to him. He detailed his camp contentment:

> We are lying up in camps here doing nothing at all. [W]e have a nice place to camp. [W]e have a plenty to eat now but we dont get it from the government. [W]e buy it. [W]e have roasting ears and irish potatoes aplenty. [W]e had a nice turkey [the] day before yesterday and such another mess we did have. [W]e had turkey and dumplings and irish potatoes all mixed together.

Garrett grew quite content with the nice weather and the comfortable camp surroundings near Orange Court House. "[W]e have beautiful weather now. [T]he prettiest I ever saw in Virginia." He continued, "[T]here is no prospect for a fight here for some time yet. [W]e are cleaning our camps to day. I expect we will stay here a good while. [T]hey are giving furloughs now to the well men. [T]here is not a yankee in twenty five miles of us as I know of and their force I dont think they will be a fight soon.[13]

Garrett launched into a diatribe against Private Theldred Lay, who apparently returned late from a furlough home:

> [Y]ou wrote to me that Theldred Lay would tell me all the news. Theldred has not made his appearance hear yet and it now the twenty second day of the month. [Y]ou write that he started on the eleventh of the month. [H]e is not coming as long as there is any chance to get out of it on any terms honorable or dis honorable. [I]t is strange that men will so ineffably base. [S]o lost to all honor. [S]o steeped in disgrace that [he] would skulk the coward or cringe with the slave Rather than fall with the free and sleep with the brave. Theldred has acted badly. [A]ny young man that will stay back in this trying time and this hour of his countrys need is a coward and ought to be [??unreadable] [E]very man that could come ought to come for the great decisive blow is soon to be struck and we ought to have every man that we could possibly get.[14]

The condition of the men improved after several weeks around Orange Court House. James Garrett detailed some of the ways the soldiers improved their situation. "I am in better health now than I ever was in my life. [T]he health of the whole regiment is in better health than I ever have seen. [W]e are getting a plenty to eat here but we dont draw it from the government. [T]he boys get it about through the country. We are having fine fun fishing hear now. [W]e had a fine mess yesterday." He urged his mother not to sell their family horse for too little. A neighbor had offered Garrett's mother $550 for "Jane," but Garrett urged her not to take less than $800. "[I]f I had her here I could get a thousand for her very easy. [E]verything here is very high. [H]ere watermelons is worth from five to ten dollars a piece. [B]utter is worth four dollars and a half a pound. [W]e have to buy salt here and pay a dollar a pound for it. [W]e pay twenty five cents a pound for flour but roasting ears and irish potatoes we get for nothing. [T]he boys go to the cornfields and get them. I want you to eat a big watermelon for me. I am sorry I cannot get home to help you eat them but I will have my share of roasting ears and potatoes as long as they last."[15]

Many men turned to God for solace amidst the growing concern for their country. Garrett noted, "[W]e have meeting day and night hear now. I saw eight baptized day before yesterday. [T]he meeting has been going on for the last two weeks. [T]here is a right sum of interest taken in it. [N]early fifty have join the church since the meeting commenced. [W]e have had no chaplain for our regiment yet."[16]

Some soldiers turned their backs on any type of spiritual development. Other men exhibited an open defiance toward authority. Arrogance even infected some Georgians who professed themselves Christians. Garrett described a similar mind-set in himself:

> I have got so here lately that nothing dont hurt me and I dont care for nothing nor the half of that so I go where I please and do what I please. [W]e all do pretty much what we please here lately. [W]e go foraging and stay all night and all day and our officers don't pester us. [S]ometimes we bring back [??unreadable] and peas sometimes pumpkins and irish potatoes and roasting ears. [T]he boys got two turkeys the other night. We intend to live here. [I]f Jeff Davis dont feed us we will feed ourselves and we will last off of the people of Virginia.[17]

Garrett reported that on September 6 tempers flared during a disagreement between two soldiers from Company A. "Two men of company A got to fighting and one stabed [stabbed] the other twice once between the eyes and on the left nipple. [T]he later [latter] place reached the hollow. [H]e is not dead yet but I think he will die. [T]he vile perpetrator of the deed is kept under a strong guard night and day. [H]e will be shot I expect." He provided more graphic insight into the men of his Company D when he wrote, "[W]e have some of the best preaching you ever heard. [G]ood preaching is greatly needed here for we have got the wickedest company in the whole regiment and every one of my mess swears except me. [W]e have not got a single man in the company that prays in public except Lieutenant [Benjamin W.] Morton and he is at home."[18]

A 45th Georgia officer noted that on September 1 there was a division parade, and General Wilcox deemed the 45th Georgia the sharpest-looking regiment in the division. Several days later, members of the same regiment mobbed a sutler in the brigade area. The sutler reported to the provost marshal that these wayward men stole all the pies and bread off his wagon. History failed to recall Cadmus Wilcox's reaction to this incident. This crime and many other instances of bad behavior convinced the officers to tighten discipline. The pie and bread thieves faced a court-martial two days later.[19]

First Lieutenant Solomon G. Johnson, Company C, faced a court-martial on August 28. The court-martial convened to try Johnson on a charge of conduct unbecoming an officer and a gentleman. The alleged misconduct had occurred a year earlier in September 1862 when Johnson obtained furloughs for two of his soldiers and then sold the furloughs to other soldiers. Captain William T. Nicholson, 37th North Carolina, prosecuted the case as the Judge Advocate. Lieutenant Colonel R. P. Lester, 14th Georgia, provided counsel for Johnson during the proceedings. Nicholson and Lester presented evidence and questioned witnesses for several days.[20]

The evidence revealed that Private Thomas J. Daniel, Company C, had fallen ill in August 1862. Lieutenant Johnson had procured a furlough for him, but Daniel died on September 3, 1862. The lieutenant sold the unused furlough to another man for twenty dollars. The defendant later told a fellow officer, Lieutenant John E. Steed, that he had sent the twenty dollars to Daniel's impoverished wife.

Another soldier in Company C, Private Harbird Cook, received a furlough from the Medical Board. The Secretary of War's office approved a second furlough for Cook at the same time. Cook stated in court that Johnson did not give him the Secretary of War furlough; thus Cook had gone home on the Medical Board furlough. Lieutenant Johnson then gave the unused furlough to Corporal William Burran, Company C. Burran stated to the court that a man in Richmond owed him twenty-five dollars, and he told Johnson to collect the debt and keep the money as payment for the furlough. Burran recalled that in February or March 1863, Johnson gave him the twenty-five dollars. The officer told Burran that he never intended to keep the money.

The jury of officers, after deliberating over the evidence and testimony, found Johnson guilty and ordered his dismissal from the service. Robert E. Lee signed his approval to the bottom of the court-martial paperwork.

Lieutenant Johnson, apparently, was very popular with his enlisted men and his fellow officers. His guilty verdict created uproar throughout the regiment and in particular Company C. Most of the officers in the 35th Georgia signed a two-page letter of protest on September 27, and sent it to General Samuel Cooper, the Adjutant and Inspector General for the Confederacy. The Georgia officers wrote, "We most earnestly petition his restoration to his rank and position in this Regiment. We are induced to do this from personal knowledge of Lt. Johnson's uniform gallantry upon the field and his complete discipline in his company in both of which his character is unexceptionable." The letter further stated that the undersigned did not want to besmirch the decision of the court, but if they knew Lieutenant Johnson the way the undersigned knew him, the decision of the court would have been different. "We are also conversant with the facts of this case and give it as our candid belief that Lt. Johnson acted in the premises more from an *ignorance* of military law and usage, and a want of proper discretion than any intention to do wrong or violate the law."[21]

On October 1, the enlisted men of Company C forwarded a letter in support of Johnson. "We know him to be tried and true in the hour of danger, a good disciplinarian in Camps and every way worthy to Command us in the position of 1st Lieutenant." The names of forty enlisted members of Company C appeared at the bottom of the letter including the names of Private Harbird Cook and Corporal William Burran. Captain James McElvany, Company F, apparently penned the letter and he certified in a statement at the bottom of the page that on his honor he had read the petition to the men whose names appeared on the letter.[22]

It was impossible to tell what weight these letters carried, but it was interesting that a notation made during the first week of October indicated that both Cadmus Wilcox and A.P. Hill each disapproved the court-martial. Unfortunately, a subsequent notation by General Lee was completely illegible. This flurry of paperwork possibly aided Johnson's case because he received a lighter sentence. The officer remained in the service, but he apparently received a reduction in rank because a year later he signed a pay statement as a second lieutenant. He survived the war and surrendered at Appomattox.(see Appendix D for more detail)[23]

Private Woodson D. Moon, Company G, wrote to his wife, Charlotte, on September 11. He warned her about Confederate money:

> Anything you want you had as well buy it if you have the money, as I don't expect the money will be any good in a short time from this, for there is so much of it afloat and it buys such a little. If you go to buy anything you will have to give a measure of money for a measure of anything you buy. You may use what money you please, and live as well as you can, for that is all that is allotted to man in this world, and you had as well enjoy it as for to lay it up and let it go down on your hands, which it undoubtedly will do.

Moon reported on life around Orange Court House. "The army here is in good health at this time, but is small. The companies will not average more than thirty-five men, and that makes the regiment about 350 men. . . ." Rumors abounded in camp that another corps might follow Longstreet's men to Tennessee to assist Braxton Bragg's army. The vanguard of Longstreet's corps had departed on September 9.

Moon described how some of the men grew bored eating the same food. "Times are very hard here now; things [prices] are so high and the men are so tired of meat and bread that they will pay any price asked. They have to pay from fifteen to twenty dollars per bushel for Irish potatoes, one dollar a pound for dried fruit and two dollars a plug for tobacco, and everything else in proportion." He figured he had enough clothes to survive the winter, and he urged his family not to send him any more, "for if I have to move I will have to throw them away." The holes in the bottom of his shoes created a problem. "The shoes that I have would do to wear in dry weather if they were half-soled. If you have the leather I want you to send me two half-soles and I will put them on myself." He closed this letter with a short poem. "When this you see remember me, though seven hundred miles between us be."[24]

James Garrett reported on September 7 that he foresaw no prospect of a fight. He stated that the pickets stood many miles away. "[T]he weather is very cool for the time of year. [T]he nights especially we need more cover than we have got. [Y]ou had better send me a light blanket by James Dunson if you can get it for me. I have got a plenty of other clothing." He needed socks along with a special request. "You spoke of sending me some brandy by James Dunson. I would be very glad to get some good brandy but you must not load him down with things for me for they are some trouble to bring."[25]

Wagonloads of equipment, food and clothing reached the men over the next several weeks. These items helped to bolster the well-being and morale of the troops. The ranks continued to swell as conscripts and recuperated veterans arrived at their units. Revivalism again swept through camp. The chaplains held daily meetings, and many soldiers who had turned their backs on Christianity during the winter of 1862–63 seemed ready to listen.

Edward Thomas inspected his brigade on Sunday, August 23. Most of the men in the four regiments then walked down to the Rapidan River to witness the baptism of a number of converts. Lieutenant Josiah B. Patterson, 14th Georgia, reported, "There is considerable interest on the subject of religion in our Army at present and many are connecting themselves with the church. Our chaplains are very active and zealous and their labors appear to be signally blessed."[26] Captain McElvany wrote in his diary that thirty-nine men were baptized on September 13.[27] A 45th Georgia officer reported that on September 21, he attended an evening baptism for fourteen men. This group of baptized men included Colonel Robert W. Folsom, 14th Georgia, and Lieutenant Colonel William H. McCullohs, 35th Georgia.[28]

Each company drilled every morning from 7–8 A.M., before it became too hot. The men held a skirmish or battalion drill each afternoon from 5–6 P.M. Then at 6:30 P.M., there was a dress parade followed by the evening meal. Two men out of every hundred received thirty-day furloughs.[29] The Georgians participated in a corps review on Friday, September 11. Generals Robert E. Lee, A.P. Hill, Richard Anderson and Henry Heth attended. The three divisions formed in three separate lines about one hundred yards apart. Each line stood about a mile in length. The entourage of officers and aides galloped on their horses the length of the lines. The generals then dismounted and stood along an incline as the columns of soldiers marched past. Martial music filled the air.[30]

On September 22, the brigade marched six miles west to Liberty Mills to guard several bridge crossings along the Rapidan River. The men lined up as pickets along the south bank. They listened to sounds of an intense cavalry skirmish in the direction of Madison Court House. Two days later, the Georgians marched back to Orange Court House.[31]

The discipline problem in Lee's army manifested itself during the fall of 1863. Numerous soldiers faced courts-martial hearings. Some of these men soon faced execution. McElvany noted in his diary that a firing squad shot two deserters from Lane's Brigade on September 19. His next entry provided a stark contrast. It showed that on September 21, a chaplain baptized ten soldiers in the 35th Georgia.[32]

On Saturday, September 26, every soldier in Wilcox's Division witnessed an event that remained etched in their memories. Sergeant Marion Hill Fitzpatrick, 45th Georgia, stated that at 11 A.M., the units formed in a U-shape (referred by soldiers as a hollow square) on a nearby parade field. Another witness, with the initials T.C.E., stood near the front of the formation. He reported that only Thomas' and Scales' brigades stood in a half-circle on two hills. Soldiers hammered two stakes with crosspieces into the ground between both hills. An officer ordered the men to attention as the band from the 13th North Carolina played the "Dead March" in the distance. Fitzpatrick described the solemn scene: "The procession then moved out of a skirt of woods near by, and was composed of a band of music, three chaplains, the two prisoners, two or three officers and twenty men that done the shooting. They marched around the whole line the band playing the dead march which was the most solemn music I ever heard. I shall never forget the impression it made on me."[33] T.C.E. described the marked difference in the demeanor of each condemned prisoner:

> The North Carolinian had his head down, but the Georgian was erect, kept a firm step to the music, and peered fearlessly into the men's faces as he passed by. He was a handsome fellow, well set, of round and ruddy face, and black hair and eyes. When they reached the stakes the North Carolinian fell down with his face in his hands, and remained in that position. Not so the Georgian, he showed not the least fear. The chaplain prayed over them, and then they were asked if they had anything to say. The Georgian stood up, asked permission to pull off his overcoat, and then said substantially as follows,
>
> 'I want to say that my sentence is a just one; I did wrong to leave my colors, and I want all you soldiers to take warning at my fate. The

only thing that I regret is that it will bring my old father's gray hairs to the grave in disgrace; but I want you sir, (to the chaplain), to write my wife and tell her that I died like a brave man and soldier.'

He then asked for a drink of water, and his captain, leaving the company to go to him, handed him a canteen. After drinking, and returning the canteen, he seized his officer's hand and said,

'Good-bye, Captain; I want you to promise to meet me in heaven.'

The officer was so much affected he did not reply; but he [prisoner] held to his hand, saying, 'Promise me, Captain, promise me, to meet me in heaven!'

The captain, sobbing as a child, pulled loose and returned to his company, but so urgent were the continued cries of the soldier of 'Captain, promise me, promise to meet me in heaven,' that he turned, when about half way, and made some reply, but I could not catch it.[34]

Fitzpatrick recalled these final moments as the guards formed in two ranks about ten steps in front of the prisoners:

> There were ten men to shoot at each prisoner. Six guns out of the ten were loaded with balls, the others with powder only, but none of the guard knew whether his gun contained a ball or not. After arranging the guard and prisoners, they sung a hymn and went to prayer. The prisoners were then tied to the stakes. They were kneeling with their faces toward the guards and had their arms tied to the crosspiece and were blindfolded.

The Georgia prisoner did not want a blindfold, but the officer in charge refused his request:

> The command was then given to fire and they were launched into eternity. The crosspiece to which one was tied was shot to pieces. He raised himself perpendicular, fell forward and turned over on his back and died instantly. He was pierced through with six balls. The other was struck with only one ball. He turned to one side and was some time dying.

T.C.E reported the end of the Georgian. "But he died without a quiver: the bravest man I ever saw, and he was *shot to death for cowardice.*" This soldier further defended the Georgia soldier's reputation, "He had been a gallant soldier all before this, and wore honorable scars on his person."[35]

Both prisoners had received convictions for desertion, cowardice and disobedience of orders. The man shot six times was Romulus Dixon, 14th Georgia. Dixon had a wife and two children back home. A court-martial had convicted and sentenced Dixon to death on September 1. The specification for cowardice stated that he left the 14th Georgia for two days during the Battle of Chancellorsville. Then he feigned a wound at Gettysburg. The specification for disobedience stated that Dixon failed to obey the order of a surgeon at the Battle of Gettysburg to go back into battle. Dixon forged the surgeon's certificate of disability. The other soldier executed alongside Dixon was a North Carolinian from Scales' Brigade. The whole division marched by the blood-soaked corpses. The army leadership believed that public scenes like these would stave off future desertions, which the army could ill afford.[36]

Three days after the execution, James Garrett reported, "I am well at present though I have been very sick since I wrote to you last. [W]e have been marching about a little but we have got still again." He expressed thanks for the Confederate victory at Chickamauga, Georgia. "[W]e have heard that Longstreet and Bragg have driven the Yankees out of Georgia. [T]his is good news to me for they were getting most too close to our homes. [T]he Yankees have all cool down here again and we are having a fine time eating beans and roasting ears & pumkin. We are still having meetings every day and knight and a great deal of interest is felt. I saw forty two men baptized at one time the other day. [I]t was one of the most beautiful sites that I ever witnessed in all the days of my life. [T]wo have join the church and have been baptized in my mess viz BF Cassels and Alen White. [I]t is the greatest revival that I ever saw." The two messmates he mentioned were Privates Benjamin F. Cassels and Henry A. White.[37]

Private James Dunson, Company D, returned to Orange Court House from furlough on October 8. He carried a disturbing letter for James Garrett from Garrett's mother. Garrett's sixteen-year-old brother, William (Bud), had apparently abandoned the family farm. The frustrated soldier immediately scribbled a letter back to his mother. "[Y]ou wrote to me that bud was at Kingston Ga. [Y]ou never wrote to me how come him there nor nothing about it. [A]ny way I want you to sit rite down as soon as you get this letter and tell me all about it. I want to know whether he ran away or if you was willing for him to go or not." Garrett then adopted a scolding tone. "I want you to be sure to write all about bud. [H]ow he come to go off. [Y]ou did very wrong if you consented for him to go. I wanted [him] with me if he went off. [I]f he has gone off with frank formby he will never be any account in the world. [H]e will learn him to be a gambler for it is the greatest place to learn to gamble in the world."[38]

Two more 35th Georgians found themselves in trouble during the waning months of 1863. A court-martial panel found Private Seaborn J.M. Sizemore, Company H, not guilty of desertion on October 1. A note from his trial paperwork stated that his case was dismissed because "the Proclamation of the President was not published in GA [Georgia] 20 days before he was arrested." President Davis had issued this proclamation granting amnesty to deserters if they returned to their units. Authorities had captured Sizemore in Georgia, however the proclamation had failed to make the local papers in time for him to return to the 35th Georgia. Sizemore harbored no allegiance toward his comrades from his close call because a year later he deserted to the enemy while manning the Petersburg lines in October 1864.[39]

Another court-martial panel, on November 1, 1863, found Lieutenant Josiah Barber Scott, Company G, guilty of conduct unbecoming an officer. The specifications of his charge claimed that he forged a medical certificate to seek relief from ulcers—one on his foot and two more on his leg. Then he apparently forged another medical certificate. The last specification stated that he wrote an untruthful letter to his captain outlining his medical problems. His sentence was dismissal from the service. General Lee noted on his paperwork to "publish his crime in his hometown newspaper." Scott still favored the Southern cause because records revealed that he enlisted as a private in Company A, 11th Battalion, Georgia Light Artillery, three days later.[40]

The Adjutant and Inspector General's Office in Richmond issued General Order #131, on October 3, 1863. This Roll of Honor recognized those soldiers "conspicuous for courage and good conduct on the field of battle." The following members of the 35th Georgia received this honor: Corporal Jackson Baggett, Co. A (posthumous); Private Algernon S.W. Bass, Co. B (posthumous); 2nd Sergeant James E. Cochran, Co. C; Private Rolla Willingham, Co. D; Private David P. White, Co. E; Private Richard D.B. Holt, Co. F; Private William E. Moon, Co. G; Private Absalom Martin, Co. H (posthumous); Private Lewis Millican, Co. I (posthumous); Corporal Davis M. Pierce, Co.K.[41]

George Meade's Army of the Potomac still represented a threat to Lee. Meade's troops camped around Culpeper Court House, only seventeen miles away. Lee wanted to move the enemy out of the war-torn Virginia countryside, and he reasoned that if he turned Meade's right flank, this would force the enemy to withdraw closer to Washington.

James Garrett wrote on October 8, "You kneed not be surprised to hear of our being in a fight at any day for we are cooking up three days rations to be ready to leave at six oclock this evening. [T]he general opinion is that we are going to attack the yankees tomorrow or next day so you kneed not be in a hurry to send me any thing else at present untill the move is over."[42] Lee's army left Orange Court House in the cool darkness the next morning and headed northwest. The column cautiously wound around the bases of hills to avoid detection. As evening approached they camped near Madison Court House. Officers permitted the men to only build small fires.[43]

By October 11, Lee's army approached Culpeper Court House undetected. Surprised Yankee pickets scattered from their posts and ran east. That night the 35th Georgia halted about six miles northwest of Culpeper. Meade's army started a retreat to the northeast. Both Hill's and Ewell's corps paralleled the Federal army. Two days later, the Georgians reached Warrenton, Virginia, and it appeared the next day would bring a battle. The following morning, the 35th Georgia received orders to guard a wagon train. The remainder of the Georgia brigade double-quicked ahead and endured heavy enemy artillery fire. When the 35th Georgia moved forward later, the Battle of Bristoe Station had ended. On October 15, the Federals completed their withdrawal across Broad Run.[44]

Corporal Stephen L. Moon described the move from the foot soldier's perspective. "We have been near Manassas and drove the Yankees from the Rappahanock river to Manassas, and they did not stop to give up any fight; only the cavalry, as we would push on them so close that they could not get away without making the attempt until we were in two or three miles of Manassas. Then we had ten brigades of infantry engaged. . . ." Moon failed to mention the dismal results of the hasty attack ordered by A.P. Hill. Several Confederate brigades endured huge casualties after being lured into a Federal trap.[45]

Private William T. Formby, Company D, wrote a letter to James Garret's mother and reported the move toward Bristoe Station:

> We have taken another short trip up to manassas after the yanks but they went too fast for us. [W]e run them from near Orange CH to centervill taking 20 or 25 hundred prisoners with but verry little fighting. Our division was not engaged in a fight. [D]uring the trip we fell back from there and tore up the railroad to that place. James [Garrett] is well and hearty. [H]e has been complaining of his knees hurting him which was from cold and fateague though they have quite hurting him.

The Garrett family rented cropland from Formby. Formby wanted to make a change to the rental agreement because of the devalued Confederate currency. "I received a few lines from you yesterday stating that you wanted to rent my land again next year. I will rent it to you but I must have part of the crop. [T]he confederate money is depreciated that it wount [won't] pay me to rent at $100 dollars. [F]ive dollars is not worth as much as one at the present times. [Y]ou can have the land at the third and fourth or the customary rates for rent."[46]

The following week, Thomas' Brigade marched south along the Orange and Alexandria Railroad. They pulled up rails and attempted to burn the railroad ties amid torrential rains. The work was cold and tedious. To prevent enemy reuse of the rails, groups of soldiers struggled through the mud to carry the iron to the south side of the Rappahannock River. A pontoon bridge erected on October 18 broke because of the high water. This prevented the brigade from crossing until the following day.[47] Stephen Moon curiously failed to mention the difficulty crossing the Rappahannock. He wrote, "we then fell back across the Rapahanock river burning the railroad bridges as we went."[48]

Once across the river, the troops bivouacked between Brandy Station and Rappahannock Station. James Garrett described his money problems to his mother. "[T]he reason I have not wrote to you sooner is because I did not have any paper nor no money to get any with. I borrow a little from Lieut Mitchell to get me some paper and soda with." He then complained of the chilly weather and described some of his colleagues in Company D:

> It is tolerable cool here now. [W]e have had several rite heavy frost hear lately. [W]e are suffering for blankets. [W]e have got plenty of other clothing. [W]e ly on the ground and cover with our blankets. [W]e have no tents only some little yankee tents though with all this we are all well generally. Bill Formby is complaining a little. I have been sick a few days myself but I have got over it again. Jim Dunson & Theldred Lay and Bill Williams & Peter are all complaining. Theldred Lay says he knew he would not stand it. [H]e never will be any count here. Jim Dunson will make a verry good soldier.[49]

Garrett's thoughts constantly returned to his family difficulties in Heard County. Garrett's mother tried to run the family farm without any adult male help. His sixteen- year-old brother had still not returned home. This situation left eighteen-year-old Sophronia, fourteen-year-old Mary (Ellen), and eleven-year-old John to help their mother. A frustrated James Garrett did not know where or how to write to his missing brother, Bud. He urged his mother: "I want you to write to me as soon as you get this letter and give me all the news. [W]rite how much corn you have made and how your hogs are getting along and also if your colt is fat. [Y]ou have never wrote to me what Mrs Allen planted in that field you rented her. [I]f she planted it in cotton and it makes anything you will get a rite smart rent as cotton is fifty cents a pound." Garrett feared his family's ability to manage the land they rented from William (Bill) Formby. "I dont know how you are going to manage about cultivating the land. [A]re you going to keep that negro that you had or are you going to hire one. I will try to send you all the money I can spare. I will send you about seventy five dollars the next time we draw. I dont know when that will be. [W]e are looking for it every day." He requested that his family send him a box as soon as possible with a bed quilt, some butter, a bottle of brandy and some socks. Everything else he needed could be drawn from the government.[50]

By the end of October 1863, camp debate centered on whether the army would spend winter quarters at their present location. One officer in the brigade reported, "Water is very convenient but we have burned up all the wood in reach and will have to haul our future supplies. Some of the officers have built very neat and comfortable chimneys to their tents but we delayed building one to ours for fear we might move and thus lose our labor. The reflection that we are permanently located for the winter is too pleasant to indulge as yet, the season not being sufficiently advanced to make a military movement impossible."[51] Another Georgian remarked on the uncertainty of winter camp location when he wrote, "Soldiers would always provide themselves very comfortable quarters for winter, were they only assured they would be permitted to enjoy the fruits of their labor, but repeated disappointments leave but little encouragement to work."[52] James Garrett's opinion was, "I dont think we will stay here all the winter. I think we will go back towards Orange Court House again."[53]

An active rumor still circulated through camp that more of Lee's troops would leave Virginia to go assist in the western theater. Stephen Moon wrote on October 20:

> I think we will take up winter quarters some where near where we did last winter, if we don't go west. It is the chat here now, that three divisions of the army will go west and General Lee will go also, and leave Hill and Ewell here to defend Virginia. I think if Lee goes with his men he will show the western boys how to fight and would drive the last Yankee back on their own soil. I heard today that [Confederate General Braxton] Bragg was still fighting them and they [Bragg's men] were still falling back. I also heard that the Yankees said that as soon as our men charged them they knew that some of the army from the Potomac [Army of Northern Virginia] was there, for they did not fight like the [Confederate] troops that they had been used to fighting. I dont think there will be any more fighting here this winter.[54]

The latter part of October 1863, found Colonel Bolling H. Holt on a thirty-day furlough at his parent's home in Columbus, Georgia. His father,

Hines Holt, was extremely ill. Hines Holt wrote a letter on November 1 to Confederate Secretary of War James A. Seddon requesting a furlough extension for his son. The elder Holt believed his death was imminent and he needed his son to help take care of family affairs. He ended the letter with a request that if he died his son be allowed to resign from the army to attend to a family that consisted of all females and one young boy. It was not known whether Seddon granted a furlough extension to the young colonel.[55]

The pessimists in the brigade received their reward when orders arrived to move. On November 5, they marched five miles southwest, closer to Culpeper Court House. Soldiers in the 14th and 45th Georgia regiments started construction for their winter quarters at the new site. Soon several shanties with oak log walls awaited roofing. A grove of persimmons stood nearby and many troops, willing to try anything to change their diet, scurried around gathering the fruit.[56] Soldiers in the 35th Georgia probably started construction on their winter quarters because of the frosty weather. The following day remained cold and windy.

About midnight on November 7, the soldiers in Thomas' Brigade awoke and they marched in the darkness about a mile from camp and formed into line of battle. They remained there in the cold all day until 6 P.M., when they withdrew south and marched toward Orange Court House. Many of the soldiers suffered as the weather deteriorated, especially those without shoes. The first snow of the season fell on the morning of November 9, as the Georgians arrived at their old Orange Court House bivouac site from the previous month.[57]

Many soldiers speculated on another move during the middle of November. A short time later, the men received the unpopular order to cook two days rations. Some thought the army would move toward Fredericksburg. Then on the evening of November 15, shouts of alarm sounded and the Georgians grabbed their weapons, marched out about a half mile, and halted. The soldiers returned to camp after reassurances from the cavalry that the enemy was no closer than twenty-five miles. James Garrett predicted, "I think we will have a fight yet before the winter sets in."[58]

Garrett provided some insight on local vegetables and the money that could be earned with a little effort:

> I am well and as hearty as a pig. I am nearly as fat as I was when I left home the last time. I have been living on cabbage for the last week or two. I get them at fifty cents a head. [W]e buy a head every day. [T]here is three of us in a mess which makes about sixteen cents a peace for us. I saw a turnip sell for one dollar and seventy cents. [I]t would have weighed about three lbs. William Formby said he

Tombstone of Private Warren H. Brand, Co.G

This Walton County soldier was captured near Culpeper Courthouse, Va. on November 14, 1863. He probably was captured by Federal cavalry while on picket duty. He died of smallpox at a Federal hospital in Washington, D.C. on January 23, 1864. Federal authorities buried Brand in the Confederate section at Arlington National Cemetery.

Photo by the author

> saw one the other day as large as a peck measure [four pecks = one bushel]. [H]e bought a bushel and lug them seven miles on his back. [H]e give four dollars a bushel and brought them to camp and sold three pecks for eight dollars. [S]o you see he doubled his money and had a peck left to eat himself. I could make five dollars a day here if I would speculate on little things but I have got no turn for such business though I expect to try them turnips if I stay here long enough.[59]

Lieutenant Jerry R. Winchester, Company D, told James Garrett on November 17 that the men would draw their regular pay soon, but their money for clothing allowance would be delayed until January. Garrett then wrote his mother that he would not be able to send her much money. "I cannot send you but about twenty dollars this time. I am going to send you all that I can spare. I have some money to buy something to eat for I tell you we dont get enough to eat here." He then illustrated the critical decision-making that must go into the simplest things of camp life. "Three of us have got two cups full of flour to last untill to morrow night. [W]e can eat it all today."[60]

Garrett took the opportunity to complain about Theldred Lay again. "[W]e are all well. [T]here is not a sick man in our company except Theldred Lay. [H]e is moping about here like a sick hen. He is not worth a cent to this confederacy nor ever will be. [H]e is so lazy he cannot hardly [??illegible]."[61]

Garrett still expressed concern about his younger brother. He questioned how the young man had avoided military service after abandoning the family farm to go to Kingston, Georgia. "I want you to write to me how Bud got out of the war or whether he was ever mustered in or not and if he got any pay for his service. [Y]ou can tell him if he got sick for that little he is no man at all. [I]f he cant stand that little he had better stay out of the war. [I]f they would let me go to Kingston I would stand guard every night." He also issued some directives to his family to send him some clothes. He expressed his disdain for the poor quality of some government manufactured clothing:

> I want you to be sure to knit me a pair of gloves. [I]f you cant get wool take cotton. [T]hey are better than none. I dont want you to buy wool to make me any clothes for I can get them cheaper here than you can make them at home. I have got two coats and a vest that will do me this winter. I want you to make me two shirts and two pair of draws by next spring. I can draw them here but they are not half made and will last no time.[62]

Ten days later, Garrett asked that his family send a box of provisions. He repeated his pressing need for gloves. "I need them [gloves] bad. [T]hese nights are too cool to stand guard without gloves. I had to stand few hours this morning bare handed." The young Georgian described his success with his own turnip sales. "I bought a bushel of turnips the other day for $4.00 and sold four of them for a $1.00 a piece which made my money back and I ate the balance myself. They eat very well with beef."

Garrett and his fellow soldiers spent a lot of time thinking about food. Many of the men devised schemes to gather food outside of the sparse military commissary channels:

> I would like very well to be at home now to eat hog jowl and turnips, spare rib and back bone. I had a mess of fresh pork yester-

> day morning. I got it from a fellow that got it by the slite of hand but you need not say anything about that. The boys get corn somehow or other and carry it to mill and get some meal. I dont know how they got it. They go off with a sack and come back with it full of corn. But dont you say anything about that for it is not a terrible thing. It is not for everybody to know but dont understand me to say that I do that that way. For I do not. I cant blame them for it for we do not get enough to eat. One pint of flour a day is not enough for us and it is all we get. And salt we do not get half enough we have it to buy. The boys cant find it and we pay $1.00 a pound for it but we will come out of that some day I hope if we live long enough.[63]

At 4 A.M., on Friday, November 27, the Georgians marched east along the Orange Plank Road toward Fredericksburg to counter another Federal move. The boom of cannons grew louder with each step. By the end of the day, the brigade formed in line of battle to the right and left of the Orange Plank Road. Stretcher-bearers carried numerous wounded soldiers toward the rear. Others limped toward a safe haven. The scene underscored a hard fight ahead. A cold rain pelted the soldier's backs as they prepared their position. One Georgian wrote, "The cold was very severe and as wagons with baggage could not come near many suffered exceedingly from cold. Fortunately, all were allowed to have large fires notwithstanding the enemy's line was but four to five hundred yards distant."[64]

The brigade withdrew two miles just prior to daybreak on a cold, rainy November 28. Several soldiers deemed the new position on the west side of Mine Run easier to defend.[65] The soldiers scraped at the ground to prepare their new line. Wilcox's Division occupied the right flank. His troops extended north of the Orange Plank Road and south to the Catharpin Road. Anderson's Division stood sandwiched between Wilcox and Ewell's Second Corps to the north.[66] The brigade lines shuffled forward several more times during the day. [67] The following morning, Thomas' Brigade occupied the extreme right wing on the western edge of the Wilderness. The men could see only a few yards ahead in the dense, impenetrable undergrowth. Edward Thomas feared a flank attack. He sent a portion of the brigade forward to reconnoiter. A thick fire from Federal pickets greeted them and they returned to their lines without any casualties.[68] That night an icy wind tore at tree limbs and penetrated soldiers' clothing. The men on the skirmish line, without a warming fire, found themselves in a difficult spot.[69]

The thick area occupied by the brigade lacked hardwood trees. A 45th Georgia officer described the scene. "Nearly all the time we were in a pine thicket and had no wood to burn but the green pines, which we used freely; the wind blew nearly all the time and we were smoked (with the black pine smoke) until the whites of our eyes would shine like those of a 'gentleman just from Ethiopia'."[70]

The Light Division shifted farther right, before daylight on November 30. That night the bitterly cold wind threatened to uproot trees again as the troops moved even farther right. When they halted, the right flank of Thomas' Brigade rested in the yard of Antioch Church. A Confederate attack on December 2 quickly ended when pickets reported that the enemy had retreated. The next morning, Lee's relieved troops marched back to winter quarters at Orange Court House. It appeared that the winter campaign was over.[71]

The difficult conditions had taken their toll. A combination of bad weather, bad food, and what some considered a futile war served to lower morale among the Confederates. The approach of a third Christmas away from family added to this burden. James Garrett stressed, "[W]ar is not the thing it is cracked up to be. I have found that out long ago and to my sorrow at that."[72] Another Georgia soldier wrote, "[W]e were verry tired, sore and worn out, and glad to get back to our comfortable quarters once more."[73]

Private John R. Thomas, Company G, missed the misery of the Mine Run trek because he returned from furlough on December 9. He brought a letter and a package of food for Woodson D. Moon from Moon's family. An ecstatic Moon wrote to his family the following day: "I received some little articles from you and we stewed up the fruit today and baked some pies. I took the best 'bait' I have had since I have been in Virginia, for I was tired of one diet all the time. I have a craving appetite for something nourishing."[74]

Moon then described the hardships of the most recent campaign:

> We have had a hard time from the 27th of November to the 2nd of December. The Yankees crossed the Rapidan on the 26th in force which we had to meet. They crossed at Ely's Ford about twenty miles below this place and about ten miles above Chancellorsville, and there we met them and fortified against them and remained in line of battle for five days and nights in five hundred yards of the Yankee pickets, and in the coldest weather that I ever saw, in an old field and no wood to burn. As to my part, I shivered the worst that I ever did in my life, but the Yankees took a hint and left the night before we intended to attack them the next morning, and I don't think there were many that cared. As to my part, I did not, for I was not anxious to engage them for they had five corps while we had but two, but if they would have stayed till the next morning we would have tried them.

Moon's pent up frustration spilled out when he penned:

> I am awfully tired of this war and would like the best in the world to be at home, but I see no chance for me to get there. I would give my interest in the Confederacy to be relieved of it, for we are whipped anyway, for I see no chance for us to hold our own, for our army is growing weaker everyday and we have no course to go to, while the Yankees have plenty; they have the world open to them, and if we can whip them we can whip the world.

He also mentioned the rumors circulating in camp that the Yankees recruit 15,000 foreigners a week into their army. While untrue, this tale certainly did not improve Confederate morale around Orange Court House in December 1863.[75]

Notes

Abbreviations:

CSR—"Compiled Service Records of Confederate Soldiers Who Served In Organizations From The State of Georgia," Thirty-fifth Infantry Regiment (National Archives Microfilm Publication M266) National Archives Building, Washington, D.C.

GDAH—Georgia Division of Archives and History, Morrow, Ga.

NMP—National Military Park

OR.—*War of the Rebellion: A Compilation of the Official Records of the Union and Confederate Armies.* 130 Vols.

SHSP—Southern Historical Society Papers

1. "Letters and Journal of Major James T. McElvany of the 35th Georgia Infantry Regiment," p.17.
2. "Diary of George W. Hall, 14th Georgia Volunteers, CSA, 1861–1865," Hargrett Rare Book and Manuscript Library/ University of Georgia Libraries, Athens, Ga. p.45.
3. Draughton Stith Haynes, *The Field Diary of A Confederate Soldier-Draughton Stith Haynes-While Serving With the Army of Northern Virginia, CSA.* (49th Ga.)(Darien, Ga. 1963) p.32 (Edited by William G. Haynes, Jr.)
4. McElvany. p.18; Hall, p.45.
5. Ibid. McElvany, p.18; Ibid. Hall p.16, 45.
6. Letter of JT McElvany to "Dear Sisters and Bro. from Camp 35th GA Regt Bunker Hill VA July 19th 1863," James T. McElvany Collection, microfilm, GDAH.
7. Letter of JM Garrett to "Dear Mother from Camp Near Bunkers Hill Va July the 18 1863," James M. Garrett Collection. The identity of Mr. Cumby was not known.
8. McElvany Letters and Journal, p.18–19; OR ., Vol. 27, Pt.II, p.609.
9. Anita B. Sams, *Wayfarers In Walton.* (Atlanta, Ga., 1967) p.169–172.
10. McElvany Letter, July 19th, 1863.

11. Robert E. Lee, *Lee's Dispatches to Jefferson Davis.* (New York, 1957) p.115–116. Douglas S. Freeman and Grady McWhiney, editors.
12. Letters of Private George B. Pass to "Dear Francis & children from Camp Lee Richmond Va June 23 1863," and to "Dear Francis from Camp Lee Richmond Va August 8th/63," and to "Dear Wife & children form Camp Lee August 11th/63," copies of letters sent to author courtesy of Bill Smedlund, Sharpsburg, Ga.- Gene Chatham of Dacula, Ga. and Edwina Pass Bryan of Cleveland, Al. have the originals.
13. Letter of James M. Garrett to "Dear Mother from Camp Near Orange Court House, Saturday August the 22, 1863," James M. Garrett Collection
14. Ibid.
15. Ibid.
16. Ibid.
17. Ibid.
18. Letter of James M. Garrett to "Dear Mother from Camp near Orange Court House VA, Monday Sept the 7th 1:10P 1863," James M. Garrett Collection.
19. Diary of Captain Daniel S. Redding, Co.D, 45th Georgia, March-December 1863, "Confederate Diaries of the War: Soldiers and Citizens, 1860–65," collected and bound by Georgia Division UDC, Vol 5, 1940, p.26–27, located at GDAH.
20. "Letters Received By The Confederate Adjutant and Inspector General, 1861–1865," (National Archives Microfilm Publication M474, roll #69, numbers 16–1165, Jan.-Dec. 1863, Document #859J). National Archives and Records Administration Building, Washington, D.C.
21. Letter of 35th Georgia officers to "Gen'l. S. Cooper A & I Gen'l., CSA, Richmond Va. from Camp 35th Ga. Regt., Sept. 27th 1863," "Letters rec'd. by the Confederate Adjutant and Inspector General 1861–1865," (National Archives Microfilm Publication, M474, roll #69, document #859J) National Archives and Records Administration Building, Washington, D.C.
22. Letter of Company C, 35th Georgia enlisted men to unlisted officer from "Camp 35th Ga Regt Near Poplar Run, Va. Oct 1st 1863," "Letters rec'd. by the Confederate Adjutant and Inspector General 1861–1865," (National Archives Microfilm Publication, M474, roll #69, document #859J) National Archives and Records Administration Building, Washington, D.C.
23. "Army of Northern Virginia General Orders, August 11, 1861- March 27, 1865", National Archives microfilm M921, roll 1, file 0935.
24. Letter of Woodson Daniel Moon, Co.G, 35th Georgia, to "My Dear Charlotte, Camp Near Orange Court House, Va. Sept. 11, 1863," Wm H. Moon, *History of the Moon Family,* (Conyers, Ga. 1920) p.25–26. Note that this letter was already typescripted with punctuation/spelling errors corrected by the editor. This letter and the Moon letter in note #74 are also found in "Reminiscences of Confederate Soldiers and Stories of the War, 1861–65," collected and bound by the Ga. Div. UDC. Vol. 8, p.101–104. located at GDAH.
25. Garrett Letter, September, 7th, 1863.
26. Josiah B. Patterson, "The Incomplete Correspondence of Lt. Josiah B. Patterson, 14th Georgia Infantry," Atlanta Historical Society, Atlanta, Ga. p.49.
27. McElvany. p.19.
28. Redding, p.34.

29. Patterson, p.49.
30. Marion Hill Fitzpatrick, *Letters to Amanda.* (Macon, Ga., 1998) p. 88 (edited by Jeffrey C. Lowe and Sam Hodges).
31. Ibid. p.89.
32. McElvany, p.19.
33. Fitzpatrick, p.90.; *Southern Bivouac,* "The Georgia Deserter," by T.C.E., June 1886-December 1886, Vol.V, reprinted by Broadfoot Publishing Company, Wilmington N.C., 1993, p.196. Note: This article appeared in the actual magazine in the August 1886 edition.
34. Ibid., *Southern Bivouac.*
35. Fitzpatrick, p.90; Ibid, *Southern Bivouac;* McElvany Letters and Journal, p.20; Redding, p.35; Hall, p.25.
36. Ibid., Fitzpatrick, p.90; Ibid., *Southern Bivouac;* Ibid, McElvany, p.20; "Army of Northern Virginia General Orders, August 11, 1861- March 27, 1865," (National Archives microfilm M921, roll 1, file 0935).
37. Letter of James M. Garrett to "Dear Mother from Camp Near Orange Court House Va September the 29th 1863," James M Garrett Collection.
38. Letter of James M Garrett to "Dear Mother from Orange Court House Va Oct the 8th 1864," James M. Garrett Collection.
39. "Army of Northern Virginia General Orders, August 11, 1861-March 27, 1865," National Archives publication M921, roll 1, file #anv0019. National Archives, Washington, D.C. I wish to thank Dr. Thomas Lowry with "The Index Project, Inc." (Woodbridge, Va.) for providing me with all the court-martials on file for Thomas' Brigade.
40. Ibid., file#anv0975.
41. "Confederate Adjutant and Inspector Generals Office-General Orders 1861–65," National Archives, Washington, D.C.
42. Garrett Letter. October 8th, 1863.
43. McElvany Letters and Journal, p.21; Hall, p.26.
44. Ibid. McElvany, p.20–22; Ibid. Hall, p.26–28; Redding, p.33–35; Letter of James Garrett to "Dear Mother from Camp Near Rappahanoc River Va October 30th 1863," James M. Garrett Collection.
45. Letter of Stephen Lafayette Moon to "Dear Father and Mother from Camp near Brandy Station Virginia—October 20," in "Reminiscences of Confederate Soldiers and Stories of the War 1861–65," Volume XIII. Collected by Ga. Division, United Daughters of the Confederacy, , p.108–109. located at GDAH. There is no year listed for the letter but it was most definitely written in 1863 right after the Battle at Bristoe Station.
46. Letter of WT Formby to "Mrs EJ Garrett Dear Friend from Camps Near Brandy Station Oct 25th 1863," James M. Garrett Collection.
47. McElvany, p. 20–22; Garrett Letter. October 30, 1863; Redding, p.39.
48. Stephen Lafayette Moon Letter, October 20.
49. Garrett Letter. October 30, 1863.
50. Ibid. Garrett.
51. Patterson, p.51.

52. Letter of Ivy W. Duggan (49th Georgia Infantry) to "Editor, *Central Georgian* (Sandersville, Ga), Camp Near Orange CH, Va., November 18, 1863."
53. Garrett Letter, October 30, 1863.
54. Stephen L. Moon Letter. October 20. There is no year listed for the letter but it was most definitely written in 1863 right after the Battle at Bristoe Station. With Longstreet's corps already in Tennessee, Lee would never strip his army and Virginia of the equivalent of another corps to send to the west. If he did so, it would only leave one Confederate corps (three divisions) plus a cavalry division to face Meade's Army of the Potomac. However, a good camp rumor was usually never swayed by logic. The derision that many of Lee's men held for the poor fighting prowess of their counterparts in Major General Braxton Bragg's Army of Tennessee was apparent in Moon's letter.
55. "Letters Received by the Confederate Adjutant and Inspector General and the Quartermaster General, 1861–1865," (National Archives Microfilm Publication M474, roll 68, document 1941) National Archives Building, Washington, D.C.
56. Redding, p.42; Hall, p.30.
57. McElvany. p. 20–22; Ibid., Redding, p.42–43; Ibid., Hall, p.29–30.
58. Letter of James M. Garrett to "Dear Mother, Camp Near Orange Court House Va, November the 17th 1863," James M.Garrett Collection.
59. Ibid.
60. Ibid.
61. Ibid.
62. Ibid.
63. Letter of James M. Garrett to "Dear Mother, Camp Near Orange Courthouse Va, November 26, 1863," James M. Garrett Collection.
64. Letter of Ivy W. Duggan (49th Georgia Infantry) to "Editor, *Central Georgian* (Sandersville, Ga), Camp Near Orange CH, Va., December 8, 1863."
65. Redding, p.46; Hall, p.31–32; *OR* ., Vol.29, Pt.I, p.895–896.
66. Ibid., Vol. 29, Pt. I, p.895–896.
67. Redding, p.41; Hall, p.32.
68. Ibid., Redding p.41–42; Ibid., Hall p.32.
69. J.F.J. Caldwell, *The History of a Brigade of South Carolinians Known As 'Gregg's', and Subsequently As 'McGowan's' Brigade.* (Philadelphia, 1866) (Morningside Press reprint, p.166).
70. Letter of Charles A. Conn to "Miss Carrie Fair from 'Camp Pleasant' near Orange C.H. Va. Dec.9,1863,"(45th Ga.). *The Georgia Historical Quarterly.* Vol.XLVI 1962, p.191–192.
71. OR ., Vol. 29, Pt.I, p.896.
72. Garrett Letter, November 17, 1863.
73. Hall, p.32.
74. Letter of Woodson D. Moon to "Dear Wife and Children from Camp Near Orange C.H. Va. Dec.10, 1863." *History of the Moon Family,* p.26–27. See notes accompanying #24 above. This letter and the Moon letter in note #24 are also found in "Reminiscences of Confederate Soldiers and Stories of the War, 1861–65," collected and bound by the Ga. Div. UDC. Vol. 8, p.101–104. located at GDAH.
75. Ibid.

Chapter Eleven

A Tough Winter in the Valley

"Send me some fried chicken if you have got it."
Private James M. Garrett

Several officers in the 35th Georgia received promotions in late 1863. Captain Lee A.J. Williams, the Company D commander, moved up to major on December 23. He succeeded Major William L. Groves, from Chattooga County, who had been elected to serve in the Georgia Legislature. First Lieutenant John M. Mitchell became captain and replaced Williams at the helm of Company D. First Lieutenant Ezekial Mason Roberts moved to captain of Company H.

The forty-one-year-old Groves had been involved in a tragic situation at the beginning of the war. Fortunately for his family, this situation had a humorous and happy ending. In July 1861, even before he formed Company I in Chattooga County, Groves received the first casualty reports of the Battle of First Manassas. One of the dispatches reported that Groves' brother-in-law, Captain Dunlap Scott, had been killed. Scott served in the brigade commanded by Colonel Francis Bartow, who received mortal wounds in the same fight. Groves immediately departed for Virginia to bring the young captain's body back to Georgia for a proper burial. Groves stopped in Rome, Georgia and purchased a metal coffin and then continued by train on the sad trip to Virginia. A protective box encased the coffin. Written on top of the box was the name "W.L. Groves." When Groves arrived in Richmond, he received a pleasant surprise. Captain Scott was very much alive and back with his unit at Manassas. Groves hastily left the coffin on the railroad platform in Richmond and boarded a train to Manassas. The depot agent assumed the coffin contained a dead soldier. After several days, numerous people complained to the station agent about the offensive smell emitting from the coffin. The agent sent a letter to the Richmond mayor about the situation and asked him to have it removed. The mayor failed to send a speedy reply, so the agent reluctantly opened the coffin and received a surprise to find it empty. Groves finally returned to claim his box as well as a good laugh.[1]

At Orange Court House everybody prepared huts for a winter that had already arrived. Private James Garrett described his shelter: "I am building myself a house to live in this winter. [I]t is twelve feet long and ten wide. James Dunson is going to live with me. [W]hen I get in it will be all write for the winter if we don't have to move again."[2] A soldier in the 14th Georgia recorded, "[W]e are now verry comfortable situated. [A]ll the co [company] has very warm shanties." By the second week of December, frustration and indignation mounted as rumors circulated of another move.[3]

Garrett reported on December 12, "I am as well as any body could wish at present. [T]he company is well generally. [W]e have but two sick men in the company and one of them is going to get a furlough and the other a transfer to work in a government shop." He apologized for not putting a stamp on the letter because of a stamp shortage in camp.[4]

The growing Confederate food shortage and its resultant exorbitant food prices had a grave consequence—gnawing hunger for many soldiers. James Garrett wrote his mother for her help:

> [T]he reason I am writing this letter so soon is because Captain Virgil L. Hopson is at home (LaGrange) & I thought maybe you could get him to bring my things from home. [H]e is Quartermaster of the Regiment now. James Dunson wrote his father to send him a box by Hopson and told me to write to you and tell you to put my things in the box with his. [Y]ou had better go up and see Mr Dunson and see if he is going to put up a box. [I]f so you put my things in with his. [A]nything would be acceptable from home now if it was nothing but a potato or two or three biscuits or even a pone of corn bread. [F]or something to eat is scarce here as sure as you are born. Look a hear now dont you forget that bottle of brandy now whatever you do. [B]randy is worth twenty dollars a quart here.

Garrett then repeated a request from a previous letter, "I kneed my gloves worse than anything else. [M]aybe Hopson will bring them if nothing else." He apologized for not sending her any money:

> Ma I have been writing to you that I would send you some money but I tell you I believe it will take all that I get to buy something to eat with. [W]e have to pay two dollars a gallon for meal and meat is not to be found at any price. You had better see Hopson rite away for his furlough will be out pretty soon about the last of this month.

> [D]ont forget the brandy. Send me some fried chicken if you have got it. Some butter anyhow.[5]

During this period, several soldiers in Company G went on a night adventure under the protection of darkness. Corporal Thomas A. "Dink" Harmon led Privates Augustus J. Moon and James H. Nunnally on a mission to alleviate some of their hunger. They left camp without the required pass. Each soldier lugged seven canteens slung over his shoulder to "Juice somebody's cow and get a load of milk. They ran upon a Provost Marshall and had to flee to keep from being caught, but James Nunnally had a cripple leg and was caught." There was no mention of what happened to the slow moving private for this midnight cow caper, but he probably spent some extra time on guard duty or worse.[6]

Private Dock Knight, Company G, provided fodder for his hilarious reputation at this time of scarce provisions. The quartermaster issued rations for several days. Dock found a comfortable place to sit down and he

Major William Lorcas Groves, Co.I

The Chattooga County native was the first commander of Company I. He received a promotion to major in late-1862. A year later he resigned after the citizens of his county elected him to the Georgia legislature.

From *Sunny South,* Atlanta, Ga. May 2, 1891

ate all his food at once. He reasoned "he was going to get the good of it while he had it."[7]

Branches of the Moon family from Walton County provided twelve members to the 35th Georgia—eleven of them in Company G. Interesting situations in the company usually involved a Moon. The small stature of DeKalb Moon came in handy in an undated incident. "One day they could not locate the Yankees and the commanding officer called for a volunteer to climb a tall tree to see if any could be seen. DeKalb volunteered and climbed the tree and shouted back that he could see Yankees everywhere closing in on them. As he hastened down a command was given to fall in at once." Wherever this occurred, they must have pushed the enemy back because officers reportedly called on his tree climbing skills thirty-nine times at the same spot. Another series of Moon stories starred Corporal Edom T. Moon. Edom developed a reputation as a camp prankster:

> He made as fine a clown as you ever saw. He and two or three of his friends built a bush arbor and ran a regular theater while in Camp. Although he weighed over 200 lbs he could turn a summersault and catch on his feet, walk on his hands with his feet above his head. He was walking about one day alone, and happened to have his gun, when he came to an old house with fifteen Yankees in it. He knew he would be captured if he did not do something quick—He yelled out 'Surround the House boys'—He then went to the door and said–'Throw down your guns and march out double quick.' They all obeyed his orders and marched out—he got behind them and marched them into camp single handed.[8]

The movement rumors became a reality on December 15. At 4 P.M., the brigade marched to the Orange and Alexandria Railroad depot and stood in the cold awaiting a train. One officer in the 45th Georgia echoed a common disappointment when he wrote, "We regret to leave our quarters to go up into the mountains."[9] They climbed aboard the boxcars around 10 P.M., and rolled south to Gordonsville. There they changed to a Virginia Central train bound for the Shenandoah Valley. The men again crowded into boxcars, but some suffered the misfortune to ride in open cars through the chilly night air as the train moved slowly west. Just before daylight, on December 16, the train passed through Charlottesville. The following day they reached Staunton. After a lengthy wait, the train continued ten miles west to Buffalo Gap and stopped. There the cramped, restless soldiers spent an uncomfortable night in the cars. While the men tried to sleep, a sleet storm sculpted a spectacular ice display for the morning sun. The rain froze as fast as it touched the ground. Tabs of ice hung from everything. The troops again boarded the train and returned to Staunton. The 35th and 49th Georgia regiments remained on the train, which then reversed direction again and proceeded through Buffalo Gap southwest to Millboro, Virginia. The following morning, Saturday, December 19, the men of the 45th and 14th Georgia regiments joined their sister regiments at Millboro. In the driving wind and snow, the soldiers used every bit of wood in the area to fuel campfires. They even tore down an elderly man's wooden fence and burned it. The following morning, the commander of the 45th Georgia paid him $133 because the hungry soldiers also stole his axes, cabbage and potatoes.[10]

Major General Jubal A. Early commanded the Confederate forces in the Shenandoah Valley. Early's mission was to counter a Federal onslaught of cavalry and infantry led by Major General William W. Averell. The infantry brigades of Thomas and Henry Harrison Walker strengthened Early's force. Averell's men had raided the East Tennessee and Virginia Railroad near Salem, Virginia during the third week of December. Some Confederates believed that Averell's force would try to slip back into the Shenandoah Valley via Millboro. Thomas' Georgians hoped to head them off, but the enemy took a different route.[11]

At 11 A.M., on December 20, Thomas' Brigade climbed on the train and rode back to Staunton. Reports soon reached town of another Federal force located near Harrisonburg, Virginia. The Georgians, now on foot, marched twenty-four miles north along the Valley Pike. Early's force comprised a home guard of about one hundred mounted men, two pieces of artillery and the infantry brigades of Thomas and Walker. On December 21, the Union troops at Harrisonburg withdrew as Early approached. The Confederates continued an exhausting pursuit for thirty-two miles in a biting wind. An officer in the 45th Georgia wrote:

> Altogether I think this is the severest campaign we've ever passed through. Having experienced during the past week, rain, sleet and snow, with keen and bitter winds, but the boys have stood it like heroes. On the severe march Monday, which was twice the distance we usually march, I did not have a straggler, and there were very few from the Brigade. Although hundreds were limping with sore feet and legs everyone seemed to press forward and determined, if possible to keep up.[12]

Another Georgian described his exhaustion. "[M]y feet was so sore I could scarcely put them to the ground and the cold weather had nearly used me up. [W]hen we got to camp I could scarcely put one foot before the other."[13] The march continued again the following day, but halted at the abandoned Yankee campsites at New Market. The Southern force soon moved east and occupied New Market Gap on Massanutten Mountain, two miles from New Market.

Thomas' Brigade celebrated their third Christmas of the war on the outskirts of New Market. One officer wrote he had bought some pies and had eaten well, but would rather have spent the day at home with his family.[14] Another soldier described the day as "[A] dull time to us in the cold wind among the ice." He expressed more optimism in a diary notation the following day. "I go out foraging and get butter, milk and cabbage. [H]ave a dinner that is good to the taste of a poor soldier, a luxury we seldom have. [W]e fair a good deal better in regard to something in the valley than we did with the main army."[15]

James Garrett wrote a hastily scribbled short note on December 26. Christmas failed to make an impression on him because he did not even mention it. He described their difficult journey of the past two weeks. "[W]e have been lying out ever since with out any tents. [I]t rained all day and it frozed as fast as it fell and continued to rain until in the night. [W]e went on the rail road to Staunton and then we marched to this place a distance of forty three miles in a day and a have [half]." With the numerous movements, he feared that his mail might get misdirected or even worse—stolen. He urged his mother, "[D]ont send my things if you have not done it until I write again."[16]

Despite this winter campaign of hard marching amidst the brutality of winter there was one positive constant. The soldiers received a warm reception from most of the Shenandoah Valley residents. George W. Hall, 14th Georgia, described his experience while foraging for food. "[T]he people of this valley are the kindest and most benevolent of any place I have ever known."[17] Captain Daniel S. Redding, 45th Georgia, wrote, "The people of New Market treat us liberally."[18]

Thomas' Brigade marched north on the last day of 1863 and camped on Fisher's Hill, a high prominence two miles south of Strasburg. The thermometer on New Year's Day hovered near zero.[19] A Confederate cavalry brigade commanded by Colonel George H. Smith occupied Winchester. These troopers rode north and attacked the B&O Railroad seizing a large cache of supplies. On January 2, 1864, Thomas' Brigade received orders to move north toward Colonel Smith to guard the wagon train of captured supplies. Edward Thomas wrote to General Early the same day and stressed, "A great many of my men are without shoes, so I hope we will have as little marching as possible."[20] George Hall wrote the same day that, "[I]t is affirmed by citizens that the weather was colder last night than in five years before."[21]

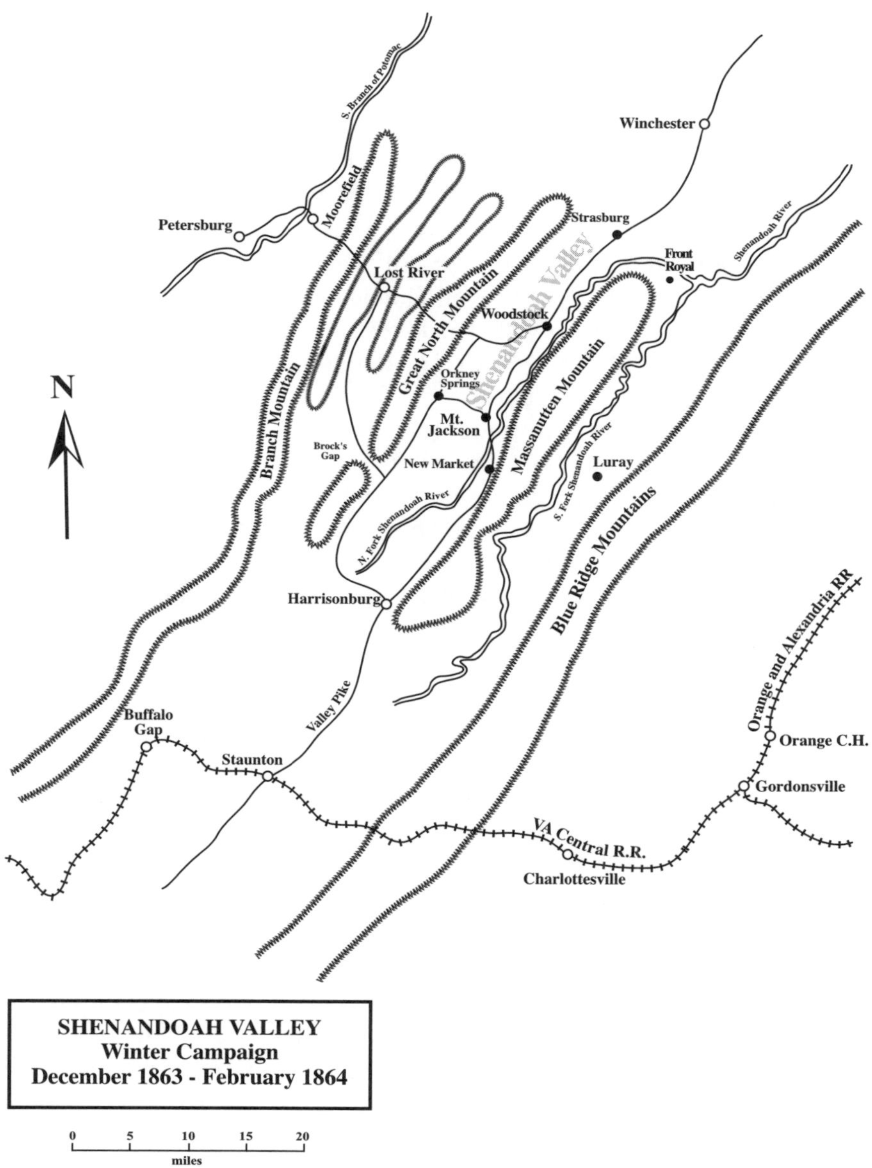
S. Branch of Potomac
Winchester
Moorefield
Petersburg
Strasburg
Shenandoah Valley
Front Royal
Shenandoah River
Lost River
Great North Mountain
Woodstock
Branch Mountain
Orkney Springs
Mt. Jackson
Massanutten Mountain
Brock's Gap
New Market
Luray
S. Fork Shenandoah River
N. Fork Shenandoah River
Blue Ridge Mountains
Harrisonburg
Orange and Alexandria RR
Valley Pike
Buffalo Gap
Orange C.H.
Staunton
Gordonsville
VA Central R.R.
Charlottesville
N
SHENANDOAH VALLEY
Winter Campaign
December 1863 - February 1864
0 5 10 15 20
miles

The Georgians continued their northward march. They passed through Middletown and halted on the north side of the village. Edward Thomas reported that the enemy remained in considerable force at Front Royal. He sent the 14th and elements of the 49th Georgia regiments back to Strasburg to block an enemy crossing of the Shenandoah River. On January 4, the 35th and 45th Georgia regiments reversed course and marched through a heavy snowfall back to Fisher's Hill. The next morning nearly a foot of cold powder covered the ground.[22]

It snowed in spurts until the brigade moved all the way back to Staunton on January 9. Early described the difficult conditions the men endured and he saluted their mettle. "While we were at Fisher's Hill, there were two heavy snows, and there was very hard freezing weather all the time. The men had no tents and their only shelter consisted of rude open sheds made of split wood, yet, though Thomas' was a Georgia brigade, they stood the weather remarkably well and seemed to take a pleasure in the expedition, regretting when the time came to fall back."[23]

As the column headed south along the Valley Pike, the men slipped and slid along the road, but the wagon trains had an even tougher time. The teamsters harnessed extra horses to pull the wagons through the snow and ice. Shoeless soldiers hitched rides in the wagons, but this did not help ease the aching cold. Four days later they had covered the seventy-two miles, but illness and exhaustion gripped two-thirds of the brigade.[24] In a letter written from Staunton, James Garrett described the trying conditions for an infantryman:

> I have been suffering for several days with that pain over my eye again. [T]he Doctor gave me twelve grains of Quinine this morning. [I]t don't seem to do me much good. I am well all but that. [W]e are camped two miles from Staunton. [W]e marched seventy two miles in four days. I was bare footed and got to ride all the way. [T]he snow was six inches deep. I have got shoes now. I want you to get me a hat and send me. [T]he hat I got was not much account. [I]t is worn out aready. I want you to get me as light a one as you can and a good one.[25]

Another Georgian described the arduous trek of the shoeless infantrymen up and down the macadamized Valley Turnpike. "And now you have heard of Our Revolutionary Soldiers marching through the snow and you could trail them by the blood. This I saw with my own eyes. It was impossible to get shoes until we got to Staunton."[26]

Supplies failed to reach the troops, even around Staunton with its rail connection. James Garrett asked his mother to send the items he had requested in mid-December. He perhaps figured they would stay put in Staunton for some time. Garrett suggested his mother take his requested items to Private Green Gatlin's (Lemuel G. Gatlin) home because Gatlin was there on furlough. If that failed, he suggested that Corporal Rholly Willingham (Rolla H. Willingham) could return with the supplies since he was due for a furlough.[27]

Garrett, James Dunson and James Newton Craig messed together for eating and sleeping in Staunton. "Peter cooks for us and does our washing. I would send you more money but I am obliged to have money here to buy something to eat with for we dont draw enough. I can take all the flour that we draw for a days rations and eat it all at one meal." The unidentified Peter was probably a servant for either Dunson or Craig.[28]

Many soldiers assumed the brigade would board a train in Staunton and return to Orange Court House. A week passed as each regiment rotated as provost guard for the city of Staunton. Because of General Order #1, issued on January 1, 1864, most soldiers tried to arrange a furlough. The order authorized a furlough of up to thirty days for every enlisted man who furnished to any company in the Army of Northern Virginia an able-bodied recruit for the duration of the war. Able-bodied meant the recruit had to be healthy, not already enlisted, and not a deserter. The order inspired numerous attempts, both honorable and dishonorable, for a furlough. James Garrett figured his younger brother would be conscripted anyway so he repeatedly wrote home to his mother and asked that his brother, William A. (Bud), be sent to Company D so that James could come home.[29]

The brigade again marched north on January 19. Garrett wrote a letter on January 25 from Taylor Springs, four miles east of Harrisonburg. Jonathan and William Taylor had purchased Taylor Springs in 1814. The clean, cool tasting water and picturesque setting of the area had made this place a popular meeting site for Indians and early Valley settlers.[30]

The paymaster caught up with the men on their trip back down the Valley. The soldiers received pay on January 24, and Garrett drew ninety-six dollars. He reported that after he paid his debts he still had seventy-five dollars left. He promised to send some of it home via a soldier on furlough. Garrett headed into Harrisonburg after drawing his pay and he reported, "I went to town yesterday and weighed. I weighed a hundred and sixty pounds." He pleaded with his mother to send the requested box of items back with Rolla Willingham if she had not already sent them. He reported imbibing one of his favorite things from home:

> I got a few swallows of good old Georgia peach Brandy the other knight. [I]t made me feel tolerable sick. I want you to send me a

> bottle before yours is all gone and some butter to. I tried to buy some butter in town yesterday and what do you reckon they ask me for it. [F]ive dollars a pound. [T]hat is a little more than I can afford to pay. I went to a citizens home yesterday and eat dinner. [I]t cost me a dollar & a half. I had a very good dinner. [W]e dont draw anything but flour & pork & a little salt. [W]e are camp[ed] twenty five miles from the railroad and have not got any tents yet nor dont know when we will get any. I don [doing] fairly. I have got a little yankee tent that I carry on my back.

Garrett mentioned that several men in Company D from Hogansville, Georgia would soon start home on a furlough. They were Corporal Hiram J. Franklin, Sergeant William T. Scogin, Private George W. Redding, and Corporal Rolla H. Willingham.[31]

Imagine James Garrett's excitement when Private John R. Mooty walked into camp from furlough. Mooty held in his hands Garrett's box filled with provisions from home. Garrett wrote:

> [H]e brought my things through all right. [M]y pants are two [too] long for me. I traded them to Segt John B Hester for two pair of government pants. So I will have pants enough to do me all year. I have got a new pairs of pants now. [M]y things come in a bad time. [W]e had orders to leave this morning [January 26] but the order is countermanded. [W]e will leave in the morning at 8 o clock.

Garrett worried about having to carry these new items and described his solution. "I got Quincy Moore [Sgt. Wilson J. Moore] to carry my quilt and cape. [H]e is an ambulance driver. So I am all right." All of Garrett's friends watched with interest as he opened the box. "[M]y brandy and honey went well here. I eat my biscuits for breakfast this morning. [I]f ever I get home again I will learn you all how to cook. I will show you how to bake biscuits with out burning them up." Newly flush with money, he visited some of the area farmers to purchase food. "I went a forageing yesterday. I bought: two dollars worth of meal; two cabbage heads; one chicken; quart of butter milk; quart of apple jelly; seventy five cents worth of soap. I got my chicken for 50 cents. I have got soap enough to do me a long time to wash my clothes with." Garrett again urged his mother to send his brother to the 35th Georgia so he could get a thirty-day furlough. Around the campfires that night, soldiers speculated about where the men would march the following morning. "I dont know where we will go to from here," Garrett wrote. "Some of the boys think that we will cross the aleganiy [Allegheny] mountains. I for my part I dont know where we will go and dont much care. I have trudged about so much untill I dont care for which way we go."[32]

On January 27, Thomas' men marched north, at a rapid pace, past Harrisonburg and New Market to rendezvous with the rest of Early's troops. The following day the Georgians joined with Brigadier General Thomas L. Rosser's cavalry brigade, Captain Harry W. Gilmor's and Captain John H. McNeill's Partisan Rangers, and four guns of Captain John H. McClanahan's Battery. Jubal Early left John D. Imboden's cavalry brigade and Henry Walker's infantry brigade at Mount Jackson to guard the Valley. He ordered the horse-mounted troops to move from Mount Jackson through Brock's Gap in the Allegheny Mountains into the Lost River Valley. Edward Thomas' infantry trekked through the steeper pass at Orkney Springs into the same valley.[33] They moved toward Moorefield in Hardy County in western Virginia, but the real objective was the capture of the Federal garrison at Petersburg (not the same Petersburg south of Richmond). This area represented the most rugged country that the Georgians encountered during the war.[34]

On the same day, a Federal column comprised of eighty wagons loaded with supplies rolled south from New Creek. They carried supplies for the garrison at Petersburg, about forty-eight road miles distant. Federal officers halted the supply train because of citizen warnings of Confederate troops in the area. These wagons turned back toward New Creek for fear of attack. On January 29, Federal authorities increased the number of guards and the wagons rolled again under the watchful eyes of infantry and cavalry commanded by Colonel Joseph Snider, 4th West Virginia Cavalry. The following day, Thomas Rosser's Confederate troopers attacked and captured the wagon train. The confused defenders and wagon drivers ran off into the mountains.[35]

Edward Thomas' men had followed a narrow muddy road across numerous foggy peaks for three days. They halted within eight miles of Petersburg on the evening of January 30.[36] Many soldiers wondered why they had tramped around the rugged mountains in such horrible weather. General Early knew of his soldier's sentiment. Early wrote, "Thomas' Georgians, moving along the summit of Branch Mountain with nothing but wild inaccessible mountains and deep ravines on each side as far as the eye could reach, could not understand why they were carried over such a route at this season. . . ."[37] Private Frank Edwards, Company D, had some ideas. "Don't you know we dreaded that wild chase through the sleet and snow? That was a great place for applejack, and General Early drank a great deal. We decided that was the greatest reason for going over there. General Early claimed there was a great quantity of sugar, coffee, meat, flour, and fish

Captain Ezekiel Mason Roberts, Co.H

Roberts originally enlisted in the 8th Georgia. He transferred to the 35th Georgia and the men soon elected him to a lieutenant's position. He eventually replaced Captain Charles Tuggle as commander of Company H. Tuggle was captured at Gettysburg and died at the Federal prison camp at Johnson's Island, Ohio. Roberts tendered his resignation on February 3, 1865, on grounds he was incompetent to be the captain. The resignation became effective March 1, 1865.

From *Sunny South,* Atlanta, Ga. May 2, 1891

there, but did not mention applejack. We learned from old citizens that there was a large distillery at the foot of the mountain." Edwards claimed that Jubal Early placed a guard at the distillery with orders that no private soldier was to enter. This preferential treatment angered the troops as officers went in and filled their canteens. Generals Thomas and Early received their share and the pair rode on down the road. "The boys decided to go into that distillery. The guard ordered us to halt, but the boys went right in. I think there must have been twenty-five barrels of apple-jack in that building. The boys knocked the heads out of a great many of the barrels, and everybody drank all they wanted, filled up their canteens and went to the camp. All the officers were drunk, and the whole brigade of soldiers. I never saw so many drunk men as I saw there."[38]

Early claimed that his men's spirits soared when they looked down on the beautiful Moorefield valley. Things improved "by the sight of a large number of beautiful girls rushing out to see and welcome 'our' infantry, as they called it . . . ." He recalled, "The Georgians were ready then to go anywhere."[39]

Colonel Joseph Thoburn, 1st West Virginia Infantry, commanded the Union detachment at Petersburg. Thoburn tried to make sense of the numerous reports that reached him of the converging Confederate columns. One of the reports informed him that the wagon train with their much-needed supplies had been captured. He described what happened then: "A little after dark a scouting party brought in a prisoner taken from Early, as he was going into camp on the Moorefield road, 6 or 7 miles from Petersburg, from whom we learned that we would be attacked the following morning at daylight. At midnight, every preparation being completed, the command moved off quietly, taking with us, with some trifling exceptions, all our stores and Government property."[40]

A thick cold fog greeted the Georgians on the morning of January 31. The 49th Georgia took the direct road toward Petersburg. This road passed through a narrow defile with the South Branch of the Potomac River on the left and a steep vertical precipice on the right. The rest of the brigade ascended a steep craggy mountain and crept along a narrow, seldom used path covered in underbrush. They followed the path along the ridge crest and hoped to descend in a surprise attack from the north of town. Everybody anticipated complete surprise due to the veil of fog, but their hopes shattered when they discovered the enemy had evacuated during the night.[41] Jubal Early reported, "The works at Petersburg were found to be very strong with a ditch around them and very strong abatis. There were large bomb-proof shelters, and appearances indicated that a good deal of work had been done lately."[42] James Garrett expressed frustration that despite their efforts the enemy escaped:

> [W]e made a pretty good haul on them the other day but we had some very hard marching to do it. [W]e marched eighty miles in four days. [W]e came very near capturing the whole garrison if it had not been for the bridge breaking down with us we would have got the whole of them. [W]hile we was fixing up the bridge they found us and left in double quick time leaving all there baggage in our hands together with a lot of bacon and corn, sugar, coffee, soap, and everything else that you could want. [S]ome of the Yankees had their wifes there with them and they went off in such a hurry that they left them. [Y]ou may know they were in a big hurry to get off.[43]

Entrance To Petersburg, West Virginia

View looking NE down road toward Moorefield, W.Va. The South Fork of the Potomac River flows through the pass just right of the road. The 14th Georgia followed this road into Petersburg while the 35th, 45th and 49th Georgia Regiments climbed the rocky mountain on the left to attack the Federal garrison at Fort Mulligan.

photo by author

The Georgians discovered the bomb-proof shelters held a large quantity of ammunition as well as supplies. The men jubilantly seized the commissary stores and ammunition and then destroyed the enemy fortifications and winter quarters.[44]

Frank Edwards expressed thanks for the captured supplies. "We had all we wanted to eat. There were a great many pretty girls over there; before we came they claimed to be yankees; when we made our appearance they were Southern. The people in this valley were very intelligent, had plenty to eat and drink. None of the men belonged to the army. They were for both sides."[45]

Colonel Thoburn proudly wrote that his blue-clad troops reached New Creek, on February 1, after a cold tiring trek through the mountains. "The column arrived in good condition, without casualty or disaster on the way, with the exception of a few stragglers that were picked up by the enemy while in a state of intoxication." These drunken stragglers included two captains.[46]

Captain Washington T. Irvine, Company I, wrote that the brigade-size Federal garrison would have inflicted a number of casualties on the Geor-

Federal Fort Mulligan at Petersburg, West Virginia

This aerial view looks west. Note the large bombproof in the middle of the photo. The diminished walls in the middle of the largest bombproof perhaps came from explosive charges placed by the Georgians. Federal soldiers built winter huts along the wooded hill side at the upper left of photo. This extensive fort is quite well preserved.

photo courtesy of Kenneth R. Shobe, South Branch Valley Civil War Society, Inc.

gians if the enemy had not abandoned their strong position. Irvine claimed that their good fortune to not have to fight their way into Petersburg was because of a captured soldier in Company C. "The evening before, however, while crossing the stream on a log or footbridge, private John N. Smith of Company C [Corporal John W. Smith], the 35th, fell into the water, and getting out on the side next [to] the enemy, went up to a house to warm himself. There he was captured and conveyed to the general commanding the Post. When Smith was asked about Early's force, he gave such an exaggerated account of the number of infantry, artillery and cavalry, that the commander [Thoburn] beat a retreat that night."[47] Smith probably was the captured Confederate soldier that Colonel Thoburn described in his report.

On February 1, the Georgians marched back toward Moorefield with the fifty-one wagons captured by Rosser's cavalry. Rosser's Brigade had spurred on to Romney to capture some cattle and sheep. The following day, the spirits of the weary infantrymen soared because the commissary officers issued the captured rations. The hungry soldiers sampled beans, rice, pickled pork, bacon, sugar, coffee, salt, black pepper and cornmeal.[48]

Rear Wall of Federal Fort Mulligan

View looking NE. This precipice commands the whole area overlooking Petersburg, West Virginia. Federal troops under command of Colonel James Mulligan constructed this impressive fort from August-December 1863.

photo by author

Early's command began the arduous trek back to the Shenandoah Valley in the early morning darkness of February 4. The 14th Georgia headed the column. They led a parade that included the 51 wagons, 1200 beef cattle, 500 sheep, and the rest of Thomas' Brigade with Rosser's cavalry guarding the rear. The soldiers of the 35th, 45th and 49th Georgia regiments gingerly stepped around and over the numerous animal droppings. The stench was terrible. Two and a half hours later the rumble of cannon fire echoed off the hills. A Federal cavalry brigade, commanded by Lieutenant Colonel Fitz Simmons, had appeared just north of Moorefield on the Romney Road. Edward Thomas rapidly reversed the march of his infantry and rushed toward Moorefield. By noon, the blue horsemen failed to make a move so Jubal Early ordered Thomas' troops to return up the mountain where the 14th Georgia had remained with the rest of the column.[49]

On February 5, the wagon train rolled through Brock's Gap west of Mount Jackson. One soldier expressed his jubilation over returning to the Valley in a diary notation. "As we descend the last range of mountains between us and the Shenandoah Valley the most beautiful view I ever saw presents it self to us. [T]he wide extensive valley dotted over with a hun-

Rear Wall of Fort Mulligan
View looking SW showing formidable rear wall of Federal fort. Interior of fort housed four large bombproofs. The outside dimensions of one of these thick bombproofs was 200 feet by 55 feet.
photo by author

dred towns and villages. [T]he broad fields and beautiful farm houses extending away from Winchester to Staunton, brings vivid to my memory happier scenes of by gone days."[50]

The column reached the Shenandoah Valley without any further incident. During the entire operation, the 35th Georgia had two men killed. General Early reported, "We found the people of Moorefield and the adjoining valley very true to our cause, and exceedingly kind and hospitable to our men."[51]

The Georgians reached Taylor Springs, east of Harrisonburg, on the evening of Sunday, February 7. To the consternation of the brigade chaplains, members of the 35th Georgia threw a party even though it was the Sabbath. James Garrett described the celebration: "[W]e had a gay time of it last night after we got back. [T]he boys drunk about two hundred dollars worth of whisky. I was out of it my self. I would like to have a little once in a while but it takes two much money." His hangover the following morning left him in sad shape. "I feel pretty smartly jaded this morning."[52] Perhaps this party spurred the search for a regimental chaplain to help quell the wayward men. A week later, Chaplain John H. Taylor arrived for his assignment with the 35th Georgia.

Garrett described the difficult ordeal of the previous eleven days:

> I have marched one hundred & sixty miles since I wrote to you last. [W]e got back last night. [W]e marched across home of the highest mountain in Va. [W]e captured one hundred and fifteen wagons. [T]welve hundred head of beef cattle. Six hundred head of sheep and run the Yankees off [and] burnd thare camps and never lost but two men killed. [W]e captured some old rye coffee & sugar. I had coffee for breakfast this morning.

He closed his letter with, "Mother I am so fateagued that you will have to put up with a short letter. I hope you will excuse me. Tell Sapphronia I wrote her a letter and she never has answered it. [T]hat is not treating me rite." Whether Garrett was fatigued from the long march or the exuberance of the night before was unknown—perhaps it was a combination of the two. He mentioned that he had some money he wanted to send home, but there was nobody leaving on furlough that he could trust.[53]

Word reached Thomas' men that the remainder of Wilcox's Light Division, encamped at Orange Court House, had reenlisted for the war. Garrett accepted the reality of his situation when he wrote:

> I guess we will all reinlist as soon as our time is out. [T]here is no use tring [trying] to get out of it for if we dont reinlist we will be conscribed. [S]o we just as well reinlist and be done with it. [W]e have got to have an army as long as the war lasts. [T]his war is getting to be a desperate thing. [I]t cant last much longer.[54]

He then complained of the immediate economic effect of the war. "[E]very things so high that poor people cant live. [T]his sheet of paper that I am writing on cost me fifty cents. [F]lour is worth two hundred dollars a barrel here. I dont see for my part how the poor class of people is to live." He inquired about the corn planting back home and again asked about his brother Bud:

> [I]f there is any chance for you to keep Bud at home I want you to do it. [I]f there is know [no] chance I would like for him to come here for if he comes here I can get a thirty days furlough. [H]e had just as well come here as to go in State service for he will be turned over to Jeff Davis before long any how and so he might as well come here and be done with it but I want you to keep him at home as long as you can. John [youngest brother] is old enough to begin to learn to plow. [Y]ou ought to have him at it if you havent before now. [H]e and the girls can make enough corn to do you if they will try.[55]

Garrett reported from Taylor Springs on February 14: "The wind is blowing very hard today and the fire has got out of the camp. [T]he boys are putting it out." The other problem of this day was empty stomachs. "[H]ave not had anything to eat today and will not get any untill evening. [W]e dont get enough in camp know [no] how."[56]

Frank Edwards related a humorous story that probably occurred in the Shenandoah Valley. He and a friend left camp one day during a snowstorm to search for two necessities they lacked—salt and soap:

> We could not get our hands clean unless we made up dough or rubbed them in the sand; and, of course, the boys preferred the latter. We could scarcely get salt to put in anything. A tremendous snow was falling when we started and we could hardly see our way, and we became very cold. We called at different houses and finally about four miles from where we were camped we came to a very fine house. The old Dutchman came out and asked us to come in and warm. I went out on the porch to get a drink of water, thinking maybe I would find a piece of soap. I found a piece of soap, slipped it into my pocket and went on into the house. In a few minutes both of us began to turn sick; we had been so cold the sudden change to the good warm room made us sick. The old man seemed to have a good deal of sympathy; he stepped to the closet and brought out a large jug of brandy. I was a little slow, perhaps, in taking mine. There were two girls there, and one of them said,
>
> 'We all take a toddy here every morning.'
>
> I thought I would not refuse under the circumstances. We both drank a very good drink, and it seemed to be all we wanted; even the soap and salt were forgotten. We remained a few minutes and one of the young ladies brought out two bottles, one for each of us. We were now thoroughly warm and started on our journey. We came to another nice place. I stepped up to the dining room window and asked them if they had any pies or anything of that kind to sell. The young lady laughed very heartily and said,
>
> 'No, sir, we haven't anything for sale.'
>
> We went back to camp. All the boys were very anxious for a bath. I told them to come up and take a bath, that I had found a piece of soap. I passed the water to them while they bathed. I came last. I saw they were laughing, but I did not know what was the matter. I scrubbed away, scratched the soap a little and found it was a slick rock. You never heard boys holler so loud in your life. The boys notified the whole army to look out for the man that stole the rock. The first letters I received from home after that stated they regretted that I had left the army and gone to stealing rocks. Along in the night some one would wake up and yell, 'Who stole the rock.' And about five hundred would answer, 'Edwards'.[57]

On February 19, the Georgia brigade moved a short distance. Rumors spread that the trek back to Orange Court House would begin soon. Packages and letters sent from home months before finally caught up with the brigade. Some soldiers marveled at the fine condition of the Georgia peaches, syrup, fried chicken, corn etc. Others, like Sergeant Marion Hill Fitzpatrick, 45th Georgia, did not fair as well. Fitzpatrick found "The potatoes and cakes were rotton. The butter is sound, but taste pretty rank. The meat Ma sent me kept nice enough. Last winter it would have been worth a great deal to me, but now we are drawing more meal, rice, pork than we can eat, so I sold it. I got $2.00 per pound for it from a citizen."[58]

The return to Orange Court House began the first day of March amidst a falling rain. The Georgians crossed the icy Shenandoah River in shifts, on two flat boats with long poles. This crossing probably occurred at Conrad's Ford east of Harrisonburg. Fitzpatrick recounted a humorous incident:

> There was considerable excitement in the Brigade there and along before we got there, in consequence of two young girls that were with some soldiers in the 49th Georgia. They were dressed in men's clothes or rather in a soldier's garb and were following the Brigade on foot. It was soon rumored all through the Brigade that they were of the fair sex and their face and hair also betrayed them, and everybody wanted to get a look at them. After they crossed the river, General Thomas found it out and had them put back on the other side with orders to remain there. Of course they were of disreputable characters."

As evening approached, the rain turned to sleet and then snow. The brigade halted near a mountaintop on the Blue Ridge after hiking twenty-two miles.[59]

The following morning, the brigade moved toward Charlottesville to confront Federal cavalry raiders. They arrived in the area on March 3, and found the bridge across the Rivanna River in smoldering ruins. The local population told stories of abuse by the enemy. "They carried off a great many negroes. In one instance they made the negroes hitch up the horses to their master's carriage right before their master's and mistress's faces and drive them off and they took the rings off the ladies fingers, slapped their jaws, struck them with their sabres and took all their meat, corn and horses, and acted mean generally."[60] After assurances that the raiders had departed, Edward Thomas led his men northeast toward Orange Court House. They waded the Rivanna and reunited with the rest of Robert E. Lee's army on March 5.

NOTES

Abbreviations:

CSR—"Compiled Service Records of Confederate Soldiers Who Served In Organizations From The State of Georgia," Thirty-fifth Infantry Regiment (National Archives Microfilm Publication M266) National Archives Building, Washington, D.C.

GDAH—Georgia Division of Archives and History, Morrow, Ga.

NMP—National Military Park

OR.—War of the Rebellion: A Compilation of the Official Records of the Union and Confederate Armies. 130 Vols.

SHSP—Southern Historical Society Papers

1. Rev. Groves H. Cartledge, "Sketches of the Early History of Madison Co.," Georgia, typescript in Georgia Room, Hargrett Rare Book and Manuscript Library/University of Georgia Libraries, Athens, Ga. After Bartow's death, several Georgia companies honored the fallen colonel by naming their units after him. This included Newton County's Company B, the Bartow Avengers.
2. Letter of James Garrett to "Dear Mother from Camp of the 35th Georgia Regiment Near Orange Court House Va. December the 12th 1863," James Garrett Collection
3. "Diary of George W. Hall, 14th Georgia Volunteers, CSA, 1861–1865," Hargrett Rare Book and Manuscript Library/ University of Georgia Libraries, Athens, Ga. p.33.
4. Garrett Letter, December 12th, 1863.
5. Ibid.
6. "Reminiscences of Confederate Soldiers and Stories of the War 1861–65," Volume XIII, pg.104–107. Compiled by the Georgia Division, United Daughters of the Confederacy located at GDAH. While there was no specific date attached to this incident, it most probably occurred while 35th Georgia was in camp around Orange Court House because Augustus Moon didn't enlist until March 1863 and he was captured on May 3rd, but was exchanged after only ten days.
7. Ibid.
8. Ibid.
9. "Diary and Memorandum Kept By Captain Daniel S. Redding, Co.D, 45th Georgia, March-December 1863," in "Reminiscences of Confederate Soldiers and Stories of the War 1861–65," collected and bound by Georgia Division UDC, Vol 5, 1940, p.44, GDAH; Hall, p.33–34.
10. Ibid. Redding, p.44–45.
11. Letter of Charles A. Conn to "My Dear Sister from Bivouac near New Market Va. Wednesday Dec. 23, 1863" (45th Ga.), *The Georgia Historical Quarterly.* Vol.XLVI, 1962, p.193.
12. Hall, p.34; Ibid., Conn.
13. Ibid. Hall.
14. Redding, p.45–46.
15. Hall, p.35.
16. Letter of JM Garrett to "Dear Mother from Camp Near New Market Va December 26 1863," James M. Garrett Collection.

17. Hall, p.1.
18. Redding, p.46.
19. Jubal A. Earl, *General Jubal A. Early: Autobiographical Sketch and Narrative of the War Between the States,* (Philadelphia and London, 1912) p.333.
20. *OR* ., Vol.33, p.1060.
21. Hall, p.1.
22. *OR* ., Vol.33, p.1062; Ibid., Hall, p.1.
23. Early, p.333.
24. Hall, p.2.
25. Letter of James Garrett to "Dear Mother from Camp Near Staunton Va Jan the 16th 1864," James Garrett Collection.
26. Letter of Jasper A. Gillespie (45th Ga) to "My Dear Wife from Camp Near Staunton VA Thursday Jan. 14th 1864," Jasper A. Gillespie Civil War Letters (photocopies), AC 65–404, GDAH.
27. Garrett Letter. January 16, 1864.
28. Ibid.
29. *OR* ., Vol.33, p.1059; Ibid., Garrett.
30. Letter of James Garrett to "Dear Mother from Camp 35th Georgia Regiment Near Harrisonburg Rockingham County Va, Jan. 25th 64," James Garrett Collection; "The Story of Massanetta Springs", information sheet available at the Massanetta Springs Conference Center near Harrisonburg, Va. This springs area remains popular to this day. The present day site is now called Massanetta Springs and it is owned by the Presbyterian Church and used as a conference center, children's camp and a retirement community. Massannetta Springs is located off Rt. 33 several miles east of Harrisonburg, Virginia.
31. Ibid., Garrett. Note: Both forks of the Shenandoah River tend to flow from south to north. For this reason "down the Valley" refers to movement from south to north and "up the Valley" refers to movement from north to south.
32. Letter of JM Garrett to "Dear Mother from Camp 35th Georgia Near Harrisonburg Rockingham County Virginia January the 26th 1864," James M. Garrett Collection.
33. Early, p.334.
34. *OR* ., Vol. 33, p.43.
35. Ibid. Vol 33, p.30.
36. Hall, p.4; Ibid., Vol. 33, p.43.
37. Early, p.336.
38. John Frank Edwards, *The Red Book—Army Life of Frank Edwards—Confederate Veteran 1861–65*. 1906, p.89.
39. Early, p.336.
40. *OR* ., Vol 33, p.38–39.
41. Hall. p.4; Early. p.336–337.
42. *OR* ., Vol.33, p.43–44.
43. Letter of James Garrett to "Dear Mother from Camp Near Harrisonburg Va Feb 14th 1864," James Garrett Collection.
44. Hall, p.4; Early, p.337.

45. Edwards. p.90.
46. *OR* ., Vol. 33, p.39.
47. W.T. Irvine, "Old 35th Georgia", *The Sunny South,* Atlanta, May 2, 1891.
48. Hall, p.5; *OR* ., Vol. 33, p.45
49. Ibid., Vol.33, p.44; Ibid., Hall, p.5–6; Early, p.335–338.
50. Ibid., Hall, p. 5.
51. *OR* ., Vol.33, p.44.
52. Letter of James Garrett to "Dear Mother from Camp of 35th Georgia Regiment Near Harrisonburg Rockingham County, Va., Feb 8th 1864," James Garrett Collection.
53. Ibid.
54. Garrett Letter, February 14, 1864.
55. Ibid.
56. Ibid.
57. Edwards. p.103–104.
58. Marion Hill Fitzpatrick, *Letters to Amanda.* (Macon, Ga., 1998) p.118. (edited by Jeffrey C. Lowe and Sam Hodges)
59. Ibid. p.124.
60. Ibid. p.125.

Note: all Fort Mulligan information courtesy of Fort Mulligan walking tour brochure sponsored by South Branch Valley Civil War Society, Inc.; McNeill's Rangers Camp #582 SCV; 7th W.V. Camp #7 SUV; Civil War Preservation Trust. I want to especially thank Kenny Shobe of Petersburg, W.Va., for taking his valuable time to answer my many questions on such short notice. These groups have done an outstanding job preserving a real jewel of a civil war fort.

Chapter Twelve

Chaos In the Wilderness

"We have had the hardest fight that has bin fought."
Private Woodson D. Moon

Many members of Edward Thomas' Brigade expressed sorrow after leaving the fertile Shenandoah Valley as patches of lush green plants began to peek through the ground. Most soldiers found food in abundance in the Valley, while the same did not hold true for soldiers with the main army. A common feeling of contentment in the Valley existed among the Georgians. A 45th Georgian remarked, "I had rather stay here in the Valley for the remainder of the winter. We are living high now. Our tricks from home have not given out yet and we draw plenty of good pork and have some fine eating sure."[1] The Georgians realized another benefit to life in the Valley. Senior officers did not require regular inspections of the troops nor require the men to participate in parades. Thomas' men knew to expect less food, more parades and more fighting upon their return to central Virginia.

Lieutenant S.B. David, 14th Georgia, expressed his lack of enthusiasm with their return to Orange Court House. He wrote, "We left our pleasant and delightful quarters at Harrisonburg in the valley of Virginia three weeks ago tomorrow morning, and have come back to our old camp near Orange Courthouse. We left the Valley with great reluctance, as we fared most sumptuously over there." He further reiterated the great appeal of the valley: "the whole of the Brigade would rather stay there than anywhere in the Confederacy." He described the positive reception the residents of Harrisonburg gave his soldiers. "The people were just as kind to me and my company as we could have desired."[2]

Sergeant Marion Hill Fitzpatrick, 45th Georgia, contrasted the plentiful food while in the valley with the provisions available to the army at Orange when he wrote, "My health is excellent at this time, but I tell you eating is scarce especially in the meat line. If I had the meat now that I sold in the Valley I would not take four prices for it."[3]

James Garrett had remained behind near Harrisonburg on some type of duty. He apparently was successful at finding his share of food because he reported on March 8 that his weight had climbed to 172 pounds. On January 25, he had tipped the scales at 160 pounds. One essential item he needed again was shoes. "I expect to make Jeff Davis furnish me in Shoes or I wont do duty for him. I get them from the government at ten dollars a pair. [I]f you have got leather you had better save it for next winter for you will sure kneed it."[4]

By mid-March, Garrett rejoined the regiment at Orange Court House. Incredibly, he had added another nine pounds in only nine days. He again urged his mother to send his younger brother to the regiment. "I see the act is passed for the inrollment of all men between the ages of 17 & 50. [I]f so bud will have to come the first of May but if you can keep him at home you had better do it and let him make you a crop but if you cant keep him send him along hear and I will [get] a furlough and come home. Bill Formby has drawed a furlough. [H]e sent it up but it has not come back yet. [I]f he come home you can send bud along with him." He also sent a warning to his mother. "This Confederate money has gone down to nothing hear. [I]t is hardly worth a cent. [I]f you have got any on hand you had better get shut of it for it will be nothing."[5]

The Georgians experienced some of the heaviest snowstorms of the war shortly after they arrived at Orange Court House. A blizzard at the end of March dumped fourteen inches over the Virginia countryside. Another heavy snowfall began the night of April 1 and continued throughout the following day. The deep snow created the opportunity for a number of brigade-size snowball fights. With Brigadier General Samuel McGowan's South Carolina brigade camped next to Thomas' Georgians, the two groups frequently battled each other. A soldier described the frivolity. "It is all in fun but rather rough-some with black and swollen eyes, noses, etc. It generally costs a fellow a good lick to poke his head out of his tent door."[6]

Three years of fighting throughout the fertile countryside of Virginia plus a fairly effective Federal blockade of Southern ports began to have a telling effect on the supplies reaching Lee's army in the spring of 1864. Sergeant Ivy W. Duggan, 49th Georgia, summed up the situation with some humor:

> Rations are short now, but there is little complaint made. We draw corn meal, out of which we make bread, mush, 'cush', etc. and though unsifted, I guess it is healthy. We very much prefer flour and it is probable we will get it when we begin to march. We draw one-fourth pound of bacon, but we reckon what is lacking in quantity is made up in quality for they say it often 'out ranks' Gen. Lee. We occasionally get just enough coffee, sugar and rice to remind us of home before the war. Officers draw their rations now and get no more than privates.[7]

Another Georgian described his ideas on corn meal versus flour. "We also get meal instead of flour. I don't like cornbread but manage to do very well on it. I believe it is best that meal is issued as our biscuit would have to be made without grease."[8]

By the end of March, James Garrett was desperate to get home. He perhaps realized that the improving weather would bring renewed fighting and a corresponding decrease in furloughs. William Formby had headed home on furlough, and Garrett wrote his mother:

> I wanted him [Formby] to tell you to have [B]ud mustered in at Atlanta or some where close by so he would not have to pay his every way. Jim Strickland can muster him into this company and then he can get transportation from LaGrange or Atlanta to Orange CH. I am going to send this letter by Mr William C. Scogin. [H]e got a furlough by furnishing a recruit. I would like for Bud to come before William Formby comes back. [Y]ou go to Bill Formby. [H]e will tell you all about it. I hope you will not think that I am homesick. [T]he reason I am so particular about it is because Bud will have to come any how and he just as well come a little sooner and let me go home as to wait until he gets seventeen and then have to come.

Then, to reassure his mother of his good health he wrote:

> I have not been home sick a day since I left home the last time. I am well and injoying the best of health. I dont want you to think that I am boasting or flashing myself at all but I am [??unreadable word] the best looking man in the company. I dont say that my self only but the boys all say so. So you can guess about how I look. I drew my self a new coat yesterday. I have got one that will fit Bud. I have it all the winter but it is good yet. I sent my cape home by Bill Formby. I am about to get out of socks. I want you to have me some knit by the time I come home and also some drawers if you have got the cloth. I cant get a pair that will stand me here. [W]rite to me immediately. I dont expect to write any more untill I come home. [I]t is twenty cents a letter know [now].[9]

In mid-March 1864, Thomas' Brigade received orders to establish a sharpshooter battalion. Two to four volunteers joined from each company per regiment. Their mission was to screen the flanks as well as push forward when a battle was imminent. When the regular engagement erupted, they would fall back behind the main line unless the situation was desperate. These men drilled together and were released from regular camp chores including picket duty.[10] Captain James M. Mitcham, Company B, commanded the 35th Georgia sharpshooters. On April 2, the sharpshooters received an order from Light Division headquarters forbidding any target practice until after the soldiers drilled on judging distance. Major General Cadmus Wilcox issued a similar directive a week later that the sharpshooters had to exhibit proficiency in judging target distance before actual target practice could begin.

The instructions issued for judging distance became quite detailed. Men stood at fixed points in a field. Then each sharpshooter stepped forward to guess the distance to each point. The sharpshooter learned to notice the position of the sun, the visibility, and the type of background to understand how a change in these items could affect distance perception. Over a period of days, the men learned what parts of a soldier such as firearms, clothing and accoutrements they could distinguish at the various distances.[11]

Division headquarters, after almost three weeks, finally issued a circular on April 19 detailing the parameters for target practice. It read:

> The Corps of Sharpshooters will upon the receipt of this order, commence the target practice drill with ball cartridges. Twenty two rounds will be issued to each man, and the drill will be in accordance with the following schedule—
>
> At 100 yards 3 cartridges
> At 300 yards 5 cartridges
> At 600 yards 10 cartridges
> At 900 yards 4 cartridges
>
> The men will be permitted to fire with a rest, and much care should be taken to ascertain the accuracy with which each Rifle shoots.
>
> The practice at 100 yards will require but *one* day; at 300 yds, *two* ; at 600 yds, *three* ; and at 900 yards two days. At the different distances every shot will be measured and the average of the *five* best marksmen of each Brigade will be reported to these Hd. Qtrs. in the order of their merit. In reporting the average of each man, the report should state whether the fire was to the right or left, above or below, the object aimed at.
>
> Arms should be carefully inspected before each drill, and at 600 and 900 yards the practice should not take place on a windy day.
>
> While the target practice drill is going on, those not so engaged will be exercised in the judging distance drill and the reports heretofore required in this drill will continue to be sent into Division Hd. Qtrs.
>
> By command of Maj. Gen. Wilcox
> (signed) Jas. A. Engelhard
> A.A.G.
>
> official
> Wm. Norwood
> A.A.G.[12]

Captain William S. Dunlop, commander of Samuel McGowan's sharpshooter battalion, wrote that the men constructed a small wooden tripod with a sandbag on the fork for the shooter to rest his rifle. A one-inch thick, 2x6 foot pine plank target stood at 100 yards. Another one-inch thick, 4x6 foot pine plank stood at 500 yards, not 600 yards as specified in the orders. The men increased the size of the 900-yard target to a one-inch thick, 6x6 foot pine plank. They painted bull's-eyes on all the targets. The sharpshooters fired different types of rifles at the planks. The drills revealed the superiority of the Enfield rifle at long range from 600 to 900 yards. The shooters found the Austrian, Belgian, Springfield and Mississippi rifles accurate out to only 500 yards.[13]

Edward Thomas' sharpshooter battalion did fire their weapons at the 600-yard range. Sergeant Marion Hill Fitzpatrick, 45th Georgia, described the discouraging results of the initial target practice at that distance. "We shot two rounds apiece at the distance of 600 yards. Out of 98 shots, only five hit the board. I was one of the five and I missed the cross some distance."[14]

The soldiers all knew the improving weather would bring a move by the Federal army with its new commander. Abraham Lincoln had brought Lieutenant General Ulysses S. Grant from the western theater and placed him in command of the entire Union army. Although George Meade still commanded the Army of the Potomac, Grant placed his headquarters with Meade's army and assumed overall control. Robert E. Lee faced his most dangerous adversary.

The persistent James Garrett wrote his mother on April 3 to inform her that she should expect a visit from a furloughed officer to try to recruit Bud Garrett:

> Lieut Winchester is going home also to day and I told him to go to see you about sending Bud here. I dont want you to send him unless you are perfectly satisfied. I would not have him come here against your will for a hundred furloughs. I dont [want] him to come unless you are perfectly satisfied for nothing in the world for I know that I am not home sick. Dont you start him by himself. [I]f you can help it let him stay until Bill Formby come if you cant do any better. Know mother if there is any other company that you rather Bud would go to let him go. I will not think bad if you let him go where he is best satisfied.[15]

The chaplains continued to hold prayer meetings every day in camp. On Good Friday, April 8, large numbers of soldiers attended the numerous meetings for this special day. James Garrett wrote, "[W]e had the largest congregation on fast day that I have ever seen since I have been in service.

I fasted for the first time in my life. I am willing to do anything in my power to promote the welfare of our country. I think it is every mans duty to do all in his power for his country."[16] A soldier in the 14th Georgia noted in his diary this day was "[A] day of fasting humiliation and prayer. I attend 3 prayer meetings and one sermon, a verry solumn occasion and I hope we will all profit by it and the blessed Lord will hear our prayers and deliver us."[17] Many men attended a brigade Easter meeting on April 10. Chaplain John Hyman preached, and the Reverend Thomas H. Stewart closed the service. Stewart had been appointed as a missionary to Lee's army and had recently been assigned to assist in Thomas' Brigade.[18] The prayers for peace would go unheeded. As the warm sunshine gave rise to new plant life throughout central Virginia, the two armies prepared for the most bitter campaign of all.

Twenty-one-year-old James Garrett wrote his last letter home on April 14, 1864. He thanked his mother for her letter written on April 3 and delivered to his hand on April 13-a quick transit time. He expressed optimism about his health and his resolve:

> I am still injoying the best of health. I wish you could see me now. I look better than I ever did in my life. You stated that William Formby had got home safe. I sent my cape by him and he lost it. I would not have taken fifty dollars for it. I have been offered thirty for it. I have got plenty of clothing for the preasant [present] except socks. I have got a very nice suit of cloths now so if I do get home I will have a very nice suit to wear though I shall not feel disappointed if I dont get to come. I am doing very well here better than you would think. I will not attempt to tell you at preasent if I get to come home. I will tell you if Bud is coming at all he will be on the [way] before this get there. I understand Jim Dunson has a recruit coming on so he will get a furlough. [H]e is very anxious to come home. [I]t makes him mad to tell that he is home sick.

Dunson boasted in camp which drew the ire of Garrett:

> [H]e thinks that he is the most popular man in the company but I tell you he is sadly mistaken. [H]e told some of the boys if he knew a little more about military tactics he would run for Lieutenant if there should hapen to be a vacancy now. I tell you there is men in this company that could beat him to death. [N]ow I never thought of running for Lieutenant even if there should be a vacancy but I can beat a thousand such men as he is. I stand as high as any man in this company now.[19]

There was talk in camp that Longstreet's corps would soon rejoin the rest of Lee's army. Garrett knew that if the rumor was true then:

> [W]e will have lively times soon. [I]f the battle has to be fought hear I dont care how soon it comes off. I am getting very tyred of this war but am willing to stay here three more years and live off of bread and water before I will submit to an abolition dynasty. I never thought of any thing else but that we will gain our independence. Oh how I long to see the Sun of peace and the banner of liberty float in triumphantly over the green fields of the Sunny South. Oh how I long to see the day when we can all go home and peace, happyness, and prosperity reign through out our beloved land. I hope the day is not far distant when we will be permited to see our homes and loved ones again. We are preparing our selves for one decisive effort.[20]

On April 27, Edward Thomas wrote a letter to General Samuel Cooper, the Adjutant and Inspector General in Richmond, to increase the number of soldiers under his command. He said that the 12th Georgia Infantry Battalion was located at Tallahassee, Florida and their commander desired a transfer to the Army of Northern Virginia. Since Thomas' Brigade had four regiments with only 1,297 muskets, he wanted this battalion transferred to his command. This letter went to General Lee's headquarters first. Lee noted on April 29 that if this battalion could be spared from duty in Florida then the transfer to Thomas' Brigade was fine with him. For whatever reason, this transfer never occurred.[21]

As if to foreshadow the coming violence of battle, a horrendous storm passed over the Orange Court House area on May 2. The winds flattened tents, and the clouds dropped a deluge of water until well after dark.[22]

Many soldiers in the 35th Georgia attended a prayer meeting on May 4. A courier interrupted the meeting with orders for the men to strike the tents and to cook two day's rations. The soldiers marched out of camp at 10 P.M. Hill's corps moved through Orange Court House and turned east onto the Orange Plank Road toward Fredericksburg. The march ended near Verdierville after a trek of fifteen miles.[23]

The following morning, Henry Heth's Division followed by Wilcox's Division led A.P. Hill's Third Corps past the old Mine Run entrenchments. They approached the overgrown area of the Wilderness. Later in the morning, sporadic gunfire broke out to the east. The column soon passed several wounded Confederate cavalrymen. The bodies of a few dead enemy troopers lay scattered in the dust of the road. The men moved farther east and they soon encountered the smell, the smoke, and then the flames of a brush fire that snapped and crackled on both sides of the road.[24]

Before noon, Wilcox's Division left the untangled safety of the Orange Plank Road. They filed to the left and north into the unknown brambles and briers of the Wilderness. James Lane's Brigade led the division followed by Thomas, Scales and McGowan. They hoped to link with Ewell's corps that paralleled their movement along the Orange Turnpike to the north. One soldier wrote, "We march through an old field and through a dense thicket of undergrowth and through a swampy boggy ravine."[25]

It was not known if Lane's troops actually located Ewell's right flank before the sounds of heavy fighting erupted to the east in the direction of Heth's Division. Orders soon arrived for Scales and McGowan to retrace their steps and move east along the Orange Plank Road to assist Heth. A short time later, the same orders reached Thomas and then Lane. The situation in front of Heth became dire, despite the addition of McGowan and Scales. At Hill's Third Corps headquarters near the Orange Plank Road, many officers expressed concern whether Thomas' and Lane's brigades would show up in time to halt the Federal push. Shortly before dark, relieved officers noted these last two brigades running along the road past the headquarters. The Georgians moved into the woods to the left of the road to relieve Joseph Davis' Mississippi brigade, commanded by Colonel John M. Stone. The Federals had battered Davis' men and Thomas' timely arrival cancelled the start of a suicidal bayonet charge by the 55th North Carolina.

The setting sun cast murky shadows throughout the woods. Thomas' left anchored the left of Hill's corps. This position stood about a half-mile northeast of the Widow Tapp's farmhouse. While the Georgians prepared their new line, the sounds of battle erupted from the Orange Plank Road to the south and the Orange Turnpike to the north. The Georgia pickets, suddenly, crashed back through the lines followed by a hail of lead. It was shortly after 7 P.M. A strong four-brigade column commanded by Brigadier General James S. Wadsworth from the Union Fifth Corps had sliced southward from the Orange Turnpike hitting Hill's exposed left flank.

This formidable force flanked the Georgians and threatened their rear. Thomas promptly faced the brigade to the left and rear. His men concentrated their fire, but the unseen enemy appeared to weaken only to hit another portion of the brigade line. Thomas' men repeatedly repulsed the enemy, but the Union lines kept attacking.[26] In the dim light, confusion reigned. The strong Federal fire on both of Thomas' flanks pinned down the Georgians. They found themselves fighting back to back not knowing which direction to go.

A.P. Hill had already committed all his reserves to other portions of the line. The situation became desperate as Thomas' men fought the enemy from three directions. After what seemed like an eternity, there was a loud "rebel yell" and a thin line of 5th Alabama Battalion men, scrounged from a prisoner detail, swept onto the scene. They miraculously pushed back Wadsworth's first line. By the time the Union officers restored order to their ranks, it was dark and hopes of destroying Hill's left would have to wait until the light of morning.

Woodson D. Moon, Company G, described the chaos of the day. "We went into the fight about 12 oclock and was in the fight off and on un till dark and one time we were surrounded and it rained balls as thick as thay commonly do. [T]he yankeys was firing in to us in front and rear and we had to give back and form again and the next morning the 6th [May] we're in the same fix." Moon heard some of his officers say "that on the 5th we were under the heviest musketry that had [??illegible word] during the war. [A]s to my part I could not hear as well as some might exspect for it was worse than thunder."[27]

Darkness found Hill's corps still intact, but units had intermixed and large gaps existed in the line. It was impossible in the tangled darkness to see where the lines began and ended. The enemy lay within a few yards of the Confederates, but each side remained invisible to the other because of the thick foliage. Smoke fouled the air from several brush fires that cremated whatever stood in their path.

At some point during the night, a portion of Thomas' men shifted from their position on the left and moved south across the Orange Plank Road. Davis' Brigade after a respite moved to their previous position. Confusion existed about Thomas' exact position after this move. Edward Steere stated in his book, *The Wilderness Campaign,* that Thomas' men moved to cover the right flank with Scales' men on their left. Several reports, however, indicated that Thomas' Georgians or at least portions of them formed on the south edge of the Orange Plank Road to support McGowan on the left and Scales on the right. Captain Washington Irvine, Company I, recalled that the 14th Georgia remained in a position northwest of the Orange Plank Road while the 35th Georgia moved to the south side of and parallel with the road.[28] Captain James McElvany, Company F, wrote that the 35th Georgia "Fell back to Plank Road about dark. Formed on it and lay there all night."[29] A South Carolina officer in McGowan's Brigade stated, "Thomas's brigade was immediately on the right of the road. A part of his command had spent the night there, the rest were joined with them at daylight. The line of our brigade, struck the road at an acute angle, making a salient with Thomas's brigade. Besides the latter brigade, there were no troops in line on the right of the road, as far as I have been able to learn, except, perhaps, Scales' brigade."[30]

Several accounts from soldiers in the 14th Georgia do not mention any movement from their position north of the road after darkness fell. One 14th

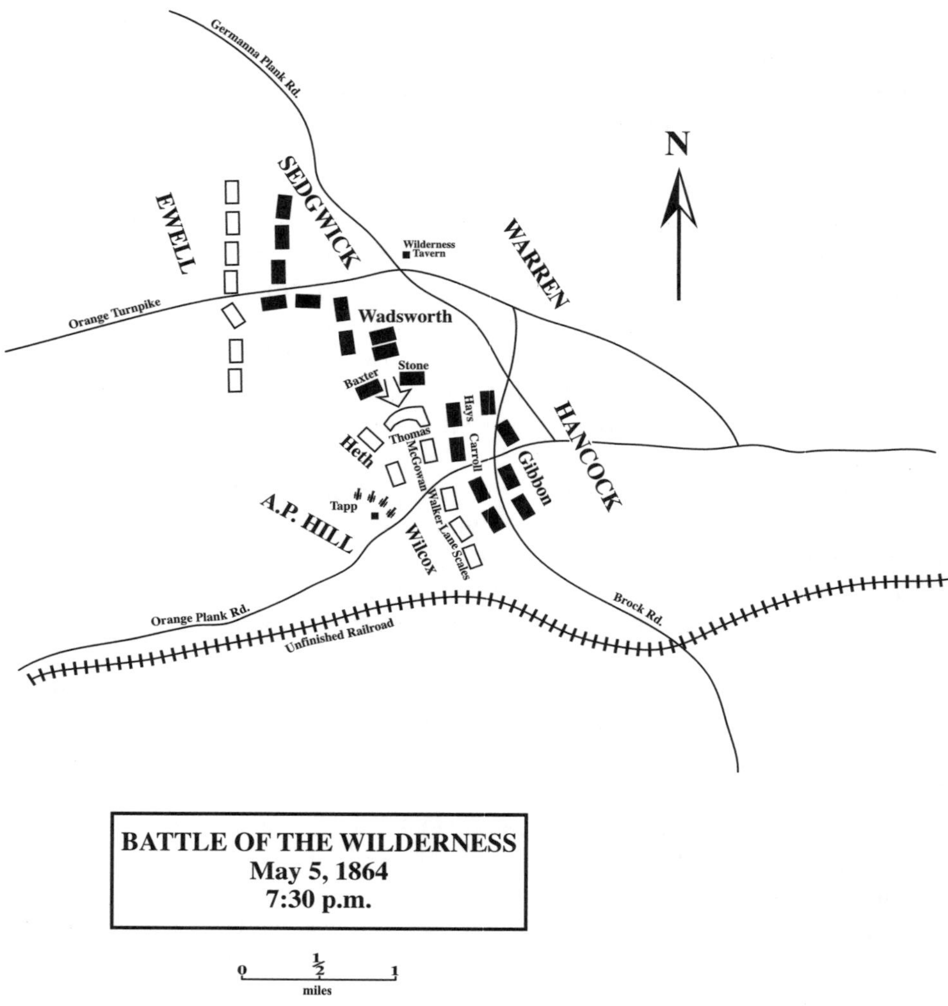

BATTLE OF THE WILDERNESS
May 5, 1864
7:30 p.m.

0 ½ 1
miles

Georgia lieutenant, while checking his men, stumbled into a group of soldiers huddled together in the darkness. Unsure of their allegiance, he inquired of their unit and they informed him they came from the 49th Georgia. The 14th Georgia pointed in a 'V' or horseshoe shape toward the enemy. Their commander, Colonel Robert Folsom, voiced his misgivings about his position, but he was ordered not to straighten his line.[31] On several occasions that night, both Heth and Wilcox approached A.P. Hill about pulling the troops back to organize lines and to consolidate scattered units. Hill re-

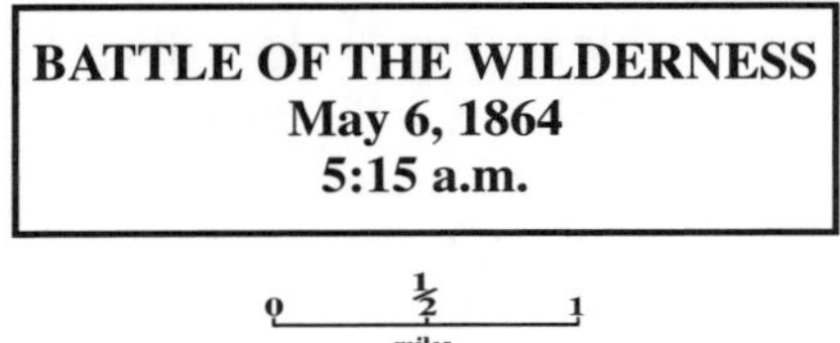

fused. He wanted the men to rest because he believed Longstreet's corps would soon relieve them.

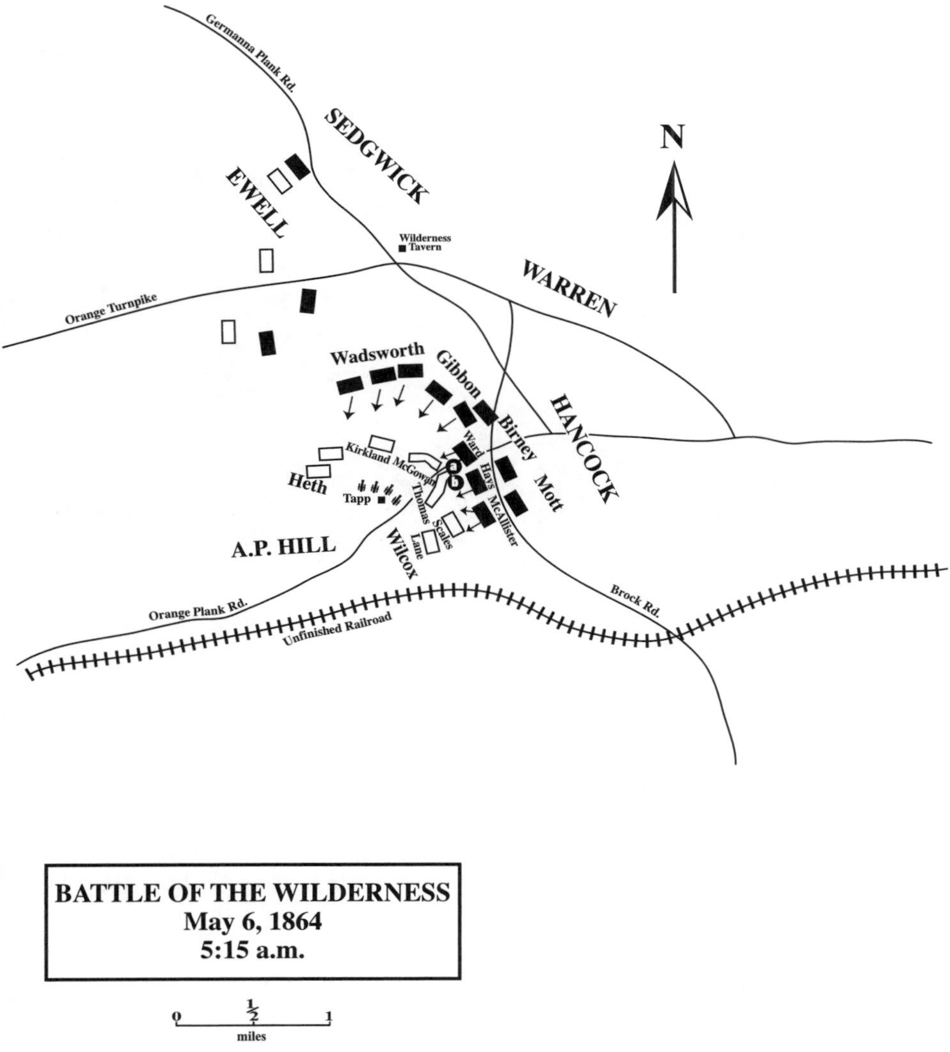

Based on the available evidence, it remained unclear exactly where in the line the 14th Georgia stood after nightfall on May 5. It was certain that Thomas moved the remainder of his brigade across the Orange Plank Road under cover of darkness that night. Based on the words of Captains McElvany and Irvine, the 35th Georgia assumed a position on the right side and

a. Orange Plank Road
Looking east on Orange Plank Road toward Federal position. This road was dividing line between Thomas' and McGowan's brigades on early morning of May 6, 1864.
photo by author

parallel with the road with their line extended in a salient toward the enemy. Scales' North Carolinians then anchored the right flank.

The fighting resumed at sunrise on May 6. Shortly after daylight, the Union infantry line moved forward pushing back Scales' Brigade. This created a dangerous void on Thomas' right. Colonel Robert McAllister's brigade from Winfield Hancock's Second Corps probably attacked the Georgians. The 5th, 6th and 11th New Jersey regiments held the brigade right while the 1st Massachusetts and the 115th Pennsylvania occupied the left. The 7th New Jersey manned a second line on the left flank.[32]

George W. Hall, 14th Georgia, described the difficulties along his line. "The enemy advanced on our Brigade from three directions from the front, right flank and rear, and we withstood the terrible fire for a considerable time and had nearly exhausted our ammunition when our right flank was nearly all captured or killed and we were ordered to fall back which we reluctantly done."[33] Captain McElvany wrote, "A column of the enemys force attacked our right flank and another our front, [we] fell back again in confusion."[34] Woodson Moon described the continued unpleasantness that greeted the regiment at first light. "[A]t sun up they pored a heavy fire in to us from boath [both] ways and Thomas Brigade had to turn tale and get

b. Thomas' Position
View of dense Wilderness woods along Georgia line looking east toward Federal line. Spring foliage would have reduced visibility to only a few yards.
photo by author

up or the last one of us would of bin taken prisoner and as god would have it Longstreet come up just as we fell back." A soldier in the 45th Georgia reported, "The second days fighting our Brigd [brigade] was badly managed so much so that the enemy succeded in braking the line and causing it to give back where a good many were taken prisoner."[35]

This chaotic withdrawal began by the left flank as the Georgians blindly stumbled through the foliage. Other Confederate units joined their dash rearward with thirteen Union brigades close on their heels. Around 7 A.M., the lead elements of Longstreet's First Corps appeared along the Orange Plank Road. They passed through Hill's disorganized lines and helped to halt the blue wave. Brigadier General Thomas rallied the Georgians and they went forward again on Longstreet's left. The Confederates pushed the Union attackers back and regained the lost ground. The Georgians quickly clawed breastworks out of the ground, but the men soon moved farther forward. They spent another anxious night in line of battle.[36]

Earlier that morning, Sergeant David H. Mobley, Company G, wore a pair of knee boots he had swapped prior to the departure from Orange Court House. Mobley recalled, "[A]bout sunup they opened fire on our lines and I was wounded in my right leg between my knee and ankle. I went down to the ground dropping my gun. It occurred to me at once what I had said to my Uncle Johnny [John Ephraim David Mobley, Co. G] on leaving camp—that I might be wounded, and if I did have a wound the boots had probably helped to weaken the force of the ball." The boots apparently lessened the damage. Doctors sent Mobley to a hospital in Lynchburg and he returned after forty days to become the regimental commissary sergeant.[37]

After the battle, the men in Company G laughed about the antics of Private Dock Knight on the morning of May 6. When the Georgians made their desperate run to escape being surrounded and captured, Dock fell behind the others. "Dock being a low man and short-legged could not run very fast. He was bringing up the rear and shouting, 'Oh Lordy', at every step." Somehow, he avoided capture or death.[38]

Lieutenant David Champion, 14th Georgia, noted an advantage Lee's army had while fighting in the dense woods and undergrowth. "We found the 'Rebel Yell' a terror to the enemy in close quarters, and especially so in the wilderness. Yelling repeatedly at the tops of our voices and charging at a run through the thick undergrowth, we no doubt deceived him as to our numbers."[39]

Both armies glared at each other for the next two days amid sporadic skirmishing. Each side suffered extremely high casualty figures for the two-day Battle of the Wilderness. The 35th Georgia reported 4 killed, 22 wounded and 23 missing.[40]

Federal soldiers actually captured the missing 35th Georgians. Union authorities sent most of these unfortunate Southerners to the notorious prison camp at Elmira, New York. Elmira became infamous for having the highest prisoner mortality rate of any Northern prison camp. Most of the inhabitants referred to the place as "Hellmira." Ten of these twenty-three men, including Private John Rigby, Company D, would not walk out of their prisons alive. Rigby died of acute bronchitis on May 4, 1865 at Elmira, almost a month after the Appomattox surrender. An inventory of Rigby's scant possessions at his death included one blanket, one pair of socks, one vest and one shirt. His wife, Nancy, never knew what had happened to her husband. Since Rigby was the only member of his company captured at the Wilderness, his family never learned of his exact fate. His wife always believed he would come home and she refused to apply for a government veteran's pension until 1893. She died in 1897. The family buried her at Liberty Cemetery in Bremen, Georgia, with an empty spot next to her grave, for John.[41]

On May 7, the brush fires continued to try to cleanse the battleground of its grisly sites. The acrid smell of wood smoke filled the air. This

Private John Rigby, Co.D

This Troup County sharecropper was shot twice at the Battle of Mechanicsville in June 1862. Doctors sent him home to convalesce for six months. On the morning of May 6, 1864, he was again wounded and then captured when the Confederate lines broke at the Battle of the Wilderness. He died at the notorious Federal prison camp at Elmira, N.Y., almost a full month after Robert E. Lee's surrender at Appomattox. His wife died in 1897 never knowing her husband's actual fate.

Photo courtesy of Mark Pollard, McDonough, Ga., and Patricia Mullinax, Villa Rica, Ga.

smoke frequently blotted out sunlight. That night, a spontaneous unforgettable vocal display occurred in the woods of the Wilderness. Far to the south at the right end of Lee's line a distant noise broke the night air. All along the line men paused to determine its source. The sound soon grew louder. The noise was the shouts of Confederate soldiers. More men joined the roar as it rolled from regiment to regiment along the line from right to left. The sound echoed northward until it reached the far end of Ewell's corps:

> Again the shout arose on the right—again it rushed down upon us from a distance of perhaps two miles—again we caught it and flung

> it joyously to the left, where it only ceased when the last post had huzzahed. And yet a third time this mighty wave of sound rang along the Confederate lines. The effect was beyond expression. It seemed to fill every heart with new life, to inspire every nerve with might never known before. Men seemed fairly convulsed with the fierce enthusiasm; and I believe that if at that instant the advance of the whole army upon Grant could have been ordered, we would have swept it into the very Rappahannock.[42]

The following day, Cadmus Wilcox's Division moved to the right over the hard fought battlefield of the previous days. An officer in McGowan's Brigade provided a vivid description of the devastation:

> The spectacle was most distressing. From a thick wilderness of stunted saplings, unbroken by a hog path, the place had become a charred, torn, open woods, cut up with numerous wagon roads. Every tree seemed to be riddled with balls. Small arms, mostly broken or bent, strewed the ground, with every conceivable damaged article of accoutrement or clothing, and graves, filled with the dead of both armies, were fearfully frequent. Horses lay unburied. The stench of burning vegetable matter and clothing, and the gases steaming up through the thin covering of the graves, almost suffocated me in the hot, close air of the forest.[43]

Woodson Moon wrote a letter on May 8 describing the Wilderness. He apologized for the poor handwriting because he had scribbled so quickly expecting orders any moment to move to the right where "the battle is still raging . . . ." The lined paper he wrote his note on was of interest. "[T]his is yankey paper got off the battlefield. [E]ver[y] one has got as much clothing and blankets as thay can toate [tote]. We have had the hardest fight that has bin fought."[44]

On May 8, an ill A.P. Hill turned temporary command of the Third Corps over to Jubal Early. The same day, Grant surprised Lee when he moved his troops south toward Richmond.

Notes

Abbreviations:

CSR—"Compiled Service Records of Confederate Soldiers Who Served In Organizations From The State of Georgia," Thirty-fifth Infantry Regiment (National Archives Microfilm Publication M266) National Archives Building, Washington, D.C.

GDAH—Georgia Division of Archives and History, Morrow, Ga.

NMP—National Military Park

OR.—War of the Rebellion: A Compilation of the Official Records of the Union and Confederate Armies. 130 Vols.

SHSP—Southern Historical Society Papers

1. Marion Hill Fitzpatrick, *Letters to Amanda.* (Macon, Ga., 1998) p. 120 (edited by Jeffrey C. Lowe and Sam Hodges).
2. Letter of Lt. S.B. David to "My Dear Mother, Camp 14th Ga. Regt. Near Orange C.H., March 21 1864," in "Reminiscences of Confederate Soldiers and Stories of the War 1861–65," collected and bound by Georgia Division, UDC, Vol II, 1940, p.159, located at GDAH.
3. Fitzpatrick, p.126.
4. Letter of JM Garrett to "Dear Mother from Camp Near Kreezel Town Va March the 8th 1864," James M. Garrett Collection. The name of the town is actually Keezletown located north of present day Rt.33 to the east of Harrisonburg, Va.
5. Letter of JM Garrett to "Dear Mother from Orange CH Va March 17th 1864," James M. Garrett Collection.
6. Letter of Francis S. Johnson, Jr. (45th Georgia) to "Dear Father from Camp 45th Ga. March 25th, 1864," in "Reminiscences of Confederate Soldiers and Stories of the War 1861–65," Vol. II, 1940, p.375, compiled by Georgia Division, UDC, located at GDAH.
7. Letter of Ivy W. Duggan (49th Georgia) to "Editor, *Central Georgian* (Sandersville, Ga) from Camp 49th Georgia Regt. Near Orange CH, Va., April 25th, 1864."
8. Johnson Letter, March 25, 1864.
9. Letter of James M Garrett to "Dear Mother from Camp Near Orange CH Va March the 30th 1864," James M. Garrett Collection.
10. Fitzpatrick, p.128–129; William S. Dunlop, *Lee's Sharpshooters or the Forefront of Battle.* (Little Rock 1899) (reprinted by Morningside House, Dayton, Oh. 1988) p.361.
11. Ibid., Dunlop, p.365.
12. James A. Engelhard Civil War Army Orders, mf 181, ac 00–272, GDAH.
13. Dunlop, 21–22.
14. Fitzpatrick, p. 141.
15. Letter of James M. Garrett to "Dear Mother from Camp Near Orange CH Va April the 3d/64," James M. Garrett Collection.
16. Letter of James M. Garrett to, "Dear Mother, Camp Near Orange CH Virginia, Apr the 14th 1864," James M. Garrett Collection.
17. "Diary of George W. Hall, 14th Georgia Volunteers, CSA, 1861–1865," Hargrett Rare Book and Manuscript Library/ University of Georgia Libraries, Athens, Ga. p.13.
18. Fitzpatrick, p.133; Harold Lawrence, *Methodist Preachers In Georgia, 1783–1900,* (Tignall, Ga., 1984) p.529–530.
19. Garrett Letter. April 14, 1864.
20. Ibid.
21. "Letters Received by the Confederate Adjutant and Inspector General and the Quartermaster General, 1861–1865," (National Archives Microfilm Publication M474, roll 113, document 674-G-1864) National Archives Building, Washington, D.C.
22. Letter of Jasper A. Gillespie, Co.B, 45th Georgia, May 3rd 1864, Jasper A. Gillespie Civil War Papers (photocopies), AC 65–404, GDAH.

23. "Letters and Journal of Major James T. McElvany of the 35th Georgia Infantry Regiment," p.23; Hall. p.15.
24. J.F.J. Caldwell, *The History of a Brigade of South Carolinians Known As 'Gregg's', and Subsequently As 'McGowan's' Brigade.* (Philadelphia, 1866) (Morningside Press reprint 1992, Dayton, Oh. , p.174).
25. Hall, p.16.
26. James Folsom, *Heroes and Martyrs of Georgia;-;Georgia's Record In The Revolution of 1861.* (Macon, Ga., 1864) p.121. (reprint by Butternut and Blue, Baltimore, 1995, p.119)
27. Letter of Woodson D. Moon to "Charlotte, On the Battle Field, Chancellorsville, May the 8th 1864," Civil War Miscellany, Personal Papers (Record Group 57-1-1), Woodson D. Moon Folder, GDAH.
28. W.T. Irvine, "Old 35th Georgia", *The Sunny South,* Atlanta, May 2, 1891.
29. McElvany, p.23.
30. Caldwell, p.179.
31. Report of Lt. David Champion, Co. G, 14th Georgia, "Confederate Reminiscences and Letters, 1861–65," Georgia Division UDC, Vol. 1, p.16–17, 1995, located at GDAH; Hall, p.16
32. *OR* .,Vol. 36, p. 498–499.
33. Hall, p.16.
34. McElvany. p.23
35. Moon Letter, May 8, 1864; Letter of Francis Solomon Johnson to "Darling Emmie, Near Spotsylvania C.H. May 17th/64," Francis Solomon Johnson, Jr., Co.F, 45th Ga. to Emily Hutchings-Special Collections, MS 243, Hargrett Rare Book and Manuscript Library/University of Georgia Libraries, Athens, Ga.
36. McElvany. p.23; Caldwell, p.183; "R.E. Lee to C.S. War Dept., May 7, 1864", *Robert E. Lee: Official Telegrams, 1862–65.* Duke University.
37. D.H. Mobley, "War History of David Harrison Mobley, Co.G, 35th Georgia," microfilm 283/34, GDAH; Anita B. Sams, *Wayfarers In Walton.* (Atlanta, Ga., 1967) p.436.
38. Moon Anecdotes, "Reminiscences of Confederate Soldiers and Stories of the War 1861–65," Volume XIII, pg.104–107. Compiled by the Georgia Division, United Daughters of the Confederacy, located at GDAH.
39. Champion, p.17.
40. Folsom, reprint p.134-note: Folsom only listed those soldiers killed/wounded. I derived the 23 missing men from doing roster searches of CSR as well as a search through Lillian Henderson, *Roster of the Confederate Soldiers of Georgia 1861–1865,* Vol.III, (Hapeville, Ga., 1960) p.843–929. It was impossible to determine the Union casualties specifically inflicted by the Georgians during the two days of fighting because Thomas' men fought against numerous enemy brigades that also fought against other Southern units during the fluid battle.
41. Rigby Family records courtesy of Mr. Mark Pollard, McDonough, Ga.
42. Caldwell, p.184; Dunlop, p.43–44.
43. Ibid., Caldwell, p.186.
44. Moon Letter. May 8, 1864.

Chapter Thirteen

Spotsylvania to Cold Harbor

"Thinking you would be glad to hear from me of the last moments of your son . . . ."
Chaplain John H. Taylor

A.P. Hill's corps, now commanded by Jubal Early, took a circuitous route south to obstruct Ulysses Grant's army. Edward L. Thomas' Brigade arrived near Spotsylvania Court House around noon on May 9. The rapid all-night march had been successful. Lee's army squarely blocked Grant's movement toward Richmond.

Cadmus Wilcox placed James Lane's Brigade about four hundred yards east of town and north of the Fredericksburg Road. The three remaining brigades, including the Georgians, extended their lines to the south forming the right end of Lee's defense. A short time later, Lee pulled two nearby divisions out of line and moved them to the west flank. This move left Wilcox's Light Division to face two divisions from Ambrose Burnside's Federal Ninth Corps. Thomas' troops stretched further apart to cover the vacated line.[1]

The sounds of battle broke out to the north and south of the line. Late in the afternoon a brief crescendo of rifle fire erupted to the right. Federal cavalry attacked the right rear of Wilcox's position trying to determine Confederate strength. The Southerners quickly repulsed the enemy troopers.[2] The following day, around 5 P.M., Burnside ordered the Ninth Corps artillery to open fire on Wilcox's position in preparation for a Federal advance. The blue-clad soldiers soon moved forward. Wilcox's men turned back several half-hearted Union assaults. An accurate sharpshooter's bullet felled Union Brigadier General Thomas G. Stevenson, commander of the 1st Division of the Ninth Corps.[3] Captain James McElvany, Company F, reported that the firing to his front and right continued all night. "Got to sleep about one or two o'clock but slept very little. One third of the men required to be awake all the time."[4] Then at 3 A.M., sergeants awakened any sleeping soldiers because of a rumored dawn attack by the enemy. This attack failed to occur. The spirits of the tired men rose when the food wagons finally arrived. A commissary detail cooked the rations about two miles behind the line and then sent the food forward in wagons to the men in the trenches. The men ate corn bread, bacon and a small amount of coffee.[5]

The skirmishing continued on May 11, but then faded away. The entire Ninth Corps mysteriously withdrew north across the Ny River at about 3 P.M. Some Confederates misread this move. Wilcox wrote, "For several hours in the afternoon of May 11 the enemy were seen to be in motion towards Fredericksburg. Large masses of infantry were seen. This continued till near dark, inducing the belief that the enemy were again moving to our right."[6]

The western sky grew ominously dark as evening approached. Jagged strokes of lightning crisscrossed the horizon followed by the clap of nature's artillery. Torrents of rain driven sideways by the wind attacked the troops. Then, inexplicably, the soaked Union soldiers crossed the Ny again and sloshed back into their previously vacated positions. Shortly after the Union men reached their old breastworks, they received orders for an attack early the following morning.[7]

Edward Thomas received new orders just as the storm passed. Under the blanket of darkness, Thomas and Alfred Scales marched their brigades west toward Shady Grove Church to help repel a Federal demonstration. A steady rain began to fall and continued throughout the night. In the early morning darkness of May 12, Confederate commanders determined that this Federal movement was a feint. Generals Thomas and Scales thus turned their wet, muddy soldiers around and retraced their path.[8]

Burnsides' 2nd Division, commanded by Brigadier General Robert B. Potter, stepped forward into the misty darkness at 4 A.M., on May 12. The 1st Division provided support on the left while the 3rd Division remained in reserve. This large Union force aimed directly toward the works of Lane's North Carolinians. Further to the north, Winfield Hancock's Second Corps troops moved against Richard Ewell's position in the salient that history has dubbed the "Mule Shoe."[9]

A chilly fog clung to the ground as the Thomas-Scales column approached Spotsylvania Court House. Most of these men anticipated some sleep even if it was back in the trenches. The sounds of a pitched battle suddenly erupted north of town. The time was approximately 5 A.M. Wilcox correctly assumed that an assault had begun near Lane's front. He immediately dispatched these two brigades north to support Lane. Wilcox's adjutant, Major Joseph Engelhard, led the column.[10] They raced for about three-quarters of a mile "through a dense wilderness of undergrowth, sometimes through marshes and ponds over our knees."[11]

Burnside described the initial success of his Union men. "The fire of the enemy was drawn about 4:30 A.M, and at 5 A.M. the engagement had become very severe. Two lines of detached rifle-pits had been carried, and an assault was ordered upon the main line by the First and Second Divisions. The latter division succeeded in carrying a portion of the line, and capturing a battery of two guns, with a large number of prisoners." Burnsides' success would be short-lived because in the ensuing confusion, the Ninth Corps' right flank had lost contact with the Second Corps' left flank.[12]

Lane's Brigade had steadfastly succeeded in repulsing an attack from Union Second Corps units on their left flank and Ninth Corps units to their front. The brigades of Thomas and Scales deployed to Lane's left rear in timely fashion. This increased firepower pushed Burnsides' men back. The Georgians and North Carolinians climbed over the Confederate breastworks and chased the enemy down a steep hill. At the bottom, they slogged across a marsh and creek in their pursuit of the enemy.[13] Two hundred yards to the east, Burnsides men slid back behind their entrenchments and watched as the Confederates struggled across the wet marsh. When the pursuers came within one hundred yards, Federal troops unleashed a torrent of grape, canister, and minie balls. This concentrated fire tore huge holes in the Confederate lines. Private James Garrett, Company D, gasped for breath as he dropped to his knees with a bullet through a lung. Before he completed his fall, another projectile ripped into his hip.[14]

Thomas' and Lane's men hugged the ground in front of Burnsides' position for some two hours. The murderous enemy fire continued to weaken the Confederate effort. Enemy soldiers flanked Thomas' right side. This prompted the Georgians to hustle back across the boggy morass and up the steep incline. The accurate enemy fire dropped many Georgians on the slope. Federal soldiers pushed forward on Thomas' right flank and captured about thirty men from the 14th Georgia.[15]

Captain James McElvany reported that Company F suffered seven casualties in this charge. Enemy fire struck Corporal Isham G. Rawlins in the leg and he died two days later. Private J.H. Whitworth was left on the field dead. Private Alfred S. Jenkins, wounded the week before at the Wilderness, was hit in the left arm and hip. "After falling back to our breast works we lay nine hours under a severe fire." Since only about four hundred yards separated the main lines "Every head raised above the works drew fire from the enemy."[16] Private Charles H. Farmer, of Company B from Newton County, had sensed a foreboding premonition the day before the battle and he had given his pocket-book to Lieutenant James M. Mitcham. Farmer died in the charge on May 12—his twentieth birthday. He was

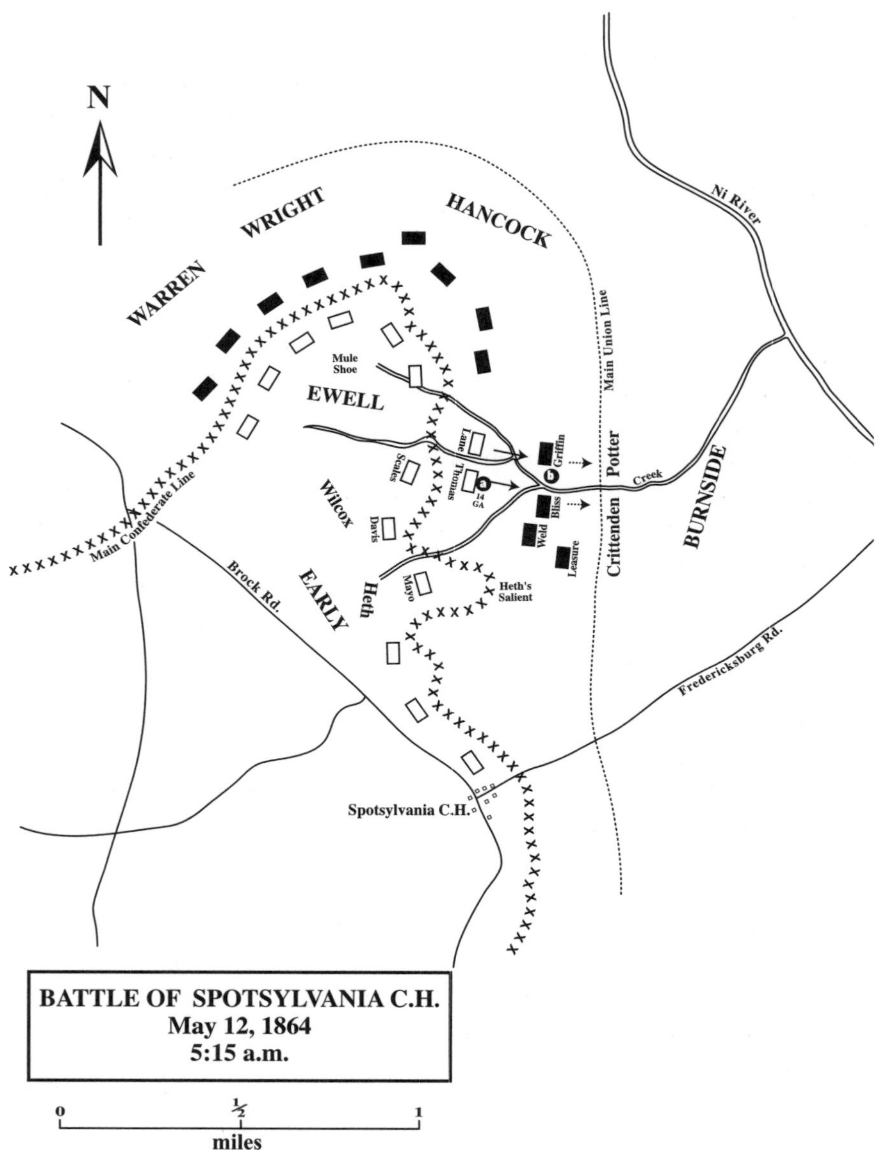

BATTLE OF SPOTSYLVANIA C.H.
May 12, 1864
5:15 a.m.

"[S]hot through the Bowels the Bawl [ball] entering about the 3rd Rib on the Right side and came out about the left hip. [H]e lay six days on the Battle Field before he was got by our men."[17]

Sergeant James M. Kimbrough, up front with the color guard, hit the ground at the right moment. He looked up to see the color bearer on his left dead. Another member of the color guard on his right writhed on the ground with a bloody hole through his arm.[18]

a. Direction of Thomas' Charge

View looking east downhill toward boggy creek bottom. Thomas' men chased Federals down this steep hill across the creek and up the opposite hill to the main enemy line 250 yards ahead. This area was more open in 1864 providing less cover for the attacking Georgians. A slight undulation along the hillside stands about 125 yards from the Federal works. This would have provided cover to the Georgians and was probably the eastern limit of their charge due to the heavy enemy artillery and small arms fire. Federal soldiers who flanked Thomas' right would have flushed the Georgians off the protective shelf.

photo by author

Corporal Hiram W. Hammond, Company E, miraculously escaped death. He lay on the battlefield shot in the head. His unconscious body remained where he fell, without water or medical treatment, for the entire day. When the litter bearers finally found him, they glanced at his bloody head and deemed his wound mortal. They abandoned him and attended to those less seriously injured. His name found its way onto a list of those fatally wounded. Hammond, somehow, survived and lived to fight again until he was wounded once more at Petersburg.[19] The staff of the 35th Georgia suffered a blow this day when Major Lee A.J. Williams fell. He died a week later of his wounds.

Sergeant Major James Payne Johnston described the fighting in a letter of condolence to James Garrett's mother outlining her son's bravery:

> As a soldier his character was unblemished and unstigmatized. I do not recall at this time how many Battles he was in; but I do recollect that when he was there, and a charge was ordered he was always in

b. Steep Hill On Confederate Side of Creek

This view looks west across creek toward main Confederate line. Thomas' Georgians charged down this hill in the face of tremendous fire from the enemy main line 200 yards behind the photo spot. When Brigadier General Edward Thomas ordered a withdrawal many Georgians were killed or wounded racing back up this steep hill toward the safety of the Confederate works. The spot where numerous 14th Georgians were captured was probably a short distance to the left of this area.

photo by author

> the van, and among the first to mount the works of the Enemy. He was thus charging after we had drove the Enemy from our works the Brigade mounted the works, with the object to charge the Enemies works, after charging several hundred yards about this point James rec'd a wound in hip and through the lung. We were unable to hold the position thus gained therefore we fell back to our works thereby leaving the wounded between our lines and that of the Enemy, but as soon as night came the ambulance corps found him and carried him to the field hospital where he died, after several days suffering excruciating pain, which I am informed by the chaplain of our Reg't he bore with great fortitude. He was perfectly conscious of his condition and often remarked to Chaplain Taylor how glad his mother would be to know he died a Christian.[20]

Thomas' troops reoccupied the breastworks that faced east. Scales' Brigade stood on their left and Joseph Davis' Brigade to the right. Just south of Thomas' position a bulge in the Confederate line protruded east-

Corporal Hiram W. Hammond, Co.E

The twenty-one year-old Hammond was shot in the head and left for dead at the Battle of Spotsylvania Court House. His name appeared on a list of those killed. He survived only to be wounded again at Petersburg during the fateful Federal breakthrough on April 2, 1865. Enemy soldiers captured him the following day as he lay in a Richmond hospital bed. He was a nephew to Captain George Washington Hammond.

Courtesy of Carl Summers, Jr. West Point, Ga.

ward. This area became known as Heth's Salient.[21] Around 2 P.M., Lane's and Colonel David Weisiger's brigades received orders to move forward through some woods. They hoped to turn Burnside's left flank. This turning movement combined with artillery and infantry fire from Thomas' line coincidentally thwarted the beginning of another Federal attack. General Lee observed nearby as these Confederate efforts drove Burnside's men back to their own lines. After darkness, Thomas' Brigade withdrew and marched to the center of Spotsylvania Court House for some rest.[22]

An officer in the 7th Rhode Island described the night along the Ninth Corps line. "Darkness had hardly put an end to the carnage on the 12th before we were throwing up intrenchments, and, by working all night with

Captain James Payne Johnston, Co.D

Edward L. Thomas appointed this Troup County native to be the 35th Georgia sergeant major in July 1862. At the time of his appointment, Johnston was just shy of his twenty-first birthday. He remained sergeant major until the men of Company D elected him to be their captain in September 1864. He replaced Captain John M. Mitchell who retired to the Invalid Corps. Johnston moved to Mississippi after the war and eventually became the mayor of Amory, Mississippi.

From *Confederate Veteran,* December 1916.

bayonets, cups, wooden shovels, and a few intrenching tools, morning found us behind friendly works, which we occupied . . . ."[23]

An interesting article about a member of the 35th Georgia appeared in the *Daily Columbus (Georgia) Enquirer* on June 3rd, 1864.

> Attached to the 35th Georgia Regiment as orderly, (and a more efficient and reliable one is not in our army), is a very small man, indeed almost a dwarf, known by no other name than 'Beauregard'. Amongst other things, Beaurie, being too small to walk or run very fast, has a great passion for a fine horse, and is generally mounted on a Yankee charger. During the recent battles in Virginia he captured a very fine horse, saddle and bridle in front of the skirmish lines of his regiment. The Yankees fired at him by platoons, but he

> brought off his horse. On the battle field he had also picked up a small pistol, and while making off with his horse he came upon two well armed Yankees. Nothing daunted, he presented his pistol, and ordered them to surrender; which they promptly did, and Beaurie made safe his retreat with his prize and prisoners. The best part of the incident is, that upon examination of the pistol it was found to be not loaded.[24]

This humorous incident probably happened near Spotsylvania Court House. A roster check revealed nobody named Beauregard in the regiment. Beauregard was no doubt an orderly or body servant brought along by a soldier to help with daily camp duties. Beauregard may have belonged to Lieutenant William C. Goggans from Company A. This officer wrote a letter to his father in November 1862 and mentioned a person named Boregard. Goggans, however, died from disease in February 1862. If Beauregard had been his orderly, then perhaps the small man elected to remain with the regiment rather than return to Georgia.[25]

Sergeant Marion Hill Fitzpatrick, 45th Georgia, described the efforts of the brigade sharpshooters during the recent battles. "I have not been in any of the regular fights but have been hard down skirmishing day and night. I have run sum pretty narrow risks but not near like being in the regular fighting. They won't let the sharpshooters go into the regular fights but form us in the rear to stop straglers."[26]

James Garrett lingered on in a nearby hospital for three days. Sergeant Wilson J. Moore, Company D, maintained a bedside vigil with his young friend until right before Garrett died. Moore wrote a letter three months later to Garrett's mother describing her son's final days:

> [H]e gave mee his Pockett Book and Ambrotype and askd mee to take care of them and send them to you if he dide. I told him that I wold do so. I was with him every day after he was wonded up to the eavening he died. I was not present at his last moments. I wanted to Bee But my buisiness was so that I could not bee. [H]e told mee to write to you the eavning before his deth and tell you that he died like a Christian. [H]e talked a great deal with mee that eavning and seemed to be perfectly satisfied to die.

Moore described the situation on the battlefield when the soldiers of the ambulance corps found Garrett:

> [H]e was brought out to the Hospitle in the knight. [T]he men that brought him off of the field said that they could not find his knap sack. [T]he clothes he had on hat, shoes, and a yankee tent was all

he had with him. Som[e] person stoled the tent. [I]t was some fellow kowdard [coward] that was playing off lying around the hospitle Pertending to bee sick and nothing the mater [matter] with him. [T]he hat I have got it with mee yet. [T]he Pockett Book and Ambrotype I sent to you By Capt John M Mitchell whitch I hope you have got it by this time."

Moore described his friends generosity:

> [I]t is a great satisfaction to mee to do any thing for a friend as possible. [F]or sutch a friend as your son was to me. I do miss him more than any one that ever belong to the company. [Y]ou are not alone to mourn the loss of your son. [Y]ou never sent him any thing from your hands in the way of something to eat but what I had to share it with him. [T]he chaplain of our Regiment was with James all the time up to the last of his moment.[27]

Chaplain John H. Taylor wrote a letter to Garrett's mother eight days after Moore's letter:

> August the 27th 1864
> Field Infirmary Near Petersburg
>
> Mrs Garrett,
>
> Thinking you would be glad to hear from me of the last moments of your son, I take this occasion to write to you and although late yet I hope it will be no less satisfactory. I should have written to you soon after his death but I was taken sick soon after and have not been able to do anything until within the last week or so. Your son James received on that bloody day the 12th of May 1864 two wounds either of which would probably have proven mortal. He was brought in to our hospital and as well cared for as could be under the circumstances. But all the care of friends and skill of physicians could not avail to save his life. He lived I think 2 or 3 days after he was wounded, and then quietly fell asleep in Jesus. It was my privilege to be with him in his last moments, and it is my happy privilege to bear testimony to the truth that, 'Jesus can make a dying bed feel soft as downy pillows and while on his breast I lean my head and breathe my life out sweetly thence.' It was certainly true in his case. I had several very satisfactory conversations with him, and he always expressed his willingness to depart, and the most perfect resignation to the will of God. He was perfectly resigned to the will of God. So I would talk to him of the 'glories' of that better world his

face would brighten with a smile, and he seemed by 'faith to have a view of brighter scenes on high.' I never heard him murmur or complain once, about his sufferings he bore them with the greatest Christian resignation and fortitude. He told me that he was converted just before the commencement of the campaign and so far as I know he conducted himself in his daily walk and conversation as a Christian. When conversing with him a short time before his death about his prospects of heaven he exclaimed, 'Oh how glad my mother will be to hear I died a Christian.' It is great consolation indeed to know that he passed away so well preparing with such bright prospects of heaven. Let that fact fill your heart with gratitude to God. I know it is hard to part from our dear children, but if they depart in Jesus we know our loss is their eternal gain. They can never come to us but we can go to them. May the God of all love fill your heart with peace and comfort. And remember that you have a treasure in heaven which should be an additional motive to make you think more of that blessed place. We wrapped him in his blanket and buried him as best as we could under the circumstances. You may rest assured that all that could be done was done. Hoping that these lines will be of great comfort to you, I remain your humble servant.

John H. Taylor, Chaplain 35th Ga.[28]

The 35th Georgia resumed their place in line on the Confederate right during the following week. Sporadic skirmish and artillery fire erupted as each side tried to determine the other's motives. On May 16 and 17, Federal troops launched several half-hearted attacks against the works of Thomas and Scales. The Southerners quickly repulsed these efforts.[29] The rain became an unwelcome yet constant companion.

Francis S. Johnson, 45th Georgia, expressed his fatigue and unease in a letter written from the trenches on May 17. "This is the fourteenth or thirteenth day this fight has been going on. I never was as tired of a thing in my life. Am pretty well worn out from fatigue and loss of sleep and am on the front line all the time with my sharpshooters who are continually banging away at the enemy who are not more than three hundred yards off. The Yanks are about as fond of shooting as we are and their balls whistle through the pines over my head even while I am writing."[30]

Grant gradually shifted his units to the southeast. This lengthened his left flank beyond Spotsylvania Court House. A sticky wet fog hugged the ground early on the morning of May 18. The soldiers could not see beyond thirty yards. The ground shook as Union artillery launched a barrage at 4 A.M. The noise grew as the Confederate guns answered the fire. A short time later, four Ninth Corps brigades stepped forward for the attack. Union

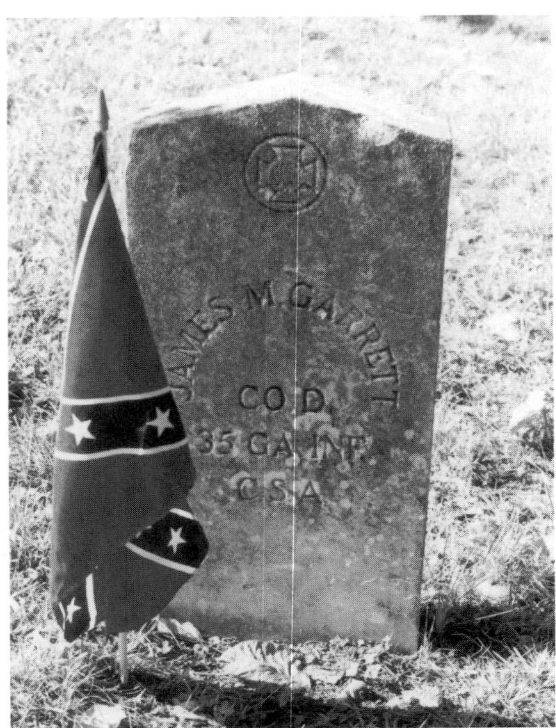

Tombstone of Private James Marion Garrett, Co.D

This is the final resting place for this twenty-one-year-old Heard County native. Garrett received a gunshot wound to the chest and hip. Hospital orderlies buried his body near the field hospital. Years later, Confederate bodies in the area were disinterred and re-buried at Spotsylvania Confederate Cemetery. Keith Bohannon located this grave for the author.

Photo by the author.

Colonel Simon Griffin's brigade occupied the right flank that struck the Georgian's position. A Georgia skirmisher reported, "We saw them coming in one direction and thought it was only a line of skirmishers. We opened fire on them hot and heavy and fought like tigers, it being the order not to fall back until we saw the line of battle. The line of battle came in by flank through a thick wood and was in twenty steps of where I was before we saw them. We poured a fire into them and retreated to our breastworks in all possible speed, while the balls came thick and fast by us."[31] Confederate artillery and infantry unleashed a decimating fire that stymied three enemy charges. The attackers vanished in the fog after a short time. When the Georgian skirmishers returned, they found the ground littered with Federal weapons. Scars in the dirt leading eastward indicated where Union comrades had dragged off their dead and wounded. Dark pools of blood stained the ground everywhere.[32] Ambrose Burnside summed up the futility of the Union assault in his report: "a general attack was made on the enemy's line, and after two or three charges by the divisions of General Crittenden and Potter, which resulted in considerable loss, it was concluded that it could not be carried by assault."[33]

On May 19, the brigades of Thomas and Scales moved forward across an open field. They created a diversion to allow Ewell's corps to attack the enemy's right flank. Thomas' Brigade led the way as the Southerners drove the Federal skirmishers out of their rifle pits. The Georgians found their new position a hot place as enemy artillery fire rained down. Wilcox wrote, "the skirmishers of this brigade acted handsomely." These two brigades withdrew a short time later when the firing on the left in the direction of Ewell's corps stopped.[34]

Two days later, Confederate commanders discovered that Grant had again slipped out of his lines and moved toward Richmond. The weary Georgians marched south a short distance on the evening of May 21. They left many of their fellow soldiers behind. The 35th Georgia reported 10 killed, 37 wounded and another 10 missing during the Battle of Spotsylvania Court House.[35] The Union casualties in both brigades of Potter's division from May 8 to 21 amounted to 184 killed, 830 wounded and 78 captured/missing.[36]

Thomas received orders on May 22 to send the skirmishers forward to locate the enemy. The Georgians moved south to Fredericksburg Road and they captured twenty to thirty prisoners. The men marched a short distance farther to the Massaponax Church Road intersection. Wilcox ordered the brigades of Lane and Scales to form in line of battle and move eastward. They stumbled into Union troops southeast of Spotsylvania Court House. A short brisk fight erupted during a violent thunderstorm. The high wind felled several trees. Later that evening, A.P. Hill returned from his illness to assume command of the Third Corps. His corps continued to move south.[37]

Thomas' Georgians reached Anderson's Station at noon on May 23. This small hamlet on the Virginia Central Railroad stood about five miles northwest of Hanover Junction. The Georgians sat down in a pine thicket to rest. One soldier pulled out his pen and paper to write a letter to his family. He described the twenty-five mile march from Spotsylvania Court House as, "weather warm, water scarce and dust in profusion." He continued, "I think I am nearer worn out, dirtyer and more in want of rest than I have been since I can recollect." He hoped to "recruit" some rations for his thin frame, but he lamented that the short rest breaks prevented this.[38]

Hill's corps anchored the Confederate left at Anderson's Station. Three miles northwest, a trail crossed the North Anna River at Jericho Mills. Confederate cavalry surprisingly had failed to secure this crossing. Earlier in the afternoon, lead elements of Major General Governour K. Warren's Fifth Corps had sloshed through the waist-deep water while Union engineers constructed a pontoon bridge for the artillery. Cadmus Wilcox received orders from A.P. Hill to move his division toward Jericho Mills to investigate Union intentions. Wilcox met with Brigadier General William H.F. "Rooney" Lee. The cavalry commander mistakenly informed Wilcox that only two brigades of Federal cavalry had forded the river. Lee reported that these enemy troopers had halted to cook their evening rations.[39]

Cadmus Wilcox really faced three enemy divisions plus at least six batteries that had already crossed the river. Federal Brigadier General Samuel W. Crawford's division deployed on the Union left with Brigadier General Charles Griffin's division on the right. Brigadier General Lysander Cutler's division remained to the rear in reserve near the river ford. Numerous Federal batteries dotted the high ground on both sides of the river.

At 4:30 P.M., Wilcox's column marched out of Anderson Station northwest along a road that paralleled the railroad tracks. Two miles later, they reached the dirt road at Noel Station that led to Jericho Mills. Three of the Southern brigades formed a line of battle perpendicular to the dirt road. Thomas' Brigade occupied the left with McGowan's Brigade, now commanded by Colonel Joseph N. Brown, in the middle and Lane's men on the right. Scales' brigade, led by Colonel William Lowrance, remained behind the rear of Thomas' left flank to envelop the Federal line if the opportunity arose. The time was near 6 P.M. As the troops crossed the railroad tracks and headed north along the dirt road, they came under a vigorous artillery bombardment followed by sporadic skirmish fire. Thomas' men found themselves in woods at the foot of a slope. They crossed a boggy stream and slogged uphill into scattered pines and then a thick forest.[40] The undergrowth made it difficult to maintain a straight line of battle. The sudden appearance of the Georgians in the dense woods surprised the skirmishers of the 95th New York and the 22nd Massachusetts. The Southerners captured several enemy skirmishers while the remainder tore away through the woods. The commander of the 22nd Massachusetts expressed frustration as he watched Thomas' and Scales' troops march diagonally toward the undefended Union right. He had feared a turning movement from that direction and had expressed his worries all the way up through his chain of command to Fifth Corps headquarters—all to no avail. Faced with danger, Cutler's blue division received orders to move from their reserve position toward the Union right, but it proved to be too little too late.[41]

Edward Thomas urged his Georgians forward with a yell. In the excitement of the charge, Thomas' men angled toward the left creating a gap with McGowan's men to the right. Colonel Jacob Sweitzer's Union brigade, astride the dirt road, offered stiffer resistance in front of the South Carolinians. This prevented the Palmetto State soldiers from moving forward to maintain the line with the Georgians.

As Thomas' men charged forward, they slammed head on into Colonel William W. Robinson's famous Iron Brigade from Cutler's division. Robinson's Midwesterners had just arrived on the line and his 6th Wisconsin linked with the right of Sweitzer's 9th Massachusetts. This location became a hot place because Scales' men had maneuvered around west of the Union line and now drove into the exposed right flank of the Iron Brigade. Hit from the front and right, most of Robinson's men broke. Major Merit Welsh, 7th Indiana, wrote, "While forming in line, but before the troops on the right got into position, we were attacked by the enemy in overwhelming numbers and forced to retire some 200 yards . . . ."[42]

Lieutenant Colonel Rufus R. Dawes, 6th Wisconsin, experienced much frustration as he tried to extend the Union line to the right of Griffin's division. The thick underbrush proved troublesome as his men formed into line of battle. "I immediately threw forward skirmishers to cover my front. In a few moments I heard sharp musketry and the peculiar cheer of a charging column of the enemy on my right. My skirmishers also commenced firing and falling back. When my front was cleared, I ordered the regiment to kneel and fire right oblique through the bushes in direction of the cheering." Dawes expressed concern when the firing to his right slackened. He sent his adjutant to find out why. Moments later the startled staff officer returned with a dire report—all the Federal units on the right had run off. Simultaneously, an enfilade fire from the right zipped amongst his men. Dawes ordered a partial change of front to meet this new threat, but he needed more men. "Finding the enemy in rear of my right, I changed front again so as to throw my line at right angles to the front of the First [Griffin] Division." Dawes soon faced another problem. The 9th Massachusetts on his left abandoned their position. He reluctantly ordered his Wisconsin men back.[43] This threat to the Fifth Corps right flank threatened to roll up the line and push the blue infantry into the river. As jubilant Confederates shoved the Federal line rearward, an overconfident Cadmus Wilcox sent a courier to find A. P. Hill and report "that the engagement was going on well and that the enemy would be whipped."[44]

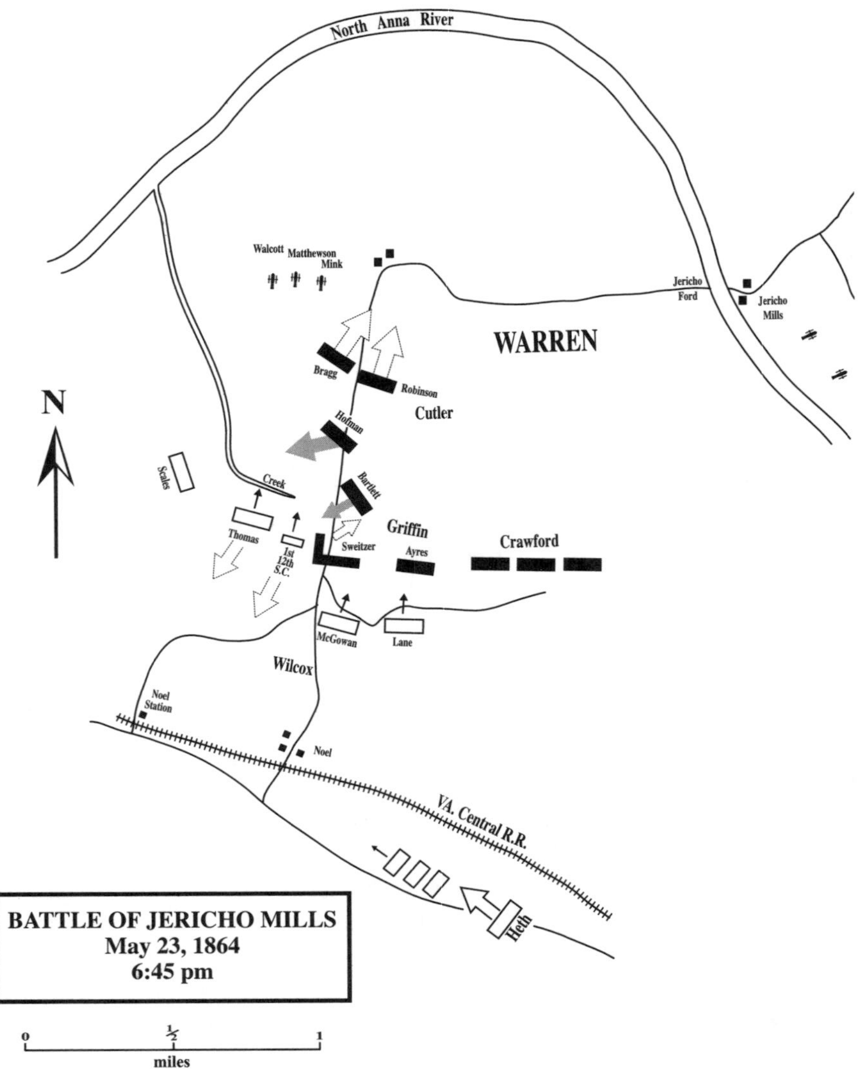

Three Federal batteries on a ridge behind the right part of the main line now grimly attempted to hold the Confederate tide. Frantic Union officers rallied the retreating infantry around the cannons. These three batteries manned the line from left to right respectively: Battery H, 1st New York Light Artillery commanded by Captain Charles E. Mink; Battery D, 1st New York Light Artillery commanded by Captain Angell Matthewson; Battery C, Massachusetts Light Artillery commanded by Lieutenant Aaron F. Walcott.

McGowan's two left regiments, the 1st and 12th South Carolina, moved through the woods on the right of Thomas' men as the pressure in their front disappeared. Thomas' men found themselves in the open along a small creek at the base of a hill. Atop the hill sat the three Union batteries and these cannons turned their full attention on the Georgians. At this critical moment, Charles Griffin had only one Union brigade left at his disposal. The Federal commander immediately ordered this reserve, commanded by Brigadier General Joseph J. Bartlett, forward to patch the opening on his right flank. The situation suddenly turned. Bartlett's men opened a deadly enfilade fire into the open right flank of the 1st and 12th South Carolina regiments. The shock of this attack halted the Southerners in their tracks. The commander of the 1st Michigan described the impact his men, accompanied by the 16th Michigan and 83rd Pennsylvania, made against the South Carolinians and then the Georgians. "We moved on a double-quick to the support of Sweitzer, and forming rapidly on his right flank poured stunning volleys into the enemy's ranks, which, with a severe fire of grape and canister from our batteries, very much demoralized his troops."[45] Federal fire struck both commanders of the two South Carolina regiments. In the ensuing confusion, blue-clad soldiers captured Colonel Joseph Brown, the South Carolina brigade commander. The deadly combination of enemy infantry and artillery fire became too much and the South Carolinians retreated. This move uncovered the Georgians right flank, and as they charged forward from their dense cover, Bartlett's oblique fire from the right stunned them too. At the same time, canister and case shot from the Union batteries just ahead tore holes in their front lines.

Captain Mink described the devastating effect his twelve-pounder cannons had upon the on-rushing Georgians and South Carolinians:

> I brought the battery in position, and as soon as our retiring troops could be cleared from our front, I opened upon the enemy with canister, and supported by Colonel Hoffman's brigade, of Cutler's division, repulsed their charge and drove them from the field, firing case-shot into them until they were driven into the woods. We then kept up a fire of solid shot through the timber until the field was cleared, and our troops held a position about 1,000 yards in advance of the ground where the battle opened.[46]

Private Augustus J. Moon, Company G, vividly recalled the carnage of this artillery fire. He watched as an artillery explosion knocked his company commander, Captain John Y. Carter, through the air. The officer's broken body flopped down upon a stump. Moon rushed over and tried to talk to him but received no response. Moon dragged the severely wounded officer off the stump and straightened his body out on the ground. He placed a hat over Carter's face to shield it from the sun and then he dashed off toward the safety of the railroad tracks. Just as he reached a railroad cut, a shell exploded nearby showering him with dirt as he slid down the slope.[47]

Captain Washington T. Irvine wrote that the numerous enemy cannons "vomited shell and canister on the devoted band there present." He recalled that "The 35th was in open field in a hollow, while the other regiments were partially protected by a hill. A halt was made but no men could halt long under such fire. To move forward alone without support was folly. Col. Holt endeavored to move them, but his men refused, and finally broke to the rear in a railroad cut."[48]

Cadmus Wilcox's face grew long as the confidence of certain victory disappeared. He stared in disbelief as Thomas' Georgians and McGowan's

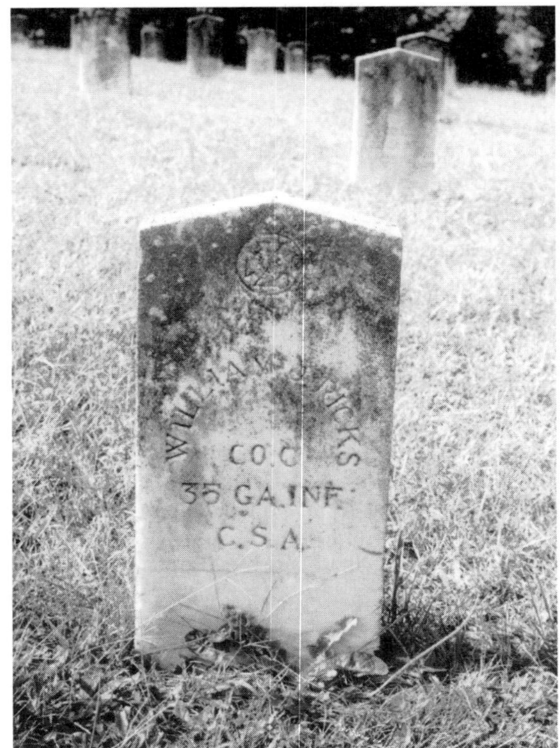

Tombstone of Private William J. Ricks, Co.C

This Campbell County veteran died a week after suffering wounds at the Battle of Spotsylvania Court House on May 12, 1864. He was buried at Spotsylvania Confederate Cemetery.

Photo by the author

1st and 12th South Carolina regiments broke rearward. In their worst performance of the war, Thomas watched helplessly as his men dashed back toward the railroad. Confederate soldiers in other units noted the poor showing and voiced some criticism of the Georgians. Sergeant Marion Hill Fitzpatrick, 45th Georgia, described the withdrawal of the brigade sharpshooters:

> We soon ran up with the yankee skirmish line, and fought them hot and heavy, drove them in and fought the line of battle for awhile. But they got too strong for us and we fell back, expecting to find the Brigade in our rear ready to go on and whip them out. But we had inclined to the right and the Brigade to the left, so where I was I found no support atall in my rear. Several of us fell back to the railroad where started from. The fight then opened in earnest. They drove the Yanks a good ways but fell back about a mile last night.[49]

A fellow 45th Georgian wrote, "We had to run like anything one time but it was unavoidable the enemy throwing seven colums against one. I hated to run but thought prudence the better part of valor especially as I saw every body else running the same way."[50]

Wilcox expressed frustration because Thomas' men had driven in the enemy line, but then they had broken rearward themselves. The gap created when Thomas' and McGowan's men broke for the rear destroyed the Confederate momentum and caused the rest of the attack to collapse. The Light Division commander placed the blame for the debacle on Thomas' men. He wrote of the Georgia brigade, "The conduct of this brigade hither to of good reputation is inexplicable." He claimed that the rest of McGowan's Brigade had almost reached the enemy's batteries when "The breaking of the Georgia brigade on its left threw the South Carolina brigade into disorder."[51]

An officer in the 1st South Carolina stated that as they chased enemy skirmishers up and over the crest of a hill they came to within two hundred yards of the three batteries. "It would not have been difficult to capture them by a brisk charge; but Thomas's brigade did not come up, and the connection with the other three regiments of McGowan's brigade was broken by a gap of at least a hundred or more yards." He claimed that it was at this point that a severe enfilade fire from the right forced the two South Carolina regiments back.[52]

Whether the South Carolinians or Georgians broke rearward first was unknown. Edward Thomas' perspective on the situation at Jericho Ford remained a mystery because no written report by the Georgia commander ever surfaced. Cadmus Wilcox's report left no doubt that he blamed Thomas for the disaster. In reality, the day might have turned out better for

Wilcox if he had received better cavalry intelligence, a more timely arrival of Henry Heth's reinforcements, and a more aggressive push by Scales' (Lowrance) Brigade against the Union right flank.

At darkness, an angry Wilcox found the Georgians huddled in a railroad cut and he ordered them back forward. He reportedly berated Thomas there. The division moved back to Anderson's Station a short time later. The Battle of Jericho Mills resulted in over 600 casualties in Wilcox's Division. The 35th Georgia lost 10 killed and 28 wounded with another 21 missing.[53] One of those killed was Company G's Captain John Carter. Private William McElvany, Company F, also died. This youngest brother of Major James McElvany had enlisted only one month before. He became the third brother that Major McElvany buried during the war. Thirty-one-year-old Private Woodson D. Moon was also killed. He belonged to the large Moon clan from Company G. Augustus Moon had stood next to his relative when he died and he described to George Moon the location of the body. George crept back that night "to search for him to see if he was dead. He could hear the Union soldiers talking all around him. He found Woodson Moon's body and got his pocket knife and comb."[54]

Governeur K. Warren's men suffered light casualties during this fight. The Fifth Corps casualty returns represented the period from May 22–June 1 and thus were not specific to the fighting on May 23.[55]

The campaign had taken a toll on many of Thomas' men. The constant fighting for weeks with no relief had drained many men both physically and mentally. There had not been a mail call in over two weeks. One Georgian reported that he had just taken his boots off for the first time in three weeks to sleep. "We all look very much like a horse after a weeks hard riding on the shortest kind of rations." For many days, the men had survived on hard crackers and bacon. The gaunt stares and thin frames betrayed their hunger. The soldiers knew that if they could just halt for a short time, form a camp, then the supply wagons with food could reach them. Many, however, wondered when that time would come as Grant seemed determined to move his army to Richmond.[56]

Both armies reached a stalemate by May 26. Grant then moved around Lee's army again. By May 29, the Confederates blocked Grant's access to Richmond. As Hill's corps secured the left from Totopotomoy Creek west toward the Virginia Central Railroad, his soldiers scraped defensive positions and waited. Grant again sidestepped to the southeast toward Bethesda Church and then Cold Harbor, where both armies jockeyed for control of the crossroads settlement. There, Wilcox's Light Division anchored the Confederate right on the Chickahominy River. None of Edward Thomas' four regiments took an active part in the Battle of Cold Harbor on June 3 although Lieutenant Wyatt V. Liner, Company A, was wounded the following day and he died three days later.

The men of both armies maintained a stressful but dull vigilance over each other for the next nine days. The stench of rotting flesh engulfed everything as thousands of Union bodies roasted under the sun where they had fallen in front of the Confederate entrenchments. Hundreds of buzzards circled overhead. On the morning of June 13, the Federal lines stood empty.

Notes

Abbreviations:

CSR—"Compiled Service Records of Confederate Soldiers Who Served In Organizations From The State of Georgia," Thirty-fifth Infantry Regiment (National Archives Microfilm Publication M266) National Archives Building, Washington, D.C.

GDAH—Georgia Division of Archives and History, Morrow, Ga.

NMP—National Military Park

OR.—*War of the Rebellion: A Compilation of the Official Records of the Union and Confederate Armies.* 130 Vols.

1. Major General Cadmus Wilcox, "Report of Operations Around Spotsylvania, May 1864," Virginia Historical Society, Richmond, Va.; Major James T. McElvany, "The Letters and Journal of Major James T. McElvany of the 35th Georgia Infantry Regiment." p.24.
2. Ibid. McElvany, p.24.
3. *OR* ., Vol 36, Pt. I, p.908–909.
4. McElvany, p.24.
5. J.F.J. Caldwell, *The History of a Brigade of South Carolinians Known As 'Gregg's', and Subsequently As 'McGowan's' Brigade.* (Philadelphia, 1866) (Morningside Press reprint, p.202).
6. Wilcox.
7. *OR* ., Vol.36, Pt.I, p.909, 928.
8. J.A. Early, *General Jubal A. Early: Autobiographical Sketch and Narrative of the War Between the States.* (Philadelphia, 1912) p.355.
9. *OR* ., Vol. 36, Pt.I, p.909.
10. Early, p.355; Wilcox.
11. "Diary of George W. Hall, 14th Georgia Volunteers, CSA, 1861–1865," Hargrett Rare Book and Manuscript Library/ University of Georgia Libraries, Athens, Ga. p.17.
12. *OR* ., Vol. 36, Pt.I, p.909.
13. Wilcox; McElvany, p.24.
14. Hall. p.18; Letter of Sergeant Major James P. Johnston to "Mrs. E.J. Garrett from Near Port Walthal, Virginia July 20th, 1864," James Garrett Collection.
15. Hall, p.18.
16. McElvany, p.24–25.

17. Letter of R.H. and Elizabeth Farmer to "dear Daughter from Newton Co. ga. June 18th 1864," Civil War Miscellany, Personal Papers, R.H. and Elizabeth Farmer Folder, GDAH.
18. J.M. Kimbrough, "My War History 1861–65," typescript at Chickamauga-Chattanooga NMP, Ga.
19. Hiram W. Hammond, "Confederate Diary of Hiram W. Hammond, Co.E, 35th Georgia Regiment Volunteers."
20. J.P. Johnston Letter. July 20th, 1864.
21. Wilcox.
22. Ibid; Early, p.355–356; McElvany, p.25.
23. *OR* ., Vol. 36, Pt.I, p.931.
24. *Daily Columbus Enquirer,* Columbus, Ga., June 3, 1864, "An Incident of the Battlefield."
25. Letter of Lieut WC Goggans to "Mr. Josiah Goggans from Camp Hill near Buryville Northern Va. Nov 5th 1862," William C. Goggans Civil War Letters, courtesy of Hargrett Rare Book & Manuscript Library/ University of Georgia Libraries, Athens Ga.
26. Marion Hill Fitzpatrick, *Letters to Amanda.* (Macon, Ga., 1998) p. 143–144. (edited by Jeffrey C. Lowe and Sam Hodges).
27. Letter of W.J. Moore to "Mrs Garrett from Camp Woods Agust 19th 1864," James M. Garrett Collection.
28. Letter of John H. Taylor, Chaplain 35 Ga to "Mrs Garrett from Field Infirmary Near Petersburg August the 27th 1864," James M. Garrett Collection.
29. Wilcox.
30. Letter of Francis Solomon Johnson to "Darling Emmie, Near Spotsylvania C.H. May 17th/64," Francis Solomon Johnson, Jr., Co.F, 45th Ga. to Emily Hutchings-Special Collections, MS 243, Hargrett Rare Book and Manuscript Library/University of Georgia Libraries, Athens, Ga.
31. Fitzpatrick, p. 145.
32. Ibid; *OR* ., Vol.36, Pt.I, p.232.
33. Ibid. Vol. 36, Pt. I, p.910–911.
34. Wilcox.
35. James Folsom, *Heroes and Martyrs of Georgia-Georgia's Record In The Revolution Of 1861.* (Macon, Ga., 1864) p.121. (reprint by Butternut and Blue, 1995, p.134)-note: Folsom only listed dead and wounded. I derived the missing soldiers from a roster search through CSR, as well as a search through Lillian Henderson, *Roster of the Confederate Soldiers of Georgia 1861–1865,* Vol.III, (Hapeville, Ga., 1960) p.843–929.
36. *OR* ., Vol. 36, Pt.I, p.148.
37. Fitzpatrick, p.146–147; Wilcox.
38. Letter of Francis Solomon Johnson to "Dearest Emmie, Near Hanover Junction, May 23rd 1864," Francis Solomon Johnson, Jr., Co.F, 45th Ga. to Emily Hutchings-Special Collections, MS 243, Hargrett Rare Book and Manuscript Library, University of Georgia Libraries, Athens, Ga.
39. Caldwell, p.204.
40. Wilcox.

41. *OR* ., Vol. 36, Pt.I, p.563.
42. Ibid., Vol.36, Pt. I, p.617.
43. Ibid., Vol. 36, Pt.I, p.621.
44. Wilcox.
45. *OR..,* Vol. 36, Pt.I, p. 582, 589.
46. Ibid., Vol. 36, Pt.I, p. 655–656.
47. Augustus J. Moon anecdote, "Reminiscences of Confederate Soldiers and Stories of the War 1861–65," Collected by Ga. Division, United Daughters of the Confederacy, Volume XIII, p.106. located at GDAH.
48. W.T. Irvine, "Old 35th Georgia", *The Sunny South,* Atlanta, May 2, 1891. Irvine's description of the " . . . vomited shell and canister. . . ." in describing the intensity of the Union artillery is almost verbatim from Folsom's 1864 book. Irvine obviously refreshed his memory from Folsom's book prior to writing his 1891 article; Folsom, p.142. (Butternut & Blue reprint p.140)
49. Fitzpatrick, p.147.
50. F.S. Johnson Letter. May 23, 1864.
51. Wilcox.
52. Caldwell, p.205.
53. Folsom, p.134. See above endnote #35 as missing soldiers were derived from the same sources.
54. Moon. pg.104–107. A records search provided no record of a George Moon. However, of the twelve Moons that served in the regiment, eleven of them were in Company G. My guess is that George was a nickname. I have narrowed the list down to three possible soldiers that could be George Moon: Private John A. Moon, Private M.L. Moon, or First Sergeant Joseph D. Moon.
55. *OR.*, Vol. 36, Pt.I, p.156–157. The casualty return from May 23–June 1 showed Jacob Sweitzer's entire brigade lost only 14 killed, 77 wounded and 13 missing for a total of 104. William Robinson's Iron Brigade lost 20 killed, 95 wounded and 17 captured/missing for a total of 132. Joseph Bartlett's brigade reported 12 killed, 88 wounded and 5 captured/missing for an aggregate of 105 men.
56. F.S. Johnson Letter. May 23, 1864.

Note: The Jericho Mills Battlefield is on posted private property and there was no opportunity to walk the terrain and get pictures.

Chapter Fourteen

Total War Around Petersburg

"We ar still holding old Grant in check and will as long as old Bob has got a man but that army will whip us yet I fear."
Corporal Robert A. Jackson

Robert E. Lee immediately sent James Longstreet's First Corps, now commanded by Richard H. Anderson, in pursuit of the elusive U.S. Grant on June 13. A.P. Hill's Third Corps joined the chase. The Confederate commander did not know whether Grant had moved southeast along the Peninsula or had looped toward the James River and Richmond. Hill's troops waded the Chickahominy River and passed west of White Oak Swamp. That evening they ran directly into cavalry and infantry from Major General Gouvernour K. Warren's Fifth Corps at Riddell's Shop along the Charles City Road just north of the 1862 Malvern Hill battlefield. The Georgia brigade sharpshooters formed a skirmish line. The remainder of Edward Thomas' men deployed into another line about two hundred yards behind. Both lines moved forward and pushed the enemy off a wooded hill. The blue troops reformed and made a strong stand aided by artillery. The Confederate persistence finally forced the Union troops from the field. The 35th Georgia lost two killed and six wounded.[1]

Enemy fire severely wounded Private Andrew J. Moon of Company B. He was a brother of seven Moons from Company G. George Moon, apparently went berserk when told of the wounding of his brother. "His comrades had to hold him to keep him from going right on to the Yankee Line. He [George] was a brave and fearless soldier and did not mind a close call."[2]

As darkness settled over the area, the 35th Georgia bivouacked on the fields of the 1862 Frayser's Farm battlefield. By June 16, Confederate leaders discovered that many of Grant's troops had crossed the James River. Several Confederate divisions raced off in pursuit. A.P. Hill's corps remained in a blocking position to protect Richmond. Hill's line extended from the James River north past Malvern Hill to the Riddell's Shop area. The tactical situation left Lee in a difficult position because he still did not know the location of three Union corps. Also worrisome was the poor physical condition of many of the men. The constant exposure to all of nature's elements had taken its toll. The men constantly grumbled. Muddy trenches and muddy roads had been their continuous companions for forty-three long days since they had left Orange Court House. The requirement for maximum manpower on the front line coupled with constant anxiety kept the men from getting adequate rest. The minimal and poor quality of the rations further frustrated the men. All of these conditions plus the numerous swampy water sources in the area helped to aggravate the many cases of disease. During this period, Confederate medical personnel reported numerous cases of indigestion, fever, dysentery and diarrhea.[3]

Early on June 18, Lee ordered Hill's corps, to cross the James River near Chaffin's Bluff and move toward Petersburg. This major rail junction and second largest town in Virginia obviously was Grant's objective. Thomas' Georgians entered Petersburg by late afternoon. They marched out of town to the southwest and assumed positions near the Petersburg Railroad. Both sides dug in for the longest campaign of the war.

Thomas ordered his men to halt their digging and prepare to move on June 21. Grant had dispatched two corps to capture the Petersburg Railroad, the main Confederate supply line that ran south out of Petersburg. The Confederate divisions of Cadmus Wilcox and William Mahone marched south and then turned east to punch into the Federal flank. The next day, in the thick woods, Mahone made contact and rolled back the Federal left. His troops captured 1,700 prisoners and everlasting fame. Wilcox's efforts were uncoordinated, either through misunderstanding of orders or unfamiliarity with the terrain, and consequently of little help. The Light Division returned to the Petersburg defense line. The 35th Georgia reported three wounded and three missing.[4]

As the Georgians dug their trenches, concern grew for their families as Major General William T. Sherman's Union army advanced toward Atlanta. Letters from home slowly trickled in for Thomas' men because "the Yanks tore up the railroad and stopped communication, and it has been useless to write."[5] Many of the soldiers elected to send their letters home via friends headed south on furlough. Some of these letters and their couriers failed to make it to Georgia because they were captured enroute.

Back in the Petersburg trenches, an occasional soldier fell victim to a sniper's bullet after exposing himself above the walls too long. After dark, eyes and ears strained to pick out any enemy movement that might signal an attack. With the opposing lines as little as one hundred yards apart, exchanges of gunfire were frequent. Disease still took its toll on many Georgians. Desertion became another problem as many soldiers tired of the war

Captain Nathan C. Carr, Co.B

The men of his company elected this Newton County veteran to be their captain in June 1864. He replaced Captain Graves B. Almand who had died of typhoid fever. Carr was wounded on March 25, 1865 at the Battle of Jones Farm. He surrendered two weeks later at Appomattox.

From *Sunny South,* Atlanta, Ga. May 2, 1891

and the horrendous conditions in which they lived. Some deserters, worried about their families, attempted to return to war-torn Georgia. Federal reports commonly mentioned desertions by members of Thomas' Brigade from June to August 1864.[6] A search through the records revealed twenty-one 35th Georgia soldiers listed as deserters during the Petersburg campaign.

Thomas' Brigade crossed the Appomattox River and occupied a defense line several miles northeast of Petersburg on July 4. The right wing of their skirmish line rested on the Appomattox River. The enemy line stood only a short distance away. Each side had reached an amicable agreement not to fire on each other unless an advance was made. Some soldiers defied orders and traded food, newspapers, knives and tobacco with their enemy counterparts. Evidence indicated that the brigade sharpshooter battalion occupied a separate camp from the rest of the brigade as indicated by a letter written by Sergeant Marion Hill Fitzpatrick, 45th Georgia. He wrote on July 18 that his skirmishers still camped in the same place and that cordial trading relations with the enemy had ceased. "We sharpshooters have not been relieved since we came here, and do not want to be as we have a better position than back at the Brigade." The sharpshooters probably remained in this position until at least the middle of August.[7]

After July, the 35th Georgia occupied an area around the Dunlop House. This area was located six miles north of Petersburg between Fort Clifton on the Appomattox River and Swift Run. The Georgians periodically marched a short distance away to provide support along the line.[8] The Georgians did not participate in the rout of the Federal Second Corps at Reams Station south of Petersburg on August 25. Cadmus Wilcox stated that he entered the fight with the brigades of McGowan, Lane and Scales.

Colonel Bolling H. Holt became ill in mid-summer of 1864. Lieutenant Colonel William H. McCullohs assumed command of the 35th Georgia. Holt received a certificate of disability dated July 7 and signed by a surgeon named R.S.J. Peebles. This paper admitted Holt to private quarters in Richmond for treatment. After several days of treatment there, Holt received another certificate of disability. This new certificate, signed by three surgeons, stated that his chronic diarrhea, catarrh and debility required a six-week furlough from duty. The young colonel forwarded his certificates of disability to division headquarters on a regular basis. He then requested a thirty-day leave. Light Division officials, however, disapproved the certificate of disability dated August 12 and forwarded the paperwork to the corps hospital. This apparent misunderstanding turned into a serious problem for Holt because he had already left for Georgia. An investigation began when the Light Division staff discovered that Colonel Holt no longer resided at the corps hospital and had gone for treatment to Richmond. Colonel Joseph A. Engelhard, the division assistant adjutant general, sent a letter to Colonel T.J. Simmons of the 45th Georgia, the acting brigade commander. Engelhard demanded to know why and how Holt got to Richmond.[9]

The regimental muster rolls from September-October 1864, listed Holt as absent without leave. The November-December 1864 documents listed him "absent, sick without leave." A lengthy notation in an inspection report dated November 29, 1864 said:

> Absent since July 16, 1864. He received a furlough from hospital in Richmond at that time, but it is not known how Colonel Holt got to Richmond as the books at the Corps Hospital show that he was ordered to rejoin his regiment from there: but he did not return. Certificates of disability have been forwarded in his case but it is not known what action was taken on them at superior Hd.Qrs. Colonel Holt is now reporting at a Hospital in Columbus, Georgia.[10]

When Holt returned to the regiment in January 1865, the matter remained unresolved because the January-February 1865 muster roll listed him present in arrest.

A mysterious court martial proceeding against Brigadier General Edward Lloyd Thomas added additional confusion to the leadership ranks during the summer. The court recommended a formal reprimand for Thomas. A thorough search through numerous records failed to divulge the charges filed against Thomas and by whom. Perhaps Cadmus Wilcox preferred charges against Thomas based on the division commander's perception of the poor showing by Thomas' Brigade at the Battle of Jericho Mill on May 23. No doubt, relief swept over the officers and men of the Georgia brigade when the Adjutant and Inspector-General's Office in Richmond issued Special Orders #216 on September 12. Item VII read, "The proceedings of the military court for the Third Corps of the Army of Northern Virginia in the trial of Brigadier-General E.L. Thomas, Provisional Army Confederate States, having been transmitted to the Secretary of War, and by him laid before the President, the sentence of reprimand pronounced by the court against him is, by order of the President, remitted. Brigadier-General will be released from arrest and returned to duty."[11]

Major James T. McElvany assumed temporary command of the regiment during September 1864 because of Lieutenant Colonel William McCullohs' absence. As both sides harassed each other with cannon and small arms fire, morale in Lee's army sank lower each day. Inadequate food and poor sanitation in the trenches promoted widespread disease. As the difficulties mounted, many soldiers realized they needed to strengthen their devotion to God, and the spirit of revivalism grew again and remained present until the end of the war.

On September 19, a Federal report stated "A deserter from the Thirty-Fifth Georgia, Thomas' brigade, came into the lines of the Tenth Army Corps at 10 A.M. yesterday. He reports that his brigade (Thomas') extends from the Appomattox at a point opposite Beauregard's line to Pickett's division, a distance of four miles."[12] This was the area near Fort Clifton.

One morning during the first week of October, the brigade sharpshooters manned a forward skirmish line. They began to fire in rapid succession. The soldiers along the main line peered ahead with their rifles at the ready. More shots rang out as a fat cow came crashing through the undergrowth toward the rear. The twentieth shot dropped her to the ground. The sharpshooters immediately butchered the animal and divided the meat. For many, this cow became the first fresh meat seen in a long time. A colonel of one of the regiments became extremely upset when he found that the adversary was a cow and not the Yankees. "He sent us back and that night sent us word that he would acquit us but we must do so no more. The boys said they would not unless another cow came over."[13]

Some supplies did succeed in reaching the Georgians during the fall of 1864. During this time, the quartermaster received and issued ammunition for .54, .58 and .69 caliber rifles.[14] The supply wagons also brought pants and shirts for the men. In some cases these supplies came too little too late. Many soldiers wrote home requesting clothes, probably for the better fit and color selection. One man even gave directions in a letter to his wife for sewing seams together on pants to prevent hiding places for lice, commonly referred to as "neighbors." Since shoe supplies were low, twenty-three-year-old Corporal Robert A. Jackson, one of three brothers from Company E, became the shoemaker in the 35th Georgia. He received this position after he was wounded in the right knee in May 1864 and had trouble walking. The brigade officially detailed one man from each regiment to repair shoes.[15]

Corporal Jackson expressed his good fortune to be away from the front lines and living with Quartermaster Captain Virgil L. Hopson. He wrote, "Know I am not in the wether, I have a good house to stay in and I am in a good mess. I am messing with the quartermaster of our regiment and you no they have the best that going to eat." Jackson indicated that he could make from ten to fifty dollars a day fixing shoes.[16] He reflected on the grim prospects of the Confederacy and his personal frustration with not receiving mail from home because of the swath Sherman's troops had cut across Georgia. Four days before Christmas, Jackson wrote, "I had give out ever hearing from you all eny more. I had written 8 letters sence I got a word from you but I know you never got my letters. I don't blame you a tall Ma. We ar still holding old Grant in check and will as long as old Bob has got a man but that army will whip us yet I fear. Old Hood is just letting the Vandles envade our own State Georgia the land of my birth."[17]

By at least the first week of November 1864, the 35th Georgia and the rest of the brigade moved their line to the Covington House on the bank of the Appomattox River. This area sat about one mile south of Fort Clifton. Here they dug defensive positions.[18] All soldiers between the ages of 18 and 45 who had previous assignments to rear echelon details were ordered back to their units. This order represented an attempt to increase the number of rifles on the front line.[19]

The outlook remained bleak as the Confederate soldiers prepared for their fourth Virginia winter. Many had lost hope and the ability to cope with the harsh conditions. Water and mud filled the ditches. Dry weather created a layer of dust that covered everything. Frequent enemy artillery and mortar fire interrupted the boredom in the trenches. In November 1864, a large number of soldiers from Thomas' Brigade tossed down their weapons and walked into Federal lines. The most common complaint they aired to their captors was a lack of winter clothing.[20] For those that remained, November's chilly winds brought the need for winter quarters. During November 3–4, both sides reached an agreement to halt the skirmishing in front of Thomas' Brigade so construction of quarters could safely begin. Sergeant Marion Hill Fitzpatrick, 45th Georgia, described the type of quarters many Georgians built. "Instead of building huts as formerly, they dug a hole in the ground about six feet deep and ten feet square, put over the top a layer of large logs. On that a layer of boughs and leaves, and cover the whole with dirt which they pile on till it is shaped like a potatoe hill. They then fix a chimney and are not only very comfortable but protected from the enemy's shells."[21]

During the latter portion of 1864, Private Frank Edwards, Company D, and another soldier received an order to man a listening post near enemy lines. Edwards dubiously claimed that Lieutenant General A.P. Hill specifically selected and briefed him for this mission. A courier guided the two soldiers as they slogged through the knee-deep mud and water of a swamp to reach their posts. Edwards described his sentiments after the courier dropped him by a tall pine tree and then left to take the other soldier to another post:

> Do you have any idea how I felt? That pine seemed to be the tallest tree I ever saw, about a hundred feet to the first limb. I did as I was ordered, and stood very, very close to that pine. I could see a flash of lightning occasionally, and it was misting rain a little, just enough to make it very lonely; my feelings were such that I can not describe them. No one near. The man with whom I came was a mile away, and the enemy within about one hundred and fifty yards of my post, but I can't say that the enemy was any consolation to me. I stood there listening, thinking. I could not tell you all I thought, only my thoughts were such that my hair seemed to stand straight up.

A short time later, Edwards heard the clanking movement of artillery and wagon trains and officers giving orders in hushed tones. A closer sound soon drew his attention:

> About that time I heard a rustle in the leaves just in front of me, about ten steps away. I did not look. I simply stood and listened. The undergrowth was oak and hickory, very thick. I will say this much, I don't think my breathing was ever so short. It seemed I could 'swallow my throat'. That something kept moving towards me. It moved

> something like a hog in the leaves. It moved to my right and then to my left, just a little closer every time. I began to think. I decided to risk one eye anyway. My face was very close to the pine and my hat off. I looked very close to my right and saw a bulk of something about five paces from the pine. That was my pine yet. I was satisfied that that something was a yankee. But I could not tell what he wanted to do; but I had it fixed in my mind what I was to do. I heard him make about three steps toward my pine. He came to a standstill as though he thought, 'Nobody here.' I was very close to that pine, indeed. I thought, 'Now was the time to act.' A great deal depended on that first move. If I fired and killed him, the enemy would hear and come at once. I made ready. He was about two paces from the pine. I jumped right in his front; I had the drop. I said, 'Surrender.' He jumped and threw down his gun, and said, 'Yes, yes, yes! I will! I will! Don't shoot!'

Edwards claimed he escorted his prize back through Confederate lines all the way to A.P. Hill's command tent. Hill informed Edwards that he had been the only successful soldier out of five men placed at that post. The other four had been captured or killed.[22]

On Sunday, December 4, a special visitor came to the brigade area and broke the monotony of the trench lines. This man came to talk about his invention that he believed could win the war for the South. While many men laughed at his idea, he was actually quite farsighted and only slightly ahead of his time. R.O. Davidson talked about his mechanical bird operated by steam that carried a pilot and a number of shells that could be dropped on fear-stricken Yankees. The Confederate government had denied his request for aid on the project. Ebbing with confidence, Davidson asked the troops to contribute to his effort. He passed a hat and collected $116 from the Georgians. He planned to make five hundred birds that would be ready for active operations the following February.[23]

An article from the *Charleston News and Courier* that was reprinted in the *Southern Historical Society Papers* described a similar visit to McGowan's Brigade during the same time period at Petersburg:

> One cold, raw day the brigade was called out, without arms, to hear a speech from a scientific personage, who was introduced as 'Professor' Blank. The old soldiers crowded around and took their seats on the ground and he unfolded his scheme for demoralizing and driving away Grant's army. He had just invented an airship. In shape, it was something like a bird. And for that reason he had called it 'Artis Avis', or, 'The Bird of Art', which was the meaning of the two Latin words. The frame was made of hoop-iron and wire. It was covered

> with white-oak splints. It was to be run by a one-horse-power engine, and flown by a single brave man. The engine was to be in the body and to furnish power for keeping the wings in motion. A small door at the shoulder was opened or closed to control the direction of the Bird of Art. A door under the throat was opened when it was desirable to descend and a door on top of the neck when the operator wished to go higher. There was machinery by which the tail could be spread out or closed. In the body of the bird there was a room for a number of shells, and the operator, by touching a spring with his foot, could drop them upon the enemy from a safe distance. The 'Professor' claimed that he had completed one bird and made a test of its speed and how it would work. He had tied it to a flat-car, which was coupled to a fast engine. It was then attached to the flat-car with a long, strong rope. The word was given, and the railroad engine started off at great speed. The Bird of Art did the same, and had no trouble in keeping up with the iron horse without pulling on the rope. The 'Professor' concluded his remarks by saying he needed a little more money to make birds enough to destroy Grant's army, and asked the old soldiers to contribute one dollar each to the cause. Many of them did, and the 'Professor' moved on and disappeared.[24]

This was no doubt the same man who spoke to and solicited money from the Georgians. Apparently, this man was Roderick O. Davidson, who had developed his flying machine idea for several years. Confederate Senator Brown from Mississippi had previously presented information on Davidson's idea to the first session of the First Confederate Congress on February 27, 1862. The idea was referred to the Committee on Military Affairs and obviously did not get very far with the politicians, which explained why Davidson solicited monetary donations from soldiers on the front line two and a half years later. A *Confederate Veteran* article listed a Dr. Roderick O. Davidson on the roster of Company E, 11th Mississippi Infantry Regiment. Davidson worked a brief stint in the infantry and then found a position as a clerk in the Confederate Treasury Department in Richmond. The article mentioned that he was a well-educated man with an interest in air navigation.[25] While Davidson appeared sincere about his idea, the fact that he solicited donations from soldiers caused some to question his real motive.

A month after Davidson's visit, Frank Edwards received a plush assignment. A local plantation owner had complained to Confederate authorities that his livestock and property were being pillaged by nearby soldiers. About the first week of January 1865, Edwards arrived at the family's doorstep as their guard. He must have been the envy of every other soldier in Company D. Edwards claimed this assignment was his reward for capturing and bringing a prisoner to A.P. Hill.[26]

The first two months of 1865 found Thomas' Georgians still manning the line along the Appomattox River north of Petersburg. This period found the 35th Georgia staff undermanned. Colonel Bolling Holt had returned from his apparent unauthorized hospital stay in Columbus, Georgia. The regimental muster roll listed him as present and under arrest. Lieutenant Colonel McCullohs and Major McElvany were both on sick furlough. This left Captain John Duke as the acting regimental commander. Surgeon William P. Hill was on furlough. The muster roll listed several staff non-commissioned officers as absent without leave, including Sergeant Major George H. Dozier. Quite possibly this AWOL listing resulted from the men's inability to return from furloughs in Georgia due to widespread enemy movement throughout the South.[27]

By the first week of March, Phil Sheridan's Federal troops had defeated Jubal Early at Waynesboro in the Shenandoah Valley. Sheridan's men moved towards Petersburg to reinforce Grant. The 35th Georgia, still commanded by Captain Duke, received orders detaching them from the brigade. They moved north to man the earthworks along the Richmond, Fredericksburg and Potomac Railroad at Richmond.

The rest of Thomas' Brigade moved from their position north of the Appomattox River. They joined A.P. Hill's corps in the lines southwest of Petersburg. Later in the month, the 35th Georgia headed back to Petersburg and reunited with the rest of the brigade on this line.

Confederate lines extended for nearly forty miles from Richmond to Petersburg and then southwestward to Hatcher's Run. Lee had an army of probably less than 60,000 men to man this long line. He faced two well-fed and well-supplied Union armies of more than 100,000 troops. These enemy surpluses required the Confederate commander to be efficient in positioning his units. The Confederates strengthened likely Union avenues of attack with impregnable defensive works. They manned these spots with many soldiers. Unlikely areas of attack conversely received fewer men. The engineers in Cadmus Wilcox's sector had built a dam across Old Town or Rohoic Creek. The resultant backflow of water turned a portion of the area into a quagmire that rendered it an unlikely area for attack. This effort freed soldiers to plug another part of the line.[28]

During the period from February 15 to March 5, 923 men deserted from Hill's corps. This represented an average of fifty-one desertions per day. Prospects indeed seemed dim for the Confederacy as another spring bloomed in Virginia.[29] Thomas' entire brigade had dwindled to 78 officers and 958 men present for duty—barely more than a full-strength regiment.

Casualties from fighting, disease and desertion had taken their toll. What few green recruits trickled in further lowered the morale of the veterans.[30]

Frank Edwards, meanwhile, still guarded the plantation near Petersburg. This Virginia family had welcomed him like a son. Their only son had died at the Battle of First Manassas in 1861. It did not take long for Edwards to fall in love with the younger of the two daughters. Edwards wrestled with his situation because he knew he would soon receive orders to return to the front. "Now my friends, I was surely between two fires. There was that good family and my great love for Miss Emma, the sweetest and best girl in all the world to me; and I was compelled to turn my back and follow my duty, go to the front, not knowing what would be the result; not knowing but what I would be at Petersburg dead before the sun rose again. It certainly would change your minds to something more than sadness." The two lovers tried to spend as much time together before the inevitable day arrived. When that difficult day came Edwards wrote: "She was sitting on the sofa. Her great emotion was uncontrollable. I began to think I would never leave her. I bid them all farewell. That was the greatest trial of my life. The family were all in tears. I passed on. The old gentleman had his carriage ready. I went out and took my seat in the carriage. I went to the front March 24, 1865. I had spent two and a half months at the home of the kind old gentleman."[31]

At 10 P.M., on March 24, the soldiers in Thomas' and Lane's brigades marched northeast along the Boydton Plank Road toward Petersburg. They passed the leadworks along the Petersburg Railroad. The march continued until early the following morning when the tired soldiers moved into position to support Major General John Gordon's Division on the east side of Petersburg. Thomas' Brigade remained in reserve for the ill-fated attack against part of the Union Ninth Corps at Fort Stedman. The Confederate attackers seized the Union fort, several artillery batteries and a portion of the enemy line. A heavy Federal counterattack, however, drove Gordon's men back to their line.

The weary soldiers in Lane's and Thomas' brigades marched back to their former positions. As soon as they returned they faced a Union attack there. Their line paralleled the Boydton Plank Road on the south side of the road. The buildings of the Jones farm stood just west of Church Road between the Confederate picket and main lines. Lane's men occupied a position astride the Church Road. On Lane's right stood McGowan's Brigade while Thomas' Georgians held the left. The Georgian's portion of the main line lay just north of Rohoic Creek. This marshy area to their front created a good defensive position. Confederate pickets huddled in their entrenched lines about a half-mile south. Pickets from Major General Horatio Wright's Union Sixth Corps manned a line no more than one-half mile south of the

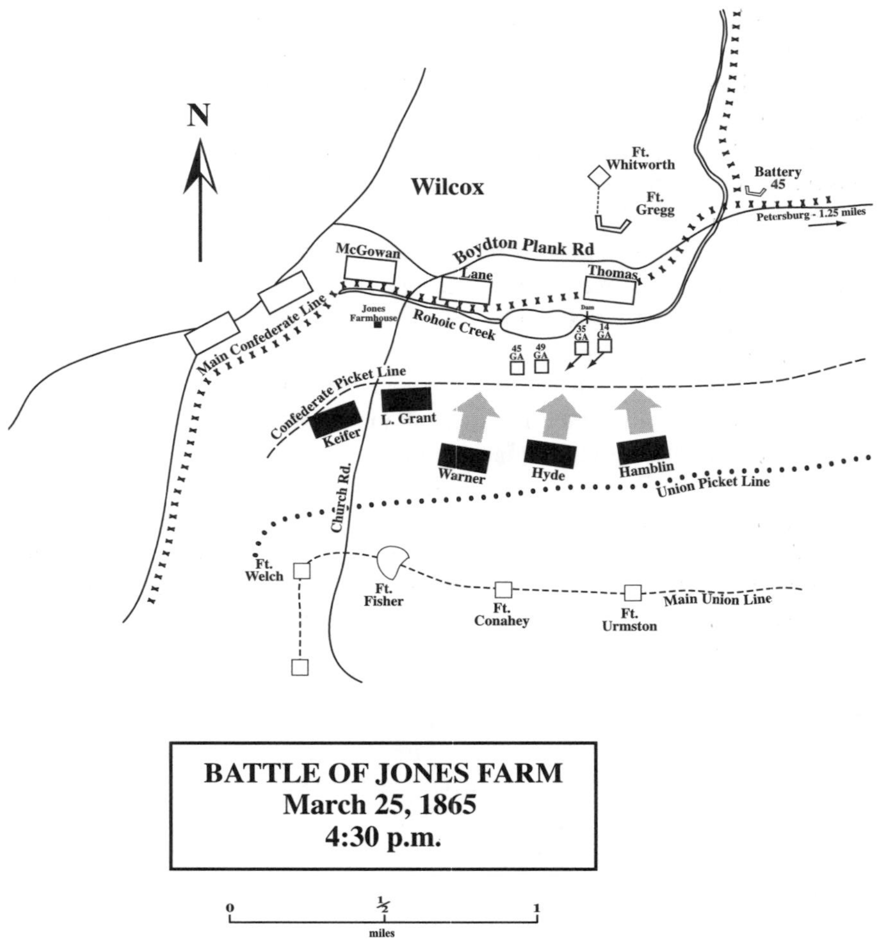

BATTLE OF JONES FARM
March 25, 1865
4:30 p.m.

Confederate picket line. The Union main line, anchored at intervals by forts, stood south of the picket position. Union Forts Conahey, Fisher, Welch and Gregg occupied the sector ahead of Wilcox's Light Division.

A portion of Wilcox's soldiers had repulsed an undermanned Union assault against the entrenched Confederate picket line at around 1 P.M., on March 25. A short time after Lane's and Thomas' men had returned to their old positions the soldiers of the Union Sixth Corps renewed their assault. It was shortly before 3 P.M. when the Union infantry began to maneuver.

Union Colonel J. Warren Kiefer commanded a brigade in Brigadier General Truman Seymour's division. Two of his regiments had received considerable casualties in the previous failed assault on the heavily defended picket line. Kiefer received new orders to take the same picket line. Kiefer pushed his regiments forward toward his own entrenched picket line in preparation for the assault. This movement drew the interest of Confederate gunners. A severe fire of artillery projectiles rained down upon his men. The brigades in the Federal assault line from left to right belonged to Kiefer, Colonel James M. Warner, Brigadier General Lewis Grant, Colonel Thomas Hyde, and Colonel Joseph Hamblin. At 3 P.M. a signal gun roared, and Kiefer reported that the troops leaped out of their holes and charged forward without stopping to fire. Enthusiastic Union infantrymen quickly inundated and overran the Confederate picket line.[32]

Edward Thomas ordered the 45th and 49th Georgia regiments forward to recapture the picket line. Shortly thereafter he sent the 35th and 14th Georgia regiments to help. Soon the full weight of the Georgia brigade forced the Unionists to withdraw. A witness in McGowan's Brigade reported that as the Georgians moved near the Jones house, they came forward in line of battle almost at a right angle to their captured picket line and the enemy maneuvered to front them. This move exposed the enemy left flank to a severe enfilade of rifle and artillery fire from McGowan's line.[33] The Georgians most likely encountered Hyde's mixed brigade composed of the 1st Maine, 43rd New York, 49th New York, 77th New York, 122nd New York, and 61st Pennsylvania. The Georgians did not remain long at the recaptured picket line, however, as a large Union counterattack soon overwhelmed them. When the blue-clad infantry again swarmed into the rifle pits, those Georgians that could not escape found themselves swinging their rifles as clubs, but this was really to no avail. A ball hit Private Theldred S. Lay, Company D, in the left leg. He fell to the ground in excruciating pain. The 35th Georgia's temporary commander, Captain John Duke, lay dead on the ground nearby. Broken bodies sprawled all along the Confederate picket line. Union soldiers killed or captured those Southerners who remained in the ditch. Theldred Lay fell into the captured category. Union authorities sent Lay to a Washington, D.C. hospital to treat his severely fractured leg. He died there from his injuries and Union soldiers buried him in the Confederate section at Arlington National Cemetery.

Colonel James Warner described his Union counterattack:

> At 5 P.M. was directed by General Getty to carry the enemy's skirmish pits in our front. The line was formed in the following order from left to right: One hundred and second Pennsylvania Veteran Volunteers, One hundred and thirty ninth Pennsylvania Volunteers, First Maine

Tombstone of Private Theldred S. Lay, Co.D
Lay was shot in the left leg at the Battle of Jones Farm on March 25, 1865. The blow severely fractured the leg and he was captured. Federal authorities sent him to a hospital in Washington, D.C., but he died. His final resting place is in the Confederate section at Arlington National Cemetery.
Photo by author.

> Veteran Volunteers, Ninety-third Pennsylvania Veteran Volunteers, and about fifty of the One Hundred and twenty-second New York Volunteers. The behavior of the troops was admirable. The pits and a crest about 300 yards beyond was carried, capturing many prisoners.[34]

Captain Washington T. Irvine reported that the soldiers in the 45th and 49th Georgia regiments found themselves almost surrounded by a large enemy force. The 35th and 14th Georgia soldiers moved in to help prevent their capture. As the enemy reinforced their position, he described the fight as "short and bloody." All four Georgia regiments just barely escaped. The enemy forced them back in confusion. The Georgians raced across the narrow causeway atop the Rohoic Creek dam toward the protection of their main defense line. The blue infantry occupied the area of the Jones farmhouse and then fell back to the captured picket trenches just south of the house. Soldiers from the 2nd Vermont torched the large structure to prevent the home's use by Confederate sharpshooters. Smoke and flames leaped into the air and illuminated the sky shortly after dark.[35]

Frank Edwards described his version of the back and forth fight. "Our command was ordered in double quick to meet them. I was a member of the sharpshooters. The line of battle halted. The sharpshooters charged the enemy and drove them back to their works. We fell back a short distance. They charged with their entire line. We fell back some distance again. Our line of battle held them back and finally drove them to their works with heavy loss on both sides."[36]

Irvine described the 35th Georgia's losses at the Battle of Jones Farm as 150 killed, wounded and captured. Irvine claimed this was the most severe fight for the brigade during the entire war. He believed the 35th Georgia entered the fray with over 300 men and lost about half of the regiment. These casualty figures could not be verified via any other official sources. Since Irvine issued his report twenty-six years after the fight he possibly overstated his casualty figures.[37] An unofficial roster count showed 6 killed, 8 wounded and 39 captured. Due to poor and inaccurate Confederate records keeping, these numbers are probably low. Sergeant Major Marion Hill Fitzpatrick, 45th Georgia, evidenced the severity of the fight. He recorded that his regiment lost 6 killed, 25 wounded and another 118 captured.[38]

During the fight, a spent ball struck Edward L. Thomas, but he refused to leave the field.[39] Private John C. Jackson, formerly first sergeant of Company E, was killed.[40] The totals for the Jones Farm fight coupled with the earlier losses at Fort Stedman brought the day's casualties in Lee's army to 4,000 killed, captured and wounded.

Notes

Abbreviations:

CSR—"Compiled Service Records of Confederate Soldiers Who Served In Organizations From The State of Georgia,"—Thirty-fifth Infantry Regiment (National Archives Microfilm Publication M266) National Archives Building, Washington, D.C.

GDAH—Georgia Division of Archives and History, Morrow, Ga.

NMP—National Military Park

OR.— War of the Rebellion: A Compilation of the Official Records of the Union and Confederate Armies. 130 Vols.

SHSP—Southern Historical Society Papers

1. *OR.,* Vol. 36, Pt. I, p.1035; James Folsom, *Heroes and Martyrs of Georgia-Georgia's Record In The Revolution Of 1861.* (Macon, Ga., 1864) p.142, (reprint by Butternut and Blue, 1995, p. 135, 140); J.F.J. Caldwell, *The History of a Brigade of South Carolinians Known As 'Gregg's', and Subsequently As 'McGowan's' Brigade.* (Philadelphia, 1866) (Morningside Press reprint, p. 211; William S. Dunlop, *Lee's Sharpshooters.* (Dayton, Oh. 1988) p. 101.
2. "Reminiscences of Confederate Soldiers and Stories of the War 1861–65" Volume XIII, pg.104–107. Compiled by the Georgia Division, United Daughters of the Confederacy, Georgia located at GDAH. A records search provided no record of a George Moon. However, of the twelve Moon's that served in the regiment, eleven of them were in Company G. My guess is that George was a nickname. I have narrowed the list down to three possible soldiers that could be George Moon: Private John A. Moon, Private M.L. Moon, or First Sergeant Joseph D. Moon.
3. Caldwell, p.213.
4. John D. Smith, *The History of the Nineteenth Regiment of Maine Volunteer Infantry 1862–65.* (Minneapolis, Mn., 1909) p.211; Folsom, p.140–141.
5. Marion Hill Fitzpatrick, *Letters to Amanda.* (Macon, Ga., 1998) p. 156. (edited by Jeffrey C. Lowe and Sam Hodges).
6. *OR .,* Vol.40, Pt.III, p.168, 762.
7. Fitzpatrick, p. 158, 161, 164.
8. W.T. Irvine, "Old 35th Georgia," *The Sunny South,* Atlanta, May 2, 1891.
9. CSR of Colonel Bolling Hall Holt, M266; "Letters Received by the Confederate Adjutant and Inspector General and Quartermaster General 1861–1865," (National Archives Microfilm Publication M474, roll 118, document 2075; roll 113, document 1017) National Archives Building, Washington, D.C.
10. Ibid, CSR; Ibid, "Letters recv. by Confed. AI&QG."
11. Orders, Adjutant and Inspector-General's Office, Richmond, Va., September 12, 1864. Special Orders No. 216, item VII.
12. *OR .,* Vol.42, Pt.II, p.913.
13. Fitzpatrick, p. 176–177.
14. CSR., Colonel Bolling Hall Holt.
15. Daniel A. Jackson Collection of Letters, microfilm, GDAH; Fitzpatrick, p.179
16. Jackson
17. Ibid., Letter of Robert Jackson from Petersburg, December 21, 1864. Jackson Collection, microfilm, GDAH.
18. Irvine.
19. Fitzpatrick, p. 182.
20. *OR .,* Vol.42, Pt.II, p.913.
21. Fitzpatrick, p.181.
22. John Frank Edwards, *Army Life of Frank Edwards—Confederate Veteran—Army of Northern Virginia 1861–1865.* 1906. p.10–16.
23. Fitzpatrick. p.187–188
24. *SHSP,* Vol. XXVII, 1900. "A Confederate Airship-The Artis Avis Which Was To Destroy Grant's Army," p. 303–305.

25. Ibid. Vol. 44, June 1923, p.64–65; *Confederate Veteran,* Vol. 33, February 1925, No.2, p.50–52.
26. Edwards. p.16.
27. "Compiled Service Records—Captions and Records of Events," National Archives, Washington, D.C./ also at GDAH on microfilm 279/84.
28. Caldwell, p.251; Dunlop, p.219–220.
29. Letters of Robert E. Lee to "John C. Breckinridge, Feb. 28 and Mar. 8, 1865," in "Lee Papers," Virginia Historical Society, Richmond, Va.
30. Carroll R. Patterson, "The 14th Georgia Volunteer Infantry—An Outline of Its History," Atlanta Historical Society, p.64; *OR* ., Vol.46, Series I, Pt. I, p.389.
31. Edwards. p.36–38.
32. *O.R* .,Vol. 46, Pt.I, p.309.
33. Caldwell, p.265.
34. *OR* ., Vol. 46, Pt. I, p.302–303.
35. Irvine; Caldwell, p.265; Ibid, Vol. 46, Pt. I, p.304–305.
36. Edwards. p.38.
37. Irvine.
38. Fitzpatrick, p.207.
39. *Columbus Daily Sun,* "In the Trenches Near Petersburg", March 28th, 1865, Columbus, Ga.
40. Letter of John C. Jackson to "Dear Susan March 7th 1864," Daniel A. Jackson Collection of Letters, microfilm, GDAH. Jackson was reduced in rank, loss of six months pay, and six months labor from court martial proceedings for being absent without leave. The specific date of his court martial was not known.

Note: the Confederate picket line at the Battle of Jones Farm has been decimated by the construction of a huge steel plant which unfortunately even sticks up well above the horizon.

Chapter Fifteen

LAST GASP AT FORT GREGG

"Our ammunition gave out. I don't think there was a cartridge left. I never saw such heroism as was shown there. I saw we were gone."
Private Frank Edwards

The last week of March 1865 saw the command of the 35th Georgia bestowed upon Captain Washington T. Irvine following the death of Captain John Duke. Illness and furloughs had depleted the command structure of the regiment. Colonel Bolling H. Holt's location and status remained unknown. He probably still remained under arrest for the 1864 illness/furlough/AWOL situation.

Cadmus Wilcox discovered a problem on the eastern end of his Light Division line when the light of day dawned on March 26. Thomas' Georgians held this part of the line. The ground captured by the Federal Sixth Corps the previous day included McIlwaine's Hill. This small hill, located just southeast of Thomas' position, presented a commanding position for Federal artillery to fire down upon the exposed Confederate line. For this reason the hill could not be allowed to remain in Union hands.

All the sharpshooter battalions in Cadmus Wilcox's Division assembled at approximately 1:30 A.M., on March 27 to launch a night assault. When informed of the mission, Captain William S. Dunlop, commanding McGowan's sharpshooters, recalled his anxiety as he reflected on Thomas' Brigade fight over the same terrain two days prior. "The persistent gallantry of the Georgia brigade in their heroic efforts to recover and hold the hill, and the heroic and successful defense of the Federals to retain its possession, which we had witnessed, together with the conditions of the order of our assignment, impressed us with the importance and peril of the undertaking . . . ."[1]

McGowan's sharpshooters occupied the left and Lane's sharpshooters the right in the first assault line. In the second line stood Scales' sharpshooters on the left and Thomas' on the right. At 5 A.M., under a cloudy sky, both lines crept forward. About one hundred yards from the Federal line, the Confederates encountered a deep ditch, covered on both sides with briars and thorns. After the men crossed this obstacle, they adjusted their ranks and moved forward again. Suddenly at thirty paces from the enemy position, a shot from an alert Union picket broke the inky stillness. The sharpshooters uttered a loud yell as they rushed forward. They pushed the surprised pickets from the brigades of Brigadier General Lewis Grant and Colonel Thomas Hyde backwards. McGowan's men jumped into the enemy trenches and then wheeled their line to the left and stormed along the ditch. Lane's sharpshooters wheeled right and rolled the enemy line up in the opposite direction. The sharpshooter battalions of Scales and Thomas rushed forward and seized the middle part of the enemy works. They fired into the rapidly retreating enemy. The flashes of gunfire from the summit of McIlwaine's Hill provided quite a show for the rest of Wilcox's men, still manning the main Confederate line. Once the sharpshooters secured the hill, more infantry scrambled forward to occupy the line in case of a Union counterattack. The Union leadership accepted the loss of this hill and formed a new picket line several hundred yards south of McIlwaine's Hill. Union losses this day proved much greater than the ten to fifteen Confederate sharpshooters lost from all four battalions. A short time after this clash, leaders from both sides declared a truce so stretcher-bearers could retrieve the wounded and bury the dead.[2]

On March 30, Lee extended his line southwest of Petersburg to meet a growing Federal threat as Ulysses Grant tried to maneuver around the Confederate right flank. This move stretched the razor thin Southern line even more. Private Frank Edwards noted, "It seemed that the enemy was reinforcing all the time and moving to our right. Our commanders were somewhat confused."[3]

McGowan's Brigade had already shifted to the right on the previous day. Now Scale's men received orders to depart their works and move west. The Georgians still held the left flank of Wilcox's Division just south of the Boydton Plank Road. Lane's North Carolinians remained on the right of Thomas. All along the division line men spread further apart to fill in the gaps. They waited in their soggy wet trenches as the rain that had begun to fall the night of March 29 continued unabated, adding to their misery.

Then on April 1, Grant dealt Lee a devastating blow. Union forces defeated George Pickett's Division at Five Forks, a strategic road junction nine miles southwest of McIlwaine's Hill. This loss uncovered the direct route to the Confederate supply line along the South Side Railroad. Grant tasted victory and he assumed that Lee would pull other Southern units from elsewhere on his line to protect the railroad. The Federal commander scheduled a massive climactic assault for the following morning. Grant ordered the assault to extend from Jerusalem Plank Road west to Hatcher's Run to locate Lee's weakened line.

Major General Horatio G. Wright's Sixth Corps received orders to participate in the attack. Wright's men assembled their equipment and waited along their line south of the burned Jones farmhouse. Directly across the way, Wilcox's Southerners unknowingly stood behind their works.[4]

That night at approximately 10 P.M., Union artillery all along the line unleashed a tremendous fusillade designed to soften up the Confederate defenders. Not to be unheard, Confederate artillery crews sprang into action. For about three hours, the unnerving missiles soared back and forth over the lines shaking the ground and momentarily illuminating the woods. Under cover of the darkness and artillery, Wright's blue clad infantry moved north out of their lines to forward assault positions just behind their pickets. Then the pickets began to trade shots that added to the noise. After 1 A.M., the firing finally faded away and a tense eerie silence fell over the field.[5] Union infantrymen lay on the ground and knew what would soon come while their counterparts on the other side could only guess what the next several hours might bring. A Federal signal cannon fired after 4 A.M., on April 2. Anxious Union infantrymen pulled themselves off the ground to launch the momentous attack. In Wright's Sixth Corps, the right side of the Union line faced the brigades of Lane and Thomas. Brigadier General Frank Wheaton's division moved forward with Colonel Joseph E. Hamblin's brigade on the right flank. Hamblin's front comprised the 2nd Connecticut Heavy Artillery and the 65th New York. To their rear followed the 121st New York and the 95th Pennsylvania. Sharpshooters from the 49th Pennsylvania, armed with Spencer repeating rifles, guarded Hamblin's vulnerable right flank. As the line moved forward, these sharpshooters enfiladed the Confederate picket line and captured about sixty-five Georgians.[6] Union pioneers armed with axes interspersed with the infantry in the first line to hack open passage through the abatis.

Each Georgian in Thomas' Brigade stood ten paces apart to extend the thin defense line. The exact regimental alignment was unknown. When Hamblin's blue infantry charged forth out of the misty darkness, the overwhelmed Southerners fell back in confusion. The scene alarmed even the most seasoned veteran. Private John O. Andrews, 14th Georgia, wrote, "The whole country was blue with them as far as we could see and I lost hope right then and there. It was plain that we were overpowered and was useless to go to battle with that army that was advancing rapidly."[7]

Hamblin reported confusion in the misty darkness as his Unionists reached the enemy lines. The Confederate small arms and artillery fire increased the disorder in the blue ranks. A portion of Hamblin's brigade moved north toward the South Side Railroad after flooding through the line of Lane and Thomas. Another group composed of men from the 65th New York and the 95th Pennsylvania "turned to the right and passed down the line of works, capturing guns and prisoners for nearly a mile from the point of entrance."[8]

These two Union regiments created a stampede of Georgians as the Unionists bolted along the main part of Thomas' line. If the Union infantry in fact moved along the Confederate trenches for a mile then this would have encompassed most if not all of Thomas' position. Some Georgians stayed to fight and were killed while some were captured. The rest escaped northeastward. The commander of the 65th New York bragged that one of his men planted the first colors in Hamblin's brigade on the enemy works. This spot belonged to one of the right flank Georgia regiments. As the exuberant New Yorkers poured into the trenches and moved northeast, they captured four artillery pieces and swung them around and fired into the backs of the retreating Georgians.[9] The commander of the 121st New York reported that his men captured about two hundred prisoners.[10] Wheaton described the difficulty in controlling the excitement amongst the men of his division. "The troops were perfectly wild with delight at their success in this grand assault, and with difficulty could be restrained and the brigades reformed after the works, guns, prisoners, and camps were indisputably ours."[11] A Sixth Corps dispatch from Horatio Wright to Army of the Potomac headquarters at 5:15 A.M. described the success. "The corps has carried the works in front and to the left of the Jones house. Prisoners are now coming in."[12]

A 14th Georgia sharpshooter reported his trying experience starting on the night of April 1. He had just returned to the picket line from cooking his rations of corn bread and two slices of bacon. It must have been around 10 P.M., because he reported the enemy artillery barrage had just begun:

> At the picket line I found the men all in the rifle pits expecting a charge from the Yankee lines. After night set in and no advance had been made, I was informed by the officer in command that he wanted me about an hour before day the next morning to go on vedette duty in front of the pit where he was stationed. I saw, and so did he, that a general advance of the enemy next morning was a foregone conclusion. Sleep was weighing my eyelids down, and I retired about fifty yards from the rifle pits, rolled myself up in my blanket by a smoldering fire, and slept to the music of shrieking shot and shell from Yankee batteries. The officer awoke me the next

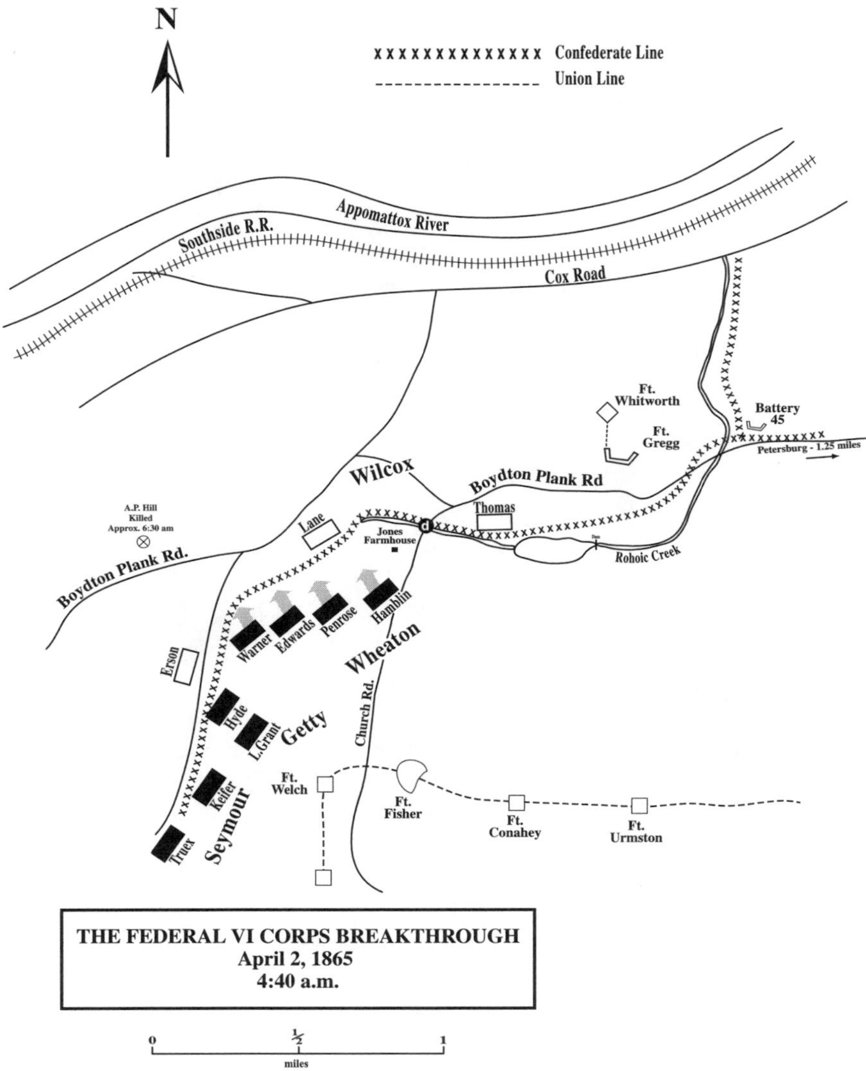

THE FEDERAL VI CORPS BREAKTHROUGH
April 2, 1865
4:40 a.m.

morning about four o'clock; and as I passed out into the dense darkness in front of his position to the vedette post, I cautioned him not to allow the men to fire until I could get in when the advance of the enemy was made. Advancing nearly two hundred yards in front of the skirmish line, I nervously awaited developments. I could distinctly hear the enemy in my front preparing for the charge, although they had not begun to advance, when suddenly to my right perhaps a

Rohoic Creek and Thomas' Main Line
Looking east from Church Road along Rohoic Creek toward Thomas' left on the fateful morning of April 2, 1865. This area had few trees in 1865. Hamblin's Union soldiers pierced the Confederate line in Lane's area and then turned east and rolled right into the Georgia line. The Georgians who survived this attack raced away toward Fort Gregg.
photo by author

> mile below, our skirmish line began a rapid firing which came steadily up the line until our men behind me caught the infection and began pouring a fusillade into the woods behind me. I crawled on my hands and knees back to the pits, while bullets hissed above me too uncomfortably close to be at all pleasant or assuring. How I escaped I could never tell, and I gave my excited comrades a piece of my mind in not very complimentary terms.[13]

Daylight enabled this soldier to see his true situation. "When day dawned we saw that our works below had been captured, and our troops were scattered badly and were retreating up their works toward the city of Petersburg. We left our position on the skirmish line and fell back to the works, only to find them deserted and the enemy, line after line with colors flying, close in pursuit of our decimated and now scattered column." As he stared aghast at the swarming hordes of blue clad soldiers from the 65th New York and 95th Pennsylvania he too turned to run and cleverly recalled, "Our skirmish line commander no longer tried to keep us in ranks, and each man constituted himself a committee of one to look out for his own safety."[14]

The men of one obstinate Confederate battery, previously abandoned by their infantry support, refused to relinquish their cannons. As several Georgians approached along the trench line from the southwest they were struck by the heroism exuded by these men in the face of such trying odds. "One defiant fellow, who seemed to be in command, was walking along the parapets around his gun with hat off and hurling anathemas loud and deep at the advancing foe, while the air was vocal with the hiss of their bullets. We stopped for a while at his earnest solicitation to help defend his guns, although there was no shadow of a chance for a successful resistance." As these Georgians gazed back southwestward along their trench lines, the scene indeed looked grim. "Line after line of Federal troops were seen as far as the eye could reach, and the front line was now within two hundred yards of the battery." The bedraggled infantrymen then turned and sprinted toward the raised walls of Fort Gregg a short distance away. When they looked back at the gallant battery its guns had succumbed to the inevitable and had been silenced.[15]

Private Frank Edwards, Company D, had stood in line that morning with the brigade sharpshooters. He described the initial withdrawal. "I outran everything on our line, and got to the fort ahead of all of them. We lost about fifteen men going to the fort. I outran bullets, men and all and did not receive a scratch; but I lost my old shoes. I regretted this, and would have turned back, but I reflected that I had no time for shoes just then. About half of our ammunition was out, and my gun was hot."[16]

Aroused by the noise and then reports of the breakthrough on his right, A.P. Hill had hurriedly dressed. He had raced to Lee's headquarters, where he spent only a few moments before he galloped off to the southwest to try to patch his line. Hill and an accompanying sergeant stumbled upon a small group of enemy soldiers a short time later, about three-quarters of a mile north of the Boisseau house. One of the Union men shot the general dead from the saddle.

Streams of soldiers from Thomas' and Lane's brigades retreated northeast along the Boydton Plank Road. Cadmus Wilcox met scattered groups of men from his division near Fort Gregg and they informed the major general that the line had been overrun with Yankees. Most of Wright's Sixth Corps had moved left toward Hatcher's Run after piercing Lane's position. This gave the Confederates an opportunity to mount a counterattack. Wilcox recorded, "Lane's and Thomas' men were reformed—in all about 600—moved forward in good spirits, and recaptured the lines to the vicinity of Boisseau's house, together with the artillery in the different batteries along it."[17] The two Confederate brigades moved back southwest for possibly one mile with Lane on the right of Thomas. Wilcox probably exaggerated or mistook the depth of his counterattack. His men did not reach the Boisseau house located just west of Church Road and about one-quarter mile southwest of the charred Jones farmhouse. James Lane reported the counterattack cleared the Confederate works to a point where the left end of the 33rd North Carolina rested on the previous night. This point lay a short distance east of Church Road.[18]

Lieutenant Henry H. Beard, Co.H
Beard's service record noted that this veteran was captured in 1865. Federal soldiers probably captured him on April 2, 1865. Federal officials held him at Libby Prison in Richmond until his parole on April 20.
From *Sunny South,* Atlanta, Ga. May 2, 1891

Federal Brigadier General Frank Wheaton meanwhile worked desperately to get his exuberant men into an effective combat line after their successful capture of the Confederate works. With two of his brigades headed toward Hatcher's Run, only Hamblin's brigade remained to defend what they had captured. Reports from the Federal skirmishers soon reached Wheaton that a strong Confederate force marched his way. This force comprised the counterattacking line of Lane and Thomas returning to retake their old position. Wheaton wrote:

> but a force of some 600 of them [Confederates]came down the line of works, driving a detachment of some eighty men from the Sixty-fifth New York Volunteers, Ninety-fifth Pennsylvania Volunteers, and division sharpshooters out of a fort they had captured some three-quarters of a mile to our right. They soon opened an enfilading fire upon us with two rifled guns from this work, and at the same time the tower signal officer reported a column of some 600 of the enemy as having passed through the woods between us and the Appomattox, apparently to attack the left of the Second [Hamblin] Brigade as it faced toward Petersburg.[19]

The arrival of Brigadier General Nathaniel H. Harris' Mississippi brigade with about 500 rifles represented this second column. Harris' men marched forward to support the right flank of Lane. Wheaton expressed concern because he did not have the men to meet the Mississippians maneuvering around on his left flank. "More than three-quarters of this [Union] brigade was already deployed in the line of works and skirmishing, and there were but few troops in reserve for any emergency. In a very short time, however, a column of our troops arrived from near Fort Fisher, and the Second Brigade was relieved by a division of the Twenty-fourth Corps." The Twenty-Fourth Corps commander, Major General John Gibbon, had received orders at 6:50 A.M. that morning from Army of the James commander, Major General Edward Ord, to send all of his available force to support the Sixth Corps breakthrough. In reality, Cadmus Wilcox probably had ordered the Confederate counterattacking force to withdraw toward Forts Gregg and Whitworth prior to the arrival of Gibbon's corps.[20]

Hamblin's brigade suffered surprisingly light casualties considering the frontal assault they launched against a dug-in foe. The casualty return showed 2 killed and 50 wounded. Darkness was a Union ally as it prevented the Confederate defenders from launching any type of accurate fire before swarms of blue-clad infantry inundated their works.[21]

Cadmus Wilcox realized the seriousness of his situation as he watched the heavy Union force move forward. Union Colonel Thomas O. Osborn's brigade from Brigadier General Richard S. Foster's division led this force northeast along the Boydton Plank Road. Wilcox ordered Harris' Mississippians to delay the Federal troops while the remnants of Thomas and Lane moved toward Fort Gregg. The Georgians and North Carolinians halted at times to fire at their attackers. Wilcox ordered the men of these two brigades to form a pair of defensive lines. One line extended across the Boydton Plank Road with its left anchored near Rohoic Creek. The other line formed along the west bank of the creek just to the east of Fort Gregg. The remainder of Thomas' and Lane's soldiers received orders to man Fort Gregg and support two artillery crews already there. Harris' Mississippians soon joined the contingent at the fort.[22]

Forts (Battery) Gregg and (Battery) Whitworth (also referred to as Fort Baldwin) stood atop a ridge about two-and-a-half miles west of Petersburg and just north of the Boydton Plank Road. Whitworth sat approximately six hundred yards north of Gregg. Each was open on one side; therefore, one fort could not survive in battle if the other fell to the enemy. The crescent shaped Fort Gregg, built in the fall of 1864, faced south overlooking the Boydton Plank Road. A defensive trench that connected both forts ran from north to south. The angled walls of Gregg towered fifteen feet over a rain-filled moat. The ground beyond the moat gently sloped down to the Boydton Plank Road.

Confederate soldiers poured into the protection offered by the earthen and log walls. They scrambled along the parapets for firing positions. One North Carolina officer in Lane's Brigade claimed there were about twenty Georgians from Thomas' Brigade inside the fort, including two Georgia lieutenants and Thomas' adjutant, Captain William Norwood. Other reports indicated the fort held forty soldiers from Thomas' Brigade. Captain Washington Irvine stated after the war that the 35th Georgia lost 40 killed and/or captured at Fort Gregg. No other source corroborated Irvine's figures. A roster search revealed that the regiment had 1 killed, 3 wounded and another 29 captured (2 of whom were listed as wounded too) on April 2. The roster, however, does not specify whether the casualties occurred at Fort Gregg or earlier in the morning when Union troops breached the Confederate defense line.[23]

The North Carolina officer believed that about twenty-five Mississippians occupied Fort Gregg while Captain A.K. Jones of the 16th Mississippi stated that his regiment and the 12th Mississippi mustered about 190 men. Jones' figure was probably more realistic. Several other North Carolina officers indicated that approximately eighty to eighty-five soldiers from Lane's Brigade defended Gregg's earthen walls.[24] Two gun crews, one from Lieutenant Francis McElroy's Battery of the New Orleans Washington Artillery and the other from Captain Walter Scott Chew's 4th Maryland Battery, manned the pair of three-inch Parrot field rifles. Jones believed these artillerists added about 15 more men.[25] Cadmus Wilcox claimed that the detachment inside Fort Gregg numbered about two hundred. A more correct estimate would place the total closer to 300 men.[26] Several Federal commanders believed that Fort Gregg held about 300 men as well.[27] Wilcox agreed that the number of men from Thomas' Brigade fell below the other two brigades. The evidence failed to reveal with certainty the actual number of Georgia or Confederate troops that actually fought inside Fort Gregg. Nathaniel Harris and the 19th and 48th Mississippi regiments occupied Fort Whitworth and joined the three artillery pieces there.[28]

Jones recorded that when the Mississippians reached Fort Gregg they found two three-inch rifles, about twelve to fifteen artillerymen, and about 100 other infantrymen.[29] These 100 infantrymen, "begged to go to the rear, and we hesitated whether to let them go or make them stay and help to defend the fort; but concluded that in their demoralized condition it was better to let them go, provided they left their guns with us, which they readily consented to do."[30] Jones failed to mention what unit these infantrymen belonged to. Perhaps some of these soldiers did leave, but records indicated that members of Lane's and Thomas' brigades stayed to fight at Fort Gregg. A member of the 14th Georgia defended his premature withdrawal from the fort. "I went into Fort Gregg and found it crowded with miscellaneous troops, three brigadier generals among the number. I soon saw that there were more men in there than could well be fought, and I left it before its capture." He moved to a defense line about five hundred yards east of Fort Gregg and watched the terrific scene that soon unfolded.[31]

Cadmus Wilcox rode into the entrance of Fort Gregg and remained on his horse. In a loud voice he addressed the soldiers, "Men, the salvation of Lee's army is in your keeping; you must realize the responsibility, and your duty; don't surrender this fort; if you can hold the enemy in check for two hours, Longstreet, who is making a forced march, will be here, and the danger to the army in the trenches will be averted." Suddenly the ground shook and a close artillery burst blocked his words. The garrison members then turned to Wilcox and shouted, "Tell General Lee, Fort Gregg will never surrender."[32] Other explosions quickly rocked Fort Gregg. Wilcox recalled, "I was in Gregg about 10 minutes. Saw that it had as many men as could fire conveniently. Extra ammunition was supplied, and the little detachments ordered to hold these two batteries to the last."[33]

Attention turned from Wilcox to the southwest. Two blue battle lines stretched to the horizon and the sunlight glinted off thousands of bayonets. The enemy artillery fire lasted about thirty minutes. It was so accurate and heavy that the gunners from Chew's and McElroy's batteries abandoned their guns and sought shelter in the fort's bombproof.[34] To the north, dark smoke swirled skyward as Confederate soldiers torched some of the old winter quarters around Fort Whitworth to improve their fields of fire.

A gun section commanded by Lieutenant William Sears, 1st New York Light Artillery, unlimbered their cannons across Rohoic Creek south of the forts. They created quite a problem for the defenders by sending a rapid and accurate enfilade fire into both bastions. When this day ended, these guns had fired 611 rounds at the two forts.[35]

With most of Wright's Sixth Corps guarding his left flank, John Gibbon assembled his assault force on a wooded ridge about 800 yards southwest of the Confederate forts. The first line of Union troops comprised two brigades from Foster's division—that of Osborn and Colonel George B. Dandy. Around 1 P.M., Gibbon ordered the assault of Fort Gregg to commence. Osborn started his men forward several hundred yards at quick time and right shoulder shift arms. They moved downhill and at the bottom struggled across a boggy area. When his line cleared this morass, he ordered the soldiers to charge and the men cheered and "swept up the ascent at the double-quick, under a terrible fire of grape, canister, and minie-balls tearing through the ranks." The 199th Pennsylvania anchored the far right and they moved toward the eastern wall angle. Next in order came the 62nd Ohio, 39th Illinois, 67th Ohio. Two regiments from Dandy's brigade, the 10th Connecticut and the 100th New York, occupied the left flank of this first line. Colonel Harrison S. Fairchild's brigade formed a second supporting line. Gibbon also dispatched the brigade of Brigadier General Thomas Harris to attack Fort Whitworth.[36]

As the thousands of blue-clad infantry stepped forward, Captain Jones remarked from his vantage point on the parapet at Gregg that they marched forward in beautiful order.[37] Fearing that the artillery pieces at both forts would certainly be captured, the gun crews received urgent orders to evacuate their guns. The guns from Whitworth escaped eastward, but by the time the order reached the gun crews in Gregg the Federal infantry was too close to commence a safe withdrawal. At the height of the fighting the approximately 200 Confederates in Fort Whitworth and another estimated 300 Confederates in Fort Gregg faced some 5,000 soldiers from six Federal brigades.

The defenders of Fort Gregg, side by side along the parapet, strained for a better view as thousands of enemy soldiers moved forward from the wood line about 800 yards away. As the enemy came into range, Confederate small arms fire accompanied by canister belched forth from both garrisons. Gaps appeared in the blue ranks, yet they quickly filled. Frank

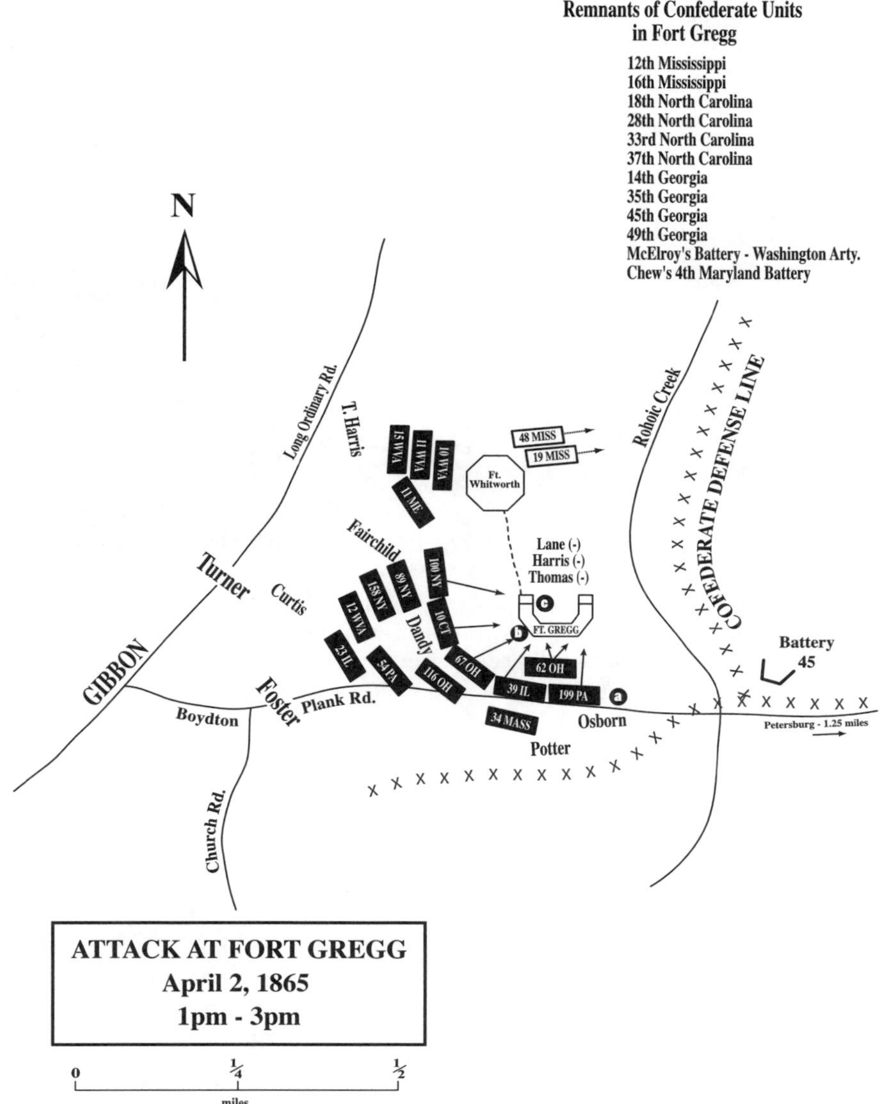

ATTACK AT FORT GREGG
April 2, 1865
1pm - 3pm

a. Fort Gregg

This view of earthen walls of Confederate fort taken from the Boydton Plank Road looking NW (330 degrees). On April 2, 1865, approximately three hundred Southerners held off about five thousand Federal soldiers for some two hours. This delay allowed Robert E. Lee to bolster his line and escape with the remnants of the Army of Northern Virginia that night.

photo by author

Edwards wrote, "Just as fast as they would come up we would shoot them down. We had abatis in our front, and we would shoot them down before they could get through."[38] Through the sheer weight of numbers, the Union line sloshed into the moat and reached the walls of Fort Gregg. Many Federal soldiers pressed against the base of the thick walls because the Confederate soldiers could not see downward to fire at them. Jones recalled, "When they got in twenty-five or thirty yards of the fort they were safe, for we could not see them again until they appeared upon the parapet."[39] The Federal troops clawed and scaled the walls. One Georgian remembered the first Yank he was sure he killed. "I got ready to shoot through a port hole and as I raised my gun to shoot a Yank stuck his face in the hole. I fired in his face and he fell."[40] Captain Jones described a similar recollection: "but no sooner was a head seen than it was withdrawn with a minnie ball in it."[41]

The 199th Pennsylvania, on the right flank, suffered the second highest number of Union casualties for the day. Their commander, Colonel James Briscoe, described his difficult task on the right flank. "The ground in front

b. Moat Along Front Parapet
This view to the east shows the depth of the moat at the base of the parapet walls.
photo by author

of the southeast salient of the work forms a perfect natural glacis for about 300 yards; passing over this space my regiment suffered its severest loss-canister, shot, and minie bullets tore through the ranks, yet not a man faltered. I was struck down by a glancing ball about seventy-five yards from the work, and although I lost but a moment in recovering myself, the men were already in the moat and clambering up the exterior slope. . . ."[42] These Pennsylvanians lost 16 killed and 65 wounded. The commander of the 100th New York was killed as he tried to climb the parapet on the fort's left side. The commander of the 10th Connecticut fell with a severe wound. This unit received the distinction for losing the most men on this day with 10 killed and 79 wounded.[43] Union officers screamed for reinforcements and Harrison Fairchild ordered his 89th New York forward followed by the 158th New York. They rushed ahead toward the west wall of Fort Gregg. Here the wall was vulnerable because it sloped down to the trench that connected to Fort Whitworth. The blue infantry finally stormed across the moat and over the trench into the exposed rear of Fort Gregg. Here the commander of the 89th New York was killed while the 158th New York lost three of their color corporals.[44]

Two more brigades supported the first line and as the attack stalled, these men moved into the fray. Both brigades came from Brigadier General

c. Western Parapet Wall

View from wall looking WSW (240 degrees) with Boydton Plank Road running from left to right in middle of photo. Soldiers from John Gibbon's Twenty-Fourth Corps assembled in the distant wood line and then launched their assault across the open field. The tree on the parapet wall obviously was not present in 1865.

photo by author

John Turner's Independent Division. Lieutenant Colonel Andrew Potter maneuvered his brigade, composed of the 116th Ohio and 34th Massachusetts, to the right. The other brigade, commanded by Colonel William B. Curtis, moved into the left portion of the line. This brigade comprised the 12th West Virginia, 54th Pennsylvania and 23rd Illinois. Curtis joined several other Union brigade or regimental commanders who each argued that one of their men first planted a flag on the ramparts of Gregg. The confusion of battle simply prevented the certainty of that honor. One thing remained certain though. Those first Federal soldiers over the parapets paid a heavy price in blood. Sergeant James P. Ryan, the 54th Pennsylvania's color sergeant, fell dead as he planted the colors on the wall. Major Nathan Davis, also of the 54th Pennsylvania, received severe wounds in the charge, but he refused to leave his men. He was killed as he climbed across the top of the parapet. Lieutenant Joseph Caldwell, 12th West Virginia, was one of the first to rush into Fort Gregg, and he dropped dead to the ground with a bayonet wound. Colonel Curtis wrote, "The resistance of the enemy was desperate. Those who were foremost in entering the fort were shot down or bayoneted, and several were killed on the top of the parapet in the act of leaping inside."[45]

A Louisiana artilleryman recalled what he saw and heard below the artillery piece he manned. "For some time we could hear the federal officers ordering their men on the top of the fort; the officers several times got on the parapet, with their colors in their left hands and their revolvers in their right, and demanded of us to surrender; but many of those brave officers were slain before we turned our musket butts up." He then described the heroics of a gun crew member named Berry:

> It was then that the brave and gallant No. 4 on the gun nearest the stockade, which was double-shotted with canister, was ordered by the federals, who had by then swarmed on the parapet, not to pull the lanyard which he held, but quick as a flash the brave Berry, of the Third Company, Washington Artillery, shouted back, 'Pull and be damned'. Useless to say that all in front of that gun were swept off, and our gallant artilleryman was shot down at once, and thus the heroic Berry sold his life dearly.[46]

The Union attack against Fort Whitworth was not concentrated. This enabled most of the defenders to concentrate their fire into the flanks of the numerous blue regiments that assaulted the ramparts of Gregg. Union Brigadier General Thomas M. Harris reported that as he moved his men forward toward Whitworth, they received harassing fire from sharpshooters. They continued far enough to receive an enfilade fire on their right flank from the defenders of Fort Gregg, and his men sought shelter behind some old Confederate winter quarters located just west of Whitworth.[47]

The numerous reinforcements John Gibbon called on to aid the attack was a luxury the men inside Fort Gregg lacked. Wounded Confederates, with their blood staining the ground inside the fort, loaded rifles and passed them to their colleagues along the walls. The Confederate artillery crews worked with precision as the walls shook with each pull of the lanyard. Against great odds the garrison fought for over an hour and a half. The unequal balance finally tilted toward the Federals when the brigades of Curtis and Potter joined the fray.

Federal troops struggled to stand up in the frothy water of the moat. They stuck bayonets in the walls for footholds so they could clamber upward while others surrounded Fort Gregg. Some soldiers climbed up the backs of their comrades to try and reach the top. Bitter hand-to-hand fighting erupted all along the parapets as blue clad soldiers reached the top and then struggled to stay there. Members of the Confederate garrison threw hand grenades or lit artillery fuses and tossed them into the blue masses.[48]

Federal soldiers finally forced open the entrance along the north side. Throngs of Northerners poured into Fort Gregg. Twenty-five more minutes of the most desperate kind of fighting ensued. Numerous Federal flags unsteadily wavered on top of the parapet as their defiant bearers received the brunt of the remaining Confederate fire.

Sergeant James Howard, Company K, 158th New York, grabbed the flagstaff out of the dying hands of the third color bearer shot down that day. He planted the staff on the parapet. The wooden pole immediately splintered-shot in half. Howard snatched the pole stub to keep the flag up. He received the Congressional Medal of Honor for his efforts.[49]

A 14th Georgian who had previously vacated Fort Gregg reported, "I saw some five separate and distinct lines of Yankees charge the gallant fort. The slaughter was terrible, and not until the walls of the fort were scaled was the garrison silenced."[50] Men swung rifle butts as clubs. The garrison members who ran low on ammunition hurled rocks at the invaders.[51]

Captain Jones remembered the numerous enemy assaults:

> There were six of these assaulting columns, and they followed each other about every thirty minutes, and when the fort was finally captured the parapet was covered with dead men in blue. I am satisfied that the last assaulting column walked on the heads of the other columns, who were packed in the ditch like sardines in a box, for they made no halt at all, but rushed on over the parapet into the fort. Before the last assault was made the battle flags of the enemy made almost a solid line of bunting around the fort. The noise outside was fearful, frightful and indescribable, the curses and groaning of frenzied men could be heard over and above the din of our musketry. Savage men, ravenous beasts![52]

The Fort Whitworth defenders evacuated their position with the apparent demise of Fort Gregg. Thomas Harris' Federal soldiers took this as a cue to move forward to seize Whitworth. Inside they found 2 dead and 2 wounded Confederates. They captured another 4 officers and 65 enlisted men in the fort. The attackers seized an additional 16 Confederates after a short foot chase.[53]

As the frenzied blue hoard swarmed over the walls of Fort Gregg, Jones believed many of them were under the influence of whiskey. He reported that many exasperated Union infantrymen started shooting the Confederate survivors on the spot. Blue-clad officers with cocked pistols halted this misconduct. The men of both sides were jammed into the fort so tightly that "it was impossible almost to shoot a Confederate without hitting a Federal. We lost about forty men killed in the fort after its capture, and fully that many Federals were killed by their own men."[54]

"Our ammunition gave out," wrote Frank Edwards. "I don't think there was a cartridge left. I never saw such heroism as was shown there. I saw we were gone. All our hand grenades were exhausted." Edwards did not feel optimistic with death lying all about. "Although we had holes to shoot through we lost a great many men. There was not one among us that thought we would escape from the fort alive. I just give up. They left a few of us, and we surrendered." Edwards' captor grabbed him by the left sleeve of his jacket tearing it almost off and nearly pulling him down to the ground. The angry Federal soldier demanded everything of value:

> I gave him a half plug of tobacco. I thought that would quiet him. He was proud of that tobacco and bit off about half at one chew. He said, 'What else." I gave him my pocket knife. 'What else.' I gave him all the money I had, $40 in Confederate currency, and told him that was all. He saw my pipe stem in my coat pocket, caught hold of it, gave it a jerk and nearly threw me down again. I saw he intended to kick me or hit me with his gun. He caught me by the shoulder and shoved me. He certainly intended to kick me as he shoved me, but I made the greatest jump then that I ever made. He missed me about an inch. I felt the breeze, that was all.[55]

Cadmus Wilcox adamantly praised the beleaguered garrison when he wrote, "The heroism displayed by the defenders of Battery Gregg has not been exaggerated by those attempting to describe it. A mere handful of men, they beat back repeatedly the overwhelming numbers assailing them on all sides."[56]

By 3 P.M., the surviving members of the Fort Gregg garrison had dropped their weapons. Colonel Curtis claimed that Captain William A. Smiley, of the 12th West Virginia, took the surrender of Lieutenant Colonel James Duncan, a Mississippian and the senior officer inside Gregg. Gruesome carnage littered the ground inside and out. Jones, another Mississippian and a witness to many horrific battlefields, described the view in front of the walls of Gregg. "The dead of the enemy lay literally in heaps, much thicker than they were in front of the stone fence at Fredericksburg, or in the angle at Spotsylvania Courthouse."[57]

Major General Gibbon said of the attack on Fort Gregg: "This assault, certainly one of the most desperate of the war, succeeded by the obstinate courage of our troops, but at a fearful cost."[58] Gibbon's men found the parapet and grounds inside Gregg littered with the dead, bloody bodies of 56 defenders and another 250 prisoners some 200 of who lay wounded.[59] Gibbon's own casualty figures were simply staggering. His losses during the day, most of which occurred around the two forts, amounted to 10 officers and 112 enlisted men killed with another 27 officers and 565 men wounded.[60] These figures totaled 714 soldiers and included:

Dandy's Brigade	10th Connecticut 10 KIA, 79 WIA
	100th New York 12 KIA, 41 WIA
Osborn's Brigade	199th Pennsylvania 16 KIA, 65 WIA
	62nd Ohio 3 KIA, 27 WIA
	39th Illinois 20 KIA, 45 WIA
	67th Ohio 7 KIA, 56 WIA
Fairchild's Brigade	89th New York 4 KIA, 11 WIA
	158th New York 13 KIA, 26 WIA
Potter's Brigade	17 KIA, 63 WIA (no regimental breakdown)
Curtis' Brigade	no casualties given[61]

Gibbon stated the Confederate prisoner total from both forts was three hundred. Most of these Southerners spent a difficult next several months at Point Lookout Prison in Maryland. The previously mentioned April 2 casualty figure of 33 men from the 35th Georgia was certainly a low number. These numbers failed to detail at what point on this climactic day the casualties occurred.

Although the Fort Gregg garrison's sacrifice was great, they had accomplished their mission. They had delayed Grant's assault long enough for Longstreet's reinforcements to cross the Appomattox River and shore up Lee's lines. This enabled the beleaguered Army of Northern Virginia to withdraw under cover of night north across the Appomattox River. This momentary escape postponed the inevitable showdown for another week.

The evening darkness of April 2, 1865 fell on the thousands of disgruntled men of Lee's army as they departed Petersburg. The Georgians along with the remains of Hill's Third Corps crossed the Appomattox River on the Battersea Bridge at the northwest corner of town. With the fall of Petersburg, Richmond soon followed. Frenzied soldiers, government officials and civilians clogged Richmond roadways as they hastily departed the capital. Hospital workers even abandoned the immobile wounded.

Brigadier General Edward L. Thomas assembled the few remaining members of his Georgia brigade. They joined other Third Corps units under Longstreet's command for the trek westward. Lee planned to move west and then turn south to link up with Joe Johnston's army in North Carolina. However, two columns of jubilant Federal soldiers paralleled the Confederate march. Food supplies for the weary army became scarce. Lee hoped to resuscitate his men with a supply train at Amelia Court House, Virginia. Every mile, more Confederate soldiers dropped out of the march, unable

35th Georgia Infantry Regimental Battle Flag

The few remaining Georgians surrendered this standard and their weapons at Appomattox Court House on April 12, 1865. The enemy's hand never touched this banner until this day. The battle campaigns listed on the visible three quadrants read: Seven Pines, Mechanicsville, Cold Harbor, Frazier's Farm, Cedar Run, Manassas, Fredericksburg, Chancellorsville. This flag was similar to the battle flags of the 14th and 49th Georgia. The campaigns painted on the missing quadrant probably were Ox Hill, Harper's Ferry and Shepherdstown. See Appendix F for further information. This flag has been partially restored and is part of the excellent flag collection at the Georgia State Capitol.

Photo courtesy of Georgia Capitol Museum, Office of Secretary of State, Atlanta, Ga.

to continue. Those that still had some stamina reached Amelia Court House on April 4. The anticipated food failed to arrive. The weary column staggered west toward Farmville as Federal troops pressed them from the south. The weakened, starving shells of men straggled. Many more fell out to rest, find food or flee. On April 6, Grant's men captured the Confederate rear guard east of Farmville. This loss at the Battle of Sayler's Creek amounted to approximately 9,500 Confederates. It sliced Lee's fighting strength almost in half.[62]

Lee realized that continued fighting was useless. When Grant made overtures for a Confederate surrender Lee agreed to meet with him. On April 9, Generals Lee and Grant met at the McLean House at Appomattox Court House to work out the conditions of surrender. At that momentous point, Thomas' entire brigade only numbered 57 officers and 456 men—much less than a full strength regiment.[63] Captain Irvine reported that the 35th Georgia Regiment lost 25 men in the retreat from Petersburg.[64] The deceased Corporal Benjamin Moody's prediction, made on April 9, 1862, that the war would last three years had come true to the exact day for his Georgia friends.[65]

Sergeant David H. Mobley reported seeing his beloved commanding general, Robert E. Lee, after Lee signed the surrender paperwork. "I was among the number who pressed their way to him with tears in their eyes and told him good-bye, shaking his hand. As we turned away from him he said, 'Go home, boys, and be men'."[66]

The formal ceremony took place on April 12. This delay gave the leaders of both armies time to draw up conditions of surrender and parole. Only 15 officers and 121 men stood in the ranks of the 35th Georgia to stack their arms and furl their tattered battle flag (see Appendix C). While many of their missing comrades laid in graves, hospitals and prison camps, these few dedicated men had somehow survived the war. The longest and loneliest trek of all had just begun for them—back to their families in war-ravaged Georgia.

Notes

Abbreviations:

CSR—"Compiled Service Records of Confederate Soldiers Who Served In Organizations From The State of Georgia,"—Thirty-fifth Infantry Regiment (National Archives Microfilm Publication M266) National Archives Building, Washington, D.C.

GDAH—Georgia Division of Archives and History, Morrow, Ga.

NMP—National Military Park

OR.— War of the Rebellion: A Compilation of the Official Records of the Union and Confederate Armies. 130 Vols.

SHSP—Southern Historical Society Papers

1. William S. Dunlop, *Lee's Sharpshooters.* (Dayton, Oh. 1988) p. 251.
2. J.F.J. Caldwell, *The History of a Brigade of South Carolinians Known As 'Gregg's', and Subsequently As 'McGowan's' Brigade.* (Philadelphia, 1866) (Morningside Press reprint, p.266–267; Ibid. p.252–255.
3. John Frank Edwards, *Army Life of Frank Edwards—Confederate Veteran—Army of Northern Virginia 1861–1865.* 1906. p. 38.
4. *OR* ., Vol. 46, Pt.I, p. 902.
5. Ibid., Vol.46, Pt. I, p.1009–1010.
6. Ibid., Vol. 46, Pt.I, p.930–931, 940.
7. Recollections of John O. Andrews Co.I, 14th Ga*.,* "Reminiscences of Confederate Soldiers—Stories of the War 1861–65," Vol.3, p.261, 1940. Collected and bound by Georgia Division—United Daughters of the Confederacy. Located at GDAH.
8. *OR* ., Vol.46, Pt.I, p.931.
9. Ibid., Vol.46, Pt.I, p.935.
10. Ibid., Vol.46, Pt.I, p.936.
11. Ibid., Vol.46, Pt.I, p.910.
12. Ibid., Vol.46, Pt. III, p.478.
13. J.S. Kimbrough, "From Petersburg To Hart's Island Prison," *Confederate Veteran,* Vol.XXII, #11, Nov. 1914, p.498–500.
14. Ibid.
15. Ibid.
16. Edwards, p.40.
17. Cadmus M. Wilcox, "Defence of Batteries Gregg and Whitworth, and the Evacuation of Petersburg," *SHSP,* Vol IV, 1877, p. 26.
18. A Wilson Greene, author of the definitive book *Breaking the Backbone of the Confederacy: The Final Battles of The Petersburg Campaign,* advised this author that he does not believe that the Lane/Thomas counterattack reached Dr. Boisseau's house. Adding to the confusion is the fact that there were two Boisseau houses located in the area. One of the houses, referred frequently as Tudor Hall, Samuel McGowan had used as his South Carolina brigade headquarters. This house has been preserved at present day Pamplin Park. This is the site referenced in relation to the spot of A.P. Hills death. The second Boisseau house was located one-quarter of a mile southwest of the burned Jones farmhouse and no longer exists; James H. Lane, "The Defence of Battery Gregg-General Lane's Reply to General Harris," *SHSP,* Vol.IX, 1881, p.104–105; *OR.,* Vol 46, Pt.I, p. 1285, the depth of the counterattack described by Lane here was more realistic.
19. *OR* ., Vol.46, Pt. I, p910–911.
20. Ibid. Vol. 46, Pt.I, p.910–911, 1174.
21. Ibid. Vol. 46, Pt.I, p.912.
22. Wilcox, *SHSP,* p.26; James H. Lane, *SHSP,* p.104–105; Ibid, Vol.46, Pt.I, p.1285.
23. Letter of Lieutenant D.M. Rigler, 37th North Carolina Regiment to "General James H. Lane from Charlotte, N.C., June 17, 1867," *SHSP,* Vol. III, 1877, p.27; W.T. Irvine, "Old 35th Georgia", *The Sunny South,* Atlanta, May 2, 1891; Lillian Henderson, *Roster of the Confederate Soldiers of Georgia 1861–1865,* Vol.III, (Hapeville, Ga., 1960) p.843–929.

24. Rigler Letter. June 17, 1867.
25. *SHSP,* "The Battle at Fort Gregg," Vol.XXVIII, 1900, p.266. Originally printed in the New Orleans *Picayune,* April 1, 1900.
26. *OR* ., Vol.46, Pt.I, p.1217.
27. Ibid., Vol.46, Pt.I, p.1219.
28. Wilcox, *SHSP,* p.27–28.
29. Captain A.K. Jones (16th Miss.), "The Battle of Fort Gregg," *SHSP.* Vol. 31, 1903, p. 57–58; *OR* ., Vol. 46, p.1217.
30. Ibid., Jones, *SHSP,* p.58.
31. Kimbrough, *Confederate Veteran,* p.499. note: Nathaniel Harris and his Mississippians created quite an uproar after the war because many of them wrote articles that failed to mention the presence of infantry from other Southern states inside of Fort Gregg.
32. Jones, *SHSP.* p.58
33. Wilcox, *SHSP,* p.27–28.
34. Jones, *SHSP.* p.58
35. Wilcox, *SHSP,* p.28; *OR* ., Vol. 46, Pt.I, p.1010–1012. A side note of interest: Major Andrew Cowan, who commanded the VI Corps artillery brigade reported that of the twenty artillery pieces captured along the Confederate entrenchments fully half of them were stamped on the barrel 'J.R.A.' which identified the manufacturer as the Tredegar Iron Works in Richmond owned by the former Georgia brigade commander, Joseph R. Anderson.
36. Ibid., Vol. 46, Pt.I, p.1186.
37. Jones, *SHSP,* p.58.
38. Edwards, p.41.
39. Jones, *SHSP,* p.58.
40. Andrews.
41. Jones, *SHSP,* p.59.
42. *OR* ., Vol. 46, Pt.I, p.1190.
43. Ibid., Vol 46, Pt.I, p.1186, 1195.
44. Ibid., Vol. 46, Pt.I, p.1203, 1209.
45. Ibid., Vol. 46, Pt.I, p.1217, 1219–1220.
46. "The Battle at Fort Gregg-Louisiana Survivors Tell the Story of the Fight," *SHSP,* Vol. XXVIII, 1900, p. 265–267. The 7–8 members of a cannon crew had numbers that corresponded with their positions and duties. The number 4 stood behind the left wheel of the gun carriage. He attached the lanyard to a friction primer and placed the primer into the tube vent. When the gunner gave the command to "fire" the number 4 pulled the lanyard thus firing the cannon.
47. *OR* ., Vol. 46, Pt.I, p.1221–1222.
48. Edwards, p.41.
49. *OR* ., Vol. 46, Pt. I, p.1209.
50. Kimbrough, *Confederate Veteran,* p.499.
51. E.P. Alexander, *Military Memoirs of a Confederate.* (New York, 1907) p.592–593; *OR* ., Vol.46, Pt.I, p.1179.

52. Jones, *SHSP.* p.59.
53. *OR* ., Vol.46, Pt.I, p.1222.
54. Jones, *SHSP,* p. 57–58.
55. Edwards, p.41–42.
56. Wilcox, *SHSP,* p.29.
57. *OR* ., Vol.46, Pt.I, p.1219; Jones, *SHSP,* p.60.
58. A.A. Humphreys, *The Virginia Campaign of 1864–65.* (New York, 1883) p.370.
59. *OR* ., Vol.46, Pt.I, p.1217.
60. Ibid., Vol.46, Pt.I, p. 1174, 1179, 1217; Alexander, p.593.
61. Ibid., Vol.46, Pt.I, p.594–595,1186, 1195, 1206, 1209, 1217–1220.
62. Ibid., Vol.46, Pt.I, p.1265.
63. Carroll R. Patterson, "The 14th Regiment Georgia Volunteer Infantry—An Outline of Its History," p.65, Atlanta Historical Society, Atlanta, Ga.
64. Irvine.
65. Letter of Benjamin F. Moody to "Dier Wife and Childrin, Camp near Fredericksburg Va, April the 9th 1862," Benjamin F. Moody Folder, Civil War Miscellany, Personal Papers (Record Group 57-1-1), GDAH.
66. Anita B. Sams, *Wayfarers In Walton.* (Atlanta. 1967) p. 436

Appendix A

From Hell to Home

"One blanket, one vest, one shirt, and one pair of pants." Remaining personal effects of Private John Rigby upon his death at Elmira Prison Camp.

As Lee's army surrendered, some less fortunate soldiers fought for their lives and their humanity in Union prisoner of war camps. For those men who were captured in the closing days of the Petersburg campaign—a new kind of hell on earth awaited them. Others like John Rigby had endured this hell for even longer. Rigby had been captured at the beginning of Grant's Overland Campaign in May 1864. He endured the harsh New York winter of 1864–65 at Elmira only to succumb to disease less than a month after the Appomattox surrender. Federal officials logged, "One blanket, one vest, one shirt, and one pair of pants," as his remaining possessions at his death. Rigby had used these few items for protection during the previous winter when the thermometer frequently dropped below zero degrees.[1]

When Richmond authorities abandoned the city, they also abandoned numerous wounded Confederate soldiers in the area hospitals. As the Federal army swept into town on April 3 amidst the flames of the burning buildings, these wounded soldiers became prisoners of war. This did not sit well with Company G's Sergeant Stephen L. Moon. Privates James M. Knight and Ezekiel D. Harris were also in a Richmond hospital. It was not known if all three were in the same place or if they even planned their escape together. Harris left the hospital without permission and escaped on April 25. Knight also left the hospital, but was apparently recaptured because records indicate that Federal officials released him from captivity on June 26. Moon left his hospital without permission on April 28 and headed for home.[2]

Frank Edwards, captured at Fort Gregg on April 2, 1865, wrote of his trepidation when black Union soldiers harassed the Confederate prisoners at City Point. He was relieved when he was near white Union soldiers. "After we found our way up to the white troops we were treated very nicely as prisoners of war. They knocked up some barrels of 'hard tack' and pickled pork, and we certainly did justice to that."[3]

Guards ushered the prisoners down to the City Point docks on April 4. Edwards recalled, "we went out on the boats toward hell, if you will excuse the expression. It proved to be a veritable hades." The disgruntled prisoners were unsure of their destination as the boat weighed anchor and steamed down the James River. Uncertainty weighed heavily on the twenty-two-year-old Edwards. "Those seemed to be the darkest days of my life, hard fighting, thirsty, hungry, half clad, no future, our army almost gone, so many of our brave heroes killed on the battlefield, our homes burned, our cities destroyed and we prisoners of war, out on the waters of the great ocean, and did not know where we would land." He did not believe the written word could really describe how black that night really was. His only consolation, which he called a privilege, was his ability to pray to God for protection.[4]

On the afternoon of April 5, the boat docked at the wharf for Point Lookout, Maryland. Black soldiers in blue uniforms came on board and ordered the prisoners into a formation. Roll was called and two prisoners were missing. Upon interrogation it was discovered that these two prisoners had jumped overboard in the darkness of night—no doubt to a watery grave. The guards then stripped the men of all their personal items and marched them off the boat toward the looming walls of the prison.

Point Lookout, Maryland, was established on a long sandy point where the Potomac River ran into the Chesapeake Bay. The first prisoners arrived shortly after the Battle of Gettysburg in July 1863. The camp was almost at sea level thus drainage was poor and the area was subjected to high winds and temperature extremes. It was the largest Union prison camp of the war. During its two-year existence, the tall walls held more than 52,000 military and civilian prisoners. Some 3,000 of these prisoners perished due to the squalid conditions.

A fifteen foot high wooden fence surrounded the prison. Frank Edwards received a close call shortly after his arrival:

> We found about twenty-five thousand prisoners on ten acres of land, which of course, made it very much crowded. I passed on to the lower side. I thought I would step up to the wall and see how far it was to the Chesapeake Bay. I heard several of the men saying, 'Come back! Come back! You will get killed. Don't you see that ditch; don't step across that ditch or you will be killed.' I was just in the act of stepping over the ditch; only two more steps to carry me over. I looked up and saw a negro guard ready to shoot me when I stepped over. They said nothing to a prisoner. If one stepped over that ditch he was shot without a word. I was in there only ten minutes and came very near getting shot.[5]

When Point Lookout opened, Union officials housed the first prisoners in large tents. However, the population soon exceeded the tent capacity. Thus when Edwards arrived in April 1865 the soldiers lived wherever they could find or improvise shelter. He and two other prisoners found some canvas and raised a rickety tent that could be blown over at the first puff of wind. Gathering water was also difficult. The six small well pumps frequently malfunctioned. There was a constant line to get the small dribbles of water the pumps spit out.[6]

One of the gates opened to the bay and some of the prisoners were allowed to wade into the water to bathe. Edwards watched one day as a man waded too far out and suddenly was pulled underwater. He thrashed back to the surface and screamed as a large shark dragged him back under. Back inside the walls of the prison the constant threat was always the black guards. "At all times through the night you could hear a gun shoot. Those negroes shot at random, it seemed. As our boys were close together they hardly ever missed striking someone. Late one night I had just gotten from my pallet and was sitting in my tent. I was cold and had nothing to spread over me. I heard a gun fire. The ball struck the tent pole just above my head, glanced and struck my tent mate's canteen, close to his head." They found sleep difficult for the remainder of the night.[7]

The bread wagons arrived every morning around 10 A.M. A crowd of prisoners always gathered in advance, anxious to get a good spot in line. Any soldier that stood too close to the gate was kicked by the guards. "Sometimes our boys would be very hungry and weak, standing and looking for the bread wagon, and would sometimes reel as they walked; and when they could not get out of the way as quick as the others, the negroes would send them over on their head." Edwards described the sad spectacle when the wagons were late. "The poor fellows would crowd up all around for two hundred yards back, surging, pushing, to see. They were so hungry and weak, and their anxiety so great, it seemed they were almost crazy for bread."[8]

The quest for food became an all encompassing existence for these prisoners. This desire for the slightest morsel, the means to stay alive for perhaps one more day, brought the men down to their lowest level of existence-survival of the fittest. Edwards described the scene: "I saw men stand and look so wistful and get so weak that they would sink right down to the ground and be stepped on by others surging to see the bread wagon come in. After awhile it would come, bringing in the 'glad tidings of great joy'. Notwithstanding the small amount that was issued, that was our life, our greatest desire; one little morsel would be so sweet. It did seem to me that the greatest strains of my life, mentally and physically, were the times when the bread wagon was delayed." He further described the mental anguish of starvation. "You place a man where there is no water and where there is scarcely anything to eat and keep him there, and I know of no greater punishment. I saw men standing around there trembling. Sometimes they would fall and had to be helped to their feet. I saw a man going around with bone scurvy; these boys were nothing but skin and bones. It seemed that all love and sympathy for any one was gone. If you were sick or happened to an accident, you got very little assistance."[9]

The prisoners lined up twice a day to file through the mess building. "Two meals a day, morning and night. The breakfast was a small piece cut across a five-cent loaf of bread, a small cup of beef water, which made me sick when I drank it. I would take my bread and go out. We would get this twice a day, nothing else. We saw no meat of any kind. The beef water was very filthy, being covered with bugs and flies, but our boys would eat anything, as any man will when he gets hungry enough. We would rake the insects out and drink it, and go on and think about the next time and how long it would be before we would get the next meal." Edwards had another close call once after eating some rancid corn meal. "Several times they would give us half a pint of raw meal, and we were not allowed fire with which to cook it. We just mixed it with a little water, stirred it up and drank it down. It gave us all cholera morbus. The first raw cup of meal I ate came very near taking my life. It seemed to me I was never so sick. At midnight I began to vomit. There was a small ditch about three feet away and I put my head over in that ditch, and I think I must have fainted. The guard came along and said, 'Take that head back in that tent.' I vaguely heard him, but I never moved. He repeated the command. The man that was with me jerked me by the heels back into the old tent." The following morning several prisoners lay dead from the effects of the corn meal. "I saw men go around the tent, pick up fish bones or any kind of bone thrown away, and beat them up fine, empty the bones in a tin cup with water in it, let it stand awhile and then drink it."[10]

It was difficult for a Point Lookout prisoner to relax because death could come in so many ways. In addition to starvation, illness and the trigger-happy guards, some prisoners were forced to draw for their lives. On May 12, 1865, a large number of men were marched to camp headquarters to face a firing squad. Out of this group twenty men were chosen. The guards claimed this was in retaliation for some Federal prisoners killed in North Carolina. John O. Andrews, 14th Georgia, recalled the situation: "I drew blank, for which I have always been thankful, but was scared almost to death. No battle I was ever in excited me as that did. Prison life is horrible."[11]

Each day twelve prisoners were detailed to march a distance away from the prison to cut wood. The wood was then used to stoke the fires for the bread kitchen. The work was difficult and tedious for the starved men. Whenever a prisoner stumbled he could be sure a guard's boot was not far behind. No prisoner looked forward to his name being called for this detail. One day a prisoner from Houston, Texas earned a posthumous hero status. He stumbled while on the wood detail. When the black guard stepped forward and kicked him the angry Texan jerked the guard's gun out of his hands and shot him. He turned and plunged the bayonet into another nearby guard before the remaining guards shot him dead. Frank Edwards noted: "That put a stop to the kicking. It seemed to bring about a little more quiet at the barracks also, and more especially our side."[12]

One day Edwards was called to the commandant's quarters. One of the Union officers had spent a recent night at the home of the family that Edwards had protected during the first two months of 1865. The family had heard that Edwards was either dead or captured. On the chance that he was still alive and incarcerated at Point Lookout the youngest daughter had given the Union officer a gold five dollar piece to give to Edwards. "That money saved my life," Edwards recalled. "I used five cents every day for bread; that kept me on my feet. I was so much relieved, and it was bliss to know it came from that sweet girl; to know she thought of me."[13]

Edwards decided to use fifty cents of the money to buy material to make gutta-percha rings. He purchased ten cents of silver and stamped it out very thin. He then made silver dominoes and hearts to inlay the rings. He worked almost every day on the rings for two months and was quite proud of them. His biggest fear was they would be stolen. Local residents and even those from as far away as New York would come to visit the prison to get a glimpse of the prisoners. One day a carriage with three men and three ladies drove through the gate and stopped. Edwards happened to be nearby and he approached the carriage and inquired if the ladies would like to buy any of his rings. Thousands of prisoners looked on. When one of the ladies expressed interest he handed a stick with six rings through the window of the carriage. The ladies all agreed that they were beautiful. Suddenly one of the ladies urged the driver to take off and the carriage raced away. Enraged, Edwards and many of the prisoners ran to try to stop the carriage before it escaped through the gate. The guard ordered the prisoners to halt. When this failed he hurled a small explosive device toward the front of the group. It exploded and injured one prisoner who died the following day.[14]

Another problem for the prisoners was body lice. Soldiers lay awake at night and cursed and scratched the vermin until sleep finally took over.

In the morning, each man awakened and began to scratch himself bloody. Edwards recalled, "The white officers would not come near the prison walls. The doctors would redress every time they visited the sick, and they made only one visit a day, and that a very short one."[15]

Finally, Federal officials offered the prisoners the oath of allegiance to the United States. Official records showed that Frank Edwards was released on June 26 while Edwards claimed the date was July 10. However, when the release process started Edwards was tantalized for a while longer. "They called our names alphabetically. They then commenced at A and went down to E. They then began at Z and went back up to E. When my name was called there were just a few in the prison. Nearly all had gone home." He drew some rations for the trip home and then sat down and stuffed all the food down his throat—two pounds of pickled pork and two large pones of cornbread.[16]

Edwards boarded the boat hatless and shoeless. His long hair flowed in the breeze. The boat ride south along the Chesapeake Bay was an emotional one. As the outline of Point Lookout slowly disappeared, the physical and mental scars remained forever in the minds of the surviving prisoners. Edwards reflected on that time:

> You will never know what our boys suffered at that terrible prison. I wish that I had command of language sufficient to write that you might understand what the boys suffered there. Before I was released from that prison, it seemed that the days and nights were all the same; it seemed that the sun shone no brighter than the moon. I felt that my life was nothing but misery and woe; that I would never meet another friend. My whole thought was, just give me something to eat and drink and I would spend my whole life there. No one but those who were there will ever know what our eyes saw and what our hearts felt. Our heart, soul and body would plead to be released from that place. The prayers that went up from that prison were from the heart. If I ever prayed, it was at Point Lookout, and nothing but the mercy of our Lord released us alive from that prison.

He believed he was the happiest man in the world when he walked beyond the prison gate. "No one can appreciate the life of a free man, unless he has been in prison." After further thought he wrote, "There is no word in the English language, or any other, that will compare with the word freedom."[17]

Peril still stalked these bedraggled soldiers as they scanned the expanse of blue water and soaked in the warm sun and ocean breezes. As the boat approached Cape Hatteras, North Carolina, the gentle wind increased and the waves grew. To the south the sky darkened. Waves of frothy water broke over the boats gunwales. The boat pitched and yawed as all hands held on for their lives. Most of the men became violently sick. The storm finally subsided and ahead in the water floated some debris. A lone man violently waved his arms from the middle of the debris field. He was the captain of another full prisoner boat. Its boiler had exploded in the storm killing everyone except this lone seaman.[18]

Edwards' boat finally docked at Charleston, South Carolina. "I know we looked pretty tough going along the public highway—no hat, in our bare feet, with our hair long and uncombed, and our hands and faces tanned by long exposure; we were very much the color of an Indian. The railroads were not running any trains, and we started home on afoot. We began our march through the country for home. We drew rations from the government in Charleston, hard tack and pickled pork, which we thought was very fine. We had drawn our rations on the boat regularly, but I wasn't hungry for three days after I ate that two pounds of meat and two pones of cornbread at the prison."[19]

Edwards and two travel companions, one from Alabama and the other from Louisiana, started toward home without a map. After some wrong turns they finally reached the Savannah River, the boundary between Georgia and South Carolina. There was no bridge. They finally found a small boat and paddled across to the other side. Frank Edwards was jubilant to be back in his home state. "We were now in Georgia—Georgia, the grandest old state in the Union; thank God we were in Georgia."[20]

They were wary though as an older black man approached from a nearby house. The kind man offered them some food his wife had just cooked. "The negro was our greatest enemy at Point Lookout. We said when we left that prison we could never notice another negro. But that old negro, I believe, had a good heart. We were his bitter enemies, but he caught all three of us by that kind act of his. His was the first kind act we saw from a negro after we got out of prison. That old negro gave us old-time ash cake and buttermilk, and you know that is pretty hard to get around any time, and we were tired and hungry. When we had finished that one of the boys said, 'If I had fifty dollars, I would give it to you for this act of kindness.' We bade the old negro and his wife farewell."[21]

The three men continued their journey on foot to Washington, Georgia. They hopped on the next train bound for Atlanta. Edwards found the view of Atlanta a shock:

> The whistle blew for Atlanta, our home city. How often during the past years I had thought of Atlanta, Georgia. I had sure been around

> the world in warfare. When we pulled under the old carshed, I can't describe my feelings. When I looked out I saw nothing but the skeleton, the ashes of our beloved city of Atlanta. We learned the West Point train would not leave until the next morning. I looked about the city and saw the long letters, the old 'Trout House'—it had been burned. I thought of the misery the war had caused to leave it like this; the city had almost been swept off the map. We all loved Atlanta. When I bade Atlanta farewell in August, '61, I left it well clad, well fed and everything in good shape. I thought of the great change in both Atlanta and myself from '61 to '65. I came back with no hat or shoes, just an old dirty shirt and pants. But I could at least thank God I was a free man out from under the terrible negro rule at Point Lookout.

While walking about Edwards came upon some scales and he weighed himself. "My average weight was about one hundred and fifty pounds; my weight then was one hundred and four."[22]

The following morning at Hogansville, Georgia, Edwards bade his friends goodbye. "We parted in tears. How strong are the ties of genuine friendship. The friendship that springs up between men who have had all things in common; who have had the sorrows and the joys of life together." He then started on the final twelve miles of his journey to his house on the Chattahoochee River. He cut two walking sticks to help him amble along on his sore feet. He stopped at a house along the way to ask for water. He knew the family from before the war, but they did not recognize him. Because of his appearance they refused his request until they realized who he was. "It seemed to me I would never get home. It was three miles yet. My feet were very sore, and I only kept up with my sticks. I went through the woods; I did not care to meet any one. About four o'clock in the afternoon I arrived at home, the old home, sweet home. No one ever expected to see me again. They had been told by several parties that I had been killed at the battle of Petersburg. I am satisfied you can realize how I felt to some extent. Mother fainted two or three times. When she would look at me she would faint nearly every time. No one in the family recognized me at all until I went to the well to get water."[23]

After reflection on his total war experience Edwards admitted that he had many close calls during the war. He believed that his prison experience came the closest to killing him. "I don't think the commander of the post could have been aware of the terrible condition of everything, of the thirst, the hunger, the body pest, no tents, no place to sleep except on the muddy ground, and you had to sit up and sleep, if you could; and worse than all, were the curses and kicks from the negro guards. At night, the guards, while walking about the streets, would shoot at random, you would hear some soldier yell with pain, and the next morning he would be carried to the hospital."[24]

However, at least Edwards made it back to the soil of his beloved state. He was able to look into the eyes of his parents and siblings and hold them in a sobbing embrace. He had survived a long fight to protect his loves ones. This twenty-two-year-old had a chance to pick up the pieces of his devastated life.

Fate painted a different picture at other homes. A few miles away, the family of young James Garrett knew he was not ever coming home. They did not even know where he was buried. John Rigby's wife never gave up hope that her captured husband would return. She waited for thirty-two years until her death in 1897. An empty spot next to her grave still waits for John.[25]

Notes

Abbreviations:

CSR—"Compiled Service Records of Confederate Soldiers Who Served In Organizations From The State of Georgia," Thirty-fifth Infantry Regiment (National Archives Microfilm Publication M266) National Archives Building, Washington, D.C.

GDAH—Georgia Division of Archives and History, Morrow, Ga.

NMP—National Military Park

OR.— War of the Rebellion: A Compilation of the Official Records of the Union and Confederate Armies. 130 Vols.

SHSP—Southern Historical Society Papers

1. John Rigby Family records courtesy of Mark Pollard, McDonough, Ga.
2. Anita B. Sams, *Wayfarers In Walton.* (Atlanta. 1967) p.197.
3. John Frank Edwards, *Army Life of Frank Edwards—Confederate Veteran—Army of Northern Virginia 1861–1865.* (1906). p.42.
4. Ibid., p.41–42.
5. Ibid., p.46.
6. Ibid., p.46.
7. Ibid., p.49.
8. Ibid., p.50.
9. Ibid.
10. Ibid., p.51, 63.
11. Reminiscence of John O. Andrews, Co.I, 14th Georgia, "Reminiscences of Confederate Soldiers and Stories of the War," collected and bound by Georgia Division, Daughters of the Confederacy, Vol.3, 1940, p.262. available at GDAH.
12. Edwards. p.54–55.
13. Ibid., p.57–58.

14. Ibid., p.59.
15. Ibid., p.62–63.
16. Ibid., p.64, 67.
17. Ibid., p.67–69.
18. Ibid., p.70.
19. Ibid., p.72.
20. Ibid., p.75.
21. Ibid.
22. Ibid., p.80–81.
23. Ibid., p.85.
24. Ibid., p.104.
25. Rigby Family records.

Appendix B

CASUALTY FIGURES FOR 35TH GEORGIA INFANTRY REGIMENT

The November 1, 1861 muster roll for the regiment lists 47 officers and 655 enlisted men present. Of these numbers about 112 men were absent in hospitals or on furlough due to sickness. In James Folsom's book, *Heroes and Martyrs of Georgia—Georgia's Record in the Revolution of 1861,* he reported that 740 men originally enlisted in the regiment in 1861. He also mentioned that another 535 men were recruited or conscripted during the next four years which means that some 1,275 Georgia men served during the war in this regiment. Folsom's book, published in 1864, ends in mid-June 1864 as the 35th Georgia arrived to defend Petersburg. Therefore, it does not list any casualty figures for the longest campaign of the war. Folsom does mention that three soldiers were wounded near Petersburg during the initial fighting. His figures up to the Petersburg Campaign reflect that 128 men were killed and 429 wounded as a result of battle.

After doing further research of Lillian Henderson's extensive *Roster of the Confederate Soldiers of Georgia 1861–1865* (Vol. 3 pages 843–929) and research through the military records of soldiers not listed in Henderson's book, I realized there were definitely more soldiers that served in the 35th Georgia than Folsom showed. I compiled 1,330 soldiers names. Due to oversight and poor war time record-keeping there were undoubtedly more who served. The figures below list the number of deaths by battle and disease that I was able to locate. The records of some soldiers only reveal that they were wounded, sent to a hospital and not heard from again. They possibly died, but their death was not reported back to their unit, or their death was reported to the wrong unit, or their name was listed incorrectly or any other number of confusing combinations could have occurred. Some soldier's records show they were listed as "absent without leave, no further record". Also, some soldiers were listed as AWOL in late 1864–65. Many of these men went to Georgia on furlough and then were unable to return to Virginia because they could not get through Sherman's Federal lines after his capture of Atlanta and subsequent march to Savannah. Numerous other soldiers were wounded severely and discharged. Due to the difficulty in determining who was wounded and who wasn't I have decided not to include the number of soldiers who were wounded and survived.

Breakdown of Company Deaths Through Battle and Illness In the 35th Georgia Volunteer Infantry Regiment

35th Georgia Volunteer Infantry Regiment

Total members—1,330
Death by battle—162
Death by illness—361
Total deaths—523
Death percentage—39.32%

STAFF: Total members—19
Death by battle—1
Death by illness—0
Note: more than 19 people served during the period of the war on the regimental staff, however some of the members were brought up from the companies. To prevent confusion, the number of 19 represents only soldiers that served on the staff and did not spend any time at the company level.

Company A, Haralson County (Haralson Brown Guards):
Total members—136
Death by battle—22
Death by illness—46
Total deaths—68
Death percentage—50.00%

Company B, Newton County (Bartow Avengers):
Total members—163
Death by battle—27
Death by illness—48
Total deaths—75
Death percentage—46.01%

Company C, Campbell County (Campbell Rangers)
Total members—144
Death by battle—30
Death by illness—41
Total deaths—71
Death percentage—49.30%

Company D, Heard & Troup Counties
Total members—129
Death by battle—14
Death by illness—36
Total deaths—50
Death percentage—38.75%

Company E, Campbell County (Campbell Volunteers)
Total members—104
Death by battle—16
Death by illness—22
Total deaths—38
Death percentage—36.89%

Company F, Gwinnett County
Total members—131
Death by battle—13
Death by illness—30
Total deaths—43
Death percentage—32.82%

Company G, Walton County (Walton Sharpshooters)
Total members—136
Death by battle—9
Death by illness—41
Total deaths—50
Death percentage—36.76%

Company H, Gwinnett & Hall Counties (County Line Invincibles)
Total members—122
Death by battle—11
Death by illness—31
Total deaths—42
Death percentage—34.42%

Company I, Chattooga County (Chattooga Mountaineers)
Total members—117
Death by battle—11
Death by illness—29
Total deaths—40
Death percentage—34.18%

Company K, Harris County (Harris Guards)
Total members—129
Death by battle—8
Death by illness—37
Total deaths—45
Death percentage—34.88%

Appendix C

35TH GEORGIA VOLUNTEER INFANTRY REGIMENT PAROLEES AT APPOMATTOX

The 35th Georgia surrendered with a weary force of 15 officers and 121 men. Members of the unit that were sick or wounded in hospitals, on furlough, or on other duties were not counted at the surrender.

These figures, when added to the numbers in the 14th, 45th and 49th Georgia Regiments meant that Thomas' Georgia Brigade comprised only 57 officers and 456 men at Appomattox.

Brigadier General Edward Lloyd Thomas was present and the remainder of his troops are as follows:

35th Georgia Staff: B. H. Holt, Col.
W. M. McCollum, Adj't.
W. P. Hill, Ass't. Surg.
W. B. Penn, Ass't. Surg.
H. W. Thomas, Q. M. Sergt.
W. G. Roberts, Hosp. Steward

Company A (Haralson County)
Henry C. Head, Corp.
Jas. R. P. Camp, Pvt.
J.M. C. Gibony, "
L. L. New, "
T.M. B. Stripling, "
J. L. Pike, "
W. E. Ray, "

Company B (Newton County)
N. C. Carr, Capt.
J. G. Cooper, 1st Lt.

J. M. Mitcham, 2nd Lt.
G. W. Simonton, 2d Sergt.
G. A. Lucas, 3rd Sergt.
W. T. Butler, Pvt.
W. H. Hinton, "
J. C. Kimbell, "
W. D. Lard, "
B. A. Mertett, "
W. F. McDaniel, "
R. Duncan, "
J. D. Michum, "
J. T. Parker, "
W. T. Turner, "
J. A. Mann, "

Company C (Campbell County)
J. E. Steed, Capt.
S. G. Johnson, 2nd Lt.
G. T. Cochrane, 1st Sergt.
J. B. Smith, 3rd Sergt.
B. A. Smith, 5th Sergt.
A. J. Hughes, Corp.
L. F. Cochrane, Corp.
W. Daniel, Pvt.
J. L. Hearne, "
C. D. Hopkins, "
R. C. Johnson, "
Henry Bond, "

Company D (Heard & Troup Counties)
W. C. Scogin, 1st Lt.
W. J. Moore, Sergt.
D. A. Martin, 3rd Sergt.
J. G. Frieland, Pvt.
J. E. Ring, "
E. W. Redding, "
J. W. Williams, "
G. F. Hicks, "
C. W. Furgerson,"
R. A. Jackson, "

Company E (Campbell County)
T. W. Latham Capt.
J. B. Lewis, Corp.
D. A. Jackson, Pvt.
J. W. Silvey, "
J. J. Shadix,"
H. Thomas, "
J. H. Williams, "
J. R. Smallwood,"

Company F (Gwinnett County)
T. J. Davis, Capt.
J. F. Pruitt, 1st Sergt.
W. B. Harbin, 3rd Sergt.
P. W. Wiley, 5th Sergt.
David Pruitt, 1st Corp.
W. F. Shirley, Pvt.
J. R. Bom, "
W. R. Bond, "
D. J. Brand, "
J. Campbell, "
W. H. Ellis, "
J. R. Harbin, "
J. M. Humphries,"
J. B. Campbell, "
R. D. Holt, "
W. A. Jones, "
R. D. Johnson, "
W. J. Knight, "
O. S. Longley, "
M. Minor, "
J. W. McDaniel, "
J. P. Phillips, "
W. J. Rollins, "
J. F. Rollins, "
C. D. Summerlin,"
J. C. Whitworth,"

Company G (Walton County)
W. S. McBean, 1st Sergt.
T. M. Bland, 3rd Sergt.

D. H. Mobley, 5th Sergt.
J. M. Griffin, 3rd Corp.
E. T. Moon, 4th Corp.
W. H. Boker, Pvt.
B. J. Fields, "
G. W. Harris, "
J. H. Johnson, "
J. E. Mobley, "
C. R. Moon, "
Lewis Swords, "
M. L. Moon, "
Peyton Manham, "
H. L. Mitchell, "
James Nunnally,"
H. M. Kemp, "

Company H (Gwinnett & Hall Counties)
L. S. Puckett, Corp.
B. F. Duncan, Pvt.
H. H. Gresham, "
J. D. Mikler, "
Thomas Orr, "
W. H. Orr, "

Company I (Chattooga County)
W. T. Irvine, Capt.
J. L. Groves, 1st Lt.
W. W. Parker, Pvt.
J. B. Fox, Pvt.
J. R. Green, Pvt.
James Hobbard, Pvt.
J. H. Jackson, Pvt.
J. M. Jackson, Pvt.
W. P. Perry, Pvt.

Company K (Harris County)
W. Boswell, 1st Lt.
Henry Hayes, Sergt.
William Jenkins, Sergt.
J. C. Conrad, Sergt.
David Roril, Corp.

R. M. Davis, Pvt.
J. W. Donald, Pvt.
W. G. Grant, Pvt.
J. H. Grant, Pvt.
Sidney Hale, Pvt.
H. B. Hamer, Pvt.
J. T. Hines, Pvt.
J. H. Hudson, Pvt.
T. H. Kimbrough, Pvt.
L. M. Lafield, Pvt.
C. H. McFarland, Pvt.
J. S. Moore, Pvt.
D. M. Pearse, Pvt.
Seaborn Pollard, Pvt.

Appendix D

Court Martial of Lieutenant Solomon G. Johnson, Co. C, 35th Georgia Infantry Regiment

The following is the transcript of the court martial proceedings against Lieutenant Solomon G. Johnson from Company C:

Charges and Specifications against Lieut. S. G. Johnson, Co. "C" 35th Ga. Regt.

Charge: conduct unbecoming an officer and gentleman.

Specification, 1st: In this that the said Lieut. S. G. Johnson Co. "C" 35th Ga. Regt. having obtained a furlough from the Secy of War for Harbird Cook a Private Co. "C" 35th Ga. Regt. did sell the said furlough to Corp. Burran Co. "C" 35th Ga. Regt. the said Corp. Burran having been in the Hospital, and being reported for duty, and the said Lieut. Johnson being aware that the said Burran intended to proceed to Ga. upon the papers above mentioned. All this in the City of Richmond in or about September 16th 1862.

Specification 2nd: In this that the said Lieut. S. G. Johnson Co. "C" 35th Ga. Regt. having procured a furlough for Thomas J. Daniel Privt. Co. "C" 35th Ga. Regt. from the Surgeon of Same Hospital in Richmond, Virginia on or about the 1st Sept. 1862, and the said Daniel dying shortly thereafter the said Lieut. S. G. Johnson Co. "C" 35th Ga did sell the said furlough to a Confederate Soldier. All this in Richmond, Virginia.

Witnesses
Privt. Harbird Cook
Corp.Wm. Burran
Sergt. J. B. Smith
Lieut. John E. Steed

Signed, B. H. Holt
Col. 35th Ga. Regt.

Sergt. J. S. Moore
Corp. T. M. Shannon

Case No. 79

Proceedings of a General Court Martial convened at the camp of Wilcox's Division (late Pender's) by virtue of the following order:

Special Order	HeadQurs. Dept Northn Va
No. 197	August 11th 1863

A General Court Martial is hereby appointed to meet at the camp of Pender's Division on the 13th day of August 1863 or as soon then after as practicable for trial of such prisoners as may be brought before it.

Detail for the Court

Col. Wm. M. Barbour	37th N.C.T.
Lt. Col. J. Ashford	38th " " "
Lt. Col. J. N. Brown	14th S. C. Vols.
Major M. L. Groves	35th Ga. "
"J. I. Hunt	13th S. C. Vols.
Capt. C. A. Corn	Co. "G" 45th Ga. Regt.
" E. D. Brailsford	Co. "I" 1st S.C.
" N. E. Armstrong	Co. "A" 38th N.CT.
" J. I. Poisson	Co. "G" 18th N.C.T.
Capt. Wm. T. Nicholson	Co."E" 37th N.C. T. Judge Advocate

A larger number of members could not be convened without manifest injury to the service. Should any member be absent the Court will nevertheless proceed to business, provided the members be not less than the minimum prescribed by law. The court will sit without regard to days or hours.

By Command of Genl Lee
signed W. H. Taylor
A. A. Genl

Wilcox's Division (late Pender's) Court Martial, 8 O'clock A.M.
Aug. 28th 1863.

The Court met pursuant to the above order. Present:

Col. Wm. M. Barbour	37th N.C.T.
Lt. Col. I. N. Brown	14th S. C. Vols.
Major W. L. Groves	35th Ga. "
Major J. F. Hunt	13th S. C. "
Capt. C. A. Corns	Co. "G" 45t Ga. Regt.
Capt. E. D. Brailsford	Co. "I" 1st S.C.
Capt. N. E. Armstrong	Co. "A" 38th N.C.T.
Capt. J. J. Poisson	Co. "G" 18th N.C.T.

Capt. Wm. A. Nicholson Co. "E" 37th N.C. T. Judge Advocate

Absent:

Lt. Col. J. Ashford, 38th N.C. T. "at home on leave of absence"

Lieut. S. G. Johnson Co. "C" 35th Ga. Regt. the accused, also present.

The Judge Advocate having read the order the court asked the accused Lieut. S. G. Johnson if he had any objection to any men so named above, to which he replied, "I have none".

The Court was then duly sworn by the Judge Advocate and the Judge Advocate was duly sworn by the presiding officer of the Court in the presence of the accused.

The accused here asked the permission of the court to introduce his Counsel Lt. Colonel R. P. Lester 14th Ga. Regt. which was granted.

Charges & Specifications against
Lieut. S. G. Johnson Co. "C" 35th Ga. Regt.

Charge—Conduct unbecoming an officer & gentleman.

Specification 1st—In this that the said Lieut. S. G. Johnson Co. "C" 35th Ga. Regt. having received a furlough from the Secretary of War for Harbird Cook a private Co. "C" 35th Ga. Regt. did sell the said furlough to Corp. Wm. Burran Co. "C" 35th Ga., the said Corp. Burran been in Hospital, and being reported for duty, and the said Lt. Johnson being aware that the said Burran intended to proceed to Ga. upon the papers above mentioned, all this in the City of Richmond on or about Sept. 16th 1862.

Specification 2nd—In that the said Lieut. S. G. Solomon Co. "C" 35th Ga. Regt. having procured a furlough from Surgeon of some Hospital in Richmond Va. Thom. I. Daniel Private Co. "C" 35th Ga. Regt. on or about 1st Sept. 1862 and the said Daniel dying shortly thereafter, the said Lt.

S. G. Johnson Co."C" 35th Ga did sell the said furlough to a Confederate soldier, all this in Richmond Va.

Witnesses:
Private Harbird Cook
Corp. Wm.Smith
Lieut. John E. Steed
Sergt. J. S. Moore — signed, B. H. Holt
Corp. T. M. Shannon — Col., 35th Ga. Regt.

The charges were then read aloud by the Judge Advocate. The Judge Advocate then said, "Lieut. S. G. Johnson, you have heard the charges preferred against you, how say you—guilty or not guilty"?

To which the accused Lieut. S. G. Johnson pleaded as follows—"Not Guilty".

Lieut. John E. Steed, Co. "C", 35th Ga. Regt. a witness on the part of the prosecution, entered court and was duly sworn.

By Judge Advocate—

Quest.—State what Lieut. Johnson told you about what he did with a furlough which he had procured for one Daniels of your company?

Ans.—Last September Lt. Johnson came up from Richmond and while talking to me about different members of my company he told me that Daniel was dead, that a day or two before he (Johnson) did a furlough for him which he afterwards sold for $20 (to best of my recollection that was the amount) and that he sent the money to Daniels' wife.

Quest—What did he tell you had become of Burran?

Ans—I asked him if Corp. Burran had left Richmond and he said he had gone home on furlough.

Quest—Did he state how or from whom he had procured his furlough?

Ans.—He did not as I recollect.

Quest.—Did he mention having procured furloughs from the Secy. of War for any of your company?

Ans.—He did., he said he had procured furloughs for Sergt. J. S. Moore, Corp. T. W. Shannon and J. I. Hopkins.

Quest.—Did he mention having procured one for Harbird Cook?

Ans.—He did not as I recollect.

By Counsel for Accused—

Quest.—What reason did Lt. Johnson give for selling the furlough which had been procured for Daniel?

Ans.—I had heard him say that as Daniel was a poor man, he thought he wouldsell the furlough and send the money to his wife, as she would need it.

Quest.—Were not the men for whom he said he had procured furloughs paroled prisoners?

Ans.—Moore and Hopkins were, Shannon had been captured but I don't know whether he had been exchanged or not.

Quest.—How long have you known Lt. Johnson?

Ans.—About three years.

Quest.—What has been his character in ordinary transactions of life, is it that of a gentleman?

Ans.—I have always considered him a gentleman and honorable man, and that is his general character.

Quest.—What is his general character as an officer?

Ans.—It is very good.

Quest.—Did he manifest any disposition to conceal any part of this transaction?

Ans.—None at all about Daniel's furlough, about the other case I have never talked with him.

By Judge Advocate—

Quest.—About his character as an officer, have you never heard anything against him?

The counsel for the accused objected to this question and the Judge Advocate did not insist on an answer.

Ans.—I know of only one, it was said of him that he behaved in a manner unbecoming an officer at the battle of Seven Pines.

Quest.—Have you heard any general charge against his character as a gentleman?

Ans.—I have not.

Quest.—You state that he manifested no desire to conceal what what he had done with Daniel's furlough, but that he talked freely about it. State to the court whether he was as open and frank as regards his connection with Cook's furlough and Burrans going home?

Ans.—He never told me anything about Cook's furloughor Burrans going home, except that Burran had a furlough.

Private Harbird Cook Co. "C", 35th Ga. Regt. a witness on the part of the prosecution, entered court and was duly sworn.

By Judge Advocate:—

Quest.—Did Lieut. Johnson tell you that he had procured a furlough for you from the Secy of War last Sept.?

Ans.—He did.

Quest.—Did he deliver it to you?
Ans.—He did not.
Quest.—Why did not he deliver it to you?
Ans.—I don't know.
Quest.—What did he do with it?
Ans.—He did not tell me.

By Counsel for the Accused:—
Quest.—Did you go home on a furlough about that time?
Ans.—I did.
Quest.—When did you get the furlough from which you went home on?
Ans.—The Medical Board at Camp Winder gave it to me and I had it when Lieut. Johnson told me he had got one for me.

The Court adjourns, as other important witness were absent, until tomorrow at 8 o'clock A.M.

Wm. T. Nicholson, Capt.	Wm. M. Barbour
Co. "E" 37th N. C. Troops	Col. & President
Judge Advocate of GCM	GCM

Wilcox's Division (late Pender's) Court Martial

8 o'clock A. M. Aug. 29th 1863

The Court Martial pursuant to aformentioned. Present:

Col. Wm. M. Barbour 37th N.C.T
Lt. Col. I. N. Brown 14th S. C. Vols.
Major M. L. Groves 35th Ga. "

Major I. J. Hunt	13th S. C. "
Major J. F. Hunt	13th S. C. "
Capt. C. A. Corns	Co. "G" 45t Ga. Regt.
Capt. E. D. Brailsford	Co. "I" 1st S.C.
Capt. N. E. Armstrong	Co. "A" 38th N.C.T.
Capt. J. J. Poisson	Co. "G" 18th N.C.T.

Capt. Wm. T. Nicholson Co. "E", 37th N.C. T. Judge Advocate

Absent:

Lt. Col. I. Ashford, 38th N.C. T. (at home on leave of absence)

Lieut. S. G. Johnson Co. "C", 35th Ga. the accused, with his counsel also present.

Corp. W. Burran, Co. "C", 35th Ga. Regt. a witness on the part of the prosecution enters court and was duly sworn.

By Judge Advocate—

Quest.—Did you go home from Richmond last September?

Ans.—I did.

Quest.—How did you get a furlough?

Ans.—I got it from Lieut. Johnson of my company.

Quest.—When, and for whom did he procure it?

Ans.—From the Secy of War for Harbird Cook.

Quest.—What did he charge you for it?

Ans.—A man in Richmond owed me $25 and I gave him an order or note for him to get that money.

By Counsel for accused—

Quest.—Did Lieut. Johnson pay it over to you?

Ans.—He did in about six months afterwards.

Quest.—How long did you stay at home?

Ans.—I was gone about 45 days, and remained in Richmond about 14 days. I left for home Sept. 17th.

Quest.—How long after you saw Lieut. Johnson before he paid you the money?

Ans.—He paid me about three months after I returned. I got back to the regiment in October or Nov. and he paid me in Feby. or March.

Quest.—Didn't Lieut. Johnson tell you at the time he gave you the furlough, or at any other time, that he didn't expect to charge you for it.?

Ans.—He told me this when he gave me the money back in Feby. or March.

Quest.—Hadn't you been in the Hospital since the battle of Seven Pines?

Ans.—I had been there since the battle of Malvern Hill.

Quest.—then you not staying in the Hospital under a detail?

Ans.—I was not but I was nursing in the Hospital.

Quest.—Did not you tell him that you were detailed?

Ans.—I don't remember that I did.

The Judge Advocate declared the prosecution closed.

Capt. G. B. Almand Co. "B" 35th Ga. Regt. a witness for the defense entered court and was duly sworn.

By counsel for accused:—

Quest.—What is the position of your company as composed with Lieut. Johnson?

Ans.—It is the next one on the right.

Quest.—How long have you known him?

Ans.—Since Sept. 1861.

Quest.—What is his general character as an officer and a gentleman?

Ans.—It is good.

Quest.—How long has he commanded his co.?

Ans.—Since last October.

Quest.—Didn't he command it during the battle of Richmond?

Ans.—He must have commanded at Gaines Mill Frazers Farm.

Quest.—What has been his conduct as an officer as to discipline and management of men, and on the battlefield?

Ans.—So far as I have observed, it has been considered good.

Private John J. Miles Co. "C" 35th Ga. Regt. a witness on the part of the defense entered court and was duly sworn.

By counsel for accused:

Quest.—How long have you known Lieut. Johnson?

Ans.—Ever since I could recollect.

Quest.—What is his general character as a gentleman in his neighborhood?

Ans.—He has always been considered a gentleman.

Quest.—What is his general character as an officer?

Ans.—He has always been at his post and doing his duty so far as I know.

Quest.—Were you at the battle of Seven Pines?

Ans.—I was.

Quest.—Did you have opportunities for observing him in that battle?

Ans.—I was with him al of the time.

Quest.—What was his conduct on that occasion?

Ans.—He went in with his company and staid with it as long as any of it was on the field, and he was the last of it to come out. I was with him myself at the time.

Capt. J. T. McElvany Co. "F", 35th Ga. Regt. a witness for the defense, entered court, and was duly sworn.

By counsel for accused:

Quest.—How long have you known the accused?

Ans.—I first knew him 1857 and I have been with him in the Regt. ever since it was formed.

Quest.—What is his general character as an officer and gentleman?

Ans.—I look upon him as a brave and efficient officer, and as a gentleman. He sustains a very good character so far as my acquitance extends.

Col. B. H. Holt, 35th Ga. Regt. a witness for the defense entered court and was duly sworn.

By counsel for accused:

Quest.—How long have you known the accused?

Ans.—Since November 1861.

Quest.—What is his general character as an officer and gentleman?

Ans.—Very good.

The counsel for the accused submitted his argument (Exhibit "A") and the Judge Advocate submitted his (Exhibit "B")

The statement of the parties being thus in possession of the Court, the Court was cleared for deliberation, and having maturely considered the evidence addressed, find the accused Lieut. S. G. Johnson Company "C" 35th Georgia Regiment as follows:

Of the first specification of the charge: "Guilty"

Of the second specification of the charge: "Guilty"

Of the Charge: "Guilty"

And the Court do therefore sentence the said Lieutenant S. G. Johnson Company "C" 35th Georgia Regiment to be dismissed the service.

Wm. T. Nicholson, Capt.	Wm. M. Barbour
Co. "E" 37th N. C. Troops	Col. & President
Judge Advocate of GCM	G.C.M.

The proceedings, findings and sentence in the case of Lieutenant S. G. Johnson Co. C 35th Georgia Regiment are approved. The sentence is confirmed and Lieut. Johnson ceases from this date to be an officer of the Confederate States Service.

R. E. Lee

Genl

Note: A card next to this info on the microfilm noted that the court martial of Johnson was "Respectfully forwarded and disapproved".

Signed C. M. Wilcox

HQ 3rd Army Corps

October 5, 1863

Respectfully forwarded and disapproved

Signed A. P. Hill

Lt. Genl

Hqtrs A.No. Va

7th Oct 1863

Res. Forwarded
Not recommended
The proceedings in the case are [????unreadable]
Signed R. E. Lee
Genl.

Notes: the above court martial proceedings were located in—(National Archives Microfilm Publication, Letters Received By The Confederate Adjutant and Inspector General, 1861–1865, M474, roll #69, numbers 16–1165, Jan.-Dec. 1863, Document #859J) National Archives and Records Administration Building, Washington, D.C)

A search through Johnson's service records does not shed any light on what his punishment was. Apparently he was not cashiered out of the service, but reduced in rank. At the time the court martial proceedings occurred he was a first lieutenant. A year later, he received pay on 10/3/1863 for $114. 66 and signed the pay statement as 2nd Lt. S. G. Johnson.

Then to add more confusion, there is a discharge certificate in his service records dated January 3, 1865. It said he was 38 years old, 5'10" tall, dark eyes, dark complexion, dark hair and had been a farmer. Then the certificate said, "entitled to discharge for promotion to 2nd Lt. on August 18th 1864." However, he is included in a list of soldiers in the 35th Georgia who surrendered at Appomattox.

Additional items I located in his service records can be used to show the honesty and trustworthiness of Lieutenant Johnson. There are copies of three letters Johnson wrote in December 1862 to Colonel A. C. Myers refunding payroll money he had drawn for absent soldiers when unbeknownst to him the same soldiers had drawn their money while in Richmond due to illness or furlough. In the first letter dated 18 December 1862 Johnson refunded $205 to the Confederate government. In another letter dated 19 December 1862 he refunded $70. In the final letter date 29 December 1862 he refunded $44.

Appendix E

The Real Hec Ramsey

The youngest member of the 35th Georgia went on to become a famous member of the Texas Rangers and then a U.S. Marshal out west after the war. Heck Thomas served as the role model for the 1970's NBC television series "Hec Ramsey" starring Richard Boone. Henry Andrew Thomas was born in 1850 in Athens, Georgia. He was the son of Captain Lovick Pierce Thomas and the nephew of Brigadier General Edward L. Thomas. Captain L. P. Thomas was wounded during the Seven Days Battles in June 1862. He was sent home to Georgia to recover. Upon his return to the 35th Georgia he brought two of the family servants as well as his twelve-year-old son Henry, nicknamed Heck. They returned to the unit shortly before the Battle of Second Manassas erupted in August 1862. The young Thomas claimed that his uncle charged him with caring for Union Major General Phil Kearny's horse, saddle and accoutrements after Kearny was killed. The one-armed Kearny mistakenly had ridden too close to the Georgia line at the Battle of Chantilly and he was shot from the saddle. His bewildered horse ran into Thomas' line. Several weeks later Heck Thomas brought the horse and saddle forward to be sent through the lines to Kearny's widow.

Some veterans acknowledged that Heck Thomas was the youngest soldier in the Confederate army. Reflecting on the war he said, "Well do I remember when I wrote home the pride I took in writing my address: "Henry A. Thomas, 35th Regiment Georgia Volunteers, Thomas' Brigade, A.P. Hill's Division, Stonewall Jackson's Corps."

After the war, Heck Thomas came to Atlanta and remained for a number of years. Then in his mid-twenties he pushed westward. He accepted a job in Texas riding shotgun for bank shipments. He was locked inside a railroad car with $22,000 when the train suddenly stopped. He heard shots and then fists banging on the door. A number of shots struck the door, and the lock fell off. The robbers forced him to unlock the safe, and they took off with what appeared to be the money. After they had climbed aboard their horses they fired shots back at Heck standing in the doorway of the car. He fell to the floor with a head wound. Unbeknownst to Sam Bass and his feared gang, Heck had torn up stacks of newspaper clippings and then sandwiched them between a few real bills. He had hidden the rest of the real money inside the railroad car stove. For several days Heck hovered near death, but then made a miraculous recovery.

He wanted revenge, so he joined the Texas Rangers. Soon after he joined, they ambushed the Bass Gang, and Sam Bass was killed in the shootout. Heck spent ten years as a Ranger and gained a famous reputation as a hard-nosed, but honest lawman. He heard that there were real problems in the Oklahoma Territory, so he headed north and joined forces as U.S. Marshal with Judge Isaac Parker, known as the Hanging Judge. Heck was instrumental in bringing peace to the territory at a time when more settlers were arriving from back east. He was invited to form and head the police department in the town of Lawton, Oklahoma. "He was still police chief of the well-behaved town when he died in office, with his boots on, in 1912 at the age of 62. By then Oklahoma had been a state for five years." Both his father and brother served as chief of police for Atlanta.

Notes: see Chapter 5 for another Heck Thomas photo.

1. "The Real Hec Ramsey" *The Atlanta Journal and Constitution Magazine* by C. Winn Upchurch, February 18, 1973.
2. *The Constitution,* "Bruffs Column" Atlanta, GA. Monday, March 9, 1909.

Henry Andrew "Heck" Thomas

This photo shows Thomas dressed as a U.S. Marshal. Thomas was the youngest son of Captain Lovick P. Thomas and the nephew of Brigadier General Edward Lloyd Thomas. He served in the 35th Georgia as a twelve-year-old courier and drummer boy. His war experiences helped him in the law enforcement field. A newspaper wrote, "'Gentle' Heck Thomas from Georgia was one of the most feared lawmen in the Old West."

From *The Atlanta Journal and Constitution Magazine,* February 18, 1973

Appendix F

A Remnant of the Battle Flag of the 35th Georgia

In 1910, a Mrs. Charles Hill of Waterville, Maine sent a letter to A.J. Scott, Adjutant for a United Confederate Veterans Camp in Atlanta. Enclosed with the letter was a small piece of faded bunting. In her letter she wrote that when Lee surrendered at Appomattox the Confederate flags were taken and stacked. On top of the stack was the flag of the 35th Georgia. Union Lieutenant Charles Shoney [Shuey] of the 1st Maine cut a blue portion from this flag containing a star and the name '35th Georgia' to keep as a war souvenir. When he died, his sister Mrs. Hill, mailed the piece of history to Scott. A close inspection of the flag, stored in the Georgia State Capitol, reveals where somebody sewed the swatch back onto the banner.

Note: *The Confederate Veteran,* XVIII, p. 204; *Confederate Flags in the Georgia State Capitol Collection,* Paul Ellingson editor, 1994.

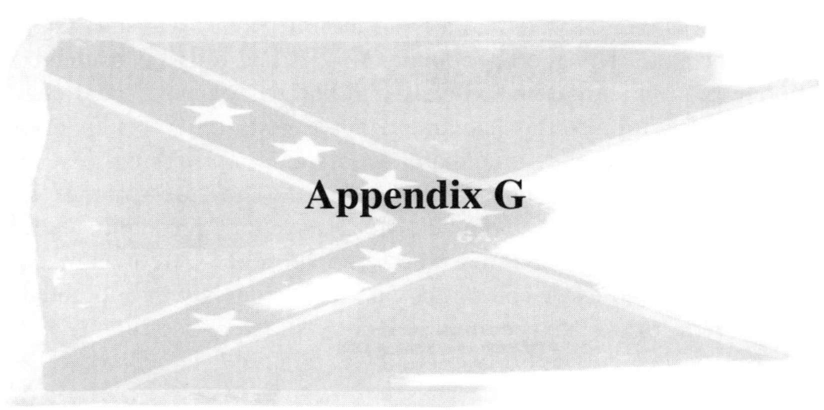

Appendix G

The author discovered the following newspaper article in a stack of research material. Unfortunately, the source and date are unknown. Scribbled at the bottom of the article is the date July 26, 1888. The article probably appeared in an Atlanta area newspaper. The article reads as follows:

A Grand Reunion

Of the Thirty-Fifth Georgia at Conyers Yesterday

Conyers was the scene of great enjoyment yesterday. The occasion was the reunion of the veterans of the 35th Georgia regiment, and may be pronounced to be one of the happiest and most successful ever held in the state.

About forty or fifty people in all left Atlanta on the 8 o'clock train, and were accompanied by the reception committee which had been sent from Conyers. The military company of Conyers met them at the train, and, together with the veterans who were in line there, escorted them to the courthouse, the band playing sweet and inspiring music as they marched.

Colonel T. W. Latham, of Fairburn, president of the association, called the veterans to order, and Colonel E. M. Roberts, of Atlanta, registered all who were present.

They then went to the academy park, where the crowd was seated under the shade of the large and beautiful trees. Prayer was then offered by Rev. G. W. Yarbrough, former chaplain of the regiment. The address of welcome was delivered by the mayor of Conyers, in a graceful and dignified manner, and was responded to by Colonel T. W. Latham.

In the absence of General Gordon, Colonel Perry, of Conyers, was substituted in his place, and made an excellent speech.

Dinner was then served, and a more tempting feast was never spread before in the state. The good people of Conyers had fully determined that every one present should be fed well, and had barbecued a great deal of meat; and in addition to this had an elegant basket dinner. Fruits, grapes, melons and every delicacy imaginable were there in profusion. After dinner the old officers were unanimously elected. They are Colonel T. W. Latham, president; Major James T. McElvany, vice-president; Colonel E. M. Roberts, secretary and treasurer. Short speeches were then made by several of the veterans. A committee on arrangements was appointed on speaking, etc., for the next reunion, which is to take place July 22, 1869, at Lawrenceville, Ga. The Forty-second Georgia holds its reunion there at the same time.

A vote of thanks was tendered to Hon. W. L. Peck, officer of the day to the military company, and to the kind citizens of Conyers and of Rockdale county for their successful efforts in making the occasion one of the highest enjoyment. The reunion broke up at four o'clock, and the day so happily spent was past. It was a remarkable fact that not even the smell of whisky was to be found in the large crowd of 2,500 persons assembled there.

The veterans of this valiant regiment look forward with a great deal of pleasure to their next meeting together.

Appendix H

35TH GEORGIA RELICS FROM CAMP FRENCH AT EVANSPORT, VA. 1861–1862

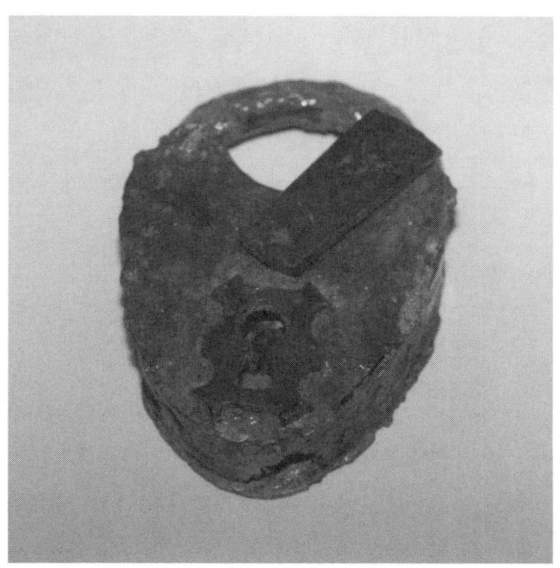

1. Padlock
photo by D. J. Bender, Winchester, Va.

2. Pair of Shoe Heels and Sewing Thimble

These heels were found in a hut site sitting upright just as the Georgia soldier had left them. The leather had rotted away, but the attaching nails still stuck upward. The sewing thimble came from a different hut. This was a handy tool to aid soldiers with clothing repairs.

photo by D. J. Bender, Winchester, Va.

3. 22" Bowie Knife

This very large blade length is 18 inches long. The hilt is another 4 inches long.

photo by D. J. Bender, Winchester, Va.

4. Assorted Artillery Fuses and Large Iron Grape Shot

All these items were found next to the large ammunition magazine that was torched when Confederates withdrew from Camp French in March 1862. Notice the middle fuse shows evidence of damage from the heat and flames.

photo by D. J. Bender, Winchester, Va.

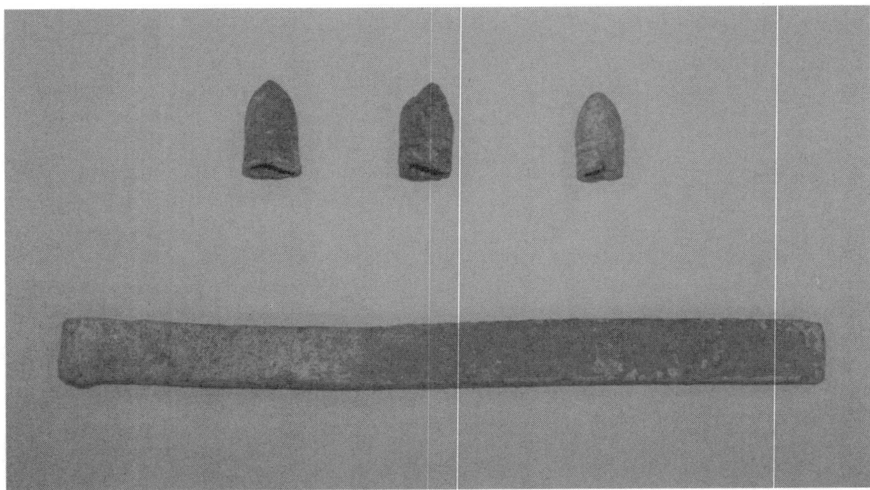

5. Field Lead Bar and .58 Caliber Macon (Ga.) Arsenal Bullets

Soldiers used the field lead bar to melt and hand-mold their own bullets. These three bullets were discovered next to the ammunition magazine.

photo by D. J. Bender, Winchester, Va.

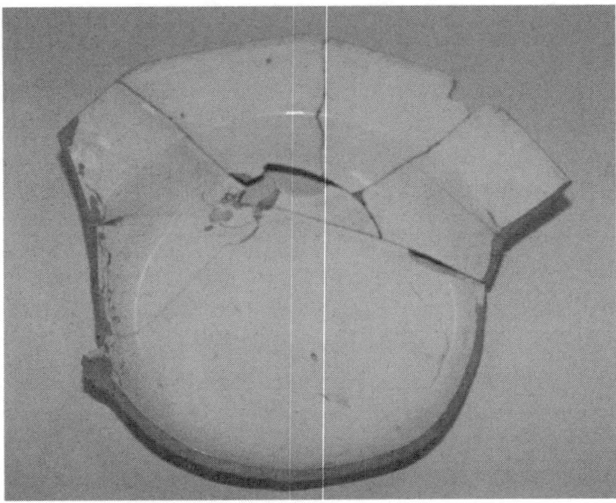

6. English Ironstone Plate (top view)

Found in hut site next to old wagon road. This plate was probably smashed by Union soldiers after the Confederate evacuation in March 1862. The back mark is legible.

photo by D. J. Bender, Winchester, Va.

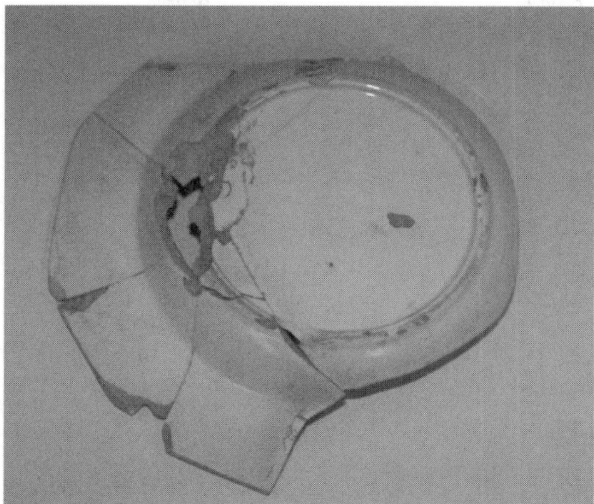

7. English Ironstone Plate (bottom view)

This is the bottom of the same plate that was meticulously reconstructed from the pieces that could be found. The back mark is in the middle. The top of the mark reads "TR Boote." The bottom reads "Sydenham. Shape." There are several letters and numbers in the middle of the mark that indicate the date of manufacture was September 5, 1850.

photo by D. J. Bender, Winchester, Va.

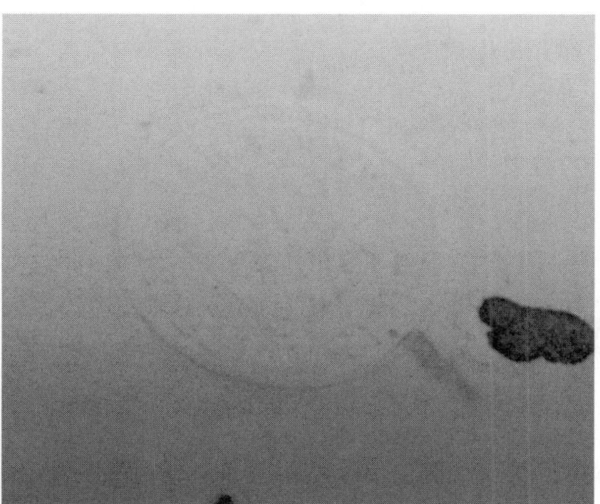

8. Close Up of English Ironstone Plate Back Mark

photo by D. J. Bender, Winchester, Va.

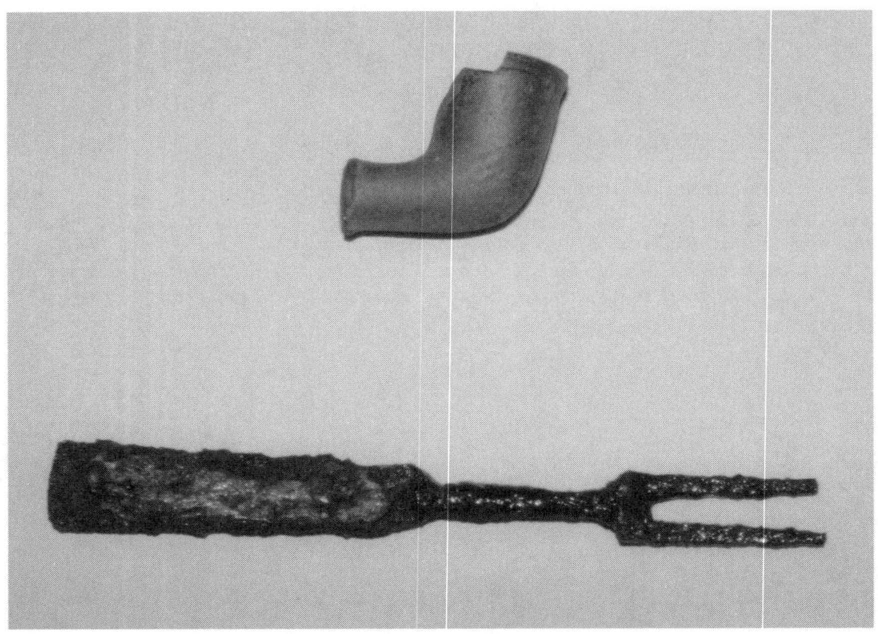

9. Fork and Clay Pipe Bowl

The fork was found in an officer's hut site near the top of the ridge. The pipe bowl was found next to the old wagon road near the ammunition magazine.

photo by D. J. Bender, Winchester, Va.

10. Bible Cover Cross

This cross came from a hut site. It stands about one-and-a-half inches tall. The backside has several sharp angled edges. The owner would have dampened both the back of the cross and the leather Bible cover and then pressed the cross into the leather cover. When the leather dried it would have held the cross in place. This cross probably fell off the Bible since there were no leather remnants left on the sharp edges of the back.

photo by D. J. Bender, Winchester, Va.

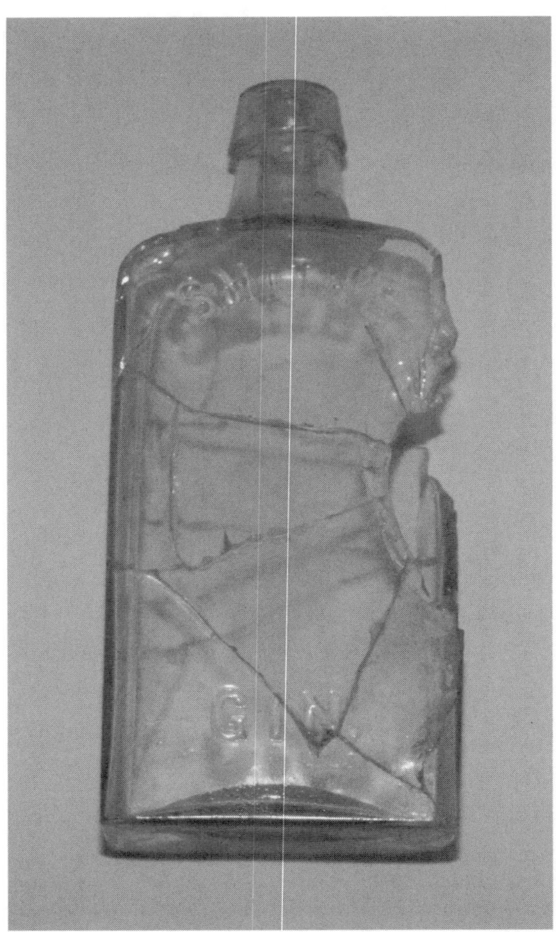

11. Smith's Gin Bottle (aqua)
This bottle came from an officer's hut site.
photo by D. J. Bender, Winchester, Va.

12. Cathedral Bottle (aqua)

This bottle came from the same officer's hut as the gin bottle. The soldiers normally used this type of bottle as a food container.

photo by D. J. Bender, Winchester, Va.

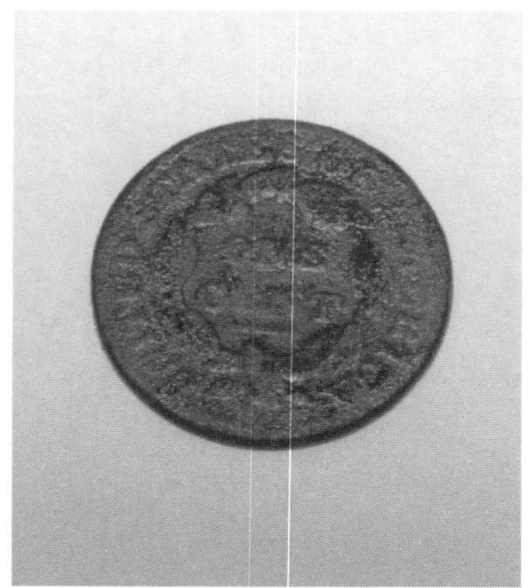

13. Large U.S. Penny (unknown date)

This coronet type coin was minted from 1816–1857. The actual date of this coin has worn away.

photo by D. J. Bender, Winchester, Va.

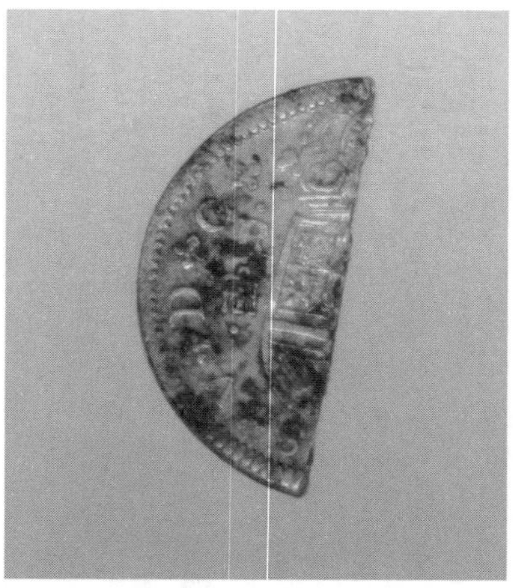

14. Half of Spanish 2 Reale Silver Coin (1761)

This coin was cut cleanly in half and was commonly used by the soldiers to buy items from sutlers or for gambling. Cut in half, this coin represents four bits of silver.

photo by D. J. Bender, Winchester, Va.

15. Seated Liberty Half Dime (1854)
This coin was found just south of the ammunition magazine.
photo by D. J. Bender, Winchester, Va.

16. Sash Buckle
U.S. Militia Eagle surrounded by "Pollack Bros. N.Y." This might have been used as an advertising disk or coin and given to a soldier by a sutler. It very well could have been dropped by Union soldiers investigating the Confederate camps during the second week of March 1862.
photo by D. J. Bender, Winchester, Va.

17. Back of Liberty Half Dime
photo by D. J. Bender, Winchester, Va.

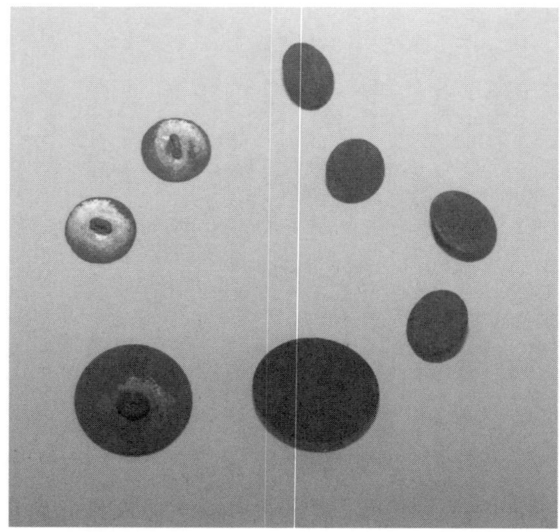

18. Group of Flat Buttons (type 1B)
These assorted fasteners came from throughout the camp.
photo by D. J. Bender, Winchester, Va.

19. Georgia State Seal Cuff Button
Found in hut site near south end of camp. Written on the back is "W.G. Mintzer Phile. Pa."
photo by D. J. Bender, Winchester, Va.

20. Blank Waist Belt Plate
This plate was bent in half and was located just south of the ammunition magazine.
photo by D. J. Bender, Winchester, Va.

35TH GEORGIA VOLUNTEER INFANTRY REGIMENT ROSTER

ROSTER ABBREVIATIONS

ACS—Acting Commissary of Subsistence
Adj—Adjutant
ANV—Army of Northern Virginia
AQM—Assistant Quartermaster
ART—Artillery
b—born
BG—Brigadier General
Bde—brigade
Bn or Battn—battalion
bur—buried
CAV—Cavalry
CIA—captured in action
Co—Company
COL—Colonel
CPL—Corporal
CPT—Captain
Cty.—county
d—died
Dsh.—discharged
frl.—furlough
GEN—General
Hsp.—Hospital
Inf—infantry
KIA—killed in action
LT—Lieutenant
LTC—Lieutenant Colonel
MAJ—Major
MIA—missing in action
NLR—no later record
Ord—Ordnance
PVT—Private
QM—Quartermaster
Regt—regiment
SGTor SG—Sergeant
SGM—Sergeant-Major
trn.—transfer
WIA—wounded in action

*Note—All dates are from the 1800's unless so indicated. A major source for this information was Lillian Henderson's *Roster of Confederate Soldiers of Georgia, Vol 3;* the National Archives' "Compiled Service Records of Confederate General and Staff Officers and Non-regimental Enlisted Men"; "Compiled Service Records of Confederate Soldiers in Organizations From the State of Georgia"; "Reference File Relating to Confederate Medical Officers." Other information for this roster came from Georgia Veteran Pension Records and 1850/1860 Georgia Census Records plus numerous other sources.

Roster A

Adair, William Henry—PVT Co.E 8/12/61. Discharged for disability 11/16/61. NLR.

Aderhold, John C. Sr.—PVT Co.E 2/15/62. Appointed 2SG 6/28/63. CIA at Farmville, Va. 4/6/65. Released at Newport News, Va. 6/25/65. B. in Georgia 2/9/43. NLR.

Akin, Andrew J.—PVT Co.G 7/25/62. CIA at Spotsylvania C.H. 5/12/64. D. of smallpox at Fort Delaware, Del. 7/29/64. NLR.

Alford, George W.—PVT Co.K 3/4/62. WIA at Manassas 8/29/62. WIA at Fredericksburg 12/13/62 requiring amputation of leg. Roll for 2/28/65 lists him as absent, wounded since 12/13/62. NLR.

Algood, Coleman C.—PVT Co.G 2/28/62. CIA at Spotsylvania C.H. 5/12/64. D. in prison. NLR.

Algood, Job B.—PVT Co.G 2/28/62. D. of measles at Winchester, Va. 10/11/62. Widow pension 1891–1901. A soldier named Joseph Algood from the same company is bur. in Georgia section, grave #132, Stonewall Confederate Cemetery (Mount Hebron), Winchester, Va. This is probably same soldier.

Algood, William F.—PVT Co.G 2/28/62. WIA at Seven Pines 5/31/62. D. from wounds at Richmond 6/3/62. Widow pension 1891.

Allen, David R.—PVT Co.G 9/16/61. Discharged on 7/25/62 for serious affliction of the legs due to a burn of seven years before. NLR.

Allen, Harrison—PVT Co.G 2/28/62. CIA at Wilderness 5/6/64. Released at Elmira, N.Y. 6/14/65. B. 3/22/1841. D. 9/22/1914 and bur Jersey Methodist Ch. Cem. in Walton Cty., Ga. Widow pension 1919.

Allen, Henry A.—PVT Co.E 2/13/62. CIA at Wilderness 5/6/64. D. of acute diarrhea at Fort Delaware, Del. 1/19/65. NLR.

Allen, Hiram W.—PVT Co.E 8/12/61. KIA at Cedar Mountain 9/9/62. NLR.

Allen, James—PVT Co.F 5/3/62. CIA at Petersburg, Va. 2/2/65. Released at Point Lookout, Md. 6/22/65. Pension roll 1895. B. 5/21/1829 in Walton Cty., Ga.

Allen, Jesse—PVT Co.G 9/16/61. D. at Dumfries, Va. hospital 1/11/62. NLR.

Allen, Presley M. PVT Co.F 2/1/62. Discharged on 7/29/62 for chronic rheumatism in left hand and arm caused by being run over by a government wagon. B. in Gwinnett Cty., Ga. 3/19/36. Pension roll 1904. D. 10/3/1914.

Allen, Richmond D.—PVT Co.G 2/28/62. D. of disease at Augusta, Ga. in 1862 while on way home on frl. Widow, Nancy, pension 1891–96.

Allen, Thomas V.—PVT Co.F 2/1/62. CIA at Wilderness 5/5/64. Paroled Elmira, N.Y. 10/11/64 and exchanged 10/29/64. Received at Venus Point at Savannah, Ga. 11/15/64. B. in Georgia 10/4/30. NLR.

Allen, William E.—PVT Co.G 2/16/62. CIA 1865. Released at Point Lookout, Md. 6/22/65. NLR.

Allen, William L.—PVT Co.G 9/16/61. Discharged 10/23/61. Possibly bur Jersey Methodist Ch. Cem in Walton Cty., Ga.

Alums, William H.—PVT Co.D 2/3/62. CIA Petersburg, Va. 4/3/65. Released at Hart's Island, N.Y. 6/15/65. NLR.

Almand, Graves Bennett—2LT Co.B 9/21/61. Elected CPT 6/13/62. D. Lynchburg, Va. 6/6/64 of typhoid fever. Bur. in Confederate Cemetery #9, 2nd line, lot 201-College. B. 6/12/27.

Almand, James F.—2SG Co.B 9/21/61. Enlisted at Conyers, Ga. Discharged for disability 4/15/62. NLR.

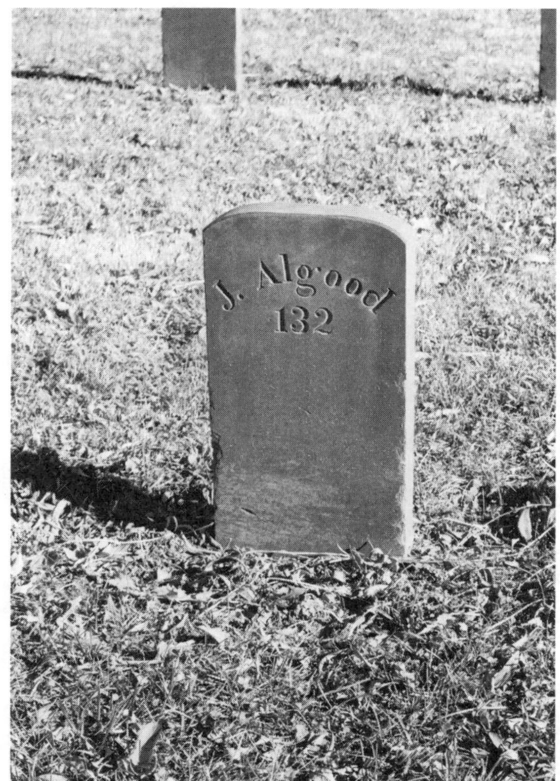

Tombstone of Private Job B. Algood, Co. G Stonewall Confederate Cemetery (Mount Hebron) at Winchester, Va.
photo by author

Almand, James T.—4SG Co.B 9/21/61. Enl. at Conyers, Ga. Appointed 1SG 6/13/62. On 4/3/63 he received commutation of rations while on detached duty from 1/27/63 to 3/24/64. D. of typhoid fever in Ga. 1864. B. 5/12/1823.

Almand, John B.—PVT Co.B 9/21/61. Enlisted at Conyers, Ga. CIA 5/7/64 at Wilderness. Released at Elmira, N.Y. 5/16/65. NLR.

Almand, Henry F.—2CPL Co.B 9/21/61. WIA Mechanicsville, Va. 6/26/62 and d. from wounds the next day.

Almand, Peter B.—PVT Co.B 9/21/61. Enlisted at Conyers, Ga. D. typhoid fever at Dumfries, Va. 1/3/62. NLR.

Anderson, Richard—PVT Co.B 2/20/62. Discharged for disability 6/25/62. NLR.

Anderson, Supre H.—PVT Co.B 9/21/61. Appointed 4CPL 1864. WIA (shot in left arm) at Petersburg 4/2/65. Captured in Jackson Hospital at Richmond 5/3/65 and was still in that hospital 5/28/65. Pension roll 1889–1911.

Anderson, William A.J.—PVT Co.B 9/21/61. Detached as steward in 3rd Georgia Hospital at Richmond 12/21/61. Discharged for disability 3/23/62. NLR.

Anglin, Henry D.—PVT Co.H 9/24/61. WIA Seven Pines, Va. 5/31/62. WIA at Fredericksburg 12/13/62. Permanently disabled due to wounds in right leg and finger of left hand. Half of fingers on left hand shot off at Seven Pines. Disabled at close of war. Pension roll 1890–1904

Armor, William Robert—PVT Co.C 9/17/61. WIA at Fredericksburg 12/13/62. D. from wounds 12/25/62. NLR.

Athey, William M.—PVT Co.B 2/15/62. WIA near Richmond 6/62. WIA at Wilderness 5/5/64. Appointed 2CPL 1864. Roll for 2/28/65 shows him AWOL since 2/15/65. B. Walton County, Ga. 1/1833. Pension roll 1905.

Avery, Charles W.—2LT Co.A 8/15/61. WIA Battle of Seven Pines 5/31/62. One bullet in shoulder and another pierced both lungs. Resigned for disability 10/10/62. B. in 1830. Carpenter. Wrote letter to Sec'y of War on 10/25/62 asking for a blacksmith to be returned to his county (Haralson) from the army because there was a "real distress". NLR.

Aycock, Francis T.—PVT Co.B 2/28/62. WIA 1862. D. of measles at Ashland, Va. 5/10/62. NLR.

Aycock, George W.—PVT Co.B 4/11/64. Roll for 2/28/65 shows him AWOL in Georgia. Pension records show he was at home at close of war on sick furlough. NLR.

Aycock, William T.—4CPL Co.B, 3rd Bn., Ga. State Troops 11/61. Mustered out of this unit 5/62. PVT Co.B, 35th Ga. Inf. Rgt. 5/4/62. Roll for 2/28/65 shows him AWOL in Georgia. Pension records show he was trying to rejoin his unit from a furlough at the close of war. NLR.

Ayers, Reuben—1CPL Co.A 8/15/61. D. at Richmond 7/5/62. NLR.

Roster B

Bachelor, James N.—PVT Co.G 9/16/61. CIA at Wilderness, Va. 5/6/64. D. Ft. Delaware Prison, Del. 7/28/64. Another source reports he d. at Pt. Lookout Prison, Md.

Baggot, Jackson (or Bagget)—PVT Co.A 8/15/61. WIA, shot in right thumb, Manassas, Va. 8/29/62. KIA at Chancellorsville 5/3/63. Listed in Gen'l Order #131 10/3/1863 as a corporal.

Bailey, David—PVT Co.H 8/62. CIA at Gettysburg, Pa. 7/3/63. D. of debility in USA General Hospital at Chester, Pa. 8/2/63.

Bailey, Eli—PVT Co.H 9/24/61. D. at Fredericksburg, Va. 3/11/62.

Bailey, Elijah P.—PVT Co.H 9/24/61. KIA at 2nd Manassas, Va. 8/30/62.

Bailey, George W.—PVT Co.F 9/23/61. CIA at Petersburg, Va. 4/2/65. Released from Point Lookout, Md. 6/9/65. NLR.

Bailey, Mansfield—PVT Co.D 9/23/61. WIA through both thighs at Fredericksburg 12/13/62. On detail duty in government shop at Columbus, Ga. from 1864 to 2/28/65. B. in Newton Cty., Ga. in 1824. Pension roll 1895–99.

Bailey, Martin V.—PVT Co.H 9/24/61. Dsh. at Richmond prior to 12/31/61.

Bailey, Newton J.—PVT Co.H 9/24/61. D. of disease in Richmond hospital 6/8/62.

Bailey, Noah S.—PVT Co.H 9/21/61. CIA at Gettysburg, Pa. 7/2/63. Prl. at Pt. Lookout, Md. and sent to City Point, Va. for exchange 4/27/64. Roll for 2/28/65 shows him AWOL. NLR.

Bailey, Worthy O.—PVT Co.H 8/30/62. CIA at Petersburg, Va. 4/3/65. Released at Hart's Island, N.Y. Harbor 6/15/65.

Baker, Charles N.—PVT Co.D 9/23/61. Appointed 4SG 12/15/61. WIA and permanently disabled at Seven Pines, Va. 5/31/62. Appointed 2SG 9/62. WIA, shot in arm, Fredericksburg, Va. 12/13/62. PVT 9/30/64. Roll for 2/28/65 reports him absent as sub-enrolling officer. B. Patrick Cty., Va. 1837. D. 1918 at Newnan, Ga.

Baker, Jordan J.—PVT Co.G 3/4/62. WIA Spotsylvania C.H., Va. 5/12/64. D. of wounds in Camp Jackson Hospital at Richmond 6/13/64. Bur. there at Hollywood Cemetery—grave U-222. Widow, Millie, pension 1891–1907.

Baker, Thomas L.—PVT Co.D 9/23/61. KIA at Seven Pines, Va. 5/31/62. Younger brother of Charles N. B. Patrick Cty., Va. 1839.

Baker, William H.—PVT Co.G 9/16/61. WIA 1864. Surrendered at Appomattox C.H. 4/9/65. NLR.

Baker, William W.—PVT Co.I 9/25/61. WIA at Hawe's Shop, Va. 6/14/64. Roll for 2/28/65 shows him present. B. 6/16/1840 in Chattooga Cty., Ga. D. 11/9/1909 at Umatilla, Fl. and bur there at Glendale Cem.

Baldwin, William H.—PVT Co.K 8/14/62. CIA near Jericho Ford, Va. 5/24/64. D. at Pt. Lookout Prison, Md. 2/10/65.

Banks, Abram C.—2CPL Co.E 8/12/61. Discharged from General Hospital at Farmville, Va. on 10/13/62 for rheumatism which caused contraction of right leg and effusion in knee joint. B. at Coweta Cty., Ga. 6/6/35. NLR.

Barfield, Henry Hawes (or Barefield)—PVT Co.C 9/17/61. Pension records show he was on furlough 2/65. When furlough expired he was cut off from his unit by the enemy. He enlisted in 9th Rgt. Ga. Militia Artillery (Glenn's Battery) 2/65. Surrendered at Atlanta 5/65. NLR

Barnes, Henry S.—PVT Co.A 2/23/62. WIA at Fredericksburg 12/13/62. D. of wounds 12/14/62. Bur. at Spotsylvania Confederate Cemetery at Spotsylvania C.H., Va. NLR.

Barnes, Walter T.C.—PVT Co.D 9/23/61. D. at Mrs. Carter's home near Brooks Station, Va. 1/3/63. NLR.

Barrett, William S.—CPT Co.G 9/16/61. Resigned for ill health 6/11/62. B. 12/17/1819. Pension 1900–04. Medical doctor before and after war. D. 12/11/1904 and bur Social Circle City Cem., Social Circle, Ga.

Bass, Algernon S.W.—PVT Co.A Cobb's Legion Ga. Inf. 8/1/61. Trn. Co.B, 35th Ga. Inf. Rgt. in exchange for Milton C. Mitchum in 1862. KIA at Chancellorsville 5/3/63. NLR.

Bass, W.N.—PVT Co.B 1861. D. at Richmond 6/24/62. Bur. there at Hollywood Cemetery. NLR.

Bays, Nathaniel D.—PVT Co.D 2/28/62. CIA 1865. Released from Point Lookout, Md. 6/24/65. NLR.

Beall, Josiah B.—PVT Co.E 8/12/61. WIA at Fredericksburg 12/13/62. Roll for 12/31/62 shows him, "absent and at a hospital somewhere." NLR.

Beam, James—PVT Co.B 2/24/62. CIA 1862. Sent to Ft. Delaware, Del. 7/9/62 and later exchanged. Roll for 2/28/65 shows him present. NLR.

Beam, Jesse—PVT Co.G 9/16/61. WIA 1864. Deserted near Petersburg, Va. 12/8/64. Took oath of allegience to U.S. Government at City Point, Va. 12/13/64 and at Washington, D.C. 12/15/64.

Beam, Thomas M.—PVT Co.G 3/9/63. WIA, left eye at Chancellorsville, Va. 5/3/63. Resulted in loss of sight. Admitted to Chimborazo Hospital #2 at Richmond 5/28/63. Furloughed for 50 days 6/10/63. Discharged for disability 12/13/63. Pension 1897–1905.

Beam, William E.—PVT Co.G 9/16/61. Admitted to General Hospital #21 at Richmond 4/4/63 for chronic diarrhea. Transferred to hsp. at Scottsville, Va. 4/12/63. NLR.

Beard, Henry H.—2SG Co.H 9/24/61. Elected 2LT in 1864. CIA 1865 probably at Petersburg, Va., on 4/2/65. In Libby USA Prison at Richmond 4/18/65. Paroled 4/20/65. Appears as witness on widow pension application of Matilda Cole, widow of I.B. Cole, in Newton Cty., Ga. 6/4/1891.

Bell, Arthur A.—PVT Co.C 4/28/62. WIA probably Seven Pines, Va.5/31/62. D. from wounds near Richmond 6/16/62.

Bellah, Amos A.—PVT Co.B, Cobb's Legion Ga. Inf. 8/5/61. Trn. Co.A, 35th Ga. Inf. Rgt. 9/5/61. WIA at Manassas 8/29/62. D. of wounds at Lynchburg, Va. 9/20/62. NLR.

Benafield, Hardy J.—PVT Co.F 9/23/61. WIA 7/64. Roll for 2/28/65 lists him as AWOL since 8/1/64. Reported to have joined Graham's Scouts in Georgia. B. 1839. Pension roll 1899–1907.

Benafield, James—PVT Co.F 9/23/61. WIA Spotsylvania C.H. 5/12/64. Roll for 2/28/65 shows him, "Sent to hospital, wounded, 5/12/64. Never heard from." NLR.

Benafield, Robert—PVT Co.F 5/5/62. CIA 1862. Paroled 8/5/62. Roll for 2/28/65 shows him present. NLR.

Bentley, Andrew J.—4SG Co.A 8/15/61. Elected Jr. 2LT 7/3/62. WIA in the head at Manassas 8/28/62. Elected 1LT. WIA Jericho Ford 5/23/64. Discharged from Talladega, Al. hospital 11/4/64 and ordered to company. AWOL 2/65. NLR.

Bentley, Isham J.—PVT Co.A 8/15/61. Discharged for chronic rheumatism and debility 7/26/62. NLR.

Bentley, James—PVT Co.A 8/15/61. KIA at Chancellorsville 5/3/63. NLR.

Bentley, J.J.—PVT Calhoun Sharpshooters (Thomas Bush's Co.), Alabama Volunteers. Trn to Co.A, 35th Ga. Inf. Rgt. 9/30/61. NLR.

Bentley, William M.—PVT Co.A 8/15/61. KIA at Cedar Mountain 8/9/62. NLR.

Billingsly, James—PVT Co.D 9/23/61. D. of pneumonia in CSA General Hospital at Danville, Va. 7/15 or 8/2/62. NLR.

Bird, Bluford T.—PVT Co.B 2/24/62. Appointed 4SG 6/13/62. WIA at Seven Days Battles near Richmond 6/62. KIA at Wilderness 5/5/64. NLR.

Bird, William—PVT Co.B 8/11/63. WIA at Hanover Junction, Va. 5/23/64. Admitted to Jackson Hospital at Richmond 5/25/64. CIA at Petersburg, Va. 4/2/65. Pension roll 1904–25. D. at Oxford, Ga. 2/20/1925. Probably bur. Byrd family cemetery in Newton County.

Bishop, John—PVT Co.A 3/20/62. In hospital probably at Liberty, Va. (now called Bedford) near Lynchburg, Va. 9/62. Discharged for tuberculosis 10/14/62. D. of diease at Bartow Cty., Ga. 1862.

Black, Doctor F.—PVT Co.A 9/19/61. WIA at Gettysburg in left forearm 7/3/63. Dsh. for wound disability 3/21/64. NLR.

Black, Jasper L.—PVT Co.H 9/24/61. D. at Richmond, Va. 5/16/62 of typhoid fever. Probably buried there at Oakwood Cemetery in grave 3-J.

Black, John N.—PVT Co.I 9/25/61. D. of pneumonia at Fredericksburg, Va. 12/24/61.

Black, John T.—PVT Co.H 2/8/62 and 44 years old. D. in Camp Winder Hospital at Richmond 7/18/62. Bur. there at Hollywood Cemetery.

Blackstock, Daniel D.—PVT Co.A 8/15/61. Appointed CPL. Discharged for rupture of right side and being over-age. 7/25/62. NLR.

Blackstock, James N.—PVT Co.A 8/15/61. D. at Richmond 10/5/61.

Boatright, William V.—PVT Co.E 8/12/61. WIA at Spotsylvania C.H. 5/12/64. Broken right arm and shot through lungs. Wounds resulted in paralysis and deafness. B. in Ga. 8/3/33. D. in Douglas Cty., Ga. 1/3/1904.

Boggs, Stephen B.—PVT Co.F 7/30/62. WIA in arm at Gettysburg 7/3/63. Roll for 2/28/65/shows him AWOL since 2/15/65. NLR.

Boggs, William M.—PVT Co.F 9/23/61. D. of pneumonia/typhus on either 9/19 or 9/28/62 at Winder Hospital at Richmond. Bur. there at Hollywood Cemetery—grave H-18.

Bohannon, Benjamin F.—PVT Co.D 2/25/62. Discharged for disability at Richmond 5/28/62. Pension roll shows WIA, in arm, 2/63 and sent to hsp in Americus, Ga. Pension roll 1907. B. 3/11/1841 in Meriwether Cty., Ga. D. 12/30/1909.

Bohannon, John O.—PVT Co.B 9/21/61. WIA at Fredericksburg 12/13/62. CIA near Petersburg, Va. 3/25/65. Released from Point Lookout, Md. 6/24/65. NLR.

Bohannon, William T.—PVT Co.B 9/21/61. KIA at Turkey Ridge, Va. just east of Richmond 6/2/64. NLR.

Bolton, Marcus L.—PVT Co.B 2/12/62. Roll for 2/28/65 shows him AWOL since 1862. NLR.

Bomar, Armistead R.—Musician Co.E 8/12/61. Discharged, under-age at Camp Gregg near Fredericksburg 1/19/63. NLR.

Bond, Henry—PVT Co.C 7/30/62. Surrendered at Appomattox. NLR.

Bond, William—PVT Co.C 9/17/61. Discharged due to disability at Richmond 7/25/62. NLR.

Bonds, William R.—PVT Co.F 5/5/62. Surrendered at Appomattox C.H. 4/9/65. NLR.

Borders, Isaac J.—PVT Co.B 2/26/62. D. at Richmond 5/19/62. NLR.

Born, Charles W.—PVT Co.B 9/21/61. Appointed 1CPL 4/15/62. KIA at Gettysburg 7/3/63. NLR.

Born, James K.P.—PVT Co.F 2/25/64. Surrendered at Appomattox C.H. 4/9/65. NLR.

Born, John A.L.—PVT Co.B 5/15/62. WIA at Manassas 8/30/62. Detailed Enrolling Officer for Clarke Cty, Ga. 6/64 and served in that capacity for remainder of war. NLR.

Boss, Henry J.—PVT Co.G 2/28/62. WIA Fredericksburg, Va. 12/13/62. D. of wounds the following day.

Boss, James J.—2SG Co.G 9/16/61. Elected Jr. 2LT 1/14/62. 2LT 6/11/62. 1LT 10/11/62. CIA at Wilderness, Va. 5/6/64. Released FT. Delaware, Del. 6/16/65. NLR.

Boss, Miles N.—PVT Co.G 9/16/61. D. of typhoid fever at Camp Winder at Richmond 6/22/62.

Boswell, William—PVT Co.K 7/4/61. Elected 2LT 2/28/62. 1LT 10/12/62. WIA at Hanover Junction, Va. 5/27/64. WIA two other times in unknown battles. Surrendered at Appomattox, Va. 4/9/65. Married to Missouria McCullohs sister of Lt. Colonel William McCullohs. She died in 1874 and he remarried Rebecca Jane Randolph Morgan the same year. In 1886 moved to Mansfield, Texas (Tarrant County). Became justice of the peace and d. there on 2/22/1906. Farmer in Ga. at start of war.

Bowen, A.—PVT Co.A 8/15/61. D. at Richmond 7/12/64 and bur. there at Hollywood Cemetery grave u-309. NLR.

Bowles, James M.—PVT Co.I 9/25/61. D. in camp at Evansport, Va. 2/16/62.

Bowman, James W.—PVT Co.I 2/25/62. WIA at Mechanicsville, Va 6/26/62. On detail duty in QM Dpt. at Columbus, Ga. 11/15/62–2/28/65. NLR.

Bowman, Joel H.—PVT Co.I 10/10/61. WIA at Mechanicsville, Va. Discharged for wound disability 6/27/63. NLR.

Bowman, Thomas J.—PVT Co.I 9/25/61. Appointed 1SG 12/28/62. CIA at Richmond 4/3/65. Released at Newport News, Va. 6/26/65. NLR.

Bradford, Joshua—PVT Co.F 5/5/62. Detailed as a nurse 1862. Roll for 2/28/65 shows him AWOL since 10/31/64. Pension records show he was at home for sick furlough and never recovered. B. in South Carolina 1832. NLR.

Bragg, Benajah H.—PVT Co.H 9/24/61. WIA during Seven Days Battles near Richmond. D. of wounds at Richmond 7/12/62. Bur. there at Oakwood Cemetery—grave 81-M.

Bramblett, Henry M.(or Bramlett)—PVT Co.H 11/25/63. CIA near Petersburg, Va. 3/25/65. Released at Pt. Lookout, Md. 6/24/65.

Brand, David J.—PVT Co.F 9/23/61. WIA in left shoulder at Mechanicsville 6/26/62. Surrendered at Appomattox C.H. 4/9/65. B. in Gwinnett Cty., Ga. 1841. Pension roll 1895–1907.

Brand, Doctor C.—PVT Co.B 2/28/62. Roll for 2/28/65 shows him AWOL from 2/24/65. B. in Ga. 1841. Pension roll 1897. Suffered from numerous foot problems he claims were caused from being barefoot in the winter of 1863–64. D. 5/30/1920.

Brand, James W.—3CPL Co.F 9/23/61. CIA 1865. Released at Point Lookout, Md. 6/24/65. NLR.

Brand, Thomas—PVT Co.G 10/30/62. Roll for 2/28/65 shows him AWOL. NLR.

Brand, Thomas M.—4SG Co.G 9/16/61. Appointed 3SG 1/14/62. Surrendered Appomattox, C.H. 4/9/65. B. 11/25/1834. D. 8/17/1916 and bur Loganville Memorial Gardens in Walton Cty., Ga.

Brand, Warren H.—PVT Co.G 3/4/62. CIA at Culpepper, Va. 11/14/63. D. of variola (smallpox) in Kalorama USA General Hospital at Washington, D.C. 1/23/64. Bur. in Arlington National (Va.) Cemetery.

Brand, William—PVT Co.G 1862. WIA, shot in elbow, 1864. B. 7/20/1828 in Walton Cty., Ga. D. 2/1872 in Newton Cty., Ga. Widow pension 1901–04.

Brannon, Fletcher J.—PVT Co.K 3/4/62. Captured at Hanover Junction, Va. 5/24/64. D. of chronic diarrhea at Elmira, N.Y. 3/30/65. Bur. at Woodlawn National Cemetery—grave #2520.

Brannon, J. Caprel—PVT Co.K 8/10/61. CIA at Gettysburg, Pa. 7/3/63. Took oath of allegience to US Govt. at Pt. Lookout, Md. and released 1/24/64. B. in Meriwether Cty., Ga. in 1839. Pension roll 1895.

Braswell, William W.—PVT Co.G 9/16/61. D. of disease 3/21/63.

Brewer, George W.—PVT Co.F 9/23/61. CIA at Gettysburg 7/3/63. Paroled at Point Lookout, Md. 2/18/65. NLR.

Brewer, John B.—PVT Co.F 9/23/61. KIA Seven Pines 5/31/62.

Brewer, Joseph A.—PVT Co.F 1/25/64. CIA Petersburg, Va. 4/2/65. Released at Point Lookout, Md. 6/24/65. NLR.

Brewer, William H.—PVT Co.F 9/24/61. Deserted or captured on picket line near Petersburg, Va. 10/11/64. Union records show he was, "Captured, and to go to Indianapolis, Ind." NLR.

Brewster, George M.—3CPL Co.A 8/15/61. D. at Gordonsville, Va. 8/12/62. NLR.

Brewster, William T.—PVT Co.A 9/19/61. Discharged for disability 3/6/62. NLR.

Briscoe, George W.—PVT Co.G 2/21/62. KIA Fredericksburg, Va. 12/13/62.

Briscoe, Henry—PVT Co.C, 25th Battn. Ga. Provost Guard Inf. (Lee's Battn.) 2/10/63. Trn. to Co.G, 35th Ga. Inf. Rgt. 5/20/64. CIA Petersburg, Va. 4/2/65. Released at Hart's Island, N.Y. Harbor 6/16/65. Applied for pension in Texas 1899. D. 10/18/1904 in Grayson Cty., Tx. Widow, Margaret, applied for pension in Cooke Cty., Tx. 1910 and Newton Cty., Ga. 1919.

Briscoe, John P.—PVT Co.G 9/16/61. Roll for 2/28/65 shows him present. B. 7/17/1835. D. either 4/13/1904 or 7/1905 and bur Rest Haven Cem. in Walton Cty., Ga.

Briscoe, Phillip D.—PVT Co.G 9/16/61. Appointed 4CPL 1864. 3CPL 7/8/64. 2CPL 1864. Roll for 2/28/65 shows him home on furlough of indulgence. B. 7/10/1840 and d. 1/13/1882. Bur. New Hope Methodist Ch. Cem. in Walton Cty., Ga.

Brock, John—3CPL Co.E 8/12/61. D. at Fredericksburg 12/29/61. NLR.

Brooks, Phillip Allston—PVT Co.F 5/3/62. WIA Fredericksburg 12/13/62. KIA Jericho Ford 5/23/64. Widow pension 1891. B. 2/4/32. Grave marker in Garrett Cem near Menlo, Ga. in Chattooga Cty., Ga.

Brooks, William R.—PVT Co.F 5/5/62. D. in Chimborazo Hospital at Richmond 6/26/62.

Brooks, Thomas A.—PVT Co.B 9/21/61. D. of measles 4/28/62. NLR.

Brown, John L.—PVT Co.C 4/27/62. WIA at Mechanicsville, Va. 6/26/62. D. of wounds at Richmond 7/3/62. NLR.

Brown, John T.—PVT Co.B 9/21/61. CIA near Petersburg, Va. 3/25/65. Released at Point Lookout, Md. 6/24/65. NLR.

Brown, Moses D.—PVT Co.C 5/2/62. WIA at Mechanicsville, Va. 6/26/62. CIA at Petersburg, Va. 4/2/65. Released at Point Lookout, Md. 6/24/65. NLR.

Brown, Sheldrick—PVT Co.K 3/4/62. KIA at Fredericksburg, Va. 12/13/62. Bur. at Confederate Cemetery at Spotsylvania C.H., Va. In a letter written by John W.S. Morgan he was referred to as Slade Brown.

Brown, Robert V.—PVT Co.D 2/28/62. Received pay at Petersburg, Va. 1/31/65. NLR.

Brown, Swan H.—PVT Co.C 5/2/62. KIA at Fredericksburg 12/13/62.

Brown, William T.—PVT Co.F 9/23/61. Paroled at Lynchburg, Va. 4/13/65. Pension 1897. D. 5/1901. Widow pension 1910.

Brown, Willis S.—PVT Co.C 5/2/62. WIA at Fredericksburg 12/13/62 and sent to General Hospital #19 at Richmond. Transferred from Receiving and Wayside Hospital, or General Hospital #9, to Chimbarazo Hospital 5/3/63. Pension records show he was captured near Saltville, Va. in 1864 and released at Point Lookout, Md. 6/1/65. B. in Ga. 9/30/37. On pension roll 1897–1901. D. 7/20/1901 and bur. at Sardis Baptist Church Cemetery in Hall County near Gainesville, Ga.

Browning, James—PVT Co.K 7/4/61. KIA at 2nd Manassas, Va. 8/29/62.

Bryan, Almon R.—2SG Co.F 9/23/61. D. in Chimbarazo Hospital at Richmond 8/24/62.

Bryan, John L. (Bryant)—PVT Co.F 2/8/62. CIA at 2nd Manassas 8/29/62. Roll for 2/28/65 shows him AWOL since 10/8/64. Reported to have joined Graham's Scouts in Georgia. Attended a 1922 Confederate veteran reunion at Walhalla, S.C.

Bryan, J.R.—PVT Co.G 5/15/64.

Bryant, Augustus B.—PVT Co.I 9/25/61. On 4/4/63 he received commutation of rations while on sick furlough from 11/8/62 to 3/24/63. D. 9/30/1863, age 20 years, and bur in Bethel Presbyterian Cem. in Chattooga Cty., Ga.

Bryant, John Wesley—PVT Co.K 3/4/62. CIA at Gettysburg, Pa. 7/3/63. D. of chronic diarrhea at Pt. Lookout, Md. 8/22/64.

Bryant, Reuben Richardson—PVT Co.K 7/4/61. D. prior to 4/62.

Bryson, Silas H.—PVT Co.I 9/25/61. D. in General Hospital at Richmond 4/5/62.

Bull, Gustavus Adolphus—Jr. 2LT Co.B, 4th Ga. Inf Rgt. 4/26/61. Resigned 10/17/61. Elected LTC 35th Ga. Inf Rgt. 10/17/61. WIA, gunshot in side, and CIA by 20th Massachusetts at Seven Pines, Va. 5/31/62. Taken to Federal Hsp and d. of wounds 6/1/62. Bur in unmarked grave near battlefield. B. at LaGrange, Ga. 2/16/1835 or 3/18/35. Graduated from Franklin College 1854. Marker at Hillview Cem on Franklin Rd in LaGrange, Ga. Lawyer.

Bullard, William H.—PVT Co.E 8/12/61. WIA and CIA at Seven Pines, Va. 5/31/62. Sent to Ft. Delaware Prison. Exchanged at Aikens Landing, Va. 8/5/62. Admitted to Episcopal Church Hospital of moribund the next day. D. at South Carolina Hospital at Petersburg, Va. 8/9/62 age 48 or 39.

Buntt, William E.—PVT Co.I, 3rd Alabama Inf. Rgt. 4/27/61. Trn. to Co.G, 35th Ga. Inf. Rgt. 4/1/64. Roll for 2/28/65 shows him on sick furlough. NLR.

Burk, James C.—PVT Co.G 3/18/62. D. at Richmond 7/15/62.

Burran, William A.—3CPL Co.C 9/17/61. 2CPL 5/12/64. Roll for 2/28/65 reports he was absent on furlough of disability at Palmetto, Ga. since 2/11/65. NLR.

Burson, Ausburn J.—PVT Co.E 8/12/61. KIA at Seven Pines, Va. 5/31/62. NLR.

Butler, John D.—PVT Co.B 2/20/62. WIA and died of wounds in hospital 8/30/62. NLR.

Butler, Martin G.—PVT Co.B 2/28/62. CIA 7/12/63 Exchanged at Point Lookout, Md. 2/13/65. NLR.

Butler, William T.—PVT Co.B 3/1/62. Surrendered at Appomattox 4/9/65. NLR.

Buttrell, Marcus A.—PVT Co.D 9/23/61. Appointed 1CPL 9/62. WIA at Chancellorsville 5/3/63 and died of wounds at Richmond 5/15/63. NLR.

Roster C

Callahan, John T.—PVT Co.I 9/25/61. D. of diarrhea in General Hospital #2 at Lynchburg, Va. 8/29/62. Bur. there in Confederate Cemetery No.2, 5th line, lot 176-Christian's Factory.

Camp, James K. Polk—PVT Co.A 3/18/63. Surrendered at Appomattox, Va. 4/9/65. NLR.

Camp, Joel C.—PVT Co.B 11/2/61. D. of measles at Evansport, Va. 12/3/61.

Camp, Robert B.—PVT Co.F 4/4/64. D. of fever in Jackson Hospital at Richmond 6/23/64. Bur. there at Hollywood Cemetery—grave U-592.

Camp, Thomas C.—2CPL Co.G 9/16/61. Roll for 5/64 lists him as PVT and wagoner. WIA, both shoulders and back, at Cold Harbor, Va. 6/3/64. Sent to Jackson Hsp. at Richmond. Roll for 2/28/65 shows him at home on wounded furlough. B. 10/1/1836. D. 10/15/98 and bur Camp Family Cem. in north Walton Cty., Ga.

Camp, William—PVT Co.G 9/16/61. WIA 1864. Roll for 2/28/65 shows him present. NLR.

Campbell, George A.—PVT Co.F 5/5/62. WIA at Mechanicsville, Va. 6/26/62. Roll for 2/28/65 shows him present. NLR.

Campbell, H.B.—PVT Co.F 1/25/62. D. of fever in Jackson Hospital at Richmond 6/15/64. Bur. there at Hollywood Cemetery—grave U-186.

Campbell, James—PVT Co.H 9/24/61. WIA 1862. CIA at Petersburg, Va. 4/3/65. Released at Hart's Island, N.Y. 6/15/65. NLR.

Campbell, James B.—PVT Co.F 9/23/61. Surrendered at Appomattox, Va. 4/9/65. NLR.

Campbell, Joseph B.—PVT Co.F 9/23/61. WIA 1862. Surrendered at Appomattox, Va. 4/9/65. NLR.

Camps, Abner J.—PVT Co.A 7/1/62. Admitted to Lynchburg Hsp. #3 for fever 6/63. D. 6/10/63 and bur. there at Old City Cemetery.

Cannon, William Augustus—PVT Co.B 9/21/61. WIA in right leg below knee and permanently disabled at Mechanicsville, Va. 6/26/62. Discharged for disability. B. in Georgia. D. 2/26/1926.

Carley, Joseph—PVT Co.D 2/22/62. D. at Richmond 5/13/62.

Carlisle, Joseph T.—PVT Co.H 9/24/61. CIA at Gettysburg, Pa. 7/1/63. Released at Ft. Delaware, Del. 5/5/65. B. in Jackson Cty., Ga. 4/26/1844. Pension roll 1904–07. D. in 1920 and bur. at Duluth Methodist Cemetery near Duluth, Ga.

Carr, Nathan C.—Jr. 2LT Co.B 9/21/61. Elected 1LT 6/13/62. CPT 6/5/64. Granted sick furlough in 1864. Delayed returning to unit by Sherman's activities in Georgia until 12/64. WIA near Petersburg, Va. 3/25/65. Surrendered at Appomattox, Va. 4/9/65. B.

in Newton Cty, Ga. 1/11/36. Indigent pension roll 1909–1921. D. 2/26/1921 at Piedmont, Al. and bur. in Covington, Ga. City Cemetery.

Carr, Wiley H.—PVT Co.I 2/15/62. On detail duty in QM Dept. at Dalton, Ga. 8/16/63 to 2/28/65. NLR.

Carter, John Y.—2LT Co.G 9/16/61. Elected 1LT 6/11/62. CPT 10/10/62. KIA at Jericho Ford, Va. 5/23/64.

Carter, Robert D.—PVT Co.G 9/16/61. Appointed 4SG 1/14/62. Elected Jr. 2LT 10/11/62. WIA and CIA at Gettysburg, Pa. 7/2/63. Trn. from Pt. Lookout, Md. to Ft. Delaware, Del. 6/25/64 where he was released 6/12/65. NLR.

Carwile, Addison F.—2SG Co.I 9/25/61. Demoted to PVT 1864. Roll for 2/28/65 shows him AWOL in Abbeville District, S.C. since 2/23/65. NLR.

Carwile, Madison M.—2LT Co.I 9/25/61. Resigned for disability, ill health, 6/16/62.

Casey, Ausburn J.(or Carey)(or Asbury J.)—PVT Co.E 8/12/61. D. of measles in a Richmond hospital 10/15/61.

Casey, Elisha B.—PVT Co.E 8/12/61. Appointed 3CPL 12/29/61. 2CPL 1862. 1CPL 1863. Roll for 2/28/65 shows him AWOL since 2/21/65. NLR.

Cash, Charles A.—PVT Co.H 9/24/61. D. at Ashland, Va. 5/11/62.

Cash, John W.—PVT Co.H 9/24/61. Discharged for chronic gastritis 6/23/63. Re-enlisted 2/1/64. Admitted to Jackson Hospital at Richmond 5/28/64. Trn. to Huguenot Springs, Va. 7/8/64. AWOL 10/13/64 to 2/28/65. NLR.

Cash, Rufus—PVT Co.K 7/4/61. D. 7/20/62.

Cassels, Benjamin F.—PVT Co.D 3/10/62. KIA at Riddle's (Riddell's) Shop, Va. 6/13/64.

Cassels, Robert H.—PVT Co.D 9/23/61. WIA, shot in chest, at Cedar Mtn., Va. 8/9/62. D. of wounds 8/19/62. Bur. at Confederate Cemetery at Charlottesville, Va. Widow applied for pension 1891–1907.

Cato, James A.—PVT Co.D 9/23/61. D. at Richmond 12/4/61.

Causert, William Jackson (or Cowsert)—PVT Co.G 9/62 or 9/63. Admitted to Jackson Hospital, Division #4 in Richmond 6/14/64 and d. of diarrhea and fever 6/20/64. Bur. there at Hollywood Cemetery—grave U-9.

Chambers, P.W.—PVT Co.K 3/4/64. Detailed as nurse at Columbus, Ga. hospital 1864.

Channell, William M.—PVT Co.A 9/19/61. WIA through right hip at Seven Pines, Va. 5/31/62. WIA with broken right leg at 2nd Manassas, Va. 8/28/62. AWOL 10/1/64–2/28/65. Pension records show he was at home, permanently disabled by wounds at end of war. On invalid pension roll 1895–1905.

Childs, Daniel P.S.—PVT Co.E 4/26/62. Appointed 1SG 1864. KIA near Petersburg, Va. 3/25/65.

Childs, James M.—5SG Co.E 8/12/61. Appointed 4SG 1863. CIA near Petersburg, Va. 3/25/65. Released at Pt. Lookout, Md. 6/24/65. NLR.

Cleland, John M.—PVT Co.B 9/21/61. WIA during Seven Days Battles near Richmond 6/62. Appointed 2CPL 7/25/62. 4SG 6/64. CIA at Petersburg, Va. 4/2/65. Released from Pt. Lookout, Md. 6/26/65.

Cleland, William P.—PVT Co.B 9/21/61. Admitted to CSA General Hospital at Farmville, Va. with acute rheumatism 5/6/64. Furloughed for 40 days 8/9/64. Roll for 2/28/65 shows him on sick furlough in Ga. NLR.

Cobb, Samuel—PVT Co.D 2/21/62. D. at Richmond 8/2/62. Possibly bur at Farmville, Va.

Cochran, Felix Frank—PVT Co.C 4/27/62. Appointed CPL. Surrendered at Appomattox, Va. 4/9/65. B. 2/12/37 and d. 2/3/98 bur. at Bethlehem Baptist Church at Fairburn, Ga. in Fulton Cty. Widow, Susan A., received indigent widow pension 1902–17 until her death 2/13/1918.

Cochran, Francis M.—PVT Co.C 5/1/63. Admitted to Jackson Hsp. at Richmond 4/17/64 for rubella. CIA in Richmond hsp. 4/3/65. Sent to Libby Prison in Richmond and then trn. to Newport News, Va. NLR.

Cochran, George T.—PVT Co.C 9/9/62. Detailed in Ord. Dpt. 9/17/63. Appointed 1SG 8/64. Surrendered at Appomattox, Va. 4/9/65. NLR.

Cochran, James E.—PVT Co.C 4/24/62. Appointed 2SG 1863. Detailed to Richmond hospital 1864. CIA Petersburg, Va. 4/2/65. Released at Pt. Lookout, Md. 6/5/65. Pension for infirmity and old age 1900–08. B. 1/9/35. D. 6/8/1918 bur at Antioch Methodist Cem on Rivertown Rd near Fairburn in Fulton Cty., Ga.

Cochran, John A.—PVT Co.C 4/20/62. WIA at Gettysburg, Pa. 7/3/63. CIA 1863. Exd. at City Point, Va. 9/8/63. Appointed 2SG 1864. Roll for 2/28/65 lists him as, "Absent, forage-master for Division." NLR.

Cochran, Orlando S.—2LT Co.C 9/17/61. WIA with a compound fracture of left ankle at Mechanicsville, Va. 6/26/62. Elected CPT 6/26/62. Resigned for wound disability 6/10/63. NLR.

Cockrell, James M.(or Cockrel)—PVT Co.A 8/15/61. Appointed 3CPL 1863. 2CPL 8/64. CIA near Petersburg, Va. 3/25/65. Released at Pt. Lookout, Md. 6/26/65. NLR.

Coffin, Price P.—2CPL Co.I 9/25/61. Appointed 4SG 12/19/61. Dsh on for disease of left leg at Rome, Ga. 3/4/63.

Cofield, David L.—PVT Co.F 9/23/61. D. in General Hospital #2 at Lynchburg, Va. 9/24/62. Bur. there at Confederate Cemetery No. 10, 3rd line, lot 180-Reid's Factory. Widow, Rebecca, widow's pension 1891–1904.

Cole, Isaac B.—PVT Co.H 3/12/64. D. of disease in Jackson Hospital at Richmond 8/3/64. Bur. there at Hollywood Cemetery. Widow, Matilda, pension 1891–1900. See Henry H. Beard.

Coleman, Minor—PVT Co.G 5/62. D. of disease in hsp at Liberty, Va. (now Bedford) 7/13/62. Widow pension 1891–1900.

Collier, William B.—PVT Co.H 9/24/61. WIA Seven Pines, Va.5/31/62. Appears last on roll for 12/62. NLR.

Compton, Welcome J.—PVT Co.C 4/28/62. CIA at Spotsylvania C.H., Va. 5/12/64. Paroled at Ft. Delaware, Del. 2/65. Received at Boulware & Cox's Wharves at James River, Va. 3/10/65. NLR.

Condor, Cyrus E.(or Conder)—1SG Co.C 12/16/61. Elected 2LT 7/27/62. WIA at 2nd Manassas, Va. 8/30/62. D. of wounds 9/27/62.

Cook, Alfred—PVT Co.I 9/25/61. Discharged for deafness 10/4/62.

Cook, Francis M.—PVT Co.C 9/17/61. D. at home at Palmetto, Ga. 1/30/64.

Cook, Harvard (or Cook, Harbird)—PVT Co.C 9/17/61. Deserted near Petersburg, Va. 8/24/64. Took oath of allegience to US Govt. 10/21/64. Received at Military Prison at Chattanooga, Tn. 10/22/64. NLR.

Cook, Richard M.—PVT Co.H 9/24/61. CIA near Petersburg, Va. 3/25/65. Released at Pt. Lookout, Md. 6/4/65. NLR.

Cook, Thomas—PVT Co.C 9/17/61. Deserted near Petersburg, Va. 8/26/64. Took oath of allegience to US Govt. 10/21/64. Received at Military Prison at Chattanooga, Tn. 10/22/64. NLR

Cook, William H.—PVT Co.H 9/21/61. Discharged, disability and under-age 5/30/62.

Cooley, Stephen B.—PVT Co.D 9/23/61. Appointed 1CPL 12/23/61. Demoted to PVT 2/62. WIA during Seven Days Battles near Richmond 6/62. D. of wounds in Camp Winder Hospital at Richmond 9/17/62. Bur. there at Hollywood Cemetery—-grave C-135.

Cooper, George W.—PVT Co.F 9/23/61. Sent to Winder Hospital at Richmond 6/18/62. Admitted to CSA General Hospital at Danville, Va. with typhoid fever 7/23/62. Returned to duty 8/22/62. NLR.

Cooper, James C.—PVT Co.G 9/16/61. Detailed with Pioneer Corps 1864. CIA at Petersburg, Va. 4/2/65. Released at Pt. Lookout, Md. 6/26/65. B. in Ga. 11/3/1826.

Cooper, James G.—1SG Co.B 9/21/61. Elected Jr. 2LT 7/21/62. WIA during Seven Days Battles near Richmond 6/62. Elected 1LT 6/5/64. Suffered from night blindness. Surrendered at Appomattox, Va. 4/9/65. Bur. at Corinth Church near Loganville, Ga.

Cooper, John H.—PVT Co.D 3/4/62. Appointed SGT. KIA at Spotslyvania C.H., Va. 5/12/64. Widow pension 1891–1923.

Couch, James Green—PVT Co.E 8/12/61. CIA near Petersburg, Va. 3/25/65. Released at Pt. Lookout, Md. 6/26/65. NLR.

Couch, James T.—PVT Co.E 8/12/61. D. of measles in hospital 10/9/61 in Richmond.

Couch, William Ira—PVT Co.A 8/15/61. KIA at Seven Pines, Va. 5/31/62.

Cowan, J.W.(or Conine)—PVT Co.E 8/12/61. CIA, date and place unknown. D. at Camp Chase, Ohio 3/22/65. Bur. there at Confederate Cemetery—grave #1733.

Cowen, George W.—PVT Co.B 9/21/61. D. of disease 10/12/62.

Cox, James M.—PVT Co.K 7/4/61. Dsh 11/20/61.

Craig, James Newton—PVT Co.D 9/23/61. Roll for 2/28/65 shows him present. B. 7/3/1844. D. 3/27/1915 and bur Corinth Cem in Heard Cty., Ga.

Craig, John H.—PVT Co.D 9/23/61. D. in camp at Evansport, Va. 1/21/62.

Crawford, William C.—PVT Co.B, 18th Ga. Inf. Rgt. 4/30/61. Trn. Co.B, 35th Ga. Inf. Rgt. 9/1/62. WIA at Chancellorsville, Va. 5/3/63. CIA at Mine Run, Va. 11/23/63. Sent to Pt. Lookout, Md. Exd. 2/13/65. NLR.

Crews, George T.—PVT Co.K 7/4/61. D. in General Hospital #17 at Richmond 1/5/63.

Crittenden, Christopher C.—PVT Co.D 9/23/61. Detailed as nurse 12/61. D. of chronic diarrhea at Chimborazo Hospital #2 at Richmond 1/16/62.

Crittenden, William E.—PVT Co.D 9/23/61. D. of variola (smallpox) in General Hospital #21 at Richmond 12/6/62.

Cook, Lewellen (or Crook)—PVT Co.C 3/10/62. CIA at Petersburg, Va. 4/2/65. Released at Hart's Island, N.Y. 6/15/65. NLR.

Croon, Henry J.—1CPL Co.F 9/23/61. Appointed 4SG 10/62. 3SG 11/1/62. 2SG 1864. KIA near Petersburg, Va. 3/25/65.

Cross, John W.—2CPL Co.H 9/24/61. Demoted to PVT in 1862. Roll for 2/28/65 shows him AWOL since 7/18/64. NLR.

Crouch, James A.—PVT Co.D 2/25/62. WIA at Gaines Mill, Va. 6/27/62. D. of wounds at home in Georgia 10/6 or 11/6/62.

Crow, Alfred M.—PVT Co.H 9/24/61. Appointed 4CPL 7/7/64. CIA near Petersburg, Va. 3/25/65. Released at Pt. Lookout, Md. 6/24/65.

Crow, Jonathan W.—PVT Co.H 9/24/61. Discharged for disability 4/12/64.

Crow, Samuel J.—PVT Co.H 2/7/63. CIA near Petersburg, Va. 3/25/65. Released at Pt. Lookout, Md. 6/26/65. B. in Ga. 1842. Pension roll 1910–11.

Roster D

Dailey, John—PVT Co.C 9/17/61. CIA at Gettysburg, Pa. 7/3/63. Paroled at Pt. Lookout, Md. 5/3/64. Admitted to Chimborazo Hospital #3 at Richmond with chronic diarrhea 5/8/64. Frl. for 20 days 5/20/64. Roll for 6/64/ shows him absent on furlough of disability at Palmetto, Ga. NLR.

Dailey, John W.—PVT Co.C 9/17/61. D. at Camp Winder Hospital at Richmond 6/19/62. Buried there at Hollywood Cemetery.

Dailey, Russell—PVT Co.C 9/17/61. Elected 1LT 6/10/63. CIA at Spotsylvania, Va. 5/12/64. Paroled at Ft. Delaware, Del. 9/28/64 and delivered at Varina, Va. for exchange 10/5/64. Pension records show he was frl. for fever 3/3/65. Pension roll 1911–15. D. 8/13/1915.

Dailey, Stephen Richards—PVT Co.C 9/17/61. Appointed 1SG 7/22/62. WIA at Cedar Mtn, Va. 8/9/62. Admitted to CSA General Hospital at Charlottesville, Va. 8/11/62 and d. of wounds 8/24/62. Buried there in Confederate Cemetery.

Dailey, Wesley—PVT Co.C 9/17/61. WIA at Cedar Mtn., Va. 8/9/62. WIA at Fredericksburg, Va. 12/13/62. Surrendered at Appomattox, Va. 4/9/65. On pension roll 1901. B. 6/10/42. D. 10/19/1904 bur at Antioch Methodist Cem on Rivertown Rd near Fairburn in Fulton Cty., Ga.

Dailey, William—PVT Co.C 4/24/62. Admitted to General Hospital at Camp Winder in Richmond with typhoid fever on 6/5/62. D. there 6/23/62.

Dailey, William J.—PVT Co.C 9/17/61. D. of disease in Dumfries, Va. hospital 1/8/62.

Daniel, Alfred David—PVT Co.C 2/13/62. WIA near Petersburg, VA 3/25/65. CIA at Richmond 4/3/65 and d. there in hospital 4/18/65. B. 4/4/45.

Daniel, Josiah Hankins—PVT Co.C 5/5/62. D. of disease at Richmond 6/9/62. B. 9/10/42.

Daniel, J.B (or I.B.)—PVT Co.C 9/17/61. D. at Richmond 4/65 and bur. there at Hollywood Cemetery.

Daniel, Moses M.—PVT Co.C 4/28/62. WIA at 2nd Manassas, Va. 8/30/62. CIA near Petersburg, Va. 3/25/65. Released at Pt. Lookout, Md. 6/26/65.

Daniel, Thomas J.—PVT Co.C 4/5/62. D. of disease at Richmond 9/3/62. Bur. there at Hollywood Cemetery—grave C-116. B. in Fayette Cty, Ga. 1839.

Daniel, William—PVT Co.D 10/25/61. D. in Dumfries, Va. hospital 1/17/62.

Daniel, William Columbus—PVT Co.D 9/23/61. Dsh at Petersburg, Va. 6/62. Enl. as PVT in Co.K, 56th Ga. Inf. Rgt. 2/64. CIA at Nashville, Tn. 12/16/64. Released at Camp Chase, Oh. 6/12/65. B. in Heard Cty, Ga. NLR.

Daniel, William M.—PVT Co.H 4/13/64. WIA Petersburg, Va. 4/1/65. CIA while being taken to hsp and held at Manchester, Va. until surrender. B. 1846. Lived in Dacula, Ga. after war. Pension roll 1915. Possibly bur. at Duncan Creek Congregational Cem. off State route 124 in Gwinnett Cty., Ga. Tombstone indicates death on 7/17/1913.

Dansby, Robert D.—PVT Co.D 9/23/61. Appointed 5SG 9/62. WIA Fredericksburg, Va. 12/13/62. D. of wounds 12/16/62.

Davenport, Charles W.—PVT Co.C 8/1/62. Trn. to Co.E. CIA at Gettysburg, Pa. 7/3/63. D. of acute diarrhea at Ft. Delaware, Del. 9/22/63.

Davenport, William H.A.—PVT Co.C 9/17/61. Appointed Ord. Sgt. 7/2/62. D. at Lynchburg, Va. 12/31/62. Bur. there at Confederate Cemetery #5, 2nd Line, Lot 101-Christian's.

Davidson, J.M.—PVT Co.E 2/10/62. Absent, sick 4/62. NLR.

Davis, Andrew J.—PVT Co.I 5/13/62. WIA at 2nd Manassas, Va. 8/29/62. Deserted 9/12/64. Received by Provost Marshal General at Washington, D.C. 9/22/64. Took oath of allegience to US Govt. and furnished transportation to New York City.

Davis, Elemuel W.—PVT Co.G 5/11/62. D. of disease 5/6/63. B. 6/22/1824. Bur. Shiloh Primitive Baptist Ch. Cem. in Walton Cty., Ga.

Davis, Henry T.—PVT Co.F 9/23/61. WIA in leg at Fredericksburg, Va. 12/13/62. D. of wounds at Moore Hospital, or General Hospital #24, at Richmond 1/3/63.

Davis, Jesse—PVT Co.I 5/12/62. On detail duty as shoemaker in QM Dpt. at Columbus, Ga. 10/15/62-2/28/65. NLR.

Davis, Reuben P.—PVT Co.C 9/17/61. D. of typhoid fever in Camp Winder Hospital in Richmond 7/13/62. Bur. there at Hollywood Cemetery—grave C-209.

Davis, Robert M.—PVT Co.K 3/4/62. Appointed Hospital Steward. WIA Fredericksburg 12/13/62. Surrendered at Appomattox, Va. 4/9/65.

Davis, Thomas J.—2LT Co.F 9/23/61. Elected 1LT 5/19/62. CPT 5/19/64. Surrendered at Appomattox, Va. 4/9/65.

Davis, William S.—PVT Co.A 4/64. Roll for May-June 1864 shows that on 6/15/64, LT Smith from Co.A, 1st Confederate Inf. Rgt. claimed that W.S. Davis belonged to his company, and upon certificate of this fact was permitted to take him. NLR.

Davison, John J.—PVT Co.I 2/21/62. CIA 1862. Received at Aiken's Landing at James River, Va. 9/27/62. Exchanged there 11/10 /62. Absent, sick 12/31/62. Widow pension 1891–1925. His widow claims in her application he never returned from the war.

Davison, Robert J.—PVT Co.I 9/25/61. Appointed CPL 1863. WIA at Jericho Ford, Va. 5/23/64. D. of wounds in Jackson Hospital at Richmond 6/7/64. Bur. there at Hollywood Cemetery—grave U-491 just west of pyramid. Born 4/20/41.

Dean, Benjamin F.—PVT Co.D 9/23/61. WIA at 2nd Manassas, Va. 8/30/62. Roll for 2/28/65 shows him absent as a pensioner of war. NLR.

Dean, Samuel H.—1LT Co.B 9/21/61. Resigned 6/13/62. D. at Richmond 7/20/62.

Dearing, Francis M.—PVT Co.A 3/4/62. WIA 1862. D. in Richmond hospital 8/4/62.

Dearing, Simeon N.—PVT Co.A 8/15/61. KIA at Chancellorsville, Va. 5/3/63.

Deaton, Andrew J.—PVT Co.H 9/24/61. Appointed 3CPL 1864. Roll for 2/28/65 shows him AWOL since 8/26/64. Said to have joined Home Guard Cavalry in Hall Cty., Ga. B. in Hall Cty., Ga. 12/27/34. Widow pension 1910. D. 7/29/1909 and bur. at Union Baptist Church Cem. near Chestnut Mountain in Hall County, Ga.

Deaton, Levi T.—PVT Co.H 9/24/61. CIA Gettysburg, Pa. 7/3/63. Paroled at Pt. Lookout, Md. 2/13/65. At home on parole at surrender. Lived in Dacula, Ga. Pension roll 1913–28. D. 1/8/1928 in Gwinnett Cty., Ga.

Denney, James A.—PVT Co.D 3/4/62. WIA at Seven Pines, Va. WIA, shot in shoulder, Petersburg, Va. 3/25/65. D. 4/27/1886. Widow pension 1894–1907.

Devite, John—PVT Co.H 9/24/61. Deserted 7/6/63 near Gettysburg, Pa. and arrested by US Army near Waynesburg, Pa. Admitted to USA General Hospital at York, Pa. 12/1/63. Forwarded to Ft. McHenry, Md. 1/25/64 where he was released on oath of allegience to US Govt. 12/28/64.

Dial, John B.—PVT Co.G 9/16/61. WIA at Wilderness, Va. 5/6/64. CIA near Petersburg, Va. 3/25/65. Released at Pt. Lookout, Md. 6/26/65. B. 7/4/1830 in Walton Cty., Ga. D. 3/4/1898 and bur Walnut Grove Cem. in Walton Cty., Ga. Widow, Linda, pension 1901–07.

Dial, Jonathan Jackson, Jr.—PVT Co.G 3/3/63. WIA 1863. D. of disease in General Hospital #1 at Richmond 12/8/63. Bur. there in Hollywood Cemetery—grave I-62.

Dial, Jonathan Jackson, Sr.—PVT Co.G 2/27/62. WIA and left leg permanently disabled at 2nd Manassas, Va. 8/29/62. CIA at Louisa C.H., Va. 4/5/65. Released at Pt. Lookout, Va. 6/26/65. B. in Ga. 10/2/1821. D. 10/14/1892 and bur Walnut Grove Cem. in Walton Cty., Ga.

Dial, Martin M.—PVT Co.G 9/16/61. Appointed 2CPL 1863. CIA Gettysburg, Va. 7/2/63. D. of typhoid fever at Ft. Delaware, Del. 1/16/64.

Dial, Patrick—PVT Co.B 9/21/61. D. of typhoid fever in General Hospital at Camp Winder at Richmond 9/23/62. Bur. there in Hollywood Cemetery, probably in grave S-154, listed under P. Dailey.

Dial, William M.—PVT Co.G 7/26/62. WIA 1864. Roll for 2/28/65 shows him AWOL. NLR.

Diggs, Berry S.—PVT Co.E 8/12/61. WIA at Jericho Ford, Va. 5/23/64. Roll for 2/28/65 lists him AWOL since 8/22/64. NLR.

Diggs, George—PVT Co.E 8/12/61. D. of measles at Richmond 11/12/61.

Dimmock, James—PVT Co.B 9/21/61. D. of typhoid fever at Dumfries, Va. 12/15/61.

Dobbs, Martin—PVT Co.A 8/15/61. Dsh 12/6/61. NLR.

Dobbs, Moses K.—PVT Co.A 8/15/61. Appointed 3SG 9/26/61. Roll for 12/62 shows him present. NLR.

Dollar, Arch—PVT Co.K 3/4/62. CIA at Petersburg, Va. 4/2/65. Released at Ft. Delaware, Del. 6/16/65.

Donald, Thomas—PVT Co.K 3/4/62. Surrendered at Appomattox, Va. 4/9/65.

Dorsey, Hezekiah C.—PVT Co.G 3/2/64. Deserted while on picket duty near Petersburg, Va. 12/8/64. Took oath of allegience to US Govt. at City Point, Va. 12/13/64 and furnished transportation to Utica, N.Y. the same day.

Dorsey, William C.—PVT Co.G 9/16/61. Deserted while on picket duty near Petersburg, Va. 12/8/64. Took oath of allegience to US Govt at City Point, Va. 12/13/64. and furnished transportation to Utica, N.Y. the same day. Probably b. 10/23/1842 and d. 4/15/1915. Possibly bur Mt. Creek Baptist Ch. Cem. in Walton Cty., Ga.

Downs, Thomas—PVT Co.K 7/4/61. Discharged for disability 11/18/61.

Dozier, George H.—PVT Co.K 2/26/64. WIA 1864. Appointed SGM 11/1/64. Pension records show he was frl. for 30 days 3/1/65. Unable to return to his command after frl. expired due to intervention of enemy in Ga. D. in Morgan Cty., Ga. 1/1899.

Drummond, James H.—PVT Co.I 9/25/61. D. in Dumfries, Va. hospital 2/26/62.

Drummond, John P.—4SG Co.I 9/25/61. D. of pneumonia at Fredericksburg, Va. 12/19/61.

Duke, John—2LT Co.A 8/15/61. Commanded Co. B from approximately 5/29/62 through Battle of Seven Pines, Va. 5/31/62. This was due to all officers in Co.B being ill. Elected CPT 7/3/62 of Co.A. Commanded regiment during Battle of Chancellorsville 5/63 and in command during 2/65 and 3/65. WIA, left shoulder by solid shot, Spotsylvania C.H., Va. 5/12/64. Admitted to Jackson Hsp. in Richmond on 5/16/64. Returned to duty 9/1/64. Roll for 2/28/65 shows him present. KIA at Battle of Jones Farm near Petersburg, Va. 3/25/65. B. in 1832. Lawyer from Tallapoosa.

Duke, Marion—PVT Co.C 9/17/61. Appointed SGT 9/17/61. Dsh 1861. NLR.

Duncan, Benjamin F.—PVT Co.H 9/24/61. Surrendered at Appomattox, Va. 4/9/65.

Duncan, Edward Y.—PVT Co.D 9/23/61. D. at Evansport, Va. 12/11/61.

Duncan, Lewis G.—PVT Co.G 3/4/62. D. in Richmond hospital 4/20/64.

Duncan, Robert S.—PVT Co.B 9/21/61. Wagonmaster detailed in Quartermaster Dpt. of Ordnance Train Artillery of 3rd Corps 6/64 until war end. Surrendered at Appomattox, Va. 4/9/65. B. in Ga.

Dunlap, Jeptha—PVT Co.E 8/12/61. Dsh for tuberculosis at Richmond 8/23/62.

Duren, William B.—PVT Co.H 9/24/61. KIA at Seven Pines, Va. 5/31/62.

Dunn, Henry H.—PVT Co.K 3/4/62. Admitted to CSA General Hospital at Danville, Va. with pneumonia 6/21/62. Roll for 12/31/62 shows him on sick frl.

Dunson, James M.—PVT Co.D 9/28/63. Roll for 2/28/65 shows him AWOL. Indigent pension roll 1900–07. Possibly bur. Old Mt. Olive Church Cem. in Heard Cty., Ga.

Durrett, A.L.—Ast. Surgeon 35th Ga. Inf Rgt. 11/16/61. Resigned, disability 11/24/62.

Dutton, James G.L.—PVT Co.F 9/23/61. D. in Chimborazo Hospital at Richmond 5/29/63. Widow, Mary Ann, pension 1891–1914 until her d. 2/8/1914.

Roster E

Eason, John—PVT Co.D 9/23/61. WIA Seven Pines, Va., arm amputated, 5/31/62. Roll for 12/31/62 shows him, "Absent, wounded." NLR.

Edison, Enoch—PVT Co.B 9/21/61. D. at Richmond 4/18/62.

Edwards, John Frank—PVT Co.D 9/23/61. In Richmond hospital for measles 2/62. WIA Fredericksburg, Va. 12/13/62. WIA Chancellorsville, Va. 5/3/63. CIA near Petersburg, Va. 4/2/65. Released at Pt. Lookout, Md. 6/26/65. Wrote "Red Book—Army Life of Frank Edwards: Confederate Veteran." Indigent pension 1900–07. B. 10/8/1842. Bur Hillview Cem on Franklin Rd. in LaGrange, Ga.

Edwards, L.B.—PVT Co.G 9/12/62. D. in Jackson Hospital at Richmond 4/21/64. Bur. there at Hollywood Cemetery—grave I-135.

Edwards, Solomon Dabney—PVT Co.G 9/12/62. CIA at Gettysburg, Va. 7/3/63. Released at Ft. Delaware, Del. 6/16/65. Pension 1898–1906. Bur. Mt. Creek Baptist Ch. Cem. in Walton Cty., Ga.

Edwards, Thomas A.—PVT Co.G 3/1/62. WIA and permanently disabled at Mechanicsville, Va. 6/26/62. Dsh. for disability at Orange C.H., Va. 9/30/63. B. 1830. Pension 1889–1900. D. 1880 and bur Old Alcovy Cem. in Walton Cty., Ga.

Edwards, William—PVT Co.K 8/14/62. D. of disease at Fredericksburg, Va. 1/63.

Ellis, Richard P.—PVT Co.F 9/23/61. Roll for 11–12/62 shows him, "Absent, sick. Sent to rear on march 9/10/62." D. 10/2/62 and bur. in Georgia section, grave #103, Stonewall Confederate Cemetery (Mount Hebron), Winchester, Va.

Ellis, Walter H.—PVT Co.D, 25th Battn. Ga. Provost Guards 9/29/62. Appointed 1CPL 1862. Trn. Co.F, 35th Ga. Inf. Rgt. in 1862. Surrendered at Appomattox, Va. 4/9/65. Probably born 11/9/1844. D. 7/6/1922 and probably bur. Mt. Carmel Methodist Ch. Cem. in Norcross, Ga.

Estes, Cicero—PVT Co.F 3/26/62. Dsh. for disability 11/10/62.

Estes, Jasper—PVT Co.F 9/23/61. Appointed 4CPL 5/2/62. WIA at 2nd Manassas, Va. 8/29/62 and sent to Lynchburg, Va. Admitted to General Hospital #9 at Richmond for wounds on 11/23/63 and remarks were, "Discharged when admitted." Presumed to have returned to unit.

Estes, Marion—PVT Co.F 9/23/61. CIA 10/62. Prl. 10/17/62. WIA in hand at Gettysburg, Pa. 7/3/63. Admitted to General Hospital #9 at Richmond on 11/23/63 and "Discharged when admitted."

Estes, Newton—PVT Co.F 9/23/61. WIA at Fredericksburg, Va. 12/13/62. Roll for 2/28/65 shows him AWOL since 2/1/65. Reported to have joined Graham's Scouts in Ga.

Everett, Buinum F.—PVT Co.C 4/23/62. WIA and CIA at Seven Pines, Va. 5/31/62. D. of wounds at USA General Hospital at Fortress Monroe, Va. 6/17/62. Bur there on south side of creek.

Ewing, Samuel J.—PVT Co.F 9/23/61. Appointed 2CPL 1864. Paroled at Farmville, Va. 4/11–21/65. B. in Gwinnett Cty, Ga. 1836. Pension roll 1900–1917. Widow, Mary, pension 1917 until her death 1933. D. 2/10/1917 and bur. Mt. Zion Baptist Ch. Cem. in Snellville, Ga.

Tombstone of Private Richard P. Ellis, Co. F Stonewall Confederate Cemetery (Mount Hebron) at Winchester, Va.
photo by author

Roster F

Farmer, Andrew J.—PVT Co.A 9/19/61. Appointed 4Cpl 1863. 3CPL 1864. WIA at Hagerstown, Md. 7/5/64. WIA in right leg near Petersburg, Va. 3/25/65. Captured in Richmond, Va. hospital 4/3/65. Released at Richmond 8/7/65. B. in Ga. 8/24/37. Disability pension 1888 until d. 8/8/1903.

Farmer, Charles H.—PVT Co.B 9/21/61. KIA, gunshot wound to stomach, at Spotsylvania, C.H., Va. 5/12/64 on his birthday. B. 5/12/44.

Farmer, James M.—PVT Co.B 2/28/64. CIA near Petersburg, Va. 3/25/65. Released at Pt. Lookout, Md. 6/25/65.

Farmer, James W.—PVT Co.A 3/4/62. D. at Ashland, Va. 4/21/62.

Farmer, Shadrack G.—PVT Co.B 2/11/62. WIA at Fredericksburg, Va. 12/13/62. CIA near Petersburg, Va. 3/25/65. Released at Pt. Lookout, Md. 6/27/ 65.

Fell, John L.—PVT Co.A 8/15/61. D. 11/3/61.

Ferrell, Bowlen M. (or Bolling)—PVT Co.C 10/31/61. Appointed Musician. WIA, Seven Days Battles near Richmond 6/62. D. in Richmond hospital 7/18/62.

Ferrell, James A.—PVT Co.C 10/31/61. Appointed Musician. Dsh. 7/30/62 for spinal affliction and old age. B. 1/13/1819. D. at Mt. Sylvan, Tx. 10/15/1889.

Ferrell, Laten—PVT Co.C 10/30/61. Appointed Musician. WIA at Seven Pines, Va. 5/31/62. Dsh. 7/30/62 for "aberration of mind produced by concussion of bomb."

Ferrell, Nicholas—PVT Co.C 9/62. D. in service.

Fields, Bartley J.—PVT Co.G 2/15/64. Surrendered at Appomattox, Va. 4/9/65.

Fields, Bluford H.—PVT Co.H 9/24/61. D. at Evansport, Va. 12/1/61.

Fields, John B.—PVT Co.G 9/21/61. CIA at Wilderness, Va. 5/6/64. D. of fever at Elmira, N.Y. hospital 9/16/64. Buried there at Woodlawn National Cemetery—grave #165.

Fields, Sylvester—PVT Co.H 8/28/62. D. of typhoid fever 11/12/62 at Staunton, Va. Bur. there at Thornrose Cemetery.

Fields, William—PVT Co.G 9/16/61. D. in camp 12/4/61.

Fisher, A.J.—PVT Co.E date unknown. Tr. from Jackson Hsp. at Richmond to Camp Winder 6/28/64. NLR.

Fitzsimmons, Henry—PVT Co.K 8/4/62. Substitute for W.A. Whitehead. Deserted in 1862. Under arrest 11 and 12/62 for absence. Captured at Culpepper, Va. 11/9/63. Took oath of allegience to US Govt. at Old Capitol Prison, Washington, D.C. Released and sent to Philadelphia, Pa. 3/15/64.

Foote, John D.S.—PVT Co.A 10/12/61. Elected Jr. 2LT 10/10/62. Resigned due to disability of hemorrhaging from lungs 9/12/64.

Ford, Jesse Stanley—Fifer Co.A 3/4/62. D. 8/1/62.

Ford, William Follett—PVT Co.A 3/4/62. D. at Richmond 8/29/62. Bur. there at Hollywood Cemetery.

Formby, Noah L.—PVT Co.D 9/23/61. WIA at Seven Pines, Va. 5/31/62. Appointed 4SG 7/28/62. 2SG 9/30/64. 1SG 11/8/64. Sick in hospital 2/28/65. CIA 1865. Received at USA General Hospital at Pt. Lookout, Md. 5/6/65 and released there 7/25/65. B. in Heard Cty., Ga. 7/2/1840.

Formby, William Thomas—PVT Co.D 3/4/62. WIA in face at Spotsylvania C.H., Va. 5/12/64. Appointed 3SG 11/8/64. WIA in hip near Petersburg, Va. 3/25/65. Captured in hospital at Richmond 4/3/65. Sent to Pt. Lookout, Md. hospital 5/6/65 and released there 7/25/65. Trn. to General Hospital at Washington, D.C. 7/27/65. B. in Ga. 5/8/1831. Pension roll 1896. D. 12/22/1919 bur Mt. Zion Baptist Cem 15 miles southeast Franklin in Heard Cty., Ga.

Forrester, John W.—PVT Co.G 2/28/62. WIA Seven Days Battles near Richmond 6/62. D. of wounds at Richmond 6/30/62. Widow, Jerusha, pension 1891–1907.

Forrester, William P.—PVT Co.G 2/28/62. CIA at Spotsylvania C.H., Va. 5/12/64. Paroled at Ft. Delaware, Del. for exchange 2/65. Received at Boulware and Cox's Wharves on the James River in Va. 3/10–12/65.

Foster, Abner J.—4CPL Co.E 8/12/61. Appointed 1CPL 1862. PVT 10/62. CIA at Petersburg, Va. 4/2/65. Released at Pt. Lookout, Md. 6/8/65.

Foster, Francis M.—PVT Co.D 9/23/61. WIA at Seven Pines, Va. 5/31/62. CIA at Gettysburg, Pa. 7/3/63. Received at Ft. Delaware, Del. 7/30/63. Took oath of allegience to US Govt. and enlisted in 3rd Rgt., US Maryland Cavalry 9/22/63.

Foster, John O.—PVT Co.E 7/30/62. D. at Winchester, Va. 11/17/62. Bur. in Georgia section, grave #215, Stonewall Jackson Cemetery (Mount Hebron), Winchester, Va.

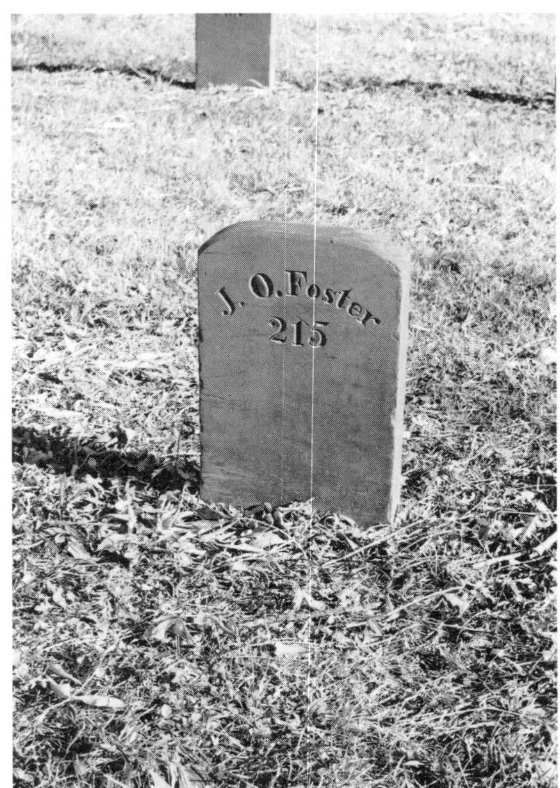

Tombstone of Private John O. Foster, Co.E Stonewall Confederate Cemetery (Mount Hebron) at Winchester, Va.
photo by author

Foster, Moses R.—PVT Co.E 7/30/62. Dsh. for disability at Decatur, Ga. 10/29/62. B. 5/8/43 and d. 3/2/1925 bur at Mt. Vernon Baptist Ch Cem on Hwy 92 west of Fairburn in Fulton Cty., Ga.

Fox, James—PVT Co.H 9/24/61. Dsh. 10/23/61.

Fox, John B.—PVT Co.I 2/21/62. Surrendered at Appomattox, Va. 4/9/65.

Fox, John M.—PVT Co.H 9/24/61. WIA Seven Pines, Va.5/31/62. Pension records show he was discharged for sickness 6/63. B. in Hall Cty., Ga. 5/9/37. D. 12/6/1923 and bur Redwine Methodist Ch. Cem in Hall Cty., Ga.

Franklin, Hiram T.—PVT Co.D 9/23/61. Appointed 2CPL 12/15/61. WIA, arm, Fredericksburg, Va. 12/13/62. Recovered at General Hsp at Charlottesville, Va. CIA at Spotsylvania C.H., Va. 5/12/64. Roll for 2/28/65 shows him, "Absent, POW." NLR.

Fraser, John M.—PVT Co.H 9/24/61. Appointed 4SG 1864. D. of disease at home in Hall Cty., Ga. 9/8/64. Widow, Isabella, pension 1891.

Fraser, Joseph A.—PVT Co.H 9/24/61. Dsh. 12/20/62.

Free, Henry G.L.—PVT Co.D 9/23/61. D. at Dumfries, Va. hospital 12/15/61.

Freeland, Isaac J.—PVT Co.D 9/23/61. Roll for 2/28/65 shows him present. NLR.

Freeman, Joseph—PVT Co.F 9/14/62. D. of disease at Fredericksburg, Va. 5/24/63. Widow, Elizabeth, pension 1891–1907.

Furgerson, Charles W. (or Purgason, Charles W.)—PVT Co.D 9/23/61. Surrendered at Appomattox, Va. 4/9/65.

Roster G

Gaddy, Robert B.—PVT Co.C 2/25/63. CIA at Petersburg, Va. 4/2/65. Released at Pt. Lookout, Md. 6/27/65.

Gaines, Edward—PVT Co.I B. 3/11/25 and d. 2/9/1912 and bur Summerville Cem Near Summerville, Ga. Chattooga Cty.

Gaines, James—PVT Co.K 7/4/61. Dsh. 11/6/61.

Gaines, Richard F.—PVT Co.I 2/15/62. WIA at Fredericksburg, Va. 12/13/62. Frl. for 30 days from 1/26/63. Dsh. for wounds.

Galamore, Joseph James—PVT Co.A 3/4/62. WIA in right shoulder at Seven Pines, Va. 5/31/62. Dsh. for shoulder disability and typhoid fever at Richmond 6/23/62. B. in Paulding Cty., Ga. 8/27/1833. Pension roll 1894–1904.

Garner, Masters—PVT Co.A 8/1/62. CIA at Spotsylvania C.H., Va. 5/12/64. Received at Ft. Delaware, Del. 5/20/64. Indigent pension roll 1895–1904.

Garrett, James Marion—PVT Co.D 9/23/61. WIA, gunshot to chest and hip, at Spotsylvania C.H., Va. 5/12/64. D. of wounds 5/15/64. Bur. at Spotsylvania Confederate Cemetery at Spotsylvania C.H.,Va. B. in Ga. 1843.

Garrett, Lemuel—1CPL Co.E 8/12/61. PVT 1862. Appointed 4CPL 1862. CIA at Wilderness, Va. 5/6/64. Paroled at Elmira, N.Y. 10/11/64. Received at Venus Point at Savannah, Ga. for exchange 11/15/64. However, his wife reported he never returned home. Wife received widow's pension 1895–1898. She d. 1900.

Gary, Harlam J.—PVT Co.E 7/3/62. Appointed 5SG 7/31/64. CIA at Petersburg, Va. 4/2/65. released at Ft. Delaware, Del. 6/16/65.

Gatlin, Lemuel G.—PVT Co.D 9/23/61. Appointed 3CPL 9/30/64. CIA at Farmville, Va. 4/6/65. Released at Newport News, Va 6/25/65.

Gentry, Bartley M.—PVT Co.A 8/15/61. D. 10/5/61.

Giles, James F.—5SG Co.G 9/16/61. D. at Richmond 5/10/62.

Giles, James M.—PVT Co.E 8/12/61. D. of measles at Richmond 10/9/61.

Giles, John—PVT Co.I 5/9/62. KIA at Mechanicsville, Va. 6/26/62.

Giles, Thomas O.—PVT Co.G 7/20/62. D. from measles and chronic diarrhea at Lynchburg, Va. 1/16/63. Widow, Martha, 1891–1920.

Giles, William—PVT Co.I 9/25/61. WIA at Jericho Ford, Va. 5/25/64. Roll for 2/28/65 shows him AWOL since 8/1/64.

Givens, Jefferson M. (or Jefferson J.) PVT Co.B 2/11/62. D. 7/16/62. Possibly bur at Farmville, Va.

Gladden, J.A.—PVT Co.A 1861. Disabled by shell 5/64.

Gladden, Robert G.—PVT Co.A 9/19/61. WIA with skull fracture at Seven Pines, Va. 5/31/62. Dsh. for wounds 9/29/62. "Report of Sick and Wounded" for 10/62 lists dsh for effect of gun shot wound on 10/4/62.

Glover, John W.—Fifer Co.A 9/19/61. Appointed CPL 1861. Sick in Gordonsville, Va. hospital 12/62. Trn. to an Alabama Battalion.

Goggans, William C.(Carey?) (Goggins)—Jr. 2LT Co.A 8/15/61. Elected 1LT 7/3/62. In Richmond hospital 1/63 for typhoid fever. D. at Richmond of chronic diarrhea 2/27/63. Born in 1838.

Gorham, Willis Jackson—PVT Co.K 4/20/62. Appointed SGM 6/24/62. Elected Jr. 2LT 7/21/62. CPT in AG Dept and ordered to report to Gen. Lee 11/19/63. CPT and Inspector General on Gen Thomas' staff. CIA at Spotsylvania, Va. 5/10/64. Initially held at Ft. Delaware Prison. One of the famous "Immortal 600." Paroled at Charleston Harbor, S.C. 12/15/64. Attended University of Ga. and Harvard Law School. Harris County lawyer before war. Became a teacher and Baptist minister after war. D. 12/26/81 and bur. Oak Hill Cemetery in Griffin, Ga.

Graham, Thomas—PVT Co.K 7/4/61. D. at Richmond 11/10/61.

Granade, Joseph C.—PVT Co.B 2/1/62. WIA at Fredericksburg, Va. 12/13/62. Appointed 3CPL 1864. CIA at Petersburg, Va. 4/2/65. Released at Pt. Lookout, Md. 6/27/65.

Granade, Timothy—PVT Co.B 2/19/62. CIA at Gettysburg, Pa. 7/3/63. D. at Pt. Lookout Prison, Md. 1/22/64.

Granger, Charles W.—PVT Co.B 4/12/64. WIA at Hanover Junction, Va. 5/27/64. Roll for 2/28/65 shows him AWOL in Newton Cty., Ga. NLR.

Grant, George A.—PVT Co.K 7/4/61. WIA and permanently disabled at Fredericksburg, Va. 12/13/62. Retired from service. On pension roll for disabled leg.

Grant, James Henry—PVT Co.K 7/4/61. Dsh. 11/8/61. Reenlisted 11/28/64. Surrendered at Appomattox, Va. 4/9/65. B. in Chester Dst., S.C. 9/26/1836. Pension 1895.

Grant, John A.—PVT Co.K 7/4/61. Dsh. 11/25/61. Admitted to Chimborazo Hospital #2 at Richmond 12/16/62 for compound fracture of thigh received at Fredericksburg, Va on 12/13/62. Trn. to Hamilton, Ga. 5/1/63. No record of reenlistment found. NLR.

Grant, John H.—PVT Co.D 2/24/62. MIA 2nd Manassas, Va. 9/30/62. CIA at Gettysburg, Pa. 7/3/63. D. of inflammation of lungs at Ft. Delaware, Del. 9/20/63.

Grantham, John T.—PVT Co.C 9/17/61. CIA at Spotsylvania C.H., Va. 5/12/64. Paroled at Ft. Delaware, Del. 2/65. Received at Boulware and Cox's Wharves on James River in Va. 3/10–12/65.

Grant, Joseph C.—PVT Co.K 7/4/61. Appointed 4SG 1864. Surrendered at Appomattox, Va. 4/9/65. Pension roll 1917. D. 5/29/1927.

Grant, Thomas Pressley—PVT Co.K 3/4/62. Roll for 2/28/65 shows him AWOL. Pension records show he was at home on 20 days furlough and was enroute to command at close of war. B. in Ga. 1841.

Grant, William G.—PVT Co.K 3/4/62. Surrendered at Appomattox, Va. 4/9/65. B. in S.C. 1836. Pension roll 1899.

Grant, Washington G.—Co.K, rank/enlistment unknown. Married Sarah E. Grant 11/1/1850. He d. 1912. Widow's pension 1912 and she d. 1/28/1924. It is possible William G. and Washington G. Grant are the same person.

Gray, Baswell C. (or Braswell, or Basil)—PVT Co.I 5/9/62. WIA at Fredericksburg, Va. 12/13/62. WIA and CIA Gettysburg, Pa. 7/4/63. D. at Pt. Lookout Prison, Md. 1/31/64.

Gray, James H.—PVT Co.E 8/12/61. KIA at Mechanicsville, Va 6/26/62.

Gray, Miles—PVT Co.I 9/25/61. WIA Fredericksburg, Va. 12/13/62. CIA at Richmond 4/3/65 and paroled 5/18/65.

Green, John R.—PVT Co.I 2/20/62. CIA Gettysburg, Pa. 7/5/63. Paroled and exchanged at Camp Lee near Richmond. Entered Hospital #9 at Richmond 3/6/64. Returned to duty 3/7/64. Surrendered at Appomattox, Va. 4/9/65.

Gregory, Benjamin, Jr.—PVT Co.B 9/21/61. WIA at Spotsylvania C.H., Va. 5/14/64. Roll for 2/28/65 shows him AWOL in Newton Cty., Ga. NLR.

Griffin, Jesse M.—PVT Co.G 3/1/62. Appointed 3CPL. D. in camp near Petersburg, Va. 12/7/64.

Griffin, John M.—PVT Co.G 9/16/61. Appointed 4CPL 11/17/64. 3CPL. Surrendered at Appomattox, Va. 4/9/65. B. in Walton Cty., Ga. 4/1/42. Pension roll 1899–1907. D. 10/5/1914. Widow, Francis, pension 1914.

Griffin, William W.—PVT Co.A 8/15/61. D. 7/27/62.

Griffith, James R.—PVT Co.I 2/15/62. Roll for 2/28/65 shows him detailed in Medical Dept. at Richmond since 3/15/63. NLR.

Griggs, Edward B.—PVT Co.D 2/28/62. WIA at Cedar Mtn., Va. 8/9/62. D. of wounds at home 9/9/62.

Grissom, Elijah S. (or Gresham)—PVT Co.H 9/24/61. CIA at Williamsport, Pa. 7/12/63. Sent to Pt. Lookout, Md. Exchanged at Aiken's Landing, Va. 9/18/63. D. of disease in Jackson Hospital at Richmond 10/3/64. Buried there at Hollywood Cemetery.

Grissom, Harrison H. (or Gresham)—PVT Co.H 9/24/61. Surrendered at Appomattox, Va. 4/9/65. B. 3/12/1832.

Grove, J.B.—PVT Co.A 8/15/61. D. at Richmond 8/8/62. Buried there at Hollywood Cemetery—grave Q-73.

Groves, John Thomas—PVT Co.I 5/16/62. Elected 2LT 11/1/62. 1LT 12/28/62. Surrendered at Appomattox, Va. 4/9/65.

Groves, William Lorcas—CPT Co.I 9/25/61. Elected MAJ (to rank from 11/1/62) 12/30/62. Apparently stricken by pneumonia. Resigned after being elected to Ga. Legislature from Chattooga Cty. 12/21/63. D. 5/17/1873 and bur. at Bethel Presbyterian Cemetery in Chattooga Cty., Ga. near Summerville. B. 11/1/1820.

Gullatt, Augustus—PVT Co.K 7/4/61. D. 10/17/61.

Gullatt, Robert B.—PVT Co.K 9/5/61. Appointed 4CPL 1862. CIA near Petersburg, Va. 3/25/65. Released at Pt. Lookout, Md. 6/28/65.

Roster H

Hale, A.F.—PVT Co.K 7/4/61. D. 10/19/61.

Hagan, J.B.—PVT Co.K 7/4/61. Dsh. 11/6/61.

Hale, John H.—PVT Co.K 7/4/61. CIA Petersburg, Va. 4/2/65. Released at Pt. Lookout, Md. 6/28/65.

Hale, Sidney—PVT Co.K 3/3/64. WIA 1864. Surrendered at Appomattox, Va. 4/9/65.

Hale, West—PVT Co.K 7/4/61. D. of disease at Winder Hospital in Richmond 9/8/62.

Hall, John M.—PVT Co.A 8/15/61. Dsh. 12/6/61.

Hall, William A.—PVT Co.I 2/22/62. Appears last on roll for 6/30/64.

Hambleton, James Poindexter—Surgeon 4th Ga. Inf Battn. 10/14/61. Trn. to 35th Ga. Inf Rgt. 1862. Assigned to temporary duty at Atlanta 3/19/62. Resigned for ill health 12/19/62. D. 5/97 in Washington, D.C.

Hamer, Henry B.—PVT Co.K 7/1/64. Surrendered Appomattox, Va. 4/9/65.

Hamilton, A.D.—Asst. Surgeon 6/5/62. Assigned 35th Ga. Inf Rgt. 12/17/62.

Hamilton, James A.—PVT Co.I 9/25/61. CIA Frederick Cty., Md. 9/1/63. Forwarded from Harper's Ferry, W.Va. to Provost Marshall, 8th U.S. Army Corps 10/9/63.

Hamilton, James O.—PVT Co.I 3/3/62. KIA Mechanicsville, Va. 6/26/62.

Hamilton, John G.—PVT Co.I 9/25/61. Appointed 1CPL 1862. WIA Mechanicsville, Va. 6/26/62. Roll for 2/28/65 shows him, "Absent, detailed Medical Dept. at Atlanta, Ga. 1/31/64. now in Augusta, Ga. resigned as 1CPL 2/2/65." NLR.

Hamilton, John W.—PVT Co.I 9/25/61. Appointed 3SG 5/1/64. CIA near Petersburg, Va. 3/25/65. Released at Pt. Lookout, Md. 6/28/65.

Hamilton, Samuel J.—PVT Co.I 9/25/61. Roll for Jan-Feb 62 shows, "Absent, sick in private house." Dsh., furnished substitute 3/24/62. B. in Ga. 1/5/46. Pension roll 1919. D. 3/17/1920 and bur Subligna Methodist Cem. in Chattooga Cty., Ga. Widow pension 1920.

Hammond, George W.—1LT Co.E 8/12/61. Elected CPT 1/23/63. Resigned for disability from chronic diarrhea 6/10/63. B. 12/5/1826. D. 2/26/1869 and bur. at Campbellton United Methodist Church Cem near Fairburn in Fulton Cty., Ga. His wife, Martha E. Hammond, applied for a widow's pension in 5/1891. They were married on 9/28/54.

Hammond, Hiram Warner—PVT Co.E 8/12/61. Appointed 4CPL 1863. 3CPL 1864. WIA, gunshot wound to head, Spotsylvania C.H., Va. 5/12/64. WIA, Petersburg 4/2/65. Captured in Richmond, Va. hospital 4/3/65. Released at Newport News, Va. 6/26/65 and sailed to Savannah aboard steamer named 'Peritt'. B. 5/7/43 in Carroll Cty., Ga. Nephew of George W. Hammond. Moved to Alabama in 1867 and married Edatha Naomi Abernathy. D.2/18/1933.

Hammond, Joel F.—PVT Co.E 8/12/61. Roll for 2/28/65 reports, "Absent, Hospital Steward, Augusta, Ga." NLR.

Hammond, John M.—PVT Co.E 8/12/61. CIA near Petersburg, Va. 3/25/65. Released at Pt. Lookout, Md. 6/27/65.

Haney, Hiram H.—PVT Co.A 8/15/61. WIA Mechanicsville, Va. 6/26/62. AWOL after furlough expired 10/31/64. NLR.

Harbin, James R.—PVT Co.F 9/23/61. Surrendered at Appomattox, Va. 4/9/65.

Harbin, Wiley B.—PVT Co.F 9/23/61. In 2nd Div. CSA Gen'l. Hospital at Farmville, Va. with pneumonia 4/8/65. B. 1/29/1838. D. 11/23/1906. Bur. Haynes Creek Primitive Baptist Ch. Cem. in Loganville, Ga.

Harbin, William B.—PVT Co.F 9/23/61. Appointed 5SG 10/62. 4SG 11/1/62. 3SG 8/64. WIA in arm at Gettysburg, Pa. 7/3/63. Surrendered at Appomattox, Va. 4/9/65.

Harmon, Thomas A.—PVT Co.G 9/16/61. Appointed 4CPL 10/1/62.WIA Petersburg, Va. 4/2/65. Admitted to CSA General Hospital at Danville, Va. 4/3/65 and furloughed for 30 days on 4/9/65. B. 1840 in Newton Cty., Ga. Pension 1900–05.

Harp, John H.—PVT Co.E 8/12/61. D. at Fredericksburg, Va. 12/29/61.

Harris, Clark M.—Pvt Co.H 9/24/61. Dsh. for old age (56 years old) and exhaustion and problems related to an old gunshot wound to right hip disability at Richmond 6/62. Received at Louisville, Ky. as Confederate deserter 6/18/64. Took oath of allegience to US Govt there and released to remain north of Ohio River during war.

Harris, Cornelius W.—PVT Co.G 3/1/62. Roll for 2/28/65 shows him present. NLR.

Harris, Ezekiel D.—PVT Co.G 5/26/64. Captured at Richmond, Va. hospital 4/3/65. Union records show he, "Left hospital without permission 4/25/65."

Harris, George F.—PVT Co.G 9/16/61. WIA in right shoulder and permanently disabled at Spotsylvania C.H., Va. 5/12/64. Dsh. for wounds 12/16/64. B. in Ga. 1/1839. Pension roll 1891–1913.

Harris, G.W.—PVT Co.G 9/16/61. WIA Hanover Junction, Va. 5/64. Surrendered at Appomattox, Va. 4/9/65. B. 1836 in Walton Cty., Ga. Pension roll 1897–1903.

Harris, Henry L.—PVT Co.D 9/23/61. Appointed 3CPL 9/62. WIA, shot in leg breaking it, Fredericksburg, Va. 12/13/62. CIA Farmville, Va. 4/7/65. B. in Ga. 12/9/1841. Pension 1890–1913. D. 9/21/1915 in Heard Cty., Ga.

Harris, Henry R.—PVT Co.G 9/16/61. CIA Jericho Ford, Va. 5/23/64. Paroled at Elmira, N.Y. for exchange 3/2/65. Sent to James River, Va. 3/65.

Harris, Thomas C.—PVT Co.H 9/24/61. Appointed 5SG 9/8/64. CIA near Petersburg, Va. 3/25/65. D. 4/10/65 at Pt. Lookout Prison, Md. Also shown to have been released at Pt. Lookout, Md. 6/28/65.

Harris, William—PVT Co.F 2/28/62. Dsh. for disability 7/29/62. B. in Gwinnett Cty., Ga. 1835.

Harrison, Edward—PVT Co.H 9/24/61. Dsh. 10/29/61.

Hatfield, General W.—PVT Co.A 8/15/61. Trn. to Co.B, Cobb's Legion Ga. Inf. 9/5/61. KIA at Sharpsburg, Md. 9/17/62.

Hawkins, Thomas J.—PVT Co.F 2/25/64. WIA, left arm and side, at Petersburg, Va. 7/22/64. At home on wounded furlough 2/28/65. Pension 1890–1906. Bur. Mt. Zion Baptist Ch. Cem. in Snellville, Ga.

Hayes, Daniel J.—PVT Co.H 9/24/61. CIA Fredericksburg, Va. 5/3/63. Paroled at Headquarters, Army of Potomac and forwarded to Washington, D.C. 5/4/63. Sent to City Pt, Va. for exchange 5/10/63. Received there 5/13/63. CIA Gettysburg, Pa. 7/3/63. Sent to Ft. McHenry, Md. 7/6/63 and trn. to Ft. Delaware, Del. same day. Forwarded to Pt. Lookout, Md. 10/20/63 where he was paroled and trn. to Aiken's Landing, Va. for exchange 9/18/64. Received at Varina, Va. 9/22/64. NLR.

Hayes, Henry J.—PVT Co.K 7/4/61. Appointed 1SG 1862. WIA Wilderness, Va. 5/6/64. Surrendered at Appomattox, Va. 4/9/65.

Hayes, James M.—PVT Co.K 7/4/61. D. 11/15/61.

Hayes, William S.—PVT Co.K 7/4/61. WIA at Fredericksburg, Va. 12/13/62 shot in ankle. NLR.

Haynes, John—PVT Co.A 8/15/61. Dsh. 7/28/62. Ren. 7/20/64. Roll for 2/28/65 shows him present. NLR.

Hays, Ezekiel J.—PVT Co.A 8/15/61. D. 11/7/61.

Hays, John W.—PVT Co.A 3/25/64. WIA Wilderness, Va. 5/5/64. Roll for 2/28/65 shows him AWOL after furlough expired on 11/1/64.

Head, Charles P.—PVT Co.A 7/1/62. D. at Berryville, Va. 11/7/62 probably from typhoid fever.

Head, Emanuel—PVT Co.D 7/3/62. Substitute for James M. Ponder. WIA 2nd Manassas, Va. 8/30/62. Roll for 2/28/65 shows him AWOL. NLR.

Head, Henry C.—PVT Co.A 7/1/62. Appointed 1CPL 9/8/62. Surrendered at Appomattox, Va. 4/9/65. D. 5/1904 in Buchanan, Ga.

Head, James C.—PVT Co.D 4/25/62. CIA Petersburg, Va. 4/2/65. Released at Pt. Lookout, Md. 6/28/65.

Head, James K.—PVT Co.C 4/24/62. Roll for 2/28/65 shows him sick in Macon, Ga. hospital. NLR.

Head, Noah Hill—PVT Co.D 4/8/63. CIA Petersburg, Va. 4/65. Released at Hart's Island, N.Y. 6/16/65.

Head, Singleton A.—PVT Co.C 9/17/61. B. 6/15/31. D. on 10/3/62 bur Antioch Methodist Cem on Rivertown Rd near Fairburn in Fulton Cty., Ga.

Head, William Jefferson—CPT Co.A 8/15/61. Resigned for illness and fatigue 7/3/62. B. in 1828. Lawyer.

Hearn, Henry M.—PVT Co.D 9/23/61. Detailed as Provost Guard in Wilcox's Div in 1864. Appointed 4CPL 1864. 1SG 1864. Roll for 2/28/65 shows him AWOL. NLR.

Hearn, James L.—PVT Co.C 9/17/61. Appointed Musician. WIA 1862. Surrendered at Appomattox, Va. 4/9/65.

Hearn, Joseph L.—PVT Co.C 8/28/62. WIA Gettysburg, Pa. 7/3/63 and d. of wounds 7/5/63.

Heath, James A.—PVT Co.D 9/26/62. WIA in left arm and leg at Wilderness, Va. 5/5/64. Dsh. 9/17/64. B. in Ga. 1845.

Hembree, Isaiah—1SG Co.E 8/12/61. WIA Mechanicsville, Va. 6/26/62. WIA Wilderness, Va. 5/6/64 and d. of wounds 5/8/64.

Henderson, David—PVT Co.I 9/25/61. D. of disease at Evansport, Va. 12/27/61.

Henderson, James M.—PVT Co.G 9/16/61. D. at Richmond 7/29/62.

Henderson, James T.—PVT Co.C 9/17/61. Deserted near Petersburg, Va. 8/26/64. Took oath of allegience to US Govt. 10/21/64. Received at Military Prison at Chattanooga, Tn. 10/22/64.

Henderson, John M.—PVT Co.I 9/25/61. WIA and CIA Petersburg, Va. 4/2/65. Released at Pt. Lookout, Md. 6/13/65.

Henderson, Samuel—PVT Co.C 2/19/62. D. at Fredericksburg, Va. 4/11/62.

Henderson, Thomas J.—PVT Co.G 2/28/62. D. at Richmond 5/3/62.

Hendrix, David—PVT Co.I 5/9/62. D. at home in Chattooga Cty., Ga. 8/21/63.

Hendrix, John H.—PVT Co.I 9/25/61. D. of pneumonia at Dumfries, Va. 12/23/61.

Hendrix, William—PVT Co.H 9/24/61. D. of phthisis at Petersburg, Va. 4/17 or 6/17/62.

Henry, David B.—CPT Co.C 9/17/61. KIA at Mechanicsville, Va. 6/26/62 and apparently buried in an unknown grave on the field.

Henry, J.T.—PVT Co.B 9/21/61. CIA, date and place unknown. D. at Camp Douglas, Ill.

Henry, William—PVT Co.A, 1st City Battn., Ga. Inf. 5/5/64 (also known as Co.A, 19th Battn., Ga. State Guards Inf.). No record of trn. to Co.F, 35th Ga. Inf. Rgt. found. His name appears on signature to parole of prisoners that surrendered at Greensboro, N.C. 4/26/65.

Herndon, Cyrus M.—PVT Co.I 2/22/62. Roll for 2/28/65 shows him AWOL since 1/1/65. B. 1/25. D. 12/92 and bur at Trion Cem at Trion, Ga. in Chattooga Cty.

Herndon, John H.—PVT Co.F 2/12/62. D. in Winder Hospital at Richmond 8/29/62. Buried there at Hollywood Cemetery—grave S-40.

Herndon, William M.—PVT Co.F 5/5/62. D. near Richmond 7/1/62.

Herren, John W.—PVT Co.H 9/24/61. WIA Seven Pines, Va.5/31/62. CIA Gettysburg, Pa. 7/3/63. Paroled at Pt. Lookout, Md. 2/18/65. B. in Clarke Cty., Ga. 12/11/1839. Pension 1914. D. 5/3/1916.

Herren, William—PVT Co.H 9/24/61. CIA Gettysburg, Pa. 7/1/63. D. of inflammation of lungs at Ft. Delaware, Del. 7/19/63.

Herring, Hiram F.—PVT Co.F 8/28/61. WIA Fredericksburg, Va. 12/13/62 necessitating amputation of arm. At home on furlough at end of war. B. 12/30/1836. D. 4/24/1913. Bur. Chestnut Grove Baptist Ch. Cem. in Grayson, Ga.

Herring, Jesse J.W.—PVT Co.F 9/23/61. D. of smallpox at Camp Gregg, Va. near Fredericksburg 4/4/63.

Hester, John B.—PVT Co.D 9/23/61. Appointed 5SG 12/61. Regimental Ensign 1862. 1SG 7/22/62.

Hestleage, Elisha—PVT Co.C 9/17/61. KIA at Gaines Mill, Va. 6/27/62.

Hicks, Davis Jr.—PVT Co.I 10/64. D. at Lynchburg, Va. 10/64.

Hicks, Davis W.—PVT Co.I 9/18/62. D. of erysipelas in Confederate Hospital at Winchester, Va. 12/10/62.

Hicks, Gilham T. (or Gillam F.)—PVT Co.D 3/10/63. Surrendered at Appomattox, Va. 4/9/65.

Hicks, Henry B.—PVT Co.I 2/22/62. D. of measles at Richmond 4/29/62. Widow pension 1891–96.

Hicks, Henry Jackson—PVT Co.I 2/18/62. WIA in fingers necessitating amputation at Fredericksburg, Va. 12/13/62. CIA near Petersburg, Va. 3/25/65. Released at Pt.

Lookout, Md. 6/28/65. B. in Ga. 12/5/1842. Lived near Trion Factory, Ga. Pension roll 1904–07.

Hicks, James C.—PVT Co.I 2/22/62. Detailed as forage master for A.P. Hill's division train. CIA at Greencastle, Pa. 7/5/63. Trn. from Ft. Delaware, Del. to Pt. Lookout, Md. 10/63 and paroled there 2/21/65. B. in Chattooga Cty., Ga.

Hicks, William—PVT Co.I 3/3/62. Admitted to General Hospital at Camp Winder in Richmond 6/5/62. Dsh., furnished a substitute 6/22/62.

Hicks, Wyatt J.—PVT Co.D 3/2/64. CIA at Petersburg, Va. 6/24/64. Released from Pt. Lookout, Md. 6/5/65. Indigent pension 1900–07. B. 7/18/1829 in Pike Cty., Ga.

Hill, James H.—PVT Co.A 8/15/61. D. at Ashland, Va. 4/22/62.

Hill, John A.—PVT Co.I 9/25/61. WIA Mechanicsville, Va. 6/26/62. Admitted to General Hospital at Camp Winder at Richmond 8/18/63. Returned to duty 9/4/63. Dsh., disabled by wounds 4/14/64.

Hill, Wiley—PVT Co.B 2/15/62. WIA Cedar Mtn., Va. 8/9/62. D. of wounds 8/10/62.

Hill, William J.—1SG Co.I 9/25/61. Elected 1LT 11/1/62. Resigned 12/23/62.

Hill, William P.—Asst. Surgeon 9/27/61. Assigned to 35th Ga. Inf Rgt. 1/20/62. CIA Gettysburg, Pa. 7/5/63 and sent Ft. Delaware, Del. Paroled at City Pt., Va. 8/63. Surrendered Appomattox, Va. 4/9/65

Hines, Clayton W.—PVT Co.K 3/4/62. WIA Spotsylvania C.H., Va. 5/12/64. Roll for 2/28/65 shows him, "Absent, wounded." Pension roll 1890.

Hines, James T.—PVT Co.I 7/4/61. Surrendered Appomattox, Va. 4/9/65.

Hinton, John N.—PVT Co.B 2/28/62. D. of disease 8/3/62.

Hinton, William H.—PVT Co.B 9/21/61. Surrendered at Appomattox, Va. 4/9/65.

Hitch, Benjamin F.—PVT Co.C 9/17/61. Appointed QM SGT 1861. D. at Petersburg, Va. 11/7/64.

Hogan, Cordy W.—PVT Co.G 3/1/62. CIA Gettysburg, Pa. 7/3/63. D. of chronic bronchitis at Ft. Delaware, Del. 2/21/64.

Hogan, Isaiah J.—PVT Co.G 9/16/61. KIA Mechanicsville, Va. 6/26/62.

Holcombe, Reuben J.—PVT Co.A 8/15/61. KIA Seven Pines, Va. 5/31/62.

Holcombe, William Martin, Jr.—PVT Co.A 8/15/61. Appointed 1CPL 7/5/62. WIA Cedar Mtn, Va. 8/9/62 and d. of wounds 9/7/62. Bur. in Confederate Cemetery at Lynchburg, Va. Body disinterred and sent to Cartersville, Ga. for Burton Watson.

Holcombe, William Martin, Sr.—PVT Co.A 8/15/61. Roll for 2/28/65 shows him present. Pension records show he was sent to hospital on 4/1/65. B. in Carroll Cty., Ga. 9/12/1844. Indigent pension roll 1900–1907.

Holder, William S.—PVT Co.A 9/19/61. D. 10/13/61.

Hollingsworth, Joseph—1CPL Co.B 9/21/61.Appointed 2SG 4/15/62. D. of disease at Richmond 7/10/62.

Holmes, Hiram R.—PVT Co.H 9/24/61. Dsh. from service at Chimborazo #3 Hospital at Richmond 6/13/62.

Holt, Bolling Hall—PVT Co.G, 2nd Ga. Inf Rgt. 4/16/61. Dsh. 10/14/61. Elected MAJ 35th Ga. Inf Rgt 10/14/61. LTC 6/1/62. Regimental commander 7/15/62 when E.L. Thomas promoted to brigade command. COL 11/1/62. Surrendered Appomattox, Va. 4/9/65. Born 11/10/40. Attended Univ. of Va. (from Ohio). D. 9/27/67 and buried at Linwood Cemetery, Lot 622, Section C, in Columbus, Ga.

Holt, Richard D.B.—PVT Co.F 9/23/61. Surrendered at Appomattox, Va. 4/9/65.

Holt, W.S.—PVT Co.F 1/25/64. D. in Petersburg, Va. hospital 6/24/64.

Hopkins, Collin D.—PVT Co.C 9/17/61. Dsh. 8/1/62. Re-enlisted.WIA at Gettysburg, Pa. 7/3/63. Surrendered at Appomattox, Va. 4/9/65.

Hopkins, Elijah—PVT Co.C 9/17/61. Dsh. 9/5/62.

Hopkins, James Frank—PVT Co.C 9/17/61. Roll for 2/28/65 shows him AWOL since 9/12/64. NLR.

Hopkins, John F.—PVT Co.C 9/17/61. WIA and CIA Petersburg, Va. 4/2/65. Released at Pt. Lookout, Md. 6/13/65.

Hopkins, William—PVT Co.K 9/5/61. D. 5/14/62.

Hopson, Virgil L.—Acting Commissary of Subsistence (ACS) 35th Ga. Inf Rgt. 10/14/61. CPT and Ast QM 10/24/63. Relieved from duty with 35th Ga. and assigned to Richardson's Art. Battn. as Ast. QM 3/5/65. From LaGrange, Ga. NLR.

Hopson, W.B.—PVT Co.B, 4th Ga. Inf. Rgt., 4/26/61. Dsh 8/14/61. Joined Co.D, 35th Ga. WIA. Sent to Butts Cty., Ga. as enrolling officer. Pension 1905. B. 1834 in Troup Cty., Ga.

Horn, O.H.—PVT Co.I 3/62. Enlisted at Summerville, Ga. B. 2/28/1843 in Chattooga Cty., Ga. Pension roll 1901–07.

Houston, Jesse—PVT Co.A 8/15/61. WIA Mechanicsville, Va. 6/26/62. Appointed 2CPL 1863. 3SG 5/6/64. Captured in Richmond hospital 4/3/65 and paroled there 4/22/65.

Howard, G.W.—PVT Co.K 7/4/61. Appears last on roll for Sept-Oct. 62. D. in service.

Howard, Hiram—PVT Co.K 7/4/61. D. 10/6/61.

Howard, H.T.—PVT Co.K 7/4/61. D. 10/9/61.

Howard, William S.—PVt Co.C 2/18/62. D. in Fredericksburg, Va. hospital 4/7/62.

Howard, Zebulon L.—PVT Co.C 9/17/61. CPL 1861. D. of disease at Evansport, Va. 11/27/61.

Hubbard, James—PVT Co.I 3/3/62. WIA/CIA near Hagerstown, Md. 7/12/63. Later paroled and rejoined unit. Surrendered at Appomattox, Va. 4/9/65.

Hubbard, John—PVT Co.I 9/25/61. D. of pneumonia at Fredericksburg, Va. 12/25/61.

Huckaby, James T.—PVT Co.H 9/24/61. AWOL 2/9/65–2/28/65. NLR.

Hudson, Charles C.—PVT Co.B 9/21/61. WIA Seven Pines, Va. 5/31/62 and d. on battlefield same day. Widow, Mabelle, filed for widow's pension 1891–1900.

Hudson, David Judson—PVT Co.B 2/20/62. WIA at Seven Days Battles near Richmond, Va. 6/62. WIA Gettysburg, Pa. 7/3/63. Roll for 2/28/65 shows him, "Absent in Ga., wounded since 7/63." NLR.

Hudson, James A. (or James H.)—PVT Co.K 3/4/62. Surrendered at Appomattox, Va. 4/9/65.

Hudson, Joshua B.—PVT Co.B 9/21/61. CIA at Wilderness, Va. 5/6/64. D. of smallpox at Elmira, N.Y. 2/19/65.

Hughes, Andrew J.—PVT Co.C 9/17/61. WIA 1862. Appointed 4CPL 1864. Surrendered at Appomattox, Va. 4/9/65.

Hughes, Guilford Columbus—PVT Co.C 9/17/61. Dsh. 1862.

Hughes, Pinkney T.—PVT Co.A 8/15/61. Appointed 5SG 9/23/61. D. at Fredericksburg, Va. 4/2/62.

Hughes, Rufus K.—PVT Co.A 8/15/61. D. at Richmond 11/8/61.

Hull, Francis Oscar—PVT Co.B 9/21/61. CIA Gettysburg, Pa. 7/3/63. Prl. at Pt. Lookout, Md. 3/16/64. Received at City Pt., Va. for exchange 3/20/64. CIA near Petersburg, Va. 3/25/65. Released at Pt. Lookout, Md. 6/27/65.

Hulsey, H.—PVT Co.A 8/15/61. D. at Richmond 4/25/64. Bur. there at Hollywood Cemetery.

Hulsey, William—PVT Co.A 11/1/63. Roll for 2/28/65 shows him present. NLR.

Hulsey, William T.—PVT Co.A 8/15/61. Dsh. 12/15/64.

Humphries, Charles B.—PVT Co.B 2/28/62. WIA at Mechanicsville, Va. 6/26/62. D. at Farmville, Va. 7/16/62.

Humphries, J.M.—PVT Co.F 9/23/61. Surrendered at Appomattox, Va. 4/9/65.

Humphries, Shadrick H.—PVT Co.B 9/21/61. WIA at 2nd Manassas, Va. 8/30/62. D. from wounds 9/26/62.

Humphries, Stephen—PVT Co.F 9/23/61. Roll for 2/28/65 shows him present. NLR.

Hutchinson, Robert (or Hutcherson or Hutchins)—PVT Co.I 2/18/62. WIA, shot in eye, resulting in loss of sight at Wilderness, Va. 5/6/64. Roll for 2/28/65 shows him AWOL in Floyd Cty., Ga. since 1/1/65. Pension roll 1889–1894.

Hyatt,—PVT Co.B. D. at Lynchburg, Va. Bur. there 5/31/62 in Confederate Cemetery No.3, 5th line, lot 171-College Hospital.

Hyatt, John P.—PVT Co.B 9/21/61. WIA at Mechanicsville, Va. 6/26/62. D. of wounds at Richmond 7/14/62.

Hyatt, Thomas J.—PVT Co.B 9/21/61. WIA at 2nd Manassas, Va. 8/30/62 and d. of wounds 9/14/62.

Roster I

Ingraham, Russell—PVT Co.K 7/4/61. D. 10/28/61.

Ingram, Thomas J. (or Thomas W.)—PVT Co.A 8/15/61. Sick in Fredericksburg, Va. hospital 2/62. Dsh. 7/29/62.

Irvin, David—PVT Co.G 9/16/61. WIA 1862. Admitted to General Hospital #21 at Richmond 11/19/62. Trn. to Howard's Grove General Hospital at Richmond 12/16/62. Dsh. for disability 8/24/63 at age 34. Measles and smallpox caused ulceration of right leg and amputation. farmer. Pension roll 1888–1907.

Irvin, Eli B. (or Irwin)—PVT Co.B 9/21/61. WIA at Gettysburg, Pa. and died there same day 7/3/63.

Irvine, Washington T.—1LT Co.I 9/25/61. Elected CPT 11/1/62. Surrendered at Appomattox, Va. 4/9/65. B. 1/5/1836. D. 2/10/1908 and bur. at Bethel Presbyterian Cemetery at Chattooga Cty., Ga. near Summerville.

Irwin, W.J.—PVT Co.E 8/12/61. WIA, date and place unknown.

Roster J

Jackson, Andrew M.—PVT Co.I 9/25/61. Dsh., disability 2/10/65.

Jackson, Benjamin F.M.—PVT Co.E 8/12/61. WIA Chancellorsville, Va. 5/3/63. D. of wounds in General Hospital #23 at Richmond 5/16/63.

Jackson, Daniel A.—PVT Co.E 8/12/61. Appointed CPL. Surrendered at Appomattox, Va. 4/9/65. Living in Springdale, Tx. in 1897.

Jackson, John C.—PVT Co.E 8/12/61. Appointed 3CPL 1862. 1SG 1863. Reduced in rank, loss of six months pay, and six months labor from court martial proceedings for being absent without leave. KIA near Petersburg, Va. 3/25/65.

Jackson, John P. (or John H.)—PVT Co.I 5/9/62. WIA Jericho Ford, Va. 5/25/64. Surrendered Appomattox, Va. 4/9/65.

Jackson, John Warren—PVT Co.D 2/28/62. D. at Ashland, Va. 4/13/62. Bur. at Richmond, Va. at Hollywood Cemetery—grave W-668.

Jackson, Joseph M.—PVT Co.I 1/30/64. Surrendered Appomattox, Va. 4/9/65.

Jackson, Martin V.—3SG Co.K 7/4/61. CIA Petersburg, Va. 4/2/65. Released at Hart's Island, N.Y. 6/15/65. Widow, Cornelia, pension 1919.

Jackson, Noah—PVT Co.D 4/2/63. WIA, probably at Petersburg, Va. on 3/25/65. Admitted to Richmond hsp. for leg amputation 3/27/65. CIA at Richmond 4/3/65. Escaped from hospital 5/4/65. D. 1865. Bur. at Richmond at Hollywood Cemetery—grave W265. Widow filed pension application 1891 stating her husband shot in right thigh and leg amputated after gangrene set in. She states he died 4/19/65 in Jackson Hsp in Richmond.

Jackson, Robert A.—PVT Co.E 8/12/61. Appointed 4CPL 1862. 3CPL 1863. 2CPL 1864. WIA in May 1864. Became regimental shoemaker. Surrendered as a PVT Co.D, 35th Ga. Inf. Rgt. At Appomattox, Va. 4/9/65. No Record of company trn. found. B. 9/28/41.

Jackson, Simeon—PVT Co.D 2/28/62. D. at Richmond 5/6/62.

Jackson, Warren J.—PVT Co.E 8/12/61. D. of chronic diarrhea in Richmond hospital 11/17/62.

Jackson, William E.—PVT Co.A 8/15/61. D. at Richmond 4/62.

Jackson, William J.—PVT Co.E 8/6/62. D. in Winchester, Va. hospital 10/14/62. A soldier named J.W. Jackson from same company died on 10/13/62 in Winchester and was bur. in Georgia section, grave #135, Stonewall Jackson Cemetery (Mount Hebron), Winchester, Va. This grave marker actually says J.N. Jackson. This is probably the same soldier.

Jeffres, Uriah W. (or Jeffries)—PVT Co.C 4/28/62. KIA Battle of Second Manassas, Va. 8/28/62.

Jenkins, Albert—PVT Co.D 2/20/62. WIA, shell wound to knee, Malvern Hill, Va. 7/1/62. Absent, sick 12/62. NLR.

Jenkins, Alfred S.—PVT Co.F 2/12/62. WIA, left shoulder, at Wilderness, Va. 5/6/64. WIA, left arm and hip, Spotsylvania C.H., Va. 5/12/64. Roll for 2/28/65 shows him AWOL since 10/31/64. reported to have joined Graham's Scouts in Ga. Resident of Ga. since 10/15/1842.

Jenkins, T.W.—2CPL Co.K 7/4/61. D. at Richmond 6/27/62.

Jenkins, William W.—2SG Co.K 7/4/61. Surrendered Appomattox, Va. 4/9/65. D. at Midland, Ga. 7/31/1916.

Jennings, Jonathan—3SG Co.C 9/17/61. WIA/CIA Seven Pines, Va. 5/31/62. D. of wounds in Chesapeake USA General Hospital at Fortress Monroe, Va. 6/13/62.

Jennings, Martin Van Buren—PVT Co.C 9/17/61. D. in Gate City Hospital at Atlanta, Ga. 1/5/63. Buried there at Oakland Cemetery.

Jennings, Peter E.L.—Ast. Surgeon 35th Ga. Inf Rgt. 11/16/61. Resigned for rheumatism and chronic diarrhea 7/31/62. From Hogansville, Ga.

Jett, Stephen L.—PVT Co.A 8/15/61. D. 12/7/61.

Johnsey, James T. (or Johnsie, T.)—PVT Co.K 2/25/62. CIA Gettysburg, Pa. 7/3/63. D. of smallpox at Ft. Delaware, Del. 7/11/64.

Johnsey, L.H. (or Johnsie, L.W.)—PVT Co.K 2/28/62. Dsh. prior to 8/31/62.

Johnson, Cephas R.—2SG Co.D 9/23/61. Appointed SGM 10/14/61. D. 6/62.

Johnson, George A.—PVT Co.B 2/28/62. WIA during Seven Days Battles near Richmond 6/62. CIA Petersburg, Va. 4/2/65. Released at Pt. Lookout, Md. 6/28/65.

Johnson, Isaac H.—PVT Co.H 2/23/62. Appointed 3CPL 11/1/62. Records of Medical Director's office at Richmond from General Hospital #16 show that he was poisoned by impure virus 4/17/63. He was frl. for 40 days 6/17/63. Admitted to CSA General Hospital at Charlottesville, Va. 11/3/63. and trn to Lynchburg, Va. 12/3/63. Dsh., disability at Orange C.H. 4/30/64.

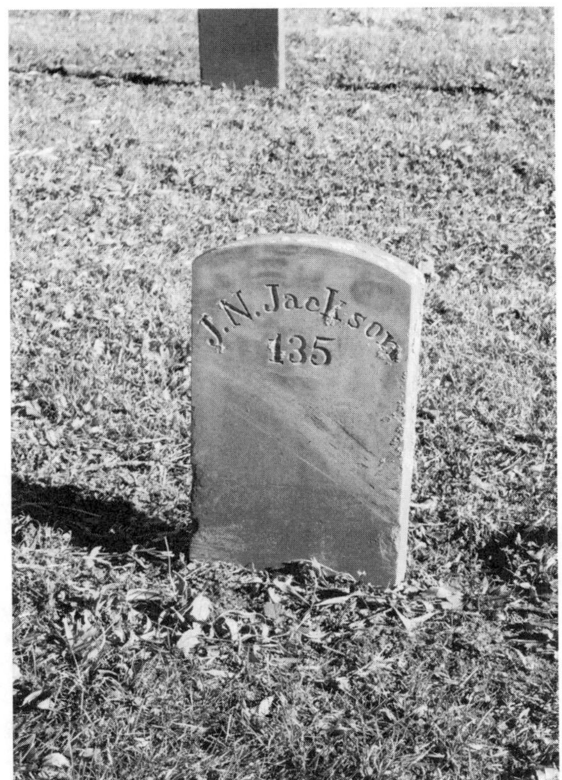

Tombstone of Private William J. Jackson, Co. E Stonewall Confederate Cemetery (Mount Hebron) at Winchester, Va.
photo by author

Johnson, Jackson H.—PVT Co.G 7/26/62. Surrendered Appomattox, Va. 4/9/65. D. 1/1872. Widow, Francis, pension 1910–33.

Johnson, James J.—PVT Co.G 2/11/62. Union POW records show he was paroled at Farmville, Va. 4/11 to 4/21/65.

Johnson, James J.—PVT Co.H 9/24/61. WIA Seven Pines, Va.5/31/62. Appointed 5SG 8/9/62. 1SG 1862. WIA Jericho Ford, Va. 5/23/64. D. from wounds in lung at Jackson Hospital in Richmond 4/6/65.

Johnson, John W.—PVT Co.B 2/28/62. WIA 2nd Manassas, Va. 8/30/62. Roll for 2/28/65 shows him absent in Georgia on wounded furlough. NLR.

Johnson, Joseph T.—PVT Co.H 9/24/61. KIA at Jericho Ford, Va. 5/23/64.

Johnson, Josiah Marshall—5SG Co.B 9/21/61. Appointed 1SG 6/64. On sick furlough in Ga. 2/28/65. NLR.

Johnson, Nathan Z.—PVT Co.B 2/24/62. WIA (shot in back and shoulder) Seven Pines, Va. 5/31/62. Roll for for 2/28/65 shows him absent in Georgia on wounded furlough. Invalid pension 1887–1907.

Johnson, Perry—PVT Co.I 5/22/62. Admitted to Chimborazo Hospital #2 at Richmond with dysentery 5/2/63. Returned for duty 5/19/63. D. of dysentery at Richmond 7/28/63. Bur. there at Hollywood Cemetery.

Johnson, R.D.—PVt Co.F 9/23/61. Surrendered at Appomattox, Va. 4/9/65. B. in Ga. Pension roll 1919.

Johnson, Riley C. PVT Co.C 3/8/64. Surrendered at Appomattox, Va. 4/9/65.

Johnson, Solomon G.—Jr. 2LT Co.C 9/17/61. Elected 2LT 6/26/62. 1LT 10/62. Surrendered at Appomattox, Va 4/9/65.

Johnson, Thomas Linsey—PVT Co.B 9/21/61. D. 12/6/61 at Evansport, Va.

Johnson, William H.—PVT Co.I 2/22/62. Frl. 1/65. Roll for 2/28/65, last on file, shows him AWOL in Chattooga Cty., Ga. since 2/9/65. Pension roll 1898–1907. Possibly d. 1924.

Johnson, William R.—PVT Co.H 9/1/63. CIA Petersburg, Va. 4/3/65. Released at Hart's Island, N.Y. 6/15/65. B. at Aiken, S.C. 6/14/1823. Pension roll 1902–07.

Johnson, William S.—PVT Co.G 3/4/62. In hospital 12/62. D. in Richmond 12/31/62 and possibly bur. there at Hollywood Cemetery—grave M195.

Johnston, George W.—PVT Co.E 8/12/61. WIA at Gettysburg, Pa. 7/3/63. CIA there 7/5/65. Received at City Pt., Va. 9/27/63. NLR.

Johnston, James Payne—3SG Co.D 9/23/61. Elected 2LT. Appointed SGM by Col. E.L. Thomas 7/28/62. Elected CPT of Co.D 9/13/64. Roll for 2/28/65 shows absent with leave of indulgence. B. in Troup Cty., Ga. 9/13/1841. In 1867 he moved to Pontotoc, Mississippi and in 1868 married Elmira L. Simmons. Worked there as a farmer, teacher, tax assessor, sheriff. Assisted in surveying for new town of Amory, Miss. and became Amory mayor in 1897. D. at his home in Amory, Miss. 7/17/1916.

Johnston, William J.—PVT Co.D 9/23/61. WIA. Dsh. 10/12/62. "Report of Sick and Wounded" in 10/62 show dsh date of 10/4/62 for chronic rheumatism. D. 11/26/1915 in Chambers Cty., Al.

Jones, G.W.—1SG Co.K 7/4/61. Elected Jr. 2LT 10/15/62, age 22. WIA, in head, Fredericksburg, Va. 12/13/62. Resigned, giving as his reason that some of the officers and men of the company objected to his holding the position, 4/29/63.

Jones, Isaac A.—PVT Co.H 9/24/61. Dsh. for accidental gunshot wound to left hand 6/26/62.

Jones, J.J.—PVT Co.E 4/23/62. KIA Seven Pines, Va. 5/31/62.

Jones, Larkin—4CPL Co.F 9/23/61. D. in Richmond hospital 5/2/62. Widow, Elizabeth, widow's pension 1891–1907.

Jones, Lewis D.—PVT Co.K 7/4/61. Appointed 3CPL 1864. CIA Petersburg, Va. 3/25/65. Released Pt. Lookout, Md. 6/28/65.

Jones, Randle (or Rundle)—PVT Co.K 3/4/62. D. 5/12/62.

Jones, Robert I. (or Robert J.)—PVT Co.K 7/4/61. CIA Petersburg, Va. 3/25/65. Released Pt. Lookout, Md. 6/28/65.

Jones, Thomas B.—1SG Co.H 9/24/61. Elected 2LT 7/23/62. Elected 1LT 11/12/62. WIA, skull fractured, CIA, Gettysburg, Pa. 7/2/63. Trn. from Johnson's Island, Oh. to Pt. Lookout, Md. 4/22/64. Trn. to Washington, D.C. 8/9/64. Admitted to Hammond USA Hospital at Pt. Lookout, Md. 4/26/65. Sent to General Hospital 5/20/65. B. 1/29/1826. Pension roll 1887. D. 12/18/1901 in Hall Cty., Ga.

Jones, Thomas S.—PVT Co.H 9/24/61. Deserted 1864. Arrested near Petersburg, Va. 7/29/64.

Jones, Warren—PVT Co.F 9/13/61. WIA 3/25/65 at Petersburg, Va. D. 11/20/1868. Wife, Lucinda, pension 1910.

Jones, Warren A.—PVT Co.F 9/23/61. Surrendered at Appomattox, Va. 4/9/65. B. in S.C. 1/1846. D. in Gwinnett Cty., Ga. 1/20/1915. Pension roll 1904. Widow, Ophelia, pension 1937. B. 1/17/46. Bur. at Bethesda United Methodist Church Cem. near Lawrenceville, Ga.

Jones, William J.—PVT Co.F 5/31/62. WIA, left leg, at Seven Pines, Va. 5/31/62. CIA Gettysburg, Pa. 7/3/63. Exchanged at James River, Va. 3/10 to 3/12/65. Captured in Richmond, Va. hospital 4/3/65. Trn. Pt. Lookout, Md. 5/2/65. B. in Ga. 9/4/1839. Pension roll 1892–1929. D. 10/13/1929 in Gwinnett Cty., Ga.

Jordan, Alfred—PVT Co.A 2/24/62. WIA at 2nd Manassas, Va. 8/29/62. and died near there from wounds 9/1/62.

Jordan, James H.—PVT Co.F 8/17/63. Dsh. for disability 9/12/64.

Jordan, John A.—PVT Co.F 9/23/61. Appointed 5SG 11/1/62. 4SG 1864. Roll for 2/28/65 shows him, "Home on leave of indulgence; time out 3/16/65." D. 1/19/1909 in Gwinnett Cty., Ga. Widow, Sarah, pension 1915 to her death 1/7/1928.

Jordan, Reuben J.—PVT Co.A 9/19/61. D. at Camp French at Evansport, Va. 1/22/62.

Jordan, William—PVT Co.A 8/15/61. D. at Richmond 4/18/62.

Roster K

Karr, John A.—PVT Co.E 8/12/61. WIA, left eye resulting in loss of sight, and CIA at Gettysburg, Pa. 7/3/63. Paroled Ft. Delaware, Del. 10/30/64. Received at Venus Pt. near Savannah, Ga. for exchange 11/15/64. Pension records show he lost hearing from explosion of shell and was dsh. B. in Ga. 4/8/1842.

Karr, William P.—PVT Co.E 8/12/61. Dsh. for disability 12/8/62. B. in Ga. 1844.

Kelly, William H.—PVT Co.C 9/17/61. D. of pleurisy at Richmond 4/8/62.

Kemp, H.M.—PVT Co.G 9/16/61. Surrendered Appomattox, Va. 4/9/65.

Kidd, Alpheus—PVT Co.C 9/17/61.

Kidd, James H.—PVT Co.C 9/17/61. Appointed SGT. WIA Fredericksburg, Va.12/13/62. D. from wounds 12/15/62.

Kidd, James Milton—PVT Co.C 4/23/62. WIA and CIA Wilderness, Va. 5/5/64. D. of chronic diarrhea at Elmira, N.Y. 4/20/65. Bur. there at Woodlawn National Cemetery—grave #1381 WNC.

Kidd, John E.—PVT Co.C 2/24/62. D. of measles in Richmond hospital 4/30/62.

Kidd, John M.—4SG Co.C 9/17/61. Appointed 2SG 7/22/62. Elected Jr. 2LT 10/62. D. at Atlanta, Ga. 4/2/63.

Kidd, Milton P.—PVT Co.C 9/17/61. D. in camp of pneumonia 3/23/64.

Kidd, William LaFayette—PVT Co.C 9/17/61. Roll for 2/28/65 shows he was absent on leave of indulgence at Fairburn, Ga. since 2/5/65. NLR.

Kilgo, William B.—PVT Co.I 9/25/61. Roll for 2/28/61 shows him AWOL in Chattooga Cty., Ga. since 1/1/65. NLR.

Kilgore, Dotson B.—PVT Co.A 9/19/61. Roll for 2/28/65 shows him AWOL after furlough expired on 5/31/64. NLR.

Kilgore, James J.—PVT Co.A 4/1/62. On sick frl. in Ga. 12/62. NLR.

Kilgore, William J.—PVT Co.A 8/15/61. D. 12/24/61.

Kilgore, Wilson—PVT Co.A 8/15/61. Appointed 5SG 4/2/62. KIA Gettysburg, Pa. 7/3/63.

Kimbrough, James M.—PVT Co.K 7/4/61. Appointed 5SG 1862. Regimental Ensign. Sick furlough 1/65 until end of war. B. in Ga. Pension roll 1919. D. 6/25/1925. Widow, Sallie, pension 1925.

Kimbrough, Jesse W.—2LT Co.K 7/4/61. elected 1LT 2/13/62. CPT 10/12/62. Roll for 2/28/65 shows him AWOL since 2/24/65. Permission for 24 day absence issued by Gen. Lee 2/30/65. NLR

Kimbrough, T.M.—5SG Co.K 7/4/61. Appears last on roll for 12/31/62. Trn. to Co.F, 12th Alabama Inf. Rgt. 1/29/63.

Kimbrough, Thomas E.—Ordnance SGT. NLR.

Kimbrough, Thomas Hugh—PVT Co.K 11/28/62. Surrendered Appomattox, Va. 4/9/65. B. 12/6/1844 in Ga. Lived in Cataula, Ga. Pension roll 1919. D. 5/20/1927 and bur Pierce Chapel Methodist Ch. Cem. in Harris Cty., Ga. There is a postwar picture of him in History of Harris County, Ga., p. 361.

Kimble, Francis M.—PVT Co.B 2/24/62. WIA 1862. KIA Petersburg, Va. 4/2/65.

Kimble, Joseph Fannin—PVT Co.B 2/28/62. Surrendered Appomattox, Va. 4/9/65.

King, Jesse C.—PVT Co.H 11/25/63. Roll for 10/31/64 shows he, "Deserted Jackson Hospital at Richmond, Va. 8/10/64." Widow, Elizabeth, pension 1894–1905. She claimed in her application that her husband never returned from war.

King, John Thomas—PVT Co.K 7/4/61. CIA near Petersburg, Va. 3/25/65. Released Pt. Lookout, Md. 6/28/65.

King, John W.—PVT Co.C 4/23/62. CIA Jericho Ford, Va. 5/24/64. Released at Elmira, N.Y. 5/29/65.

King, William M.—PVT Co.C 9/17/61. Absent, sick at Richmond 11/61. Dsh. 12/12/61. NLR.

Kinsey, Lazarus F.—PVT Co.K 3/4/62. WIA Gettysburg, Pa. 7/3/63. Admitted to General Hospital #9 at Richmond 7/14/63, and trn to Camp Winder Hospital at Richmond. Detailed Sub-Enrolling Officer for Harris Cty., Ga.

Kirk, Andrew J.—PVT Co.D 9/23/61. Dsh. for chronic bronchial disease 12/7/62.

Kirk, George T.—PVT Co.F 5/5/62. WIA, in arm, Battle of Second Manassas, Va. 8/29/62. Dsh. for wounds 9/7/63.

Kirk, John H.—2CPL Co.F 9/23/61. PVT. WIA, right hip, place unknown. CIA Gettysburg, Pa. 7/3/63. Paroled Pt. Lookout, Md. 2/18/65. Received at Boulware and Cox's Wharves on James River near Richmond for exchange 2/20 to 2/21/65. B. 1836 in Gwinnett Cty., Ga. Pension 1900–06. Bur at Mountain Creek Baptist Ch Cem in Walton Cty., Ga.

Kirkland, Wade—PVT Co.B 2/21/61. Roll for 2/28/65, last on file, shows him AWOL in Newton Cty., Ga. Pension records show he was frl. for 90 days for sickness 4/64. The frl. was extended an additional 90 days. He was never able to return to his unit. B. in 1843. D. in Walker Cty., Ga. in 1916.

Knight, Doctor O.—PVT Co.G 9/7/62. Roll for Nov.-Dec. 1864 shows stoppage of pay for 12 months for general court martial. Roll for 2/28/65 shows him present. NLR.

Knight, James M.—PVT Co.G 9/16/61. WIA 1864. Captured in Richmond hospital 4/3/65. Released at Newport News, Va. 6/26/65.

Knight, Jesse—PVT Co.F 3/13/62. Admitted to Receiving and Wayside Hospital at Richmond 3/12/65. Frl. for 30 days 3/13/65.

Knight, John T.—PVT Co.F 11/10/62. Roll for 2/28/65 shows him present. Surrendered at Appomattox, Va. 4/9/65. B. in Ga. 1842.

Knight, Joseph N.—PVT Co.F 9/23/61. WIA at Riddle's Shop, Va. 6/13/64. Roll for 2/28/65 shows him AWOL since 9/9/64.

Knight, Josiah—PVT Co.G 9/16/61. D. 4/8/62.

Knight, Nathaniel D.—PVT Co.D 5/10/62. Listed as disabled and sent on detail duty at Govt. Shops at Atlanta, Ga. as blacksmith 1/11/63. Indigent pension 1897. B. 2/12/1828 in Chesterfield, S.C. D. 8/99 in LaGrange, Ga. Widow pension 1901.

Knight, Robert W.—3SG Co.F 9/23/61. Elected Jr. 2LT 6/6/62. WIA Mechanicsville, Va. 6/26/62. WIA, right thigh, at Malvern Hill, Va. 7/1/62. Resigned on account of wounds 10/29/62. Pension 1889–94. D. 11/10/1894 in Gwinnett Cty., Ga.

Knight, Thomas B.—PVT Co.F 9/23/61. AWOL 8/21/64 to 2/28/65. Pension records show he was captured and carried to Baltimore, Md. where he was a POW for 6 months. B. in Gwinnett Cty., Ga. 1833.

Knight, Thomas W.—PVT Co.F 9/23/61. Roll for 12/62 shows him, "Absent, sick, sent to hospital 9/25/62." NLR.

Knight, William J.—PVT Co.F 9/23/61. Surrendered at Appomattox, Va. 4/9/65.

Knight, William R.—4SG Co.F 9/23/61. Appointed 3SG 9/62. WIA and CIA Gettysburg, Pa. 7/3/63. D. of wounds.

Roster L

Lane, Joel B.—PVT Co.C 9/17/61. D. at Richmond 6/20/62.

Lane, John A.—4CPL Co.C 9/17/61. KIA Seven Pines, Va. 5/31/62.

Lane, Richard Q.—PVT Co.C 9/17/61. WIA Seven Pines, Va. 5/31/62. D. in General Hsp.#2 at Lynchburg, Va. from wounds and chronic diarrhea 9/17/62. Bur. there at Confederate Cemetery No.3, 3rd Line, Lot 179-Miller's.

Langley, Enoch—PVT Co.F 2/12/64. At home on sick frl. 2/28/65. NLR.

Langley, Oswell T.—PVT Co.F 7/8/64. Surrendered Appomattox, Va. 4/9/65.

Langston, James O.—PVT Co.C 4/23/62. Appointed CPL. KIA Spotsylvania C.H., Va 5/12/64.

Langston, Robert E.—PVT Co.C 4/23/62. D. of measles in Richmond hospital 7/13/62. Bur. there at Hollywood Cemetery—grave M200.

Langston, Thomas M.—PVT Co.C 9/17/61. D. in Winder Hsp. at Richmond of typhoid fever 6/28/62.

Langston, William F.—2CPL Co.C 9/17/61. 1CPL 12/16/61. PVT 12/1/62. Detailed for hsp. duty at Augusta, Ga. 4/16/64. D. in service.

Lanier, David S.—PVT Co.F 9/23/61. WIA Seven Pines, Va. 5/31/62. Dsh., disability, at Atlanta, Ga. 2/25/63. B. 11/24/41 and d. 12/22/1908 and bur. Friendship Primitive Baptist Ch. Cem. on Dogwood Rd. in Gwinnett County, Ga.

Laird, George M.—PVT Co.B 11/1/61. D. of measles at Richmond 12/29/61. Bur. there at Hollywood Cemetery, probably in grave B170.

Laird, John E.—PVT Co.B 9/21/61. D. at Richmond 6/2/62.

Laird, Thomas C.—PVT Co.B 3/5/62. D. 4/23/62.

Laird, Winfield D.—PVT Co.B 9/21/61. WIA Jericho Ford, Va. 5/23/64. Surrendered Appomattox, Va. 4/9/65. B. in Newton Cty., Ga. 5/31/1839.

Latham, Thomas W.—PVT Co.E 8/12/61. Elected 2LT 9/25/62. 1LT. CPT 6/10/63. Surrendered Appomattox, Va. 4/9/65.

Latimer, William Thomas—PVT Co.I 9/25/61. Appointed 4CPL 1862. WIA Mechanicsville, Va. 6/26/62. Roll for 12/62 shows him absent on sick frl. in Chattooga Cty., Ga. NLR.

Lawless, John T.—PVT Co.I 9/25/61. WIA Seven Pines, Va. 5/31/62. On wounded frl. 8/31/62. Wound was in left hand and after an extensive operation the hand was considered useless plus he had a fever. Dsh. for disability at age 35, 10/18/62. NLR.

Lawrence, Anderson—PVT Co.I 9/25/61. Dsh. for hernia at Richmond prior to 8/31/62.

Lawrence, Andrew J.—PVT Co.D. Deserted. Took oath of allegience to US Govt. at Louisville, Ky. and sent north of Ohio River 12/20/63.

Lawrence, Ira L.—PVT Co.I 9/25/61. WIA Seven Pines, Va. 5/31/62. Appointed 3CPL 6/26/62. WIA and CIA Gettysburg, Pa. 7/3/63. D. of wounds in DeCamp General Hospital at David's Island, N.Y. Harbor 8/23/63.

Lawson, A.S.—PVT Co.K 7/4/61. D. 10/24/61.

Lay Theldred S.—PVT Co.D 9/25/63. WIA and CIA near Petersburg, Va. 3/25/65. Severe fracture of left leg from gunshot wound. D. of wounds in Lincoln USA General Hospital at Washington, D.C. Bur. in Confederate section of Arlington National Cemetery.

Layfield, John W.—PVT Co.K 8/14/62. D. of typhoid fever in General Hospital #1 at Lynchburg, Va. 2/12/63. Bur. there in Confederate Cemetery No. 10, 1st Line, Lot 195-Ferguson's.

Layfield, Seth M.—Musician Co.K 7/4/61. Surrendered at Appomattox, Va. 4/9/65.

Layfield, Urba H.—PVT Co.K 7/4/61. CIA Wilderness, Va. 5/5/64. Released at Elmira, N.Y. 7/7/65. D. at Chipley, Ga.

Leatherwood, William J.—PVT Co.C 9/17/61. D. at Richmond 11/27/61.

Leatherwood, William Y.—PVT Co.C 2/16/62. KIA Seven Pines, Va. 5/31/62.

Lee, Joseph—PVT Co.D 9/23/65. Roll for 2/28/65 shows him present. NLR.

Lester, Francis M.—PVT Co.B 2/28/62. WIA Fredericksburg, Va. 12/13/62. D. from wounds at Chimborazo Hospital at Richmond 12/18/62.

Lester, Henry—PVT Co.B 2/28/62. WIA Seven Pines, Va. 5/31/62. D. at Camp Winder near Richmond 7/2/62.

Lester, Robert—PVT Co.B 2/28/62. WIA Seven Pines, Va. and d. on battlefield same day 5/31/62.

Lewis, Jesse L.—PVT Co.E 4/23/62. KIA 2nd Manassas, Va. 8/29/62 and bur. there.

Lewis, Samuel Bailey—PVT Co.E 4/23/62. Appointed 4CPL 1864. Surrendered Appomattox, Va. 4/9/65. B. in Campbell Cty, Ga. in 1841. After war returned to Fayette County and married Lucy Hilsman in 1867. Served as postmaster and a judge after war. D. 12/2/1924 and bur. in Fayetteville Cemetery.

Lindley, John—PVT Co.E 8/12/61. Dsh. 7/30/62.

Lindley, Jonathan—PVT Co.E 8/12/61. Dsh., disability and over-age (age 60) 11/14/61. B. in S.C.

Lindsey, Thomas, Jr.—PVT Co.B 9/21/61. D. at Evansport, Va. 12/18/61.

Liner, James M.—PVT Co.A 5/1/62. Roll for 2/28/62 shows him AWOL since frl. expired 11/20/63. NLR.

Liner, John M.—PVT Co.A 5/1/62. D. at Gordonsville, Va. from typhoid fever 8/8/62.

Liner, Wyatt V.—2SG Co.A 8/15/61. Appointed 1SG 10/11/62. Elected 2LT 1863. WIA Cold Harbor, Va. 6/4/64. D. of wounds 6/7/64.

Little, John W.—PVT Co.A 9/19/61. WIA Seven Days Battles near Richmond. WIA 2nd Manassas, Va. 8/29/62. Trn. to Co.H, 1st Ga. Cav. Rgt. 6/1/63. Roll for 12/64 shows him AWOL. NLR.

Livingston, G.W.—PVT Co.K 3/4/62. D. 5/5/62.

Livsey, Robert T.—PVT Co.F 5/3/62. WIA 2nd Manassas, Va. 8/29/62. Roll for 2/28/65 shows him AWOL since 2/21/65. NLR.

Long, William J.T.—PVT Co.E 8/12/61. Appointed 3CPL 1862. CIA Petersburg, Va. 4/3/65. Released at Hart's Island, N.Y. 6/15/65.

Longshore, Young W.—PVT Co.A 8/15/61. D. at Fredericksburg, Va. 12/21 or 12/27/61.

Lowery, Jiles Jasper—PVT Co.A 8/15/61. KIA Gaines Mill, Va. 6/27/62.

Lucas, George A.—PVT Co. B 2/23/62. WIA Fredericksburg, Va. 12/13/62. Appointed 5SG for gallantry in battle 1864. 3SG 1864. Surrendered Appomattox, Va. 4/9/65. B. in Newton Cty., Ga. 1/15/1841.

Lucas, James K.P.—PVT Co.B 2/11/62. D. from typhoid fever at Guinea Station, Va. 6/11/63.

Lucas, Jefferson J.—PVT Co.B 2/11/62. D. 4/23/62.

Lucas, John F.—PVT Co.B 9/21/61. WIA, in arm necessitating amputation, Seven Pines, Va. 5/31/62. Dsh. 6/24/62.

Lyons, James H.—PVT Co.K 11/28/61. Dsh. 12/6/62.

Lyons, Nathan—PVT Co.K 7/4/61. Dsh. 12/5/61. Reenlisted. Admitted to CSA General Hospital at Danville, Va. for debility 7/11/63. Returned to duty 8/4/63. NLR.

Lyons, Robert C., Jr.—PVT Co.K 7/4/61. D. of diarrhea in Jackson Hospital at Richmond 7/27/64. Bur. there at Hollywood Cemetery—grave V299.

Lyons, Robert C., Sr.—PVT Co.K 7/4/61. Sick in Richmond hospital 2/28/65. NLR.

Roster M

MacFarlane, Charles Heard (or McFarland or McFarlan)—PVT Co.K 7/4/61. Surrendered Appomattox, Va. 4/9/65. Pension roll 1910. B. 11/1843 and d. 9/1/1912, bur Hillview Cem on Franklin Rd in LaGrange, Ga. Wife, Lantha Ada Amoss b. 5/27/49 and d. 4/19/1935.

Maddox, Jacob N.—PVT Co.B 2/28/62. WIA Seven Pines, Va. 5/31/62 and d. on battlefield same day.

Maddox, William Jackson—PVT Co.B 9/21/61. CIA near Petersburg, Va. 3/25/65. Released at PT. Lookout, Md. 6/15/65.

Mann, Jesse A.—PVT Co.A 8/15/61. Roll for 2/28/65 shows him AWOL after frl. expired on 12/20/63. NLR.

Mann, John A.—PVT Co.B 2/16/62. Surrendered Appomattox, Va. 4/9/65.

Mann, William T.—PVT Co.B 9/21/61. WIA Seven Pines, Va. 5/31/62. D. in 3rd Ga. Hospital at Richmond same day.

Marbut, Burr Johnson—PVT Co.B 2/24/62. Roll for 2/28/65 shows him present. NLR.

Marshall, John—PVT Co.I 2/18/62. D. at Ashland, Va. 4/30/62.

Martin, Absalom—PVT Co.H 9/24/61. KIA Chancellorsville, Va. 5/3/63.

Martin, Dallas A.C.—PVT Co.D 10/11/61. Appointed 4SG 9/30/64. 3SG 12/64. Surrendered at Appomattox, Va. 4/9/65.

Martin, Josiah P.—PVT Co.D 9/17/62. CIA Jericho Ford, Va. 5/24/64. Paroled at Pt. Lookout, Md. and trn. to Aiken's Landing, Va. for exchange 3/14/65.

Martin, Philo B.—PVT Co.H 2/28/63. Appointed 4CPL 1864. D. of disease in Howard's Grove Hospital at Richmond 7/7/64.

Masser, J.S.—PVT Co.A 8/15/61. D. at Richmond 10/17/62. Bur. there at Hollywood Cemetery—grave V129

Masters, James B.—PVT Co.G 9/16/61. Admitted to Chimborazo Hospital #2 at Richmond for debility 6/14/63. Trn. to Camp Jackson, Va. 8/5/63. Pension records show he was dsh. for disability 3/64. B. 1815 in Spartanburg, S.C. Pension 1895–1902.

Mattox, William M.—PVT Co.A 8/15/61. Appointed 4SG 1863. WIA at Riddle's (Riddell's) Shop, Va. 6/13/64. Roll for 2/28/65 shows him AWOL since 10/31/64. NLR.

Mayfield, William W.—PVT Co.K 3/2/62. Roll for 2/28/65 shows him AWOL. NLR.

McBean, Daniel S.—3SG Co.G 9/16/61. Elected 2SG 1/14/62. 1SG 4/62. Surrendered Appomattox, Va. 4/9/65. B. 10/19/1832. Doctor after war. D. 7/19/1877 and bur Loganville Memorial Gardens in Walton Cty., Ga.

McBride, Samuel L.—PVT Co.A 8/15/61. WIA Mechanicsville, Va. 6/26/62. CIA Rapidan Station, Va. 11/4/63. Paroled at Pt. Lookout, Md. Took oath of allegience to US Govt. and released 2/18/64. Enlisted in US service 2/64.

McCalla, Charles R.—3CPL Co.B 9/21/61. Appointed 1CPL 1864. WIA, arm and left shoulder near Petersburg, Va. 3/25/65. In field hospital at Petersburg, Va. at close of war. B. in Newton Cty., 4/5/1845.

McCart, John—PVT Co.F 9/23/61. Roll for 2/28/65 shows him AWOL since 9/17/63. Pension 1895. D. 3/1908.

McCollum, William M.—PVT Co.I 9/25/61. WIA Chancellorsville, Va. 5/3/63. Elected Jr. 2LT 6/30/64. Appointed Acting Adj. 1864. Adj. Surrendered Appomattox, Va. 4/9/65. D. 3/3/1921 and bur South Carolina Campground Cem on Ga. Hwy 100 north of Holland, Ga in Chattooga Cty., Ga. B. 1/27/42.

McCormick, George W.—PVT Co.E 8/12/61. WIA at Seven Pines, Va. 5/31/62 and taken to 1st Georgia Hsp in Richmond. D. 10/21/62.

McCullohs, Daniel N.—PVT Co.K 3/4/62. Appointed Ord. SGT 1862. Roll for 2/28/65 shows him AWOL. NLR.

McCullohs, William H.—CPT Co.K 7/4/61. Elected MAJ 7/3/62. LTC 11/1/62. On sick frl. 2/28/65. B. Talbot Cty., Ga. 11/1839. Married Martha Maria Lowe. D. at Waverly Hall in Harris Cty., Ga., and bur there, 7/18/1912, age 73.

McCutcheon, James—PVT Co.H 9/24/61. Admitted to General Hospital at Farmville, Va. 11/14/62. Returned to duty 12/19/62. Frl. for 60 days from 12/20/62. NLR.

McDaniel, Daniel R.—PVT Co.F 9/23/61. WIA, left arm, requiring amputation, 2nd Manassas, Va. 8/29/62. Captured and paroled, Warrenton, Va. 9/30/62. Dsh. for disability 10/12/62. Pension 1879–1907.

McDaniel, James P.—PVT Co.B 2/28/62. Captured while sick in Richmond hospital 4/3/65. D. 4/18/65.

McDaniel, James W.—PVT Co.F 12/23/63. Surrendered Appomattox, Va. 4/9/65.

McDaniel, John J.—PVT Co.F 9/23/65. Appointed 5SG 12/17/61. 1SG 11/1/62. WIA, in leg requiring amputation above knee, Fredericksburg, Va. 12/13/62. Retired to Invalid Corps 3/15/65. Pension roll 1893–1907. B. 7/24/31 and D. 6/3/1917 and bur. at Bethesda United Methodist Ch. Cem. near Lawrenceville, Ga.

McDaniel, William Franklin—PVT Co.B 8/8/63. Surrendered Appomattox, Va. 4/9/65.

McDonald, Young—PVT Co.B 9/21/61. Dsh., disability and over-age 1863.

McElvany, James Thomas—1LT Co.F 9/23/61. Elected CPT 5/9/62. WIA, struck in head (left temple) by shell fragment, Cedar Mtn., Va. 8/9/62. Elected MAJ 5/19/64. On sick frl. 2/28/65 to end of war. B. in Gwinnett Cty., Ga. 12/3/1834. Pension roll 1899–1901. D. 2/4/1901. School teacher at beginning of war. Gwinnett County Sheriff 1868–1870. Elected from Gwinnett Cty to State House of Representatives 1882.

McElvany, William A.—PVT Co.F 4/12/64. KIA Jericho Ford, Va. 5/23/64. B. 4/16/1846 in Ga.

McGaha, Joseph—PVT Co.A 8/15/61. Arrested for desertion 12/63 and sent to Camp of Instruction at Decatur, Ga. Deserted 6/21/64.

McGehee, James T.—PVT Co.K 3/4/62. WIA Spotsylvania C.H., Va. 5/12/64. Sick in Columbus, Ga. hospital with measles 2/28/65. Afterward, on sick frl at home. D. 6/1919 in Harris Cty., Ga. Widow pension 1919.

McGiboney, Jeremiah—PVT Co.G 5/12/62. Trn. to Co.A in 1863. Surrendered Appomattox, Va. 4/9/65. B. 1830 in Green Cty., Ga. Widow, Sarah, pension 1901–07.

McGuffey, John W.—PVT Co.D. Pension records show he enlisted in spring 1862. WIA, head and right arm and right leg, Spotsylvania C.H., Va. 5/12/64. At home on frl. at close of war. Pension 1923. B. in Ga. 1847. D. 12/30/1936 and bur Mt. Vernon Cem. at Monroe, Ga.

McHargue, William—PVT Co.A 2/25/62. D. of lung congestion and measles 4/24/62.

McKibbin, James E.—PVT Co.E 2/24/62. Admitted to Chimborazo Hsp #4 at Richmond with gunshot wound to right fingers 7/13/63. Trn. to Jackson Hsp. at Richmond 8/7/63. D. of chronic diarrhea in Lynchburg, Va. hospital 6/11/64. Bur. there in Confederate Cemetery No.5, Line ?, Lot 201-Knight's.

McKinzey, Dolphin T.—PVT Co.H 9/24/61. WIA Mechanicsville, Va. 6/26/62. D. from wounds at Richmond 7/27/62.

McKinzey, George W.—PVT Co.H 9/24/61. WIA Seven Pines, Va.5/31/62. D. of disease at Richmond 7/17/62.

McKinzey, William L.—3CPL Co.H 9/24/61. PVT. On sick frl. for 40 days from 1/23 to 3/3/65. NLR.

McLure, Charles P.—PVT Co.E 8/12/61. KIA at Seven Pines, Va. 5/31/62.

McMahan, Robert—PVT Co.E 8/12/61. D. of disease at Evansport, Va. 12/7/61 and bur there.

McWhorter, Arthur W.—PVT Co.A 7/1/62. CIA near Petersburg, Va. 3/25/65. Released at Pt. Lookout, Md. 6/29/65.

McWhorter, Masselona (Loney)—PVT Co.A 7/1/62. CIA near Petersburg, Va. 6/22/64. Paroled at Pt. Lookout, Md. for exchange 3/15/65. Received at Boulware & Cox's Wharves on James River near Richmond 3/18/65.

McWhorter, William M.—PVT Co.C 2/20/62. WIA 2nd Manassas, Va. 8/30/62. Deserted. Took oath of allegience to US Govt. at Wash. D.C. and furnished transportation to Cairo, Ill. 3/30/65.

McWright, John W.—PVT Co.H 3/1/64. Appointed 3CPL 1864. Paroled at Burkeville Junction, Va. 4/14 to 4/17/65. B. in Gwinnett Cty., Ga. 5/1838. Pension roll 1900. Probably d. 8/1905 and bur Buford City Cem. in Buford, Ga.

Meadows, A.T.—PVT Co.K 2/16/64. D. of chronic diarrhea in Jackson Hospital at Richmond 6/25/64. Bur. there at Hollywood Cemetery.

Meadows, James M.—PVT Co.E 8/12/61. Roll for 12/62 shows him, "Absent at hospital." NLR.

Mercer, Alexander H.R.—PVT Co.D 9/23/61. D. of disease at Fredericksburg, Va. 4/8/62.

Mercer, Madison—PVT Co.D 3/4/62. CIA at Williamsburg, Va. 5/6/62. Exchanged. WIA during May-June 64. D. of wounds 10/16/64.

Meriwether, Henry A.—PVT Co.B 5/1/63. Detailed courier for BG Thomas 1864. D. at Dunlap Station, Va. 2/5/65. B. 1845. Bur. at Oxford Historic Cemetery in Oxford, Ga.

Mertett, B.A.—PVT Co.B 2/28/62. Surrendered Appomattox, Va. 4/9/65.

Mickler, James D.—PVT Co.H 9/24/61. Appointed 5SG 6/20/62. Surrendered Appomattox, Va. 4/9/65.

Miers, David C.—PVT Co.B 9/21/61. CIA Wilderness, Va. 5/6/64. Released Pt. Lookout, Md. 1865.

Milam, Wiley B.—PVT Co.E 8/12/61. WIA Seven Pines, Va. 5/31/62. CIA Gettysburg, Pa. 7/3/63. D. at Pt. Lookout Prison, Md. 11/17/63.

Miles, John F.—PVT Co.K 7/4/61. Dsh. for disability 9/23/61. D. in 1862.

Miles, John J.—PVT Co.C 4/23/62. WIA Seven Pines, Va. 5/31/62. WIA Gettysburg, Pa. 7/3/63. WIA Wilderness, Va. 5/6/64. Appointed 3CPL 5/12/64. WIA, left hand shattered, Spotsylvania C.H., Va. 5/12/64. Retired 2/8/65. B. in Coweta Cty., Ga. 11/5/41.

Miles, Lewis P.—PVT Co.C 9/17/61. Detailed nurse at Camp Winder Hospital at Richmond 10/62. D. of pneumonia at Staunton, Va. 1/15/64.

Milford, John W.—2LT Co.E 8/12/61. KIA 2nd Manassas, Va. 8/30/62.

Miller, Alexander—PVT Co.C 9/17/61. CIA Falling Waters, Md. 7/14/63. Sent to Pt. Lookout, Md. where he d. 2/19/64.

Miller, Simeon—PVT Co.C 4/25/62. Trn. to Co.A 5/31/64. AWOL 2/16 to 2/28/65. NLR.

Miller, William—PVT Co.I 9/25/61. D. of pneumonia at Dumfries, Va. 12/21/61.

Millican, Lewis J.—PVT Co.I 3/3/62. KIA Chancellorsville, Va. 5/3/63. His body may have been shipped home for burial since there is a marker in Bethel Presbyterian Cem. in Chattooga Cty., Ga. B. 2/6/1827.

Millican, Robert A.—PVT Co.I 2/22/62. WIA Seven Pines, Va. 5/31/62. CIA Wilderness, Va. 5/5/64. Released Elmira, N.Y. 6/23/65.

Minor, Americus Miles—PVT Co.F 8/12/63. WIA Spotsylvania C.H., Va. 5/12/64. Roll for 2/28/65 shows him AWOL since 10/31/64. B. at Stone Mtn., Ga. 8/6/45. NLR.

Minor, Coleman—PVT Co.G 3/1/62. D. of disease at Liberty (Bedford), Va. 7/13/62.

Minor, Marcus M.—PVT Co.F 2/8/62. WIA Spotsylvania C.H., Va. 5/12/64. Surrendered Appomattox, Va. 4/9/65. B. in Ga. 8/22/1842. D. 2/15/1926. Bur. Nash, Walker Cem. in Lilburn, Ga.

Minor, William D.—PVT Co.F 2/16/62. D. in Winder Hospital at Richmond 7/2/62. Bur. there at Hollywood Cemetery—grave M174.

Mitcham, James M.—PVT Co.B 9/21/61. Appointed 2SG 11/62. Elected 2LT 2/7/63. CPT of Sharpshooters 1864. WIA Spotsylvania C.H., Va. 5/12/64. In charge of Rgt. Litter Corps 1864. Surrendered Appomattox, Va 4/9/65. D. 11/8/1908. Widow filed for pension 1919.

Mitcham, Joseph D.—PVT Co.B 2/24/62.WIA Spotsylvania C.H., Va. 5/12/64. Roll for 2/28/65 shows him present. NLR.

Mitcham, Milton C.—PVT Co.B 2/24/62. Admitted to CSA General Hospital at Danville, Va. 6/29/62. Returned to duty 7/23/62. Sick in Camp Winder Hospital at Richmond 5/31/62. Trn to Co.A, Cobb's Legion Ga. Inf. in exchange for Algernon S.W. Bass in 1862. Roll for July-Aug. 1864 shows he deserted.

Mitcham, Thomas J.—PVT Co.B 9/21/61. WIA Seven Pines, Va. 5/31/62. D. of wounds 6/27 or 7/2/62.

Mitcham, William J.—PVT Co.B 2/28/62. D. of disease at home in Ga. on 6/29/63.

Mitchell, Elisha—PVT Co.B 3/5/62. Roll shows, "Deserted, or rather failed to join company by 4/4/62." NLR.

Mitchell, H.L.—PVT Co.G 4/18/64. Surrendered Appomattox, Va. 4/9/65.

Mitchell, John M.—1LT Co.D 9/23/61. Elected CPT 12/21/63. Retired to Invalid Corps after numerous illnesses like chronic hepatitus and chronic diarrhea 8/3/64.

Mitchell, Reuben L.—PVT Co.C 2/27/62. Dsh. for disability 5/12/62.

Mitchell, Thomas C.—PVT Co.G 5/18/64. Roll for 2/28/65 shows him at home on frl. of indulgence. B. 2/12/1845 in Walton Cty., Ga. Pension roll 1902.

Mobley, David Harrison—1CPL Co.G 9/16/61. Home on sick furlough 5/62 and missed Battle of Seven Pines. WIA Wilderness, Va. 5/6/64 in right leg between knee and ankle.Appointed 5SG 1864. Detailed as Commissary Sgt. Surrendered at Appomattox, Va. 4/9/65. B. 6/16/40 in Walton Cty., Ga. Pension roll 1898–1901.

Mobley, Daniel I.—PVT Co.G 9/16/61. D. at Richmond 6/13/62. Brother of D.H. Mobley.

Mobley, Henry C.—PVT Co.G 9/16/61. D. at Richmond 7/24/62. Bur. there at Hollywood Cemetery—grave O326. Uncle of D.H. Mobley.

Mobley, John Ephraim David—PVT Co.G 5/12/62. Surrendered Appomattox, Va. 4/9/65. B. 8/17/1831. D. 7/1/1888 and bur Mobley Family Cem. in Walton Cty., Ga. Uncle of D.H. Mobley.

Moody, Benjamin Franklin—PVT Co.E 8/12/61. Brigade wagoner for short period 12/61to 1/62. Color-Corporal 6/10/62. KIA Mechanicsville, Va. 6/26/62 and buried on field in unknown grave by brigade burial detail. B. 1/3/29. Wheat/cotton farmer in Georgia.

Moon, Andrew J.—PVT Co.B 2/28/62. WIA Spotsylvania C.H., Va. 5/12/64. WIA on Charles City Rd. east of Richmond 6/13/64. D. from wounds 6/15/64. Son of Joseph Moon in Walton Cty.

Moon, Augustus J.—PVT Co.G 3/63. Frl 2/65 and on frl at surrender. CIA Chancellorsville, Va. 5/3/63 and exchanged 10 days later. B. 3/15/1842 in Walton Cty., Ga. Pension 1908. D. 12/5/1922. Son of Joseph Moon in Walton Cty.

Moon, Charles Knox Polk—PVT Co.G 4/18/64. Surrendered Appomattox, Va. 4/9/65. B. 1847 in Walton Cty., Ga. Pension roll 1899–1906. D. at Atlanta, Ga. 8/16/1925. Bur. at Hillcrest Cem. in Walton Cty., Ga. Son of Joseph Moon in Walton Cty.

Moon, Edom T.—PVT Co.G 9/16/61. WIA 5/62. Appointed 4CPL 1864. Surrendered Appomattox, Va. 4/9/65. Son of Joseph Moon in Walton Cty. B. 12/14/1845. D. 11/1908 and bur. Haynes Creek Primitive Baptist Church Cem. in Gwinnett Cty., Ga.

Moon, George W.—PVT Co.G 1863. Son of Joseph Moon in Walton Cty.

Moon, John A.—PVT Co.G 4/8/64. CIA Petersburg, Va. 3/25/65. Released Pt. Lookout, Md. 5/14/65.

Moon, Joseph D.—PVT Co.G 9/16/61. Appointed 1SG 7/21/62. Roll for 2/28/65 shows him at home on frl. of indulgence. This soldier was possibly referred to as 'DeKalb' Moon and was possibly another son of Joseph Moon in Walton Cty. NLR.

Moon, M.L.—PVT Co.G 9/16/61. Surrendered Appomattox, Va. 4/9/65.

Moon, Stephen LaFayette—3CPL Co.G 9/16/61. Appointed 5SG 1864. Elected Jr. 2LT 7/64. WIA on left arm during Seven Days Battles near Richmond 6/62. WIA Petersburg, Va. 7/3/64. Captured in Richmond hospital 4/3/65. Reported to have escaped from the hospital 4/28/65. B. 10/28/1834. D. 3/18/1911 at Loganville, Ga. and bur Hillcrest Cem. in Walton Cty., Ga. Widow pension 1919. Son of Joseph Moon in Walton Cty.

Moon, Thomas L.—PVT Co.G 9/16/61. D. of disease at Winchester, Va. 11/10/62.

Moon, Thomas Monroe—PVT Co.G 4/18/64. Roll for 2/28/65 shows him present. B. 5/25/1845. D. in Walton Cty., Ga. 6/1/1890.and bur Corinth Memorial Gardens in Walton Cty., Ga. Son of William E. Moon.

Moon, William E.—PVT Co.G 2/28/62. Roll for 2/28/65 shows him at home on frl. of indulgence. Thomas Monroe Moon was his son. Son of Joseph Moon in Walton Cty. NLR.

Moon, Woodson D.—PVT Co.G 5/8/62. KIA at Jericho Ford, Va. 5/23/64. B. 2/15/33 in Walton Cty., Ga. Farmer.

Moore, Elliott J.—PVT Co.C 2/28/62. WIA Fredericksburg, Va. 12/13/62. Trn. Co.K. KIA near Petersburg, Va. 3/25/65.

Moore, Green W.—PVT Co.B 9/21/61. D. of disease at Bunker Hill, Va. 6/5/63.

Moore, Jesse Spencer—5SG Co.C 9/17/61. Trn. to Co.K, 35th Ga. Inf. Rgt. Surrendered at Appomattox, Va. 4/9/65.

Moore, John J.—PVT Co.G 9/21/61. Served as wagoner. Roll for 2/28/65 shows him present. B. 8/16/1829 in Walton Cty., Ga. Pension roll 1897–1907. D. 5/30/1914 and bur Hillcrest Cem. in Walton Cty., Ga.

Moore, Micajah C.—PVT Co.B 9/21/61. D. from typhoid fever at Fredericksburg, Va. 1/8/62.

Moore, Robert—PVT Co.D 2/21/62. Deserted 3/10/62.

Moore, Thomas F.—PVT Co.B 2/28/62. CIA Chester Gap, Va. 7/23/63. Took oath of allegience to US Govt. at Old Capitol Prison at Washington, D.C. 9/23/63. Released and sent to Philadelphia, Pa. 9/24/63.

Moore, Wilson J. (Quincy)—4CPL Co.D 9/23/61. Appointed 5SG. WIA Gaines Mill, Va. 6/27/62. Ambulance driver January 64, May–June 64. Surrendered at Appomattox, Va. 4/9/65.

Mooty, John R.—PVT Co.D 9/23/61. Roll for 2/28/65 shows him present. NLR.

Morgan, David W.—PVT Co.B 9/21/61. CIA 7/12/63. Paroled 9/63. CIA Petersburg, Va. 6/64. Roll for 2/28/65 lists him as POW. NLR.

Morgan, John William Sharp—PVT Co.K 7/4/61. Appointed Color SGT 6/1/62. KIA Gettysburg, Pa. 7/2/63.

Morris, John F.—Jr. 2LT Co.E 8/12/61. Roll for 8/31/62 last on record. Found not guilty of cowardice during court-martial on 3/1/63. NLR.

Morris, Thomas J.—2CPL Co.A 8/15/61. D. in Haralson Cty., Ga. 9/12/62.

Morse, Samuel F.—PVT Co.E 8/12/61. Appointed 1CPL 10/62. WIA Fredericksburg, Va. 12/13/62. In Lynchburg, Va. hospital 12/31/62. WIA, date/place unknown. Dsh. for paralyzed arm, resulting from wounds, 3/22/64.

Morton, Azariah—PVT Co.I 2/1/62. D. in Richmond 6/23/62. Bur. there at Hollywood Cemetery.

Morton, Benjamin W.—2LT Co.D 9/23/61. Elected 1LT 12/21/63. Retired to Invalid Corps 4/30/64. Assigned to Commandant of Conscripts in Georgia 5/6/64.

Morton, J.—PVT Co.D 9/23/61. D. at Richmond 6/22/62. Bur. there at Hollywood Cemetery—grave O170.

Morton, Thomas D.—PVT Co.D 6/17/64. Roll for Sept.-Oct. 1864 shows he was dsh.

Morton, Thomas F.—PVT Co.I 9/25/61. Appointed 2SG 1861. D. in Richmond hospital 5/9/62.

Morton, Thomas R.—PVT Co.I 9/25/61. WIA Cedar Mtn., Va. 8/9/62. CIA Spotsylvania C.H., Va. 5/12/64. Exchanged at Ft. Delaware, Del. 3/7/65. Received at Boulware & Cox's Wharves on James River 3/10–12/65. B.4/2/1839. Pension roll 1902. Lived near Subligna, Ga. D. 2/14/1915 and bur in Subligna Methodist Ch. Cem. in Chattooga Cty., Ga.

Morton, Zachariah T.—PVT Co.I 9/25/61. D. in Ashland, Va. hospital 4/17/62.

Moughon, Peyton—PVT Co.G 9/21/61. Surrendered Appomattox, Va. 4/9/65.

Moughon, William A.—4CPL Co.G 9/16/61. Dsh. 7/25/62.

Murdock, John R.—PVT Co.I 2/19/62. WIA, 2 fingers shot off, Gaines Mill, Va. 6/27/62. CIA near Petersburg, West Virginia 2/64. Roll for 6/64/ shows him present. Pension roll 1890. D. 2/26/1928 and bur in Little Sand Mountain Baptist Cem. in Chattooga Cty., Ga. near Summerville. B. 4/7/40.

Murdock, Joseph M.—PVT Co.I 3/3/62. D. while home on sick frl. 5/2/63.

Murdock, Richard F.—PVT Co.I 3/4/62. CIA Spotsylvania C.H., Va. 5/12/64. Paroled at Ft. Delaware, Del. 2/65. Received at Boulware & Cox's Wharves on James River, Va. for exchange 3/10/65.

Murphy, Hugh A.—PVT Co.K 7/4/61. Admitted to General Hospital at Howard's Grove in Richmond with smallpox. 3/6/63. D. 3/12/63. Widow, Mary, pension 1891.

Roster N

Nash, Amos B.—PVT Co.F 9/23/61. D. of disease in 3rd Hospital at Dumfries, Va. 1/27/62.

Needham, Samuel L.—PVT Co.G 3/1/62. Roll for 2/28/65 shows him home on sick frl. NLR.

Needham, William B.—PVT Co.G 2/3/64. CIA Petersburg, Va. 4/3/65. Released at Hart's Island, N.Y. Harbor 6/15/65.

Neely, Andrew J.—PVT Co.C 9/17/61. D. at Evansport, Va. 12/27/61.

Neely, James Henry—PVT Co.C 5/5/62. Roll for 2/28/65 shows him AWOL at Palmetto, Ga. since 2/9/65.

Neely, John W.—PVT Co.C 9/17/61. KIA at 2nd Manassas, Va. 8/29/62.

Neely, Mathew W.—PVT Co.C 10/31/62. CIA at Richmond 4/3/65. Released from General Hospital at Pt. Lookout, Md. 7/7/65.

New, Elijah B.—PVT Co.I 2/15/62. D. of chronic diarrhea in General Hospital #12 at Greensboro 12/1/64.

New, Henry K.—PVT Co.A 8/15/61. D. at Ashland, Va. 5/2/62.

New, James M.—PVT Co.A 8/15/61. D. 3/14/62.

New, Jesse W.—PVT Co.I 10/1/62. Roll for 12/31/62 shows him present. Possibly MIA.

New, John W.—PVT Co.A 3/4/62. Roll for 2/28/65 shows him AWOL since 5/1/64. NLR.

New, John W.—PVT Co.I 9/25/61. Received pay at Richmond 3/28/64. NLR.

New, Luke L.—PVT Co.A 8/15/61. Surrendered Appomattox, Va. 4/9/65.

Newsome, James A. (or Newsom)—PVT Co.F 3/13/62. Roll for 2/28/65 shows him AWOL since 2/10/65. B. in Morgan Cty., Ga. 11/17/44. NLR.

Newsome, James O.—PVT Co.B 3/8/62. CIA at Falling Waters, Md. 7/14/63. Paroled at Pt. Lookout, Md. for exchange 3/3/64. Received at City Pt., Va. 3/6/64. Roll for 2/28/65 shows him AWOL in Georgia. NLR.

Newsome, John W. (or Newsom)—PVT Co.F 9/23/61. D. of typhoid pneumonia in Winder Hospital at Richmond 8/2/62.

Nix, Francis W.—PVT Co.B 2/13/64. CIA Harper's Farm, Va. 4/6/65. Released at Newport News, Va. 6/26/65. D. 7/1865 from exposure and hardship. Widow, Martha, filed for widow's pension 1891–1898.

Nix, Riley J.—PVT Co.F 9/23/61. WIA Gaines Mill, Va. 6/27/62. D. of wounds 6/28/62.

Nixon, John F.—PVT Co.E 8/12/61. KIA 2nd Manassas, Va. 8/30/62.

Noblitt, William M.—PVT Co.A 3/25/64. Dsh. prior to 6/30/64 for being under-age.

Norris, James W.—PVT Co.D 2/28/62. Appointed 1CPL 1864. CIA Milford Station, Va. 5/24/64. D. of disease at Pt. Lookout, Md. 9/21 or 9/24/64.

Nunnally, James H.—PVT Co.G 9/16/61. Surrendered Appomattox, Va. 4/9/65. Pension roll 1889–1907.

Roster O

O'Bryant, Cornelius A.—PVT Co.I 2/22/62. D. in Ashland, Va. hospital 4/1/62.

Odom, Elkanah—PVT Co.B 2/15/64. CIA near Petersburg, Va. 3/25/65. Released Pt. Lookout, Va. 6/29/65.

Odom, John H.—PVT Co.B 9/21/61. WIA Mechanicsville, Va. 6/26/62. CIA Wilderness, Va. 5/6/64. D. of phthisis (tuberculosis of the lungs) at Elmira, N.Y. 10/11/64. Bur. there at Woodlawn National Cemetery—grave #577 WNC.

Oliver, Richard B.G.—PVT Co.D 2/25/62. AWOL from 12/31/62. NLR.

O'Neal, Jesse M.—PVT Co.A 9/19/61. WIA Mechanicsville, Va. 6/26/62. D. from wounds 8/8/62.

Orr, Thomas W.—PVT Co.H 2/1/64. Surrendered Appomattox, Va. 4/9/65. B. in Ga. 1845.

Orr, William H.—PVT Co.H 5/10/63. Surrendered Appomattox, 4/1865.

Osborn, C.R.—PVT Co.G 3/2/64. CIA Jericho Ford, Va. 5/23/64. Exchanged at Elmira, N.Y. 3/14/65. Received at Boulware & Cox's Wharves at James River, Va. 3/18–21/65.

Overby, William—PVT Co.H 9/24/61. KIA accidently at Yorktown, Va. 4/20/62. He was on night advance picket outpost in front of woods when false alarm was given and he was shot by own troops. Widow, Sarah, pension 1891–1905.

Owen, John (or Owens)—PVT Co.A 8/15/61. On 4/1/63 he, "Received commutation of rations while on indulgent furlough—30 days." NLR.

Owens, William R., Sr.—PVT Co.B 9/21/61. CIA Wilderness, Va. 5/6/64. Released Elmira, N.Y. 5/18/65.

Roster P

Page, F.A.—PVT Co.K 3/4/62. Sent to Winchester, Va. for sickness 10/9/62. D. at Staunton, Va. of erysipelas 10/29/62. Bur. there at Thornrose Cemetery.

Page, Reuben—PVT Co.K 3/4/62.

Pannell, Benjamin F.—PVT Co.C 9/17/61. WIA, date and place unknown. D. at Richmond of typhoid fever 11/1/62.

Pannell, William A.—PVT Co.C 9/17/61. CIA Jericho Ford, Va. 5/23/64. Paroled at Pt. Lookout, Md. and trn. to Aiken's Landing, Va. for exchange. Received at Boulware & Cox's Wharf at James River, Va. 3/18/65.

Park, Alonzo Thomas—PVT Co.I 9/25/61. Detailed in Medical Dept 1861. Pension records show he was appointed Hospital Steward in Chattanooga, Tn. hospital 3/63. Surrendered with Hospital Corps at Enterprise, Miss. 1865.

Parker, Asbury G.—PVT Co.C 3/11/62. D. at Ashland, Va. hospital 4 or 5/19/62.

Parker, H.L.—PVT Co.K 7/4/61. Dsh. 11/25/61.

Parker, Joshua F.M.—PVT Co.B 2/19/62. Surrendered Appomattox, Va. 4/9/65.

Parker, Matthew—PVT Co.H 9/24/61. Jan-Mar 1862 on extra duty as butcher. WIA, left leg requiring amputation, and CIA Gettysburg, Pa. 7/3/63. Paroled 9/8/63. Admitted to General Hospital at Petersburg, Va. 9/8/63. Frl. for 60 days 9/16/63. Pension roll 1879.

Parker, Parks W.—PVT Co.C 4/23/62. Roll for 2/28/65 shows him sick in Augusta, Ga. hospital.

Parker, W.W.—PVT Co.I 2/25/62. Surrendered Appomattox, Va. 4/9/65.

Parks, Johnson J.—PVT Co.D 9/23/61. D. of disease at Berryville or Winchester, Va. 11/18/62.

Pass, George B.—PVT Co.H, 1863. D. of chronic diarrhea at General Hospital #3 at Lynchburg, Va. 11/10/63. Bur. there in Old City Cemetery plot 200, row 1, grave 3. The initials "G.P., 35 Ga." are on his marker. B. 3/3/1826 in White County, Tenn. His wife, Frances L. (Green) Pass moved family to Blount Cty, Alabama in 1871. She is buried in the Methodist Cemetery in Cleveland, Al.

Passmore, A.M.—PVT Co.K 7/4/61. Appointed CPL. Dsh. 11/9/61. Reenlisted 3/4/62. KIA 2nd Manassas, Va. 8/29/62.

Passmore, John F.—PVT Co.K 3/4/62. D. 6/26/62.

Passmore, Nathan S.—1CPL Co.K 7/4/61. PVT. CIA Petersburg, Va. 7/21/64. Paroled at Pt. Lookout, Md. and trn to Aiken's Landing, Va. for exd. 3/14/65. Received at Boulware & Cox's Wharf at James River, Va. 3/16/65.

Passmore, W.H.—PVT Co.K 6/11/63. Dsh for deafness and lameness in left leg at age 23, 6/27/63. B. 1841.

Pate, Jesse—PVT Co.K 7/4/61. D. at Fredericksburg, Va. 3/22/62.

Patterson, Jesse C.—PVT Co.C 4/24/62. D. of disease 7/25/62.

Patterson, John W.—PVT Co.C 9/17/61. CIA Wilderness, Va. 5/5/64. D. of chronic diarrhea at Elmira, N.Y. 12/30/64. Bur. there at Woodlawn National Cemetery—grave #1312 WNC.

Patterson, Thomas Elbert—PVT Co.C 9/17/61. Appointed 4SG 7/22/62. Admitted to Ocmulgee Hospital at Macon, Ga. for ulcers 2/4/65. Returned to duty 3/28/65.

Paulett, Henry T.(or L)—PVT Co.E 8/12/61. D. at Lynchburg, Va. 8/17/62. Bur. there in Confederate Cemetery—Longhorne's Factory. Disinterred and sent to Atlanta, Ga.

Payne, Sanford V.—PVT Co.H 9/24/61. D. of pneumonia at General Hospital #14 at Richmond 1/4/63.

Payne, Warren C.—PVT Co.H 9/24/61. D. in Chimborazo Hospital #5 at Richmond 5/29/62.

Payne, William J.B.—PVT Co.H 9/24/61. WIA Seven Pines, Va. 5/31/62. Appointed 2CPL 11/62. CIA Gettysburg, Pa. 7/3/63. D. at Pt. Lookout, Md. 11/10/63.

Peavy, Robert L.—PVT Co.B 2/28/62. CIA Petersburg, Va. 4/2/65. Released Pt. Lookout, Md. 6/17/65.

Peek, William L.—PVT Co.B 2/28/62. Elected 2LT 6/13/62. WIA 2nd Manassas, Va. 8/30/62. Resigned, disabled by rheumatism at Belleview Hospital in Richmond 1/24/63.

Penn, William B.—Appointed Asst. Surgeon 49th Ga. Inf Rgt. 3/9/62. Serving in Medical Dept. in Florida under General Finegan 9/63. Reassigned back to 49th Ga. 11/18/64. Trn. To 35th Ga. Inf Rgt. 1/65. Surrendered Appomattox, Va. 4/9/65.

Pennington, James O.A.—PVT Co.C 9/17/61. Appointed 1SG 10/10/62. Deserted in 7/14/64. Received at Fortress Monroe, Va. as a Confederate deserter 7/19/64. Took oath of allegience to US Govt. Released and sent to Philadelphia, Pa. 7/21/64.

Perry, James A.H.—3SG Co.I 9/25/61. Roll for 12/62 shows him absent on frl. Dsh and d. of disease 1862.

Perry, Lovick P.—PVT Co.I 2/22/62. Roll for 2/28/65 shows him AWOL in Chattooga Cty., Ga. since 1/1/65. NLR.

Perry, W.P.—PVT Co.I 9/25/61. Surrendered Appomattox, Va. 4/9/65.

Peters, Pendleton L.—PVT Co.K 3/4/62. WIA Seven Pines, Va. 5/31/62. WIA 2nd Manassas, Va. 8/29/62. Roll for 2/28/65 shows him absent, wounded. NLR.

Petty, John P.—PVT Co.C 2/24/62. D. in Ashland, Va. hospital 4/11/62.

Petty, Isaac J.—PVT Co.F 8/3/63. CIA Petersburg, Va. 4/1/65. Released Pt. Lookout, Md. 6/17/65.

Phillips, J.P.—PVT Co.F 9/23/61. Surrendered Appomattox, Va. 4/9/65. D. 7/6/1911 in Gwinnett Cty., Ga. Widow, Mahala, pension 1912–1927.

Phillips, Jackson H. (or Jackson A.)—PVT Co.C 11/9/61. D. of chronic diarrhea in General Hospital at Danville, Va. 8/12/62.

Phillips, James H.—PVT Co.D 3/3/62. D. of typhoid pneumonia in Chimborazo Hospital #3 at Richmond 4/11 or 4/18/62.

Phillips, John T.—PVT Co.G 8/24/61. Roll for 12/62 shows him home on frl. NLR.

Phillips, Richard—PVT Co.H 9/24/61. D. at Richmond 4/30/62.

Phillips, Richard J.—Co.H B. 11/28/41 and d. 9/14/1910 bur Warsaw United Meth Ch Cem near Dultuh in Fulton Cty., Ga.

Phillips, Thomas J.—PVT Co.C 4/23/62. WIA, in head, Fredericksburg, Va. 12/13/62. Roll for 6/30/64 shows him present. B. 2/4/38 and d. 2/17/1904 bur Antioch Methodist Ch Cem on Rivertown Rd near Fairburn in Fulton Cty., Ga.

Phillips, William F.—1CPL Co.D 9/23/61. D. of disease at Fredericksburg, Va. 12/23/61.

Pierce, Davis M.—PVT Co.K 7/4/61. Appointed 3CPL 1862. WIA, date/place unknown. Surrendered Appomattox, Va. 4/9/65.

Pierce, George W.—PVT Co.C 9/17/61. WIA, in thigh, at Mechanicsville, Va. 6/26/62. Dsh., disabled by wounds 11/5/63.

Pierce, Joel Harper—PVT Co.K 7/4/61. D. at Richmond 10/19/61.

Pierce, John J.L.—PVT Co.K 7/4/61. CIA near Petersburg, Va. 3/25/65. Released Pt. Lookout, Md. 6/17/65.

Pike, John L.—PVT Co.A 8/15/61. WIA Mechanicsville, Va. 6/26/62. Surrendered Appomattox, Va. 4/9/65.

Pirkle, Andrew J.—PVT Co.H 9/4/63. WIA Spotsylvania C.H., Va. 5/14/64. Roll for 2/28/65 shows him AWOL since 9/16/64. B. in Ga. in 1823. Pension roll 1894.

Pitts, John—PVT Co.B 9/21/61. WIA 2nd Manassas, Va. 8/30/62. D. from wounds 9/1 or 9/17/62.

Plummer, James S.—PVT Co.F 5/5/62. WIA Frederickburg, Va. 12/13/62 and d. there of wounds 12/14/62.

Plummer, John M.—PVT Co.F 9/23/61. KIA Seven Pines, Va. 5/31/62.

Plunkett, David F.—PVT Co.B 9/21/61. D. 4/24/62.

Pollard, Joseph—PVT Co.K 3/4/62.

Pollard, Seaborn—PVT Co.K 3/4/62. Surrendered Appomattox, Va. 4/9/65

Pollard, William—PVT Co.K 3/4/62. CIA Frederick, Md. 10/3/62. Exchanged at Fortress Monroe, Va. 12/8/62. KIA Spotsylvania C.H., Va. 5/12/64.

Ponder, James M.—PVT Co.D 2/28/62. Dsh., furnished Emanuel Head as substitute 7/3/62.

Ponder, James W.—PVT Co.B 9/21/61. D. of disease at Ashland, Va. 4/18/62.

Ponder, Joseph A.—PVT Co.B 2/28/62. D. of disease at Huguenot Springs, Va. 10/30/62. Bur. at Huguenot Springs Confederate Cemetery, Powhatan Cty., Va.

Pope, John C.—PVT Co.B 2/18/62. Listed as MIA after Seven Days Battles 6/62. Dsh. for debility from long attack of typhoid fever from General Hospital at Farmville, Va. 10/13/62. D. in Henry Cty., Ga. and death claim filed by family on 4/3/63.

Powell, Andrew J.—PVT Co.F 1/24/62. D. in Chimborazo Hospital at Richmond 4/1862.

Powell, Charles—PVT Co.F 2/17/62. MIA at Williamburg, Va. 5/5/62. Apparently, he was CIA and sent to USA Hospital at Williamsburg, Va. 5/10/62. D. 6/22/62 while a POW and bur at Congressional Cemetery grave 65R 85CC in Washington, D.C.

Power, Charles R.—PVT Co.D 2/19/62. Appointed 2CPL 9/30/64. CIA Petersburg, Va. 4/1/65. Released Pt. Lookout, Md. 6/16/65.

Pratt, Charles F.—PVT Co.I 9/25/61. Detailed Hospital Steward 12/8/61. Roll for 2/28/65 shows him AWOL in Chattooga Cty., Ga. since 2/18/65.

Price, Henry J.—PVT Co.F 8/25/64. CIA Petersburg, Va. 4/2/65. Released Pt. Lookout, Va. 6/16/65.

Price, James R.—PVT Co.B 9/21/61. Dsh. for disability 7/22/62.

Prichard, W.J.—4CPL Co.K 7/4/61. PVT 1862. Pension records show he was dsh. 1863. Enlisted in Waddell's Battery (Alabama) 1863. Surrendered at Columbus, Ga. 1865. B. in Harris Cty., Ga. 5/31/1833. Pension roll 1898.

Pritchett, E.H.—PVT Co.K 5th Alabama. Appointed Surgeon 35th Ga. Inf Rgt. 5/30/63. Resigned for disability, chronic rheumatism and failing eyesight 2/13/64. Age in mid-40s.

Pruett, David—PVT Co.F 9/23/61. Appointed 3CPL 10/1/62. 1CPL 1864. Surrendered Appomattox, Va. 4/9/65.

Pruett, John F.—PVT Co.F 9/23/61. Appointed 3SG 10/62. 2SG.1SG 1864. Surrendered Appomattox, Va. 4/9/65.

Puckett, Asa W.—PVT Co.H 2/15/63. D. of disease at Winder Hospital at Richmond 6/19/64. Bur. there at Hollywood Cemetery—grave U188.

Puckett, David H.—PVT Co.H 9/24/61. WIA, left arm, Seven Pines, Va. 5/31/62. Dsh., permanent disability 1/22/64. B. in Ga. 1841. Pension roll 1889–1920. From Buford, Ga.

Puckett, Elias S. (or L.S.)—PVT Co.H 9/24/61. Appointed CPL 5/64. Surrendered Appomattox, Va. 4/9/65.

Puckett, George T.—PVT Co.H 9/24/61. D. of disease at Evansport, Va. 3/7/62.

Puckett, James B.—PVT Co.A 7/1/62. WIA Wilderness, Va. 5/6/64. Roll for 2/28/65 shows him AWOL since 2/18/65. NLR.

Puckett, John H.—PVT Co.H 7/62. D. 11/2/62 in Hall Cty., Ga. of typhoid fever. Widow, L.C., pension 1893–94.

Puckett, William G.—PVT Co.H 9/24/61. Dsh. prior to 12/31/61.

Roster R

Ragan, Josiah R. (or Reagin)—PVT Co.G 5/18/64. CIA Petersburg, Va. 4/2/65. Released at Pt. Lookout, Md. 6/17/65.

Ramey, Christopher—PVT Co.H 9/24/61. D. in Receiving Hospital at Fredericksburg, Va. 4/16/62.

Ramey, Miles W.—PVT Co.H 9/24/61. Roll for 12/61 shows he was dsh., date not given.

Ratliffe, John A.—PVT Co.I 9/25/61. Appointed 1CPL 9/63. 3CPL 1864. CIA Petersburg, Va. 3/25/65. Released Pt. Lookout, Md. 6/17/65.

Rawlins, David S.—PVT Co.F 9/23/61. Roll for 2/28/65 shows him present. Probably b. 5/17/1841. Pension 1910. D. 2/21/1913 and probably bur. Snellville City Cem. in Snellville, Ga.

Rawlins, Isham G.—PVT Co.F 9/23/61. Appointed CPL 1864. WIA in leg Spotsylvania C.H., Va. 5/12/64. D. of wounds 5/14/64.

Rawlins, James A.—PVT Co.F 9/23/61. D. in camp near Orange C.H., Va. 11/19/64. Author's note: the death date here is most likely 1863 as the regiment was in camp around Orange C.H. then but in late 1864 the regiment was around Petersburg, Va.

Rawlins, James F.—PVT Co.F 9/23/61. Surrendered Appomattox, Va. 4/9/65.

Rawlins, Mathew H.—PVT Co.F 10/10/63. CIA Petersburg, Va. 4/2/65. Released Pt. Lookout, Md. 6/17/65.

Rawlins, Robert M.—CPT Co.F 9/23/61. D. of disease at Richmond 5/19/62.

Rawlins, S.F.—PVT Co.F 1862. WIA 1862. D. of typhoid pneumonia and wounds in General Hospital at Howard's Grove near Richmond 7/2/62.

Rawlins, William J.—PVT Co.F 9/23/61. Surrendered Appomattox, Va. 4/9/65. Pension 1919.

Rawlins, William M.—Jr. 2LT Co.F 9/23/61. Elected 2LT 5/19/62. 1LT 5/19/64. WIA in hip at Gettysburg 7/3/63. Roll for 2/28/65 shows him AWOL since 2/10/65. NLR.

Reagin, Oliver—PVT Co.B 2/19/62. WIA, permanently disabled, Fredericksburg, Va. 12/13/62. Roll for 2/28/65 shows him in Ga. on wounded frl. NLR.

Reagin, William—PVT Co.B 9/21/61. Appointed 4CPL 4/62. WIA 1862. Appointed Color Bearer. 3SG 6/64. KIA Petersburg, Va. 3/25/65.

Reagin, Wilson—PVT Co.B 9/21/61. WIA Chantilly, Va. 9/1/62. MIA Gettysburg, Pa. 7/3/63. NLR.

Redding, E.W.—PVT Co.D. Surrendered Appomattox, Va. 4/9/65.

Redding, George W.—PVT, Trn from Co.E, 28th Ga. Inf Rgt, on 9/9/62. Surrendered Appomattox, Va. 4/9/65.

Reed, George W.—PVT Co.E 12/18/61. WIA, permanently disabled, Seven Pines, Va. 5/31/62. Recommended for retirement 10/17/64 to Invalid Corps, right leg shortened 5 inches from wound.

Reed, John V.—PVT Co.G 9/16/61. D. at Richmond 7/10/62.

Reed, Wiley J.—PVT Co.E 8/12/61. WIA Seven Pines, Va. 5/31/62 and taken to 1st Georgia Hospital in Richmond. D. of wounds at Richmond 6/23/62.

Reed, William P.—Chaplain 12/8/62. Declined appointment as chaplain. NLR.

Reeves, William H.—PVT Co.C 7/30/62. Appointed CPL. WIA Fredericksburg, Va. 12/13/62 and d. there of wounds 12/14/62.

Reeves, William W.—PVT Co.C 4/28/62. CIA Five Forks, Va. 4/1/65. Released Pt. Lookout, Md. 6/17/65.

Rich, James S.—PVT Co.G 4/23/64. CIA Petersburg, Va.4/2/65. Released Pt. Lookout, Va. 6/17/65.

Richardson, Aaron K.—CPT Co.H 9/24/61. Resigned 11/12/62.

Richardson, Baylis—PVT Co.E 4/19/62. CIA Petersburg, Va. 4/2/65. Released Hart's Island, N.Y. Harbor 6/15/65.

Ricks, Andrew M.—PVT Co.C 9/17/61. Dsh. for disability 1/22/62.

Ricks, Charles W.—PVT Co.C 9/17/61. Dsh. disability 8/64. Wife, E.J., on indigent widow pension roll 1907–20. She died 10/25/1920.

Ricks, Jesse B.—PVT Co.C 1/23/64. WIA Spotsylvania C.H., 5/12/64. Roll for 2/28/65 shows him present. NLR.

Ricks, John H.—PVT Co.C 9/17/61. Dsh. disability 1/3/62.

Ricks, William J.—PVT Co.C 9/17/61. WIA Spotsylvania C.H., Va. 5/12/64. D. from wounds 5/20/64. Bur. there at Spotsylvania Confederate Cemetery.

Ridgeway, Hewlett S.—PVT Co.C 2/20/62. D. of measles at Richmond hospital 4/6/62.

Ridley, Charles A.—PVT Co.D 8/28/62. WIA, through right thigh and knee, Wilderness, Va. 5/6/64. Roll for 2/28/65 shows him AWOL. NLR.

Rigby, John—PVT Co.D 9/23/61. WIA Mechanicsville, Va. 6/26/62. Shot in right thigh and left breast resulting in collapsed left lung. Sent home to convalesce. Returned to unit 12/62. WIA/CIA Wilderness, VA. 5/6/64. D. of acute bronchitis at Elmira, N.Y. 5/4/65. Bur. there at Woodlawn National Cemetery—Grave #2756 WNC. Wife, Nancy, applied for a veterans pension in 1893. She died in 1897 and was bur at Liberty Cemetery in Bremen, Ga. Sharecropper from Hogansville, Ga.

Riley, Edward O.—PVT Co.E 8/12/61. CIA Wilderness, Va. 5/5/64. Released Ft. Delaware, Del. 5/11/65.

Riley, William S.—PVT Co.E 8/12/61. KIA Mechanicsville, Va. 6/26/62.

Riley, William T.—PVT Co.B 2/28/62. WIA (broken right leg) Gettysburg. CIA near Petersburg, Va. 7/22/64. Paroled at Pt. Lookout, Md. 3/15/65. Received at Boulware & Cox's Wharf at James River, Va. 3/18/65. Pension 1900–07.

Ringer, William N.—PVT Co.D 9/23/61. Ambulance driver Mar-Apr 62. WIA 6/64. CIA near Petersburg, Va. 3/25/65. Released at Pt. Lookout, Md. 6/17/65.

Ringo, J.E.—PVT Co.D 2/28/62. Surrendered Appomattox, Va. 4/9/65.

Roberts, Albert C.—PVT Co.H 9/24/61. Appointed 5SG 1862. 3SG 6/64. CIA Petersburg, Va. 4/3/65. Released at Hart's Island, N.Y. Harbor 6/15/65.

Roberts, Charles B.—PVT Co.G 9/16/61. CIA Gettysburg, Pa. 7/2/63. Paroled at Ft. Delaware, Del. 2/65. Exchanged at Boulware & Cox's Wharves at James River, Va. 3/10/65. B. in Fulton Cty., Ga. 11/44.

Roberts, Cornelius H.—PVT Co.H 9/24/61. Deserted to enemy 9/14/64. Received at Hdqtrs. Provost Marshal General, Washington, D.C. 9/24/64 where he took oath of allegience to US Govt.

Roberts, Ezekiel Mason—PVT Co.F, 8th Ga. Inf Rgt. 5/22/61. Trn. to Co.H, 35th Ga. Inf. Rgt. 9/24/61. Elected Jr. 2LT 12/2/61. 1LT 11/12/62. CPT 11/6/63. Roll for 2/28/65 shows him AWOL. Permission for his absence was granted by Gen. Lee 2/14/65. Tendered his resignation on grounds he was incompetent to fill position on 2/3/65. Resignation was effective 3/1/65.

Roberts, Hardin—PVT Co.H 9/24/61. D. at Chimborazo Hsp. #3 at Richmond 4/7/62.

Roberts, Hope H.—1LT Co.C 9/17/61. KIA Mechanicsville, Va. 6/26/62 at age 20.

Roberts, James M.—2LT Co.H 9/24/61. Resigned 7/23/62.

Roberts, Martin V.B.—PVT Co.H 9/24/61. WIA 1862. CIA Jericho Ford, Va. 5/24/64. Trn. to Elmira, N.Y. 7/8/64 and released there 6/14/65.

Roberts, Melville C.—PVT Co.C 4/22/62. Appointed 1CPL 10/62. KIA Gettysburg, Pa. 7/3/63.

Roberts, Orin H.—3CPL Co.D 9/23/61. WIA, in arm requiring amputation, 2nd Manassas, Va. 8/29/62. Appointed 2CPL 9/62. Deserted. Received by USA Provost Marshal General 9/19/64. Took oath of allegiance to US Govt. (signed oath as C.H. Roberts) at City Pt.,Va. 9/22/64. On pension roll 1879–1918. D. 10/25/1918. Widow applied for pension 1919. Bur. Providence Bible Church Cem. in Smith plot in Troup Cty., Ga.

Roberts, William G.—PVT Co.C 9/17/61. Appointed Hospital Steward 11/16/61. CIA Gettysburg, Pa. 7/3/63. Paroled at Pt. Lookout, Md. 3/9/64. Surrendered Appomattox, Va. 4/9/65. B. in Campbell Cty., Ga. 7/31/1837. On pension roll 1899–1908. D. in Confederate Soldiers' home at Atlanta, Ga. 1/4/1910. Bur. there at Westview Cemetery on Gordon St in Atlanta.

Robertson, James A.—PVT Co.A 8/15/61. CIA Gettysburg, Pa. 7/2/63. Paroled At Ft. Delaware, Del. 7/30/63. Received at City Pt., Va. 8/1/63. Received at Louisville, Ky. as a Confederate deserter 7/25/64 where he took oath of allegience to US Govt. and was released to remain north of Ohio River for rest of war.

Rodgers, John N.—PVT Co.B 2/24/62. D. at Richmond 5/16/62.

Rodgers, John T.—PVT Co.B 2/25/62. CIA Wilderness, Va. 5/6/64. Released at Elmira, N.Y. 6/19/65. D. 10/14/1913. Widow, Sarah, applied for pension 1919.

Roebuck, William E.—PVT Co.H 9/24/61. Admitted to CSA Geneal Hsp. at Danville, Va. with chronic rheumatism 6/29/62. Dsh. for disability 10/8/62. B. in Ga. in 1834. Possibly d. 2/1899 and bur at Peachtree Rd. Baptist Ch. Cem. in Gwinnett Cty., Ga.

Roquemore, John M.—PVT Co.G 3/1/62. D. of typhoid fever in General Hospital #3 at Lynchburg, Va. 12/3/63. Bur. there at Confederate Cemetery, No.10, 3rd Line, Lot 200-Ferguson's. Widow, E.E., pension 1891–1907.

Rorie, David—PVT Co.K 3/4/62. WIA Seven Days Battles near Richmond 6/62. WIA 2nd Manassas, Va. 8/29/62. Appointed 2CPL 1864. Surrendered Appomattox, Va. 4/9/65.

Rowell, Adolphus D.—PVT Co.A 8/15/61. D. of fever in Jackson Hospital at Richmond 6/12/64.

Rowell, Alexander—PVT Co.A 8/15/61. WIA Mechanicsville, Va. 6/26/62. Roll for 2/28/65 shows him AWOL since 12/14/62. NLR.

Rowell, George C.(Colvin?)—PVT Co.A 8/15/61. D. of disease 4/25/62 probably at a hospital in Fredericksburg, Va..

Royal, Nevils (or Royall)—PVT Co.A, 30th North Carolina Inf. Rgt. 9/1/61. Trn. to Co.E, 35th Ga. Inf. Rgt. 1862. Roll for 6/64 shows him present. Not on subsequent rolls. "Union Register of prisoners confined at Bermuda Hundred, Va. shows that he was captured 8/9/64 at Dept. Headquarters, a deserter."

Rutherford, James—PVT Co.I 9/25/61. WIA Mechanicsville, Va. 6/26/62. Appointed 2SG 12/62. CIA Wilderness, Va. 5/5/64. Released Elmira, N.Y. 6/14/65.

Rutherford, John—PVT Co.I 3/3/62. CIA Wilderness, Va. 5/5/64. D. of chronic diarrhea at Elmira, N.Y. 3/25/65. Bur. there at Woodlawn National Cemetery in grave #2459 WNC.

Rutledge, Samuel S.—PVT Co.I 5/10/62. KIA Mechanicsville, Va. 6/26/62.

Roster S

Sanford, Martin V.—PVT Co.A 10/12/61. WIA Cedar Mtn., Va.8/9/62. Roll for 2/28/65 shows him AWOL since 4/20/64. NLR.

Sanford, William Minor—PVT Co.A 5/2/62.WIA Seven Days Battles near Richmond. Appointed teamster in Wilcox Div. train. Roll for 2/28/65 shows him AWOL. Pension records show he was frl. for 30 days 3/65. B. 6/10/1831. Indigent pension roll 1895–1907.

Sarratt, Demosthenes M.—PVT Co.I 10/23/61. WIA Seven Pines, Va. 5/31/62. CIA Frederick, Md. 9/12/62. Exchanged at Aiken's Landing, Va. 11/10/62. WIA Jericho Ford, Va. 5/25/64. CIA near Petersburg, Va. 3/25/65. Released at Pt. Lookout, Md. 6/14/65. B. at Spartanburg, S.C. 1/9/1844.

Sarratt, Leonidas—PVT Co.I 9/25/61. Received disability dsh 1861. NLR.

Sarratt, William R.—PVT Co.I 9/25/61. D. at Fredericksburg, Va. hsp. 4/1/62.

Sartor, George W.—PVT Co.I 9/25/61. Admitted to General Hsp. at Camp Winder at Richmond 7/5/63. Frl. for 30 days 9/9/63. D. in General Hsp. in Staunton, Va. 2/19/64.

Scogin, Elisha H.(or Scoggin)—PVT Co.I 9/25/61. WIA Mechanicsville, Va. 6/26/62. Roll for 2/28/65 shows, "Absent, retired under General Order #34, 1864, A&IGO Office, 4/14/64, for six months. AWOL since 10/14/64. No extension of retirement has been received." Bur. 1901 at Farmerville Cem. on Farmerville Rd. in Chattooga Cty., Ga. B. 1823.

Scogin, Gillam M. (or Scoggin)—PVT Co.D 9/23/61. On disabled frl. 6/64. NLR.

Scogin, James H.(or Scoggin)—PVT Co.I 9/4/62. Substitute for Levi S. Scogin. Roll for 2/28/65 shows him AWOL in Chattooga Cty., Ga. since 2/15/65. NLR.

Scogin, Levi Sanford (or Scoggin)—PVT Co.I 9/25/61. Dsh., furnished James H. Scogin as substitute 9/4/62. Enlisted as PVT in Co.E, 6th Ga. CAV Rgt.

Scogin, Lindsay, H.(or Scoggin)—PVT Co.I 9/25/61. On sick frl. from 10/26/62 to 2/17/63. NLR.

Scogin, Millington M.(or Scoggin)—PVT Co.D 9/23/61. KIA Cedar Mtn, Va. 8/9/62.

Scogin, Wiley G. (middle name possibly Gresham) (or Scoggin)—PVT Co.I 3/4/62. Roll for 2/28/65 shows him AWOL at Chattooga Cty., Ga. since 1/1/65. D. 11/9/1909 and bur at Farmerville Cem on Farmerville Rd in Chattooga Cty., Ga. B. 2/7/26.

Scogin, William C.—PVT Co.D 10/11/61. Appointed 1CPL 12/61. WIA Manassas Junction, Va. 8/27/62. Appointed 3SG 9/62. 1SG 9/30/64. Elected 1LT. Surrendered Appomattox, Va. 4/9/65. Pension 1898. D. 5/18/1903. Widow, Lucinda, filed for widow's pension 1903.

Scott, James H.—PVT Co.B 2/28/62. CIA Petersburg, Va. 4/2/65. Released from Pt. Lookout, Md. 6/19/65.

Scott, John D.—PVT Co.B 2/24/62. CIA Hanover Junction, Va. 5/24/64. D. of chronic diarrhea at Elmira, N.Y. 9/12/64. Bur. there at Woodlawn National Cemetery—grave #175 WNC.

Scott, John H.—PVT Co.A 8/15/61. Appointed 2CPL 9/17/61. Dsh. for disability from fever and dysentery 11/8/61.

Scott, Josiah Barber—1SG Co.G 9/16/61. Elected Jr. 2LT 6/11/62. 2LT 10/11/62. In Lynchburg, Va. hsp. 12/62. In General Hsp.#4 at Richmond 5/5/63. Found guilty by court martial on 11/1/63 of conduct unbecoming an officer. The first specification was that he forged a medical certificate for himself, citing ulcers, one on the foot and two on his leg at Macon, Ga. The second specification was that he forged a second medical certificate for himself. The third specification was that he lied about his activities in a letter to the company captain. His sentence was dismissal from the service. General R.E. Lee noted on his paperwork to publish his crime in his hometown newspaper. Enlisted as PVT in Co.A, 11th Battn., Ga. Light Artillery 11/4/63. Roll for 2/65 shows him absent on detached duty for company by order of General Lee.

Scott, William Flavius—Jr. 2LT Co.G 9/16/61. Sick in #1 Hsp. at Dumfries, Va. 12/61. Resigned 1/2/62. B. in Ga. D. at Palestine, Tx.

Sellars, William A. (or Scellars)—PVT Co.C 9/17/61. KIA Seven Pines, Va. 5/31/62.

Selman, James W.—2LT Co.I 9/21/61. Resigned for disability 6/26/62. B. 2/17/23 and d. 6/19/1907 and bur Old Armuchee Cem in Floyd Cty., Ga.

Sexton, Williamson L.—PVT Co.F 2/12/62. WIA, date/place unknown. Roll for 2/28/65 shows him home on leave of indulgence. B. 2/15/1836. D. 4/17/1900. Bur. Bethabra Baptist Ch. Cem. in Barrow Cty., Ga.

Simonton, George W.—PVT Co.B 8/28/62. WIA Gettysburg, Pa. 7/3/63. Appointed 2SG 2/20/64. Surrendered Appomattox, Va. 4/9/65.

Shadix, Green B.—PVT Co.E 8/12/61. In Jackson Hsp. in Richmond from 12/31/63 to 2/29/64. In Jackson Hsp. in Richmond 4/7/64. NLR.

Shadix, John J.—PVT Co.E 8/12/61. Surrendered Appomattox, Va. 4/9/65.

Shannon, Joel H.—PVT Co.C 4/22/62. Appointed CPL. WIA Fredericksburg, Va. 12/13/62. Sent to Richmond hsp 1862 and captured there 4/3/65. Sent to Libby Prison in Richmond and then trn. to Newport News, Va. 4/23/65. Released 6/16/65.

Shannon, Thomas M.—PVT Co.C 9/17/61. Appointed 2CPL 12/16/61. KIA Spotsylvania C.H., Va. 5/12/64.

Shaver, William—PVT Co.E 2/13/62. CIA Gettysburg, Pa. 7/3/63. NLR.

Shaw, John—PVT Co.I 5/12/62. Trn Co.K, 21st Ga. Inf. Rgt. 9/11/63.

Shell, James F.—PVT Co.C., enlistment date unknown. Probably was a patient at Mt. Jackson Hospital. D. 8/11/63 at Mt. Jackson, Va. and bur. at Mt. Jackson Cemetery (Our Soldiers Cemetery) in Mount Jackson, Va.

Shellnut, William T.—PVT Co.G 9/21/61. D. at Richmond 4/14/62.

Shippy, Joseph J.—PVT Co.K 5/14/64. CIA Petersburg, Va. 4/2/65. Released at Pt. Lookout, Md. 6/19/65.

Shirley, Abner M.—PVT Co.E 8/12/61. WIA, shot in hand, Seven Days Battles near Richmond 6/62. CIA Gettysburg, Pa. 7/3/63 and admitted to USA Hsp. at Chester, Pa. 7/31/64. Paroled. Attached to Jackson Hsp. in Richmond 4/10/64. Returned to unit 7/16/64. Deserted 7/29/64. NLR.

Shirley, Jonathan—PVT Co.E 8/12/61. Sick at Richmond 3/62. Dsh. 7/30/62.

Shirley, William F.—PVT Co.E 8/12/61. CIA 1864. Roll for 2/28/65 shows him present. Indigent pension roll 1896–1914. D. 4/12/1914.

Short, Franklin (Babe)—PVT Co. K 7/4/61. Dsh. 11/30/61.

Short, George—PVT Co.K 7/4/61. D. in service.

Silvey, James W.—PVT Co.E 7/30/62. Detailed drummer 1864. Surrendered Appomattox, Va. 4/9/65.

Sizemore, Ephraim W.—PVT Co.H 9/24/61. D. of typhoid fever at Belmont and Greve Hsp. at Belmont, Va. 8/25/62.

Sizemore, Seaborn J.M.—PVT Co.H 9/24/61. Deserted to enemy 10/3/64. Note: apparently he also deserted at some time in 1863 was arrested and was found not guilty during a court martial on 10/1/63.

Slaton, Thomas N.—PVT Co.C 4/24/62. Appointed 1CPL 1864. Roll for 2/28/65 shows him AWOL at Fairburn, Ga. since 2/15/65. Indigent pension roll 1902–06/1908. B. 8/20/33 and d. 10/22/1908 bur Antioch Methodist Cem on Rivertown Rd near Fairburn in Fulton Cty., Ga..

Slaughter, Robert W.—PVT Co.K 7/4/61. WIA Wilderness, Va. 5/5/64. CIA Petersburg, Va. 4/2/65. Released Pt. Lookout, Md. 6/19/65.

Sloper, John—2CPL Co.D 9/23/61. Appointed 2SG 12/15/61. PVT 1862. Detailed Commissary SGT 1864. CIA High Bridge, Va. 4/6/65. Released Newport News, Va. 6/26/65. B. at Oxford, N.H.

Smallwood, John R.—PVT Co.E 9/8/62. Wounded in foot 1/63. Surrendered Appomattox, Va. 4/9/65.

Smart, Thomas S.—PVT Co.C 4/24/62. Admitted to Chimborazo Hsp. at Richmond 5/3/63. CIA on retreat from Petersburg, Va. 4/65.

Smart, Titus J.—PVT Co.C 4/24/62. CIA on retreat from Petersburg, Va. 4/65.

Smith, Basil Andrew Jackson—PVT Co.C 9/17/61. Appointed 5SG 1864. Surrendered Appomattox, Va. 4/9/65. B. 3/27/43 and d. 11/31/1922 bur Ramah Baptist Ch Cem near Palmetto, Ga. in Fulton Cty., Ga.

Smith, Daniel D.E.—PVT Co.A 10/12/61. D. 4/18/62.

Smith, Elisha L.(or S.E.)—PVT Co.G 3/4/62. CIA Gettysburg, Pa. 7/3/63. D. of smallpox at Ft. Delaware, Del. 10/22/63.

Smith, Isham H.—PVT Co.G 9/21/61. D. 1/11/62.

Smith, Jackson V.—PVT Co.A 7/12/62. D. of disease in Richmond hsp. 11/15/62.

Smith, James Allen—PVT Co.I 9/25/61. WIA near Richmond 6/28/62. Dsh. 11/4/62. Pension records show he enlisted in a company of 6th Ga. CAV Rgt. and surrendered at Kingston, Ga. 5/12/65.

Smith, James E.E.—PVT Co.D 3/1/62. D. in Alabama, date unknown.

Smith, James H.—PVT Co.B 9/21/61. D. at Fredericksburg, Va. 4/9/62.

Smith, James H.—PVT Co.G 9/16/61. CIA Jericho Ford, Va. 5/23/64. Released at Pt. Lookout, Md. 6/19/65.

Smith, Joel B.—PVT Co.C 9/17/61. Appointed 3SG 7/13/62. Surrendered Appomattox, Va. 4/9/65.

Smith, John J.—PVT Co.E 8/12/61. CIA Wilderness, Va. 5/5/64. Took oath of allegience to US Govt. and enlisted in US Army 6/15/64.

Smith, John W.—PVT Co.C 9/17/61. Appointed 4CPL 5/31/62. Appointed Color Bearer. CIA near Petersburg, W.Va. 1/30/64. Sent to Camp Chase, Oh. 2/9/64. Trn to Ft. Delaware, Del. 3/14/64. Exchanged at Ft. Delaware, Del. 3/7/65. B. in Madison Cty., Ga 3/10/1840. D. at Confederate Soldier's home in Atlanta 7/15/1902. Bur. Westview Cemetery on Gordon St. in Atlanta.

Smith, John W.—PVT Co.E 8/12/61. Appointed 2CPL 1863. AWOL 2/28/65. NLR.

Smith, Joseph—PVT Co.F 2/1/62. D. at home in Gwinnett Cty., Ga 9/23/62. Widow, Julia, pension 1891.

Smith, Levi P.—PVT Co.B 9/21/61. Admitted to General Hsp. # 21 at Richmond 10/26/62. D. of smallpox 12/1/62.

Smith, Sanford C.—PVT Co.E 2/24/62. WIA, right hand, Fredericksburg, Va. 12/13/62. On detached duty at Gordonsville, Va. 2/28/65. NLR.

Smith, Thomas F.—PVT Co.E 8/12/61. Dsh. for old age (58 years old) and extreme debility 5/1/62. B. in 1804.

Smith, Thomas S.—PVT Co.B, 9th Ga. Inf Rgt. 6/12/61. Dsh., disability at Richmond 11/8/61. Enlisted as PVT Co.I, 35th Ga. Inf Rgt. 3/20/62. Dsh., disability at General Hsp.#4 at Richmond 11/18/62.

Smith, Wiley C.—PVT Co.B 2/25/62. CIA near Petersburg, Va. 3/25/65. Released from Pt. Lookout, Md. 6/30/65.

Smith, William—PVT Co.C 9/17/61. KIA Petersburg, Va. 4/65.

Smith, William A.—PVT Co.A 2/24/62. D. of disease at Ashland, Va 4/27/62.

Smith, William J.J.—PVT Co.C 9/17/61. KIA Gettysburg, Pa. 7/2/63.

Sockwell, Thomas—PVT Co.B 9/21/61. WIA Seven Pines, Va. 5/31/62. WIA Mechanicsville, Va. 6/26/62. Roll for 10/62 shows him absent, sick at a Lynchburg, Va. hsp. Dsh. for disability at age 47, 10/28/62.

Sparks, Masters H.—4CPL Co.B 9/21/61. D. of typhoid fever at Evansport, Va. 2/23/62.

Sparks, Mathew—PVT Co.B 2/24/62. D. of measles at Evansport, Va. 12/61.

Sparks, Peter B.—PVT Co.B 2/24/62. D. of heart disease at Camp Gregg near Fredericksburg, Va. 2/15/63.

Sparks, Welcome U.—PVT Co.B 3/1/62. WIA Mechanicsville, Va. 6/26/62. CIA Spotsylvania C.H., Va. 5/12/64. D. of pneumonia at Elmira, N.Y. 11/10/64. Bur. there at Woodlawn National Cemetery—grave #787 WNC.

Spinks, Hiram T.—PVT Co.B 9/21/61. WIA Mechanicsville, Va. 6/26/62. CIA Petersburg, Va. 4/2/65. Released Pt. Lookout, Md. 6/19/65.

Spinks, William R.—PVT Co.B 5/7/64. CIA Petersburg, Va. 4/2/65. Released Pt. Lookout, Md. 6/19/65.

Sprayberry, William J.—PVT Co.E 5/19/62. Deserted 6/5/63. Bur. at Bethel Presbyterian Ch. Cem in Chattooga Cty, Ga. near Summerville.

Starr, Samuel Henry—PVT Co.F 6/20/62. WIA Fredericksburg, Va. 12/13/62. CIA Gettysburg, Pa. 7/2/63. NLR.

Statham, Edward—PVT Co.A 4/22/64. Appears on rolls of Co.A, 35th Regt. Ga. Inf. With remark: "On June 15, 1864, Lt. Smith, Co.A, 1st Confederate Regt. Inf. Claimed that Ed Statham had joined his company first and took him off by order of the Colonel." NLR.

Steed, Collier A.—PVT Co.C 4/24/62. KIA Gettysburg, Pa. 7/3/63.

Stephens, Andrew A.J.—PVT Co.G 9/16/61. D. at Richmond, Va. 6/29/62.

Stephens, John—PVT Co.A 3/4/62. D. 4/24/62.

Stephens, Robert M.—PVT Co.G 9/16/61. D. at Richmond, Va. 7/21/62 and bur there at Hollywood Cemetery in grave H-134.

Stephens, Rufus—PVT Co.D 9/23/61. D. at Richmond 4/21/62.

Stephens, Wilson L.—PVT Co.G 2/15/62. D. in Chimborazo Hospital at Richmond, Va. 4/25/62.

Stevens, Benjamin F. (Stephens)—PVT Co.F 2/12/62. D. of typhoid fever in General Hospital at Danville, Va. 6/23/62. Widow pension 1891.

Stevens, Bradley H. (Stephens)—PVT Co.F 9/23/61. WIA Seven Pines 5/31/62. Roll for 2/28/65, last on file, shows him at home on sick furlough. B 1/14/42. Pension 1898. D 4/7/1900 and bur. Haynes Creek Primitive Baptist Church near Loganville, Ga.

Stevens, F.M. (Stephens)—PVT Co.F 5/5/62. D. 1862.

Stevens, John A. (Stephens)—PVT Co.F 9/23/61. D. at Staunton, Va. 3/9/63.

Stipe, John Wesley—PVT Co.C 4/28/62. CIA Petersburg, Va. 4/2/65. Released at Point Lookout, Md. 6/19/65. D. 2/2/1917.

St. John, James M.—PVT Co.B 9/21/61. Trn to Co.B, 18th Ga. Inf. Rgt. 5/14/62. WIA Seven Days Battles near Richmond. CIA Fisher's Hill, Va. 9/19/64. Paroled at Pt. Lookout, Md. 1/17/65. Received at James River, Va. for exchange 1/21/65. B. 9/9/31 in Newton Cty, Ga. Pension roll 1898–1907.

St. Johns, John B.—PVT Co.D 9/23/61. D. of chronic diarrhea in General Hospital at Staunton, Va. 4/3/64.

St. Johns, Thomas B.—PVT Co.D 5/10/62. CIA Gettysburg, Pa. 7/3/63. Paroled at Point Lookout, Md. 1865. Exchanged 2/10/65. Admitted to Jackson Hospital in Richmond with ascites 2/15/65. Transferred to Camp Lee at Richmond 3/1/65. NLR.

Street, George W.—PVT Co.B 11/18/61. WIA 1862. Detailed as nurse at Lynchburg, Va. 1864, and was paroled there 4/13/65.

Strickland, Benjamin F.—PVT Co.I 9/25/61. Left hand injured in railroad accident and discharged due to injuries.

Strickland, William—PVT Co.E 8/12/61. Sick in hospital for 13 months with measles starting in early 1862. CIA at Gettysburg, Pa. 7/2/63. Paroled at Ft. Delaware, Del. 2/65. Received at Boulware & Cox's wharves On the James River in Va. 3/10/65. Admitted to General Hospital #9 at Richmond the same day. Sent to Camp Lee at Richmond 3/11/65. D. 7/28/90.

Strickland, Wilson—PVT Co.D 9/23/61. Roll for 2/28/65, last on file, shows him present. NLT.

Stripling, Benjamin F.—PVT Co.K 7/4/61. Captured at High Bridge, Va. 4/6/65. Released at Newport New, Va. 6/15/65.

Stripling, Francis M.B.—PVT Co.A 8/15/61. Elected 2LT 8/15/61. Resigned 8/15/61. Reenlisted and appointed 2SGT 10/1/62. Surrendered at Appomattox 4/9/65. D. 10/94 at Norwood, Texas.

Stripling, James—PVT Co.K 3/4/62. Roll for 12/31/62, shows him "Absent, sick, sent to Ashland, Va. 4/4/62." NLR.

Stripling, William A.—PVT Co.K 7/4/61. Appointed 4CPL 1864. CIA Wilderness Va. 5/5/64. Released at Elmira, N.Y. 6/30/65.

Stripling, W.H.—PVT Co.K 7/4/61. D. in service.

Suggs, Elliott—PVT Co.D 3/4/62. D. of measles and pneumonia 5/4/62.

Summerlin, James C.—PVT Co.F 9/23/61. Roll for 2/28/65, last on file, shows him at home on sick furlough. NLT.

Summerlin, Syrenius D.—PVT Co.F 2/25/64. Surrendered at Appomattox, Va 4/9/65. B. 3/22/46. D. 5/2/1922 and bur Chestnut Grove Baptist Church in Grayson, Ga.

Summerville, Robert—PVT Co.A 8/15/61. Appointed 3CPL 9/1/61. WIA 1862. D. of fever in hospital 10/30/64. His widow applied for pension 1891.

Summerville, William J.—PVT Co.A 2/15/64. Roll for 2/28/65, last on file, shows him AWOL, time expired 11/1/64. NLR.

Sutton, Josiah P.—PVT Co.K 7/4/61. WIA Wilderness, Va. 5/5/64 in left knee. WIA Petersburg, Va. 4/2/65 in right eye resulting in loss of sight. Captured at hospital in Richmond 4/3/65. Paroled 5/65. B. in Ga. 6/14/45. D. 7/9/1909. Widow pension 1919.

Sutton, N.J.—PVT Co.K 3/4/62. Roll date 12/31/62shows him, "Absent, sick, left near Leesburg, Va. 9/2/62." D. in service.

Swafford, Andrew J. (Swofford)—PVT Co.H 9/24/61. appointed CPL. PVT 5/1/64. CIA Petersburg, Va. 4/3/65. Released at Hart's Island, N.Y. Harbor 6/14/65. B. 1842 in Hall Cty., Ga. D. 1877 while in Tennessee on business. Widow pension 1901–07.

Swafford, Isaac (Swofford)—PVT Co.H 9/24/61. Captured by enemy as a Confederate deserter 10/13/64. Took oath of allegiance to U.S. Govt. at Bermuda Hundred, Va. 10/14/64, remarks: "To go to New York."

Swafford, M.W. (Swofford)—PVT Co.H 2/25/63. CIA Gettysburg, Pa. 7/3/63. Sent to Pt. Lookout, Md. 10/30/63 where he died of chronic diarrhea in General Hospital 11/22/63.

Swafford, William (Swofford)—4SGT 9/24/61. Records of Chimborazo Hospital #3 at Richmond show he was discharged from service on account of nephritis 7/19/62. B. in Hall Cty., Ga. 7/9/32.

Swan, Elijah—PVT Co.B 9/21/61. WIA Fredericksburg, Va. 12/13/62. WIA Spotsylvania CH, Va. 5/12/64. Discharged near Petersburg, Va. 10/14/64. NLR.

Swan, James S. PVT Co.B 2/24/62. D. of measles in camp near Richmond, Va. 6/20/62. Bur. there at Hollywood Cemetery, grave O-231.

Swilling, John W.—PVT Co.I 9/25/61. Elected 1LT. Roll for 2/28/65, last on file, shows him AWOL in Floyd Cty., Ga. since 2/10/65. NLR

Swords, Lewis—PVT Co.G 9/16/61. WIA Mechanicsville, Va. 6/26/62, and disabled. Surrendered at Appomattox, Va. 4/9/65. B. in 5/23/33 at Walton Cty., Ga. Pension 1890–1905. Bur. McCullers Family cemetery in Walton Cty. Ga.

Roster T

Tackett, Henry T.—PVT Co.E 8/12/61. D. at Richmond 11/9/61.

Talley, Elijah W.—PVT Co.D 9/23/61. On frl. in Ga. 12/62. NLR.

Tate, David W.—PVT Co.I 2/18/62. Dsh., disability 5/30/62.

Taylor, John H.—Chaplain 35th Ga. Inf. Rgt. 2/15/64. Resigned, disability 2/10/65.

Taylor, Richard B.—PVT Co.A 8/15/61. D. at Dumfries, Va. 2/2/62.

Teal, John W.—PVT Co.C 5/19/62. Appears last on roll for 6/64 which shows him absent.

Teal, Lawson M.—PVT Co.C 7/19/62. Appears last on roll for 6/64.

Teal, Samuel F.—PVT Co.C 2/18/64. Roll for 2/28/65 shows him AWOL at Fairburn, Ga. since 8/20/64. NLR.

Terry, Stephen A.—PVT Co.K 11/28/64. CIA Petersburg, Va. 4/2/65. Released Pt. Lookout, Md. 6/21/65. B. in Harris Cty., Ga. 1832. Pension roll 1895. After receiving pension he was judged to be a lunatic and unable to take care of himself and was admitted to a lunatic asylum.

Tharp, John A.—1SG Co.D 9/23/61. Dsh 12/15/61. No record of reenlistment. Rolls show he died as a PVT at Evansport, Va. 5/19/63. Note: either this date or place of death is wrong.

Thomas, David—PVT Co.F 2/12/62. D. in General Hsp at Staunton, Va. of chronic diarrhea 10/2/62 and bur. there at Thornrose Cemetery (age 35). His dsh for illness was approved 10/5/62.

Thomas, Edward Lloyd—LTC 4th Ga. Inf. Bn. 10/14/61. COL 35th Ga. Inf. Rgt. 10/15/61. BG, commanding inf. brigade in Light Division, Army of Northern Va. 11/1/62. WIA Mechanicsville, Va. 6/26/62. Special Orders 216/7 were issued 9/12/64 from President Davis remitting a sentence of reprimand against Thomas and releasing him from arrest to return to duty. Unable to determine what the reprimand was for. Possibly for poor showing of brigade at Battle of Jericho Ford. WIA near Petersburg, Va. 3/25/65. Surrendered at Appomattox, Va. 4/9/65. B. in Clark Cty., Ga. 3/23/1825. Graduated from Emory College 1846. Appointed by President Cleveland in 1885 to serve in U.S. Land Department and in 1893 to serve in the Indian Bureau in Oklahoma Territory until his d. 3/10/1898. Bur. at Kiowa, Ok. in Oak Hill/City Cemetery. Younger brother of CPT Lovick P. Thomas and uncle of Henry Andrew "Heck" Thomas.

Thomas, Francis M.—PVT Co.H 9/24/61. WIA Seven Pines, Va.5/31/62. D. of smallpox at Richmond 3/11/64.

Thomas, George Washington—PVT Co.G 3/1/62. On detail as shoemaker from 1864 to 2/28/65. B. 6/6/1829 in Hall Cty., Ga. Pension roll 1909. D. in Gwinnett Cty., Ga. 1/28/1910. Bur. at Hog Mountain Baptist Ch. Cem near Lawrenceville, Ga.

Thomas, Henderson—PVT Co.E 8/12/61. Elected 2LT. Surrendered Appomattox, Va. 4/9/65.

Thomas, Henry Andrew (Heck)—youngest son of CPT Lovick P. Thomas. B. near Athens, Ga. 8/12/1850. Returned to war in Va. with father in 1862. Served as a courier and drummer boy. After war became a US Marshal out west and was the character that the 1970's television show "Hec Ramsey" was based on. D. in Lawton, Ok. 1912 at age 62.

Thomas, Henry W.—PVT Co.F 3/1/63. Appointed 4CPL 1864. QM SGT 1864. Surrendered Appomattox, Va. 4/9/65. B. in Gwinnett Cty., Ga. 8/9/1844. D. in Confederate Soldier's Home at Atlanta 10/11/1913.

Thomas, James—PVT Co.A 2/62. WIA 2nd Manassas, Va. 8/28/62 and d. there from wounds on 9/1/62.

Thomas, James W.—PVT Co.K 8/7/61. Roll for 2/28/65 shows him AWOL. NLR.

Thomas, J.D.—PVT Co.K 7/4/61. D. of typhoid fever in Richmond hsp. 6/17/62.

Thomas, Joel—PVT Co.E 2/24/62. D. at Fredericksburg, Va. 4/8/62.

Thomas, John R.—PVT Co.G 3/1/62. Roll for 2/28/65 shows him on frl. NLR.

Thomas, Kinnon (or Kineon)—PVT Co.A 3/12/62. WIA Cedar Mtn, Va. 8/9/62. In Lynchburg, Va. hsp. 8/31/62 where he d. 9/13/62. Bur. there at Confederate Cemetery, No.3, 2nd Line, Lot 179-Ford's Factory.

Thomas, Lovick P.—CPT and QM 4th Ga. Inf. Battn. 10/14/61. Trn to 35th Ga. Inf Rgt. WIA right lung at Mechanicsville, Va. 6/26/62. Brother of BG E.L. Thomas. Resigned, disability 10/3/63. B. in 1812 and died in 1878. Father of Henry (Heck) Andrew Thomas and father of Colonel Lovick P. Thomas Jr., commander of 42nd Georgia born in 1835.

Thomas, Thomas Jefferson—PVT Co.A 8/15/61. Roll for 2/28/65 shows him present. NLR.

Thomas, William—PVT Co.A 7/1/62. D. of debility in General Hsp. #1 at Danville, Va. 1/23/63.

Thomas, Winfield Scott—Adj 35th Ga. Inf. Rgt. 7/29/62. Elected CPT Co.K, 16th Ga. Cav. Battn. 5/2/64. Trn to Co.K, 13th Ga. Cav Rgt. 1864. Roll for 10/64 show him present. NLR. Thomason, Benjamin F.—PVT Co.G 9/21/61. KIA 2nd Manassas, Va. 8/30/62.

Thomason, Gideon A.—PVT Co.G 9/21/61. Roll for 2/28/65 shows him AWOL. NLR.

Thomason, J.B.—PVT Co.K 7/4/61. D. 6/17/62.

Thomason, William T.—PVT Co.K 7/4/61. Suffered accidental gunshot wound to left wrist rendering it useless at Evansport, Va. 12/15/61. Roll for 9/64 shows him detailed as brigade baker. Dsh and retired for disability 1/1/65.

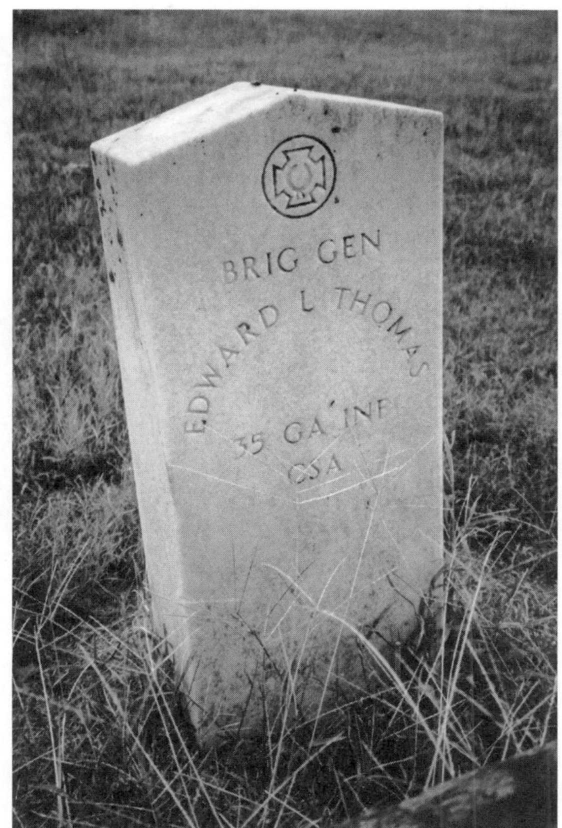

Tombstone of Brigadier General Edward Lloyd Thomas

Thomas survived the war. In 1893 he served in the Indian Bureau in the Oklahoma Territory. He died there on March 10, 1898 and was buried at Kiowa, Oklahoma in the Oak Hill/City Cemetery.

photo by Bob Price, Norcross, Ga.

Thompson, William H.—PVT Co.D 3/4/62. WIA, left thigh, 2nd Manassas, Va. 8/29/62. Dsh., permanent disability, at Atlanta, Ga. 7/28/63.

Tillerson, Spencer (or Tillson)—PVT Co.H 9/24/61. WIA Seven Pines, Va.5/31/62. On detached duty 1864. Roll for 2/28/65 reports him AWOL.

Tolbert, James C.—PVT Co.A 8/15/61. Deserted 6/21/64.

Toler, Alsey K.—PVT Co.K 5/4/62. D. of meningitis in General Hsp. #2 at Lynchburg, Va. 5/15/64. Bur. there in Confederate Cemetery, No.10, 3rd Line, Lot 195-Christian's.

Toler, William J.—PVT Co.K 3/4/62. Captured in Richmond hsp 4/3/65. Released at Newport News, Va. 6/25/65. B. 1828 in Upson Cty., Ga. D. 10/8/1866 in Harris Cty., Ga. Widow, Mary, pension 1901.

Tomblin, Solomon S.—PVT Co.E 8/15/62. CIA Spotsylvania C.H., Va. 5/12/64. Released at Ft. Delaware, Del. 6/7/65.

E.L. Thomas gravesite
photo by Bob Price, Norcross, Ga.

Torrance, David—PVT Co.E 8/12/61. Roll for 6/64 shows him present. NLR.

Torrance, Middleton—PVT Co.E 8/12/61. D. in Richmond hsp. 6/23/62.

Trimble, John—PVT Co.D 2/24/62. Dsh 5/28/62.

Trimble, John T.—PVT Co.D 2/28/62. Roll for 12/62 shows detailed as QM SGT by order LTC McCullohs. Roll for 6/64 shows QM Clerk. Dsh for poor health from measles. D. 1/15/65 of disease at hsp.

Trussell, Daniel L.—PVT Co.C 2/27/62. Roll for 2/28/65 shows him absent, detailed to work in arsenal at Atlanta, Ga. 2/13/63. NLR.

Tucker, Henry—PVT Co.H 4/30/64. WIA Spotsylvania C.H., Va. 5/12/64. Roll for 2/28/65 shows him absent, wounded, whereabouts unknown.

Tucker, James M.—PVT Co.G 9/21/61. D. of typhoid fever in Chimborazo Hsp. at Richmond 8/10/62.

Tucker, William W.—PVT Co.D 2/24/62. Roll for 12/62 shows him present. NLR.

Tuggle, Adam G.—1CPL Co.H 9/24/61. PVT 9/9/62. WIA, left hip, Spotsylvania C.H., Va. 5/12/64. CIA Jericho ford, Va. 5/24/64. Released at Elmira, N.Y. 6/16/65. B. in Ga. 1835.

Tuggle, Anderson G.—PVT Co.H 9/24/61. WIA, gunshot to left hip, at Spotsylvania C.H. 5/64. Roll for 2/28/65 shows him AWOL since 8/1/64. Probably b. 1847. Pension roll 1890. Probably d. 1920 and bur in Tuggle family cem. on south side of Thompson Mill Rd., east of Spout Spring Rd. in Gwinnett Cty., Ga.

Tuggle, Charles M.—1LT Co.H 9/24/61. Elected CPT 11/12/62. CIA Gettysburg, Pa. 7/2/63. D. of fever at Johnson's Island, Oh.11/6/63. Bur. there in grave #2CC. From Hall Cty., Ga.

Tuggle, Charles M.—PVT Co.H 3/18/63. CIA Hanover Jct, Va. 5/24/64. D. of disease at Pt. Lookout Prison, Md. 10/12/64.

Tuggle, George M.—3SG Co.H 9/24/61. PVT. CIA Jericho Ford, VA. 5/24/64. Released Pt. Lookout, Md. 6/21/65.

Tuggle, Henry H.—PVT Co.H 9/24/61. KIA Seven Pines, Va. 5/31/62.

Tuggle, Manning J.—PVT Co.H 9/24/61. CIA Jericho Ford, Va. 5/24/64. Paroled Elmira, N.Y. and sent to James River, Va. for exchange 3/2/65.

Tuggle, Russell A.—PVT Co.H 9/24/61. D. of disease while on frl. in Ga. 11/20/62.

Tuggle, Sanford—PVT Co.H 9/24/61 at age 16. CIA Gettysburg, Pa. 7/2/63. Exchanged at Pt. Lookout, Md. 3/3/64. Roll for 2/28/65 shows him AWOL since 4/20/64. Born 1/4/45. His father, James Tuggle of Gwinnett County, sent a letter to Sec'y of War on 10/25/62 asking for his son to be discharged because he had enlisted against his father's will and without his consent. This letter is located at National Archives in "Confederate Secy of War Letters Recd" on microfilm roll m437, roll 75, item 476-T-1862.

Tuggle, Woodward—PVT Co.H 5/10/62. CIA Jericho Ford, Va. 5/24/64. Released Elmira, N.Y. 5/29/65.

Turner, Dan—PVT Co.C 5/62. D. in service.

Turner, James—PVT Co.E 8/12/61. Roll for 2/28/65 shows him AWOL. Pension records show he was on sick frl. from spring 1863 until end of war. B. in Ga. 3/1834. Widow, Elizabeth, received widow's pension 1920–21 and 1924.

Turner, Richard L.—PVT Co.I 9/25/61. Dsh. due to loss of eye 5/9/62. B. 5/8/34. D. 6/28/1903 and bur Subligna Methodist Cem in Chattooga Cty., Ga.

Turner, William J.—PVT Co.B 9/21/61. WIA Yorktown, Va. 4/20/62 by own troops. Surrendered Appomattox, Va. 4/9/65. D. 4/19/1915 at Lawrenceville, Ga. Widow, Matilda, filed for widow's pension 1916.

Tyler, Allen R.—PVT Co.I 9/25/61. KIA Jericho Ford, Va. 5/23/64.

Roster U

Underwood, Henry—PVT Co.E 8/12/62. Admitted to General Hsp. at Danville, Va. with chronic diarrhea 7/12/63. Returned to duty 7/21/63. NLR.

Roster V

Van Pelt, Amsi C.—PVT Co.I 2/21/62. D. at Richmond 4/29/62.

Van Pelt, W.A.—Co.I., rank/enlistment unknown. D. 4/30/62 of pneumonia at Richmond hsp. Widow pension 1891. NOTE: the two Van Pelts may be the same soldier.

Vardaman, James A.—4SG Co.K 7/4/61. PVT. CIA near Petersburg, Va. 3/25/65. Released Pt. Lookout, Md. 7/21/65.

Vickery, John M.(or Vicery)—PVT Co.B 2/28/62. D. at Camp Winder near Richmond 6/23/62.

Vickery, Thomas M.—4CPL Co.I 9/25/61. On detail duty as blacksmith in Brigade QM Dept. at Richmond 4/14/63 to 2/28/65. He was ruptured while shoeing a horse and permanently disabled. NLR.

Roster W

Wade, William Harris—PVT Co.F 2/28/62. D. at Ashland, Va. 4/27/62.

Wade, Wilson—PVT Co.F 9/23/61. D. in Bird Island Hsp at Richmond 12/1/61.

Waldrop, John M.—Drummer Co.A 8/15/61. Appointed 1SG 1864. CIA Petersburg, Va. 4/2/65. Released Pt. Lookout, Md. 6/22/65. B. in Henry Cty., Ga. 10/24/1837. Indigent pension roll 1895–1906 for kidney problems and rheumatism.

Waldrop, Joseph M.—3SG Co.A 8/15/61. Dsh., disability 9/26/61. enlisted as PVT Co.G, 40th Ga. Inf Rgt. 3/4/62. Appears only on bounty payroll dated 3/27/62. B. in Henry Cty., Ga. 1835. Indigent pension roll shows he was dsh. 1862 for rupture in both sides. D. 7/11/1908.

Wallace, Isham J. (Wallis)—3SG Co.B 9/21/61. WIA Seven Pines, Va. 5/31/62. Roll for 2/28/65 reports "Absent, wounded, in Ga. since 5/31/62." NLR.

Wallace, James M. (Wallis)—PVT Co.B 9/21/61. D. of ulceration of bowels at Richmond 1/12/62. Bur. there at Hollywood Cemetery—grave B313.

Wallace, Jonathan—PVT Co.D 9/23/61. WIA Cedar Mtn, Va. 8/9/62. WIA, gunshot to right thigh, at Wilderness, Va. 5/6/64. Roll for 2/28/65 shows him present. NLR.

Walters, William T., Co.I Born 9/10/46 and d. 11/12/1916 and bur Subligna Methodist Cem in Chattooga Cty., Ga.

Wammock, Louis B.(or Wammack)—PVT Co.A 8/15/61. D. 8/5/62.

Wammock, Thomas A.(or Wammack)—PVT Co.A 8/15/61. WIA/CIA, left shoulder and back, Spotsylvania C.H., Va. 5/12/64. D. in Fredericksburg, Va. hsp. 5/23/64.

Ware, James H.—1LT Co.K 7/4/61. Appointed Adj 2/13/62. WIA Seven Pines, Va. 5/31/62. KIA Mechanicsville, Va. 6/26/62. Body returned to Columbus, Ga. by servant on 7/5/62 and bur there.

Watson, George W.J.—4CPL Co.A 8/15/61. WIA, in eye resulting in loss of sight in one eye, 2nd Manassas, Va. 8/29/62. Appointed 5SG 8/64. CIA/WIA, gunshot to left leg, near Petersburg, Va. 4/3/65. Released from prisoner camp 6/17/65. Married Sarah A. Jean on 1/3/67. Disappeared from wife in 1875. Wife filed for widow's pension 1910.

Watts, Hope A.—PVT Co.I 9/25/61. Dsh., disabled by disease at Camp French near Evansport, Va. 1/10/62. Enlisted as PVT Co.E, 6th Ga. Cav. Rgt. 8/6/62. Roll from 11/1/62 to 4/30/63 shows him absent, sick at Moss Creek Hsp. NLR.

Watts, Thomas J.—3CPL Co.I 9/25/61..KIA Mechanicsville, Va. 6/26/62.

Wayne, Thomas W.—PVT Co.H 9/24/61. D. of typhoid fever in General Hsp. at Danville, Va. 8/8/62.

Webb, Andrew J.—PVT Co.G 9/16/61. Appointed 5SG 10/1/62. 4SG 1864. CIA Jericho Ford, Va. 5/25/64. Paroled Pt. Lookout, Md. and trn to Aiken's Landing, Va for exchange 3/15/65. D. 6/2/1924 and bur. at Friendship Primitive Baptist Ch. Cem. on Dogwood Rd. in Gwinnett County, Ga. Widow, Mary, pension 1924–29.

Webb, Jasper—PVT Co.G 9/16/61. D. of smallpox at Winchester, Va. 11/16/62.

Webb, John—PVT Co.D 9/23/61. WIA 2nd Manassas, Va. 8/29/62. Roll for 10/62 lists him absent, wounded. NLR.

Webb, John W.—PVT Co.E 8/12/61. KIA 2nd Manassas, Va. 8/30/62.

Webb, Newton G.—PVT Co.G 9/16/61. Roll for 2/28/65 shows him AWOL. NLR.

Weeks, Joseph H.—PVT Co.D 9/23/61. CIA Gettysburg, Pa. 7/2/63. D. of anemia at Ft. Delaware, Del. 2/15/64.

Wells, George E.—PVT Co.B 2/25/62. WIA Fredericksburg, Va. 12/13/62. D. from wounds in General Hsp.#8 at Richmond 12/29/62.

Wells, Joel C.—PVT Co.B 9/21/61. KIA Seven Pines, Va. 5/31/62.

Wells, Joseph—PVT Co.B 9/21/61. Dsh. for chronic diarrhea from General Hsp. at Camp Winder near Richmond 10/15/62.

West, Robert P.—PVT Co.H 9/24/61. Appointed 3SG. KIA Jericho Ford, Va. 5/23/64.

West, W.C.—PVT Co.K 7/4/61. KIA Seven Pines, Va. 5/31/62.

Wheatley, William—PVT Co.D 2/25/62. D. at Richmond 7/24/62. Bur. there at Hollywood Cemetery—grave H157.

Wheeler, John—Jr. 2LT Co.H 9/24/61. Resigned 12/1/61. Enlisted as PVT 2/62. D. at Fredericksburg, Va. 3/8/62 from measles. Widow, Sarah, pension 1891–94.

Wheeler, Jonathan H.—PVT Co.H 11/25/63. CIA Petersburg, Va. 3/25/65. Released Pt. Lookout, Md. 6/22/65.

Wheeler, Marcus D.—PVT Co.I 9/25/61. D. of erysipelas in General Hsp.#1 at Lynchburg, Va. 6/27/63. Bur. there in Confederate Cemetery. No.8. 1st Line. Lot 192-Ferguson's.

Wheeler, Obediah N.—4CPL Co.H 9/24/61. D. of typhoid fever in General Receiving Hsp. at Gordonsville, Va. 8/15/63.

White, David P.—3SG Co.E 8/12/61. PVT 1862. WIA Gettysburg, Pa. 7/3/63. Roll for 2/28/65 shows him AWOL. B.5/10/29 and d. 4/7/1911 bur Owl Rock Methodist Ch Cem, 5800 Campbellton Rd in Fulton Cty., Ga.

White, Henry A.—PVT Co.D 9/23/61. WIA Malvern Hill, Va. 7/1/62. CIA Jericho Ford, Va. 5/23/64. Released Elmira, N.Y. 7/19/65.

White, James M.—CPT Co.B 9/21/61. On recruiting duty in Georgia 1/62 and returned 3/10/62. Resigned for debility 6/13/62.

White, North Harrison—PVT Co.I 9/25/61. KIA Jericho Ford, Va. 5/23/64. B. 2/18/41. Grave marker at South Carolina Campground Cem on Ga. Hwy 100 north of Holland, Ga. in Chattooga Cty.

White, R.A.—PVT Co.H 3/12/64. Dsh. for disease 7/25/64.

White, R.C.—PVT Co.K 7/4/61. Dsh. 11/6/61.

White, Robert E.—PVT Co.K 3/17/64. CIA Hanover Junction, Va. 5/23/64. Paroled Elmira, N.Y. and sent to James River, Va. for exchange 2/20/65. B. in Harris Cty., Ga. 1832. Pension roll 1897.

Whitehead, William Alexander—PVT Co.K 3/4/62. Dsh., furnished Henry Fitzsimmons as substitute 8/4/62. B. 7/22/1839. D. 10/3/1908 and bur Waverly Hall Cem. in Harris Cty., Ga.

Whitley, Andrew J.—PVT Co.H 9/24/61. CIA Petersburg, Va. 4/2/65. Released Pt. Lookout, Md. 6/22/65.

Whitley, Evan Riley—CPT Co.E 8/12/61. Resigned, disability 1/23/63.

Whitley, Levi A.V.—PVT Co.G 9/16/61. Dsh. 7/25/62.

Whitley, William D.—PVT Co.B 9/21/61. WIA Seven Days Battles near Richmond 6/62. CIA Spotsylvania C.H., Va. 5/21/64. Arrived at Pt. Lookout, Va. 5/30/64 and released to join US Army 6/1/64.

Whitley, Zachariah—PVT Co.B 2/17/62. Dsh. 5/1/62.

Whitworth, J.H.—PVT Co.F 2/25/64. KIA Spotsylvania C.H., Va. 5/12/64.

Whitworth, James O.—PVT Co.F 5/3/62. WIA, left eye resulting in loss of sight, Cedar Mtn., Va. 8/9/62. Surrendered Appomattox, Va. 4/9/65. Pension roll 1887–1907. D. 2/27/1908.

Wilder, James S.—PVT Co.F 5/3/62. KIA Fredericksburg, Va. 12/13/62.

Wiley, Isaac D.—PVT Co.H 9/24/61. WIA Seven Pines, Va. 5/31/62. Roll for 2/28/65 shows he was detached as shoemaker 8/20/63 and assigned to duty in Ga. NLR.

Wiley, Patrick W.—PVT Co.F 9/23/61. Appointed 1CPL 10/62. 5SG 1864. Surrendered Appomattox, Va. 4/9/65.

Wilkinson, James M.—PVT Co.B 11/2/61. Dsh. for old age and rheumatism 1/28/62.

Wilkinson, James P.—1LT Co.G 9/16/61. Elected CPT 6/11/62. Resigned 10/10/62 due to injuries suffered in a fall at Battle of Mechanicsville, Va.

Wilkinson, William H.—PVT Co.D 3/4/62. Dsh., furnished John H. Wilson as substitute 6/3/62.

Williams, Andrew J.—PVT Co.K 7/4/61. Roll for 2/28/65 shows him absent, detailed as a shoemaker at Columbus, Ga. 12/5/62. NLR.

Williams, Arch J.—PVT Co.K 7/4/61. 3CPL 11/9/61. In Hsp.#1 at Richmond 4/12/62. D. 7/14/62.

Williams, C.J.—PVT Co.K 7/4/61. Appointed 2CPL 7/20/62. D. in service.

Williams, Daniel J.—PVT Co.F 9/23/61. D. in 3rd Hsp. at Dumfries, Va. 3/3/62.

Williams, Greenbury H.—PVT Co.A 3/4/62. D. 8/5/62.

Williams, Harrison—PVT Co.A 8/15/61. CIA Wilderness, Va. 5/5/64. D. of chronic diarrhea at Elmira, N.Y. 11/7/64. Bur. there at Woodlawn National Cemetery grave #768.

Williams, Harrison—PVT Co.I 9/25/61. Sick in Richmond hsp. 8/31/62. On frl. from 6/1 to 9/3/63. NLR.

Williams, Henry—Jr. 2LT Co.K 7/4/61. Resigned, disability 7/17/62.

Williams, Henry S.—PVT Co.E 7/8/62. WIA, right arm requiring amputation, Gettysburg, Pa. 7/3/63. Retired, disability, 3/10/64.

Williams, James—PVT Co.A 8/15/61. KIA Gettysburg, PA. 7/2 or 7/3/63.

Williams, James—PVT Co.D 9/23/61. Dsh., disability and old age, at Richmond 7/28/62.

Williams, John B.—1SG Co.F 9/23/61. Elected Jr. 2LT 11/1/62. WIA, calf of right leg, Fredericksburg, Va. 12/13/62. WIA, right knee and hip, Gettysburg, Pa. 7/2/63. WIA, gunshot to thigh and leg, Wilderness, Va. 5/5/64. Admitted to General Hsp. at Farmville, Va. 5/6/64 and trn. to Oxford, Ga. 6/16/64. NLR.

Williams, John H.—PVT Co.E 3/2/64. Elected 2LT. Surrendered Appomattox, Va. 4/9/65.

Williams, John W.S.—PVT Co.D 9/26/63. Surrendered Appomattox, Va. 4/9/65. B. in Putnam Cty., Ga. 10/9/1822. Pension roll 1895–1900.

Williams, Jonathan N.—PVT Co.A 8/15/61. Dsh. 11/8/61. elected 1LT of Co.K, 40th Ga. Inf Rgt. 3/4/62. Resigned for disability 1862.

Williams, Lee Andrew Jackson—CPT Co.D 9/23/61. Elected MAJ 12/21/63. WIA Spotsylvania C.H., Va. 5/12/64 and d. of wounds 5/19/64.

Williams, Lemuel M.—PVT Co.E 8/12/61. Brigade wagoner for short period during 12/61 to 1/62. Elected Jr. 2LT 10/31/62. 1LT 1/10/63. WIA Gaines Mill, Va. 6/27/62. Roll for 2/28/65 shows him AWOL since 12/28/64. Paroled at Thomasville, Ga. with Major General Sam Smith's Florida Confederate Forces.

Williams, Leonidas—PVT Co.A 8/15/61. Appointed CPL. 3SG. WIA Wilderness, Va. 5/5/64 and d. of wounds same day.

Williams, Nathan G.—PVT Co.H 9/24/61. KIA Mechanicsville, Va. 6/26/62.

Williams, Permenus—PVT Co.H 9/24/61. Appointed 5SG 1861. WIA Seven Pines, Va.5/31/62. 4SG 7/19/62. CIA near Petersburg, Va. 7/21/64. Released at Elmira, N.Y. 6/21/65.

Williams, Robert W.—PVT Co.H 9/24/61. WIA, gunshot to leg, Mechanicsville, Va. 6/26/62. Roll for 12/62 shows him absent, sick. Dsh for leg disability 8/27/63. NLR.

Williams, William C.—PVT Co.H 9/24/61. Roll for 2/28/65 shows him absent, detailed as local guard at Staunton, Va. 4/18/64. NLR.

Williams, William H.—PVT Co.F 9/23/61. Dsh. at Camp Thomas at Atlanta 10/16/61.

Willingham, Elijah M.—PVT Co.G 9/16/61. D. in camp near Richmond 6/25/62.

Willingham, Rolla H.—PVT Co.D 9/23/61. Appointed 4CPL. 5SGT 9/30/64. 4SGT 12/64. CIA near Richmond 4/6/65. Released at Newport News, Va. 6/25/65.

Willingham, W.B.—PVT Co.G 3/1/62. KIA Fredericksburg, Va. 12/13/62.

Willis, Bradford W.—PVT Co.G 9/16/61. Appointed 3CPL, 2CPL, 1CPL 1864. WIA during Seven Days Battles near Richmond 6/62. CIA Gettysburg, Pa. 7/2/63. Sent to Ft. Delaware, Del. and then exchanged 7/31/63. WIA 1864. CIA near Petersburg, Va. 3/25/65. Released at Pt. Lookout, Md. 6/22/65.

Wilson, Esley M.—PVT Co.K 7/4/61. CIA Petersburg, Va. 4/2/65. Released from Pt. Lookout, Md. 6/22/65.

Wilson James W.—PVT Co.C 9/17/61. Appears last on roll 12/31/62.

Wilson, John H.—PVT Co.D 6/3/62. Substitute for William H. Wilkinson. WIA Seven Days Battles near Richmond 6/62. WIA, abdomen, Fredericksburg, Va. 12/13/62. Recovered at General Hsp at Charlottesville, Va. WIA, shot through hip and bowels, Chancellorsville, Va. 5/63. Roll for 12/64 shows he was retired from service. D. 5/16/1888.

Wilson, Joseph R.—PVT Co.D 9/23/61. D. of disease in General Hsp. at Danville, Va. 8/23/62.

Wilson, Newman J.—PVT Co.A, 11th Ga. Inf. Rgt. 7/3/61. Trn. to Co.H, 35th Ga. Inf. Rgt. in 1863. CIA Gettysburg, Pa. 7/2/63. Paroled Pt. Lookout, Md. 1864. Appointed 2SGT 1864. Paroled at Burkeville, Va. 4/14 to 4/17/65.

Wilson, William M.—PVT Co.D 9/23/61. WIA, gunshot to hand, Seven Pines, Va. 5/31/62. Roll for 2/28/65 shows him sick at hsp. NLR.

Winchester, Jerry R.—4SGT Co.D 9/23/61. Appointed 1SGT 12/15/61. Elected Jr. 2LT 6/16/62. WIA Spotsylvania C.H., Va. 5/12/64. D. of typhoid fever at home in Heard Cty., Ga. 9/13/64.

Winchester, Jesse D.—PVT Co.D 9/23/61. D. at Fredericksburg, Va. 12/28/61.

Winchester, William L.—PVT Co.D 9/23/61. Trn. to Co.K, 34th Ga. Inf. Rgt. 5/13/62. D. at Vicksburg, Ms. 7/11/63.

Wingo, Alford M.—PVT Co.D 9/23/61. WIA Cedar Mtn., Va. 8/9/62. Retired to Invalid Corps 5/2/64. NLR.

Wingo, John P.—PVT Co.D 9/23/61. WIA 2nd Manassas, Va. 8/30/62. Roll for 2/28/65 shows him present. NLR.

Witcher, Benjamin M.—PVT Co.D 2/28/62. WIA, date/place unknown. Dsh. for age (51), debility and an uncurable fever 8/27/63.

Wood, Daniel Y.—Jr. 2LT Co.D 9/23/61. D. at Richmond 6/14/62. Possibly bur. at Hollywood Cemetery in Richmond.

Wood, James P.—PVT Co.H 9/24/61. Appointed 1CPL 8/9/62. WIA 1862. CIA Gettysburg, Pa. 7/2/63. Paroled at Ft. Delaware, Del. 2/65. Exchanged at Boulware & Cox's Wharves at James River, Va. 3/10/65. B. near Greenville, S.C. 9/9/1823.

Wood, James W.—PVT Co.A 8/15/61. D. 8/12/62.

Wood, Luke Robertson—1SGT Co.A 8/15/61. WIA, in thigh, Seven Pines, Va. 5/31/61. Dsh. 4/15/64.

Wood, S.D.—Ast. Surgeon 35th Ga, Inf Rgt. 6/9/62.

Wood, Williams—PVT Co.A 3/18/63. CIA near Petersburg 3/25/65. Released at Pt. Lookout, Md. 6/30/65.

Woodard, James (or Woodward)—PVT Co.E 1/8/62. Dsh. for chronic rheumatism from General Hsp at Danville, Va. 10/8/62.

Word, John T.—PVT Co.C 2/19/62. WIA, left wrist, Seven Pines, Va. 5/31/62. Trn. to Co.E, 27th Ga. Inf. Rgt. 1863. WIA, left hip and abdomen 1/15/65. Admitted to CSA General Hsp.#3 at Greensboro, N.C. 1/17/65. Frl. from Pettigrew General Hsp.#13 at Raleigh, N.C. for 60 days 2/6/65. At Milledgeville, Ga. at end of war. B. in Fayette Cty., Ga. 1839.

Worthy, John H.—PVT Co.A 3/25/62. WIA Cedar Mtn., Va. 8/9/62. Dsh. 10/25/64. Signed a witness statement for pension application of William Channell in Newton Cty., Ga. on 2/9/1895.

Wray, James M.—PVT Co.A 8/15/61. Appointed 2CPL 11/10/61. WIA 2nd Manassas, Va. 8/29/62. Appointed 2SGT 5/1/64. CIA near Petersburg, Va. 3/25/65. Released Pt.Lookout, Md. 6/30/65.

Wray, William E.—PVT Co.A 8/15/61. Surrendered Appomattox, Va. 4/9/65.

Wright, Cador G.—PVT Co.I 9/25/61. Dsh. at Richmond 11/4/62.

Wright, John F.—PVT Co.A 8/15/61. Admitted to Winder Hsp for fever 6/5/62. Returned to company 6/12/62. D. of disease 6/23/62.

Wright, John H.(or James H.)—PVT Co.I 10/10/61. Appointed 2CPL 12/19/61. WIA 1862. WIA Gettysburg, Pa. 7/4/63. D. of wounds 7/6/63.

Wright, Joshua J.—PVT Co.F 9/23/61. D. in Louisiana Hsp. at Richmond of typhoid fever 6/11/62.

Wright, Samuel E.—PVT Co.F 9/23/61. D. at Bird Island Hsp. at Richmond 12/3/61.

Wynn, J.H.—PVT Co.K 7/4/61. WIA Wilderness, Va. 5/5/64. D. of wounds in CSA General Hsp. at Charlottesville, Va. 5/11/64. Bur. there in Confederate Cemetery.

Roster Y

Yarbrough, George W.—Chaplain 35th Ga. Inf Rgt. 11/16/61. Resigned, ill health 9/23/62.

Yeargan, Burton—PVT Co.I 9/25/61. CIA Petersburg, Va. Mar/Apr 65. Released Pt. Lookout, Md. 6/22/65.

Young, Andrew F.—PVT Co.H 9/24/61. WIA Seven Pines, Va.5/31/62. Appointed 5SGT 6/1/64. CIA Petersburg, Va. 4/3/65. Released Hart's Island, N.Y. Harbor 6/15/65. B. in Hall Cty., Ga. 7/17/1838. Pension roll 1902–07. D. 2/1914. Widow pension 1914.

Young, Boling G. (or Balden G.)—PVT Co.B 5/15/62. WIA Spotsylvania C.H., Va. 5/12/64. CIA near Petersburg, Va. 3/25/65. Released at Pt. Lookout, Md. 6/22/65.

Young, Haywood A.—PVT Co.B 11/8/62. D. of typhoid fever in General Hsp.#16 at Richmond 5/5/63.

Young, Jasper N.(M.)—PVT Co.C 9/17/61. CIA Gettysburg, Pa. 7/3/63. Admitted to Hammond USA General Hsp. at Pt. Lookout, Md. 10/22/63. Sent to General Hsp 12/14/63 for smallpox. Discharged from hospital back to prison 2/8/64. D. as POW of scurvy 3/14/65 at Pt. Lookout and bur. there in POW grave #1289.

Young, Samuel D.—PVT Co.B 2/24/62. WIA Seven Days Battles near Richmond 6/62. D. of disease at home in Ga. 1863.

Young, Smith J.—PVT Co.E 8/12/61. D. at Richmond 12/8/61.

Roster Z

Zachry, Alfred A.—PVT Co.B 9/21/61. Appointed 2SGT 7/25/62. WIA Gettysburg, Pa. 7/3/63. Elected CPT of Co.B, Roswell's Bn. Ga. Cavalry 9/1/64.

BIBLIOGRAPHY

Manuscripts

ATLANTA HISTORICAL SOCIETY, Atlanta, Georgia

Patterson, Carroll R., The 14th Georgia Volunteer Infantry—An Outline of Its History, Atlanta Historical Society.

The Incomplete Correspondence of Lt. Josiah Blair Patterson
14th Regiment Georgia Volunteer Infantry, annotated by
Carroll Ruffin Patterson, Atlanta Historical Society.

CHICKAMAUGA-CHATTANOOGA NATIONAL MILITARY PARK

James M. Kimbrough, Co.K, 35th Georgia, typescript copy of "My War History 1861–1865"

EMORY UNIVERSITY, Atlanta, Georgia

Edward Lloyd Thomas Letter 12/2/1861, Special Collections,
Woodruff Library, Emory University. Atlanta, Ga.

FREDERICKSBURG-SPOTSYLVANIA NATIONAL MILITARY PARK

Letters of Simeon B. David, typescript located at Fredericksburg-Spotslyvania Military Park, Fredericksburg, Va.

GEORGIA DIVISION OF ARCHIVES AND HISTORY, Morrow Georgia.

Reminiscences of John O. Andrews, Reminiscences of
Confederate Soldiers—Stories of the War 1861–65
Vol. 3 1940, collected by Ga. Division of United
Daughters of the Confederacy, Georgia Division of Archives and History, Morrow, Ga.

Edwin C. Bearss Collection, Letters of Francis Solomon Johnson 3/25/1864, on microfilm at Georgia Division of Archives and History, Morrow, Ga.

Boyce Collection, Letter of Joseph T. Johnson 1/4/1863, on microfilm at Georgia Division of Archives and History, Morrow, Ga.,

Confederate Pension Records of Georgia, Georgia Division of Archives and History, Morrow, Ga.

Letters of Simeon B. David, Reminiscences of Confederate Soldiers and Stories of the War 1861–65 Vol. 2 1940, collected by Ga. Division of United Daughters of the Confederacy, located at Georgia Division of Archives and History, Morrow, Ga..

Charles Farmer Letter, Co.B, 35th Ga. 6/18/1864, Civil War Miscellany, Georgia Division of Archives and History, Morrow, Ga.

Malachi Henry Foy Collection, Letter 6/18/1862, on microfilm at Georgia Division of Archives and History, Morrow, Ga.

Jasper A. Gillespie Civil War Papers, Georgia Division of Archives and History, Morrow, Ga.

Daniel Andrew Jackson, Sr. Collection, on microfilm at Georgia Division of Archives and History, Morrow, Ga.

Anecdote of Doctor O. Knight and Augustus J. Moon, Reminiscences of Confederate Soldiers and Stories of the War 1861–65. Collected by Ga. Division, United Daughters of the Confederacy, Volume XIII, p.106–107. Located at Georgia Division of Archives and History, Morrow, Ga.

Diary of Betty Herndon Maury 1861–1863, on microfilm at Georgia Division of Archives and History, Morrow, Ga.

James T. McElvany Collection, on microfilm at Georgia Division of Archives and History, Morrow, Ga.

War History of David Harrison Mobley, on microfilm at Georgia Division of Archives and History, Morrow Ga.

Benjamin Franklin Moody Folder, Civil War Miscellany, Personal Papers (Record Group 57–1–1), on microfilm at Georgia Division of Archives and History, Morrow, Ga.

Letters of Stephen L. Moon, Reminiscences of Confederate Soldiers and Stories of the War 1861–65. Collected by Ga. Division, United Daughters of the Confederacy, Volume XIII, p.108–109. Located at Georgia Division of Archives and History, Morrow, Ga.

Woodson Daniel Moon Letter, to Charlotte written on May 8, 1864, on microfilm at Georgia Division of Archives and History. Morrow, Ga.

Letters of Josiah Blair Patterson, Georgia Division of Archives and History, Morrow, Ga.

Diary and Memorandum Kept By Captain Daniel S. Redding, Co.D, 45th Georgia Regiment, March-December 1863. Reminiscences of Confederate Soldiers and Stories of the War 1861–65, Vol. 5 1940, collected by Ga. Division of UDC, located at Georgia Division of Archives and History, Morrow, Ga.

Minnie Robertson Smith Collection, AC 33–031, Folder 5–06; Letters of Sergeant Isham Wallis on 1/13/1862; 2/12/1862; 5/21/1862; 5/9/1863 on microfilm at Georgia Division of Archives and History, Morrow, Ga.

Wiley J. Smith Collection, Letter 5/21/1864, on microfilm at Georgia Division of Archives and History, Morrow, Ga.

Sketch of Edward Lloyd Thomas, on microfilm at Georgia Division of Archives and History, Morrow, Ga.

Letter by Captain Edward Willis, on microfilm at Georgia Division of Archives and History, Morrow, Ga.

HOLLYWOOD CEMETERY, Richmond, Virginia
Register of the Confederate Dead Interred in Hollywood Cemetery
Richmond, Va., Gary Clemmitt & Jones Printers, 1869.

Hollywood Cemetery Burial Records. Hollywood Cemetery in Richmond, Va.

MANSFIELD HISTORICAL SOCIETY, Mansfield, Texas.
William Boswell Collection.

WOODSON D. MOON LETTERS
Woodson Daniel Moon Letters, *History of the Moon Family,* William H. Moon, The Times Publishing Co., Conyers Ga. 1920.

NATIONAL ARCHIVES, Washington, D.C.
Compiled Military Service Records—Captions and Records of Events, National Archives, Washington, D.C.
Compiled Records Showing Service of Military Units In Confederate Organizations, National Archives, Washington, D.C.
Compiled Service Records of Confederate General and Staff Officers and Nonregimental Enlisted Men, National Archives Washington, D.C.
Compiled Service Records of Confederate Soldiers in Organizations From the State of Georgia, National Archives, Washington, D.C.
Reference File Relating to Confederate Medical Officers, National Archives, Washington, D.C.
Edward Lloyd Thomas Letters, Letters received by the Confederate Secretary of War. National Archives, Washington, D.C.

PRIVATE COLLECTIONS
James M. Garrett Collection, Courtesy of Mrs. Dian Stroud of Columbus, Ga. (typescript copies in possession of author)

Confederate Diary of Hiram Warner Hammond, In the possession of David Hollis of Lanett, Alabama.

Letters and Journal of Major James T. McElvany of the 35th Georgia Infantry Regiment. In possession of John and Robert Bailey, Douglasville, Ga.

Letters of Private George B. Pass, Co. H, 35th Georgia, in possession of Gene Chatham of Dacula, Ga., and Edwina Pass Bryan of Cleveland, Al.

John Rigby Family Records, in possession of Mark Pollard of McDonough, Ga.

SPOTSYLVANIA CONFEDERATE CEMETERY, Spotsylvania C.H., Virginia
Register of Names of Men Buried In the Confederate Cemetery
Spottsylvania C.H., Va. Confederate Memorial Association, Spottsylvania, Va.

UNIVERSITY OF GEORGIA, Athens, Georgia
Cartledge, Rev. Groves H., Sketches of the Early History of Madison County, Georgia, typescript in Georgia Room, University of Georgia, Athens, Ga.

William C. Goggans Letters, Hargrett Rare Book and Manuscript Library/University of Georgia Libraries, Athens, Ga.

Diaries of George Washington Hall, 14th Georgia Volunteers, CSA, 1861–1865, Hargrett Rare Book and Manuscript Library/ University of Georgia Libraries, Athens, Ga.

Letters of Francis Solomon Johnson, Co.F 45th Georgia, to Emily Hutchings, MS 243, Special Collections, Hargrett Rare Book and Manuscript Library/University of Georgia Libraries (See above Edwin C. Bearss Collection at GDAH)

VIRGINIA HISTORICAL SOCIETY, Richmond, Virginia
Report of Major General Cadmus M. Wilcox at Spotsylvania C.H., MSS3L515a, folder F.

VIRGINIA STATE LIBRARY, Richmond, Virginia.
Joseph R. Anderson Papers 1861,1862 and 1867, Letter to Lee
7/15/1862, #26167, Virginia State Library, Richmond, Va.

Published Primary Sources

Alexander, E.P., *Military Memoirs of a Confederate.* New York, 1907.

Bigelow, John., *The Campaign of Chancellorsville.* New Haven, Conn., 1910.

Blake, Henry N. *Three Years in the Army of the Potomac.* Boston: 1865.

Bryan, T. Conn., "Letters of Two Confederate Officers: William Thomas Conn Charles Augustus Conn". *The Georgia Historical Quarterly.* Vol. XLVI p.169–195. 1962.

—"Conn-Brantley Letters 1862". *The Georgia Historical Quarterly.* Vol. LV. p.437–441. 1971.

Caldwell, J.F.J., *The History of a Brigade of South Carolinians Known First As "Gregg's" and Subsequently As "McGowan's Brigade"*. Philadelphia, King & Baird, 1866—reprinted by Morningside Press, Dayton, Oh., 1992.

Confederate Military History Extended Edition—Georgia. Vol.VII. Confederate Publishing Co. 1899. Reprint: Wilmington, N.C. Broadfoot Publishing Co. 1987.

Cudworth, Warren H. *History of the First Regiment (Mass. Infantry)* Boston. Walker, Fuller and Co. 1866.

Davis, George B.; Perry, Leslie J.; Kirkley, Joseph W., *Atlas To Accompany the Official Records of the Union and Confederate Armies.* Washington: Government Printing Office, 1891–1895.

Douglas, Henry Kyd., *I Rode With Stonewall.* Chapel Hill, N.C. The University of North Carolina Press. 1940.

Dunlop, William S., *Lee's Sharpshooters or, The Forefront of Battle. Dayton,* Oh., Morningside House. 1988.

Early, Jubal A., *General Jubal A. Early: Autobiographical Sketch and Narrative of the War Between the States.* Philadelphia. J.B. Lippincott and Co. 1912.

Edwards, Frank., *The Red Book—Army Life of Frank Edwards—Confederate Veteran 1861–65.* 1906.

Fitzpatrick, Marion Hill., *Letters To Amanda.* compiled by Henry Mansell Hammock, Culloden, Ga., 1975.

—*Letters to Amanda—The Civil War Letters of Marion Hill Fitzpatrick, Army of Northern Virginia.* Jeffrey C. Lowe and Sam Hodges, editors. Mercer University Press, Macon, Ga., 1998.

Folsom, James M., *Heroes and Martyrs of Georgia: Georgia's Record In The Revolution of 1861.* Macon, Ga. Burke, Boykin & Co. 1864.

—*Heroes and Martyrs of Georgia: Georgia's Record In The Revolution of 1861.* reprint. Baltimore, Md. Butternut and Blue. 1995.

Haynes, Draughton Stith. *The Field Diary of a Confederate Soldier.* Darien, Ga. The Ashantilly Press, 1963.

Haynes, Martin A. *History of the Second Regiment, New Hampshire Volunteer Infantry in the War of the Rebellion.* Lakeport, N.H., 1896.

Hewett, Janet B. ed., *Supplement to the Official Records of the Union and Confederate Armies. Part II—Record of Events,* Vol. 6,Serial No.18. Wilmington, N.C., Broadfoot Publishing Co., 1995.

Hewett, Janet B.; Trudeau, Noah A.; Suderow, Bryce A., ed., *Supplement to the Official Records of the Union and Confederate Armies. Part I-Reports,* Vol. 6, Serial No. 6. Wilmington, N.C., Broadfoot Publishing Co., 1996.

Hotchkiss, Jedediah., *Make Me A Map of the Valley.* Dallas, Tx. Southern Methodist University Press, 1973.

Houghton, M.B. and W.R., *Two Boys In the Civil War and After.* Montgomery, Al., 1912.

Humphreys, A.A., *The Virginia Campaign of 1864–65.* New York, Charles Scribner's Sons, 1883.

Jones, J. William., *Christ In Camp.* Richmond, Va., 1887.

Lane, Mills ed., *Dear Mother: Don't Grieve About Me. If I Get Killed I'll Only Be Dead.* The Beehive Press, Savannah Ga. 1977.

Lee, Robert E., *Lee's Dispatches to Jefferson Davis.* Douglas S. Freeman and Grady McWhiney, editors. G.P. Putnam's Sons, New York, 1957.

McCrady, Edward., Gregg's Brigade of South Carolinians in the Battle of Second Manassas. *Southern Historical Society Papers.* Vol.12. 1885. p.3–39.

McDonald, Cornelia., *A Diary With Reminiscences of the War and Refuge Life in the Shenandoah Valley, 1860–65.* Nashville, Tn., 1934.

Pender, William Dorsey., *The General to His Lady: The Civil War Letters of William Dorsey Pender to Fanny Pender.* Chapel Hill: University of North Carolina Press, 1962.

Smith, Gustavus W., *The Battle of Seven Pines.* New York, N.Y., C.G. Crawford. 1891.

Smith, John D., *The History of the Nineteenth Regiment of Maine Volunteer Infantry 1862–65.* Minneapolis, Mn., 1909.

Southern Historical Society Papers. Vol. XXV. 1897. Kraws Reprint Co., Millwood, N.Y., 1977, p.99.—Vol.VI, 1878, p.279

—Vol.XXVII, 1900, p.303–305.

—Vol. XLIV, 1923, p. 64–65.

Thomas, Henry W., *History of Doles-Cook Brigade.* Atlanta. The Franklin Printing and Publishing Co. 1903.

U.S. War Department., *War of the Rebellion: A Compilation of the Official Records of the Union and Confederate Armies.* 130 Vols. Washington, D.C.: U.S. Government Printing Office, 1880–1901.

Worsham, John H., *One of Jackson's Foot Cavalry.* New York, 1912.

Published Secondary Sources

Baker, Robert S., *Chattooga County—The Story of a County and Its People.* Roswell, Ga.: W.H. Wolfe and Assoc., 1988.

Barfield, Louise C. *History of Harris County, Georgia 1827–1961.* Columbus, Ga.: Columbus Office Supply Co. 1961.

Cook, John Homer. *The History of Chattooga County.* thesis for Mercer University. 1931. located at Georgia Department of Archives and History. Atlanta, Ga.

Cornell, Nancy Jones. *Campbell County, Georgia: Miscellaneous Records.* Riverdale, Ga.: Inkwell Publications 1983.

—Campbell County, *Georgia Confederate Pension Roll 1890–1928.* Riverdale, Ga., 1980.

Crouch, Howard R. *Relic Hunter.* Fairfax, Va. 1978.

Crute, Joseph H. *Units of the Confederate States Army.* Midlothian, Va.: Derwent Books. 1987.

Dixon, Sara A. and Mary Jane, *Newton County Cemeteries, Vols.I,II, and III.* Starrsville, Ga., 1968, 1972, and 1978.

Eller, Lynda S., *Heard County, Ga.—A History of Its People.* Huguley, Al.: Genealogical Roving Press, 1980.

—Heard County, Ga., Cemeteries. 1977.

Ellingson, Paul, ed., *Confederate Flags in the Georgia State Capitol Collection.* Georgia Office of Secretary of State, 1994.

Flanigan, James C., *History of Gwinnett County, Georgia 1818–1960 Volume II.* Chelsea, Michigan: Bookcrafters, Inc. 1959.

Fox, William G. *Regimental Losses in the American Civil War 1861–65.* Albany, N.Y.: Brandow Printing Co. 1898.

Freeman, D.S. *Lee's Lieutenants Vol.I-III.* New York: Charles Scribner's Sons. 1945.

Furgurson, Ernest B., *Chancellorsville 1863—The Souls of the Brave.* New York: Alfred A. Knopf Co. 1992.

Georgia Division, United Daughters of the Confederacy. *Roster of Confederate Graves, Volumes I-V.* 1995.

Heard County Historical Society, *History of Heard County.* Dallas, Tx.: Curtis Media Corp., 1991.

Henderson, Lillian. *Roster of Confederate Soldiers of Georgia Vol. 3,* Hapeville,Ga.: Longino & Porter, 1960.

Hennessy, John J. *Return to Bull Run.* New York: Simon & Schuster. 1993.

—*Second Manassas Battlefield Map Study.* Lynchburg, Va.: H.E. Howard, Inc. 1985.

Historical Society of Walton County, *In Remembrance—Cemetery Readings of Walton County, Ga.* Monroe, Ga.: Walton Press, 1981.

Ingmire, Francis and Carolyn Ericson. *Confederate POW's—Soldiers and Sailors Who Died in Federal Prisons and Military Hospitals in the North.* St. Louis, Missouri: Ingmire Publications, 1984.

Katcher, Philip. *The Army of Robert E. Lee.* London: Arms and Armor Press. 1994.

Krick, Robert E.L. *Staff Officers In Gray: A Biographical Register of the Staff Officers In The Army of Northern Virginia.* Chapel Hill, N.C.: University of North Carolina Press, 2003.

Krick, Robert K. *Lee's Colonels: A Biographical Register of the Field Officers of the Army of Northern Virginia.* Dayton, Ohio: Press of Morningside Bookshop. 1979.

—*Stonewall Jackson At Cedar Mountain.* Chapel Hill, N.C.: The University of North Carolina Press. 1990.

—*The Smoothbore Volley That Doomed the Confederacy: The Death of Stonewall Jackson and Other Chapters On the Army of Northern Virginia.* Baton Rouge, La.: LSU Press. 2002.

Kurtz, Lucy F.; Ritter, Benny. *A Roster of Confederate Soldiers Buried in Stonewall Cemetery Winchester, Virginia.* 1962.

Lawrence, Harold. *Methodist Preachers in Georgia, 1783–1900.* Tignall, Ga.: The Boyd Publishing Co., Ltd. 1984.

Lee, Fitzhugh. *Newton County History.* Newton County, Ga. 1937.

Long, A.L. *Memoirs of Robert E. Lee.* Secaucus, N.J.: The Blue and Grey Press. 1983.

Matter, William D. *If It Takes All Summer.* Chapel Hill, N.C.: The University of North Carolina Press. 1988.

McCabe, Alice Smythe. *Gwinnett County Families.* Atlanta, Ga.: Cherokee Publishing Co. 1980.

—*Gwinnett County, Georgia Deaths 1818–1989.* Gwinnett Historical Society, Lawrenceville, Ga., 1991.

McClendon, Dorothy; Lambert, Lillie; Knight, Danny, *Family, Church and Community Cemeteries of Troup County, Ga.* LaGrange, Ga.: Family Tree, 1990.

McRay, Sybil W., *Tombstone Inscriptions of Hall County, Ga.* 1971.

Miller, J. Michael. *The North Anna Campaign—'Even To Hell Itself'—May 21–26, 1864.* Lynchburg, Va.: H.E. Howard Inc. 1989.

Minnigh, Luther W., *Gettysburg, What They Did Here.* Gettysburg, Pa. 1922.

Moon, William H., *History of the Moon Family,* Conyers, Ga.: The Times Publishing Co., 1920.

Newton County Historical Society, *History of Newton County, Ga.* 1988.

Newton, Steven H., *The Battle of Seven Pines: May 31–June 1, 1862.* Lynchburg, Va.: H.E. Howard Inc. 1993.

O'Reilly, Frank A., *Stonewall Jackson at Fredericksburg—The Battle of Prospect Hill—December 13, 1862.* Lynchburg,Va.: H.E. Howard Inc., 1993.

—*The Fredericksburg Campaign—Winter War On The Rappahannock.* Baton Rouge, La.: LSU Press. 2003.

Register of the Confederate Dead Interred In Hollywood Cemetery, Richmond Va., Gary Clemnitt and Jones Printers. Richmond, Va. 1869.

Rhea, Gordon C., *The Battle of the Wilderness—May 5–6, 1864.* Baton Rouge, La.: LSU Press. 1994.

—*The Battles for Spotsylvania Court House and the Road to Yellow Tavern—May 7–12, 1864.* Baton Rouge, La.: LSU Press. 1997.

—*To the North Anna River—Grant and Lee—May 13–25, 1864.* Baton Rouge, La.: LSU Press. 2000

Robertson, Jr., James I. *General A.P. Hill: The Story of a Confederate Warrior.* New York: Random House. 1987.

Sams, Anita B. *Wayfarers In Walton.* Atlanta, Ga.: Foote & Davies 1967.

Scott, Robert Garth., *Into the Wilderness With the Army of the Potomac.* Bloomington, In.: Indiana University Press. 1985.

Sears, Stephen W., *To the Gates of Richmond—The Peninsula Campaign* New York: Ticknor & Fields. 1992.

—*Chancellorsville.* Boston: Houghton Mifflin Co. 1996.

Smedlund, William S., *Camp Fires of Georgia's Troops, 1861–1865.* Kennesaw, Ga.: Kennesaw Mountain Press, 1994.

Smith, Clifford L., *History of Troup County.* Atlanta, Ga.: Foote and Davies Co., 1935.

Sommers, Richard J., *Richmond Redeemed—The Siege At Petersburg.* Garden City, New York: Doubleday & Co. Inc., 1981.

Steere, Edward. *The Wilderness Campaign.* Mechanicsburg, Pa.: Stackpole Books., 1960.

Time-Life Books., *Echoes of Glory: Arms and Equipment of the Confederacy.* Alexandria Va. 1991.

Trudeau, Noah A., *Bloody Roads South.* Boston: Little, Brown and Co. 1989.

Wert, Jeffry D., *Gettysburg—Day Three.* New York: Simon & Schuster. 2001.

Wheeler, Richard. *An Eyewitness History of McClellan's Peninsula Campaign.* New York: The Fairfax Press. 1986.

Wilbur, C.Keith. *Civil War Medicine: 1861–1865.* Old Saybrook, Connecticut: Old Globe Pequot Press. 1998.

Williford, William Bailey. *The Glory of Covington.* Atlanta, Ga.: Cherokee Publishing Co. 1973.

Wills, Mary Alice. *The Confederate Blockade of Washington, D.C. 1861–1862.* Parsons, W.Va.: McClain Printing Co. 1975.

Articles/Essays/Newspapers

Anderson, Terry Lynn, ed., "Faithful to the End: Letters of Lt. William Boswell, 35th Georgia." *Military Images.* Vol.9, #4, Jan-Feb 1988

"An Incident of the Battle Field." *Daily Columbus Enquirer.* June 3, 1864. p.2.

Augusta Daily Constitutionalist, Augusta, Ga. 1861–1865.

Brock, R.A. "Paroles of the Army of Northern Virginia". *Southern Historical Society Papers. Vol.XV* 1887.

"Bruffs Column". *The Atlanta Constitution.* March 9, 1908. Atlanta, Ga., p.4.

Central Georgian, Sandersville Ga., 1861–64.

Columbus Enquirer, Daily and Weekly, Columbus, Ga. 1861–65.

Columbus Sun, Daily and Weekly, Columbus, Ga., 1862–65.

Confederate Veteran. 1893–1932.

Cullen, Joseph P. "When Grant Faced Lee Across the North Anna". *Civil War Times Illustrated.* Vol.3 #10. p.16–23. Feb. 1965.

—"Cold Harbor." *Civil War Times Illustrated.* Vol.2 #7. p.11–17. Nov.1863.

—"The Battle of Gaine's Mill." *Civil War Times Illustrated.* Vol.3 #1. April 1964.

—"The Battle of Mechanicsville." *Civil War Times Illustrated.* Vol.V #6. October 1966.

—"It Was Not War - It Was Murder." *Civil War Times Illustrated.* Vol. 5 #2. May 1966.

—"The Siege of Petersburg." Eastern Acorn Press, 1981.

Daily Intelligencer, Atlanta, Ga., 1861–65.

Frye, Dennis E. "Stonewall Attacks!—The Siege of Harpers Ferry." *Blue & Gray Magazine.* Vol.V issue 1. Sept. 1987.

Garman, James E. "Bibliographical Material, Georgia CSA Units." 1960. Located at Georgia Division of Archives and History, Morrow, Ga.

"General Thomas Passes Away". *Atlanta Journal.* March 10, 1898.

Greene, A. Wilson. "Opportunity To The South: Meade Versus Jackson At Fredericksburg." *Civil War History.* Vol.XXXIII #IV. p.295–313. December 1987.

—"Artistry In August—Stonewall Jackson and the Second Manassas Campaign." *Civil War.* Vol.XIV. p.8–30.

Holden, Walter. "The Blooding of the Best." *America's Civil War.* Vol.1 #4. November 1988.

"In the Trenches Near Petersburg." *Columbus Daily Sun.* April 15, 1865.

Irvine, W.T. "Old 35th Georgia." *The Sunny South,* Atlanta, Ga., May 2, 1891.

Lowry, Thomas P. "The Index Project," Civil War Court-Martial Research 6060 Lost Colony Dr., Woodbridge, Va. 22193

Naisawald, L. VanLoan. "The Battle of Chantilly." *Civil War Times Illustrated.* Vol.3 #3. June 1964.

Norton, Herman. "Revivalism In The Confederate Armies." *Civil War History.* Vol. VI p.410–424. 1960.

Seabourne, J. Gay. "The Battle of Cedar Mountain." *Civil War Times Illustrated.* Vol.V #8. December 1966.

Sears, Stephen W. "America's Bloodiest Day: The Battle of Antietam." *Civil War Times Illustrated.* Vol.XXVI #2. August 1987.

Skoch, George. "The Last Ditch." *Civil War Times Illustrated.* Vol. XXVII #9. p.12–18. January 1989.

Smith, William F., "Longstreet to the Rescue of Thomas' Brigade." *Atlanta Journal.* September 21, 1901.

Southern Confederacy, Atlanta, Ga., 1861–65.

"Reunion of Virginia Division A.N.V. Association." *Southern Historical Society Papers.* Vol. XII Jan-Dec 1884. Millwood, N.Y. Krause Reprint Co. 1977.

Upchurch, C. Winn. "The Real 'Hec Ramsey'." *The Atlanta Journal and Constitution Magazine.* February 18, 1973.

Wert, Jeffry. "Like An Avalanche—Part I." *Civil War Times Illustrated.* Vol.XXVII. #6. October 1988.

—"At Richmond's Gates—Part II." *Civil War Times Illustrated.* Vol.XXVII #7. November 1988.

Whitehorne, Joseph W.A. "The Battle of Chantilly." *Blue & Gray Magazine.* Vol. IV issue 5. May 1987.

Author's Biography

John J. Fox, III grew up in Richmond, Virginia. He graduated from Washington & Lee University and served on active duty in the U.S. Army for seven years as an armor officer and aviator. Fox lived in the Columbus and Atlanta, Georgia areas for thirteen years. He now resides with his family in the Shenandoah Valley of Virginia.

INDEX